COMMONWEALTH CARIBBEAN LAW AND LEGAL SYSTEMS

Fully updated and revised to fit in with the new laws and structure in the Commonwealth Caribbean law and legal systems, this new edition examines the institutions, structures and processes of the law in the Commonwealth Caribbean.

The author explores:

- the court system and the new Caribbean Court of Justice which replaces appeals to the Privy Council
- the offshore financial legal sector
- Caribbean customary law and the rights of indigenous peoples
- the Constitutions of Commonwealth Caribbean jurisdictions and Human Rights
- the impact of the historical continuum to the region's jurisprudence including the question of reparations
- the complexities of judicial precedent for Caribbean peoples
- international law as a source of law
- alternative dispute mechanisms and the Ombudsman

Effortlessy combining discussions of traditional subjects with more innovative subject areas, this book is an excit and legal systems for those studying comparative l

Rose-Marie Belle Antoine is the Profess Financial Law at the University of the West-Indies.

COMMONWEALTH CARIBBEAN LAW AND LEGAL SYSTEMS

Second Edition

Rose-Marie Belle Antoine
LLB (UWI), LLM (Cantab), DPhil (Oxon)
Professor of Labour Law and Offshore Financial Law,
Faculty of Law, University of the West-Indies
Attorney-at-Law

Routledge·Cavendish
Taylor & Francis Group
LONDON AND NEW YORK

First published 1998
by Routledge-Cavendish Publishing Ltd

Second Edition published 2008
by Routledge-Cavendish
2 Park Square, Milton Park, Abingdon, Oxon OX14 4RN

Simultaneously published in the USA and Canada
by Routledge-Cavendish
270 Madison Ave, New York, NY 10016

Routledge is an imprint of the Taylor & Francis Group, an informa business

© 1998, 2008 Rose-Marie Belle Antoine

Typeset in Palatino by
RefineCatch Limited, Bungay, Suffolk
Printed and bound in Great Britain by
CPI Antony Rowe, Chippenham, Wiltshire

British Library Cataloguing in Publication Data
A catalogue record for this book is available from the British Library

Library of Congress Cataloging in Publication Data
Antoine, Rose-Marie Belle.
Commonwealth Caribbean law and legal systems / Rose-Marie Belle Antoine. – 2nd ed.
p. cm.
1. Law–Caribbean Area. 2. Law–West Indies, British. 3. Law–Commonwealth countries.
I. Title.
KGJ97.A58 2008
349.729–dc22
2007036111

ISBN10: 1–85941–853–8 (pbk)
eISBN10: 0–203–93039–8 (ebk)

ISBN13: 978–1–85941–853–6 (pbk)
eISBN13: 978–0–203–93039–7 (ebk)

CONTENTS

FOREWORD TO THE SECOND EDITION

This new edition of Professor Rose-Marie Belle Antoine's excellent *Commonwealth Caribbean Law and Legal Systems* is to be warmly welcomed. By a happy coincidence its publication comes exactly 50 years after the first focused research into the law in the Commonwealth Caribbean was initiated by Sir Roy Marshall, at the time Dean of the Faculty of Law at the University of Sheffield. Until that time, the origins and characteristics of the region's legal institutions had been the subject of almost no systematic study. The legal education and training of the relatively few West Indian practitioners was provided through studying for the English Bar and Law Society, in some cases after obtaining a law degree at an English University. Hardly surprisingly, law and practice in the Caribbean countries, all of which were still colonial possessions, drew heavily upon English law and practice, not uncommonly of an earlier date.

That the region had a distinct legal history that merited examination and distinctive social needs that were not met through the largely inherited law became apparent through such early doctoral researches as those of Nick Liverpool (on succession in the West Indies), Edwin Watkins (on the Jamaican legal system), Fenton Ramsahoye (British Guiana land law) and Adolph Edwards (Jamaican criminal law). Those themes were explored at a series of ground-breaking colloquia at Cambridge and Cumberland Lodge, in Windsor Great Park, attended by West Indian students studying in England (see my accounts in *Some aspects of Marriage and Divorce in the West Indies* (1959) 8 ICLQ 632-677 and *Law in the West Indies, Some Recent Trends*, British Institute of International and Comparative Law, 1966).

However, it was the establishment of the Faculty of Law in the University of the West Indies in 1970 and the need to provide materials for the legal education of the region's lawyers that created the opportunity for sustained legal research concerning the Commonwealth Caribbean. Acceptance by past and present members of the Faculty of that opportunity has resulted in a scholarly output that addresses an evident concern to develop law and legal institutions that effectively serve the region's specific needs and circumstances. This book is a fine example of this scholarly development, which Professor Antoine has already confidently demonstrated in her published work relating to the law of Offshore Finance in the Caribbean.

Readers of this work will find not only a careful and up-to-date account of the legal systems and the sources of law in the region but also a thoughtful and pertinent analysis of the challenges that face a system that is necessarily moving away from its derivative origins. It is refreshing to see the extent to which it has been possible for the author to illustrate so many aspects of the subject matter with locally decided cases, many of which bear testimony to a growing confidence of the judiciary to develop the law to take account of local circumstances. It is also valuable to be provided with a discussion of the issues facing the newly operational Caribbean Court of Justice and of the past role and likely future implications of the judgments of the Judicial Committee of the Privy Council, particularly those often controversial decisions relating to the death penalty that have dominated its Caribbean case load.

This work marks the considerable progress that has been made in creating law and legal institutions that are appropriate to the needs of the communities of the Commonwealth Caribbean, but it also offers insights as to where further development is called for. Those who study those institutions need a well organised and well written publication from which to acquire reliable information about their origins, sources and working, but which also encourages clear and critical thinking about what has been achieved and what may need to be changed or enhanced. Professor Antoine's book admirably serves those purposes.

Professor Keith Patchett
Dean of the Faculty of Law, UWI, 1970-1973.
Order of Barbados; LLD (Hon) (University of West-Indies)
April 2008

FOREWORD TO THE FIRST EDITION

It was clearly a daunting task to undertake the writing of a textbook on the law and legal systems of the Commonwealth Caribbean. There are no fewer than 12 independent countries in the region, and six territories which remain dependencies of Great Britain, though exercising various levels of self-government in the administration of their local affairs.

Though daunting, it was a task which had to be undertaken, particularly for the benefit of the student who needed, as early as possible, to be exposed to the diversity of legal institutions which now exist in the region and their potential for creativity and development.

Rose-Marie Antoine has successfully accomplished the task. She has been particularly effective in placing the legal institutions, and the content of the law itself, in the context of their historical and social backgrounds. This enables her to discuss the inhibiting effects that these have had, and to emphasise the opportunities which independence affords to devise solutions reflecting the new spirit of independence and nationhood.

This leads to a salutary emphasis on the Constitutions and the ideals of democratic government and the recognition and protection of fundamental rights and freedoms which the law and the legal systems of the region are designed to fulfil.

Issues of the day, such as the possible abolition of appeals to the Privy Council and the setting up of a Caribbean Court of Appeal, are addressed in detail. The way in which these issues are discussed can serve as a model, to a student, of the proper approach to the serious discussion of contentious legal problems.

The inclusion of a chapter on alternative dispute resolution is admirable. It impresses upon the student the importance not only of grasping the heritage of the past and assessing its value, but also of looking into the future to pioneer new solutions to the problems of the present.

The approach is refreshingly stimulating. There is the bedrock of accurate factual material as well as trenchant comments on chances missed when opportunities for innovations presented themselves.

Although the book is aimed primarily at students, it could be read with interest and profit by everyone interested in the social and economic advancement of the region.

The Rt Hon Philip Telford Georges, OCC
Barbados
October 1998

PREFACE

This new and revised edition appears at a time when there are exciting developments in the Law and Legal Systems of the Commonwealth Caribbean. Alternative Dispute Resolution has been given new impetus and currency. Conciliation, arbitration and case management are now familiar features of the legal process. Unquestionably, the most significant development has been the decision of the Heads of Government of the Caribbean Community to establish the Caribbean Court of Justice to replace the Privy Council as the final appellate court of the Community. This decision continues to provoke controversy and unease. Only two Member States have, to date, acceded to the appellate jurisdiction of the Court.

With these developments, it is exceedingly difficult for this revised edition to simply restate and update the law. To accommodate these and other developments as well as the weaknesses and gaps in the first edition, this new and revised edition is considerably expanded. As before, the work attempts to include the voices of those who first started writing in this area.

A book on the subject of 'Commonwealth Caribbean Law and Legal Systems' presents some unique challenges. The Commonwealth Caribbean is racially diverse with rather complex social formations. It comprises several sovereign and independent States, the majority of which are small and frankly, geographically, insignificant. In this socio-political milieux, it is debatable whether one can speak of a 'Commonwealth Caribbean Legal System' or of 'Commonwealth Caribbean Legal Systems'. In this book, a preference has been expressed for 'Legal Systems' to reflect not only the sovereign status of the majority of these States, but also, the diversity that exists within and among the States. In this sense, this work, despite having to concede to broad similarities, applies the tools of the 'comparative lawyer and academic'.

A deliberate effort has been made to maintain the philosophical underpinnings of the original text. As in the first edition, this book seeks to locate the law in its social, historical and political context. It constantly examines the interaction between law, State and society. This is a challenging undertaking because no examination of the Legal Systems of the Commonwealth Caribbean could ignore the fact that the people of the region live in a plural, and racially diverse community of States.

The early chapters focus on the identity of Commonwealth Caribbean Legal Systems. Chapter 2 turns to the history of slavery and colonialism to provide a more contextual interpretation of the functions of law in Commonwealth Caribbean Societies. The Legal Traditions which colonialism bequeathed, are examined in considerable depth and detail. This leads to a comprehensive analysis of the remaining hybrid or mixed systems of law.

The Chapters on the 'Sources of Law' have undergone significant adjustment and change. The first edition broke new ground when it treated the norms of International Law as an emerging but significant source of law. The discussion exceeded the conventional treatment of the subject in textbooks on Legal Systems. This edition confirms International Law as a major source of law but explores in greater detail, its impact on domestic law and in particular, the interpretation of the Constitutions of Commonwealth Caribbean States.

Consistent with the redefinition of the 'Sources of Law', greater primacy is given to Caribbean Constitutions as the most significant source in the hierarchy of legal sources. Inevitably, this included discussion on the evolving rules of constitutional interpretation and adjudication, particularly in Human Rights cases.

A more robust approach has been taken to the role of 'custom' in the legal systems of the Commonwealth Caribbean. The discussion is provocative, exploratory and wide ranging. It includes an analysis of the customs of the 'indigenous' populations of the region. The law governing marriages in two of the States of the Commonwealth Caribbean with mixed populations, Trinidad and Tobago and Guyana, was selected for more detailed treatment. The discussion focuses on the extent to which legal recognition has been conceded to the traditional norms and customs of Hindu and Muslim marriages in both jurisdictions. Particular attention is paid to the efforts of Caribbean judges to 'mould' or even redefine the common law to give meaning to the Caribbean peculiarity, the 'Chattel House'.

No discussion on the sources of law could ignore the complex and constantly evolving rules of judicial precedent. The likely impact of the Caribbean Court of Justice on precedent is a subject of particular interest. Chapter 8 devotes attention to this and other issues.

The chapter on 'Statutory Interpretation' has been re-conceptualized, re-worked, and considerably expanded to accommodate the growing number of judicial decisions on 'Statutory Interpretation' by the Courts of the region.

An analysis of the establishment of the Caribbean Court of Justice is preceded by Chapter 15 which focuses on the structure and jurisdiction of the traditional Courts of Law of the Commonwealth Caribbean States.

Chapter 17 explores the reasons for the creation of the Caribbean Court of Justice (the CCJ), the challenges which the court confronts and the prospects for its future viability. Inevitably, one is drawn to an examination of the jurisdiction of the Court and the unique mechanism for the appointment of judges. The creators of the CCJ granted the Court original jurisdiction in matters pertaining to the interpretation of the Treaty of Chaguaramas and appellate jurisdiction, in specified civil and criminal matters emanating from the Courts of Appeal of Member States. This twin juris-diction is analysed to determine the potential of the Court to create a jurisprudence that truly reflects the will, likeness and aspirations of the people of the Caribbean.

Chapter 18 focuses on Specialized Courts, Tribunals and their functions in the Legal Systems. The discussion ranges from Industrial Courts to Juvenile Courts to Specialized Courts such as Revenue Courts and the 'infamous' Gun Court of Jamaica. Few changes have been made to this chapter except, of course, to update the law.

The chapter on the 'Jury System' has been retained and expanded. While readers are reminded of the weaknesses of the 'Jury System', particularly in the small States of the Commonwealth Caribbean with its complex social 'mores', the value of the 'Jury System' in allowing for 'participatory justice' is re-affirmed, hopefully, with greater conviction.

The breadth and depth of this edition, like its predecessor publication, can be confirmed by the two closing chapters. Chapter 20 reviews 'The Office of the Ombudsman', the appointment and removal of its members, its jurisdiction and functions. The overall value and significance of the office to citizens is an issue which, in time, will require greater attention.

Chapter 21 looks at 'Alternative Dispute Mechanisms'. The chapter goes beyond the traditional definition of the subject, certainly as understood by lawyers, to include a discussion on 'Commissions of Enquiry'. In recent times, the region has had its fair share of such enquiries, especially in the wake of General Elections which have replaced one political party by another.

It is hoped that this edition will follow its predecessor and appeal to the interest of not only lawyers, students and academics but the citizens of the Caribbean Community and those beyond the region interested in comparative law. Already, the book has travelled as far away as Africa and Europe. After all, this book was written to suggest that law is a social phenomenon, albeit that it finds expression in norms, prescriptions and rules.

Rose-Marie Belle Antoine
Faculty of Law
Barbados
April 2008

ACKNOWLEDGMENTS

I wish to express my appreciation to my typists, Pat Worrel and Valda Maynard.

I am also indebted to Jan Yves Remy and Kimberley Polius, students at the Faculty of Law, for their research assistance.

TABLE OF CASES

TABLE OF LEGISLATION

PART I

THE NATURE OF THE LAW AND LEGAL SYSTEMS AND ITS HISTORICAL PRECEPTS

CHAPTER 1

INTRODUCTION TO LAW AND LEGAL SYSTEMS IN THE COMMONWEALTH CARIBBEAN

THE NATURE OF THE LEGAL SYSTEM

The study of law and legal systems is a diverse and intriguing subject which cannot be divorced from its proper social context. In the Commonwealth Caribbean, the law and legal systems were born out of the colonial experience. Indeed, the very nomenclature by which the region is known is evidence of this. The notion of a 'Commonwealth' betrays the historical fact of imperialism and gave the region a certain identity, which even today, still survives.

For a description with less emotive connotations, the Commonwealth Caribbean is that part of the globe known as the West Indies.[1] It comprises both dependent and independent democratic States, but the former are now few in number.[2] The independent countries of the region belong to a socio-economic grouping – a loose political community labelled the Caribbean Community (CARICOM).[3] There is a further sub-grouping of the countries of the Eastern Caribbean, known as the Organisation of the Eastern Caribbean States (OECS).

A West Indian identity?

The historical reality of colonialism is perhaps more evident in the study of 'Law and Legal Systems' than in any other legal subject. While the ex-colonies have attempted to fashion new identities since gaining independence, their legal expressions remains largely British, or, at least, neo-colonial. As Sharma JA from the Trinidad and Tobago Court of Appeal explained in *Boodram v AG and Another*:[4]

> . . . even after independence, our courts have continued to develop our law very much in accordance with English jurisprudence. The inherent danger and pitfall in this approach is that, since independence our society has developed differently from the English and now requires a robust examination in order to render our Constitution and common law more meaningful.[5]

---

1 Although the Republic of Guyana is not strictly speaking part of the Caribbean, but part of South America, it is usually included in the term 'Commonwealth Caribbean'. Bermuda is similarly included, as is Belize, although the latter is part of Central America. The term 'Caribbean' should be taken to mean the Commonwealth Caribbean. Likewise, the term 'West Indies' is used synonymously with 'Commonwealth Caribbean'.

2 These include Montserrat, the Cayman Islands, Bermuda, Anguilla, Turks and Caicos and the British Virgin Islands.

3 CARICOM further embraces the dependent territories as Associated States, and more recently, countries in the Caribbean which are not part of the Commonwealth, such as Suriname and Haiti. An exception is Montserrat which is a full CARICOM member although still a dependent territory. There are current initiatives toward formal economic integration and more formal political ties, but the principle of autonomous self-government for each one of these States is likely to be retained. The system of government identified in the region, the Westminster Parliamentary system, including its traditions of political and legal Conventions, follows closely the model set out by Britain, the former coloniser of the Commonwealth Caribbean.

4 (1994) 47 WIR 459.

5 At p 470.

Turn toward other foreign law?

More recently, Commonwealth Caribbean courts and jurists have sought to resort less to English jurisprudence, turning instead to legal thought and infrastructure from elsewhere, such as Europe and North America. The emphasis on North American and European jurisprudence is most pronounced in constitutional adjudication, largely perhaps because of the absence of a written UK Constitution and consequent jurisprudence upon which to lean. However, these foreign solutions still deny our own creativity and experience.

The convergence toward North American models of legal systems is also seen in the recent adoption of case management, court practices and rules borrowed from North America, with the aim of making court adjudication more efficient. Further, we have already seen a high degree of Americanisation of the region, aided no doubt, by geographical proximity and the dominance of American television and pop culture. That same television is a medium for transmitting models of justice, such as televised trials, racially constructed juries, new rules of evidence, and changing the locations of juries to avoid bias. These may challenge long-held assumptions about the right (English) way of doing things. Perhaps the day is not too far away when we will be electing judges!

Some options which may be borrowed from the American legal system seem more attractive than others. Contingency fees, for example, may be suitable in societies such as ours where many citizens find the cost of justice to be prohibitive and where legal aid is scarce. It may also have the effect of speeding up the process, by encouraging legal counsel to be more time-efficient.[6] In addition, as discussed in Chapter 18 ('Specialised Courts, Tribunals and Functions'), it has been argued that multicultural societies such as ours should be accurately reflected in the composition of our juries, a position which has been resisted under the traditional English jury system, but adopted in the US.

Similarly, access to court trials on television, a medium which is wholeheartedly embraced in the region, may encourage more inclusion in the adjudication system, in societies whose peoples have traditionally felt that formal channels of justice were closed to them or alienated from them. This is not a panacea, however, as television trials also have great potential to distort truth or sensationalise litigation.

The plantation paradigm

Noted economists, historians and sociologists have described the region as 'plantation societies',[7] a reference to the fact that the territories were once shaped by the dictates of the great sugar plantations. The plantation paradigm best explains the 'persistent poverty' of the region, both in terms of economics and legal innovation.[8]

The legal systems of the region cannot, therefore, be described as endogenous. The greatest divergence of this colonial outlook can be seen to be the advent of written

---

6   See the Cayman Islands case of *National Trust for Cayman Islands v Planning Appeals Tribunal Central Planning Authority and Humphreys (Cayman) Ltd* [2002] CILR 59 (Grand Court, Cayman Islands).

7   Beckford, G, *Persistent Poverty: Underdevelopment in Plantation Economics in the Third World*, 1972, New York: ISER.

8   See *ibid*, for the economic theory on persistent poverty.

Constitutions, in particular, Bills of Rights, again a product of independence. Yet, even here, we cannot say that there is complete originality. The written Constitutions of the Caribbean borrowed heavily from international human rights instruments, and were constructed with much less indigenous input than is usually expected of such defining documents.

The battles between different imperialist powers, while challenging periodically the dominance of the English common law, did not allow the development of a unique West Indian law in the interplay and consequently did not undermine the exogenous nature of the law. The region still awaits the revolution which will force capitulation of these essentially non-West Indian strains of legal dominance.

It appears that we are successful legal civilisations if we judge ourselves by how admirably we have retained and maintained the English jurisprudence that we inherited or, more accurately, was thrust upon us. However, we have exhibited failure in our inability to put our own stamp, our own face, on our justice. Ultimately, law is meant to reflect society and to engineer society. Yet our law still looks very alien and foreign to many.

Striving to be West Indian

The region's law and legal systems are still 'striving' to be West Indian. Apart from deviations from Westminster-style democracy, as evidenced by the written Constitutions, there have been experiments with socialism and democratic socialism in at least three countries: Jamaica, Guyana and Grenada. In the latter two nations, the impact of these political changes extended to their Constitutions.[9] In Grenada, the change was profound, even including a suspension of the Constitution under a revolutionary government, with a substantial change to the court structure which necessitated complex jurisprudential questions about State legitimacy.[10]

In addition, while the base of the law and legal systems remains the common law, the detail of that law has been changed according to the social, political and economic needs of the region, albeit not substantially enough in the eyes of many.

The vulnerabilities of the legal system to socio-political realities

In our examination of Commonwealth Caribbean law and legal systems, what we find is that there are common denominators in the many subject areas in this book. They are: issues of political and cultural sovereignty, economic sustainability and even of economic survival. These underline the vulnerable status and place of small developing countries in the world. An important thread running through our analyses is the extent to which small, poor, developing nations such as those in the region, have the freedom and the flexibility to fully define the legal systems therein. This may, at first blush, seem to be an alarmist, rather extreme position, but upon closer examination, we shall see that there are important truths and realities to be ascertained.

---

9   In Guyana, eg, the Constitution declared the country to be a socialist State and proclaimed the 'right to work'.

10   Under the Peoples Laws of 1979. See the discussion of the Grenada experiment in Chapter 16 ('The Privy Council'), Chapter 17 ('The Renewed Initiative Towards a Caribbean Court of Justice') and Chapter 18 ('Specialised Courts, Tribunals and Functions').

When we speak of difficulties in defining and shaping the legal systems in the region, we are not, of course, speaking of the kind of legal displacement that can occur when one country invades or intervenes in another smaller, weaker, country. That brings its own dynamics and is certainly something which occurred very early in our legal history, although the existence of the legal and political systems of the original peoples is hardly even acknowledged.[11] Instead, legal displacement may be far more subtle and may even be welcomed with open arms. Indeed, in some cases, it is self-perpetuating.

Economic and political sovereignty and the impact on law

The region's economic and political sovereignty is clearly not untouched by the dictates of larger States. For example, CARICOM was threatened with economic retaliation by the US for not voting to excuse the US from the jurisdiction of the International Criminal Court as it requested.

These political realities may have implications for the kinds of laws which we put into place. For example, they have had practical impact in the urgency with which the region has had to implement laws against terrorism. Such initiatives have hefty economical implications. While they may not be undesirable objectives in themselves, they do demonstrate the extent to which legal changes in policy may be dictated from outside of the region and the often low priority given to pressing issues of law reform in favour of external priorities. Often, these are not choices, but imperatives.

These vulnerabilities were born out of the colonial, imperialist construct in which law had an important part to play. This function of the law is the subject of the following chapter. Here, we note merely that law in the region has also served as a powerful tool of underdevelopment and dependency. Some would argue that it even cemented the economic servitude of the former colonies by notions of property that guaranteed the continued ownership and even the monopoly of vital sectors of the economy to the former colonial masters. Its notions of property and compensation were further used in the French West Indies to perpetuate unjust notions of ownership of human beings when Haiti, the first independent black nation, was made to pay millions in compensation to France for the 'loss' of the former slaves as property. This payment lasted for over 200 years, contributing to Haiti being the poorest nation in the Western hemisphere.[12]

PLURALISTIC SOCIETIES – RASTAFARIANISM AND BEYOND

The societies in the Commonwealth Caribbean have often been described as 'pluralistic'.[13] This is taken to mean that there are several diverse ethnic, religious and class groups existing within these societies. While these groups make up one society, their cultural and social differences can still be identified.

---

11   Nor did the legal systems of early European conquerors like the Spanish, French, Portuguese or Dutch endure, except in isolated cases such as in St Lucia and Guyana.

12   See Chapter 2 ('The Historical Function of Law in the West Indies – Creating a Future from a Troubled Past'), for a further discussion of this within the context of Reparations.

13   See, eg, Smith, MG, *The Plural Society in the British West Indies*, 1965, Los Angeles: California UP, who first applied the term to West Indian society. Bishop Tutu of South Africa described Trinidadians, and, by extension, West Indians, as 'rainbow people'.

Despite this sociological classification, with few exceptions, such pluralism is not evident within the law and legal systems of the region. From a legal perspective, the Commonwealth Caribbean can be seen as a homogenous entity, joined by strong British legal ties. The major deviations are the hybrid legal systems of St Lucia and Guyana, discussed below. Yet even these hybrid systems do not seriously challenge the homogeneity of Commonwealth Caribbean law and legal systems. Within each country's legal system, homogeneity is also evident.

This does not mean that areas of legal divergence between the various countries which make up the Commonwealth Caribbean do not exist. While the countries share the inheritance of the common law as the basic law, there are differences in socio-political and economic policy which are reflected within the law. In the main, these will have been effected through legislation and not case law. A good example would be the differences between offshore law countries and non-offshore law countries in the region, discussed below (p 13). As expected, there will be substantial differences in areas like foreign investment law, international tax law and company law. Another useful example is the area of labour law, which is traditionally a field that is considerably influenced by a country's particular economic and ideological orientation. Some countries, notably Trinidad and Tobago, the Bahamas and Antigua, have deviated significantly from the original common law in the industrial relations aspect of the law.[14]

Thus, while the societies of the region may be termed 'pluralistic', they are not generally recognised as containing clearly identifiable minorities. Groups which can be identified in the society and, to a limited extent, under the law, include religious and ethnic groups such as the Muslims and Hindus. These groups have a strong presence in Trinidad and Tobago and Guyana. Two other religious-social groups are worthy of mention. These are the Rastafarians and the Shango Baptists or Orisha followers.[15] The other identifiable grouping is the indigenous peoples, often called Amerindians, the original peoples of the region. These are considered separately.

These plural groups are not, however, given any or adequate recognition by the law and legal systems, even where they form significant groups in the society.

Hindus and Muslims – ethnic and religious groups

East Indians make up over 40 per cent of the populations of Guyana and Trinidad and Tobago[16] and have retained significant aspects of their culture and customs. Yet they are anglicised in the eyes of the law, with only token recognition. For example, as discussed in Chapter 3 on 'Legal Traditions', provision is made for the legality of Hindu and Muslim marriages in conformity with their respective religions.[17]

---

14 See Chapter 21 ('Alternative Dispute Mechanisms – Arbitration, Negotiation and Commissions of Inquiry') for a discussion on some of these divergences.

15 The latter is a religious group which follows African religious practices, although there is evidence that these practices have mingled with Christianity.

16 Central Statistical Office, Trinidad and Tobago, 2006. Muslims originally belonged to East Indian ethnic groups. More recently, however, persons of Afro-West-Indian heritage may also be identified as Muslims (often called 'Black Muslims').

17 See such Acts as the Hindu Marriage Act 1992 and the Muslim Marriage and Divorce Act 1980 (rev) of Trinidad and Tobago. Jamaica also makes provision for this under the Hindu Marriage Act 1973.

We can be sceptical about the acceptance of Muslims or Hindus by the legal culture even where the laws acknowledge them as identifiable groups. In a fascinating case from Trinidad and Tobago, *Mohammed v Moraine and Another*,[18] the reluctance of the law to fully recognise and accept these other cultures was demonstrated. A Muslim student was suspended for wearing her Muslim mode of dress, the hijab, to school instead of the prescribed school uniform. In judicial review proceedings challenging the decision, the court seemed to take a non-committal stance on the issue of religious plurality or discrimination. It found that the relevant regulations under the Education Act had been construed too rigidly and that the School Board had taken irrelevant considerations into account in its decision, such as the school's tradition and the student's loyalty to the school.[19] However, it failed to find that the applicant's constitutional rights to equality and against non-discrimination had been violated. This is a surprising result even if the interpretations of those particular constitutional provisions are controversial.[20] More significantly, the court engaged in no real discussion about the rights of a significant socio-religious group within the society.

Sagar also points to:

> ... the conflict between the Hindu marriage system and the legal provisions.
>
> Thus, where personal law allows a separation via a family council decree, the law does not recognise this – while the Hindu is free to remarry according to personal law, under the law it is polygamy.[21]

The case of *Henry v Henry*[22] further underlines this conflict within the law. Here, the 'wife' of one such union was held to be unmarried, for the purposes of the Maintenance and Separation Act.

The Rastafarians

Similar problems accrue to Rastafarianism, despite it being a significant cultural and religious phenomenon in the entire Commonwealth Caribbean and one which has had a tremendous impact the world over. Indeed, the law can hardly be said to have accepted the proponents of Rastafarinism when, not too long ago, at least one country placed on its statute books legislation which permitted the shooting of Rastafarians on sight. The Prohibited and Unlawful Societies and Associations Act, No 32 of 1974 of Dominica, commonly called 'The Dread Act'[23] because of the labelling of the Rastafarians as 'Dreads' in the Schedule, made certain societies, identifiable by 'their mode of dress or manner of wearing their hair',[24] in particular, the Rastafarian community, unlawful.[25] Infamously, section 9 provided:

---

18   (1995) 49 WIR 371. See also the discussion on 'The Religious Legal Tradition below' in Chapter 3 ('Legal Traditions – Types of Legal Systems in the Commonwealth Caribbean').
19   It also found that the Board had failed to take relevant considerations into account, such as the psychological effect on the pupil.
20   See the discussions in Chapter 7 ('The Written Constitution as a Legal Source') and Chapter 3 ('Legal Traditions – Types of Legal Systems in the Commonwealth Caribbean').
21   Sagar, K, 'Law and custom in the West Indies with special emphasis on East Indians', 1978, unpublished thesis, University of the West Indies.
22   (1972) 20 WIR 524.
23   The Act is still on the statute books but is not enforced.
24   Section 2.
25   Section 3.

> No proceedings either criminal or civil shall be brought or maintained against any person who kills or injures any member of an association or society designated unlawful, who shall be found at any time of day or night inside a dwelling house.

The Act further provided that any Rastafarian or other member of a prohibited society could be arrested without warrant[26] and they were prohibited from holding public office.[27]

The statute betrays intolerance to cultural and religious diversity which is perhaps not typical in the region, but nevertheless indicative of the strong adherence, legally and culturally, to dominant social groupings. It is nonetheless remarkable that the Act has never been challenged for unconstitutionality.

Rastafarians have also experienced problems before the courts in proclaiming their separateness from other groups in order to lay claim to some notion of legal identity. In particular, the courts have been reluctant to accept Rastafarianism and its distinct set of beliefs as a religion recognised and protected under the law.

In *Forsythe v DPP and the AG of Jamaica*,[28] for example, the appellant who was a Rastafarian was arrested for the possession of ganja and dealing in ganja under the Dangerous Drugs Act. He sought Constitutional redress, on the ground that the Act contravened his Constitutional right to the enjoyment of his freedom of conscience in the practice of his religion as a Rastafarian, since using ganja was a part of the sacrament and essential practices of his Rastafarian faith. The court dismissed the application, albeit on the ground that the Dangerous Drug Act had been saved by the Constitution and was enacted in the interests of public health. The reasoning, in particular, the latter element of public health, is somewhat suspect, given that the court refused to consider the health benefits or otherwise of ganja and further, did not balance the use of ganja with any harms perceived. Further, the court relied on a UK precedent which was not on Constitutional law and did not take into account the impact of a written Constitution enshrining rights of religious freedom.

Rastafariansm was in an even more precarious position in the Cayman Islands, in the case of *Grant and Chin v The Principal of John A Cumber Primary School et al.*[29] In this case, a schoolboy was expelled from school because of his failure to comply with school rules which prohibited him from wearing his hair in 'dreadlocks'.[30] His parents challenged the decision on the ground that his freedom to practice his religion was being infringed. The Grand Court inquired into whether Rastafarianism was a religion, and came up with a negative.[31] It viewed Rastafarianism more in the nature of 'socio-political movement than a religion'. More importantly, in attempting to define a religion it emphasised an approach which relied on faith and worship of a particular God or deity.[32]

---

26 Section 5.
27 Section 16.
28 (1997) 34 JLR 512.
29 (1999) CILR 307.
30 A characteristic hairstyle of the Rastafarians where hair is left uncut and uncombed.
31 As Cayman Islands does not have a Bill of Rights, the case had to be argued on judicial review grounds, in particular, the unreasonableness of the decision, as well as a breach of the International Human Rights Convention.
32 As demonstrated in *R v Registrar General, ex p Segerdal* [1970] 3 All ER 886, at 892.

An alternative approach is one which recognises religion where it embodies beliefs which are sufficiently separate and distinct (the functional approach). In *Chin*, the court acknowledged both approaches. However, it seemed to have difficulty in placing Rastafarianism as a religion under the theistic approach. It also found that there had been no discriminatory treatment.

One rationale for this decision was because the Treaty Rights upon which Chin relied were not directly enforceable in domestic law. The court, however, had to concede that the wearing of dreadlocks was 'central and fundamental to a Rastafarian's perception and expression of himself as such'. The decision is, however, not encouraging to a pluralistic approach.

However, in the same year as *Chin*, a Barbadian court seemed to suggest that Rastafarian religious beliefs should be accepted by the courts. In *Hinds v AG and Superintendant of Glendairy Prison*,[33] a prisoner of the Rasta persuasion sought an injunction to restrain the Superintendent of Prisoners from cutting his hair, on the ground that the growing of locks was a fundamental tenet of his religious beliefs. While Hinds lost his case on its facts, not having notified the prison authorities that he was of the Rasta faith,[34] the implicit suggestion was that had he given such notification, his religious beliefs as a Rasta would have been legitimate in the eyes of the law and could be protected.

It is doubtful however, whether such recognition will be given more than token effect in the eyes of the law. Concessions, such as the right to proclaim Rastafarianism on oath or to wear dreadlocks, may be made. However, as seen in later chapters, issues which conflict with majority norms of the society in a more profound way, such as the use of marijuana, are more problematic.[35]

The Orisha or Orisa

The Orisa, or Orisha Shango Baptists, an African-West Indian religious/cultural grouping found everywhere in the region, although not conforming in nomenclature, have fared somewhat better than the Rastafarians, at least in one country. In 1991, after years of intense lobbying, the Parliament of Trinidad and Tobago gave them legal recognition by enacting the Opa Orisha (Shango) of Trinidad and Tobago (Incorporation) Act.[36] The aims and objectives are:

---

33 Civ Appeal No 20 of 1997, decided 30 September 1999, CA, Barbados.
34 The court pointed out correctly that a person could wear a Rasta hairstyle without belonging to the Rasta religion.
35 See Chapter 3 ('Legal Traditions – Types of Legal Systems in the Commonwealth Caribbean'), Chapter 10 ('Custom as a Source of Law') and Chapter 7 ('The Written Constitution as a Legal Source'). Cf *R v Hines and King* (1971) 17 WIR 326 (CA), where the Jamaican Court of Appeal recognised Rastafarianism as a religion or 'faith' and the attendant right to swear an oath in the name of Rastafarianism. In *Re Chickweche* (1995) (4) SA 284 the Zimbabwe Supreme Court also recognised Rastafarianism as a religion. Rastafarianism has also been recognised by the United Nations as one of the religions of the world.
36 They now also have their own religious public holiday, the subject of which allegedly caused the downfall of one government when it refused to grant it. See also the Orisa Marriage Act, Chap 45: 04, Act 22 of 1999 of Trinidad and Tobago and the Orisa Movement of Trinidad and Tobago (Incorporation) Act of 1981 of Trinidad and Tobago. Up to 1999, in Trinidad and Tobago, laws such as the Summary Offences Act, Chap 11:02, especially ss 64(2) and 65, effectively discriminated against these African religions by banning lighted torches, drums and blow-horns in public places.

... to continue the Orisha traditions and practices as they are known in Trinidad and Tobago and are taught by approved experts of Africa and the African diaspora.[37]

Still, even these flirtations with the law are not enough to suggest that any of these groups are accorded a minority or recognisable status under the law as is done in other plural societies. In the eyes of the law, they are all uniform subjects. As we shall see in a subsequent chapter,[38] even Hindu and Muslim marriage hopefuls must also make concessions to the traditional State law procedures, for their marriages to be deemed legal.

The failure to reflect minority interests in the law

The cases above suggest a failure, or at best, a reluctance to reflect and protect minority interests in the legal system. Such cases are examined in more detail in a following chapter,[39] where we ask whether the legal system accommodates legal pluralism or legal tokenism. In the present context, we note that while our societies may be defined as pluralistic, our law and legal systems exhibit a marked uniformity with respect to their ideological and philosophical stances. Whether we are examining religious or ethnic minorities, or, as we will see in later chapters, issues such as gender or sexual orientation, the law adopts a largely Anglo-Saxon, Christian perspective.[40]

Such a perspective embodies a particular concept of morality and justice. In our next chapter, we will examine how moral and ideological positions inform law and the way in which social and cultural norms shape the law and legal system.

The indigenous peoples

If the law has largely failed to acknowledge the customs and norms of important groups in the society, such as the Muslims and Hindus, it is fair to say that it has almost entirely ignored the original peoples of the region, often called Amerindians. This is no mere historical accident, as one of the policies of the colonial powers was to annihilate and eradicate these peoples. Reception or imposition of law theories blatantly excluded their legal thought processes and institutions and refused to acknowledge that they had legitimate legal systems in place.[41] Indeed, even the nomenclature 'pluralistic' in the sociological literature seldom includes these indigenous peoples within its parameters. Yet there are vibrant indigenous communities in certain countries of the region, notably Guyana, Dominica, Belize, Suriname, St Vincent and

---

37 Opa Orisha (Shango) of Trinidad and Tobago (Incorporation) Act 1999, Act No 27, s 3. On the introduction of this law, the Attorney-General, Hon Kamla Bissessar said: 'We felt it best to bring the legislation so that we can erase the discrimination that had been practised against the Orisa faith'. The Prime Minister of the day, Hon Basdeo Banday further explained that the children of Muslims, Hindus, the Orisas, 'were bastardized at birth, because such marriages were not recognised in an Eurocentric Christian society.' *Trinidad and Tobago Hansard*, Tuesday 10 August 1999.

38 Chapter 3 ('Legal Traditions – Types of Legal Systems in the Commonwealth Caribbean').

39 Chapter 3 ('Legal Traditions – Types of Legal Systems in the Commonwealth Caribbean'). See also Chapter 10 ('Custom as a Source of Law') and Chapter 7 ('The Written Constitution as a Legal Source').

40 See, eg, Chapter 7 ('The Written Constitution as a Legal Source').

41 See Chapter 5 ('The Reception or Imposition of English Law and its Significance to Caribbean Jurisdictions').

Trinidad and Tobago. In fact, the only known 'Carib Queen' of the hemisphere resides in the borough of Arima, itself an Amerindian name, in Trinidad and Tobago.

Today, the law acknowledges the existence of indigenous peoples primarily to regulate their habitat on reservations in Guyana, Belize and Dominica.[42] There is a limited concept of self-rule. For example, s 3 of the Amerindian Act of Guyana makes provision for the establishment of Amerindian districts or villages, and s 5 restricts the entry of non-Amerindians to these areas.[43] Yet we may well argue that such laws can perhaps more accurately be described as institutional neglect. Indeed, little is known of the indigenous peoples, even within West Indian society.[44] Intriguingly, as early as 1660, the Amerindians were on reservations in Dominica and St Vincent. These two islands were treated as Amerindian strongholds, reserved to the native populations by an Anglo-French treaty of 1660.[45] This unusual status confused the issue of the reception of English law in Dominica, as it was difficult to determine the relevant date of reception.[46] In 1668, the Amerindians of St Vincent entered into a treaty under which they agreed to be subjects of the British Crown.[47]

This legal myopia may be corrected in the future, given the attention being paid to the rights and customs of indigenous peoples in international law.[48] In May 1998, the Amerindian peoples of the region, in particular, Dominica and Guyana, signed a treaty in Barbados, the Ishirouganaim (Barbados) Treaty 1998.[49] This treaty was drafted with a view to future self-governance. This gives an indication that the original peoples, like their counterparts outside of the region, are no longer prepared to accept an almost invisible status under the law. It reads in part:

> Affirming: that Amerindian peoples are the true landlords of the Western hemisphere and are equal in dignity and rights to all other peoples . . . Concerned: that as Amerindian peoples we have been deprived of our human rights and fundamental freedoms, resulting *inter alia* in our colonisation and dispossession of our lands, territories and resources which have prevented us from establishing our right to development . . . We the descendants of the Amerindian tribal nations first encountered in the Caribbean by Cristofero Colombo in 1492, in our capacities as present day leaders of our peoples, do solemnly declare our determination to achieve a sovereign Amerindian State by 1 January 2005 . . . in our ancestral homeland Ishirouganaim (Barbados).[50]

---

42 Under such laws as the Amerindian Lands Commission Act 1966 and the Amerindian Act 1953, chapter 58, as amended 1976, of Guyana, and the Carib Reserve Act 1978 of Dominica.

43 See *D'Aguair v Cox* (1971) 18 WIR 44. The law was challenged as being *ultra vires* the Constitutional protection of freedom of movement, but was saved because it was existing law, being part of the law of Guyana, in force immediately before the 1966 Constitution, since it was enacted in 1952. See Chapter 10 ('Custom as a Source of Law').

44 The West Indian Commission gives the following approximate statistics on the population of the Amerindians in the Commonwealth Caribbean: Belize 26,000; Dominica 3,000; Guyana 41,000; St Vincent and the Grenadines 6,000; and Trinidad and Tobago 400. *An Overview of the Report of the West Indian Commission* в *Time For Action*, 1992, Barbados: West Indian Commission Secretariat, p 128.

45 Burns, A, *History of the West Indies*, 1954, London: Allen & Unwin.

46 See Chapter 5 ('The Reception of English law and its Significance to Caribbean Jurisdictions').

47 *Above*, Burns, fn 45, p 222; Cal SP (Col) 1717 and 1901.

48 Discussed below, Chapter 10 ('Custom as a Source of Law').

49 The treaty is signed by the leaders of the Dominican and Guyanese tribes. I am indebted to Damon G Corrie, fifth hereditary Chief of the Eagle Clan Lokono-Arawak and Speaker of the Grand Council of Village Chiefs of the Pan Tribal Confederacy of the Amerindian Tribal Nation, for promptly making available to me a copy of the treaty.

50 This has not, however, been realised.

The rights of indigenous peoples are now being more fully recognised in international and regional spheres. One important mechanism in this endeavour is by acknowledging and incorporating indigenous historical customs and practices formally into the legal system. We discuss this phenomenon in more depth in Chapter 10 ('Custom as a Source of Law').

NEW AVENUES FOR LEGAL SYSTEMS – THE OFFSHORE LEGAL SUBCULTURE

Recently, new developments have impacted upon the legal systems of several countries in the region. This is the creation of offshore financial centres as a path to development. The offshore financial centre is now an established phenomenon in financial circles internationally. These centres have necessitated changes in the legal infrastructure and outlook of the relevant jurisdictions to cater for the foreign investors whom they serve. This new socio-economic and legal phenomenon can be appropriately described as a legal subculture and creates a level of duality in the legal system. On the one hand, the legal system continues to serve domestic investors with traditional laws. On the other, it has created new, innovative and dynamic laws and legal policy to serve exclusively non-national investors who come mainly from major industrialised countries.[51]

The existence of these offshore laws and innovative financial legal 'products' has propelled its own unique jurisprudence. It is an interesting mix of various legal disciplines such as banking law, the law of trusts, fiscal law, company law and Constitutional law. Also, it incorporates a significant hybrid element due to the originality of several key offshore legal concepts. More important, this offshore law is threatening to significantly impact on the jurisprudence of more orthodox 'onshore' legal concepts. For example, offshore legislatures have changed the traditional rules relating to the trust, such as abolishing the rule on perpetuities or by allowing purpose trusts which defy the common law rule that a trust must have an identifiable beneficiary.[52] Similarly, they have institutionalised new insurance concepts such as captive insurance, created new legislative rules on fraudulent conveyances to more adequately protect assets from creditors and against the enforcement of foreign judgments.[53]

Another important innovation is the extent to which financial confidentiality and privacy are protected under these offshore regimes. They have gone far beyond the common law notions of financial confidentiality as enshrined in the case of *Tournier v National Provincial Bank*[54] and created strict statute-based duties toward financial

---

51   Examples are financial confidentiality and trust legislation. See the Confidential Relationships (Preservation) Law, of the Cayman Islands, amended 1993 and the Trusts Act 1992, amended 2000 of Belize, respectively. See also the discussion on the offshore financial legal framework's impact on equity, in Chapter 9 ('Equity as a Source of Law'). See, for more in-depth discussion: Rose-Marie Antoine, *Confidentiality in Offshore Financial Law*, 2002: Oxford University Press.

52   See, eg, the Trust Act 1992, amended 2000, s 6, of Belize and the International (Exempt) Trusts Act 1997, s 6, of Dominica. See, also, Chapter 9 ('Equity as a Source of Law'). See too, Rose-Marie Antoine *Trusts and Tax Related Issues in Offshore Financial Law*, 2005: Oxford University Press.

53   The latter seeks to ensure that if a creditor or other claimant in the offshore country obtains a judgment attempting to reach assets in the offshore country, it will not be enforced.

54   [1924] 1 KB 461.

confidentiality. In some instances, these are backed by criminal sanctions. This is all toward encouraging offshore investors and catering to the demands of such investors.[55]

The extent to which these new legal concepts and the consequent jurisprudence are acceptable to the international community is controversial. It has already produced its own tensions and legal conflict, particularly where offshore investors take advantage of favourable offshore tax laws to the detriment of revenue authorities in onshore countries. Yet, despite the taking of countermeasures by onshore countries, the offshore industry in the Commonwealth Caribbean is steadily growing, both in number and innovation. More importantly, for our purposes, these dynamic offshore financial legal systems have made significant contributions to the body of the common law. In some cases, onshore legal systems have opted to emulate these new legal concepts. This has occurred, for example, in Atlanta, Delaware and Colorado in the United States.[56]

THE DEPENDENT TERRITORIES

The law and legal systems of the Commonwealth Caribbean dependent territories must be considered separately from those of the independent territories. While these territories share a colonial heritage and social and economic circumstances with independent Commonwealth Caribbean countries, their law and legal systems do not have an identity of their own, except in a limited sense. It may be thought that the dependent territories are of no interest in this study as they have, in theory, no independent or distinct law and legal system, but this is a false notion. A complex political and legal relationship exists between Britain and its remaining Caribbean territories.

As colonies, these territories are under the sovereignty of the British Crown. Consequently, the UK (Westminster) Parliament retains the right to legislate for them. This concept of sovereignty was described in *Tito v Waddell (No 2)*[57] as 'in the sense of government, power, ownership and belonging'. There is, however, a convention which prescribes that the UK Parliament should not legislate for the colonies without their consent.

The application of Acts of the Westminster Parliament to the colonies is limited by two constraints. First, the statute must expressly state that it is to apply to the colony or colonies, or show necessary intention. Secondly, the application of British imperial legislation is limited by the local circumstances rule[58] to the effect that it can only apply if it is appropriate to the conditions of the colony. Where Westminster legislation applies, it overrides any local statute with which it conflicts.

---

55   See, eg the Cayman Islands Act, *op cit*, fn 51.

56   These States offer financial incentives in trusts and banking in similar fashion to offshore financial centres. See, eg, The Qualified Disposition in Trusts Act 1996 of Delaware, the Banking Law of Colorado, Title 11 (Rev), the Spendthrift Trust Act 1999 of Nevada and the Alaskan Trust Act of 1997.

57   [1977] Ch 106.

58   Discussed further in Chapter 5 ('The Reception or Imposition of English Law and Its Significance To Caribbean Jurisdictions'), Chapter 14 ('The Rules Of Statutory Interpretation') and Chapter 8 ('The Common Law and the Doctrine of Judicial Precedent').

This complex scenario on the effect of legislation in the imperial context was explained by the Privy Council in the case of *Al Sabah v Grupo Torras et al.*[59] On a question as to whether UK Bankruptcy law applied in the Cayman Islands, Lord Walker said:

> The enactment of the Colonial Laws Validity Act 1865 ('an Act to remove doubts as to the validity of colonial laws') reaffirmed the superior power of the Westminster Parliament but made clear that colonial laws could depart from any non-statutory rules of common law or equity. The 1865 Act did not in terms refer to the enactment of laws with extraterritorial effect. But most colonial legislatures' had powers . . . to make laws 'for the peace, order and good government' of the territory in question and this implied (but did not clearly define) some territorial restrictions.[60]

His Lordship continued:

> But the Westminster Parliament's supreme legislative competence has in practice been more and more constrained by two factors. One has been an increasingly strong Constitutional convention . . . not to interfere, unasked, in the laws of Commonwealth countries which enjoyed representative government. The other has been the courts' long standing practice, in construing statutes of the Westminster Parliament, of presuming that their intended territorial extent is limited to the United Kingdom, unless it is clear that a wider extent is intended.[61]

In the Cayman Islands, the position is further complicated by the fact that the Cayman Islands was formerly a dependency of Jamaica.[62]

This dependent legal relationship can sometimes create a dilemma in the legal and social consciousness of the citizens who live there. While they may wish to retain their status as British territories, they also want their laws to be more representative of their own social mores, as is the case with the independent countries. As a result, they may resist what they perceive to be legal initiatives by the British which are insensitive to their concerns.

This dilemma was brought to the fore in a rather colourful incident. In late 1997 and early 1998, cruise ships containing tourists who were also homosexuals attempted to land in the Cayman Islands, Bermuda and the British Virgin Islands. Public protests were made against the landing and they were refused entry in the Cayman Islands.[63] The gay tourists complained to the British Government that they had been discriminated against. Approximately two weeks after, the British Government instructed the British Caribbean territories that they would have to remove from their statute books laws outlawing homosexuality. This sparked a great outcry from the dependent territories, where there were 'strong cultural and religious forces . . . opposed to removing any ban on homosexuality'.[64]

On the part of Britain, this is more than a moral issue. The British government has stated its intention to enforce its obligations under the International Covenant on Civil and Political Rights. To allow discriminatory laws on the statute books of British

---

59   [2005] 2 WLR 904 (CI).
60   *Ibid*, at para 12.
61   *Ibid*, at para 13.
62   *Ibid*.
63   Editorial, 'Cruise ships under attack from activists' (1998) *The Barbados Advocate*, 17 April, p 15.
64   Caribbean News Agency Report (CANA) (printed copy), 'Britain wants colonies to remove gay sex laws', 26 January 1998, Bridgetown, Barbados.

territories would be breaching those international obligations. The incident thus demonstrates the complexities involved in the legal relationship.

There has also been opposition in the dependent territories to the abolition of the death penalty, long since effected in the UK. In addition, there has been some deviation from orthodox British law both in case law and statute. Once again, the phenomenon of offshore financial centres provides interesting exceptions to the rule on legal uniformity between Britain and her territories, giving rise to perhaps the most substantial deviations in the law and legal systems. With the exception of Montserrat, British Caribbean territories are well-developed offshore financial industries. In fact, the Cayman Islands and the British Virgin Islands are two of the most established and successful offshore financial centres in the world. These dependent territories have been allowed to design and implement laws for their respective offshore regime which differ radically from, and even conflict with, those of the 'mother country', as explained above. One explanation for this legal freedom could be the tremendous financial benefits which accrue to offshore financial centres as a result of this industry.

However, deviation from orthodox English common law is not limited to decisions on the offshore sector. There have been some surprisingly radical decisions from the courts of these dependent territories, most notably from the Cayman Islands and one can discern a desire to define their legal destiny in more distinctly West Indian terms.[65]

REDEFINING LEGAL SYSTEMS

Commonwealth Caribbean law and legal systems are, as we have illustrated, diverse and complex entities, plagued with problems of both a psychological and structural nature. Yet, this is an exciting and appropriate time to be discussing Commonwealth Caribbean legal systems. We stand at the very crossroads of a Caribbean revolution in legal development. At this juncture, as we attempt to define our place in the world, we have several important choices to make, and our future will be determined by the wisdom of those choices. It is an opportune time to create an independent legal philosophy, whilst at the same time, steaming ahead to forge a unified Caribbean identity.

Caribbean legal systems can be said to be at boiling point. Perhaps there has been no other time in our history when every Caribbean man and woman has been aware of, and has had a stake in, the direction in which our laws and legal policies are going. Whether we are speaking about the retention of the death penalty, or the abolition of appeals to the English Privy Council, or the Caribbean Single Market and Economy (CSME), or changes in our offshore financial systems brought about by blacklisting attempts by the world community (which impacts directly on employment opportunities) the Caribbean citizen can relate intimately with and participate directly in these developments and debates. Thus, the Commonwealth Caribbean stands poised at the crossroads of possibility, waiting to exhale.

---

65   See, eg, *National Trust for Cayman Islands v Planning Appeals Tribunal Central Planning Authority and Humphreys (Cayman) Ltd, above*, fn 6, on the question of contingency fees.

Funding justice

Finally, we should note that issues of law reform and legal development, whether we are speaking about jurisprudence, or justice generally, cannot come to fruition without adequate physical infrastructure. For example, our courts need to be adequately funded and supported. This is as true for criminal trials as it is for civil trials and for juvenile justice. As discussed in Chapter 18, often juveniles spend nights in jail with hardened adult criminals because of a lack of special facilities in which to house them. Judicial decisions discussed further in the book,[66] declaring that undue delay on Death Row is unconstitutional, are also significantly fuelled by the lack of resources. Such decisions highlight the need to make the administration of justice more efficient and speedy.

Funding is just as important for finding the legal principles which inform the courts. This necessitates, for example, adequate and efficient law reporting. All of these things are lacking in the region because of our fragile and needy economies, economies further vulnerable to the forces of nature and to international market forces. If Commonwealth Caribbean law and legal systems are to realise their true potential, these difficulties must be overcome.

---

66 See, eg, Chapter 7 ('The Written Constitution as a Legal Source'), Chapter 12 ('International Law as a Source of Law') and Chapter 8 ('The Common Law and the Doctrine of Judicial Precedent').

CHAPTER 2

THE HISTORICAL FUNCTION OF LAW IN THE WEST INDIES – CREATING A FUTURE FROM A TROUBLED PAST

INTRODUCTION – THE GROUNDINGS OF HISTORY

There is a cruel irony in our study of law in the region. West Indian students of law are taught about Aquinas and law, and morality theories about the function of law in society, but mention is hardly ever made of the important immoral function the law played in much of the history of the Commonwealth Caribbean. This is its role in the infamous slave systems of the region. Indeed, traditionally legal analysts and jurists have not paid much attention to the historical functions of our law. Yet such a perspective is essential to a full appreciation of the values and norm-building precepts that underline law and legal systems in the Commonwealth Caribbean. While the established theories on the role and functions of law in society are important, the historical function of law in our legal system is just as significant. The role and functions of law in West Indian society have deeper dimensions which arise out of this historical connection.

Just as the study of the English common law must examine the historical evolution of that law, so too must the study of West Indian law appreciate the genesis of our own law grounded in slavery and colonialism. The legal thought processes and institutions will only have meaning when this historical perspective is understood. A discussion on the role and functions of law in West Indian society should, therefore, begin with an appraisal of the role and functions of the law and legal system in instituting and upholding the systems of slavery and colonialism which existed previously throughout the region.

The brutality of treatment meted out to black slaves and sanctioned by the law in the West Indies is well known. What is less known is the way in which the judicial system actually worked and the functions it served within that context.

The initiation of law into Caribbean society was within a colonial, imperialist and inequitable framework, as a tool to legitimise the exploitative nature of plantation society. The needs of the colonial settlers did not necessitate law for the organisation of a civilised and humane society and these were only added piecemeal at later convenient dates. Historically, therefore, Caribbean law has been imperialistic, foreign, elitist and oppressive in outlook. It was imperative that the black masses be kept in subordination, without rights and social mobility, in order to sustain the plantation and its metropolitan base.[1] The law continued to struggle to distance itself from this defining characteristic.[2]

Law was thus an instrument of social control and public order in plantation society. 'The slave laws were the most ubiquitous form of public control . . . Their primary function was to maintain the slave system by guaranteeing the economic, social and

---

1 Beckford says this about plantation society: 'The survival of the plantation is ensured if capital is in constant supply, land monopolised, the labour force in over supply, and its control standardised.' Beckford, G, *The Caribbean Economy*, 1975, London: Penguin, p 54.
2 See Chapter 5 ('The Reception or Imposition of Law and its Significance to Caribbean Jurisdictions').

racial subordination of the Negroes'.[3] The slave codes in force during the eighteenth century were the result of a long process of careful elaboration. They created an intricate and wide-ranging combination of legal restraints which served relatively simple and narrow ends, for their 'essential objective was the preservation of the public order which was to be secured by denying the slaves the means of escaping from their degraded status as the property of others – and by protecting the whites in their pre-eminent status as a ruling class'.[4]

Trading in slaves was a recognised and legal activity. Slaves were property. The law provided for their sale and purchase like any other chattel.[5] They could even be inherited and willed. If the slave-owner owed debts, they could be used as security or could be levied upon. They could be mortgaged and rented out, all facilitated by the law.[6] Yet, as a piece of property, rather than a person, the slave was incapable of legally possessing property or of legally making contracts.[7] On the basic idea of the slave as property a whole system of laws was built up. Indeed, as discussed below, it has been argued that the slave was the premise for the very creation of 'modern law'.[8]

Yet, slaves, being human beings with intelligent minds, independent will and depth of feeling, were not property in a real sense. Consequently, they rebelled both in spirit and in action. It is precisely because human beings are not chattels that the slave laws had to construct an elaborate and artificial legal machinery of oppression to force the slaves into submission.

As we discuss below, the notion of law in this artificially constructed West Indian slave society was devoid of its humanistic and rational expressions consonant with the functions of law common in more 'normal' societies concerned with justice.

Slavery thus created a duality in law and legal institutions. There was one set of laws and legal institutions for the master and another for the slave. There were even separate courts for the slave, such as that of the fiscal in Guyana, who was a magistrate. These magistrates had jurisdiction to punish offences in a summary way, as the law did not allow slaves to be tried by a jury.[9] They were also not allowed to give evidence against whites in the courts of justice.[10] Similarly, the penalties reserved for slaves were much harsher than those for whites.

Watson recounts some of these inequities in the penal system.[11] Under legislation specifically designed to control slaves, An Act for the Governing of Negroes 1688,[12]

---

3   Goveia, E, *Slave Society in the British Leeward Islands*, 1969, New Haven: Yale UP, pp 311–15.

4   *Ibid*.

5   Laws of Jamaica, St Jago de law Vaga, 1792, Vol 11 23 Geo 111 C 14, in Goveia, *ibid*.

6   See Haynes, J, 'Slavery and the Law', in *Proceedings of the International Anniversary of the Abolition of Slavery in the Anglophone Caribbean*, 1984, Georgetown: Guyana Printers, p 78, and *ibid*, Goveia, fn 3, p 312.

7   See, also Reeves, J, 'Slaves considered as property', House of Commons Accounts and Papers, Vol 1 XXV1 (1789) No 646 Part III.

8   See Patricia Tuitt *Race, Law, Resistance*, 2004, Australia: Glass House Press, Chapter 1.

9   Regulations for the Treatment of Servants and Slaves, Arts 6 and 7, made by the Ten on 1 October 1784, British Guiana, Directory, 1825, p 208.

10   See Long, E. *History of Jamaica*, 3 vols, 1774, London: Lowndes, pp 320–36, repr in *Slaves, Free Men, Citizens, West Indian Perspectives*, 1973, USA: Anchor. Even freed slaves during the slavery period could not be tried by jury. Like slaves, they were 'not supposed to have acquired any sense of morality'.

11   Karl Watson 'Capital Sentences Against Slaves in Barbados in the Eighteenth Century: An Analysis' in Alvin O Thompson (ed) *In the Shadow of the Plantation – Caribbean History and Legacy*, 2002, Jamaica: Ian Randle Publishers.

12   Richard Hall, Acts Passed in the Island of Barbados from 1643–1764, London: Inclusive.

Clause XII, 'any criminal act which caused damages in excess of 12 pence' would result in arrest and arraignment before a justice of the peace who would hold enquiry and pass sentence. The law declared that the slaves, being 'brutish', did not merit 'for the baseness of their condition' being tried by a jury of their peers. If the slave was found guilty, the death sentence was to be pronounced and executed.[13]

The death penalty was therefore effected for minor offences without benefit of a jury. Intriguingly, when a slave was executed, the owner of the slave was compensated by law in the form of damages for the loss,[14] such sum not to exceed £25.

In 1739, an amendment was passed to the 1688 Act making provision for owners to appeal the mandatory death sentence, which some believed 'in some instances hath been brought erroneous and many times by the malice or ill-will of the Prosecutor'.[15] Henceforth, mechanisms were put in place to avoid the death penalty, particularly for lesser offences. For example, the parties concerned (in this case the owner of the slave being a party) could attempt to reach an Agreement 'requisite and equitable, for saving the life of such slave or slaves'.[16] Failing such an Agreement, the case could be remitted to the Governor, who had a discretion to reverse or confirm the judgment.

However, many slaves during the period were executed for entirely minor offences, such as for 'stealing a turkey cock valued at 3s. 9d'[17] or for 'stealing bread and provisions worth £1.17s. 6d'.[18] Not surprisingly, offences by slaves against whites were visited by the most draconian punishment and horrific methods of execution, so as to serve as a 'dread and terror to the survivors that they may be deterr'd from perpetuating the like crime for the future.'[19] In such cases, the court did not accept evidence by slaves.[20]

In contrast to this harsh treatment to slaves facing the administration of justice for offences, there were little or no penalties for offences, even murder, committed against slaves by whites. In 1802, an attempt was made to introduce a law making the killing of a slave a felony, but this was defeated in the House of Assembly.[21]

It is suggested that capital punishment was used as a method to eradicate, not crime, in the strict sense, but resistance to the slave system. Such resistance took not only the obvious form of outright rebellion, but more subtle forms of resistance. Watson asks: 'At what point does an act perceived as criminal by the whites become an act of sabotage and resistance by the enslaved black group?'[22] Indeed, even mere 'insolence' was punishable by law.

Nonetheless, capital punishment for minor offences decreased during the period,

---

13 Watson, *above*, fn 11, p 198.
14 See Clause XV.
15 Watson, *above*, fn 11, p 199.
16 *Ibid.*
17 The Trial of George Dickes, *ibid.*
18 *Ibid*. Taken from Barbados Council Minutes.
19 Pinfold MSS, Library of Congress, Instructions of Governor Pinfold, 10 March 1763, Watson, *above*, fn 11, p 201.
20 See e.g., the Trial of Peter Archer, *Barbados Mercury and Bridgetown Gazette*, 26 December 1772, Watson, *ibid*, pp 53–58, where the court prosecutor said: '. . . a slave cannot give Testimony, although he should see a Murder perpetuated.' He proceeded to lament the injustices and irrationality of such a practice in the legal system, which he described as '. . . a shutting [sic] of the Door against Justice and a Toleration for all crimes whatever.' *Ibid*, Watson, p 203.
21 Watson, *ibid*, p 212.
22 *Ibid*, p 216.

not only because it came to be seen as inhumane, but also because it was an expensive and wasteful way of dispensing justice, especially in places such as Barbados, where slave 'property' was high in financial value.

Obeah Acts and Vagrancy Acts – laws to sustain inequity and dependence

Laws such as the Obeah Acts smacked of the attempts of those in power to further the acculturation process, ridding the black majority of their social identity and dignity.[23] Laws such as these, as well as Vagrancy Acts, considered below, served to ingrain the inequity of the African persona into the social psyche, exacerbating patterns of inferiority and dependency. In the *Fiscal v Willem*,[24] for example, a slave was convicted for an offence based on the *minje mama*, or water mother dance, an Obeah practice.

After the collapse of the slave system (mainly due to the fact that slavery and sugar plantations were no longer profitable),[25] slavery was abolished by the Emancipation Acts of 1833. Yet the law and legal systems continued to reflect the unequal structure of the ex-slave, colonial society. In fact, they were used deliberately to reinforce this structure.[26] Laws such as the Tenancy Acts and Vagrancy Acts, imported from England, served a clandestine function in the West Indies. They helped to force 'idle', jobless ex-slaves, devoid of land, money or opportunity, back on the plantations. They were intended to discourage small landholdings and force labour to remain on the oversupplied market. Under the Vagrancy Acts, for example, innocuous activities such as loitering were criminalised.

One writer has attempted to refute the widely accepted rationale for Vagrancy Acts in the West Indies.[27] He argues essentially that vagrancy laws in the Caribbean were mere replicas of English law, both in content and focus saying:

> The English experience and that of Barbados . . . also gives the lie to suggestions, by some legislators and historians, that vagrancy legislation in the latter country was uniquely conceived by the planter class to repress further newly emancipated slaves . . . They become particularly dangerous if treated as unequivocal fact.[28]

Indeed, it is 'dangerous' to treat assertions as fact unless historically valid. Thus, to prevent an accusation of participating in the 'use and misuse of history [which] was

---

23 Obeah is an African religious practice associated with magic. There were several attempts to outlaw it throughout the period.

24 'The Trial of Slave Willem in Berbice for Obeah and Murder of the Negress Madalon', printed by order of the House of Commons, 14 May 1823. Cited in Shahabuddeen, M, *The Legal System of Guyana*, 1973, Georgetown, Guyana: Guyana Printers.

25 See William, E, *Capitalism and Slavery*, 1964, London: Andrè Deutsch, who proved the thesis, now accepted, that the real reason for the emancipation of the slaves lay not so much in humanitarianism but in the fact that the slave sugar plantation system was no longer economically viable.

26 After emancipation, the British Government appointed special justices of the peace with exclusive jurisdiction over the newly freed slaves and ex-masters. Macmillan, W, *The Road to Self-Rule*, 1959, London: Faber and Faber, p 81. See also Bridget Brereton, *Law Justice and Empire – The Colonial Career of John Gorrie 1829–1892*, 1997, Jamaica: UWI Press.

27 Hall, CG, 'A legislative history of vagrancy in England and Barbados', in *Contemporary Caribbean Legal Issues*, No 2, 1997, Cave Hill, Barbados: UWI.

28 *Ibid.*

of course one of the primary engines for mounting this constant assault on the minds of colonial peoples',[29] it is necessary to set the record straight.

Hall's conclusion may well be inconsistent with the historical data. It appears that the weight of the historical evidence as well as a proper appreciation of law in context is against this new argument, however intriguing.[30] It is no doubt true that the Vagrancy Acts were not indigenous. Indeed, historians have never contended that such Acts were 'uniquely conceived', at least in their form.

Yet, in the same way that it is dangerous to isolate the emancipation laws from the relevant context of the time, which was the non-profitability of slavery, so it is short-sighted, and perhaps naïve, to treat vagrancy laws and other such West Indian legislation, as divorced from their historical social context. This was, in fact, the mistake made by centuries of English history taught in West Indian schools. Eric Williams successfully debunked such myths.[31] West Indian vagrancy laws may have been similar in content and form to English vagrancy laws but their focus and objectives were exceedingly different.

The notion of poverty when applied to the Vagrancy Acts assumes a certain benevolence toward the ex-slave which was simply non-existent.[32] Indeed, just as the Vagrancy Acts were 'borrowed' from England, so were the slave laws borrowed from the *Siete Partidas* of Spain and the *Code Noir* of France. Yet they assumed an entirely different character in West Indian society. It is no longer disputed that black slavery was far more heinous than white slavery. For example, under the *Siete Partidas*, the slave was treated as persona, not property, and the master had duties toward the slaves as well as rights over them.[33]

The fact that vagrancy laws were transported and borrowed from the UK does not mean that they were not imbued with their own social connotations, context and purpose. Class distinctions in the UK and the West Indies may have been similar in some aspects, but was class related to race and was law used continually in the UK, as it was in the West Indies, to subjugate sociological, cultural and legal identity and the very sense of dignity, personhood and statehood? In effect, the black masses were only accorded full citizenship status, the franchise, in the 1950s, since before, only the landed gentry, invariably white or 'light brown', owned property or otherwise met the strict qualifications imposed. What more chilling argument on the law's subversive role is needed?

Hall also fails to consider the well-documented fears and resistance of the planters as emancipation approached and the loss of their labour supply grew near. In fact, the very apprenticeship period – the initial post-slavery period that allowed the plantocracy to keep the ex-slaves on the plantation for a nominal fee – was a compromise to placate the planters. The ex-slaves were not mere 'vagabonds', or 'idle poor'. They

---

29   Shahabuddeen, M, 'Slavery and historiographical rectification', opening address delivered at the International Round Table to mark the 150th anniversary of the abolition of slavery in the English-speaking West Indies, 1984, Georgetown: Guyana Commemoration Commission, p 13.

30   He relies mostly on English historical data on the Vagrancy Acts and a passing reference to one West Indian historian.

31   *Op cit*, Williams, fn 25.

32   Hall maintains that they were 'simplistic legislative answers to perceived, contemporary, social mischiefs in the context of poverty', *op cit*, Hall, fn 27, p 22.

33   *Op cit*, Goveia, fn 3.

were valuable labourers who had kept the islands commercially viable for centuries and provided the impetus for Britain's industrial wealth. As Williams so eloquently states:

> These [Caribbean] islands were the glittering gems in every imperial diadem, and Barbados, Jamaica, Saint Domingue (today Haiti) ... were ... magic names which meant national prosperity ... Sugar was King; without his Negro slave his kingdom would have been a desert ... As Churchill declared – 'Our possession of the West Indies ... enabled us to lay the foundations of that commercial and financial leadership which, when the world was young ... enabled us to make our great position in the world'.[34]

While we may agree that the Vagrancy Acts and other similar legislation were instruments of social control, as they were in the UK, it is inaccurate to equate them with similar or even identical legislation in respect to their other functions. Even a vagrant in West Indian society today cannot be equated with the 'vagrants' of that period. Such legislation served a dual purpose. The question of 'social control' was not a simplistic one in the West Indies at this time. Translated, it meant maintaining the pre-emancipation status quo as far as possible. This included other legislative schemes and legal policies and went beyond mere Vagrancy Acts. Curtain recounts the elaborate schemes of the plantocracy to keep the freedman tied to the plantation:

> ... there was also a demand following emancipation for a 'rural code' that would force the Negroes to work for wages. Here the Assembly had to be careful ... the Colonial Office was on guard against any direct attempt to re-establish slavery in any other guise. Various coercive or anti-settler laws were passed, but they were hidden as much as possible in innocent-looking enactments. The Police Act, for example, provided ... for the arrest of any person found carrying agricultural produce without a note of permission ... This provision was ostensibly designed to prevent 'praedial larceny' ... but it could be used equally well to prevent the illiterate small settler ... from marketing his produce ... Other 'class legislation' was discovered and disallowed by the home government. In this group were the Vagrancy Acts of 1834 and 1839, which were rejected because they extended unduly the legal definition of the offence.[35]

To cement the argument on the true function of these Vagrancy Acts, it is instructive to note that attempts to introduce vagrancy laws were rejected in Guyana by the British Government because they 'showed that the old slave codes exercised a very powerful influence on their structure and character'.[36]

Other attempts to suppress the newly found independence of the black population for the benefit of the elite plantocracy included an intricate 'labour-for-rent' scheme where the freedmen forcefully became tenants at will under such statutes as the Masters and Servants Act 1840.[37] Such involuntary tenants were charged excessively high rents, forcing them to work to pay the high bills, or being charged high rents only if they refused to work on the plantation. The ex-slave was allotted a house

---

34 Williams, E, 'Slavery and the plantation system', in *The Negro in the Caribbean*, 1944, Manchester: Panaf Service, p 12.

35 Welch, A, 'Special magistrate's report', Manchester, 29 June 1836, PP, 1837, iii (521–1), 33 in Curtain, P, *Two Jamaicas*, 1955, Cambridge, Mass: Harvard UP, p 130. The control of burial grounds was also used as a bargaining chip for labour.

36 *Op cit*, Shahabuddeen, fn 29, p 74. See, e.g., Ordinance No 16 of 1838. It is not true to suggest that these Acts were imported lock, stock and barrel.

37 See Marshall, T, 'Post-emancipation adjustments in Barbados, 1838–76', in *Emancipation 1 – A Series of Lectures*, 1984, Barbados: UWI, p 91.

and land for which he paid a stipulated rent. However, he had, 'as a condition of renting, to give the estate a certain number of days' labour at certain stipulated wages . . . the labourer, fettered by the system of tenancy at will, is compelled to work . . . He is, therefore, virtually a slave'.[38] Similarly, if the former slaves failed to work on the plantation, their houses could be pulled down and their provision grounds destroyed or they could be evicted.[39]

THE CONTINUATION OF LEGAL PARADIGMS BORN OUT OF SLAVERY

The legal and economic institution which was slavery also helped to institutionalise class and race segregation which today is the focus of those who argue for the divisive nature of West Indian 'plural societies'.[40] In a somewhat vicious cycle, such segregation perpetuated an enduring imbalance within the legal system.

The law continued to be unsupportive of the large black masses. This was mainly because it failed to adapt adequately to the needs of the newly liberated peoples who were landless, powerless, largely uneducated, culturally and psychologically emascu-lated and still tied to the plantation. The white minority remained the elite and the rulers of West Indian society and continued to view the black masses as plantation labour.

Early accounts of the legal system, and in particular, the administration of justice, reveal that the disadvantaged clearly perceived that justice was out of their reach and that legal personnel were unperturbed about the status quo, even after emancipation. Brereton, in recounting the misdeeds of one Chief Magistrate, Sir Joseph Needham, (1870–85) had this to say:

> Under his long regime of official neglect, complaints about the administration of justice proliferated. The main burden of these protests was that ordinary people felt they had no access to the higher courts, and that the magistrates' courts . . . routinely handed down unfair decisions. 'If we are to judge by appearances and practice', stated a . . . local paper in 1873, 'we have here two distinct laws and customs, one for the favoured few, and the other for the common herd.'[41]

This sentiment was echoed by a villager in 1888: 'When the laws of Trinidad comes in Trinidad we poor fellows don't get none of it, don't hear none at all. When we hear the laws of any case brought before the court we don't know how to speak for ourselves, because we don't hear no laws, for it is hidden from us.'[42] Such a view was expressed more poetically in a calypso[43] by Eagle as late as 1984: 'The rich ones control

---

38   Sewell, G, *The Ordeal of Free Labour*, 1862, repr 1968, London: Sampson Low, p 32.
39   Smith to Glenelg, 10 September 1838, PP, 1839, xxxv (107), *passim*; Lord Sligo, letter to the Marquess of Normandy relative to the present state of Jamaica, 1839, London, p 16, cited in *op cit*, Curtain, fn 35, pp 129–30.
40   See Smith, MG, *The Plural Society in the British West Indies*, 1965, Los Angeles: California UP.
41   Reported in Bridget Brereton, *Law, Justice and Empire – The Colonial Career of John Gorrie 1829–1892*; 1997, Jamaica: UWI Press, 229–30.
42   Tel 16/4/73: Letter from Diogenes: Royal Franchise Commission (Trinidad) 1888: Evidence of Henry Richardson, Fifth Company Village, 33 in Bridget Brereton, *ibid*, p 230.
43   A form of social commentary in song indigenous to the Caribbean, which originated in Trinidad and Tobago.

the law. The law controls the ones wha poor. So the law and the poor always in a war.'[44]

These historical dimensions of law continue to be reborn in the legal decision-making and institutions of the region. It has imbued West Indian society with deeply conditioned attitudes which often restrict the appropriate development of the law and legal systems. The process of colonisation has been 'like a huge tidal wave. It has covered our land, submerging the natural life of our people'.[45] Whether we are discussing precedent, custom, the Constitution, or the wider society at large, for which law must function, the underlying notions of dependency and inequity are still present in many areas.

The psychological impact and longevity of brutal slave societies also encourages what can be described as feelings of insecurity and even self-hate in our societies and legal systems today. Perhaps this is the reason why today, we still send our final appeals to the Privy Council located in England and so many Caribbean people doubt that we can adjudicate final appeals for ourselves in a just manner. Interestingly, this belief that we could not be trusted to do things right for ourselves was one of the reasons why, upon Independence, we ended up with written Constitutions with entrenchment provisions and saving law clauses, instead of continuing with the pure Westminster model of unwritten Constitutions.

The eminent Caribbean philosopher Franz Fanon describes this state of self-denigration and its causes: 'My body was given back to me sprawled out, distorted, recolored . . . The Negro is an animal, the Negro is bad . . .'[46]

Another relic of our historical architecture is that the law is accused of being alien. This is perhaps because it is identified with the elite and imperial oppression.

Our ex-slave society may thus be described as apathetic in its attitude to law, as a result of the enduring alienation that Caribbean peoples, the governed, feel with those who govern. There is a sense of disconnect, a feeling that we do not and cannot control our own destiny and that our voices are not heard. Although this may be changing in relation to models of government, it is being substituted for the growing feelings of helplessness that so-called Third World countries feel in relation to international economics and politics. In those paradigms, small developing countries have little voice and little control over their destinies. We see this, for example, in the negative way in which free trade law constructs have impacted upon our banana industries, our sugar industries and even our international financial services sector.

The self-styled 'interpreter' of Rastafari doctrine in 1963, speaking on Jamaica, but in a context which could easily apply to the entire region, wrote:

> Jamaica today is independent . . . yet English customs and laws and English instructions still leads us . . . how much voice do we have in saying what laws will pass . . . politics was not the black man's lot but the white man's plot.[47]

---

44 'Law and Poor, 1984' in Louis Regis, *The Political Calypso – True Opposition in Trinidad and Tobago 1962–1987*, 1999, USA: University Press of Florida.

45 Kapi, M (Sir), 'The underlying law in Papua New Guinea', Ninth Commonwealth Law Conference, 1990, New Zealand: Commerce Clearing House, p 129.

46 Franz Fanon *Black Skin, White Masks*, Lam Markmann C (trans), 1986, *London, Pluto*, p 119.

47 Bongo Dizzy, 'Voice of the interpreter', in Nettleford, R (ed), *Mirror, Mirror: Identity, Race and Protest in Jamaica*, 1970, Jamaica: Collins and Sangster, p 44.

Imperial law and the indigenous peoples

Law during slavery was used not only to subjugate the exported African peoples. It, coupled with brute force, also played a considerable part in subordinating the original peoples, the Amerindians, and other indigenous groups. To the extent that these indigenous peoples were deprived of their lands, cultures and way of life, they were subjugated. Nor did the indigenous peoples have the benefit of Emancipation Acts to facilitate the return of their liberties. Even today, the indigenous peoples in the region, as elsewhere in the world, remain marginalised, isolated and powerless. The laws concerning the indigenous peoples reflect this marginalisation.[48]

THE LAW'S RESPONSE TO HISTORY THROUGH SOCIAL ENGINEERING – FROM REFORM TO REPARATIONS

Because of the historical function of the law that we have illustrated, a contemporary role of law must be to attempt to correct the inequities that centuries of enduring the unjust system of slavery and exploitation wrought. Today, it is no longer fashionable to speak of slavery and exploitation. Instead, the appropriate jargon is 'Third World' problems, the 'new world order', poverty alleviation and sustainable development. Yet the underlying reality remains the same, the unfair disadvantage that ex-slave/colonial societies began with.

Nowhere is the unjust disadvantage wrought on West Indian societies more apparent than in the experience of Haiti. Haiti, the first black nation in the New World, fought for and won its freedom from the French colonialists under the famous general Toussaint L'Overture. However, this emancipation was premised on the condition that the peoples of Haiti had to repay millions of dollars in compensation to the French government for the loss of its 'property' in slaves. This, of course was a direct consequence of the unjust legal construct of the African person being considered a chattel, for which loss must be compensated. Many believe that this forced compensation in large measure accounts for Haiti's unenviable status as the poorest nation in the Western hemisphere.[49]

Just as the law played its role in subjugating Caribbean peoples, so must it assist in 'liberating' them and in developing what are still young, developing nations.[50] In view of this, this writer has argued elsewhere that the Caribbean man and judge have an active role to play in 're-interpreting the legal framework to build a more

---

48   But see new developments in relation to the rights of indigenous peoples, discussed below, Chapter 10 ('Custom as a Source of Law').

49   See Dionne J Miller 'Aristide's Call For Reparations From France Unlikely to Die', Inter Press Service News Agency, 12 March 2004. Former President of Haiti, President Aristide, actually demanded that France pay Haiti over 21 billion US dollars, equivalent to the more than 90 million gold francs Haiti was forced to pay France. 'Historians say that the massive toll that France exacted on Haiti played a large part in the Caribbean country's subsequent descent into start poverty and underdevelopment.' *Ibid*, p 2.

50   Independence was attained for most States during the 1960s and 1970s, making the countries in question exceedingly young nations.

indigenous and just' society.[51] The judge and legislator must perform the role of the 'social engineer':[52]

... the legal engineer should not isolate nor ignore the historical continuum evident in the neo-colonial framework in which we exist, but must actively seek to eradicate this negative phenomenon. Thus, the law must seek to decolonise society, not merely by a 'patchwork' method of attempting to fit inadequate law into a proper social context, but by a conscious propulsion of new law, and indeed, if warranted, new legal systems, to promote a more egalitarian social, economic and political system.[53]

It is in this context that the debate on reparations for the descendants of African slaves for the injustices suffered during slavery must be understood. Undoubtedly, the developed nations of today, in particular, the former colonial nations, built their wealth substantially on the slave societies of the Commonwealth Caribbean and other slave territories. In so doing, they not only raped these lands of financial benefits during slavery, but the unequal financial relationships endured, perpetrating continued and economic exploitation, thus depriving such countries of their true financial status. These essentially political and economic paradigms were facilitated by the law and it remains the law's task to locate mechanisms, such as reparations, in the language of legal compensation and restitution, which will force a fair balance.

Legitimising the concept of reparations

The notion of reparations is not new. It has always been accepted as a rule of customary law that compensation should ensue for a tort or wrong. Ironically, those from whom reparations are sought today, the plantation and slave owners, were paid compensation for their loss of property in the slave upon Emancipation. However, the concept of reparations as used in contemporary jurisprudence embodies not merely a tort or harm, but a wrong imbued with deep immorality and repugnance to basic decency. The concept as expressed in this form was crystallised in the Nuremberg trials as embodied in the Charter of the Nuremberg Tribunal which defined crimes against humanity.

The question of reparations for peoples of the African diaspora is a volatile one. Arguments raised to contest the right to reparations include the legality of the slave trade, the remoteness of the event, the difficulty of identifying those harmed and the huge financial costs involved were a claim to be successful.

In response, a proper understanding of the legitimacy of the law, a concept well understood in international law, reveals that the formal legality of slavery within the domestic sphere does not clothe slave laws with legitimacy. International law, for example, recognises the concepts of crimes against humanity and genocide, for which slavery qualifies. The moral value of law which gives it legitimacy is also lacking in relation to the slave laws.

While slavery indeed happened a long time ago,[54] the principle of remoteness

---

51 Antoine, R-M B, 'Law and the Caribbean Man – A Means of Progress. Social Engineering in a Caribbean Context' [1986] Stud LR 24.
52 The concept of social engineering is taken from Pound, R, *Contemporary Justice Theory*, 1940, London: Banton.
53 *Above*, Antoine, fn 51.
54 Slavery was abolished in the Commonwealth Caribbean in 1838.

does not easily defeat a claim. Some heinous crimes, such as murder, have no statute of limitations and remain crimes throughout time. Such is the nature of a crime against humanity such as slavery. Further, there have been other examples of crimes against humanity for which reparations were successfully sought, despite a long period of time between the crime and the claim. Examples include the genocide against the indigenous peoples, for which reparations in the form of land rights, however modest, were paid by the Canadian, US and Australian governments, and reparations for the Jewish Holocaust by Germany and also for the internment of Japanese Americans in the USA during World War II.[55] In these reparations, descendants of the victims were granted the compensation and a similar principle should be used for African reparations. Further, the query on remoteness is not altogether appropriate if we acknowledge that some of the offences instigated by slavery still endure, notably, racial prejudice.

However, the claim for reparations is also accompanied by a pragmatic acceptance of the complexity of identifying precisely the ancestors of the victims of the slave trade who can give evidence of wrongdoing.

Yet, the argument for reparations is grounded in the self-evident truth that all displaced peoples of African heritage in the Commonwealth Caribbean had ancestors who were victims of the slave trade. As such, it is African peoples as a group who should be compensated. Thus, the claim is more in the nature of a class action, on behalf of an identifiable group. The practical result is that the expectation of reparations is not for a defined amount for each victim, but for financial compensation to the African community as a whole. For example, this may take the form of funding for educational and other developmental projects to African communities or nations, such as those in the Commonwealth Caribbean.

As to the sums involved, no doubt they are huge, but treating reparations as a type of class action makes it manageable. In any event, as Lord Gifford, an early advocate of reparations, asserts: 'Once the right to reparations is seen to be soundly established in international law, then ways of doing justice can and will be found. Difficulties of scale or procedure should not be obstacles to justice.'[56]

Ultimately, reparations are not just about compensation in monetary terms or an attempt at restitution. It is also an opportunity to express the moral outrage of the world at this heinous crime which was perpetuated on an entire race of peoples.

Judicial concerns about social engineering

Whether the reform of the law is manifested in politics or property matters, it must be emancipated from its past. In short, the law must be repatriated. Yet, not everyone agrees that the law should engage in social engineering. In *In the Estate of B*,[57] Murphy, J, in holding that illegitimate children could not share in the estate of their natural

---

55 See, e.g., the Civil Liberties Act 1988, which made restitution to Japanese Americans for the losses caused by the discriminatory actions of the US Government in interning Japanese Americans during the wartime period. The Act specifically recognises the 'fundamental injustice of the evacuation, relocation and internment of US citizens and permanent resident aliens of Japanese ancestry during World War II' and makes 'restitution'.

56 Lord Anthony Gifford 'The Legal Basis of the Claim for Reparations', Paper presented to the First Pan-African Congress on Reparations, Abuja, Nigeria, 27–29 April 1993, p 10. See also below, p 32 for a discussion of 'Reparations and Morality.'

57 [1999] CILR 460 (Grand Court, Cayman Islands).

father's estate according to the 'clear and unambiguous language' of the succession law, had this to say:

> That result may not be fair. It may point to a lacuna in our law. It may not accord with the values and mores of our society in the 21st century. It may even be perceived by some to be contrary to modern morality. Those are not my direct concerns as a judge . . . My function is not that of a social engineer or to impose my own values by creative judicial interpretation. If there is to be reform in this area that is for the legislature, not for the judge.

Certainly, the social engineer's role cannot be strained beyond the reasonable competencies of a statute. But, the law as a social engineer also presupposes a dynamic and socially centred law reform process, involving the Legislature. As Murphy J hints, the social engineering process must involve the Legislature and indeed the entire society.

LOCATING THE CONTEMPORARY FUNCTIONS OF LAW – POSITIVISM, NATURAL LAW AND WEST-INDIAN IDENTITY

Whilst our history has contributed to certain deficiencies in our law and legal systems, this cannot be the only focus of the social engineer. There must be a broader purpose. As with any society, we must be concerned with shaping our law to create a more just society. To the extent that our colonial 'shackles' obstruct this broader objective, they must be broken, whether they be rigid forms, such as precedent, or inappropriate content. Yet the law's purpose must go beyond this narrow objective. This leads us to a more philosophical discussion of the role and functions of law in society. Many distinguished legal philosophers have explored the question of the functions of law in society. However, one stock answer cannot be identified. It depends partly on the view taken of the nature of law.

Legal theorists can thus be divided into two schools of thought, those who adhere to positivism and others who subscribe to the natural law theory. The positivists, like Hart and Austin, merely attempt to define what law is, not what it should be, or its content. The natural law theorists, on the other hand, believe that rules or principles can only legitimately be called law if they conform to an acceptable code of moral behaviour. The proponents of the natural law school of thought include St. Thomas Aquinas[58] and Fuller.[59]

The Grenada revolution and Austin's sovereign

Law might simply be considered as a set of rules within the society. However, this description does not tell us much about the authoritative and coercive nature of a legal rule. John Austin responds by saying that law is different from other rules because it is a 'command' from the legitimate 'sovereign'.[60] This command is backed by sanctions. For the purposes of this theory, we must be able to identify the 'sovereign'.

---

58   Aquinas, T (St), *Summa Theologica*, 1942, London: Burns, Oates and Washbourne.
59   Fuller, R, *The Morality of Law*, 1969, London: Yale UP.
60   Austin, J, *The Province of Jurisprudence Determined*, 1954, London: Weidenfeld and Nicolson.

This thesis was tested in the Commonwealth Caribbean in the case of *Mitchell v DPP*.[61] Here, the courts had to decide whether a Supreme Court established in Grenada by the People's Revolutionary Government was legally constituted. This involved a larger question, specifically, whether this revolutionary government, which had taken power in a bloodless coup, was the 'legitimate sovereign' in the Austinian sense, such as to confer a legal status on the law and the courts. The case was decided in the affirmative on the grounds of necessity.

A similar question could have been posed in the case of *Phillips and Others v DPP*[62] when, after another coup, this time in Trinidad and Tobago, rebels seized power. Instead, the court was concerned with the validity of a pardon given to the rebels.

Limits of the command theory

As Hart points out,[63] the command theory, while authoritative, makes the erroneous assumption that all legal rules make commands or impose sanctions. There are many laws, which, for example, merely confer rights and are not backed by sanctions.

Hart proceeds to link types of rules with the legal system. He identifies two main sets of rules, primary rules and secondary rules. Primary rules are those which any society needs in order to survive. They forbid the conduct most destructive to the society, such as murder. Even simple societies contain these rules. Secondary rules are those which confer power rather than impose duties. They are divided into three types: rules of adjudication, rules of change and rules of recognition.

The first, rules of adjudication, are designed to allow the society to settle disputes such as legal offences and their sentences. Rules of change are those which promote other new rules. A developing society needs to respond to new situations and these rules accommodate this imperative. Rules of recognition are those which demonstrate the acceptance of the law by the society. They thus spell out which rules in the society have legal force. For example, Hart says, the UK has a single rule of recognition: what the Queen enacts is law. In like vein, we can say that our rule of recognition in the Commonwealth Caribbean is the Constitution, although these simple definitions do not describe accurately judge-made law.

Dworkin[64] rejects Hart's theory on rules on the basis that law contains not just rules, but a set of principles upon which these rules are based. These principles are the guidelines which inform the law but do not propose a solution. One such principle is that no one should benefit from their own wrong. These principles have a certain dimension of weight or importance that rules lack. This enables judges to weigh conflicting principles.

The naturalists and the morality of law

We need also to consider carefully the question of the appropriate functions of law in a society according to the naturalist school of thought. Should law, as the naturalists would have us believe, seek to reflect morality? This question is particularly pertinent

---

61 [1985] LRC (Const) 127; (1985) 32 WIR 241, PC.
62 [1992] 1 AC 545.
63 Hart, HLA, *The Concept of Law*, 1981, Oxford: Clarendon.
64 Dworkin, K, *Taking Rights Seriously*, 1977, London: Duckworth.

to our appreciation of law during slavery, which by any account, was immoral. Those who argue in the affirmative believe that there is some kind of 'higher law', known as 'natural law' to which we must turn for a basic moral code. There are diverging views on the source of that moral code, however. Some, like Aquinas, argue that it comes from God. Others see it merely as a question of the basic ethics of the society based on reason. The moralists believe that law should not only be moral in itself but should contain rules which prohibit 'immoral behaviour'. The law cannot divorce itself from these moral values.

The belief that law should reflect morality has spurned some interesting cases. In *Shaw v DPP*,[65] for example, the House of Lords upheld a conviction of the offence of a conspiracy to corrupt the public's morals when the defendant published a porno-graphic book. The Court found that a fundamental purpose of the law was to 'conserve not only the safety and order but also the moral welfare of the State'.[66] Similarly, in *R v Gibson*,[67] a conviction was obtained for the common law offence of outraging the public decency when the defendant artist exhibited earrings made from freeze-dried foetuses.

These decisions have engendered much controversy and have been criticised by those who believe that morality is a private concern and not the business of the law. John Stuart Mill, for example, argues that the law should not impose its concept of morality on individuals. Individuals should be free to choose their own conduct, as long as they do not harm others.[68]

Natural law, morality and our pluralistic societies

Certainly, the morality theories present difficulty. In any society there will be conflicting ideas of what is moral. This is particularly so in pluralistic societies such as ours. Muslims, for example, allow men to have more than one wife, whereas Western civilisation considers this immoral.[69] We have seen already the conflict between the UK and its territories over the issue of homosexuality, which those West Indian communities found to be immoral. Indeed, Commonwealth Caribbean societies may be described as conservative in social outlook. Debates continue to ensue on homosexuality, abortion, prostitution and even contraception. In discussions surrounding the approach to treatment for HIV/AIDS, for example, many continue to oppose giving prisoners and young people contraceptives, or legalising prostitution as a means of regulating such sexual activity, thereby potentially reducing health risks.

Issues such as gender and race equality also straddle the social morality spectrum. Here again, if one is to judge by the formal recognition of the law, the region is well behind many of its counterparts, nor is there consensus on these matters.[70] If the law is to define standards of moral behaviour, how are we to identify those standards? In

---

65   [1962] AC 220; [1961] 2 All ER 446, HL.
66   See also, *Knuller v DPP* [1973] AC 435, which was a conviction for publishing advertisements to contact others for homosexual purposes.
67   [1991] 1 All ER 439, CA.
68   JS Mill, *Utilitarianism*, 1979, USA: Hackett Publishing.
69   See Chapter 3 ('Legal Traditions – Types of Legal Systems in the Commonwealth Caribbean') for a discussion of relevant cases on polygamy.
70   See Chapter 7 ('The Written Constitution as a Legal Source').

addition, a society's morals change over time. The much talked about issue of the morality of the death penalty is one such example, although one cannot argue that there is consensus on the issue.

Less controversial functions of law include public order, social control, social cohesion, to promote change in the society, to define rights and duties and to balance conflicting interests in the particular society.[71]

When should we obey the law?

Even if we can identify what law is and what it should be, this still leaves the question, 'why do we obey law?' Is it, as Austin thought, because of the sanctions behind it, or is it, as Hart believed, because we accept it? Would we refrain from committing murder if there were no sanctions? Perhaps law is obeyed because it is the most convenient and fair way of organising any society? We may also obey law because we believe that it is right or morally correct.

This last suggestion leads us to an interesting point. Is there an obligation to obey rules emanating from the State which are immoral? There are several examples of these: the Nazi laws of Germany; the apartheid laws of South Africa; and of course, the slave laws which we discussed earlier. These were all legitimised by the relevant Parliaments. But did those laws have moral authority? The people who obeyed such laws may have believed that they were simply obeying the law. Yet they can be brought before international courts, for example, on claims that they have committed crimes against humanity, or genocide, or, as in South Africa, new national courts, for legal violations which are based on a higher moral order. This higher construct is sometimes called the 'rule of law'.[72] It suggests that we only have a duty to obey the law if it is morally just. Rules must conform to acceptable moral standards before we can consider them to be law.

In *Forsythe v DPP and the AG of Jamaica*,[73] for example, the appellant, a Rastafarian, author and Professor at Harvard University, USA, unsuccessfully sought legal validation for the utilisation of ganja as a sacrament of the Rastafarian faith. He argued against the validity of legislation which outlawed ganja in this way:

> That by defining all marijuana possession as 'criminal' . . . must cause ordinary people to loose [*sic*] respect for the law thereby. That a law is valuable not because it is 'the law' but because there is 'right' in it and laws should be like clothes; the Laws should be tailored to fit the people they are meant to serve.[74]

This was recognition not only that law should suit its society, but that it must be based on the moral values of that society which, judging from the lack of success in this case, is demonstrably subjective.

The intrinsic morality or immorality of law also leads us once again, to the discussion of reparations for the slave trade. It is precisely the immoral nature of the laws

---

71   See Funk, DA, who argues that there are seven major functions of law. He includes in the list of functions: to legitimise and to allocate power. 'Seven major functions of law' (1972) 23:2 Case Western Reserve L Rev 257.

72   Note that the term 'rule of law' has more than one meaning in the Commonwealth Caribbean. In the constitutional context, it is akin to procedural justice.

73   (1997) 34 JLR 512.

74   *Ibid*, at p 518.

which upheld the slave trade that supports the assertion that these were not legitimate laws. As such, unlawful acts of slavery were perpetrated, which had significant
adverse consequences, for which compensation is due.

ROLE OF THE SLAVE IN CREATING MODERN LAW

Our chapter ends as we began, examining closely the role the law played in slavery
and the relationship of the slave to the law. However, the historical function of law
assumes a different aspect in Tuitt's thesis on the slave and the law. She provides an
alternative construct for the historical function of law and indeed, law itself, as the
slave and slavery are seen as responsible for the very birth of modern law. Law is
portrayed as existing not merely to deny the slave rights. Rather, drawing heavily on
a notion reminiscent to relativity theory, Tuitt asserts that the slave, by the very
existence of her condition as, in essence, an antithesis to rights, was responsible for
creating human rights and indeed modern law.

Marginalised or subjugated groups in society are viewed as enduring and having
an integral relation with the 'constitution of the societies, institutions and structures
from which they have been ousted.'[75] Law plays an important role both in 'construct-
ing and maintaining these subjugated groups and figures.' Further, the slave figure
'foreshadows' many accounts of other subjugated groups:[76]

> Modern law can, therefore, be best understood through the metaphor or trope of the
> slave. The slave trope thus stands to represent the function of modern law which . . .
> serves, rather steadfastly, dominant powers.[77]

The slave was, in fact, one of the 'chief causes' of modern law, for example, the law of
contract was derived from the ancient law of chattels.[78] Similarly,

> the slave of the common law produced a notion of universal freedom – a notion sub-
> sequently and continually endorsed in law – particularly in the exemplary legal form of
> contractual relations which she could not enjoy . . . The slave's subjugation in fact and in
> law concentrated the freedom of other legal subjects. The slave as chattel produced the
> law of chattels that worked not to serve her but to bind her in subjugation.[79]

However, these subjugated groups are continually 'alienated from the law . . . that
they are integral in creating'.

Thus, the slave is seen as the law's protagonist, and one often identified in racial
terms. Yet, Tuitt's theory, if brought to its logical conclusion, suggests that oppression
is a prerequisite for enlightened law. This is indeed, the very antithesis of Rousseau's
Social Contract,[80] which sees rights as grounded in equity and self-preservation. It
therefore offers a very base, even brutish explanation for law.

We end this chapter with two calypsos, one composed and sung by slaves of
the period, the other by a well-known calypsonian of the contemporary period,

---

75 Tuitt, *above*, fn 8, p 2.
76 *Ibid*, p 3.
77 *Ibid*, p 6.
78 *Ibid*, p 11.
79 *Ibid*, pp 14–15.
80 Jean-Jacques Rosseau, *The Social Contract*, 1762, France.

demonstrating a consciousness of slavery and empathy with the slave some 150 years after its abolition:

> Tink dere is a God in a top
> No use me ill, Obisha [ie overseer]
> Me no horse, me no mare, me no mule,
> No use me ill Obisha.[81]

> I'm a slave from a land so far,
> I was caught and I was brought here from Africa.
> Well, it was licks like fire from the white slave master, everyday,
> Ah toil and toil and toil and toil so hard each day.
> I'm dying, I'm crying,
> O Lord, ah want to be free.[82]

---

81   Reproduced by Matthew Gregory Lewis, *Journal of a West-India Proprietor*, 1834, London in Orlando Patterson, *The Sociology of Slavery* 1973, London: Granada Publications Ltd, 255–56.

82   Dr Slinger Francisco – (The Mighty Sparrow), Spektakula Forum, Trinidad and Tobago, 30 August 1986, cited in Hollis (Chalkdust) Liverpool, *Rituals of Power and Rebellion – The Carnival Tradition in Trinidad and Tobago 1732–1962*, 2001, Chicago, USA: Research Associates School Times Publications/Frontline Distribution International Inc, p 27.

CHAPTER 3

LEGAL TRADITIONS – TYPES OF LEGAL SYSTEMS IN THE COMMONWEALTH CARIBBEAN

INTRODUCTION – THE DIFFICULTY IN DEFINING LEGAL SYSTEMS

In the study of law and legal systems in the Commonwealth Caribbean, perhaps the initial question to be asked is: what type of legal system is found in the region? However, it is first necessary to attempt to describe what we mean by the term 'legal system'. The term can be used very simply to mean the sum of legal rules, legal institutions and machinery which operate within the particular country or jurisdiction. This definition is not necessarily limited to a geographical jurisdiction, for within any country's legal system, there will be certain legal rules, such as rules of international law, which may originate from outside that country's geographical area, but which should be viewed as being part of its legal system.

Further, the geographical and political boundaries of a State may not indicate accurately the term 'legal system'. A legal system may actually exist apart from a State so defined. It may be less than the State. For example, Quebec and Toronto can be viewed as two separate legal systems because they have different legal rules, traditions and institutions, although both belong to the nation State of Canada. Similarly, England and Scotland can be viewed as two separate legal systems although, together with Northern Ireland, they form the State of the United Kingdom. Yet, if we were merely to define a legal system in relation to the law making power of the State as a geographical and political entity, then, in both examples above, we could say that there is a single legal system. A legal system, therefore, is not easily defined, as there is more than one approach to the description of what constitutes such a system.

Further, the above description does not tell us much about the fundamental characteristics of the particular legal system. As such, it is a limiting description. It also ignores the comparative analysis of legal systems which allows us to categorise legal systems into separate and often distinct models. As we will see, when used in this comparative sense, the term 'legal system' has come to have a more specific and deeper meaning than merely the particular collection of legal rules, institutions and machinery in a given jurisdiction.

THE CONCEPT OF A LEGAL TRADITION OR LEGAL FAMILY

The comparative study of different legal systems in the world today is the subject of comparativists. This study involves going beyond a mere examination of legal rules, institutions and machinery to determine the essential characteristics, differences and similarities which exist between various legal system models. The result is that various types of legal systems, or what are often termed legal traditions or families,[1] are seen to exist in the world today. Such legal traditions are grouped according to their defining characteristics. All legal systems in the world can be classed according to a

---

1   The term 'legal family' is attributed here to René David. See David, R and Brierley, J, *Major Legal Systems in the World Today*, 3rd edn, 1985, London: Stevens.

particular legal tradition or family. Such a classification enables us to explain the socio-legal concepts and thought processes which shape a particular legal system.

Different categories of legal traditions or families can, therefore, be identified by examining those fundamental elements of the system through which legal rules to be applied are interpreted, evaluated and discovered. This examination involves an inquiry into the technique, substance and *form* of legal rules within a particular legal system. The description legal family or tradition takes into account historically grounded values and attitudes about the nature of law, about the role of law in the society, about how the legal system should be organised and operated. The legal tradition is also shaped by the cultural identity and peculiar legal concepts of the society.

Legal families are not easily distinguishable. Very often, it is difficult to determine the appropriate criteria upon which different categories of legal families are to be based. The grouping of laws into limited and distinct categories of legal families to some extent oversimplifies the attempt to describe adequately the types of laws and legal systems which exist. It is neither a certain nor infallible exercise. Yet there is little doubt that such a method does help in the attempt to study the world's contemporary laws, legal institutions and concepts and facilitates an understanding of them. It remains, however, essentially an exercise of convenience.

Which criteria to be used?

The problem of which criteria should be used for classification into legal families is well illustrated in the Commonwealth Caribbean. Consequently, the primary question – that of which legal family best describes the legal systems of the Commonwealth Caribbean – by no means evokes a simplistic response. If we were to accept that form is the most essential criterion, we might tend toward the school of thought that there are two main existing legal traditions: the common law legal tradition or family and the civil law legal family. Since the common law legal tradition is synonymous with the particular system which originated in England and was transplanted to the Commonwealth through the process of English colonisation, an observer might easily conclude that, by virtue of the colonial history of the Commonwealth Caribbean, it belongs to the common law legal tradition. However, it can be demonstrated that if we were to base the analysis on other criteria, the answer would be surprisingly different. For example, if ideological criteria were to be used to distinguish different categories of legal systems, the countries of Grenada and the Republic of Guyana could stand apart from the rest of the Commonwealth Caribbean, at least at particular moments of their historical and social development. This is so since these two countries – the former through the promulgation of the People's Laws under the PRG socialist regime,[2] and the latter via its Constitution, which declared that Republic to be socialist – would belong to the Socialist Legal tradition, a category of legal system which has been described as a major legal tradition.

Even if we accept that there are only two legal traditions, the common law and civil law legal traditions, it would still be problematic to achieve a proper analysis of

---

2 These laws were enacted during the Grenada Revolution during the late 1970s to the early 1980s. It should be noted, however, that since the Grenada invasion, when the Revolution was prematurely halted, Grenada can no longer be considered a socialist State.

the legal systems in the Commonwealth Caribbean. This is because some jurisdictions within the region exhibit hybrid tendencies, displaying essential characteristics of both the civil law and common law legal systems. This is exemplified in St Lucia and the Republic of Guyana. These are described as hybrid or mixed legal systems, a phenomenon discussed in the following chapter, and one which, indeed, undermines the very exercise of creating clear and distinct categories of legal families or traditions.

There is no general agreement as to the method of classification. Some writers place more emphasis on the substantive social objectives of the law. For example, they may view the aim of achieving a socialist State as the most definitive characteristic of the system, hence the notion of a Socialist Legal tradition. Others are more concerned with technical differences. They place more importance on the sources or origins of the law and its structure and method. It is also becoming increasingly more important to examine the political, philosophical and economic principles upon which laws are based, for, in comparing legal systems, even if there is identity in form, technique and social objectives, philosophical and politico-economic principles make a substantial difference to the outlook of the law.

It is noteworthy that the classification into legal traditions is not static, since it may vary according to time and historical and social development. A vivid example is the former USSR. With the radical changes which took place in what used to be communist East Germany and Russia, these countries can no longer be said to belong to the Socialist Legal family, even if many socialist laws remain on the statute books. A similar situation arises in connection with Grenada since the Grenada invasion,[3] for the political changes since that time have brought a return to traditional democracy.

DISTINGUISHING CRITERIA OF LEGAL TRADITIONS

Several criteria may be offered up for selection as criteria when categorising legal traditions. Among the most common are legal technique, historical and legal sources, ideology, religion, legal institutions, economics, geography and race. Often, it is merely a question of semantics. The noted comparativists, Zweigert[4] and Kotz, advocate that the critical distinguishing criterion is simply the *style* of differing legal systems. Inherent in the element of style they identify other factors, such as distinctive institutions, ideology, legal source, historical background and development, and the predominant and characteristic mode of thought in legal matters. It is apparent that, although they do not specifically mention religion, for example, this can be considered under the heading 'historical background and development' or even 'ideology'. Similarly, the description 'characteristic mode of thought' is perhaps merely referring to the type of legal technique existent in the particular legal system.

Let us examine briefly an explanation of some of the criteria used for classification into legal systems and tradition.

First, the elements of legal technique, form, or mode of legal thinking: these criteria, which mean substantially the same, attempt to evaluate the way in which law is organised and promulgated. For example, in the civil law system, the tendency is to

---

3   In 1983, with the slaying of the popular revolutionary leader, Maurice Bishop.
4   Zweigert, K and Kotz, H, *An Introduction to Comparative Law*, Vol 1, 1977, Amsterdam: North Holland.

use highly technical codes which contain legal rules. On the other hand, the common law tradition relies on precedent or judgemade law to promulgate legal rules.

With regard to the criterion of ideology, the comparativist will be concerned with the substantive socio-economic political and philosophical principles which inform the law. Technique or form will be of little value in classification.

Similarly, if one is examining religion as a criterion for distinguishing legal traditions, the question whether the law and legal institutions are substantially influenced and supported by the factor of religion is highly relevant. This is epitomised in Islamic and Hindu countries.

The criteria of historical source and development are seeking merely to categorise legal systems by emphasising their origins. Thus the common law system grew up in England as a creation of the judges of the King's Court. Indeed, because of this, it is sometimes accused of being a tool of the upper classes on the basis that judges usually belong to that class and the legal tradition is imbued with their values. On the other hand, the French civil law system was heavily influenced by the political principles of *égalité*.

One may also inquire into the legal source of law, that is, where it gets its legitimacy or legal validity. As mentioned previously, the civil law tradition relies primarily on codification. Consequently, the principal source of validity would be the code, whereas the main legal source within common law systems would be judicial precedents, or, simply put, binding judicial principles emanating from judges.

Finally, one may look at distinctive legal institutions or concepts to determine the issue of classification. For example, the legal concepts of 'estoppel' and 'trust' are distinct, unique and peculiar to the common law legal tradition.

Identifying major legal traditions

Since it is apparent that there is no clear consensus as to the exact nature of the criteria upon which to base classification into legal traditions, it is not surprising that the same is true in attempting to outline clearly the major legal traditions or families in the contemporary world. Those who simply assert that there are only two groupings, that of the civil law and common law traditions, are arguing that *all* other legal systems can fit into these two groups. They will be no less correct than the person who includes the Socialist Legal tradition, traditions based on religion or any other legal family. However, there appears to be some measure of consensus with regard to at least three categories of legal traditions, namely, the Romano-Germanic or civil law tradition, the common law tradition and the Socialist Legal tradition. Clearly, however, in the light of the previous discussion, and although all countries may perhaps exhibit characteristics of any of these, such an economical classification cannot take into account all contemporary legal phenomena.

For the purpose of this book, other traditions which prevail in a large number of contemporary societies, and which exhibit essential characteristics outside the sphere of the three named categories, will be discussed briefly. These are the Muslim and Hindu legal traditions and the legal tradition of the Far East.[5] A grouping of legal

---

5   The legal systems of Africa and Madagascar are sometimes placed into a separate legal tradition. See *op cit*, David and Brierley, fn 1, and Zweigert and Kotz, fn 4.

traditions into only Romano-Germanic civil law, common law and Socialist Legal traditions places too great an emphasis on Western civilisation and thinking. There is no doubt that Western civilisation has, in varying degrees, influenced many of the world's legal systems, at least in modern times. Yet, in non-Western countries that have indigenous legal institutions, attitudes and concepts of law which are often based on religious belief, the European/Western concept of law has not been readily embraced. It is therefore unwise and myopic to believe that the West has a monopoly in, or superiority over, legal thought and processes. Gutteridge describes the refusal of the common law tradition to learn from other legal traditions of the world as '. . . very complete and traditionally consecrated ignorance'.[6]

THE COMMON LAW LEGAL TRADITION

For the purpose of the study of law and legal systems in the Commonwealth Caribbean, an examination of the common law system or tradition is exceedingly important. This is because Commonwealth Caribbean jurisdictions, in the main, fall squarely into this grouping. This is a direct consequence of the historical development of the countries of the Commonwealth Caribbean region. These were rediscovered by the Europeans in the 15th century, became a battleground to facilitate the then European focus of imperialism, finally being conquered and dominated by the English. Since the common law system originated in England, in form, character and substance, it should be of little surprise to learn that this system, through the process of colonisation, was imposed upon the former conquered territories, some of which now make up the Commonwealth Caribbean.[7]

The historical continuum is still evident in that, even today, when most of the countries of the Commonwealth Caribbean are politically independent, they have not in the main deviated from the common law tradition in the way some European countries have digressed from the civil law tradition, for example, to embrace the socialist tradition. The countries of the Commonwealth Caribbean continue to exhibit perhaps excessive tendencies of reliance on the form, structure, substance and content of the law as expressed in England.

The student of law and legal systems should be warned that the term 'common law' has more than one meaning. It can be used in a restricted sense to mean that aspect of the common law tradition which is concerned only with the legal rules of the tradition and not its essential characteristics in entirety. However, when one speaks of the common law as a tradition, this description includes the legal rules described above, as well as other features of the system. It would include, for example, equity, legal concepts and institutions.[8]

The term common law tradition, although originating in England and founded on English law, speaks to all the English-speaking countries and the geographical area known as the Commonwealth. There are very few exceptions. In those areas of the Commonwealth which cannot wholly be described as being part of the common law

---

6   Ratcliffe, P (ed), *The Good Samaritan and the Law*, 1966, London: Doubleday, p 142.
7   See Chapter 5 ('The Reception of English Law and Its Significance to Caribbean Jurisdictions').
8   See Chapters 8 and 9 ('The Common Law and the Doctrine of Judicial Precedent' and 'Equity as a Source of Law').

tradition, such tradition has exerted great influence on their jurists, judicial systems and substantive areas of both civil and criminal law.[9]

A study of the common law tradition is intimately linked with the study of the development of English law and history, since the path of historical development is very important to this tradition. It is essentially the history of the law of England. Today there are different strains of the common law tradition. For example, while the USA belongs to the common law tradition, it has incorporated into the system its own peculiar legal concepts and rules.[10] We may see the influence of North American and other nuances in our adoption of written Constitutions and Bills of Rights which in themselves represent a departure from the original English common law model. However, for those examining the legal systems of the Commonwealth Caribbean, it is the original character of the common law system which is most important. Essentially, the common law tradition describes the substantive and procedural legal rules, techniques, and institutions which evolved from the early courts of law in England after the Norman conquest.[11]

One of the essential characteristics of the common law is the structure and development of its legal rules. Laws or legal rules under the common law tradition were promulgated on an ad hoc basis by the common law courts as matters came before such courts. Thus, the legal rules of the common law tradition are often referred to as 'judge-made law' or 'soft law', to reflect the somewhat arbitrary and changeable origins of such legal rules.[12] This phenomenon resulted in a doctrine called judicial precedent, whereby the applicable legal rules and norms were handed down through these judicial pronouncements. This created a coherent system of rules as well as a procedure through which new legal principles could be made.[13]

Thus, the common law tradition incorporates both the legal rules of the common law courts or judge-made law and the rules of equity.[14] The legal rules of the common law and those of equity differ both in substance and application.

The common law tradition is characterised by particular legal concepts such as 'trust', 'bailment', 'estoppel', the writ of habeas corpus, 'consideration' and 'trespass', as well as concepts grounded in equity. Distinct legal traditions include the jury system. Such concepts and institutions could not easily be translated into the civil law tradition or other legal tradition.

Recent attempts to transplant trust into civil law systems to achieve greater harmony in international finance, particularly offshore finance, demonstrate this. While civil law can accommodate trust by methods of assimilation, adaptation or

---

9   Such as India, which can also be grouped under 'religious legal traditions'.
10 We may say the same for India.
11 For further discussion, see Walker, R and Ward R, *Walker and Walker's English Legal System*, 7th edn, 1994, London: Butterworths.
12 In contrast, rules of the civil law tradition, which are found in codes, are called 'hard law'. See below, p 31.
13 For an exposition of how this doctrine operates, see Chapter 8 ('The Common Law and the Doctrine of Judicial Precedent').
14 The rules of equity developed as a solution to alleviate the rigidity and harshness of the rules and procedures of the common law courts. These rules were developed by the Court of Chancery. They are essentially a collection of remedies based on equitable principles or the principles of conscience. Their function is to grant a remedy to those deserving, in circumstances where the rules of the common law restricted the courts from doing so. For a fuller discussion of equity, see Chapter 9 ('Equity as a Source of Law').

transposition, it is a tortured process which leads to conflicts of laws.[15] For example, trust in civil law systems is usually accommodated under the notion of a contract, which is broader in civil law jurisdictions. Yet a contract is not the same as a trust, which has a unique arrangement whereby duality of ownership (or more accurately, a separation between ownership and control) is recognised.[16]

Even the basic concept of a legal rule has a different meaning in the common law tradition and other legal families. In the common law family, the legal rule involves at least three judicial sources, judicial precedent, legislation and equity. In contrast, the legal rule in the civil law tradition is enumerated through a specific type of legislation called a code, which embodies legal doctrine as well as detail.

THE CIVIL LAW OR ROMANO-GERMANIC TRADITION

The civil or Romano-Germanic legal tradition has its historical base in continental Europe. Its true origins may be found in the law of ancient Rome, from which it spread throughout the world, constantly evolving, until it developed the particular characteristics which distinguish it today.

Adherents to the Romano-Germanic tradition are found primarily in continental Europe, Latin America, large parts of Africa, the countries of the Near East, Japan and Indonesia. As with the common law system, the system of transplantation from its centre in Europe to other parts of the world was mainly via the historical process of colonisation and imperialism. In the Commonwealth Caribbean, influences of the civil law tradition can be seen in St Lucia and the Republic of Guyana.

Since the expansion of CARICOM to include Haiti and Suriname, it has become more important for the region to be familiar with the civil law legal tradition. More particularly, one of the judges on the newly constituted Caribbean Court of Justice, a final court of appeal, Justice Wit, is from the Netherlands and it is to be expected that influences of civil law will come to the fore. Indeed, this process can be seen to have begun, if one is to judge by one of the first decisions from the court.[17] In this case, the differences between the civil law tradition and the common law in attitudes toward the reception of international law through treaty-making in domestic law were apparent. Under the civil law tradition, the monist doctrine prevails, whereby international law is treated as binding upon ratification by a treaty. In direct opposition, the common law tradition under the dualist tradition does not recognise the direct enforceability of ratified treaties. They are perceived as being merely influential unless incorporated into domestic law by statute.

In that case also, Justice Wit's judgment relied on no fewer than four treatises from jurists, underlining the emphasis which civilian judges place on such works, in direct contrast to the common law judges' almost total dependence on case law and precedent.

---

15   This means that there are inherent tensions of the law between the one jurisdiction and the next.

16   See, eg, *Courtois v De Ganay*, Rev Cr de dr int pr 518 (1973) Paris, CA, where the trust was recognised as a type of contract. This is an example of the tendency of modern legal traditions to borrow from each other, discussed below, p 46.

17   *AG of Barbados et al v Joseph and Boyce* CCJ Appeal No CV 2 of 2005, decided 8 November 2006, discussed in detail in Chapter 12 ('International Law as a Source of Law'). Justice Wit put forward a modified version of the dualist doctrine.

The development of the Romano-Germanic tradition was greatly influenced by the natural law school of thought. This sought to discover and teach a fully rational law, based on reason, suitable for universal application.[18]

The development of the civil law legal tradition is also 'closely linked to a rediscovery of Roman law and the creation of legal science in the 11th Century'.[19] The tradition spread throughout Europe as a result of the scholars and the emphasis on the Justinian *Corpus Juries* as a scholastic legal tradition. This is the reason for the continued reliance on legal scholars in the civil law tradition even today.

Just as it is possible to identify different variations of the common law tradition, such as the North American model, so it is possible with the Romano-Germanic tradition. One may identify, for example, German and French variations to the Romano-Germanic legal family. While the French variation grounded itself in the principles of the French Revolution, the drafting of the German Civil Code at the end of the 19th century was carried out on the basis of Pandectist scholarship. There are differences both in method and style between the two models. The French and German models also differ in terms of the possibilities for judicial interpretation, with German judges enjoying wider powers in this respect. However, the fundamental characteristics of these two models, as well as the models found in other countries which belong to the tradition, bear much more similarity than difference. As such, a discernible category of legal tradition may be identified.

The most fundamental and distinguishing characteristic of the Romano-Germanic tradition is its reliance on statute in the form of a code as the ultimate legal source and technique.

Codification is the compilation of legislation, the purpose of which is to attempt to gather together and systematically organise the legal rules and legislation on any special subject. A primordial role is attributed to legislation and it is this that essentially unites countries which belong to the Romano-Germanic tradition. Further, it is this legal technique of codification which facilitated the expansion of the Romano-Germanic tradition. Codified law is known as 'hard law', being of enduring quality by the mere fact that it is enshrined in statute. This makes it easy to be transported and retained. In the Commonwealth Caribbean, it is one of the reasons that the island of St Lucia, even after conquest and reconquest by the English, still retains elements of the Romano-Germanic tradition which were originally brought to the island by the French centuries ago. The judge-made 'soft law' of England could not entirely replace it.

This is not to say that legislation does not form part of the common law tradition. Indeed, it is an important source of law.[20] Rather, it is the extent to which emphasis is placed on legislation that makes the distinction between the common law and civil law traditions. The heavy reliance on legislation through codification to ground legal rules and concepts is characteristic of the civil law tradition rather than that of the common law, although increasingly, common law jurisdictions are making use of legislation to create legal norms. However, the use of codes is still not prevalent in common law systems. The advent of written Constitutions, in particular, Bills of

---

18 See, eg, Aquinas, T (St), *Summa Theologica*, 1942, London: Burns, Oates and Washbourne.
19 Rogowski, R, 'Civil Law' in Kritzer, H (ed), *Legal Systems of the World – A Political, Social and Cultural Encyclopedia*, Vol 1, 2002, USA: ABC CLIO, p 307.
20 See the discussion on sources of law below, Chapter 6 ('Introduction to Sources of Law').

Rights, in the Commonwealth Caribbean can, to a limited extent, be viewed as a departure from common law principles, tending toward codification. In essence, a written Constitution is supreme or parent legislation which contains both legal principle and detail. In fact, the notion of a Bill of Rights or statutory instrument setting out the fundamental rights of the citizen is derived from the civil law tradition.

The concept of the legal rule can also be distinguished in the Romano-Germanic tradition. In this tradition, the legal rule is not merely a rule to solve a judicial dispute, but achieves a higher level of abstraction primarily because of the heavy influence of doctrinal writing and scholarship.

As regards legal technique, the abstract nature or generality of the legal rule explains why the interpretation of legislation is an essential and fundamental characteristic of the tradition, as opposed to the common law tradition. In the latter, the task of judicial persona prioritises the process of distinguishing judicial decisions in finding solutions for new legal situations or deviating from precedent in old ones. Judges must be careful not to be seen to be creating law. In contrast, in the civil law tradition, the judge has more freedom to define the legal rule. Indeed, he is expected to give it substance.

Thus, whereas in the common law tradition a legal rule is promulgated in a precise manner, in the Romano-Germanic tradition such a rule simply establishes the framework of the law and merely gives the judge guidelines for decision making. The judge in the Romano-Germanic tradition can be viewed as having more judicial discretion than his common law counterpart.

The Romano-Germanic tradition places much more emphasis on the role of academic jurists, doctrinal writings and other scholarship than does the common law tradition. This is relied upon for the rationalisation, interpretation and systematisation of the law. In fact, the work of philosophers and legal scholars grounds the tradition and the abstract nature of legal rules.

There are certain legal concepts or institutions peculiar to the Romano-Germanic tradition which provide other criteria for distinguishing it as a unique category. These include cause, abuse of right, the extent to which there is strict liability in the law, tort, the notary public and the law of obligations.

In a wider dimension, the concepts of 'public law' and 'private law' have different meanings in the common law and Romano-Germanic traditions. In the latter, there is a clear dichotomy between public and private law categories. This dichotomy is based upon a fundamental philosophy which maintains that the sphere of relations between the State and its citizens calls for a different approach from that of relations between private persons. This philosophy is not evident to the same degree in the common law tradition.

The nature of legal personnel can also be distinguished when comparing different legal traditions. In the Romano-Germanic tradition there is a high level of specialised judicial branches such as notaries and advocates. There are even specialist, or career judges, a notion alien to the common law tradition.

Finally, the very nature of the judicial system is distinguishable in the Romano-Germanic tradition. The judicial system of the common law tradition is described as accusatorial or adversarial, while the judicial system in the Romano-Germanic is inquisitorial. An accusatorial system describes a method of trial where the legal parties to the dispute and their attorneys act as adversaries against each other. The judge's role is similar to an impartial umpire. He does not directly intervene in the proceedings, but allows the trial to be conducted largely by the litigants and their legal representatives. Even the way cases are reported reflect this. In the Romano-Germanic method of trial, however, the judge participates more actively in the proceedings, even examining witnesses, and commenting on the evidence given. His purpose is to inquire into the evidence.

Civil Law Systems in CARICOM

In CARICOM, one may identify Haiti and Suriname as being examples of the civil law tradition, the French and Dutch models respectively. The Dutch civil law tradition is described as being 'of old Dutch, French and Roman law descent'.[21] Interestingly, Suriname provides one of the few examples of a common law legal system being transplanted by a civil law legal system, this being the result of initial colonisation by the British in 1651. Subsequently, after battle with the Netherlands, the country was given to the Dutch under the Peace of Breda agreement in 1667. As with other civil law systems, the legal system of Suriname is dominated by a Civil Code, originally a replica of the Civil Code in use in the Netherlands. The Code incorporated indigenous elements peculiar to Suriname.

SIMILARITIES BETWEEN THE COMMON LAW AND CIVIL LAW TRADITIONS

It is easy to oversimplify and exaggerate the difference in legal technique between the Romano-Germanic and common law traditions. For instance, in the treatment of precedent: although binding precedent can be theoretically viewed as limiting, common law judges are able to perfect the process of distinguishing precedents to give themselves more freedom to avoid following unpopular precedents.[22] Similarly, there is limited use of a type of precedent within the Romano-Germanic tradition, such as in French administrative law. There is also the existence of what is termed a 'jurisprudence constant', that is, a particular line of decisions interpreting a code and emanating from the highest court. This will be accorded great respect by other judges. Indeed, the influence of previous judicial decisions is now more openly acknowledged in civil law systems.

Further, as we noted previously, it is possible to distinguish some codification in common law countries, such as Bills of Rights in written Constitutions, Sales of Goods Acts, or the Labour Code of Antigua. Nevertheless, the points of distinction between the various legal traditions lie in the extent of codification.

As legal traditions become more familiar with each other, we also see certain concepts which are characteristic of a particular legal tradition being utilised or emulated by another legal tradition. For example, the French have now introduced a concept called *la fiducie,* which is a type of trust. In turn, common law legal systems have found the concept of 'abuse of form' very attractive, particularly in tax cases.[23]

---

21   Munneke, H and Kekker, AJ, 'Suriname' in Kritzer, H (ed) *Legal Systems of the World – A Political, Social and Cultural Encyclopedia* Vol IV, ABC-CLIO, USA, 2002, p 1551.

22   See Chapter 8 ('The Common Law and the Doctrine of Judicial Precedent').

23   For example, to thwart what was considered lawful tax avoidance for being within the 'letter of the law'. Such avoidance is now seen as an abuse. Now, the intention of the law, rather than its letter, is to be prioritised.

Even the philosophical difference between public law and private law is fast becoming unimportant. This is due to the developments in administrative law which have now created such a dichotomy, particularly in relation to judicial procedure.[24]

Once again, we may see a deviation from the strictly theoretical with the increasing trend toward specialisation on the part of attorneys at law in practice, if not in training under the common law tradition. Further, with the advent of specialised courts in common law legal systems, such as family courts, industrial courts and Juvenile Courts, there has been a corresponding emergence of specialised judges to sit on these courts.[25]

THE SOCIALIST LEGAL TRADITION

The Socialist Legal tradition has its historical origin in the Bolshevist revolution of 1917. This initiated the new international political and economic order known as socialism or communism. Its main distinguishing feature is ideology, as opposed to the common law or Romano-Germanic tradition where legal technique and form are more important as distinguishing criteria. The question has often been asked whether the legal systems of socialist countries should be seen as belonging to a separate system distinct from the Romano-Germanic tradition with which it has a close affinity as regards form and technique. It is undisputed that the law in the former USSR, for example, has retained the terminology and structure of the Romano-Germanic tradition but, as socialists argue, law cannot be isolated from the social, political and economic order within which it operates. The social, political and economic forces which inform the law are therefore of fundamental importance in determining the type of legal system in existence. Indeed, because of the ideology which shapes the law in socialist countries, common legal concepts may take on new meanings. Examples are the meanings attached to notions of 'property' and 'democracy'.

In contemporary times it is difficult to state clearly which countries of the world should be definitively described as socialist or communist countries. This is because of the radical developments of 'perestroika' and 'glasnost' which are threatening to shatter the socialist world and with it, the need for a category such as the Socialist Legal tradition.

It is because of the ideological dominance over legal rules that, while recognising the diminution of the tradition in quantity, we still isolate it as a legal tradition. Some countries, such as Poland, which just a few years ago would have belonged to the Socialist Legal tradition, have now changed to democratic political and legal systems. Similar changes have occurred in Germany, while other traditional socialist countries are undergoing radical political, economic and legal reform. These developments are evidence that legal systems are not static, but are continuously in a state of flux.

Traditionally, however, the Socialist Legal tradition included the countries of the former USSR, a few countries in Europe which adhered to the Marxist-Leninist political tradition[26] and, in the Caribbean, Cuba.

---

24 See, eg, *O' Reilly v Mackman* [1983] 2 AC 237 and *Cocks v Thanet DC* [1983] 2 AC 286. There is now a dichotomy between a housing authority's public law and private law functions, as seen in *Cocks v Thanet*.

25 See the discussion in Chapter 18 ('Specialised Courts, Tribunals and Functions').

26 The countries in Europe which traditionally belonged to this tradition include Romania, Czechoslovakia, Yugoslavia, Albania, Bulgaria, Hungary, Poland and East Germany.

Not every socialist or communist State is necessarily placed under the Socialist Legal tradition. For example, China is often categorised separately under the legal tradition of the Far East.[27] It is noteworthy that the term 'socialist' has often been used imprecisely by various political parties and governments. However, the term when used in the context of the 'Socialist Legal tradition' embodies the meaning assigned to it by the Russian Revolution, which was aimed at achieving a communist State. With this came a corresponding need to fashion a legal system consistent with this ideal. This new legal framework and political order emphasised a 'dictatorship of the proletariat' in conformity with the principles laid down by political and socialist ideology such as Marxist-Leninism.

In the Commonwealth Caribbean, the Republic of Guyana has declared itself, through the Constitution, to be 'socialist'. However, it is doubtful whether, under the restricted meaning assigned to the term Socialist Legal tradition, that country can truly be considered a legitimate part of the tradition, for there has been little attempt within the legal framework to bring the country close to the ideals of its professed ideology.[28]

In contrast, Grenada, under the socialist People's Revolutionary Government (PRG) regime, with its promulgation of the 'People's Laws' could legitimately have been viewed as part of the Socialist Legal tradition before the Grenada invasion. This is so since that regime and its law were tending toward the Cuban model, a model which is accepted as being part of the Socialist Legal tradition.[29]

The development of Socialist law can be divided into three main phases. First, the period of the construction of socialism from 1917–36. This phase saw the legal enactment of some of the fundamental principles of socialism, for example, the Declaration of the Rights of the Toiling and Exploited People and nationalisation laws. The second phase began in 1936 and introduced mechanisms to strengthen the socialist State.[30] It was characterised by the promulgation of codes, such as a Civil Code, a criminal code, a family code, a new agrarian code and a code of criminal procedure. Another essential feature was the collectivisation of agriculture and other means of production in keeping with the communist ideal. Present day reality can be viewed as the third phase. This signalled the reformation or even the decline of socialism with increasing encouragement of private enterprise.

Perhaps the most essential thread running through the laws of the countries belonging to the Socialist Legal tradition is the affirmation or embodiment of the principle of 'socialist legality'. This principle reflects the attitude of socialists toward law. For socialists, laws in non-socialist countries exist only to serve an essentially

---

27 This is the formulation used by David and Brierley in their authoritative text on comparative law, *op cit*, fn 1.

28 The Constitution did declare a 'right to work' in Part I. This was adjudged to be justiciable and enforceable in the remarkable case of *AG v Mohammed Ali* [1989] LRC (Const) 474. However, as a result of this decision and its adherence to this popular socialist ideal, the Constitution was later amended to reverse the decision.

29 The PRG regime came into being in 1979 and changed the laws of Grenada by promulgating the People's Laws, a model seeking to promote socialism. Previously Grenada would have belonged to the common law tradition. Legal changes under the PRG included the abolition of the Privy Council as the final Court of Appeal and the suspension of the former Constitution. Presently, the issue of legal validity as regards the change in the legal order in Grenada is still alive, although the country's political order has been returned to democracy.

30 For an exposé of the Soviet legal system, see Hafard, J, Butler, W and Maggs, P, *The Soviet Legal System*, 3rd edn, 1977, New York: Oceana.

unjust order, by catering only to the privileged few or 'bourgeoisie'. In socialism, however, citizens obey law because it is deemed just. 'Justice' is achieved because the State, through its socialist nature, exists in the interest of all. It is, therefore, the very principle and ideals of socialism which give law its validity or authority, hence the notion of 'socialist legality'. Thus, the law only has value in relation to the economic and political structure within which it exists. This explains the socialist content of legal rules.

The existence of a special institution known as the 'Prokuratura' is a unique and distinguishing feature of the Socialist Legal tradition. This institution was created to guarantee the principle of 'socialist legality', and is a highly developed and extensive administrative body, which works alongside the courts.

It is apparent from the foregoing discussion that the legal sources of the Socialist Legal tradition are different from the common law tradition and the Romano-Germanic tradition. Since the Socialist Legal tradition relies so heavily on political ideology and content, the fundamental sources of law can be seen to be the collectiv-isation of the means of production and the establishment of the means of production. It is only in a secondary sense that one may consider technical aspects of the law, such as legislation, precedent and legal technique, to be legal sources.

The reliance on legislation as a means of promulgating legal rules is as prominent in the Socialist Legal tradition as in the Romano-Germanic tradition. Yet the similarity between these two legal traditions is only superficial, since the rationale for legislation is entirely different. In the socialist countries, the legislative method is seen merely to be the most speedy and efficient means of creating revolutionary social change, whereas, in the Romano-Germanic tradition, legislation is viewed as the most concise and clear method of expressing legal thought in the form of rules. Through legisla-tion, the fundamental principles of socialism have been declared. These include prin-ciples on education, civil law and procedure, criminal law, health and judicial organisation.

THE RELIGIOUS LEGAL TRADITIONS

Although Muslim law and the Hindu law are grouped together under the category of 'religious traditions', it is necessary to emphasise that they have little in common except that they both rely heavily on their respective religions to shape legal systems. They will therefore be discussed separately.[31]

Muslim law

The phenomenon that is Muslim law is, in essence, a fundamental part of Muslim theological thought rather than an independent branch of learning. Legal rules can therefore be ascertained from a study of the Koran, the foundation of Muslim religious learning.

Traditionally, the sources of Muslim law are the Koran (Qur'an), the Sunna, the book of the life of the Prophet, the Izma of reasoning of the Muslim scholars, and the

---

31   Jewish law may also be considered as part of the tradition, but is not explored here as there is a very small presence of Jews in the region and no legal recognition of them as a separate group.

Kiyas (or giyas), juristic reasoning by analogy. Of these, the Koran is the primary source, although it does not contain all the legal rules necessary for the operation of Muslim society, but is supplemented by other sources. The practice today is that the judge consults, not the Koran directly, but a book of 'fikh', which is a book containing interpretations of the Koran and Sunna compiled or approved by the 'Izma'. The doctrines emanating from the 'Izma' are unchangeable and binding. They form the basis of the Muslim legal system in practice. Thus, Muslim law is itself immutable. Muslim law cannot be created or changed by legislation. Muslim rulers can only make regulations within the defined limits of the authority of religious sources. These sources are viewed as infallible.

Other unique features of Muslim law include its relative lack of systematisation, the pervasive archaic nature of its legal institutions and its originality of content. The latter is due to the fact that Muslim law is founded on the Muslim religion.

Despite the apparently static nature of Muslim law, it is considered to be one of the great legal systems of the world. Its adherents can be found in several countries, some of which include Morocco, Tunisia, Syria, Iran, Afghanistan, Yemen, Pakistan, Egypt, Iraq and the Islamic republic of Mauritania.

Notwithstanding Muslim law's deference to ancient wisdom, the forces of modernisation and westernisation have managed to penetrate. Today, although Muslim law is proclaimed in principle in Muslim countries, custom and legislation have introduced changes. The result is that such countries are no longer governed exclusively by traditional Muslim law. These attempts at modernisation have produced certain tensions within Muslim society, primarily due to the wish of some Muslims to adhere to orthodox Muslim principles.[32]

This process of modernisation is facilitated by codification which seeks to introduce Western concepts of law. In addition, special courts which traditionally applied Muslim law are being eliminated in some countries. Yet it cannot be said that the contemporary law of Muslim countries has been assimilated into the Romano-Germanic tradition to which it increasingly bears resemblance. Muslim religious ideals still inform the outlook of the law and it remains correct to view Muslim law as belonging to a separate tradition.

Hindu law

Hindu law has its origins in India, but India can no longer claim a monopoly over it, since several countries, such as other south east Asian countries and parts of Africa, adhere to this legal tradition. Hindu law is based on the ancient religion of Hinduism, a religion which encompasses all aspects of the Hindu's life, going beyond spiritual and moral philosophies. Consequently, the religious doctrines of Hinduism permeate every aspect of the law and legal system.

The principles of religious and moral behaviour are contained in texts called 'Sastras'. These are divided into different subject areas and are called 'Dharma', 'Artha' and 'Karma'.[33]

---

32   This manifests itself, eg, in political parties which are separated by differing attitudes to religion as in Pakistan or Turkey. 'Pakistan proposed controversial legislative amendments which will make the legal system conform more strictly to Muslim religious doctrine.' (BBC/CNN, October 1998.)

33   These deal with virtue, pleasure, work ethic and other important areas.

Judicial decisions and legislation are not sources of law in the Hindu legal tradition in the way that they are in the common or civil law traditions. Instead, the books of Dharma, Artha and Karma form the scientific base of the law. Like Muslim law, Hindu law has been influenced by Western thinking. This was largely brought about by the English political domination of India in the 18th century. An important consequence of English colonial rule was that the application of Hindu law was restricted to a limited number of legal situations.

After the independence of India in 1947, developments in Hindu law took place. As in the Commonwealth Caribbean, a written Constitution was established as the supreme law of the land, thus creating a new source of law. Further, extensive legislative reform took place, much of which further westernised the law. Still, the fundamental norms peculiar to the Hindu faith remain in practice.

Because of the previous colonisation of India by the British and the consequent transplantation of the common law, we can discern much similarity in technique and form between the Hindu legal tradition in India and the common law tradition. However, there are substantial differences between these two traditions. For example, there is no distinction between common law and equity, as exists in England.

Another important difference between the Indian and English common law traditions is the way in which the doctrine of precedent operates. In theory, the Indian Supreme Court, like the American Supreme Court, can effect changes in precedents emanating from its own sitting. This makes the operation of precedent much less rigid than in the English common law tradition. The most significant difference, however, is the grounding of the Hindu legal tradition in the law.

EVIDENCE OF THE RELIGIOUS LEGAL TRADITION IN THE COMMONWEALTH CARIBBEAN

In some countries of the Commonwealth Caribbean, concessions are made to religious legal traditions, in particular Muslim law and Hindu law.[34] This occurs in those countries which have large Muslim and Hindu populations, specifically, Trinidad and Tobago and Guyana. In both these countries, Muslim religious adherents are not only free to practice their religion but certain important religious traditions are recognised by law. Notably, followers of the Muslim or Hindu faiths can marry according to their religious legal traditions. This is affirmed by statute.[35] The law also recognises religious divorces and holidays. Further, some acknowledgment is given to the Hindu language and modes of dress which conform to religious beliefs.

This recognition of religious legal traditions is also found in Suriname, a CARICOM Member State and a highly pluralistic society. Here, there also appears to be a recognition of religion in the law, for example, in the recognition of religious

---

34 See also Chapter 1 ('Introduction to Law and Legal Systems in the Commonwealth Caribbean').

35 See, eg, the Muslim Marriage and Divorce Act 1980 of Trinidad and Tobago, Chap 45/02, the Hindu Marriage Act 1980, and 1993 of Trinidad and Tobago, Chap 45/03 and the Hindu Midhi-Hindu Foundation of Trinidad and Tobago (Inc) Act 1990. Note that the Orisa may also be married according to their own traditions. However, mechanisms under the law are relatively undeveloped and are, therefore, not discussed further here. See, however, Chapter 1, ('Introduction to Law and Legal Systems in the Commonwealth Caribbean') for a discussion on the Orisa group.

marriage, both for Hindustanis and Islamists, as they are called there. The age permitted for religious marriage is lower than that for secular marriages and parental consent is not necessary. Islamic divorce, whereby the husband only has to say a particular formula of words, is accepted by the law.[36]

Most significantly, one may find Muslim or Islamic courts along similar lines, in terms of structure, to those found in Islamic countries. The important difference in the region, however, is that the Islamic court has no binding legal authority in the land and is not formally recognised as a legal institution. It functions like an arbitrating body and must rely on legal processes within the dominant secular legal tradition for its effectiveness. For example, the parties to a judgment of the court must sign an agreement, recognised as a formal contract, agreeing to the terms of the 'judgment' of the court. It is really that contract which is binding and recognised as a enforceable legal document.

Religious marriage and divorce

With respect to marriages, the State has been sensitive and quite facilitating. In Trinidad and Tobago, for example, not only does legislation exists which permits Muslims to marry in their own religious rites, but a system is in place which gives authority to elders of the faith to perform these rites with legal authority. Thus, Muslim marriage officers are appointed and registered by the State as marriage officers and in this way Muslim marriages are legitimised. The marriageable age for women also conforms to Muslim religious traditions (12 years). Notwithstanding, polygamy, a characteristic feature of Muslim marriage norms, is not legalised. As with secular marriages, Muslim marriages are to be registered before they are deemed legal.

The incidence of polygamy in Muslim marriages was at one time an obstacle to certain legal rights accruing from marriage, such as maintenance of the wife or children and claims to marital property. In the early case of *Henry v Henry,*[37] for example, a wife in a Muslim marriage who had been legally married under the Muslim Marriage and Divorce Ordinance Chap 29 brought a maintenance claim before the courts. The court refused the claim on the basis that only monogamous marriages in the Christian sense entitled persons to remedies, adjudication or relief in marriage claims, thereby Muslim marriages were excluded. Counsel for the applicant argued successfully that Islamic law was not part of the colony and was 'highly repugnant' to local matrimony law because of polygamy.

The same issue arose with respect to Hindu marriages in *Maharaj v Maharaj,*[38] but with contrasting results. The question was whether the Supreme Court had jurisdiction to pronounce a decree of divorce in relation to a registered Hindu marriage under the Hindu Marriage Ordinance Chap 29, that is, whether the Hindu marriage could be recognised for the purpose of relief. The court found that while Muslim marriages were limited under the law, Hindu marriages were not. Further, the court recognised the indigenous practice of Hinduism in Trinidad, finding that while in England Hindu marriages were potentially polygamous and would not be recognised by the courts, in Trinidad and Tobago the position was different and Hindu marriages were

---

36 Munneke, fn 21, *op cit*, p 1554.
37 (1959) 1 WIR 149.
38 TT 1958 HC 1.

monogamous. Further, the Hindu Marriage Ordinance expressly proclaimed the validity of such marriages when it read:

> such [Hindu] marriage shall . . . be as valid as if it had been solemnized in conformity with the provisions of the said Marriage Ordinance.[39]

The effect of this provision was to equate registered Hindu marriages with those registered under the Marriage Ordinance which applied generally.

The inequitable and intolerant position relating to Muslim marriages thus had to be changed by statute, initially by the Muslim Marriage and Divorce Ordinance 1961, the forerunner of the current legislation. This profound change in the law was recognised in *Rafique v Rafique*.[40] The question whether the newly enacted Muslim Marriage and Divorce Ordinance, No 7 of 1961 had put Muslim marriages on a par with all other marriages recognised by the law of the land was answered in the affirmative, both with respect to the status of such marriages and the remedies which were possible under the law. [41]

Significantly, however, even the new law did not recognise the polygamous aspect of Muslim marriage. Section 7(3) of the Act states specifically that polygamous marriages are not validated. This led the court in *Rafique* to observe that:

> although the Moslem religion may approve and exalt to equality as wives women other than the wife of a valid monogamous marriage, the status of such women in the eyes of the law of the land would be no different from that of paramours whose existence is condemned by the Christian religion . . . and in the Courts it is the law of the land that governs.[42]

It is clear, therefore, that the law does not recognise all facets of religious marriage but only those compatible with Christian marriages.

Similarly, rights and benefits for children born into Muslim marriages have proved litigious. The position now seems settled, however, that such children are recognised by the law as having equal entitlements to other children in the State. Their legal status is derived first from the fact that their parents are party to a marriage known and recognised by the law of the land.[43] The second basis upon which such children have recognised entitlements is through the recognition of common law marriages by the law. Consequently, although the law does not recognised polygamous marriages (and all Muslim marriages are treated as potentially polygamous),[44] children from such marriages are entitled.

As with marriages, the law makes provision for divorce according to religious legal traditions. Such divorces are typically less cumbersome than in Christian or secular divorces. Divorce officers are appointed by the State who operate under the jurisdiction of a Council of Divorce, the chairman of which is an attorney at law of at

---

39 Section 10 of the Ordinance.
40 T&T 1966 CA 132; (1966–1969) 9 T&TLR 184.
41 See, eg, s 7 of the Act: 'Every marriage effected or contracted under this Ordinance . . . shall . . . be as valid as if it had been solemnised or contracted in conformity with the provisions of the Marriage Ordinance'.
42 *Above*, fn 40, p 133.
43 See, eg, *Mohammed v Mohammed* (1960) 3 WIR 202, which also involved a successful maintenance suit on behalf of the wife.
44 See *Henry v Henry, above*, fn 37.

least three years' standing.[45] This Council functions as a quasi-divorce court, hearing and determining petitions of Muslims for divorce according to Islamic tradition.[46] For example, the standard of proof required for divorce for Muslims 'shall be that required under Islamic Law'.[47]

The issue of Muslim divorces and the differences with respect to secular divorces was examined in *Mohammed v Mohammed*.[48] It was confirmed in this case that dissolution of a marriage by the Muslim Marriage Council constituted a valid divorce.

Despite the special jurisdiction afforded to Muslim and Hindu marriages and divorces, the courts of the land are not precluded from assuming jurisdiction in such matters. In *Mohammed*,[49] for example, the court ruled that the legislative ouster clause declaring Muslim divorces determined by the Divorce Councils final and conclusive could not stand. It is clear, therefore, that the courts of the land retain inherent supervisory jurisdiction to review such decisions on marriage and divorce.

A broader point on the jurisdiction of the courts over such marriages and divorces was confirmed in the Trinidadian case of *Ali v Ali*.[50] Here the High Court examined the legal history of the Muslim Marriage and Divorce Act 1961 and the mischief that it attempted to cure, that is, to introduce status and remedies to Muslim marriages and divorces and provide for the maintenance of children in such marriages. However, the court noted that although special Divorce Councils existed to determine Muslim divorces, a petitioner's right to seek relief before the High Court was not abolished.

Notwithstanding the arrangements made for marriages and divorces, a serious defect remains in the system. Since polygamy, a characteristic trait of Muslim marriage traditions, is not recognised by the law, the status of women in such marriages in relation to property rights which typically accrue in marriage, is vulnerable. While the rules of equity can help to remedy this defect, in situations, for example, where a wife has contributed in tangible ways to marital assets,[51] this is not equivalent to a general legal entitlement. Similarly, for religious marriages which have not been registered, the status is that akin to common law marriage.

An example of an enlightened equitable judgment is found in the Guyanese case of *Rahieman v Hack*.[52] The parties had been married according to Muslim rites but never registered the marriage. In a subsequent property dispute between them, the court was willing to apply the equitable principles of the trust giving the 'wife' property rights on the basis of culture and recognition of their religion. The court found the wife to be deserving since the relationship of the parties was of 'some permanence and flows from a marriage in accordance with their religion. This view appears to be consonant not only with reason and palpable justice but also with the culture and way of life of so many of our citizens . . . many persons who are married

---

45   See the Muslim Marriage and Divorce Act, above.
46   *Ibid*. See especially reg 5(1): 'Either party to a marriage shall be at liberty to apply to the Muslim body . . . for the dissolution or annulment of the marriage by filing the application therefore with the Secretary of that body'. Further, under reg 11, the determination of the Council 'shall be final and conclusive'.
47   20 March 1998 (HC, T&T), *per* Sinanan, J.
48   *Above*, fn 43.
49   *Ibid*.
50   TT 1991 HC 175.
51   See, eg, *Khan v Khan*, 30 December 1970 (HC, Guyana). The rules relating to common law marriages for unions which are well established and qualify under the law, may also assist.
52   GY 1975 HC 24.

according to their religion appear not to be interested in registering their marriages accordingly.'[53]

Religious dress and expression

Apart from marriage and divorce, the law also acknowledges certain aspects of dress which are viewed as symbols of religious faith. We have already discussed the case of *Mohammed Moraine*[54] where a Muslim schoolgirl in Trinidad challenged the rules of a convent high school which prohibited her from attending school wearing her hijab. This was a landmark case which was won on grounds of judicial review and not constitutional redress. The school's decision was held to be unreasonable in that it took irrelevant considerations into account.[55]

There is evidence that the law recognises other forms of religious dress and religious symbolism. The issue of the beard, a religious symbol of Islam, has also been litigious. In *Mohammed v the Commissioner of Police*,[56] for example, the court upheld the provisions of the Prisons Act 1838, which acknowledged the Islamic tradition by providing that 'the hair and beard of a Mohammedan shall not be cut except on the written order of the Medical Officer . . .'.[57] Mohammed was at the time serving a prison sentence for breach of a maintenance order.

In a rare case involving African religions and religious expression, *Enyahooma et al v AG of T&T*,[58] the applicant sought constitutional redress alleging that a magistrate had breached his rights to freedom of religion and equality under section 4 of the Constitution by refusing to allow him to retain his tahj in court. He was also ejected from the court upon his refusal to take the tahj off when requested to do so. The issue turned on whether the applicant had informed the magistrate that he was dressed in religious attire and the court concluded that he had not. The court conceded however, that had it been made clear that the applicant was wearing a tahj, a form of religious attire, he should have been permitted to wear the religious garment. The court also noted that other forms of religious head dress such as the orni, worn by Hindu women, were permitted in the courts.

Indeed, in the Guyanese case of *Dick v R*,[59] the Court of Appeal noted the court's tolerance to different religious beliefs in that country, explaining that three religious books were allowed in the courts of the land for swearing in purposes, 'thus underlining that court's official cultural awareness of certain social patterns within the society.'[60]

---

53   *Ibid*, p 28.
54   (1995) 49 WIR 371; [1996] 3 LRC 475. See also Chapter 1 ('Introduction to Law and Legal Systems in the Commonwealth Caribbean').
55   The decision had important social consequences as it paved the way for Muslim school-children being allowed to go to school in religious dress, forcing a change in school policy.
56   12 January 2005 (HC, T&T). The issue has also come before the United Nations Human Rights Committee when prisoners from Trinidad and Tobago made complaints on the ground of freedom of religion. See, eg, *Boodoo v T&T* UNHRC Comm No 721/1996.
57   Rule 248.
58   TT 2002 HC 103.
59   GY 1985 CA 3.
60   *Ibid*, p 4. But contrast the court's attitude in *Dookie v The State*, TT 1989 CA 1, where a Trinidadian court treated with some disdain a defendant accused of murder when he explained in a somewhat bizarre defence as to why he had murdered his wife that he was a Hindu and believed that he and his children would be reincarnated after death and go on to a better life!

In recent times, similar issues have been hotly contested before the European courts and there appears to be a swing against the freedom to manifest one's religion. This seems to be a response to allegations of religious extremism, particularly Islamic extremism, since the terrorist events of September 2001.[61] As yet, the West Indian courts have not taken this approach.

Legal pluralism or legal tokenism?

Although the Hindu and Muslim religions are practised by these large communities and influence the cultural outlook of their respective countries, it is difficult to perceive any true corresponding penetration into the dominant legal traditions of these countries. Both Hindus and Muslims must come before the common law courts for legal remedies and redress. Similarly, their legal transactions and practices, apart from the instances mentioned above, must conform to the common law or ordinary statute applicable to the entire population. It is therefore their non-contentious social and religious beliefs, rather than general legal aspects of their traditions, which are exhibited in the Commonwealth Caribbean.

Thus, even in relation to these concessions to marriage and religious symbolism, upon closer examination of the attitude of the courts, it is difficult to discern any genuine accommodation of these religious traditions when it matters most, that is, when they appear to conflict with the dominant Christian religious beliefs of the society. The refusal to accommodate polygamy for Muslims is but one example. In other instances, while the courts have been anxious to proclaim religious freedoms, they have curiously found several other ways for denying such freedoms, in a host of technical and perhaps circuitous ways, such as in *Enyahooma*, proclaiming that a magistrate has no duty to ascertain a person's religious beliefs as manifested in dress, thereby placing the burden on an applicant to demonstrate the religious significance of his dress or beliefs. In a similar vein, in *Re Orisa Movement EGBE*,[62] the Orisa Movement, a body of African religious believers who had incorporated their group, failed in its bid to assert a violation of their rights to conscience when the national television company broadcasted a programme which they alleged presented them in a negative light. One of the arguments raised against their action was that, as a corporate body, they could not enjoy freedom of conscience.

We may argue that Rastafarianism is another minority religion in the Commonwealth Caribbean, one worthy of examining whether there are separate legal influences. However, as we have seen,[63] the courts have had difficulty accepting the religious tenets of Rastafarianism (such as the use of ganja) and sometimes have even been reluctant to regard it as a religion, on grounds such as its recent origin and non-theistic character. Here too, we see a failure to accommodate religious doctrine where it conflicts with that of Christian doctrine.[64]

The cases discussed do not necessarily demonstrate inaccurate reasoning by the various courts. They do, however, challenge the assumptions made about West Indian

---

61 See, eg, *Monribot v Société Sagem* 23 ILLR 121 (France); *Dahlab v Switzerland* 21 ILLR 13; *Shabina Begum v The Headteacher, Governor of Denbigh High School* [2004] EWHC 1389; (2006) UKHL 15.

62 TT 1983 HC 121.

63 See Chapter 1 ('Introduction to Law and Legal Systems in the Commonwealth Caribbean').

64 See, eg, *Dawkins v Dept of the Environment* [1993] IRLR 284; *Chikweche* [1995] 2 LRC 93; *Grant and Chin v Principal of JCPS et al* [1999] CILR 307.

societies, in particular, Guyana and Trinidad and Tobago, that they are pluralistic. Rather, it is evident that while different ethnic groups are given some acknowledgement by the law, the concept of legal pluralism cannot be said to exist. Any such pluralistic elements remain essentially in the social and cultural domain.

THE LEGAL TRADITION OF THE FAR EAST

Although the law in the countries of the Far East may appear to follow Western models in their form and technique, it is in the *attitudes* towards law and the role of function of law in society that substantial differences between East and West may be found. Because of this, the law of the Far East can be classified separately. The countries of the Far East do not conform to a uniform system of law. In China, for example, communism informs the political and legal order. In contrast, Japan, a close adherence to Western ideals in the form of capitalism, democracy, and a legal system based on the American model of the common law tradition may be ascertained. Nevertheless, greater assimilarity between China and Japan may be seen to exist than when compared to the former USSR and the USA, the two countries with which they appear to have political affinity. Indeed, the culture of traditional thinking in China and Japan has resulted in the formation of unique models of communism and capitalism respectively. Thus, neither the Socialist Legal nor the common law traditions fully explain the legal systems of the Far East.

The attitude towards law in the countries of the Far East is characterised by negotiation, persuasion and conciliation. These are believed to be typical Eastern attitudes for dispute solving. They can be contrasted with the spirit of adjudication or tendency toward litigation evident in Western modes of thought.[65] Law appears to be exalted in Western countries, but there is an aversion to law as a primary means of dispute solving in Far Eastern countries. The legal process is invoked primarily when other means for the resolution of conflicts have failed or been exhausted.

CONCLUSION – WHITHER COMMONWEALTH CARIBBEAN LEGAL SYSTEMS?

From the previous discussion of the various legal traditions of the world, it is not difficult to premise that the dominant legal tradition in the Commonwealth Caribbean is that of the common law tradition. Yet, this assertion by no means gives a total picture. It is necessary to make further observations about the legal systems in the Commonwealth Caribbean.

Most of the countries in the Commonwealth Caribbean have now attained independence from British domination and with it they have, in the main, re-endorsed the ideals of the common law tradition. However, these countries have deviated to a limited extent from some of the fundamental principles and characteristics of the original model of the tradition. The embrace of written Constitutions is the prime example of this deviance. With the advent of written Constitutions, the doctrine of parliamentary sovereignty, a fundamental characteristic of the English common law tradition, has been rejected in favour of the doctrine of constitutional supremacy.

---

65   See *op cit*, Zweigert and Kotz, fn 4.

This variation in Commonwealth Caribbean jurisdictions is more in keeping with the Anglo-American model of the common law tradition. In fact, the Bills of Rights which exist in Commonwealth Caribbean Constitutions have been greatly influenced by the American Bill of Rights.[66]

It is not suggested, however, that the above changes, substantial though they may be, are enough to ground the argument that the Commonwealth Caribbean exhibits deviant tendencies from the original conception of the model in the same way as do other countries of the common law world, such as the United States of America.

Evidence of competing legal traditions in the region, in principle, if not in practice, make the classification of the Commonwealth Caribbean into one particular legal tradition more complex than it first appears. Most significant is the location of legal norms of the civil law tradition in Guyana and St Lucia. This is discussed separately in Chapter 4 ('The hybrid legal systems of St Lucia and Guyana'). As we have seen, the socialist experiments of Grenada and Guyana can also produce some intellectual difficulty, at least from a historical perspective. The dilemma is even more apparent in the Republic of Guyana, where there has also been a blending together of the civilist and common law traditions. Coupled with the declaration of socialism found in that country's Constitution,[67] the problem of an apt category is intriguing. Is this identification with socialism to be viewed as another phase of hybridism or is it only cosmetic, having no real effect on the existing legal tradition?

Finally, one may make some observations on the attitudes toward law in the Commonwealth Caribbean and the way in which indigenous social norms impinge upon the law and legal tradition. It is worth re-emphasising that the classification of law into legal families and traditions is concerned not only with the organisation and operation of the legal system and its rules but also with the deeply rooted attitudes which inform the law. This includes attitudes towards the role of the law in the society and the way in which the law and legal system are related to the culture of the society within which it operates. To what extent can we identify cultural elements of West Indian society in the law? Could these be sufficient to justify a separate legal tradition, at least in the future? The justification for a separate classification for the legal systems of the Far East was based on just such a focus on societal attitudes and attitudes toward law. It is not frivolous to ask the question in relation to law and legal systems in the Commonwealth Caribbean.

West Indian attitudes toward law

By and large, the societies of the Commonwealth Caribbean are cosmopolitan societies and are made up of a miscegenation of various races and cultures. Eastern and African ideas and attitudes meet with those of the West. It is hardly surprising that some of these cultural norms are reflected in Commonwealth Caribbean attitudes towards law. For example, the African concept of the family unit as an extended family is still evident in the Commonwealth Caribbean and has even been given

---

66   Which in turn has been influenced by the natural law school of thought in the civil law tradition. See discussion on the civil law above, p 30 and Chapter 7 ('The Written Constitution as a Legal Source').

67   Constitution of the Co-operative Republic of Guyana, 1980, Art 1.

judicial recognition. In the case of *AB v Social Welfare Officer*,[68] a Barbadian court ruled that in Caribbean societies, where it is the norm for grandmothers to care for children, the English common law rule restricting legal adoption of such children could not be followed.

Cultural perspectives which are the result of societies which were once under the shackles of slavery and colonisation may also explain different attitudes toward the law. Law, associated with colonial rule and government, can easily be perceived as alien and oppressing. This may account for the lack of redress to the courts as a means for dispute solving. The relatively high proportion of children born out of wedlock has similarly been analysed as an outgrowth of slavery. This has resulted in a rejection of the concept of illegitimacy in some instances.[69] It is another example of the way in which cultural norms have shaped the law.

Legal traditions of the Amerindians

There is no legal tradition which describes the law and legal systems of the 'indigenous' or original peoples of the region, the Amerindians. This is despite the fact that it is accepted that the Amerindians – in particular, the Aztecs and Mayas – had highly developed civilisations and legal traditions of their own.[70] This omission is an historical anomaly. We have already seen that the laws of these original peoples were displaced by the colonisers. What exists today is not 'Amerindian' law, but law designed by hostile invaders and their modern-day conspirators. It exists primarily to compartmentalise the Amerindians and preserve their minority status.[71] The experience of the region's true inhabitants are not, therefore, reflected in the legal tradition ascribed to the region. It cannot even be said to form a hybrid legal construct.

---

68   (1961) 3 WIR 420.
69   Many jurisdictions in the Commonwealth Caribbean have abolished 'illegitimacy' as a legal concept.
70   The descendants of the Mayas still exist in Belize. See Chapter 10 ('Custom as a Source of Law').
71   See, eg, laws which regulate 'reservations' for Amerindians, such as the Carib Reserve Act 1991 of Dominica.

CHAPTER 4

THE HYBRID LEGAL SYSTEMS OF ST LUCIA AND GUYANA

INTRODUCTION

Not all legal systems can be classified so rigidly as to fall into distinct legal traditions. Some legal systems are a mixture of these traditions, and can thus be described as mixed or hybrid legal systems. In the Commonwealth Caribbean, the phenomenon has found a home as exhibited by the legal systems of Guyana and St Lucia.[1]

As we noted previously, the history of legal systems in the Commonwealth Caribbean is intimately related to the story of conquest.[2] It is noteworthy that the rule with the British conquerors was that they retained the laws and institutions of conquered territories, while reserving the right to change them. The experiences of Guyana and St Lucia are no exception to this rule, and best explain the phenomenon of hybrid or mixed legal systems.

CLASSIFYING HYBRID LEGAL TRADITIONS

Two central questions must be addressed in the discussion on hybrid systems. First, we can question the very nomenclature 'hybrid legal system' or tradition. What are the characteristics of such a system? Is there in existence a legal tradition with such clear, distinguishing characteristics that it is deserving of a separate classification or is it accurately placed in a more traditional classification?

Secondly, we are concerned about the sustainability or viability of a hybrid system. Even if we concede that such a legal system displays deviant characteristics, we may well ask whether it is merely in a transitory process, *en route* to becoming a more orthodox legal system. Alternatively, is the hybrid nature of the system itself a permanent or enduring one? Indeed, in a world of increased communication and openness, legal systems do not stand in isolation. The great legal traditions of the world are steadily feeding upon each other and some comparativists question the very term hybridism, arguing that all legal systems in the world today are to a certain extent hybrid.

True hybrid legal traditions should not be viewed as merely being in a stage of transformation or belonging predominantly to one legal tradition, but should be judged on their own. Thus, judicial decisions and institutions should be examined against the peculiar sociological character or pattern of the system. They have, in fact,

---

1   For a comprehensive and authoritative examination of the hybrid legal system of St Lucia, see the work of Anthony, KD, in such publications as 'Aspects of the evolution of Caribbean legal systems', in *Comparative Law Studies*, 1986, Washington: OAS, General Secretariat, p 29; 'The viability of the civilist legal tradition in Saint Lucia', in Landry, RA and Caparros, E (eds), *Essays on the Civil Codes of Quebec and St Lucia*, 1984, Ottawa: Ottawa UP, p 33; 'The reception of the common law system by the civil law systems in the Commonwealth Caribbean', in Doucet, M and Venderlinden, J (eds), *La Réception des Systèmes Juridiques*, 1994, Brussels: Bruylant, p 15; 'The identification and classification of mixed systems of law', in Kodilinye, G and Menon, PK (eds), *Commonwealth Caribbean Legal Studies*, 1992, London: Butterworths, p 179. In this chapter, the author wishes to acknowledge the reliance placed on these authorities.

2   See above, Chapter 1.

evolved a 'judicial personality' of their own.[3] The process is not merely an aspect of a legal or historical folk culture. Hybrid legal systems are often in a state of flux and could reject their mixed character and conform to a single legal tradition. This leads to problems of continuity. Still, it is often very difficult to determine whether the legal system is in the process of this transformation.

To identify the existence of a hybrid legal system we may consider the way in which structured, cultural and substantive elements interact with each other under the influence of external or situational factors pressing in from the larger society. Anthony further suggests that we examine the following specific elements of the legal system:

(a) the infrastructure of the legal system – that is, its institutional foundations;

(b) legal norms – that is, substantive rules and legal sources and their relative importance;

(c) legal methodology – the principles of reasoning relating to the discovery and application of rules of law;

(d) legal style – how legal principles and concepts are expressed;

(e) values which underpin the system, and, more specifically, the folklore which sustains it. This is to determine the beliefs about the legal system itself.

A hybrid legal system may be identified if, after examining these distinctive elements, we recognise fundamental characteristics of more than one legal tradition. We can reiterate crucial elements of this phenomenon as being the evolving nature of the system and the cross-breeding of inherited traditions. Further, the hybrid character is reinforced if any existing duality in the legal culture metamorphoses into a permanent feature.

Hybrid legal systems thus contain a plurality of legal traditions. The majority are composed of a mixture of common law and civil law. They are the products of more than one wave of reception of law because of historical events such as colonisation, double colonisation, cession, purchase or annexation by a State or power with a legal system of a different tradition than that of the jurisdiction acquired. The historical process is therefore crucial to the development or underdevelopment of the hybrid legal system.

In hybrid legal systems, the civil law is restricted primarily to the private law. In contrast, public law characteristically belongs to the legal tradition of the conquering or acquiring power. It is, essentially, an expression of sovereign power. For example, constitutional law in St Lucia belongs to the English common law tradition. Procedural law usually belongs to the legal tradition of the ultimate conquering power. Again, in St Lucia, court procedural rules and legal training conform to the English common law.[4]

Mixed or hybrid legal systems are not homogeneous in all essential characteristics. In some cases, the private law is codified, while in others, it is not. Similarly,

---

3   *Op cit*, Anthony, 'The viability of the civilist legal tradition in St Lucia', fn 1. The differences between plural legal systems and hybrid or mixed ones should also be noted. They are only superficially similar. Pluralism exists within a political entity in a State where particular clusters of rules apply only to particular groups such as ethnic or class minorities. In contrast, in hybrid legal systems there is one set of rules for everyone and every situation but these rules are themselves derived from different legal traditions and the legal system itself is cohesive.

4   This is not surprising as the conquering power expects to further undermine the 'conquered' law.

some mixed systems are independent State entities, while others are sub-legal systems, such as in Quebec.

These legal systems are constantly evolving. They are under constant pressure to alter or change their status and conform to one tradition or another. This may be either internal or external pressure. A practical but telling example is this. Legal training for West Indian students of law occurs at the University of the West Indies, which is schooled in the English common law. This exerts pressure on law students and practitioners from St Lucia, who, by and large, have to educate themselves on the civil law aspects of the legal system.

The role of indigenous law, legal attitudes and culture is even more important as a distinguishing characteristic of the legal system. The existence of hybrid legal systems may often stimulate creative legal responses, as legal rules may not always be clearly identified as belonging to a particular legal tradition.

The very existence of these deviant legal systems makes the exercise of the classification of legal traditions even more difficult. Depending on the criteria used, two different outcomes are possible. If we focus on substance or substantive rules, and the core of the legal system is identified as private law, we might conclude that the legal system is essentially civilist but with a common law overlay. This is because, as discussed previously, the private law is found in the Code. On the other hand, if we use criteria such as legal style, historical sources and concepts, we might conclude that it is essentially common law. The difficulty of classification into orthodox legal traditions underscores the need for an independent category of classification. Yet in the mere acknowledgment of the concept of a hybrid legal system, we are challenging the very rigidity of the classification exercise.[5]

THE HYBRID PHENOMENON IN THE COMMONWEALTH CARIBBEAN

Because of our peculiar historical development, all jurisdictions in the Commonwealth Caribbean could, at one time or another, have been described as mixed. All exhibited characteristics of one, or more than one, legal tradition. For example, when the Spaniards rediscovered most of the Caribbean territories, civil law was introduced by them. During the following period of English and French conquest, civil law (from the French) and the common law (from the English) would have been introduced. Trinidad, for example, had, until recently, heavy influences of Spanish civil law mingled with the English common law.[6] Yet we do not classify them all as hybrid. Today, St Lucia and Guyana are the only two jurisdictions in the Commonwealth Caribbean which can legitimately be described as hybrid. This tells us that the survivability of

---

5   See the discussion in Chapter 3 ('Legal Traditions – Types of Legal Systems in the Commonwealth Caribbean') on the artificiality of the exercise of classifying legal systems into definite traditions.

6   See, eg, Campbell, C, 'The transition from Spanish law to English law in Trinidad' (1989) 3 The Lawyer 15. Up to the 1830s, it was still possible to describe the legal system as an Anglo-Spanish system. It was not purely Spanish, nor purely English, but an uneasy concoction of both. Report of His Majesty's Commissioners of Legal Inquiry on the Colony of Trinidad, 1827. Anthony explains that, while Trinidad initially displayed certain hybrid characteristics, the Spanish civil law did not endure, and the term 'hybrid' is no longer appropriate in today's context, op cit, Anthony, 'The reception of the common law systems by the civil law systems in the Commonwealth Caribbean', fn 1.

these mixed elements through successive colonisation periods was so extraordinary as to warrant special classification.

Outside of St Lucia, Guyana and the rest of the Commonwealth Caribbean, we can group amongst hybrid legal traditions States such as Israel, Quebec, Mauritius, Scotland, Louisiana, South Africa and Sri Lanka (the latter two are a mixture of common law and Roman-Dutch law). The essential point with all these hybrid or mixed systems is that they cannot be easily placed into one single category, that is, neither the common law nor civil law traditions.

Hybrid legal systems in the Commonwealth Caribbean can be described as systems which are essentially that of the civil law tradition and which have been considerably undermined due to the influence of external pressures from the Anglo-American common law. They have, in part, been overlaid by that rival system of jurisprudence.[7] In consequence, they possess fundamental characteristics of both the civil and common law legal traditions. Such systems usually emerge out of the process of double colonisation, the change from one coloniser to another, as occurred so frequently in the Caribbean. Indeed, St Lucia, the prime example of a mixed legal system in the Caribbean, changed hands 14 times, alternating between French and English domination. This was a battle of political will which expressed itself in the law.

Anthony[8] maintains that there is a definite historical pattern which secures this process of anglicisation. He outlines certain features of the process. They include the establishment of an ultimate appellate jurisdiction to force integration into the common law structure, legislative control, adoption of the style and procedure of the common law and forced adoption of English as the official language. Today, there is still evidence of this conflict with language (albeit resolved happily), as St Lucians are bilingual, speaking both English and French patois. The colonisers were aware that one route to legal and political domination was through the control of language. Initially, the Civil Code was written in the French language.

THE GUYANESE EXPERIENCE

In Guyana, systems of Roman-Dutch law, followed by English common law, were the legacy of colonialism under the Dutch empire and Britain respectively. It is a truism that European colonists in the West Indies took their law with them. Consequently, the colonisation of Guyana by the Dutch at the end of the 16th century was accompanied by the transplantation of Roman-Dutch law there. Although Guyana was to come under Dutch, French and British rule, it was only the Dutch and English legal systems which took root.

The legal system under Roman-Dutch law comprised the law received from the colonisers and statute law enacted by legislative bodies such as the West India Company. The Civil Law of Guyana Act[9] attempts to rationalise the remaining civil law. This is a legal regime which is still evident in certain areas of the law of property, such as the law relating to the acquisition and expropriation of property, insolvency, matrimonial causes and the law of succession.

---

7   *Op cit*, Anthony, 'Aspects of the evolution of Caribbean legal systems', fn 1.
8   *Op cit*, Anthony, 'The viability of the civilist legal tradition in St Lucia', fn 1, p 8.
9   Cap 6:01 [G].

The legal tradition which took hold in Guyana via the Roman-Dutch law was itself of a civil hybrid kind. It was a mixture of Teutonic law and custom with Roman law. The combined set of principles was described as the Roman-Dutch law. Within the Netherlands there were indigenous systems in the several States. Yet, it was the Dutch law which largely took root in Guyana.

A firm statement on the application of Roman-Dutch law to the Dutch colonies was given in 1629 in an Order of the Netherlands Government. This order provided that the law applicable to all the Dutch colonies was the Political Ordinance of 1580, which codified the common custom of South Holland in relation to civil cases. It also provided the authority for the transplantation of Roman-Dutch law in criminal matters, family law, law of property, contract and regulation of government.

The legal system of Guyana continued to be totally Roman-Dutch until the cession of Guyana to the British, after which there was a steady erosion of the Roman civil tradition. This consequently gave way to the common law tradition nurtured by the English. The English capitulation of 1803 had a profound effect upon the juris-prudence of Guyana, resulting in a legal system of a hybrid nature which derived its principles from both the civil and common law and produced an Anglo-Roman jurisprudence. The new hybrid system sometimes produced conflict. After the initial formation, radical changes were introduced to the law to correct this incongruous mixture of Dutch and English legal principles.

The Roman-Dutch system still thrived during the remainder of the 19th century, but it was inevitable that it would steadily give way to the law of the English con-querors. By means of statute, much of Roman-Dutch law was replaced. For example, in 1846, 17 ordinances were passed introducing English criminal law to replace that of Roman-Dutch origin. This was followed by the introduction of English mercantile law in 1874, the English Interpretation Ordinance in 1891, the Companies Ordinance and the Sales of Goods legislation in 1913.

In 1924 the Common Law Commission of Guyana completed the final, decisive step in the process with the following recommendations:

> [The] introduction of the English common law in regard to all mercantile matters, to all domestic relations ... to the law of delicts or torts, agency, surety, liens, intestate, succession, and in fact to all the law of persons, things, obligations, inheritance, and every other description of matters whatsoever not dealt with by legislation or otherwise exempted. The English law of real property should be expressly excluded.[10]

This hybrid mixture of the common law and the Roman-Dutch legal tradition was further complicated by undertones of the socialist legal tradition as declared in the 1980 Constitution, although very little else of this influence is apparent.

Yet, in *Ramamugh and Another v Hand in Hand Mutual Life Insurance and Others*,[11] the Guyanese Court of Appeal found that although the civil law of the British Guiana Ordinance 1917 had 'sounded the death knell of the Roman-Dutch system of law', the pre-1917 Roman-Dutch law and practice relating to conventional mortgages had been preserved.[12]

---

10 As reported in Shahabuddeen, M, *The Legal System of Guyana*, 1973, Georgetown: Guyana Printers, p 203.
11 (1992) 47 WIR 198.
12 *Ibid*, p 203.

Less surprisingly, the Court of Appeal of Guyana in *Nazim v AG and Others*[13] looked to the Civil Law of Guyana Act,[14] in a case on specific performance relating to an agreement for land. The pertinent question was whether a plaintiff seeking an order of specific performance had to disclose in his statement of claim that the action was maintainable in that the agreement had to be in writing. This was to satisfy the Statute of Frauds, which was incorporated into the law of Guyana by the Civil Law of Guyana Act. Answering in the negative, the court noted that specific performance for an agreement to a sale of land is available on the principles which obtain in England by virtue of the reception of those equitable principles under the Civil Law of Guyana Act.[15]

The civil law tradition in Guyana was not as enduring as that of St Lucia's, discussed below, pp 63–72. Shahabuddeen outlines several factors which were conducive to the abolition of Roman-Dutch law: first, Roman-Dutch law 'did not enjoy the protective shield of a Code'. Since Code law is 'hard law', it is less easily amenable to interference. Further, Roman-Dutch law did not apply the doctrine of stare decisis. Hence, Roman-Dutch judges were not required to give reasons for their judgments. This practice of the civil law was a source of conflict to common law advocates, accustomed to relying on precedent as a source of law. Further, there was a 'general lack of sympathy' for Roman-Dutch law, which was 'not difficult to understand given the unfamiliarity of common law judges with the legal system'.[16]

It is of little surprise, therefore, that the legal system as it exists today in Guyana is primarily that of the common law tradition, with mere remnants of the Roman-Dutch tradition.

THE HYBRID LEGAL SYSTEM OF ST LUCIA

The legal system of St Lucia has been described by one writer as a 'fascinating blend of Quebec, French, English and indigenous law'.[17] It is this multiformity that earns the St Lucian system the classification of a hybrid legal system.

Although the phenomenon of colonialism resulted in the transplantation of the civil law tradition to other Caribbean territories such as Trinidad and Guyana, it is only in St Lucia that the substantial features and content of civil law in the form of a Civil Code survived British colonial domination. This survival is remarkable when one considers the deliberate effort made by Britain to anglicise the law of its Caribbean colonies. Unlike that of Guyana, the civil law tradition of St Lucia had a resilience so outstanding as to make the legal system of that territory truly unique. The transplantation of the common law on the civil law inheritance was the foundation upon which the hybrid character of the legal system was built.

Several reasons have been advanced to explain the survival of the civilist tradition in St Lucia. White[18] looks to the fact of codification of the civil law for an explanation.

---

13   (2004) 67 WIR 147 (CA) Guyana.
14   Cap 60:01 [G].
15   *Above*, fn 13 at p 152.
16   (1992) 47 WIR 198.
17   Floissac, V, 'The interpretation of the civil code of Saint Lucia' in R A Landry, *above*, fn 1 at p 339.
18   White, D, 'Some Problems of a Hybrid Legal System: a Case Study of St Lucia' (1981) 30 ICLQ 862.

In her view, codification 'confers a certain enduring quality on law and codified law is tough law'. The fact that a separate commercial code was adopted, which had the effect of placating French business interests, is also advanced as a reason for the civil law's survival:[19]

> ... thus, unlike Trinidad and British Guiana, St Lucian commercial interests did not have the opportunity to extend their demands beyond anglicisation of the commercial law to include the code.[20]

Anthony, while agreeing with the above arguments, believes that further analysis is necessary to explain the uniqueness of the St Lucian experience. He argues that other '... explanations are to be found ... in the politics of the legal culture'.[21]

One such explanation is the historical experience of the island. Its frequent changeovers between British and French ownership led to a real desire to protect French hegemony.[22] The result was the formation of well established civil law institutions and legal rules which formed a solid and entrenched base from which opposition to anglicisation of the law could be supported.

This was to supplement the already solid legal base which the British found in St Lucia:

> When St Lucia was ceded to England in 1814, it had firmly rooted French traditions and institutions. The British inherited a legal system based on ancient French law, before the promulgation of the Coutume de Paris.[23]

Another factor instrumental in securing the immediate future of the civilist tradition was the work of William De Voeux as the Administrator of the island and James Armstrong as Chief Justice. These two officials were determined to introduce certainly into the civil law as it existed in St Lucia. They did this through codification based on the model of the English versions of the Quebec Civil Code and the Code of Civil Procedure. This process had been completed by 20 October 1879 in the form of the St Lucian Civil Code. It is believed that the adoption of the Quebec Code represented a neat compromise, for it allowed the civil law tradition to survive, while the element of certainty within the law, and the fact that the Code was in English, pleased the British administrators. The success of this compromise sheds further light on the reason for the survival of the civil law tradition in St Lucia.

It is to be noted that the Quebec Code itself already had its share of infusion of English common law rules and remedies. This enhances the hybrid nature of the St Lucia legal system.

---

19   Both by White, *ibid*, and K D Anthony, *above*, fn 1.
20   *Op cit*, White, fn 18, p 14.
21   *Op cit*, Anthony, 'The viability of the civilist legal tradition in St Lucia', fn 1, p 14.
22   When the island was ceded under the Treaty of Paris 1814, there was an express undertaking that the French civil law would be continued. Adherence to this undertaking in spirit, if not in detail, is one reason for the endurance of the civil law.
23   Anthony, K and Ventose, E, 'St Lucia' in Kritzer, H (ed) *Legal Systems of the World*, 2002, USA: ABC-CLIO, p 1539. For further reading, see Anthony, K, *op cit*, n 1.

EROSION OF THE CIVIL LAW

The erosion of the civilist tradition in St Lucia began even before the enactment of the St Lucia Civil Code. Court procedure was anglicised as were the requirements for admission to the St Lucian Bar. The most damaging weapon of the common law, however, was the training of lawyers and judges in the common law tradition. Potent, too, was the fact that the official legislature and administrative outlook had become completely anglicised.

The infusion of common law into the civil law tradition was done in two stages. The first stage saw a definite trend toward the adoption of the common law by legislative provisions. The second stage of the process is perhaps responsible for the conversion of the Civil Code into a hybrid one. This was done by the large scale introduction of English law reception provisions. However, the alterations to the Code did not change its civilian arrangement. The Code is, therefore, part civil and part common law.

The thrust towards deliberate anglicisation of St Lucian law reached its peak with the passing of the St Lucia (Reform and Revision) Ordinance in 1954. This Ordinance gave the Law Reform Commissioner power to assimilate the Code to the law of England in accordance with the then needs of the island where they differed.

In 1956 a Civil Code (Amendment) Ordinance 1956 was enacted which replaced, repealed or amended a number of provisions in the Code. Many codal provisions were replaced with prevailing English law. This led to an importation of English law unsurpassed by no other such importations under previous amendments to that Code.[24]

This large-scale importation of English law was effected primarily by reception clauses. Through these reception provisions, the English law of contracts, quasi-contracts and torts were introduced. For example, Article 917 A of the Code, reads:

> Subject to the provisions of this Article the law of England for the time being relating to contracts, quasi-contracts and torts shall, *mutatis mutandis* extend to this Colony and the provisions of Articles 918 to 998 and 991 to 1132 of this Code shall as far as practicable be construed accordingly; and the said article shall cease to be construed in accordance with the law of Lower Canada or the Coutume de Paris.[25]

The Code also specifically proscribed the interpretation of certain articles in accordance with the Quebec Code and provided that common law interpretations should be employed as far as practicable. This was complemented by express repetition of certain English statutory provisions.

The St Lucia Civil Code is divided into Parts which are in turn subdivided into Books. The various Parts relate respectively to persons, property ownership, acquisition and exercise of rights and property, trustees and the administration of trusts. The most far-reaching legislative infusion of English law into the Civil Code was

---

24   For further discussion on the Reception of the common law into the St Lucia legal system, see Chapter 5 ('The Reception of English Law and its Significance to Caribbean Jurisdictions').

25   There then follows a number of provisos to this general reception clause such as the meaning ascribed to consideration, considered below.

the reception of the trust concept.[26] This concept was hitherto unknown to the civil law.

Other English importations included the law of evidence, agency, liability for fatal accidents and the meanings assigned to adultery, cruelty and desertion. Further, the doctrine of privity was made subject to the right of stipulation for third parties in accordance with Article 962 of the Code.

Law of contract under the Civil Code of St Lucia

The introduction of English contract law was qualified in that the term 'consideration' was not to be interpreted in like manner to that under the common law tradition but referred to the civilian concept of 'cause'. This was confirmed in the case of *Velox and Another v HelenAir Corporation & Others*.[27] In this case the Court of Appeal overturned a judgment of the High Court which had dismissed a claim for a declaration that 10,000 paid up shares in HelenAir Corporation had been owned by John Velox. Redhead JA found that the trial judge had erred in applying the English common law doctrine of consideration instead of the meaning of consideration found under the Civil Code. He ruled that the reason for the appellant being given the shares was merely to enhance the standing of the defendant company but that this was sufficient to satisfy a contract under Article 917 A, proviso (b), which prescribed a different meaning to the term 'consideration' and made the English doctrine of consideration inapplicable. The relevant article reads:

> 917A Subject to the provisions of this article . . . the law of England for the time being relating to contracts, quasi-contracts and torts shall mutatis mutandis extend to this Colony . . . Provided however, as follows:
>
> (a) the English doctrine of consideration shall not apply to contracts governed by the law of the Colony and the term 'consideration' shall have the meaning herein assigned to it;
>
> (b) the term 'consideration' where used with respect to contracts shall continue, as heretofore to mean the cause or reason of entering into the contract or of incurring an obligation and consideration may be either onerous or gratuitous.

In accordance with (b) above, the Court of Appeal easily found that the appellant was the lawful owner of the shares as the requirement for consideration had been met.

Thus, while St Lucia still enjoys the distinction of being the only country in the region which did not introduce the common law of England way of a general reception clause and date,[28] it has, nevertheless, anglicised some aspects of its law and legal system by piecemeal incorporation.

Influence of Quebec law

Despite the injection of the English common law, the importance of the Civil Code of Quebec 1865 in interpreting the St Lucia Civil Code still remains, particularly, where

---

26 With the addition of Article 916, Cap 242. For an in-depth discussion of the introduction of the trust and its interpretation in St Lucia, see K D Anthony, 'Approaches to the Common Law trust in Codified Mixed Jurisdictions' in J McBride (ed) *Droit Sans Frontieres, Essays in Honour of L. Neville Brown*, 1991, Birmingham: Holdsworth Club. See also Chapter 9 ('Equity as a Source of Law').

27 (1997) 55 WIR 179 (CA).

28 See Chapter 5 ('The Reception of English Law and its Significance to Caribbean Jurisdictions').

the Code is silent on the interpretation of a particular provision. The Quebec Code is, at the very least, highly persuasive authority, a point which was noted forcefully by the Privy Council in *Poliniere and Others v Felicien*.[29] The case concerned the appropriate formalities which were to attach to an indirect gift of property. Their Lordships advised that 'anyone attempting to interpret the Civil Code must bear in mind that it is derived, in most cases word for word, from the Quebec Civil Code of 1865, which in turn was derived from the Code Civil of France'. According to their Lordships, this could only mean that the Legislature intended that the provisions should mean what they did in Quebec. Notably, the court found that where there was no available authority on the point from Quebec, it could look to the provisions in France for meaning.

In general, their Lordships warned that 'it was unwise for the judge and the Court of Appeal to have attempted to construe them [the St Lucia provisions] without any reference to their civilian background'. Rather, the Quebec and French jurisprudence was always of 'considerable authority'. In this case, therefore, the Privy Council looked to French jurisprudence to find that both the indirect gift and its acceptance had to be authenticated before a notary.[30]

This approach was reaffirmed in the Privy Council judgment of *Noelina Maria Prospere (nee Madore) v Frederick Prospere and Jennifer Remy*.[31] The case concerned the sale of land alleged to be community property, such sale being made without the consent of one of the parties to the marriage, Mrs Prospere. While the High Court initially ruled in favour of Mrs Prospere, declaring the property to be community property and the sale null and void, the Court of Appeal overruled that judgment.[32] After the Court of Appeal, Mrs Prospere initiated other writs contesting the sale which made it necessary for the Privy Council to determine the meaning of the term *res judicata* under St Lucian law. Their Lordships held that the question of *res judicata* was to be interpreted according to Article 1171 of the Civil Code of St Lucia. In interpreting this provision, they said that:

> [i]t was common ground between the parties that, if in doubt about the interpretation of the St Lucia Civil Code, the Board should seek guidance from authority on the Civil Codes of Quebec and France.

Consequently, the Privy Council relied on a judgment from Lower Canada, that of *Roberge v Bolduc*.[33] Their Lordships concluded that the effect of the Court of Appeal judgment in the first action was to set aside the judge's declaration that the deed of sale was null and void and thus to leave the deed of sale unchallenged on the register. The appeal was consequently dismissed with costs against Mrs Prospere.

---

29 (2000) 56 WIR 264 (PC, St Lucia).
30 *Ibid*, p 267.
31 PC Appeal No 18 of 2005, dec'd 17 January 2007 (St Lucia).
32 See the Court of Appeal judgment at (1992) 44 WIR 172 (CA, St Lucia). In doing so, the Court of Appeal explored the meaning of community property under the St Lucia Civil Code, finding that property was community property only if both parties were domiciled in St Lucia at the date of the marriage. The Court of Appeal also found that Mr Prospere could not challenge his own deed and that Mr Prospere had not proved his St Lucian domicile at the time of the marriage.
33 [1991] 1 SCR 374.

DIFFICULTIES IN APPLYING ST LUCIA'S CIVIL CODE

The multiformity of the Civil Code of St Lucia, derived from its diverse sources of law, has been 'complex and perilous to the unsuspecting lawyer' and the 'equally unsuspecting common law judge'.[34] It is difficult for lawyers trained in the common law tradition to appreciate the different nuances of the civil law, while it is equally demanding to operate within a system which is neither civil nor common law, although possessing characteristics of both.

The inherent difficulties of a uniquely hybrid system such as St Lucia are further complicated by the uncertainty surrounding the exact scope of its general reception clause in the light of the specific reception of a number of English statutory provisions. This may be due to the incoherent legislative approach to the introduction of common law rules.

This was demonstrated in the case of *Spiricor of St Lucia Ltd v AG of St Lucia and Another*,[35] where the Court of Appeal had to choose between two conflicting provisions in relation to the ownership and registration of land, that under Articles 957 and 1382 of the Civil Code and the other under the newly enacted Registered Land Act 1984.

Byron CJ held that the 1984 Act had made 'significant changes to the regime of land registration and ownership. The most important is that the transfer of land, contrary to the provisions of the Articles 957 and 1382 of the Civil Code, is no longer based on the consent of the vendor but on the completion of the registration process.'[36] As such, the provisions of the Civil Code were no longer determinative of the question.

The case highlights the hidden obstacles and traps facing the St Lucia lawyer or, as in this case, the legal draftsperson. It is necessary, not only to be fully aware of the substantive content of the Code, but to be careful to make the requisite amendments to it in the legislative agenda. Similarly, practitioners must be constantly vigilant to take account of the changes to the Civil Code which have been effected by ordinary legislation.

Another noteworthy case is that of *Caplan v Duboulay*.[37] In this case, Barrow J had cause to examine Article 73 of the Code of Civil Procedure in response to the contention that the plaintiffs were tenants in sufferance and were barred from maintaining an action for possession. He relied on the fact that Article 1515 of the Civil Code of St Lucia states that persons holding real property by sufferance of the owner, without leave, are held to be lessees and rejected the argument that the plaintiffs were tenants of sufferance.[38]

---

34   *Op cit*, White, fn 18, p 17.
35   (1997) 55 WIR 123. The case went to the Judicial Committee of the Privy Council but the issues relating to the hybrid system were not in issue. See PC Appeal No 10 of 1998, dec'd 1 December 1999.
36   *Ibid*, p 129.
37   No 29 of 1999, (HC, St Lucia), dec'd 1 June 2001.
38   The main issues in the case concerned customary law in St Lucia. This aspect of the case is discussed in Chapter 10 ('Custom as a Source of Law').

Family law under the Civil Code

One area of substantial difference to the English common law is family law, in particular, the questions of divorce and matrimonial property, which have remained, for the most part, within the civil legal tradition. The issue of matrimonial property, specifically, the entitlement of a wife, under the Civil Code, to a half share of the matrimonial property, was examined in the case of *Joseph v Joseph*.[39] Such an entitlement arises from the doctrine of forced heirship, a form of mandatory succession.[40]

In *Joseph*, the High Court examined closely Article 1192(1) of the Civil Code, which provides that the property of persons married in community is divided into separate property (owned by one spouse) and community property (owned by both husband and wife). Article 1192 describes the meaning of 'separate property' and the circumstances under which a spouse may acquire separate property during the marriage. For example, separate property comprises the income and earnings of either spouse, investments in the name of one spouse and insurance policies taken out on the life of one spouse.[41]

On the facts of the instant case, the wife did not meet the burden of proof that the said property was community property and was therefore not entitled to the half-share.

Interpretation of the Civil Code

The vulnerabilities of the St Lucia Civil Code can be partly explained by the failure of the legal system and its actors to actively produce and promote relevant mechanisms to protect it. A major deficiency in this regard is the failure to proscribe indigenous or otherwise appropriate rules to interpret the Code and indeed, to understand its philosophy and content. It should be noted that the demise of the Civil law tradition in Trinidad and Tobago and Guyana is believed to have been accelerated by attendant problems of interpretation.[42]

Anthony suggests that there is 'relative absence' of relevant rules to interpret the Civil Code and the fact that the law has never applied a 'coherent philosophy of interpretation' to the Code, but instead had 'uninhibited recourse to the English common law'.[43] While he acknowledges that some rules have been identified, he also criticises what he sees as a faulty application of those rules by judges, leading to distortion and undermining of the Civil Code. He laments:

---

39   [2003] (8)(2) Carib L B 74.
40   This is directly opposed to the doctrine of the freedom of testamentary disposition, characteristic of the common law, whereby a person is free to leave his or her property to anyone or anything that he or she wishes and is not compelled to let his children or spouse inherit.
41   See also *Prospere v Prospere and Remy, above*, fn 31, para 15, quoting from Article 1190 of the Code: 'Legal community is that which the law, in absence of stipulation to the contrary, establishes between spouses by the mere fact of their marriage, in respect of certain descriptions of property. Neither spouse can alone encumber or dispose of the common property.'
42   See Campbell, C, *'The Transition from Spanish Law to English Law', above*, fn 6, p 23 and Shahabudeen, M, *The Legal System of Guyana*, 1973, Georgetown, Guyana: Guyana Printers, at p 198 respectively.
43   K D Anthony, 'The Courts and the Interpretation of a Civil Code in a Mixed Legal System: Saint Lucia Revisited' [1995] 5(1) Carib LR 144, at p 146.

Few judges saw the maintenance of the civilian system as their judicial responsibility. Thus, in St Lucia, there was no attempt like that of Quebec to protect 'l'integrité du Code Civil'.[44]

Further, the Interpretation Act, a statute intended to promulgate rules of interpretation for ordinary legislation, was applied to the provisions of the Civil Code, often with unfortunate consequences. This application further robbed the Civil Code of its distinctive character. It is to be noted too, that the Civil Code has its own rules of interpretation contained within it.[45]

Floisaac, a former Chief Justice of the Easter Caribbean Court of Appeal, has identified four principal rules of interpretation of the Civil Code:[46]

(1) the Vagliano Rule;

(2) the Vagliano Exception;

(3) the Judicial Precedent Rule; and

(4) rules relating to the importation of English law via special the statutory provisions of 1957.

The Vagliano Rule and its exception refer to a rule identified by the House of Lords[47] and used by the Privy Council to interpret the Quebec Civil Code in such cases as *Robinson v Canadian Pacific Railway*.[48] The Rule emphasises the supremacy of codal law and the natural meanings of the words contained in the Code's provisions. The exception to this rule resembles familiar exceptions found in the rules of statutory interpretation, such as where such a natural meaning will lead to an absurdity etc.[49]

It is expected too, that where a provision of the Code is ambiguous, resort should first be made to other Code provisions to interpret it. This was reiterated in *St Rose v Lafitte*:[50]

The legislative intention is an inference drawn from the primary meanings of those Articles ... consistent with the codal context. The codal ... context comprises every other Article, word and phrase in the Code.

Anthony also suggests that where the Code is silent on a point of law, custom and local usage should be employed, rather than English law, to fill in the gap. In these cases, custom should be treated as 'a more significant source of law'.[51]

The Judicial Precedent Rule requires that if the Article to be interpreted is identical to English statute which has been interpreted without challenge, that interpretation

---

44 *Ibid*.

45 See, eg, Articles 1, 9, 10 and 11.

46 Floisaac, V, 'The interpretation of the civil code of Saint Lucia' in R A Landry, *above*, fn 1 339, at p 348.

47 In the case of *Bank of England v Vagliano* [1891] AC 107 (HL).

48 [1892] AC 481 (PC).

49 See Chapter 14 ('The Rules of Statutory Interpretation').

50 (1984) 42 WIR 113 at pp 115j–116b.

51 Anthony, *above*, fn 43. [1995] (5)(1) Carib LR 144, p 157. Custom is in fact recognised under the Code, for example, under Article 1440. See, eg, *Parke v du Boulay* 8 June 1912, St L G 288, on the question of reasonable diligence in the bringing of a redhibitory action and *Cazaubon v Barnard, Peter & Co* March 1883, St L G 216, on the question of a custom of a monthly notice for termination of employment. The customs were, however, not upheld by the courts in these cases.

will apply to the Code.[52] This approach should not, however, obstruct the clear interpretation of the Code's provisions, even where the interpretation must rely on interpretations of similar provisions in the Quebec Civil Code, upon which the Civil Code relied.

Anthony complains that this rule of judicial precedent has been abused and distorted. Too much emphasis, he argues, has been placed on UK interpretations even in the face of clear meanings to be found within the Code itself. This corrupt approach to the rule has in fact been criticised by some judges. In *Mitchell v Clauzel*,[53] for example, De Freitas CJ contended that:

> Quebec decisions should first be applied in support of the interpretation sought to be established before English cases are cited.

Where aspects of the common law have been incorporated into the Code, special interpretation approaches may apply, such as those rules contained in Articles 945–953 of the Code which apply to the interpretation of a contract, a concept hitherto unknown to the civil law tradition. These rules are not always easy to apply. Indeed, the extent to which some of these essentially common law concepts, such as the trust, have been imported into the Code is contentious.[54]

We may note too, that there has been less resort to doctrinal writings in the interpretation of the Code, giving way more and more to precedent and thereby compromising the very character of a Civil Code and its interpretation.

It is evident therefore, that the interpretation of the Civil Code of St Lucia has been outward-looking, not only beyond the boundaries of the Code itself, but also beyond the civil law precepts of the legal system. This approach makes the Code more vulnerable to common law erosions.

The very existence of the hybrid system may depend on the alleviation of some of the difficulties of the system. Anthony laments:

> To allow the current situation to exist is to encourage the death of the Civil Code. But one cannot, in conscience, let the Civil Code die by attribution and neglect. If it is to be allowed, then by all means, do so mercifully and replace it by a coherent system.[55]

THE FUTURE OF THE HYBRID LEGAL SYSTEM

The future of the St Lucia legal system hinges between the renewed vigour of a uniquely hybrid system and the complete adoption of the common law. The latter choice may even be inevitable, since the process of anglicisation has been allowed to undermine the civil law tradition to such a degree that it will be difficult to reverse the process.

According to TB Smith, a writer from Scotland, which is itself a mixed jurisdiction:

---

52   Floissac, *above* fn 1.
53   24 July 1920, St LG, at p 2.
54   For a discussion on the difficulties in interpreting the Code's provisions on the trust, see K D Anthony, 'Approaches to the common law trust in codified mixed jurisdictions' in J McBride (ed) *Droit Sans Frontieres, Essays in Honour of L. Neville Brown*, 1991, Birmingham: Holdsworth Club. See also Chapter 9 ('Equity as a Source of Law').
55   *Op cit*, Anthony, 'The viability of the civilist legal tradition in St Lucia', fn 1, p 62.

In a number of mixed jurisdictions the struggle to maintain the civilian tradition will be a damn close fought business.[56]

Yet, two developments may breathe new life into the hybrid legal systems of the region, particularly that of St Lucia, where there appears to be political and social will to retain it. One such development is the formal association of two civil law countries, Haiti and Suriname, with CARICOM. This points to greater awareness and sensitivity to civilist legal norms in the region, which can give support to our hybrid legal systems. Suriname is not only a civil law country, but also has experience of borrowing from other civil law Codes, as St Lucia did.

The other development is the appointment of a judge from a civil law country to the highest final court of appeal in the region, the newly constituted Caribbean Court of Justice. It is expected that more judicial enthusiasm and understanding will be brought to bear in interpreting questions of St. Lucian and Guyanese law which have civilist influences. Such an approach can help to expand the civil law elements of the hybrid jurisprudence. This in turn will lead to more practitioners being willing and able to research aspects of civil law and thereby assist in developing the hybrid legal tradition. Indeed, in one of the first judgments emanating from the Caribbean Court of Justice, Justice Wit, the Dutch judge, displayed his civilist background in the perspective which he brought to the question of the influence of international law on the domestic legal system.[57]

There is, therefore, cause for optimism that the hybrid legal systems of the region will be treated with greater sensitivity which, in turn, will enhance their sustainability.

In addition, the dicta of the Privy Council in *Poliniere*[58] is reassuring in its reminder of the importance of the civil law to St Lucia's law. The fact that there is a rich civil law jurisprudence from France and Quebec to which the St Lucia courts are invited, and even mandated to turn to, is an important vehicle for the continued success of the hybrid legal system.

Whatever the trend will be for the future, there is little doubt that the St Lucia legal system can be described as one possessing a uniquely hybrid character. Certainly, one should not ignore the historical rationales evident in the formation of such a legal system. The survival of the civilist tradition thus far is perhaps argument enough that the uniqueness of the system should be protected and not destroyed.

Despite its difficulties, the very existence of such a Code in the Commonwealth Caribbean, with its multifaceted elements of civil, common law and indigenous law, stands as an example of law operating in its proper historical, social and cultural context. It creates an innovative and grounded St Lucian law. The hybrid phenomenon, an illustration of unification and harmony of different legal traditions of the world, is happily exhibited by the legal system of St Lucia.

---

56   Smith, TB, 'The preservation of the civilian tradition in mixed jurisdictions', in Yiannopoulas, AN (ed), *Civil Law in the Modern World*, 1965, Louisiana: Louisiana State UP, p 4.

57   See *AG v Joseph and Boyce*, CCJ App No CV 2 of 2005, decided 8 November 2006, discussed in depth in Chapter 12 ('International Law as a Source of Law').

58   *Above*, fn 29.

CHAPTER 5

THE RECEPTION OR IMPOSITION OF LAW AND ITS SIGNIFICANCE TO CARIBBEAN JURISDICTIONS

As discussed previously, the legal systems in the Caribbean belong essentially to the common law legal tradition, with some historical linkages to the civil law legal tradition.[1] These legal systems were born out of the experience of colonialism, during which law was transplanted to the region. This transplantation process is important, since it is the foundation of the doctrine of the reception of law.

The reception of law doctrine describes the process whereby legal phenomena which were developed in a given environment are consciously exported to another environment. This definition eliminates from our discussion the influences from other legal traditions in any particular country which result from mere contact or interplay with each other.[2] It also largely excludes the 'borrowing' of jurisprudence, whether by statute or case law, from countries other than the UK, the repository of the common law. Such a jurisprudence is not binding, as is the case with English common law that is received. Such foreign jurisprudence can, however, be applied, but with modifications as deemed necessary. The exception would be where a principle of the common law is said to be developed or identified in a court other than the English Court. This might be the case, for example, with respect to the Privy Council in other Commonwealth jurisdictions, or even, in some cases, principles identified by the Australian, Canadian or other Commonwealth courts. Where this occurs, the reception of law theory is relevant.

Before examining the applicability of the doctrine to Caribbean jurisprudence, the reader must be aware that some writers question the very nomenclature of the term 'reception', claiming that it should be labelled the doctrine of 'imposition' or even 'transplantation' instead. In *Nyali Ltd v AG*,[3] for example, Lord Denning used the term 'transplantation'. Indeed, the description 'imposition' is more in keeping with an accurate record of the history of the Caribbean, which was neither peaceful nor benevolent. Allot contends, for example, that the common law was forced upon the colonies:

> If we analyse the legal reasons why the common law migrated in such cases, it is that the metropolitan legal system for its own purposes and reasons declared this to be the governing meta-norm. At bottom, then, these laws migrated because they were made to migrate.[4]

This view is supported by a 1792 Memorandum by the Master of the Rolls, affirmed by Lord Stowell in *Rudling v Switch*:[5]

> When the King of England conquers a country . . . the Conqueror by saving the lives of the people conquered gains a right and property in such people; in consequence of which he may impose on them what laws he pleases.

---

1 See the discussion in Chapter 3 ('Legal Traditions – Types of Legal Systems in the Commonwealth Caribbean'). See, also, the exceptions made for 'hybrid' legal systems.

2 See Chapter 3.

3 [1955] 1 All ER 646, CA, p 653.

4 Allot, AN, *The Limits of Law*, 1980, London: Butterworths, pp 109–10.

5 (1821) 2 Hag Con 371, p 380.

Similarly, in *Kaadesevaran v AG*,[6] Lord Diplock explained that 'in the case of most former British colonies ... the English common law is incorporated as part of the domestic law of the new independent State because it was imposed upon the colony ...'. In this book, therefore, we adopt the appropriate philosophical position and use the term 'imposition' when describing the transplantation of law during colonialism. However, where the concept 'reception' is used in case law and other sources, we reproduce that term to retain the integrity of the source.

We see, therefore, that English law was imposed on the Commonwealth Caribbean. In St Lucia and Guyana, civil law was also imposed and retained. The reader should further note that in the case of Trinidad and Tobago, Guyana and Jamaica, traces of Indian law were also received. This occurred mainly during the time of Indian indentureship. The reception of other legal traditions has left some impression on Commonwealth Caribbean legal systems. For example, as we saw previously,[7] Hindus are allowed to marry according to the tradition and customs of their own law. Some of these traditions have even been incorporated into local legislation. In the main, however, this is of cosmetic effect only[8] and the English common law tradition can be seen to be the dominant one in Commonwealth Caribbean jurisdictions. The discussion on reception thus centres around the transplantation of the English common law.

The attitude toward the imposition of English law is important in deciding to what extent English law informs or should inform the law of the Commonwealth Caribbean in form and substance. In particular, the dynamic potential of legal sources in Commonwealth Caribbean legal systems is considerably influenced by the view that Commonwealth Caribbean judges and law makers take in relation to the reception question. This is particularly so in relation to judicial precedent and the Constitution, discussed in later chapters. While the original dependency and 'Britishness' of our law and legal system is accurately attributed to the colonial policy of imposition, it cannot fully excuse the continuance of these attitudes in modern, independent societies.

Rationale for imposition

We should recognise too, that the imposition of law in the colonial territories had little in common with the development of law and citizenry in other societies where law was imposed not as a result of imperialism or war, but where it sprang from the rational desires of the citizens for justice and equity.[9]

In our societies, the imposition of law was primarily to maintain social order, indeed, an unjust social order, to maintain efficiency for the benefit of the metropolitan parent country. It is not surprising therefore, that the imposition law theory embodies the basic notion, discussed below, that only so much law as was necessary to the colony was transplanted. Unsurprisingly, the 'needs' of such limited societies were few in comparison to egalitarian societies on a true developmental path. Law

---

6 [1970] AC 1111, p 1116.
7 Chapter 1.
8 With the exception of the civil law in St Lucia and Guyana. See Chapter 4 ('The Hybrid Legal Systems of St Lucia and Guyana').
9 See Chapter 1 ('Introduction to Law and Legal Systems in the Commonwealth Caribbean') for a discussion on the 'nature and functions of law'.

thus imposed was based on convenience but was also an essential instrument of dominance and oppression, forcing a 'fit' regardless of the contrasting circumstances and without regard to the consequences. This was not a participatory process, hinged on mutual respect for the governed by the governors, or a desire to shape and assimilate those governed into citizens in every sense of the word. There was no genuine attempt by the law to reflect political will, social need or values. It was an imposing of will born out of a narrow, mean-spirited economic and political necessity. As discussed in chapters 1 and 2, in these early societies, law was also used to create and perpetuate underdevelopment and dependency.

The jurisprudential debates that should inform law in every society were largely absent at the time of imposition. It is little wonder, therefore, that Commonwealth Caribbean societies appear so reluctant to enter into such debates today, having grown accustomed to a law devoid of real meaning and centred values to their societies. Further, any meaningful law that existed, such as those of the indigenous peoples, were displaced contemptuously and with violence.[10]

SETTLED COLONIES AND CONQUERED COLONIES

Since the doctrine of imposition is closely related to the historical background of the region, it is important to make a distinction between those territories which were conquered or ceded and those which were settled.[11] The process of political transformation was directly related to the manner in which law was received and implemented. This has further implications for how law is interpreted. In the case of conquered territories, for example, with few exceptions, existing local laws emanating from other foreign colonial powers would have remained in place until such time that the British overwrote them.

One interesting difference is the right to land. In *Levy and Wood v Administrator of the Cayman Islands*,[12] a case from the Cayman Islands – a settled territory, still a British colony – the Court of Appeal held, in a contest for title to land, that 'ownership by the Government was the natural consequence of the introduction of the common law of England by the first settlers of the Islands'.[13] This was precisely because the Cayman Islands was a settled colony. Accordingly, there was no evidence of land being previously occupied by anyone.

In an intriguing case on whether interveners who were not attorneys and who appeared before a regulatory tribunal were entitled to costs, *Public Counsel v The Fair Trading Commission*,[14] Blackman J chastised an intervener for querying the relevance of the UK Statute of Gloucester and by implication, the nature of the common law to the jurisprudence of Barbados.[15]

---

10 See Chapter 10 ('Custom as a Source of Law').

11 For the purposes of imposition, there is no practical distinction between conquered and ceded territories.

12 [1952–79] CILR 42.

13 *Ibid*, p. 43.

14 No 373 of 2006, decided 28 September 2006 (High Court, Barbados). Interestingly, both counsel and Blackman J relied on the earlier edition of this book to ground their arguments and reasoning respectively. See especially, pp 14, 28 and 40.

15 *Ibid*, p 39.

The acceptance of the jurisprudential implication for Barbados as a settled colony was foremost in Justice Blackman's reasoning. He noted that the:

> ... framers of the Constitution of Barbados recognised the historical linkage of the Island's colonial past ... the rights and privileges of the then inhabitants of Barbados were embodied in the Charter of Barbados, and concluded on Jan 11, 1652 ... and the political and legal developments of the country have their origin in the original settlement in the early 17th Century and the customs which came as part of that settlement ... It is erroneous therefore to dismiss as of no relevance, the historical and juridical contribution of the common law to the development of the case law of this country.[16]

Accordingly, the common law position prior to 1975, when the UK changed it by statute, was held to be applicable and the High Court found that interveners were not entitled to costs.

The settled territories of the Commonwealth Caribbean include Anguilla, Antigua, the Bahamas, Barbados, British Virgin Islands, Montserrat, and St Kitts.[17] These countries received the English common law at the end of the 17th century. A settled colony is commonly described as one where there was no previous inhabitation by indigenous or 'civilised' peoples, or which had been inhabited by peoples from imperialist countries who had subsequently abandoned the territory or had been destroyed.[18] Nevertheless, when one considers the historical reality of the Commonwealth Caribbean, which acknowledges the existence of indigenous Amerindian peoples, the very definition is suspect. Conversely, the concept of a conquered territory refers to that which was first held by one imperialist power and which was subsequently transferred to another imperialist, conquering power after battle. In the Commonwealth Caribbean, the term 'imperialist power' usually refers to the English, French and Spanish, who fought several battles for ownership of the region.[19] The total contempt with which conquerors viewed the indigenous peoples, whom they regarded as 'uncivilised' and their laws betray the biases inherent in the reception of law doctrine.

The conquered territories are Dominica, Belize, Guyana, Grenada, St Lucia, St Vincent and Trinidad and Tobago. Liverpool argues that although Dominica was a conquered territory, it was not treated as such for purposes of the imposition theory as the British refused to accept that during occupation by the French, French law was applied in the territory. Consequently, Dominica was treated as a settled colony.[20] The status of Jamaica is controversial. It can be considered as conquered since, at the time of the arrival of the British, there were Spanish settlers there, albeit without any rational institutionalisation of law. However, with regard to the reception of English law, it is best regarded as settled, as discussed below, p 78.

The imposition doctrine and process is more complex in the cases of St Lucia and Guyana. There, the common law was imposed on essentially civil law systems. This was a difficult infusion as the civil law endured. This endurance, which was

---

16   *Ibid,* pp 39–40.
17   See Patchett, KW, 'The Reception of Law in the West Indies' [1973] JLJ 17 for an authoritative historical account of the reception of law in the region.
18   See Tucker, SG (ed), *Blackstone's Commentaries 1803,* Vol 1, 1969, New York: Kelley.
19   In the case of St Lucia, ownership actually changed hands between the French and English 14 times.
20   N Liverpool, 'Dominica' in Kritzer, H (ed) *Legal Systems of the World,* Vol 1, 2002, USA: ABC-CLIO, p 446.

the impetus for the creation of hybrid legal systems, is discussed in a separate chapter.[21]

THE METHOD AND DATE OF RECEPTION

The English common law was introduced into the Commonwealth Caribbean by two methods:

(a) With respect to settled colonies, the colonists carried with them only so much of the English law as was applicable to their own situation and the condition of the infant colony. The date of the establishment of the colony was the date of reception.

(b) For conquered territories, the colonists retained the existing legal system only in so far as it was not repugnant to natural justice. The existing system was retained until such time as other arrangements could be made for English law to be introduced.[22] If we consider St Lucia, for example, it was this arrangement of convenience which made it possible for the hybrid legal system to emerge. In such cases, the date of reception is the date which the Crown directed that English law come into operation.

These are the orthodox English rules on the reception of law. In practice, the distinction between conquered and settled territories is less important, as most countries have introduced legislation defining the date and scope of the reception of the common law. Still, as we will see below, this is not without its own difficulty.

Two types of English law were imposed on the Caribbean. They were the English common law and English statute law. This imposition of English common law was achieved via two main methods:

(a) The use of the incorporation clause – this is where the legislation of a territory makes specific provision that the common law of England, existing at a particular date, shall be deemed to be in force in the territory.

(b) By way of proclamation: Dominica, St Vincent and Jamaica are examples of reception by proclamation as evidenced by the 1763 Proclamation:

All person inhabiting . . . in our colonies may confide in our royal prosecution for the enjoyment of the benefits of the laws of our realm of England . . .[23]

The existence of existing law clauses or saving law clauses in some Constitutions may also be viewed as a mechanism under the reception or imposition doctrine. This, however, is discussed in a following chapter on the Constitution.

The reception of English law was, however, subject to statutory modification, that is, that a territory may enact legislation which abrogates the common law, and the further requirement that all law received must be suited to the circumstances or needs of the colony. The latter rule is discussed further below.

---

21 See Chapter 4 ('The Hybrid Legal Systems of St Lucia and Guyana'). See, also, Anthony, KD, 'The reception of the common law by civil law systems in the Commonwealth Caribbean', in Doucet, M and Vanderlinden, J (eds), *La Réception des Systèmes Juridiques*, 1994, Brussels: Bruylant, p 15.

22 *Op cit*, Tucker, fn 13, pp 106–07. See *Campbell v Hall* (1770) 1 Comp 204, discussed further below, p 78, which affirmed this latter rule.

23 Revised Laws of Dominica 1961.

Two prerequisites must be present before English law can be said to have been received. First, the territory must have been brought within the Crown's dominion. Secondly, the settlement must have been established, that is, Crown authorisation, recognition of unauthorised settlements and annexation of inhabited areas must have been formalised.

It was also necessary to have some semblance of a legislature before one could describe a colony as established or settled. There should have been a Constitution or some authority which had the power to legislate. This is not without historical contradiction. For example, in the British Virgin Islands, colonists arrived in 1666 but the legislature was not set up until 1774. It is nevertheless accepted that this does not mean that the Islands were without law or legal authority during the interim period. The better view may be that the term 'established colony' refers to the situation where the colony had 'some adequate communal organisation to call for legal regulation and some form of governmental and legislative control was set up'.[24]

Jamaica provides a unique example, since it came into British control by force of arms which destroyed completely the previous system of government and law. It was therefore not possible for this previous system to continue until further arrangements could be made. In *R v Vaughan*[25] and *Campbell v Hall*,[26] the island was treated as settled and this historical fact has been accepted by the Supreme Court of Jamaica.[27] Part of the problem with Jamaica was that it was one of the first colonies to be conquered. As such, the Crown was uncertain how far its Prerogative or royal power extended. The Crown did assert the right to legislate for the colony even after a grant of representative institutions had been made allowing a form of self-government. Afterwards, however, the Crown conceded that its legislative power had been lost when the Representative Assembly was restored in 1680. Therefore, the common law came to Jamaica via the exercise of the Crown's Prerogative in the proclamation of 14 December 1661. From that time onward, the basic law and the right to a representative legislature could not be altered by the Crown and it was to be treated as a settled colony.[28]

The case of *Rose And Others v Chung And Others*[29] contains an exhaustive account of the application of the reception of English law doctrine in Jamaica, some of which is reproduced here. The jurisdiction of the court was questioned as to its power to grant damages either in lieu of or in substitution for specific performance. It therefore found it necessary to consider the reception doctrine, particularly as the Chancery Amendment Act, enacted in 1858 in the United Kingdom, had not been enacted in Jamaica. The court noted that Jamaica had 'received' English laws and statute by virtue of its colonial status until 1728 and that Section 22 of the statute 1 Geo II Cap 1 sets the limitations for the reception of English laws and statutes applicable to Jamaica prior to 1728. Further, the counterpart of this section is now contained in s 41 of the Interpretation Act, which reads:

---

24 *Op cit*, Patchett, fn 17, p 18. For this assertion, he relies on the legal historian, Roberts-Wray, K, *Commonwealth Colonial Law*, 1966, London: Stevens, p 151.
25 (1769) 4 Barr 2492, p 2500.
26 (1770) 1 Comp 204, p 212.
27 *Jacquet v Edwards*, (1867) 1 Jam SC Decisions 421.
28 For further discussion of the particular case of Jamaica, see Morrison, D, 'The Reception of Law in Jamaica' (1979) 2 WILJ 43.
29 (1978) 27 WIR 211.

All such laws and Statutes of England as were, prior to the commencement of 1 George II Cap 1, esteemed, introduced, used, accepted, or received, as laws in the Island shall continue to be laws in the Island save in so far as any such laws or statutes have been, or may be, repealed or amended by any Act of the Island.[30]

The court adopted the reasoning found in a judgment of the Full Court delivered by Henry J, in *R v Commissioner of Police and Others, ex p Cephas (No 2)*,[31] on the subject of the applicability of an English statute to Jamaica. In that case Henry J stated:

The Jamaica legislature has treated the year 1728 and the Act 1 Geo II Cap 1 as the year and the event which concluded the reception of English laws and statutes into Jamaica by virtue of its colonial status. This cut-off period was beneficial to the settlers in that it extended the application of these laws and statutes beyond the year 1655 and right up to 1728 and at the same time the 1728 Act 1 Geo II Cap 1 set certain limitations on the reception of English laws and statutes by enumerating the circumstances in which they were to be applicable to Jamaica.

The *Cephas* court concluded: 'It is therefore necessary to trace cases judicially decided in Jamaica in which English statutes up to 1728 "were esteemed, used and accepted" to come to a decision as to whether a particular English statute applied to Jamaica.'

The court also stated the position with respect to judge-made law. It held that, as a colony and partial self-governing colony, Jamaica continued to be bound by the development of the law and equity by the doctrine of stare decisis, until the country became an independent nation. Consequently, to ascertain what the law was in Jamaica (apart from statute), one has to examine what the law was in England.[32]

On the question of equity and damages, the court noted the adoption in Jamaica of provisions similar to the Supreme Court of Judicature Act 1873 of the UK which consolidated the courts of law and equity in England.[33] The relevant statutory provisions reproduced in the 1973 revised edition of the Judicature (Supreme Court) Act, s 48, reads:

48. With respect to the concurrent administration of law and equity in civil causes and matters in the Supreme Court the following provisions shall apply–

(a) If a plaintiff or petitioner claims . . . any equitable estate or right, or . . . relief upon any equitable ground against a deed, instrument or contract, or against a right, title or claim asserted by a defendant or respondent in such cause or matter, or to relief founded upon a legal right which before the passing of this Act could only have been given by a Court of Equity, the Court and every Judge thereof shall give him such and the same relief as ought to have been given by the Court of Chancery before the passing of this Act.

. . .

(f) Subject to the aforesaid provisions for giving effect to equitable rights and matters of equity . . . the said Court . . . shall give effect to all legal claims and demands . . .

---

30   *Ibid*, at p 218.
31   (1976) 15 JLR 3, at 8; (1976) 24 WIR 402.
32   The Chancery Procedure Amendment Act 1858, Lord Cairns' Act (21 and 22 Vict c 27) was enacted 130 years after the cut-off period, and a similar statute was never enacted in Jamaica. Nor does the Act fall among the enactments which by the words of the statute itself were made applicable to the colony, Jamaica, by imperial legislation, such as the Extradition Act 1870 (33 and 34 Vict c 52 and amendments), the Forcible Entry Act 1381 (5 Rict 2 Stat I c 7 and amendments to 1623), the Copyright Act 1911 etc. *Rose, above*, fn 29, p 218.
33   The Judicature (Supreme Court) Act, Cap 180, 1880.

existing by the common law or by any custom, or created by any statute, in the same manner as the same would have been given effect to if this Act had not been passed by any of the Courts whose jurisdiction is hereby transferred to the Supreme Court.

It was found therefore that the Act did no more than to consolidate existing jurisdictions in one Supreme Court, and to vest in the court and every judge, powers of law and equity in civil cases. No new rights were created. Rights previously existing in the courts of either law or equity were merely confirmed.[34]

After Jamaica's independence, existing laws were preserved by virtue of s 4(1) of the Constitution and thus the existing regime was saved.[35] As the Judicature (Supreme Court) Act did not confer any new rights, the court then went on to consider whether or not the old Court of Chancery [UK] (and hence the old Court of Chancery, Jamaica) had and exercised the power to award damages in lieu of or substitution for specific performance, before Lord Cairns' Act or whether this was a new power extended by that Act.

The exact date of reception has sometimes produced controversy even in the courts. In the case of Barbados, for example, Patchett suggests 1628, the date of the Montgomery Patent, which was the formalisation of Crown control, as the relevant date. Before this date, from 1625, the island was controlled by a private syndicate by the Courteen brothers. Yet, in *Blades v Jaggard*,[36] 1625 was the date accepted by the court.

Similarly, in Dominica, one view holds that the relevant date of reception is 1763, by virtue of the proclamation of that date introducing English law as a matter of convenience while the colony awaited a Representative Assembly. The other date suggested is 1775, the date of the proclamation of the Constitution.[37]

Where the date is contentious, the effect could be that English law could be ignored to prevent the anomaly of the territory being pinned to ancient statute. This occurred in *Shillingford v AG of Dominica*.[38] Here, the Court of Appeal of the West Indian Associated States found no evidence that English Acts were treated as in force in Dominica before 1775. Consequently, the Nullum Tempus Act 1769 was not part of the law of Dominica. Again, in Trinidad, in *Desmontiles v Flood*,[39] even after the 1848 Ordinance which sought to repeal Spanish civil law in favour of British law, the Supreme Court found that Spanish law still endured.

---

34 *Ibid*, at p 219.
35 Section 4(1) reads: 'All laws which are in force in Jamaica immediately before the appointed day shall (subject to amendment or repeal by the authority having power to amend or repeal any such law) continue in force on and after the day, and all laws which have been made before that day but have not previously been brought into operation may (subject as aforesaid) be brought into force, in accordance with any provision in that behalf, on or after that day, but all such laws shall, subject to the provisions of this section, be construed, in relation to any period beginning on or after the appointed day, with such adaptations and modifications as may be necessary to bring them into conformity with the provisions of this Order.' Other Constitutions in the region have similar provisions.
36 (1961) 4 WIR 207, p 210.
37 Likewise, in St Christopher (St Kitts), the date of reception is controversial. Some suggest 1713, the date of formal acquisition, while others prefer 1623, the date of rediscovery. In contrast, in Montserrat and Antigua, the date of 1682 is accepted for both islands. See *op cit*, Patchett, fn 17, p 18.
38 (1968) 12 WIR 57.
39 [1893–1910] 1 T&T SCR, 162.

Reception of English statutory law

During the colonial era the UK was considered an imperial parliament which had the power to enact laws for its colonies via statute. This law was imposed in three main ways:

(a) by express extension by the UK Parliament of particular statutes to apply generally to all territories or to a named territory. These Acts usually concerned constitutional matters and the administration of the territories;

(b) incorporation by reference in the colonial legislation. This could be specific, relating to a particular Act, or general, relating to a body of law, for example, jurisdiction in probate divorce could be incorporated by the following words:

> Proceedings shall be subject to this ordinance and to the rules of court exercised by the court in conformity with the law and practice from time to time in force in England;

(c) incorporation by repetition: this was the most common method. Here, a particular English statute was simply repeated verbatim and enacted by the local legislature.

CARIBBEAN ATTITUDES TO RECEPTION – STATIC OR CREATIVE?

Much of the discussion and debate on the reception of law in the Commonwealth Caribbean centres on the relevant dates of reception and their significance.[40] However, while this is important, particularly in considering the effect of older statutes, it is suggested here that the more significant issue should be the attitude of West Indian judges and legislatures to the doctrine of reception itself. The first emphasises the historical accuracy of the law and legal system, while the second is more concerned with taking that historical foundation and moulding it into a viable law and legal system for the future.

What effect does the doctrine of reception have on Caribbean law and legal systems? The controversial issue in relation to the reception of law is deciding to what extent independent Commonwealth Caribbean legal systems are bound to follow common law legal principles as defined by English judges. This begs the following question. What exactly did Commonwealth Caribbean legal systems receive, or what was imposed upon them? Is it the common law as a legal tradition, or is it a set of binding legal principles and legislative interpretations which only have validity as defined by English common law judges? Clearly, the first construct will give to Commonwealth Caribbean legal systems a certain flexibility to define Caribbean jurisprudence according to their own image and likeness, ie, the potential to create an indigenous jurisprudence which conforms to the characteristics of the common law legal tradition but which may differ in detail. On the other hand, conforming to the idea that Caribbean judges are bound to follow law as expressed by their English counterparts imports a definite rigidity to Commonwealth Caribbean legal systems.

The issue is even more controversial when one considers the declaratory theory which has traditionally been accepted as the underlying principle of the English common law and judicial precedent. The declaratory theory, now no longer unchallenged, assumes that judges do not make law, but only declare it. This law which is to

---

40   See, eg, *op cit*, Patchett, fn 17, and Morrison, fn 28, respectively, and the discussion above.

be 'declared' already exists within the body of the common law. The common law is thus perceived as containing immutable legal principles. This is the common law which Commonwealth Caribbean jurisdictions received.

While the theory may be a legal fiction, it does present a certain intellectual difficulty for Caribbean jurisprudence. It presumes that it is only English courts and judges which have the authority to find and declare these common law principles. Taken to its logical conclusion, Caribbean judges and courts do not possess the flexibility to adapt the common law to local needs. Rather, they are tied to these rigid principles of the common law as declared in England. This is as true for judicial precedent as it is for the interpretation of the Constitution, as we shall see later in this book. Indeed, this is the thinking behind the case of *de Lasala v de Lasala*,[41] that the reception of the English common law presupposes that there is to be a uniform or universal interpretation of the common legislative provisions in accordance with English law,[42] although provision is made for exceptions to the principle where custom, or other local conditions make the reception inappropriate, as discussed below.[43]

The difficulty inherent in the doctrine of reception, in deciding how much of the common law was transplanted to any particular territory, is ably illustrated by the abstracts from the following cases.

Ideally, although we have received English law, or rather it has been imposed upon us, this should not restrict us in our formulation of a Caribbean jurisprudence to reflect our own needs. Rather, reception of the common law should be viewed merely as a foundation upon which to build, and where necessary to deviate from, moulding the common law to suit our societies. This view has not always found favour with Caribbean judges. Consider the restrictive view of Wooding J in *Johnson v R*,[44] a trial for murder. The difficulty with the decision lies in its reasoning, which was based on an English case that the judge saw as imposing both English statute and common law, as defined by the English courts, on the West Indies. Wooding J said:

> In view of s 3 of the Offences Against the Person Ordinance and s 12 of the Judicature Act which incorporates as part of our law the common law of England, and since any decision of the House of Lords must be regarded as the prevailing law and, in so far as it interprets it, the common law of England, we must, whatever our own view, accept its judgment . . . as declaratory of the law here.[45]

The problem of Commonwealth Caribbean judges binding themselves to precedents by courts, such as the House of Lords, which lie outside the hierarchy of Caribbean courts, is discussed in Chapter 8 ('The Common Law and Doctrine of Judicial Precedent'). Here, it is enough to note that this was a post-independence case, yet the issues of the effect that political independence might have on the reception of English law, and the attitude toward accepting that English law as binding on West Indian courts, were not addressed. The *Johnson* court clearly accepted that what was received and binding was not merely a common law tradition, but common law *legal principles*, both precedent and statutory interpretation, as defined by the English courts.

---

41 [1980] 1 AC 546, discussed further in Chapter 8 ('The Common Law and the Doctrine of Judicial Precedent').
42 Followed in *Tai Hing Cotton Mill Ltd v Liu Chong Hing Bank Ltd* [1986] 1 AC 80 (PC).
43 Under the local circumstances rule.
44 (1966) 10 WIR 402.
45 *Ibid*, p 415.

Consider, further, *Jemmot v Phang*.[46] Here the issue was whether s 18 of the Gaming Act of the UK applied to Trinidad and Tobago. The court held that the Act should apply. Section 12 of the Trinidad and Tobago Judicature Act of 1962 provides that:

> Subject to the provisions of any enactment in operation on the first day of March 1848 and to any enactment passed after that date the common law doctrines of equity and statutes of General Application of the Imperial Parliament that were in force in England on that date shall be deemed to have been enacted and to have been in force in Trinidad.

This, therefore, was a reception of law clause embodied in the Trinidad and Tobago legislation. The court found that the Gaming Act was a statute of the Imperial Parliament in force in England on 1 March 1848 and that it was a statute of general application which had not been abrogated by local legislation.

The court in the case of *Persaud v Plantation Versailles & Schoon Ordinance Ltd*[47] did not agree with this restrictive view of the doctrine of reception. The relevant issue in this case was whether the remedy of unjust enrichment was part of the law of Guyana. Money was being deducted from the wages of employees to support payment of goods from a recreation club even after the club was closed down. Although the court did decide that the remedy was part of the law in Guyana, the attitude of the judges was clearly different to that exhibited in the *Johnson* and *Jemmot* cases. Crane J, for example, noted that the English courts were unclear as to whether the principle of unjust enrichment existed in English law, but also found that the duty of a court in an independent country was to formulate a jurisprudence to 'suit the needs of our ever-changing society'.[48] For him, the date or consequence of reception was secondary to this judicial duty.

The contrast between the above cases should, therefore, be noted and is a good example of the debate on the question of the relevance of reception to West Indian jurisprudence. Indeed, in 1823, the Attorney General for Dominica said that the rule relating to reception was 'so vague and so little understood in the colonies, that decisions founded upon it will be often contradictory'.[49] While he was concerned with the relevant date of reception, the substance of his complaint holds true for more general matters on reception. Whilst of historical origin, it is a debate which still rages today and the confusion is hardly different in the current jurisprudence. We are still faced with the ultimate question, to what extent has English law been received in the territories?

A CUT-OFF POINT FOR RECEPTION?

The answer to the question as to the true meaning of the doctrine of the reception of law is made even more complex by the debate surrounding the date of reception. Certainly, the date of reception is important to the discussion. When does reception of the common law or unwritten law cease? Most former colonial territories contain

---

46   (1963) 6 WIR 88.
47   (1970) 17 WIR 107.
48   *Ibid*, p 118. See the discussion of this and other cases in the context of the binding nature of case law in Chapter 8 ('The common law and the doctrine of judicial precedent').
49   Second Report of the Commissions of Inquiry on the Administration of Civil and Civil Justice in the West Indies, 1826, First Series, p 61.

express provisions for reception in their legislation via incorporation clauses, as, for example, in Trinidad and Tobago:

> The common law doctrines of equity and statutes of general application . . . that were in force in England on 1 March 1848 shall be deemed to have been in force in Trinidad as from that date and in Tobago as from 1 January 1889.[50]

Yet such clauses do not precisely determine the implications of the reception of English law. For example, we may interpret this reception clause in two ways. First, that the date qualifies all three sources of law or that the date qualifies only statutes of general application. This is a question of statutory interpretation. The second view relies on the fact that legislatures usually prescribe dates for statutes only and that the punctuation in the clause supports the argument. The question then remains, how are we to regard subsequent interpretation after the stated date of the statute? The debate continues.

In *Thompson v R*,[51] the Privy Council stuck resolutely to a cut-off date in deciding to what extent the Police and Criminal Evidence Act 1984 of the UK, on the admissibility of confessions, which had been received in St Vincent, applied. It determined that the cut-off point was 1989, the date stated in the legislation. Accordingly, ss 76 and 78 of the Act applied, but Code C, which had been added after 1989, did not.

Commonwealth Caribbean jurisdictions continue to receive specific English law by way of reception law clauses which extend certain aspects of English law, including English statute, to the territory. It is clear that these reception clauses of more modern vintage stand, in so far as they import law at the given date. For example, in *Village Cay Marina v Ackland and Others*,[52] on the question of the taxation and recovery of costs, the High Court of the BVI reaffirmed the Privy Council ruling in *Zuliani et al v Veira*[53] that the English law relating to solicitors and the taxation and recovery of costs, 'except such as where provisions in that law are unenforceable and could have no effect in the Virgin Islands or where the rules of court here provide something that modifies that English law, prevails here and must be used and followed. It would therefore be acceptable to look at English cases relating to the taxation of costs.'[54] The relevant law had been incorporated by reference into the law of the British Virgin Islands.

Reception theory and practice also permit the courts to fill in the gaps evident in local law, even allowing some flexibility in choosing which English statutes are most suitable for application. In *Marshall v Antigua Aggregates Ltd, Zilankas & Others*,[55] the High Court of Antigua and Barbuda dealt with a deficiency in the Companies Act, that is, the absence of rules for the winding up of companies, by relying on the general jurisdiction of the High Court which permitted the court to adopt the law and practice of England. The relevant provision, section 11 of the Eastern Caribbean Supreme Court Act (CAP 143) stipulates:

> The jurisdiction vested in the High Court in civil proceedings and in Probate, Divorce and Matrimonial Causes, shall be exercised in accordance with the provisions of this

---

50 The Judicature Act 1962, discussed in *Jemmot v Phang* (1963) 6 WIR 88.
51 [1998] AC 811 (PC, St Vincent).
52 Civil Suit No 198 of 1992, decided 23 March 2001 (High Court, BVI).
53 (1994) 45 WIR 188 (PC, St Christopher and Nevis).
54 *Above, Village Cay*, fn 52, p 5.
55 Civil Suit No 181 of 1999, decided 8 December 1999 (High Court, Antigua and Barbuda).

> Act . . . and where no special provision is therein contained such jurisdiction shall be exercised as nearly as may be in conformity with the law and practice administered for the time being in the High Court of Justice in England.

The Court rejected counsel's submission that the appropriate UK Act was the Insolvency Act 1986, the most recent one on the subject. Rather, as was the practice, it was the rules under the Companies Act 1948 of the UK, which were to be adopted, since that Act was closest to Antigua's Companies Act and not the more modern legislation. As Georges J explained:

> . . . it would not . . . be apposite to invoke the rules of an Act to which there is no parallel in Antigua and which is principally designed for the liquidation of insolvent companies in England and Wales.[56]

The issue is even more difficult in relation to the uncodified common law, as a cut off point is more difficult to establish. One approach could be that where there are no stated dates of reception, the closing date for equity and the common law would be the same as for statutes. Thus, if colonists take the statutes with them as they exist at the time, which statutes will not be affected by later developments of legislation, then the same should apply to the common law and equity.

However, since the declaratory theory assumes that the common law is a body of legal principles of immemorial existence, not created by judicial action, but merely declared by judges, the common law cannot be merely the rules as are interpreted at a given date. Rather, it must describe a given system or body of legal rules at whatever point of time. Thus, the reference to a particular date of reception may not be important, for the common law at whatever date had within itself all the developments which have taken place to the present time. Therefore, universal developments of the common law, for example, landmark cases containing important legal principles, such as natural justice principles, must be followed, as they contain the universal truth. These are the underpinnings of the *Johnson* decision, discussed above, p 82.

Some countries have attempted to clarify the question of a cut-off point by way of statute. This is the case, for example, in Singapore and Malaysia, as demonstrated in the Malaysian case of *Wee Lian Construction SDN BHD v Ingersol Jati Malaysia Sdn BHD,*[57] where it was noted that s 5(2) of the Civil Law Act 1956 (the CLA) has a specific cut-off date, ie 7 April 1956, for the application of the UK Common law, rules of equity and statutes, subject to the provision that such application is not to be inconsistent with local circumstances.

Similarly, the *Persaud* case, and even the *Jemmot* decision, were willing to view the reception of law as having a cut off point. After this cut off point, Caribbean judges should not be restricted to the common law as defined by the ex-colonialists. Rather, such definitions should merely be viewed as persuasive, albeit highly persuasive. This view, by implication, rejects the declaratory theory.

The traditional theory, as outlined above, however, distinguishes equity from other legal rules of the common law:

> . . . the rules of equity are not like the rules of the common law, supposed to have been

---

56   *Ibid*, at p 7.
57   [2004] MLJU 396 (High Court, Pulau Pinang) at para 31.

established from time to time. The older precedents in equity are of little value. The doctrines are progressively refined and improved.[58]

This view is supported by the case of *Ministry of Health v Simpson*[59] where the court was in no doubt that new doctrines could be invented. The view is not consistent, however. In *Re Diplock*,[60] the judges doubted the power of the courts to invent an equitable jurisdiction for the first time if justice required it, and stressed the need to ground equitable jurisdiction upon established precedent. In the Bahamas, Luckhoo, P had to consider such questions in the case of *AG (Bahamas) v Royal Trust Co (No 2)*.[61] He conducted a vigorous historical analysis of the reception of equity in the Bahamas, eventually deciding that it was the common law at the date of imposition at 2 December 1799, 'as developed by the Court of Chancery in England, which became a part of the law of the Bahamian Islands in respect of charitable trust.'[62] However, as the position had never been altered by statute nor judicial development, the only 'sensible course' was to also adopt relevant subsequent case developments in the UK on the subject.[63]

These *dicta* were followed in the Cayman Islands case of *Bridge Trust Company and Slatter v AG, Wahr Hansen and Compass Trust Co Ltd*.[64] Although accepting that the Bahamian courts had not addressed themselves to the question as to whether local circumstances, discussed below, justified a different judicial development to the equitable principles on charities, Harre, CJ, felt, somewhat regrettably, that the 'only sensible thing to do' was to apply the common law as it had developed over the intervening years from the actual date of imposition.[65]

The American view is that the common law is a set of principles and rules constantly evolving, thus reference to a date of reception is simply to refer to the common law as it had evolved up to that point.[66] An interesting development in the continuing impact of the imposition of the English common law on its former colonies is the recent dramatic twist on the evolution of the Mareva injunction in the United States. In *Grupos Mexicano de Desorollo SA v Allison Bond Fund Inc,*[67] the US Supreme Court rejected the mareva injunction, a modern creature of equity. The decision turned on the scope of the jurisdiction conferred by the Judiciary Act 1789 on federal courts over 'all suits in equity'. Decisions before this had interpreted this as jurisdiction to administer in equity suits the principles of judicial remedies which were administered by the English Court of Chancery at the time of American Independence. However, by a majority of five to four, the Supreme Court decided that the US Federal courts had no power to grant the injunction since such a jurisdiction had not been received into US law. Its rationale was that in 1789, the date of reception, there was a

58   *Re Hallet* (1880) Ch D 696.
59   [1951] AC 251.
60   [1948] 1 Ch 465.
61   (1983) 36 WIR 1 (CA, Bahamas); upheld on appeal, [1986] 1 WLR 1001 (PC).
62   N Liverpool, 'Dominica' in Kritzer, *above*, fn 20, p 446.
63   *Above, Royal Trust*, fn 61 (1983) 36 WIR 1, at p 12.
64   [1996] CILR 52 (Grand Court, Cayman Islands).
65   *Ibid*, at p 64. Harre, CJ regarded himself as 'absolved from conducting the equivalent of the interesting historical exercise carried out by Luckoo, P in the *Royal Trust Co Ltd* case, particularly as Luckoo, P had found that the common law in England applied'. *Ibid*.
66   See, eg, *Marks v Morris* 14 Va 463 (1809).
67   119 Sup SL 1961 (1999).

well-established general rule that a judgment establishing a debt was necessary before a court would interfere with a debtor's use of his property.[68]

Other Commonwealth courts have determined, after initial debate, that rather than adopting a universal or unitary concept of the common law, through a narrow view of the reception doctrine, a divergent approach is preferred. The Canadian and Australian courts have been particularly vocal in this regard. In *Fleming v Atkinson*,[69] for example, the Supreme Court of Canada finally decided that it was not obliged to follow House of Lords precedents, as they did not necessarily embody the appropriate legal principles for Canada.[70]

One view of reception would therefore be that only so much of the common law as had been received at the date of reception should be accepted as binding precedent. Thus, all subsequent developments of the common law should be of persuasive authority only. This would allow for the independent development of West Indian law.

It is not easy to say whether Caribbean judges have followed any particular theory, for they have not usually grounded their decisions on any particular doctrine of reception. Nevertheless, when one examines the attitude of Caribbean judges as revealed from the nature of their decisions, it is clear that they often view English decisions as binding. This supports the view that they conform to the less dynamic theory about the reception of English law, that is, that the common law is a given body of legal rules. We will examine this attitude when we discuss the doctrine of judicial precedent later in this book.

Undoubtedly, wide reception clauses have attracted narrow views on the capacity of Commonwealth Caribbean courts to develop the common law or to deviate from the English interpretations of the common law in any way whatsoever. In *Musa v The Attorney General et al*,[71] the Supreme Court of Belize had to decide the extent of parliamentary privileges in Belize and the power of the Speaker of the House to commit for contempt. Despite the existence of legislation on the subject, the Belize Legislative Assembly (Powers and Privileges) Act 1962, the Court looked to the English common law for the answer, finding that the Act was 'not the entire law on the subject'. The Court was assisted by a wide reception clause found under the Imperial Laws (Extension) Act 1899, which read:

> 2(1) Subject to the provisions of this or any other Ordinance, the common law of England and all Acts ... declaratory of the common law passed prior to 1st January 1899, shall extend to this territory.

Section 5 of the said Act was not given as much prominence in the court's reasoning. It said:

> (5) Wherever by this Ordinance, or any other law, it is declared that the common law of England ... shall extend to Belize, the same shall be deemed to extend thereto so far

---

68 Note that the minority agreed that the development of the Mareva injunction was based on the traditional powers of equity to remedy the abuse of legal process and was consistent with the principles which had been administered by the Court of Chancery in 1789.

69 (1959) 18 DLR (2d) 8.

70 See also *Australian Consolidated Press Ltd v Uren* [1969] AC 590 (PC, Australia), where the Privy Council itself agreed that Australia could go its own way on the question of punitive damages, thereby refusing to follow the House of Lords landmark decision in *Rookes v Barnard* [1964] AC 1129 (HL) and adopting the approach of the Australian High Court.

71 BZ 1998 SC 6.

only as the jurisdiction of the court and *local circumstances reasonably permit and render such extension suitable and appropriate* [emphasis supplied].

The Court found that it had no power to review the internal proceedings of the House of Parliament which was protected by the common law privileges and immunities. Further, the Speaker had the power to commit for contempt. Indeed, Meerabux, J emphasised the fact that Belize, unlike other countries, had *specifically* incorporated the English common law into its own law.[72]

The local circumstances rule

While the general principle remains that a received statute must be interpreted in the context of the common law in which it was enacted,[73] it should be noted that the exceptions to reception, that is, statutory modification and adaptation to local circumstances, always apply. We will discuss also the 'local circumstances rule' in the context of statutory interpretation.[74] Here, we examine the rule in its broader context of the imposition doctrine. Since the common law must generally give way to statute, it must be subject to all English statutes which modified or abrogated the common law and which were passed before the date of reception, all English statutes expressly applying to the territory after reception, and all local legislation made either before or after reception date.

The local circumstances rule is sometimes expressed specifically in the imposition clause, such as in Belize, as we saw in *Musa*.[75] In other countries, however, such clauses have been interpreted more aggressively. In *Wee Lian Construction DN*,[76] for example, a case from Malaysia, the relevant clause restricting the general application of UK law read:

> Provided always that the said common law, rules of equity and statutes of general application shall be applied so far only as the circumstances of the States of Malaysia and their respective inhabitants permit and subject to such qualifications as local circumstances render necessary.[77]

On a question on a contract of sale, Ratnam, J of the Malaysian court said: 'I do not think that it is appropriate to rely on the UCTA [English statute] and to import its provisions into local law without express local legislation allowing it, bearing in mind that existing contract law as supplemented by local decisions are more than adequate. Besides, it is for the legislature to make the move and to promulgate such a law if it is found to be necessary.'[78]

In another case, this time from Hong Kong, on a question of land law, *Kong Sau Ching v Kong Pak Yan and Others*,[79] Reyes, J gave a rigorous examination of the

---

72   *Ibid*, at p 33.
73   See *Pollock v Manitoba* (2006) 272 DLR 4th 142, which in this case meant the common law and statute law of England at the date of reception.
74   See Chapter 14 ('The Rules of Statutory Interpretation').
75   *Above*, fn 71.
76   *Above*, fn 57.
77   Section 3(1) of the CLA.
78   *Ibid*, para 34.
79   [2003] HKCU 1212.

application of the local circumstances rule, also criticising the way in which it had been applied in previous cases. He said:

> The Full Court appears to have taken it for granted that the 1832 Act formed part of Hong Kong law . . . However, [it] failed to assess whether circumstances in Hong Kong . . . justified the application of the English restriction in Hong Kong. Nowhere in its judgment does the Full Court engage in the exercise required by SCO s 5 of considering the extent to which a facet of a relevant English law has been modified by local circumstances . . . it is doubtful that mere consideration of the rule in *Wheeldon v Burrows*. . . constitutes sufficient examination of whether Hong Kong . . . circumstances call for modification of the English restriction. A wider array of relevant local factors would need to be canvassed as part of the requisite exercise.[80]

The court continued:

> The starting point for assessing the effect of local circumstances on English law must be a date . . . 1843 . . . from which reception of English law is reckoned. One cannot look at an event X occurring in 1969 and reason that, because of X, some English rule could not have been received . . . at a reception date before 1969. X may have the effect of amending or repealing an English rule as incorporated into Hong Kong law on a relevant reception date such as 5 April 1843. But evaluating the effect of the happening of X in 1969 on a received English rule is a different exercise from ascertaining whether an English rule was received into Hong Kong law on an earlier date in the first place . . .[81]

Accordingly, the court held that because of local circumstances a limited owner in Hong Kong may acquire a right of way by prescription against another limited owner.

More restrictive legislative formulas for the local circumstances rule may be found. For example, in St Vincent, the Criminal Procedure (Amendment) Act 1970 states that where not otherwise provided for, the practice and procedure of the courts in criminal cases, 'shall be that for the time being in force in England', but this is only 'in so far as the same are not repugnant to any law in force in St Vincent'. Accordingly, in *Cottle and Laidlow v R*,[82] the Privy Council found that a practice direction laid down by Lord Parker CJ in 1964[83] in operation in the UK courts, was not applicable to St Vincent as it was repugnant to ss 12 and 13 of the Jury Ordinance which made it unlawful to try a capital and non-capital offence together.

With regard to this 'local circumstances rule', the question of determining the suitability of legislation to local circumstances has conjured up its own problems. This is often difficult to apply. Further, there is controversy as to what date or time the question of the suitability of the statute must be decided. There are four possibilities on the relevant date: (a) the date of settlement; (b) the date of enactment; (c) the date at which the controversy or suitability question arose; and (d) the date at which the matter is heard.

The cases of *Cooper v Stuart*[84] and *Ruddrick v Weathered*[85] support the third approach. Other *dicta*, however, are contradictory. For example, *Brett v Young*[86] suggests the date of settlement. There is, therefore, a lack of consistency in this area.

---

80   *Ibid*, paras 81–89.
81   *Ibid*, paras 90–92.
82   (1976) 22 WIR 543.
83   (1964) 1 WIR 1233.
84   (1889) 14 App Cas 286.
85   (1882) 7 NZLR 491.
86   (1882) 1 NZLR 264.

One difficulty with adopting the date of settlement is that it may preclude the applicability of laws which were not suitable at the time, due to the infant state of the colony, but which became suitable later on. The *Cooper* approach allows for this evolutionary determination of suitability.

Legislation which has been deemed to be unsuitable for the colonies under this test include the Statute of Mortmain, in the case of *AG v Stewart*,[87] from Grenada, on the basis that it was 'wholly political' and 'wholly English' and was 'meant to have local [English] operation'.[88] *Balboa Atlantico SA v Registrar of Lands*[89] followed this ruling in the Cayman Islands. Similarly, in *Bennet v Garvie*,[90] the Statute of Frauds was held to be inapplicable because it required written evidence of certain transactions and was thus unsuitable for a largely illiterate population. In Canada, the Acts of the Prevention of Marriage of Lunatics 1742 was held to be inapplicable in *Meanwell v Meanwell*,[91] while the Vagrancy Act 1824 was held to be unsuitable in New Zealand.[92]

The rule may be used for general principles of law. The test for determining the degree of suitability was put forward in *Leong v Lim Beng Chye*.[93] Here, the Privy Council held that a rule of law should not be held inapplicable to local circumstances unless some solid ground is established to show an inconsistency with the settlers' needs. A good argument might be where the law to be received is grounded in some policy peculiar to its jurisdiction and irrelevant to the receiving jurisdiction. Such law is to be treated cautiously and may be unsuitable for reception, at least without modification. In such a case, it should be ignored to avoid incongruity.[94]

Yet, often, in the Commonwealth Caribbean, judges have failed to apply the local circumstances rule itself, instead, viewing English statute and statutory interpretation and general legal principles as binding regardless of the suitability of the statutory provision to local circumstances.[95] It is worth recalling that it is always within the power of local legislatures to create legislation which will reign supreme over English law, whether it be common law, equity or English statute.

An enlightened approach comes from the Cayman Islands in the case of *National Trust for Cayman Islands v Planning Appeals Tribunal Central Planning Authority and Humphreys (Cayman) Ltd*.[96] The court had to decide whether laws prohibiting contingent fee arrangements for attorneys should apply to the Cayman Islands. It found that decisions of the English Court of Appeal which had found such fees to be unlawful were not binding on the Cayman Islands because local circumstances were different. In particular, in reviewing the history of the English laws against conditional or contingent fees, it found that they were based on public policy relating to maintenance and champerty. Such laws were the product of particular 'abuses which arose in the

---

87 (1817) 2 Mer 143; 35 ER 895.
88 *Ibid*, p 900, *per* Sir William Grant MR.
89 [1984–85] CILR 304.
90 (1917) 7 EAPLR 48.
91 [1941] 2 DLR 655.
92 *Quan Hick v Hinds* (1905) 2 CLR 345. Presumably because that country had neither vagrants nor ex-slaves to tie to the plantation. See the discussion in Chapter 1.
93 [1995] AC 648 at 665.
94 *Meanwell, above*, fn 91.
95 See, further, on this point, Chapter 8 ('The Common Law and the Doctrine of Judicial Precedent').
96 [2002] CILR 59 (Grand Court, Cayman Islands).

conditions of medieval society'. However, public policy considerations had moved forward. Contingent fees in the Cayman Islands could not, therefore, be said to be against public policy.

The court also noted that the principle in *de Lasala v De Lasala*[97] recognised that while decisions of the House of Lords on general principles of the common law were of 'very great persuasive authority', the principle did not apply where circumstances locally 'make it inappropriate to develop a field of common law in a manner similar to England'.[98]

Receiving law from jurisdictions other than England

In modern circumstances, jurisdictions often look to jurisprudence from like-minded courts. For example, principles of law identified and developed in one Commonwealth jurisdiction may find their way into the courts of another Commonwealth jurisdiction. Whilst this is not a strict application of the reception or imposition of law theory, based on the fact that such precedents are not binding, but merely persuasive, courts often rely on these new principles of law. Thus, although this phenomenon is not the focus of this chapter, it is helpful to determine in what circumstances such principles of law are not appropriate for adoption, or need modification, before they can be applied to the receiving country. Put another way, perhaps more realistically, the question becomes, under what circumstances are our courts to accept and adopt foreign law? The local circumstances rule is particularly relevant in this discussion.

What may be termed a modified local circumstances rule for this voluntary reception of law is emerging. Thus, in addition to a different policy rationale for the legal principle, as identified in *Meanwell*,[99] courts will look to see whether the differences between the two jurisdictions are material or superficial. If the differences are substantial, the reception of the law or legal principle will not be appropriate. We have seen this kind of discussion in a line of constitutional cases dealing with the death penalty, in particular, whether the mandatory nature of the death penalty was unconstitutional. After determining that it was unconstitutional in one jurisdiction, the Privy Council looked at differences in the various Constitutions, especially the existing law clauses to see whether such a principle could be applied in other countries. In St Lucia, for example, it found the differences to be inconsequential for this purpose and the principle was applied.[100]

Important cultural social and historical differences may also make the reception of such legal principles or laws unsuitable.[101]

---

97 *Above*, fn 41.

98 *Above*, fn 96 at p 66. The court was also persuaded by the fact that the use of such contingency fees was to be used for meritorious reasons and the court should seek to encourage attorneys willing to give their services to meritorious causes.

99 *Above*, fn 91.

100 See cases like *Hughes v R* (2002) 60 WIR 187 and *Reyes v R* (2002) 60 WIR 42. Differences in Constitutions which spoke to 'due process' and 'protection of the law' were also reconciled and treated as insubstantial differences which did not prevent the application of principles developed in another country. See this discussion in Chapter 12 ('International Law as a Source of Law') and Chapter 7 ('The Written Constitution as a Legal Source').

101 See *Victoria and Alfred Waterfront v Police Commissioner, West Cape* [2004] 4 SA 444 at 450.

RECEPTION OF LAW AS A LIBERATING CONCEPT

While English law was imposed on the region in a rigid context, the doctrine of imposition contains within itself sufficient ammunition to liberate societies on the receiving end from the negative aspects of the phenomenon, leaving behind only its intrinsic value. These negative implications are wide and may culminate in the abortion of the true development of the legal system and indeed, the society. On the other hand, the value of received law, is the belonging of transplanted societies to a great legal tradition. Judges must, therefore, actively seek ways to emphasise the positive aspects of the doctrine while mitigating its negative effects.

The rule on local circumstances or conditions, for example, can indeed be an elastic concept, as broad as a court is willing to accept. The importance which a court is willing to give to cultural and social differences, policy and the like is surely linked to the value that the court places on these differences to the particular society. If sufficient worth is accorded to such differences, then the threshold of 'repugnance' or 'strong argument' outlined in the case law for disassociating or de-linking from imposed English law, will be easier to cross.

In the end, history has demonstrated, from the experiences of Canada, Australia, and even 'developing' countries such as Malaysia and Hong Kong, that as the society and legal system mature, it becomes more difficult to reconcile or submerge these differences and the courts will opt for a more divergent approach to the common law based on the peculiar local circumstances of the society. In the Commonwealth Caribbean, thus far, we have taken only timid steps toward this more liberating concept of receiving law.

PART II

THE SOURCES OF LAW IN THE COMMONWEALTH CARIBBEAN AND THEIR IMPACT ON THE LEGAL SYSTEM

CHAPTER 6

INTRODUCTION TO SOURCES OF LAW

Having examined the kind of law and legal tradition which exists in the Commonwealth Caribbean, the historical significance of that law and how that law was transplanted, we can now look more closely at the legal sources in the region.

First, we must determine what is meant by the term 'source of law'. In considering the question of what are the sources of law in the Commonwealth Caribbean, we are really asking, where does the law come from? What is its origin or basis? The answer to this question may appear to be simple to a person familiar with the history of the Commonwealth Caribbean. The short answer would be that law and legal systems in the Commonwealth Caribbean originated from the UK and its common law legal heritage. There is no doubt that the basis of law in the English-speaking Caribbean is the English common law. However, if we were to examine the above question more carefully, it would soon be apparent that the term 'source of law' has different legal meanings. Further, the origin of law and legal systems in the Commonwealth Caribbean is not only that which emanated from the UK, but also includes law and legal systems actually created within the region. Further, we should recall that at least in St Lucia and Guyana, the law originated not only from the UK, but also from France and the Netherlands respectively.

There are several types of sources of law in any particular legal system. These include (a) legal sources, (b) literary sources and (c) historical sources. Of these, only the legal sources are examined here in detail, for they shape and inform the particular legal system to a greater degree than other categories of sources of law.

The term 'literary source of law' merely describes the location of the law, where the law can be found, that is, for example, in books, legal treaties, law reports or legislation. Here, one is not concerned with content, but with method and form. These literary sources of law merely tell us what the law is. They do not confer legitimacy on rules of conduct or social arrangements.

The historical source of law refers to the causative factors behind a rule of law, its historical origin and development. For example, the historical source of our law is to be found in the colonial process by which English statute, the common law and equity were transplanted to the region under the doctrine of the reception of law. Similarly, the historical source of the law of England would be English custom.

In one sense, it may be argued that the historical source of law is particularly important in the Commonwealth Caribbean context, for our legal sources are intimately linked with the historical source through the historical experience of colonisation and plantation societies. It is clear that the historical continuum is still evident. As we saw earlier, the historical process of the reception or imposition of the English common law is important in defining Commonwealth Caribbean law. In addition, the attitude of the judiciary and legislature, the character and modus operandi of legal institutions are still imbued with the colonial experience. These permeate the legal sources and determine the way in which they will impact on the legal system. For example, even with contemporary legal systems in the region, many relics of colonial law remain on the statute books. The vagrancy laws, discussed earlier, are colourful examples.[1]

When we speak of a legal source, we are describing the basis of the law's validity, that which gives law its authority. The identification of a legal source occurs after the process by which rules of conduct acquire the character of law, becoming objectively definite, uniform and enforceable.

The legal sources of law in the Commonwealth Caribbean are (a) the Constitution; (b) legislation; (c) the common law and judicial precedent; (d) custom; (e) international law, including the law of regional treaties; and (f) equity. Of the six named sources, international law is not traditionally known as a source of law but it has become increasingly more important as a point of origin which gives law in Commonwealth Caribbean jurisdictions validity and authority. This is so particularly in relation to labour law and the law of human rights.

Apart from the written Constitution, the legal sources in the Commonwealth Caribbean are similar to those in the UK. They are even more similar to those in other common law countries. Yet while the form of the legal sources in the Commonwealth Caribbean may not differ radically from that of other common law countries, there are important differences in substance. In addition, the degree to which they impact on the legal system may vary. For example, as we will see, international law has had a significant impact on the legal system in the area of human rights; in particular, the issue concerning the punishments for capital offences. Similarly, equity has been valuable as a legal source in offshore financial jurisdictions. Even the cornerstone legal source of the common law, judicial precedent, has manifested itself differently in the region, complicated by the existence of a Privy Council which does not in theory follow the doctrine and which acts as a quasi-regional court.

Following is a discussion of each of these legal sources.

---

1   See above, Chapter 1. These statutes were first enacted during the immediate post-emancipation period in order to prevent newly freed slaves from staying away from the plantations. The ex-slaves could therefore be arrested for 'loitering'.

CHAPTER 7

THE WRITTEN CONSTITUTION AS A LEGAL SOURCE

THE NATURE AND IMPORTANCE OF THE CONSTITUTION

The written Constitution is arguably the most important legal source in the Commonwealth Caribbean. This is so for two reasons. First, the Constitution is the founding document confirming the independent status of Commonwealth Caribbean States. The Constitution represents a symbolic break with colonialism and the former British colonial masters. This is because written Constitutions in the Commonwealth Caribbean only blossomed in the post-independence period, although, of course, limited written constitutional instruments were evident before independence.[1] Indeed, the phenomenon that is the written Constitution does not exist in the UK. A Constitution should be an indigenous source of law and a true manifestation of the political will of the people. However, as we will see, Commonwealth Caribbean Constitutions may not fulfil these mandates in entirety.

The very act of writing down a Constitution is significant. It concretises the ideals of rights, democracy and nationhood and allows for interpretative expansion. By attempting to set down the parameters of democratic governance, a Constitution also gives life to judicial review, enabling the concept of *ultra vires* to flourish.

Secondly, the Constitution is the most important legal principle and source in the region because of the adherence to the theory of constitutional supremacy. This replaced the doctrine of parliamentary sovereignty, the latter being characteristic of the UK. While in form the Constitution is an example of legislation, another legal source, it must be distinguished from ordinary legislation because of its important philosophical orientation and authority.

The substantive law on the Constitution is beyond the scope of this book. Nonetheless, one cannot adequately discuss the legal system of any country without addressing the Constitution, as it is the defining source of law. Indeed, the Constitution is such an all pervasive instrument that we address many of the important, substantive issues of constitutional jurisprudence in several other chapters whilst examining various other aspects of the legal system.[2]

Constitutional supremacy

The Constitution can be defined as a body of law containing the rules which determine the structure of the State and its principal organs. It establishes the fundamental principles according to which the State is governed. It is the authority base from which a rule of law originates and derives its validity and further validates other sources. It may thus be described as the *grundnorm* or basic norm of the society from

---

1 Indeed, dependent territories, such as the Cayman Islands and Montserrat, have written constitutional instruments but do not have Bills of Rights.
2 See, eg, Chapter 12 ('International Law as a Source of Law'), Chapter 14 ('The Rules of Statutory Interpretation'), Chapter 15 ('The Court System of the Commonwealth Caribbean') and Chapter 19 ('The Jury System').

which all other norms emanate.[3] The Constitution is parent law by which all other laws are measured, or the supreme law of the land. This latter description of the Constitution is found in the celebrated case of *Collymore v AG*:[4] 'No one, not even Parliament, can disobey the Constitution with impunity.'[5] The Constitution is therefore the ultimate source of power and authority.

All other sources of law are measured against the Constitution. It is thus a yardstick by which the validity and authority of law in general are measured. It also governs the exercise of power or authority in the State.

It should be noted that a Constitution may be unwritten, as is the case in Britain. However, one should heed the kinds of problems which may arise with an unwritten Constitution, as many advocates for a written Bill of Rights for the UK have argued.[6] The important difference between West Indian Constitutions and the British Constitution is not, however, that the British Constitution is unwritten, but that, unlike Commonwealth Constitutions, it does not conform to the doctrine of constitutional supremacy.

In the preamble to the Constitution of Barbados, for example, it is stated:

> The Constitution is the supreme law of Barbados and, subject to the provisions of this Constitution, if any other law is inconsistent with this Constitution, this Constitution shall prevail and the other law shall, to the extent of the inconsistency, be void.[7]

Functions of the Constitution

The Constitution defines citizens' rights and the shape of both the legal system and the political system. For example, the principles of democracy can be found in Western Constitutions just as the principles of socialism and communism may be found in the Constitutions of communist or socialist countries.

The Constitution lays down mandatory procedures for government. It is the foundation for judicial review, States basic human rights, including avenues for redress of violations of such rights and promulgates new remedies. The latter is illustrated in the case of *Maharaj v AG of Trinidad and Tobago*.[8] It is also the fountain for procedural fairness, or due process of the law.

Other functions of the Constitutions in the Commonwealth Caribbean include:

---

3   The term 'grundnorm' is ascribed to Kelsen. It is the rule that gives legitimacy to all other rules in the legal System. Kelsen, H, *General Theory of Law and State*, 1961, Wedber, H (trans), New York: Russel and Russel.

4   (1967) 12 WIR 5. See also *Jaundoo v AG of Guyana* (1968) 12 WIR 221, at 226: 'When internal self-government was introduced and when independence was achieved, all those safeguards which had protected colonial peoples were grafted into the Constitution. The result which flowed was that Parliament became subject to the Constitution.' *Per Stoby, J*. See also the case of *Bahamas District of the Methodist Church v Symonette* [2000] 5 LRC 196; (2000) 59 WIR (PC, The Bahamas), for a discussion of the concepts of constitutional supremacy and parliamentary supremacy. The Barbadian case of *Boyce and Joseph v R* (2004) 64 WIR 37 (PC, Barbados), also contains a helpful discussion on the rationale for and nature of, constitutional supremacy.

5   *Ibid, Collymore*, fn 4, p 6.

6   See, eg, Zander, M, *A Bill of Rights*, 1975, London: Barry Rose.

7   The Constitution of Barbados. This is typical of Caribbean Constitutions. See, eg, the Constitution of St Vincent and the Grenadines, s 103, the Grenada Constitution, s 106, s 2 of the Trinidad and Tobago Constitution, Article 2 of the Constitution of the Bahamas and s 120 of the Constitution of St Lucia.

8   [1978] 2 All ER 670. Damages were held to be available as a constitutional remedy.

(a) the definition of the territory of the State;

(b) the creation and establishment of State institutions and the distribution of the functions of the State;

(c) the granting of authority to make laws;

(d) the furnishing of legitimacy to the State through the existence of an independent body of law which regulates the State.[9]

With regard to (b), the Constitutions in the region are not content to merely delineate these powers. Rather, they go into some detail. For example, provisions are made for the establishment of Public Service Commissions to appoint, discipline, transfer and fire employees of the Crown or State.

But perhaps one of the most important functions of the Constitution in the Commonwealth Caribbean, and certainly the most popular, is its role in defining and protecting fundamental human rights. Such rights are protected against violations by the State and it is the Constitution's task to balance these individual rights against the interests of the majority and the State, since no right is absolute. This function is explained clearly in the case of *Pinder v R*.[10]

The determination of such rights through the avenue of the superior courts of record has created a substantial jurisprudence in the region. As discussed below, it is a role, nonetheless, which is not as expansive as first appears. This leads to the need for constitutional reform, a process which is not the same as mere legislative amendment. Commonwealth Constitutions contain special mechanisms for change, including the existence of entrenchment provisions, discussed below.[11]

In *Hinds v R*,[12] the Privy Council made a number of other salient points about the substance and interpretation of Commonwealth Caribbean Constitutions including that they:

> . . . embody what is in substance an agreement reached between representatives of the various shades of political opinion in the State, as to the structure and organisation of government through which the plenitude of the sovereign power of the State is to be exercised in future.[13]

Further, it found that new Constitutions are evolutionary, not revolutionary, that is, grounded in basic concepts of the common law, separation of powers and the independence of judiciary, and so on.

Form and structure of the Constitution

The typical Constitution in the region contains the following chapters or sections:

(a) a preamble;[14]

(b) chapters on citizenship;

---

9   DeMerieux, M, *Fundamental Rights in Commonwealth Caribbean Constitutions*, 1992, Barbados: UWI, p 11. See also for a further discussion on the functions and purposes of Commonwealth Constitutions, particularly as they relate to fundamental human rights.

10   [2002] 3 WLR 1443.

11   See Alexis, F, *Changing Caribbean Constitutions*, 1983, Bridgetown: Antilles Publication.

12   [1977] AC 195.

13   *Ibid*, p 212.

14   An exception is the Constitution of Jamaica.

(c) a section on fundamental rights and freedoms, called a Bill of Rights;

(d) chapters defining the powers of the Head of State and Parliament;

(e) chapters defining the powers and establishment of the Executive and Judicature;

(f) chapters establishing and defining the role and functions of the Public Service and Judicial Commissions;

(g) chapters on finance;

(h) in addition, there is a statutory formula giving Parliament power 'to make laws for peace, order and good government'.

THE PROTECTION OF FUNDAMENTAL RIGHTS – A DYNAMIC LEGAL SOURCE?

On examining Bills of Rights in the Caribbean Constitutions, we see the direct influence of international sources of law on the legal systems of the Commonwealth Caribbean. The Bill of Rights provisions can be viewed as an attempt to reflect international standards of fundamental human rights, as embodied in such international instruments as the European Convention on Human Rights, the United Nations Declaration on Human Rights and the American Convention on Human Rights. The influence of international human rights opinion is also important, as will be seen in the discussion on international law as a source of law.[15]

One of the fundamental questions in relation to the importance of the Constitution as a legal source has been whether the advent of written Constitutions in the Commonwealth Caribbean has meant the creation of new rights or whether they merely codified existing rights at common law or otherwise, by ordinary statute. An answer in the affirmative, acknowledging the creation of new rights, would mean a substantial development of the character of the legal system, deviating from its traditional British, common law outlook. As we saw earlier, Commonwealth Caribbean judges have tended to view the reception of English law in a restrictive way and this has implications for the development of rights which did not exist when the common law was received.

Trevor Munroe, in examining the historical context of West Indian Constitutions, refers to the 'imperial origins of the 1944 Constitution of Jamaica'.[16] The new Independence Constitution, in contrast, was the symbol of the transition from colonialism to self-government. However, one may well ask, did the legal thinkers of the time intend to create a new creature in the Constitution? To what extent did radical change come about through the Constitution? Was the Constitution intended to be dynamic or static?

A Constitution ultimately derives its operative force and meaning from the character of the socio-political culture of the society. If the Constitution embodies alien principles and values, to what extent is it useful? On the other hand, how meaningful is a Constitution in a legal system founded upon a democracy if it is too divorced from what may be considered to be universal principles of justice? Were these universal principles embodied in our legal systems even before the advent of the Constitution?

---

15   Chapter 12 ('International Law as a Source of Law').
16   Munroe, T and Lewis, G (eds) *Readings on Government and Politics of the West Indies*, 1986, Mona, Jamaica: UWI, p 90.

Although the Constitution is the 'supreme law' and the ultimate source of power as declared in *Collymore v AG*,[17] we can see that often, it appears to be subservient to other sources of law, such as the English common law and International Law. This dilemma between theory and reality is evident, for example, in the phenomenon of 'saving law clauses' in the Constitutions.

A detailed discussion of the substantive constitutional jurisprudence on saving law clauses and of due process and the rule of law, discussed below, is not the object of this book.[18] However, these discussions impact very much upon our larger question as to what are the sources of West Indian law? It is in this vein that they are discussed.

SAVING LAW CLAUSES

Saving law clauses,[19] sometimes called 'existing law' clauses, attempt to preserve pre-independence law, often at the expense of human rights provisions in the Constitution, with the result that the Constitution is viewed as merely codifying existing rights and not creating new ones.[20] These clauses are not identical. It is the full or general saving law clause, which seeks to preserve all existing law, which has most often caused difficulty. This clause is only present in the older Constitutions such as Jamaica.[21] The other two types of saving law clauses are the partial or special saving law clause, which speaks only to a specific right[22] and the modification clause, which allows existing law to be modified so as to bring it into conformity with the Constitution.[23]

Whatever the type of saving law clause, the essential question in the debate centres around the question of whether these new Constitutions should be interpreted as having more force than existing law, that is, having the power to go beyond common law and other legal principles as expressly preserved. Have these saving law clauses undermined the creative force of Caribbean Constitutions?

In *Nasralla v DPP*,[24] the Privy Council declared that the fundamental rights which were enshrined in the new Jamaican Constitution were 'already secured to the people of Jamaica'.[25] Consequently, in interpreting the saving law clause, the court found that rights and freedoms as declared under the new written Constitution were subject to

---

17 *Above*, fn 4.

18 But see further discussion of these concepts in Chapter 12 ('International Law as a Source of Law').

19 For an early account of saving law clauses, see Alexis, F, 'When is an Existing Law Saved?' (1975) PL 256.

20 See Chapter 14 ('The Rules of Statutory Interpretation') for a discussion on how these clauses are to be interpreted.

21 See, eg, s 26(8) of the Constitution of Jamaica: 'Nothing contained in any law in force immediately before the appointed day shall be held to be inconsistent with any of the provisions of this Chapter . . .'

22 Found in the various Constitutions. See, eg, the clauses which regulate cruel and inhuman punishment, declaring pre-existing punishment as preserved as not being 'inconsistent' with the Constitution. See, eg, para 10, Schedule 2 of the St Lucia Constitution Order.

23 See, eg, the discussion in Chapter 14 ('The Rules of Statutory Interpretation'). See also, *DPP v Mollison* (2003) 64 WIR 140 (PC).

24 [1967] 2 AC 238, (PC).

25 *Ibid*, p 247, *per* Lord Devlin.

the 'existing law' or saved common law. The implication here was that the constitutional rights protected were only those which existed before the advent of the independence Constitution.

The decision therefore reveals a tension between written constitutional guarantees of fundamental rights and pre-independence rights, as expressly saved.

In *Robinson v R*,[26] an opinion from Jamaica emanating from the United Nations Human Rights Committee, the conflict between existing law and new Bills of Rights was again apparent. Robinson lost his case right up to the level of the Privy Council. The case involved an argument that his right to a fair hearing was violated when his murder trial was forced to proceed without an attorney. The United Nations Human Rights Committee, in rejecting a restrictive view of the Constitution, found that this was a violation of his right to a fair hearing, although the common law position is that there is no right to legal counsel. Although the case did not specifically refer to a saving law clause, the underlying issue, that is, the creation of new constitutional rights, not hitherto contained under the common law, was addressed.

A similar argument was raised in the case of *Collymore v AG*.[27] Although Wooding CJ stated that the Constitution was the supreme law of the land, he nevertheless went on to hold that the constitutional provisions protecting trade union rights, by providing for the rights to form and join a trade union and freedom of assembly, did not include the right to strike. This was on the ground that, at common law, there was no such right to strike. Thus, in the past, Commonwealth Constitutions have often been interpreted as merely codifying existing common law or statute law instead of creating new legal rights and indeed new law in general. It is questionable whether the Constitution was intended to be interpreted in such a stagnant, non-purposive manner.

Changes to saving law approaches

The saving law analysis has undergone considerable evolution, one might even say revolution, in recent years. The courts have not only accepted that linguistic differences between the saving law clauses in the region may mean substantial differences in their interpretation, but they have also been prepared to revisit entirely their previous generosity towards these clauses, which resulted in such narrow interpretations of Constitutions.

Happily, the *Nasralla* approach to saving law clauses has now been discredited, making way for a more coherent and meaningful relationship between existing law before independence and the values enshrined in the Constitution. Perhaps the best indication of this new approach is found in *Lambert and Watson v R*.[28] This case was one of a long line of cases which examined the constitutionality of the mandatory death penalty within the context of a saving law clause.

Lord Hope of Craighead in the Privy Council explained the correct principle found in Lord Devlin's judgment in *Nasralla* and in so doing, offered the appropriate way to construe saving law clauses in general. The court refused to accept that

---

26   United Nations Human Rights Committee Communication No 223/1987, decided 1989.
27   *Above*, fn 4.
28   [2004] 3 WLR 841; (2004) 64 WIR 241 (PC, Jamaica).

Nasralla meant to put forward a restrictive approach to a Constitution in favour of existing law. It first acknowledged, however, that, since *Nasralla*, the general consensus as to the effect of the saving law clause in the Constitution of Jamaica immunised any law in force in Jamaica immediately before the appointed day against any human rights challenge. However, the court suggested that more had 'been read into' Lord Devlin's words than he could have intended. It agreed that the Constitution proceeded upon the presumption that fundamental rights were already secured to the people by existing law. However, *Nasralla*:

> had not said that the presumption referred to was conclusive and irrebuttable. The Board did not have to consider a case in which an existing law was found to infringe a guaranteed human right ... It would in our opinion be surprising if the Board intended to treat laws in force at the time of independence as incapable of judicial development or adaptation to bring them into conformity with evolving understanding of human rights ... The Board can scarcely have contemplated that human rights in Jamaica were to be frozen indefinitely at the point they had reached in August 1962.

In the event that the *Nasralla* approach could not be explained away, the court was prepared to hold that it was wrongly decided:

> If, contrary to our view, the Board did hold in Nasralla that the effect of section 26(8) is to prohibit judicial modification or adaptation of any existing law to bring it into conformity with the human rights guarantees in Chapter 111, we respectfully think that that decision should no longer be followed.[29]

This more Constitution-centred approach has also been seen in cases involving only partial saving law clauses.[30] Even modification clauses can be overridden in favour of a clear finding of unconstitutionality, as demonstrated in *DPP v Mollison*,[31] a case involving the constitutionality of a juvenile sentence to be determined by the Governor General.

This is not to suggest that the saving law clause is now dysfunctional and will not be considered. One such case which runs counter to the trend is *Pinder v R*,[32] where the Privy Council deviated from the international approach of treating corporal punishment as cruel and inhuman punishment in favour of a special or partial saving law clause. It found that such punishment had been expressly saved and was constitutional.

Indeed, the value of a saving law clause is not to be denied. Its inclusion was necessary to ensure that there was coherence and certainty in the transition from colony to independent State. Once that legal tradition is cemented however, surely the need for such clauses, in particular, general saving law clauses, is diminished? Rather, there should exist, underlying the entire body of law in the legal system, an acceptance that constitutional values are to inform such law.

This is not so simple an exercise however, as it begs the question how to determine precisely such values and who should identify them? It is in this sense, that we ask another question. Has Commonwealth Caribbean jurisprudence overreached in placing too much authority in the hands of the judiciary in determining the identity

---

29 *Ibid* at paras 59–61.
30 See, eg, *R v Hughes* (2002) 60 WIR 156 (PC), *Reyes v R* (2002) 60 WIR 42 (PC). Cf *Pinder v R* (2002) 61 WIR 13 (PC, The Bahamas).
31 *Above*, fn 23.
32 *Above*, fn 30.

of the Constitution? To put it another way, have we unwittingly allowed our courts to hijack our Constitutions?

Modern interpretations of saving law clauses ensure that the Constitution as a source of law is not only more dynamic, but more independent of its common law origins. On the other hand, it paves the way for it to be universal in its expansion, relying more on international law as a source of law.

PURPOSIVE INTERPRETATION AND THE ATTITUDE OF THE COURTS

In 1985 Professor Carnegie concluded that 'the general picture of constitutional pro-tection of human rights in the Commonwealth Constitutions is one of modest effect'.[33] Since then, the picture has changed. Commonwealth Caribbean jurisprudence has become more liberal and dynamic, tending toward more individualistic appreciation of human rights.

A noted example is *Maharaj v AG of Trinidad and Tobago*.[34] Here, a new remedy in damages for violations of human rights was held to have been created by the Constitution. Similarly, in *Thornhill v AG*,[35] a new constitutional right to retain coun-sel was successfully promulgated. Again, in the case of *AG of Trinidad and Tobago v Whiteman*,[36] the Constitution of Trinidad and Tobago was generously interpreted so as to uphold a right to retain and instruct the attorney of one's choice without delay.

The grounding principle in these pro-rights cases is that a Constitution is a unique instrument which must be interpreted in the light of the ideals and principles which ground it. The courts should thus give life to the meaning of the Constitution by interpreting it in a broad and purposive manner. The underlying presumption of such an instrument is that the State, through its legislature, intends to secure the broadest spectrum of rights to its citizens.

For example, in the case of *Minister of Home Affairs v Fisher*,[37] the Privy Council affirmed that a purposive and generous approach should be adopted in interpreting the Constitution, avoiding the 'austerity of tabulated legalism'.[38]

The *tour de force* must be, however, the now famous *Pratt and Morgan* decision.[39] Whatever its merits in substance, that decision represents a triumph for the generous interpretation of a Constitution. The constitutional protection against cruel and inhuman punishment found in all Commonwealth Caribbean Constitutions was interpreted to include the situation where a convicted person suffers undue delay on death row.

The *Pratt and Morgan* decision also represents both an evolution and a revolution

---

33 Carnegie, ANR, 'The constitutional protection of human rights in the Commonwealth Caribbean', 1985, unpublished paper, University of the West Indies, p 15.
34 *Above*, fn 8.
35 [1981] AC 61, PC.
36 (1991) 39 WIR 397, PC, Trinidad and Tobago.
37 [1980] AC 319.
38 *Ibid*, p 321.
39 *Pratt and Morgan v AG of Jamaica* (1993) 43 WIR 340. See Chapter 8 ('The Common Law and the Doctrine of Judicial Precedent') and Chapter 12 ('International Law as a Source of Law').

in Commonwealth Caribbean jurisprudence. It is evolutionary because of the inching progress which the undue delay concept made from its mere 'possibility', as located in the haunting dissent in *Riley v AG*,[40] its acceptance in principle in *Abbot v AG of Trinidad and Tobago*,[41] to the present decision. This progression illustrates the norm-building character of the written Constitution as a source of law.

This norm-building and evolutionary character of a Constitution was alluded to indirectly in *Hobbs et al v R*.[42] Here, the Court of Appeal spoke of the 'evolving standards of decency' and the 'new sensitivities which emerge as civilisation advances' which should be reflected in the interpretation of written Constitutions. In effect, their Lordships have emphasised that the Constitution as a legal source is not static, but must constantly evolve so as to measure up to appropriate standards of human rights and other societal values. It is, as such, a dynamic and flexible legal source.

The case is revolutionary because, at one stroke, the Privy Council overruled its previous decision in *Riley*[43] and a string of related decisions, and affirmed the dynamism of the written Constitution as a source of law, and indeed, the Privy Council itself. A similar decision in terms of its path-breaking character is *Lewis et al v AG of Jamaica*,[44] a case discussed below, on the question of the attitude to international treaties and the question of due process.

There has, therefore, been a steady progression toward a development of a more purposive construction of Commonwealth Caribbean Constitutions. What might be called a modern principle of constitutional interpretation is that liberal interpretative techniques which encompass the purposes and ideals of the constitutional instrument should be employed. This interpretative technique is in line with those from international human rights bodies when examining international human rights Conventions.[45]

Commonwealth Caribbean courts seem poised to make the constitutional protection of human rights even more elastic, even in contentious areas, such as capital punishment. In *Fisher v AG of the Bahamas*,[46] Lord Steyn, in an *obiter* statement, noted that the death row litigation was 'in transition', and that just as the principle on undue delay had evolved to find such delays unconstitutional, it might further expand to include pre-trial delay.

Yet, while strides toward expansive interpretations of the Bill of Rights may be observed in relation to certain areas, such as the death penalty or in relation to freedom of expression[47] or the press, our Constitutions remain somewhat archaic in other areas, for example, discrimination in relation to sex, gender and even religion, discussed further below.

---

40 [1983] AC 719, p 726, PC; [1982] 2 WLR 557, PC.
41 [1979] 3 All ER 21.
42 [1994] CLB 45.
43 *Above*, fn 40.
44 (2000) 57 WIR 275 (PC, Jamaica); [2000] 3 WLR 1785 (PC, Jamaica).
45 See the discussion in Chapter 12 ('International Law as a Source of Law').
46 Unreported PC Appeal No 53 of 1997, decided 12 December 1997, The Bahamas, p 18.
47 See, eg, *De Freitas v Permanent Secretary of Agriculture and Fisheries* [1998] 3 LRC 62; [1998] 53 WIR 131 (PC); [1998] 3 WLR 675.

Due process and the rule of law

It is clear that the Constitution is a source for procedural fairness, called due process or 'protection of the law' in some Constitutions.[48] This notion, in turn, is to be viewed as an aspect of the rule of law. However, these fundamental concepts do not originate from the Constitution. Rather, they are reaffirmed in the written Constitutions.[49] These are principles which ground the very character of the law and legal system. Further, they are aspects of the separation of powers doctrine as they speak to the essence of the role of the courts to apply the law, in their inherent supervisory jurisdiction. These are constitutional principles in the broadest sense.

In *AG et al v Joseph and Boyce*,[50] the Caribbean Court of Justice, in considering the import and origin of due process, relied on *Ong Ah Chuan v Public Prosecutor*,[51] and explained:

> [In] . . . a Constitution founded on the Westminster model . . . the continued references to 'law' in such contexts as 'in accordance with law,' 'equality before the law', 'protection of the law' and the like . . . refer to a system of law which incorporates these fundamental rules of natural justice that had formed part and parcel of the common law of England that was in operation . . . at the commencement of the Constitution.[52]

A similar view was expressed by the Privy Council, for example, in *Thomas v Baptiste*.[53] Lord Millett described the concept in this way:

> . . . 'due process of law' is a compendious expression in which the word 'law' does not refer to any particular law and is not a synonym for common law or statute. Rather, it invokes the concept of law itself and the universally accepted standards of justice observed by civilised nations which observe the rule of law.

Due process arises independently of other rights conferred by the Constitution so that it is not necessary to invoke it alongside a substantive right.[54] Further, in *Lewis*,[55] due process was treated as an international concept standing independently of the Constitution. This allows the Constitution to reach outside of itself, to these broad notions of justice recognised in international law.[56]

Due process is ultimately a dynamic, even flexible legal concept and seems to redefine itself with changing international standards. In *Boyce*[57] and *Lewis*,[58] for example, it laid the basis for imputing new standards of fairness which required the State to allow death row prisoners to have their matters heard before international

---

48 The courts have determined that 'due process' and 'protection of the law' are in essence the same. They both mean standards of procedural fairness. See, eg, *Lewis, above,* fn 44 and *AG et al v Joseph and Boyce* CCJ Appeal, No CV 2 of 2005, decided 21 June 2006 (Barbados).
49 *Ibid.*
50 *Boyce, ibid.*
51 [1981] AC 648, *per* Lord Diplock.
52 *Above, Boyce,* fn 48, para 62.
53 (2002) 54 WIR 387 (PC) at 421.
54 *Boyce, above,* fn 48, pp 19–27.
55 *Above,* fn 44.
56 As such, the due process penalty clause further cements international law as a source of law in Commonwealth Caribbean Constitutions. See Chapter 12 ('International Law as a Source of Law').
57 *Above,* fn 48.
58 *Above,* fn 44.

human rights bodies, despite the fact that the relevant treaty instruments had not been incorporated into domestic law.[59]

Even Lord Hoffman's dissent in *Lewis*, though it objected to the use of due process to, in effect, treat unincorporated treaties as law, thereby indirectly conferring on the Executive the authority to make law, did not disagree with the intrinsic nature of due process, as part of the common law. Indeed, he referred respectfully to due process as an 'ancient concept'. His quarrel was not with due process as a principle enshrined in the Constitution, but its parameters. Thus, due process is not sufficient to dislocate the separation of powers doctrine as according to Lord Hoffman, treaty-making should remain an executive function and legislation and law-making a Parliamentary function. Paradoxically, while due process is a potentially liberating principle, embodying ever-increasing notions of fairness to the benefit of the individual, arguably, it is also a constraining principle, imposing fetters on the Constitution and ultimately, the legal system, to define itself as deemed appropriate for the particular society. Nowhere is this more apparent than in the discussion of due process on the issue of the death penalty.

THE PREAMBLE TO THE BILL OF RIGHTS

The Bill of Rights in a typical Commonwealth Caribbean Constitution contains an introductory clause, the legal status of which has caused much discussion and some litigation. The clause declares that 'every person' is entitled to 'fundamental rights and freedoms' without regard to 'race, colour, creed, political opinion and sex'. The freedoms extend to freedom of expression, assembly, conscience, privacy and equality before the law.[60]

Because the Constitution then proceeds to guarantee redress for violation of human rights as listed under individual sections other than the introductory clause,[61] there is a line of argument which suggests that only those rights which are specifically mentioned, these individual sections contained in the body of the Constitution, are protected. Consequently, where the right is only declared in the introductory clause, it may be interpreted as non-justiciable or non-enforceable. This has been the experience in relation to the right to privacy and the protection against discrimination on the grounds of sex, for example. In *Girard and the St Lucia Teachers Union v AG*,[62] the court found that no redress was available for a lack of equality on the ground of sex as it was not mentioned in the Constitution, except in the introductory clause.

The justiciability of rights mentioned only in the preamble has been declared in other Commonwealth jurisdictions, most notably in the case of *R (on the application of a Gibraltar Company) v Financial Services Comr*,[63] a case from Gibraltar concerning

---

59   *Ibid*. Discussed more fully in Chapter 12 ('International Law as a Source of Law').

60   See, eg, the Constitution of the Bahamas, s 15. Note that the clause described is absent in the Trinidad and Tobago Constitution.

61   This is because the redress clause lists the rights for which a person can seek redress before the court. The problem occurs where the redress clause does not list the Preamble but only rights provisions coming after the Preamble. Where, as in Antigua and Barbuda, the redress clause specifically includes the Preamble, then there should be no problem.

62   Unreported judgment No 371 of 1985, decided 17 December 1986, St Lucia. See also *AG of Antigua v Lake* [1990] 1 WLR 68.

63   [2003] 4 LRC 133 (Supreme Court, Gibraltar).

whether an offshore financial company was entitled to privacy. Importantly, the Gibraltar Constitution is similar to many in the region in this respect. The Constitution of Gibraltar mentioned privacy only in the Preamble to the Bill of Rights. It says:

> ... in Gibraltar there have existed and shall continue to exist ... the following human rights ... namely–(a) the right to individual life, liberty, security of the person and the protection of the law ... and (c) the right of the individual to protection for the privacy of his home and other property and from deprivation of property without compensation.[64]

The court, in finding that there was an entitlement to privacy said: '[T]his case involves consideration of the claimant's right to privacy (see s 1(c) of the Constitution). Furthermore, that a right under s 1 of the Constitution is justiciable (see *Rent Tribunal v Aidasani* (Court of Appeal Civil Appeal No 1 of 2001)).'[65]

In the Commonwealth Caribbean, there has been as yet, no reversal of the position expressed in *Girard*. However, the courts have been slowly stepping toward making the Preamble come alive, at least with respect to certain of its provisions. In both *Lewis*[66] and *AG et al v Joseph and Boyce*,[67] the Privy Council and the CCJ respectively have treated the due process or 'protection of the law' provisions in the Preambles to the Bill of Rights as not only justiciable, but instrumental to the protection of human rights.

In *Lewis*, the Privy Council did not address the debate as to the possible limits of a provision when found only in the Preamble directly. Rather, it simply treated due process, which was located in the Preamble, as an intrinsic part of the law, the common law and even the rule of law.[68] In a sense, it did not need to address the justiciability of the Preamble provisions. In *Boyce*, however, the CCJ[69] recognised that 'protection of the law' was not specifically mentioned in the body of the Constitution to which the redress clause referred, except by way of a marginal note. The CCJ viewed the body of the Constitution to which the redress clause specifically referred, and which enumerated the human rights provisions, as 'details' on the more general rights listed in the Preamble, and importantly, provisions demonstrating how such rights were to be limited where appropriate. In the case of due process/protection of the law, the CCJ appeared to think that such detailing was not only unnecessary but impractical.[70]

At the same time, this was no general principle on the justiciability of provisions found only in the Preamble, since the CCJ was clear that with respect to other Preamble provisions, unless such detailed provisions were apparent, there was no

---

64   Section 1 of the Constitution of Gibraltar.
65   *Gibraltar Company, above,* fn 63 at p 153.
66   *Above,* fn 44.
67   *Above,* fn 48.
68   See the discussion above, as to the stature of due process. The introductory clause or Preamble to the Bill of Rights is found at s 13 of the Jamaican Constitution.
69   *Above,* fn 48, at para 41: 'the respondents' right to protection of the law, one of the fundamental human rights enumerated and recognised in section 11 of the Constitution. The right of an aggrieved person to approach the Court for redress ... expressly conferred ... only in respect of breaches that run foul of the provisions sections 12 to 23.'
70   'The right to the protection of the law is so broad and pervasive that it would be well nigh impossible to encapsulate in a section of a Constitution all the ways in which it may be invoked or can be infringed.' *Boyce,* fn 48, para 60.

protection: 'There is therefore, no scope for enforcement of the relevant right outside the four corners of the detailed sections.'[71]

The decision therefore turns on the intrinsic nature of due process itself. As we saw above, due process is treated by both the CCJ and the Privy Council as being an inherent part of the law and even the rule of law. Its existence does not therefore depend on a specific provision in the Constitution, Preamble or otherwise. Indeed, many of the other provisions listed in the Constitution, such as a right to a fair trial, also impute due process. The finding in these cases that due process and protection of the law, rights specifically contained only in the Preambles, are justiciable, makes no helpful statement on the principle on the justiciability of Preamble provisions in general. Procedural justice is not to be viewed in the same light as the substantive rights mentioned in the Preambles, the latter which must be detailed in the body of the Constitution, to have effect.

HIJACKING THE CONSTITUTION AND CONSTITUTIONAL REFORM?

We may observe from our discussion above that the purposive interpretations of the saving law and due process provisions, and by extension, the rule of law, appear to be moving away from the internal logic of the Constitution and toward more external expressions of justice. Some may even argue this is merely judicial activism disguised as purposive interpretation. We may well ask, are we hijacking our Constitutions? At what point does good judicial decision-making become judicial dictatorship which ignores the legislative imperatives of the democratically elected representatives of the people, the Parliament?

In *Pinder v R*,[72] however, the Privy Council refused to bow to international influences in employing a purposive approach to corporal punishment. It recognised that the true purpose of a Constitution may be located without travelling outside of its domestic grounding. As seen earlier, it found that corporal punishment was expressly saved by the Bahamas Constitution although such punishment was out of sync with international standards on punishment.

In one case, judicial activism forced Parliament to restate the original intention of the Constitution. The Barbadian Parliament reversed the effect of *Pratt and Morgan* and its progeny to prevent the Courts from declaring the mandatory death penalty unconstitutional.

These concerns continually raise the issue as to the origin and source of the law. Are our Constitutions, in particular, the Bills of Rights, to be mere reflections of universal human rights instruments and jurisprudence without room for deviation? This is a question that concerns us further in our following chapter on 'International Law as a Source of Law'. Is this what the framers of the Constitutions intended? Are interpretations of our Constitutions which seem so far removed from their original objectives any less imperialistic than colonial laws imposed on us? Are such redefined Constitutions in sync with coherent governance initiated by sovereign nations?

These are difficult questions to answer but certainly a Constitution is a document

---

71   *Ibid*, para 60.
72   *Above*, fn 30.

which should embody the particular philosophy and even ideology of the State and its people, even if that ideology appears different to those of other peoples. Against this must be balanced the need for the Constitution to avoid atrophy, for the Constitution 'is not a sterile and lifeless document' but 'an organic and living thing'.[73] But the change envisioned is to 'respond to the changing needs of the people it governs'[74] and not some alien audience. In *Boodram*,[75] Sharma, CJ struggled to outline the balance that a court must establish in determining constitutional imperatives. He adopted the approach of a Canadian jurist who suggests that the judge must have an understanding of the 'priorities' of the peoples whom he serves, and interpret the Constitution so as to make 'the most beneficial impact' on their lives. He conceded that the task was a political one, but not in a narrow partisan sense.[76]

DIRECTIONS IN CONSTITUTIONAL JURISPRUDENCE

In recent times, a large body of constitutional jurisprudence has emerged around the death penalty, securing more and more rights for convicted persons. We may argue that this disproportionate attention to death penalty matters means that issues which are perhaps more pressing to our societies as a whole, are not being addressed, so that our constitutional jurisprudence continues to languish in other areas.

How, we may ask, has the 'ordinary' individual fared? How has the Constitution served persons not convicted of crimes, but who have implored the courts to pronounce against religious discrimination, gender discrimination, political victimisation, property rights, trade union rights and even rights associated with freedom of association and movement? In these areas, the protection afforded under the Constitution seems to be interpreted more conservatively.[77] At minimum, it would appear that the universality of values attached to the death penalty cases has not found its place as easily in other areas of human rights. There appears to be a selective appreciation of universal human rights norms when applied to our Constitutions.

Certainly, there have been glimmers of liberalism in these more troublesome areas, notably before the Belize courts. In *Wade v Roches*,[78] for example, the Belize Court of Appeal came to the opposite conclusion to *Girard*,[79] in similar circumstances, declaring the dismissal of a pregnant school teacher as unconstitutional. Similarly, the

---

73   *Boodram v AG and Another* (1994) 47 WIR 459 (Joint judgment CA and PC, Trinidad and Tobago) at p 467 *per* Sharma JA.

74   *Ibid.*

75   *Ibid.*

76   *Boodram, ibid,* at p 468.

77   See, eg, the cases on religion such as the cases discussed in Chapter 1 ('Introduction to Law and Legal Systems in the Commonwealth Caribbean'), Chapter 3 ('Legal Traditions – Types of Legal Systems in the Commonwealth') and Chapter 10 ('Custom as a Source of Law'), which failed to secure freedom of religion for Rastafarians and other ethnic groups. See also *Collymore v AG, above,* fn 4, holding no right to strike; *Banton v Alcoa Minerals of Jamaica* (1971) 17 WIR 275, finding no right to bargain collectively; *Girard, above,* fn 62, no protection against discrimination on ground of sex; no rights to salary or property in one's job. In *The Matter of Rosemond John, (Unreported) Civil Suit No. 492 of 1996,* decided March 1997, SC, Dominica; no general right to enjoyment of property: *AG of Antigua v Lake* [1990] 1 WLR 68; *Public Order Acts* deemed constitutional.

78   Civil Appeal, No 4 of 2005, decided 9 March 2005, CA, Belize.

79   *Above,* fn 62.

Supreme Court in *Selgado v AG et al*[80] found in favour of an applicant who had been dismissed from the army because of his sexual orientation. However, it is important to note that the *Selgado* case was decided on grounds of judicial review of administrative action, examining the Public Service Regulations and not on constitutional violation on the ground of sex discrimination. The Court seemed to hint that the latter action could have succeeded however, saying:

> The unwanted and unconsented homosexual acts were alleged to be disciplinary wrongs referred to generally as misconducts. Captain Selgado denied the homosexual incidents and thus homosexuality. His denial removed the case from the purview of discrimination on account of sex, a highly controversial contemporary topic when gay inclination is involved. Given the tendency of attorneys and judges in Belize of accepting without questioning, what is considered legally right in the USA, Canada and especially England, despite vast differences in social views, Captain Selgado might have put up a formidable sex discrimination case under s 16 of the Constitution of Belize, even a constitutional motion case, had he owned up to homosexuality.[81]

More typically, to cure many of the deficiencies of the Constitution with respect to discrimination and the like, aggrieved persons have had to turn to judicial review of administrative action. This occurred, for example, in *Morraine*[82] and in a line of cases before the Trinidad courts, which fought alleged race discrimination in public employment. These proceeded by way of judicial review of the decisions of the relevant Public Service Commissions.[83] Ironically, the Trinidad and Tobago courts have been more generous in recognising discrimination even in relation to the controversial sexual orientation, when employing the discrimination argument to strike down legislation seeking to promote equality and non-discrimination. This was an action initiated by the State itself to declare the legislation unconstitutional.[84]

Constitutional protection against violation of rights is secured only against the State. In the absence of ordinary legislation on discrimination and other vulnerable areas involving rights, this emphasis results in a significant lacuna in the law. Moreover, in certain areas of human rights, in particular, with respect to discrimination, the Constitution may be seen to be further deficient, either in terms of its silence with regard to certain forms of discrimination, such as sexual orientation, gender, or even sex in some Constitutions,[85] or in the weakness of some provisions or, as we have seen, in the restricted way in which such provisions have been interpreted. For example, a requirement of 'malice' has been held to be necessary to ground discrimination.[86] Similarly, the breath of the privacy protections is questionable.

McIntosh notes correctly that 'constitutional cases often raise intractable, profound questions of political morality, which means that there is an obvious role for substantive moral argument in political debate and constitutional adjudication'.[87]

---

80   BZ 2004 SC7.
81   *Ibid*, para 5.
82   *Mohammed Morraine*, (1995) 49 WIR 371; [1996] 3 LRC 475.
83   See, eg, *Rajkumar et al v Public Service Commission* (Unreported) No. 945 of 1998, decided 26 October 1999, HCA, Trinidad and Tobago. Also for challenging political victimisation as in *Camacho and Sons v Collector of Customs* (1971) 18 WIR 159.
84   *Suratt v AG of Trinidad and Tobago* TT 2004 HC 37.
85   See, eg, the Constitution of St Lucia. Sex was mentioned only in the Preamble to the Bill of Rights and was thereby not justiciable.
86   See *Smith v LJ Williams Ltd* (1980) 32 WIR 395. Cf *Wade v Roches, above*, fn 78.
87   Simeon McIntosh, *Judicial Rights and Democratic Governance – Essays in Caribbean Jurisprudence*, 2005, Jamaica: The Caribbean Law Publishing Company, p 62.

Moreover, as we suggested in Chapters 1 and 2, despite the label of pluralism in our societies, legal discourse has tended to conform to a uniform, majoritarian, ideological position based essentially on an Anglo-Saxon, Christian type of morality and governance. This morality is often used as a way of precluding minority interests, whether in terms of gender or religion. Should not the State grant equal protection to such minority interests? What is the value of constitutional protection for religious freedom and other freedoms involving 'difference' if only majority interests are to be protected? The value of the Constitution is not only diminished but rendered nugatory.

Admittedly, litigation has been sparse. This is in part due to the lack of awareness of the rights of the citizenry. More likely, however, it is due to cultural attitudes which do not perceive certain types of conduct as discriminatory, unlawful or even inappropriate. Such attitudes spill over into the interpretation of the law. One example relates to sexual harassment. In one case a male employee challenged his summary dismissal for fondling and ogling female employees at the workplace. A female magistrate viewed it as merely 'ungentlemanly conduct', insufficient to warrant dismissal.[88]

We may argue further that certain types of rights, in particular, economic and social rights, largely rights in the collective, seem poorly served by our Constitutions. As such, issues which are vital to developmental concerns, such as rights that should attach to workers and trade unions to enable them to lobby adequately for better standards of living, are poorly defined, or entirely absent.

A similar complaint is with respect to employment rights under the Constitution, rights in the collective, litigation that could challenge earlier assumptions that in our democracies, where some Constitutions specifically protect the right to form and join a trade union, there is no right to strike, bargain collectively or recognise a union.[89]

We have already seen that the very structure of some of our Constitutions can undermine the constitutional instrument as a cohesive and effective machinery for human rights. This occurs, for example, where important rights are mentioned only in the Preamble and not detailed in the body of the Constitution and have been declared unjusticiable. Notably, already vulnerable rights such as discrimination and privacy may also fall into this category.

Thus, despite the importance of the Constitution, a number of questions are increasingly being raised about the defects and omissions of Commonwealth Caribbean Constitutions, as well as the propensity of the judges to stretch them, sometimes well beyond imaginable or even desirable boundaries in particular subject areas. Not surprisingly, many countries are actively pursuing constitutional reform.

ECONOMIC, SOCIAL AND CULTURAL RIGHTS

One area of constitutional law is particularly controversial. This is the extent to which certain rights which can be categorised as economic, social or cultural rights, often called ECONSOC rights, are justiciable or enforceable.

---

88   *Jones v Bico* (Magistrate Court, Barbados) 16 February 1995, affirmed by the Court of Appeal in *Bico Ltd v Jones* (1996) 53 WIR 49.
89   Recall, eg *Collymore v AG, above,* fn 4.

ECONSOC rights, like civil and political rights, may be enshrined in a Constitution or international human rights instrument. A common example in the Commonwealth Caribbean is the right to form a trade union.[90] ECONSOC rights are usually distinguished by the fact that they relate to rights in the collective. This means that they concern, not the rights of any particular individual, but a particular class or group. Further, they often, as the name implies, have significant and obvious economic, social or cultural implications. Indeed, the factor of cost is one important reason given for their non-enforceability. Other examples of these rights are the right to education, to work, to health, to self-determination and to strike.

The question of the justiciability of ECONSOC rights has caught the attention of the Caribbean courts with inconsistent results. In one landmark case, *AG v Mohammed Ali*,[91] it was held that such rights as the right of a trade union to consultation could be enforced. The Guyanese Constitution was, however, later changed to nullify this judgment. Elsewhere in the Commonwealth, in India, there has been exciting jurisprudence affirming the justiciability of such rights. For example, in *Olga Tellis v Union of India*,[92] the right to a livelihood was held to be justiciable. Indeed, the court in *Ali* was aware of these developments in coming to its conclusion. In contrast, the *Collymore* case,[93] met earlier, is evidence that the justiciability of such rights is still difficult in the Commonwealth Caribbean, as elsewhere in the world. The implications of the failure to find ECONSOC rights justiciable have been felt largely in the area of labour law. This is because labour 'rights' tend to be formulated in the collective, the right to strike, to equal pay, to collective bargaining, to be recognised as a workers' representative, and so on. All these rights are contentious in the region. In *Banton v Alcoa Minerals of Jamaica*,[94] for example, the right to collective bargaining was denied. While not yet a subject of litigation, the question of whether a trade union could claim a constitutional right to be recognised as the lawful representative of workers in the absence of express promulgation of such a right, but with a constitutional guarantee that workers have a right to form and join a trade union, has also engaged the mind of the public in Barbados and St Lucia.[95]

SEPARATION OF POWERS

The Constitution also embodies the 'separation of powers' principle. This principle goes to the heart of our constitutional inheritance. Indeed, separation based on the rule of law is a 'characteristic feature of democracies'.[96] The principle is of particular significance to the administration of justice in the legal system. Caribbean courts have affirmed without reservation that the Constitution provides that judges are

---

90 See, also, the Guyanese Constitution, the Grenada Constitution 1973 and the Belize Constitution 1981, which incorporate the right to work.
91 [1989] LRC (Const) 474.
92 [1987] LRC (Const) 351.
93 *Above*, fn 4.
94 (1971) 17 WIR 275.
95 In Barbados, unlike several other countries in the region, there is no statute making trade union recognition compulsory. St Lucia enacted legislation to make trade union recognition compulsory only in 1999, after this issue was aired as a result of employers refusing to recognise unions.
96 Per Lord Steyn in *R (Anderson) v SOS for the Home Department* [2002] 3 WLR 1800 at 1822.

independent, impartial and separate from political interference and from the political arm of the government, so as to administer justice impartially. Further, the judiciary and the courts have a monopoly over the exercise of the judicial function. This was confirmed in the cases of *Farrell v AG*[97] and the landmark case of *Hinds v R.*[98] In *Hinds*, the attempt to establish a Gun Court was held to be unconstitutional as a court of law. Here, the Jamaica Parliament wished to establish a Gun Court giving resident magistrates jurisdiction reserved for Supreme Court judges under the Constitution. It gave a Review Board, instead of a court, the power to sentence.

The Privy Council held, overturning the Court Appeal decision, that this was a violation of the separation of powers doctrine enshrined in the Constitution.

Similarly, while the Executive can determine a fixed penalty as set by statute, it cannot transfer from the judiciary onto itself, a discretion to determine the severity or nature of a penalty. Such a discretion is reserved to the judiciary under the Constitution. Thus, the Constitution also lays down the parameters, not just for the formal sources of law, but also some of its details, such as the authority for the award of penalties. In *DPP v Mollison*,[99] on a question whether the Governor General held the discretionary power to determine the sentence of a juvenile, the Privy Council noted that such a construct could 'open the door to the exercise of arbitrary power by the Executive'.[100] The Privy Council continued:

> There is a clear distinction between the prescription of a fixed penalty and the selection of a penalty for a particular case. The presumption of a fixed penalty is the statement of a general rule, which is one of the characteristics of legislation . . . and the application of that rule is for the courts . . . the selection of punishment is an integral part of the administration of justice and cannot be committed to the hands of the Executive.[101]

Similarly, the judiciary acknowledged that it does not make law or prescribe legal policy. This is the function of the legislature.[102]

Constitutional provisions which secure security of tenure for judges, in particular, by the establishment of independent Judicial Commissions to appoint and remove judges, also buttress the independence of the judiciary. We will further explore the constitutional principle of the independence of the judiciary in Chapter 15 ('The Court System of the Commonwealth Caribbean').

ENTRENCHMENT OF CONSTITUTIONAL PROVISIONS

All the Constitutions in the Commonwealth Caribbean contain provisions for entrenchment,[103] whereby certain of their provisions may not be altered except by a special majority of Parliament or, in some cases, a referendum. This confirms the

---

97   (1979) 27 WIR 377.
98   *Above*, fn 13.
99   (2003) 64 WIR 140.
100 Relying on *Deaton v AG & the Revenue Commissioner* [1963] WIR 170, at 182–183.
101 *Mollison, above*, fn 99.
102 See Chapter 8 ('The Common Law and the Doctrine of Judicial Precedent'). See also, the Cayman Islands case of *In the Estate of B* [1999] CILR 460 (Grand Court, Cayman Islands) at p 468, where Murphy, J, in holding that illegitimate children did not share in their father's estate said: 'My function is not . . . to impose my own values by creative interpretation. If there is to be reform in this area that is for the legislature, not for me.'
103 See, eg, the Constitutions of the Bahamas, s 54; Barbados, s 49; Jamaica, s 49; and St Lucia, s 41.

special nature of the Constitution, placing it in a different category to that of ordinary legislation.

In *Hinds v R*,[104] the court noted the significance of entrenchment:

> The purpose served by this machinery for entrenching is to ensure that those provisions which were regarded as important safeguards by the political parties ... should not be altered without mature consideration by the Parliament and the consent of a larger proportion of its members than the bare majority required for ordinary laws.

The need for a referendum to effect constitutional change with respect to certain matters was raised recently in an important case on the authority of the Jamaican Parliament to enter into an Agreement to make Jamaica part of the arrangements for the Caribbean Court of Justice.[105]

MEASURING THE VALIDITY OF OTHER LAWS AND LEGAL SOURCES

A significant contribution of the Constitution to the development of the legal system is its role in testing the validity of other laws and legal sources. Thus, the Constitution is the cornerstone of the rule of law. This testing or measuring of other laws and legal sources is carried out by the process of judicial review.[106]

The judicial review process is most important in determining the validity of ordinary legislation. Such legislation may be measured against constitutional norms and declared unconstitutional or *ultra vires* if it offends these norms. The High Court (called Supreme Court in some jurisdictions, such as Belize), has been assigned this role of judicial review. Indeed, Wooding, J in *Collymore*, referred to the Supreme Court as the 'guardian of the Constitution'.[107] This judicial review role is a responsibility which the courts must not 'shirk from or attempt to shift to Parliament. Loyalty to the democratic legal order of the Constitution required the Privy Council to grapple with the question [of judicial review] and ... to decide it'.[108]

The High Court is, however, circumspect in relation to its jurisdiction and will be reluctant to hear matters if alternative remedies are available to avoid an abuse of the court's process.[109] More recently, however, it has emerged that this general principle will not prevent matters by way of a constitutional motion if the alternative remedy is not adequate or if the matter is one that should be addressed constitutionally.[110]

Where legislation is found to be in conformity with the Constitution, it is said to be *intra vires*. The concepts of *ultra vires* or, conversely, *intra vires*, are crucial to an understanding of how the Constitution can invalidate or legitimise ordinary legislation as a legal source. If legislation does not conform to the general principles protected by the

---

104   *Above*, fn 13, p 361.
105   *Independence Jamaica Council for Human Rights (1998) Ltd v Marshall-Burnett and Another* (2005) 65 WIR 268 (PC, Jamaica).
106   In the Commonwealth Caribbean, the Constitution also provides an alternative foundation for the common law principles of judicial review of administrative action and natural justice.
107   *Above*, fn 4 at p 9.
108   *Roodal v The State* (PC, Trinidad and Tobago) (2003) 64 WIR 270, at 287.
109   See *Harikissoon v AG* (1979) 31 WIR 348; [1979] 3 WLR 62 (PC).
110   See, eg, *Jaroo v AG* (2002) 59 WIR 519.

Constitution, it will be declared null and void and be struck off the law books. Thus, the Constitution presents a formidable challenge to legislation.

The challenge to legislation under the *ultra vires* principle is not only the prerogative of the citizen as against the State. Rather, the State itself can challenge and thereby test its own legislation in the courts. This occurred in *Suratt et al v Attorney General of Trinidad and Tobago*,[111] where the Trinidad and Tobago government defended an action on the ground that a Bill seeking to promote equality was unconstitutional by virtue of it being discriminatory. While a somewhat curious initiative on the face of it, it undoubtedly underscores the separation of powers principle. In practice too, as occurred in this case, the legislation may have been promulgated by a previous government which had different policy objectives.

The *ultra vires* concept was the basis of the challenge in *Collymore v AG*.[112] Here, it was unsuccessfully argued that the Industrial Stabilisation Act, which sought to reduce strikes, was *ultra vires* the Trinidad and Tobago Constitution as it violated the constitutional right to strike.[113]

As was stated in *Smith et al v Bahamas Hotel Union:*[114]

> If any other law is inconsistent with this Constitution, this Constitution shall prevail and the other shall, to the extent of the inconsistency, be void.[115]

The validation of other legal sources

The Constitution also validates other legal sources in a sense other than the *intra vires* concept discussed above. Since it gives Parliament and the legislature the authority to make law, legislation ultimately owes its legitimacy to Constitution. Similarly, the power given to the State to sign international treaties is found in the Constitution, hence the legal source of international law can be said to be validated by the Constitution. Even the authority given to the common law in independent Commonwealth Caribbean nations can be traced to the Constitution as it saves the common law, recognising as applicable law in the legal system. The Constitution is thus of prime importance in defining and shaping legal sources and, ultimately, the legal system in the region.

---

111   *Above*, fn 84.
112   *Above*, fn 4.
113   As we have already seen, the court found that there was no constitutional right to strike.
114   BS 1985 SC 66.
115   *Ibid*.

CHAPTER 8

THE COMMON LAW AND THE OPERATION OF THE DOCTRINE OF JUDICIAL PRECEDENT IN THE COMMONWEALTH CARIBBEAN

INTRODUCTION TO THE COMMON LAW

An important source of law in the Commonwealth Caribbean is the common law or case law. This describes the legal principles derived from examining the judgments of cases where there are no applicable statutes. The common law or case law is both a legal source and an historical source. It is the latter because its existence is directly linked to the experience of colonisation in the region and the consequence of the reception and transplantation of law from England.[1]

The common law as it exists in England is also linked to the historical development of that country. It can, therefore, also be considered a historical source in the English context. This is because the common law is really the outgrowth of historical custom, consolidated by the Norman Conquest when these local customs were unified into one coherent system of law 'common to all men', hence the term 'common law'.

The unique characteristic of the common law as a legal source is its ad hoc nature. This describes the way it grew up and continues to develop on a case-by-case basis. Each case or judgment of the court builds on the principles stated in the previous judgment. Its original conceptualisation was oral. This means that it was essentially a body of unwritten legal rules which were formulated by the King's courts in an informal and flexible manner. As we noted earlier, these courts, which were the Court of King's Bench, the Court of the Exchequer and the Court of Common Pleas, were collectively known as the common law courts.[2] As the body of common law developed, the common law became more rigid and identifiable. In fact, today, we cannot with accuracy state that the common law is a body of unwritten law. It has been solidified as a result of the system of case reporting.

In time, rigid procedures for administering and applying legal rules, norms and remedies by the courts developed and these also form part of the uniqueness of the common law. One such procedure is the 'writ', which regulates the initiation of legal proceedings in court. Indeed, the emphasis on procedure is one of the more criticised elements of the common law system, often appearing to be a collection of rigid procedures which serve as an obstacle to justice.

THE DOCTRINE OF JUDICIAL PRECEDENT – CHARACTER AND RATIONALE

Central to the notion of the common law as a legal source is the doctrine of precedent, in particular, binding precedent or *stare decisis*. The phrase is an abbreviation of a Latin maxim, *stare decisis et non quieta movere*. Translated, it means standing by decisions and not disturbing settled points, often simply translated as 'let the decision

---

1   See the discussion in Chapter 5 ('The Reception of English Law and its Significance to Caribbean Jurisdictions').
2   See Chapter 3 ('Legal Traditions – Types of Legal Systems in the Commonwealth Caribbean').

stand'. The doctrine provides the impetus and scientific rationale for the development of the common law on a case-by-case basis. It is, therefore, an important source of law.

Two important questions need to be considered in a discussion of the doctrine of judicial precedent in the Commonwealth Caribbean. We must first examine the nature of the doctrine itself. What are its limitations, characteristics and advantages? Secondly, we must question how the doctrine has operated in the Commonwealth Caribbean, in particular, whether it has contributed to, or undermined the development of a Commonwealth Caribbean jurisprudence? We shall see that while the English doctrine of precedent is followed closely in the Commonwealth Caribbean, historical and geo-political realities elaborate upon the rules of precedent as expressed in the English courts. It is necessary therefore for us to search for a more philosophical understanding of what judicial precedent means to our legal system.

The doctrine of judicial precedent proceeds on the assumption that where there are no appreciable statutes on a particular issue, the judge must look to the case law, that is, cases decided previously on the said issue, to find the relevant law upon which to base his or her decision. Thus, the judge reasons by analogy. These previously decided cases, or rather, the principles of law contained in such cases, are called 'judicial precedents'. There are two types of judicial precedents: 'binding precedent' and 'persuasive precedent'. Binding precedent will be seen to be the more important in the sense that it allows the preservation of case law principles.

Binding precedent

The doctrine of binding judicial precedent, *stare decisis,* is based on the premise that the function of judges is not to create law, but to find law in conformity with existing legal rules. Thus, the judge has a legal obligation to use decided cases, not merely for guidance, but is bound to apply the principles of law found in such case. This coercive character of the doctrine of precedent is a feature peculiar to the English legal tradition.

One of the first judicial pronouncements on the doctrine of binding precedent and *stare decisis* is to be found in the case of *London Tramcars Co Ltd v London County Council,*[3] where Lord Halisbury stated that 'a decision of this House once given upon a point of law is conclusive upon the House afterwards, and it is impossible to raise that question again as it if was *res integra* and could be re-argued'.

Persuasive precedents

In converse to binding precedents, persuasive precedents are those legal principles contained in judgments which merely offer guidance. The judge will refer to these precedents, but they are not binding. *Obiter dicta* decisions, for example, discussed below,[4] may form the basis of persuasive precedents. Persuasive precedents may also originate from courts lower in the hierarchy and the decisions of courts in other jurisdictions. In the Commonwealth Caribbean, for example, the decision of the Court of Appeal of Barbados is only of persuasive authority to a court in Jamaica. The status

---

3   [1898] AC 375, p 379.
4   See p 124.

of the decisions of the Privy Council, which acts as a unifying court in the region, has created its own particular difficulty. This is discussed below.[5] In the Commonwealth Caribbean, precedents from other Commonwealth Caribbean jurisdictions and the UK are usually highly persuasive. In *Boodram v AG and Another*,[6] for example, the Court of Appeal of Trinidad and Tobago, in being persuaded by a decision from the Jamaican Court of Appeal on the question of pre-trial publicity, referred to Jamaica as a:

> country which shares with us . . . a common history and jurisprudence [and] . . . a strong common bond which we share with . . . the other islands of the region.[7]

In constitutional matters, because of the similarity between the relevant constitutional instruments, precedents from the USA, Canada, India and the European Court of Human Rights are highly persuasive to the courts in the region. In cases which touch on socio-economic matters, precedents which come from other common law developing countries would usually be viewed as highly persuasive.

The degree of persuasiveness of such a precedent depends on a variety of factors. These include the jurisdiction from which it emanates, the status of the court which makes the decision and its date. Occasionally, the reputation of the judge will influence another court.

ADVANTAGES AND DISADVANTAGES OF THE DOCTRINE OF JUDICIAL PRECEDENT

The doctrine of binding precedent can be said to offer the advantages of legal certainty and precision. Lord Hoffman, in the case of *Lewis v AG of Jamaica*,[8] reminded us of this in a powerful dissenting judgment. This is particularly useful when one considers the great volume of case law which forms the basis of the common law. In *Gallie v Lee*,[9] Lord Russell refused to support the suggestion that the House of Lords, the highest court in the British legal system, 'is free to override its own decisions'. This was so despite the fact that the House of Lords had 'given itself the ability' to do so. He further declared his firm belief 'in a system by which citizens and their advisors can have as much certainty as possible in the ordering of their affairs'.[10]

A case from South Africa painstakingly explains not only the significance of the doctrine of *stare decisis* to the Commonwealth, but also its true meaning and rationale. In *Re State v Walters*,[11] Kriegler J of the Constitutional Court said, in quashing a decision of the High Court, in which it had failed to follow a precedent from the Supreme Court of Appeal:

> It [*stare decisis*] is widely recognised in developed legal systems . . . Haho and Kahn . . . describe this deference of the law for precedent as a manifestation of the general human tendency to have respect for experience. They explain why the doctrine of *stare decisis*

---

5   See below, p 148.
6   (1994) 47 WIR 459.
7   *Ibid*, p 477.
8   [2001] AC 50 (PC).
9   [1969] 2 Ch 17.
10   *Ibid*, p 41.
11   [2003] 1 LRC 493 (South Africa) at 521.

is so important saying . . . In the legal system the calls of justice are paramount. The maintenance of certainty of the law and equality before it, the satisfaction of legitimate expectations entail a general duty of judges to follow the legal rulings in previous judicial decisions. The individual litigant would feel himself unjustly treated if a past ruling applicable to his case were not followed where the material facts were the same . . . It enables the citizen . . . to plan his private and professional activities with some degree of assurance as to their legal effects, it prevents the dislocation of rights, particularly contractual and proprietary ones, created in the belief of an existing rule of law. It cuts down the prospect of litigation; it keeps the weaker judge along right and rational paths, drastically limiting the play allowed to partiality, caprice or prejudice, thereby . . . retaining public confidence in the judicial machine through like being dealt with alike . . . Certainty, predictability . . . equality . . . conformity, convenience: these are the principal advantages.

The priority given to certainty in the law is noted too in the case of *Broome v Cassel*,[12] where it was said: 'in legal matters, some degree of certainty is at least as valuable a part of justice as perfection.'

There are certain disadvantages to the system of precedent. For example, the excessive volume of reported cases makes the location of legal principles difficult. Further, there is the danger of illogical, technical distinctions in the process of distinguishing precedent which leads to excessive legalism and sometimes, absurdity. There is also the danger that beneficial legal change is avoided in favour of maintaining the status quo. In addition, the doctrine engenders a rigidity within the legal process. Indeed, this rigidity is the most serious disadvantage of the doctrine. As discussed below, it springs both from the attitude of judges and the declaratory theory.

Precedents relevant to social contexts

In *Re State v Walters*,[13] Kriegler J's endorsement of the important values underlying the doctrine of precedent is commendable. Yet, in maturing, evolving democracies such as those in the Commonwealth Caribbean, one questions whether the original rationales for *stare decisis* are more important than a recognition that such societies have very different experiences to those from which their legal principles are derived. Thus, they must find legal solutions appropriate to their own contexts and realities. These societies were born with borrowed identities and continue to search for self-definition. This is no less so in the judicial system. Indeed, it is imperative that the judicial system reflects these strivings toward identity and relevance. While *stare decisis* defers to experience, that experience must be relevant. This is the all embracing question of policy enmeshed in the law. Why this harkening after a certainty identified elsewhere, which has to be applied in a morass of uncertainties, questioning values and suppositions?

All societies deserve an expectation not only to predictability, but more fundamentally, to a 'right' answer. Where a society searches for and finds a legal solution to a problem, it is appropriate to maintain the *status quo*. The same does not apply where that society has played no part in the search for justice.

---

12   [1972] AC 1027 at p 1054.
13   *Above*, fn 11.

Recent constitutional decisions have encouraged debate about the relative worth of strictly adhering to precedent over finding new legal solutions which might better fit society's needs. The debate ensues because of a long train of constitutional law cases involving the death penalty, in which the Privy Council overruled a number of established precedents on various aspects of the issue before it. In some instances, the Privy Council not only overruled established precedents, but soon thereafter, reinstated them, causing these aspects of the law to be in a state of flux. This chain of events caused Lord Hoffman in a powerful dissenting judgment in *Lewis v AG of Jamaica*[14] to remind the court of the value of *stare decisis*. Lord Hoffman recognised that the Privy Council had the authority to overrule but felt that this authority was being exercised too readily. These cases are discussed further in the section on 'Overruling' below. Here, we note Lord Hoffman's statements on the important values underpinning the doctrine of precedent and the resulting advantages which accrue to the legal system. Indeed, he stated: 'If the Board feels able to depart from a previous decision simply because its members on a given occasion have a "doctrinal disposition to come out differently", the rule of law itself will be damaged and there will be no stability in the administration of justice in the Caribbean.'[15]

There are, therefore, both advantages and disadvantages to the doctrine of precedent. The doctrine of precedent must be flexible enough to accommodate changes in society and the needs of the legal system, but the measure employed to determine when such changes are necessary must be a strict one. There is a balance to be struck between change and consistency.

THE HIERARCHY OF COURTS

The operation of the doctrine of precedent depends on a system of hierarchy of courts. All courts stand in definite relationship to one another. In the majority of the Commonwealth Caribbean the Judicial Committee of the Privy Council sits at the apex of this hierarchy of courts. Two countries have now replaced the Privy Council with the Caribbean Court of Justice (the CCJ).[16] Consequently, decisions of judgments emanating from the Privy Council or the CCJ are the most authoritative in the hierarchy. Next in the hierarchical structure are Courts of Appeal, then High Courts or Supreme Courts (as High Courts are sometimes called) followed by intermediate courts such as the family courts and resident magistrates' courts of Jamaica. Last, and therefore of least authority, are inferior courts such as magistrates' courts and Juvenile Courts.

The resulting rule with respect to the hierarchy of courts is that each court is

---

14 *Above*, fn 8.
15 *Ibid*, at p 90.
16 Previously, the only exception was the Republic of Guyana, which abolished appeals to the Privy Council under the Judicial Committee of Privy Council (Termination of Appeals) Act 1970, 1975 Re'v Cap1:012. Grenada also abolished briefly such appeals by virtue of the Privy Council (Abolition of Appeals) Law 1979, but has now returned to the Privy Council. See the repeal of this Law No 19/1991. In April 2005, the Caribbean Court of Justice (CCJ) was instituted with the intention that appeals from the region would go to that body instead of the Privy Council. Thus far, however, few countries have accepted the appellate jurisdiction of the court. Barbados and Guyana have already done so. See further discussion of this new court in Chapter 17 ('The Caribbean Court of Justice').

bound by a decision of a court above itself in the hierarchy.[17] In addition, a court is sometimes bound by decisions of a court of equivalent status. It will be seen that the simple notion of a hierarchy of courts has met with considerable difficulty in terms of its practical operation in the Commonwealth Caribbean.

CONCEPTS IMPORTANT TO THE DOCTRINE OF PRECEDENT

Some fundamental legal concepts are essential to the understanding of the doctrine of judicial precedent. These will be discussed in turn.

The *ratio decidendi*

Not every element or facet of a decision is binding on a judge in a consequent case. Rather, it is the particular principle, rule or ruling of law contained in the decision. This element of a decision is called the *ratio decidendi*. Still, not every statement of law or legal principle contained within a decision is binding in a particular case. Consequently, one must distinguish the *ratio decidendi* (that is, the binding element) from other legal principles in any particular judicial decision. The *ratio decidendi* is not located easily but may be defined as the principle or proposition of law stated by the judge to be applicable to resolving the precise legal issue before the court. It is therefore, the legal rationale which the judge gives for the decision that he arrives at in a particular case.

Locating the *ratio decidendi*

Our definition of the *ratio decendi* is necessarily simplistic for it may be observed that the *ratio* is easily defined but less easily identified. While law students are expected to locate the *ratio* of a case with ease, such an exercise has boggled the minds of even eminent jurists. Often, for example, the *ratio* is confused with the dictum and some even maintain that there is no distinction between the two at all.[18] Even judges, perhaps desiring to reach a different conclusion, have bickered as to what was the *ratio* or true meaning of a particular case.[19] However, isolating the *ratio* is an essential task in sustaining the doctrine of binding precedent.

A much criticised but still well known and authoritative test for ascertaining the *ratio*, or as some suggest, determining what is *not* the *ratio decidendi*, is Wambaugh's test of inversion. He instructs:

> First frame carefully the supposed proposition of law. Let him then insert in the proposition a word reversing its meaning. Let him then inquire whether, if the court had conceived this new proposition to be good, and had it in mind, the decision could have been the same. If the answer be affirmative, then, however excellent the original

---

17 See, eg, *London Tramcars Co Ltd v London County Council, above*, fn 3.
18 For a good discussion of the difficulties in identifying the *ratio*, see, eg, Cross and Harris, *Precedent in English Law*, 4th edn, 1991, Oxford: Clarendon Press, Chapter 11.
19 See, eg, *Re Anisimic* [1969] 2 AC 147.

proposition be, the case is not a precedent for that proposition, but if the answer be negative, the case is a precedent.[20]

Accordingly, a proposition of law which fails the test is merely a dictum. As has been pointed out elsewhere, Wambaugh's test not only fails to fit where there is more than one *ratio* in a case, but also does not assist greatly in finding the 'ways and means of determining what proposition of law was considered necessary by the court for its decision'.[21]

Where a case is argued on more than one ground, it is even more difficult to locate the *ratio*. Despite there being more than one ground of argument, the case may be decided on only one of the grounds argued. In such situations, it is only this decisive ground which is binding, the other points of law being undecided. Notwithstanding, a case may contain more than one *ratio* where, for example, more than one reason or more than one judgment is given for the decision. A common illustration is found in the case of *Read v Lyons and Co Ltd*.[22] One *ratio decidendi* in that case was that the well known rule in *Rylands v Fletcher* was not applicable to the escape of dangerous substances which were in the defendant's control. Another *ratio* was that the rule did not apply unless the plaintiff had an interest in the land affected by the escape.

In the landmark case from the newly constituted CCJ, *AG v Joseph and Boyce*,[23] we can also discern more than one important *ratio*. Indeed, the CCJ was anxious to pronounce on important and controversial questions surrounding the death penalty. First, the Court held that decisions of the Barbados Privy Council (the Committee responsible for making recommendations to the Governor General on the exercise of mercy) could be reviewed and redress obtained for any breaches of procedural rights inherent under the protection of law clause in the Barbados Constitution.

Secondly, the CCJ held that a person on death row had a legitimate expectation in the form of a procedural right to have an order of execution stayed until such time that his application to an international body had been heard and further, that the Mercy Committee had to consider (but not adopt) the opinions coming from that international body. This expectation arose from the State having ratified the relevant human rights treaty, including the individual right to petition and further, having held itself out as being prepared to allow citizens the right to access such international bodies. Such a legitimate expectation could, however, be defeated by an expressed overriding interest by the State.

Thirdly, in circumstances where there was a legitimate expectation that the death sentence would not be carried out, for example, as a result of a precedent that the sentence was not mandatory, or that the Pratt and Morgan five-year rule was in effect, an execution would amount to cruel and inhuman punishment and the sentence of death was to be commuted.

An interesting observation in the *Joseph and Boyce* case is that the CCJ, in particular, the joint judgment of Justices de la Bastide (President) and Saunders, was grounded in arguments not introduced by counsel on either side, ie the doctrine of

---

20   *Study of Cases* (2nd edn) 17–18, cited in *Jacobs v London County Council* [1950] AC 369.
21   Cross and Harris, *above*, fn 18, p 56. Their own definition of the *ratio* is 'any rule of law expressly or impliedly treated by the judge as a necessary step in reaching his conclusion, having regard to the line of reasoning adopted by him or a necessary part of his direction to the jury.' *Ibid*.
22   [1947] AC 156.
23   CCJ App No CV 2 of 2005, decided 8 November 2006.

legitimate expectation. This raises a perhaps not insignificant point about how judges reach decisions and indeed their ability to make law (considered below). It is often assumed that the judge's reasoning which grounds the *ratio* is always informed by the arguments and principles of law raised by counsels, but this may not necessarily be the case and indeed, belies the notion of the passive judge under the common law legal doctrine.[24]

The *ratio* is to be distinguished from the mere findings of fact and the judgment itself, the latter being formed by combining the legal reasoning and the particular facts of the case. The *ratio* should further be distinguished from *res judicata* or the adjudicated matter or judgment. This refers to the binding of the particular parties to the adjudicated matter. Subsequent parties are not so bound. In contrast, the *ratio* binds all subsequent courts. Thus, *res judicata* simply means that the matter has been finally determined.[25]

Obiter dicta

More important, the *ratio* should be distinguished from those statements of law which are 'by the way' or *obiter dicta*. Different categories of *obiter dicta* may be ascertained. For example, a statement of law will be regarded as *obiter dictum* if it is based upon facts which did not in fact exist or were not material. In the Cayman case of *Re BCCI*,[26] the Grand Court viewed its earlier decision on whether a bank's interest in confidentiality included customers' transactions as *obiter* and refused to follow it.[27]

A statement of law may also be *obiter* if the decision is not based upon it, although the statement may be based on the facts. Examples are statements of law contained in dissenting judgments or where the decision is contrary to the reasoning for some extraneous reason. In the landmark case of *Hedley Byrne and Co Ltd v Heller Partners Ltd*,[28] the legal principle that the maker of a statement owes a duty of care to the listener was *obiter* since the giver of the advice in that case was protected by a disclaimer of responsibility.

Other remarks made by the judge, such as judicial pronouncements, or comments on non-legal matters like morals or public policy may also be *obiter dicta*. An example is where the judge is making an analogy between a hypothetical situation and the case before him, even where the given hypotheses is stated by the judge to be material. In *Peters v Marksman (Supt of Prisons) and AG*,[29] Mitchell, J of the High Court of St Vincent, in a case concerning cruel and inhumane punishment in prisons,

---

24   See page 36, para 77 of the judgment where it was said: 'Unfortunately, the potential use of this doctrine [legitimate expectation] was not really argued before us ... Accordingly, we were not specifically directed to the evidence on which any such expectation might be grounded. Nor were we addressed on the principles that would govern it ... Notwithstanding the dearth of argument presented to us on this issue, there is a body of relevant material before us upon which we are able to draw.'

25   Note that even where the facts of an earlier case appear to be identical with those before the court, the judge or jury may not necessarily draw the same inference as that drawn in the earlier case.

26   *In the Matter of Bank of Credit and Commerce International (Overseas) Ltd* [1994–95] CILR 56.

27   An oft-quoted example is Lord Denning's pronouncement on equitable estoppel in the defining case of *Central London Property Trust Ltd v High Trees House Ltd* [1947] KB 130, p 133.

28   [1964] AC 465.

29   (1997) Carib LB 13, p 91.

commented, *obiter*, that 'the time will come when the very overcrowding in the prison will be a basis for a constitutional challenge on the grounds that it is inhuman and degrading'. The substance of the matter concerned the constitutionality of the use of the cat-o'-nine-tails.[30]

The fact that a statement is made *obiter* does not mean that it is unimportant. Such statements often become the basis for future precedents. In particular, dissenting judgments may be used as the rationales for further decisions when precedents are overruled or, at minimum, cause future courts to re-examine significant legal questions.[31]

An *obiter* dictum which will no doubt form the basis for subsequent *rationes* is found in one of the first judgments handed down by the CCJ, *AG v Joseph and Boyce*.[32] In this case, Justices de la Bastide and Saunders took the opportunity to pronounce on a *ratio* from the Privy Council on the five-year rule in *Pratt and Morgan*[33] when opinions from international bodies were pending. This was not a live issue before the court, but the CCJ considered it important enough to pronounce upon it and did so with authority and deliberation, in so doing disagreeing with the earlier Privy Council judgments. It was clear too that the CCJ was mindful that its words had resonance, not only for Barbados, for whom, indeed, the rule was no longer applicable, but for all other Commonwealth Caribbean countries, even those which had not yet accepted the CCJ's jurisdiction. It said:

> By the amendment of section 15 of the Constitution, the State of Barbados no longer has the constraint of the Pratt five-year time-limit . . . Where *Pratt* is applicable, as it was in Barbados for these respondents, we would have been inclined to the view, if the issue of the five-year time-limit was still a live one before us, that where the time taken in processing a condemned man's petition before an international body exceeded 18 months, the excess should be disregarded in the computation of time for the purpose of applying the decision in *Pratt*. In any event, protracted delay on the part of the international body in disposing of the proceedings initiated before it by a condemned person, could justify the State, notwithstanding the existence of the condemned man's legitimate expectation, proceeding to carry out an execution before completion of the international process.[34]

The Court then went on to invite the State to impose more reasonable time limits.[35]

Another excellent example is Rattray CJ's statements in a case on labour law, *Village Resorts v Green*[36] where he spoke on the evolution of employment law principles to ameliorate labour conditions, even to the point of inferring concepts akin to

---

30   *Ibid*, p 93. Mitchell J seemed to have in mind the developments on cruel and inhumane punishment in other circumstances. See the discussion of death row prisoners, *below*, p 135.

31   Another example is the powerful dissent of Lord Hoffman in *Lewis v AG of Jamaica* [2001] AC 50 (Privy Council), on the questions whether judicial review was available for the prerogative of mercy, whether final courts had to await the determinations of international legal bodies in capital punishment cases and whether poor prison conditions could constitute cruel and inhumane treatment. Interestingly, on the latter point, the majority found that prison conditions could ground a constitutional challenge for cruel and inhumane punishment and this seemed to have been influenced by an *obiter* statement in *Peters v Marksman*, above.

32   *Above*, fn 23 (Barbados).

33   *Pratt and Morgan v AG of Jamaica* (1993) 43 WIR 340. The rule states that five years and more on death row constitutes cruel and inhumane punishment.

34   *Ibid*, para 126, p 57.

35   *Ibid*, para 139, p 62.

36   (Unreported) No 66 of 1997, decided 30 June 1998 (SC Jamaica).

unfair dismissal. This general premise can now be seen to have formed the bases for future landmark developments in labour law in Jamaica. For example, in the case of *Jamaica Flour Mills Ltd v Industrial Disputes Tribunal and National Workers Union*,[37] the Privy Council expressly adopted it in finding, in what may be labelled a judicially activist mode, a semblance of unfair dismissal doctrine in Jamaica, despite the absence of statute on the issue and in the face of what was intended to be a non-binding industrial relations Code.

Another example of a famous dissenting judgment is that found in *Riley v AG*[38] that undue delay on death row could violate the Constitution by constituting cruel and inhumane punishment. This was later to become the controversial but well established principle in the *Pratt and Morgan* line of cases.

In view of the above, Lord Steyn's remarks in *Fisher v Minister of Public Safety and Immigration et al*[39] certainly have resonance:

> A dissenting judgment anchored in the circumstances of today sometimes appeals to the judges of tomorrow. In that way a dissenting judgment sometimes contributes to the continuing development of the law.

Statements of law made *per incuriam* and *per curiam*

Certain decisions may be deemed to have been reached *per incuriam*. This means, literally, through a lack of care. It occurs, for example, where some relevant precedent, legal principle or statutory provision which would have affected the outcome of a decision, had it been considered, was not brought to the attention of the court.

Perhaps understandably, there are few examples of judgments delivered *per incuriam*. The principle is limited in operation and there is a high threshold to cross before a judgment will be declared to be *per incuriam*, hence the few decisions labelled in that way. As directed in the case of *Morelle v Wakeling*,[40] decisions are only to be considered as *per incuriam* where they have been given in ignorance or forgetfulness of some pertinent statutory provision or binding authority which leads to inaccurate legal reasoning.

The doctrine has, however, been extended to other situations, such as where a case is not fully argued, or where the court seemed to have misunderstood the law, made a manifest slip or error, or was unaware of relevant policy considerations. In *Attorney General v Financial Clearing Corporation*,[41] for example, the Bahamas court ruled on the question of self-incrimination, in a matter contesting the constitutionality of a statute designed to compel disclosure of financial information for regulatory purposes. However, the fact that under the Constitution self-incrimination is only protected against in criminal, as opposed to civil matters, was neither brought to the attention of the court nor addressed by them. These were essential aspects of the issue which should have been considered.

A court may also make statements *per curiam*. These are relevant to the issue at hand and adequately informed by the legal principles surrounding the case. They are

---

37   PC Appeal No 69 of 2003, decided 23 March 2005.
38   [1983] AC 719.
39   [1998] AC 673 (Privy Council, The Bahamas) at pp 686–687.
40   [1955] 2 QB 379, p 406.
41   (CA, The Bahamas) No 70 of 2001, decided 8 October 2002.

not, however, part of the *ratio decidendi* as these are not statements of legal principle essential to determining the case. As such, they have no binding effect. Often, these statements attempt to give direction or policy guidance for future cases. For example, in *Abbot v AG of Trinidad and Tobago*,[42] the Privy Council, in deciding that undue delay on death row did not constitute a violation of the constitutional right to life, nevertheless cautioned *per curiam*: 'The President ought not to issue his warrant for carrying out the sentence of death, until after the advisory committee has considered the case and proffered its advice to the designated Minister and the designated Minister has tendered his own advice . . . to the President. A person aggrieved by any failure to perform those duties with reasonable dispatch would be entitled to apply to the High Court for an appropriate remedy in public law.'[43]

THE IMPORTANCE OF LAW REPORTING

Because principles of law are located in decided cases, the doctrine of precedent depends on an efficient system of recording the law for its sustainability, accessibility and viability. This process is facilitated by the reporting of cases in 'law reports'. This is an important mechanism for the preservation of the common law. The lack of an adequate system of law reporting is an acute problem in the jurisdictions of the Commonwealth Caribbean, which are under-resourced with respect to this aspect of the administration of justice.[44] The problem is being alleviated, particularly by the availability of websites but, as yet, cannot be said to be adequately resolved.

Inadequate law reporting is a severe defect in the legal system, as it leads to insufficient exposition of the legal principles of Commonwealth Caribbean law which judges may have pronounced upon but which are not easily accessible. Judges in all common law jurisdictions look to other jurisdictions for useful precedents. Consequently, the lack of adequate law reporting deprives the region of opportunities to contribute significantly to the development of the common law.

With new technological advances, cases may be reported more speedily online, through the use of the Internet. This is also advantageous because of its relatively cheap cost and because it can make law more accessible to the public at large.

Yet, other common law jurisdictions may have the opposite problem. With the advent of the information age and the increased efficiency in law reporting in other jurisdictions, there is a danger that counsel and the court may be faced with too many reported decisions. One writer complains of this 'nightmarish' phenomenon:

> . . . when the number of printed cases become like the number of grains of sand on the beach, a precedent-based, case law system does not work . . . when the store of raw materials becomes too great, too varied, too confused . . . when it becomes possible to cite . . . dozens of cases nearly identical on their facts as to be indistinguishable . . . then what is the court to do?[45]

---

42   [1979] 1 WLR 1342 (Privy Council).
43   *Ibid*.
44   For an exposition of the problems faced by inadequate law reporting in the region, see Newton, V, *Information Needs and Research Practices of the Commonwealth Caribbean Legal Profession*, UWI, Barbados, 1981, and Newton, V, 'An Historical Perspective of Law Reporting in the English Speaking Caribbean: A Case for Regional Law Reporting' (1979) 7 International Journal of Law Libraries 1.
45   Gilmore, G, 'Legal Realism: Its Cause and Cure' (1961) 70 Yale LJ 1037.

Thus, the efficiency of the law reporting process might itself be a problem for the operation of precedent. In fact, it points in favour of the Code in civil law systems. Brady-Clarke relates a rather amusing story: two lawyers appeared before the High Court in St Lucia, a country with a Civil Law Code. The defence attorney was a member of the Bar in another Commonwealth Caribbean territory and had been trained only in the common law system. The prosecuting attorney was a member of the St Lucia Bar. Defence counsel cited precedent after precedent from England and the Caribbean in support of his argument and, on conclusion, sat, satisfied that his research had been completed, his argument forceful and that the decision would surely be in his client's favour. In reply, prosecuting counsel stood and said: 'might I refer your Honour to Article X of the St Lucia Civil Code?'[46]

AVOIDING PRECEDENT – THE PROMOTION OF FLEXIBILITY

It is clear that the system of binding precedent would tend toward promoting rigidity within the common law. One may well ask, how can the common retain its original characteristic of flexibility? The answer lies in the ability of courts to avoid precedent in certain circumstances in an attempt to produce desirable change to previous decisions which are considered to be outdated, irrelevant or inaccurately decided. There are several devices available for courts to avoid binding precedent and thereby promote flexibility within the law.

Overruling decisions

The process of overruling provides an avenue for legal rules to be changed, thereby importing some flexibility into the doctrine of *stare decisis*. However, in a judicial system in which deference is paid to past decisions, it is unsurprising that precedents often gain authority as time goes on and older established precedents are often treated as sacrosanct. Thus, courts, even final courts, are reluctant to disturb or overrule such precedents. This is particularly the case since overruling operates retrospectively, that is, it is deemed to have applied even before the decision to overrule the old principle. Overruling affects the rule of law, not just the decision of the case which is overruled. When it occurs, the earlier rule of law is deemed never to have existed. This is, in fact, part of the legal fiction which conforms to the declaratory theory of law, discussed further in this book.

The authority to overrule precedent is given only to higher courts in certain strict circumstances. The circumstances in which courts have the authority or may be persuaded to overrule established precedents are discussed below.[47]

Judicial precedents thought to be inappropriate may of course also be overruled by Parliament directly, through statute. Here we are concerned, however, only with the judicial overruling process.

---

46 Brady-Clarke, C, 'The Doctrine of Judicial Precedent – Cases and Commentary', 1988, unpublished paper, University of the West Indies, p 4.
47 See p 131.

Prospective overruling

In the USA, the Supreme Court has evoked the authority to overrule decisions prospectively. This means that the Court applies the earlier decision to the case before them but overrules with respect to its effect on future cases. This process has never been judicially recognised in England or in the Commonwealth Caribbean. In *Jones v SOS for Social Services*,[48] however, Lord Simon advocated an extension of the common law to include prospective overruling. Yet, he felt that any such change should be done by parliamentary enactment rather than the courts.

Exceptions to precedent in the face of *per incuriam* or *obiter* statements

Another important exception to the doctrine of precedent is that courts are not bound to follow earlier decisions where the previous decision was reached *per incuriam,* or through lack of care. The rationale of this rule is that the decision does not accurately reflect the sate of the law. While the finding of *per incuriam* in a case is a way of avoiding precedent, since judges seldom find decisions to be *per* incuriam, it is not a popular method.

In the case of *AG of St Christopher and Nevis v Payne*,[49] it was established that a Court of Appeal in the Commonwealth Caribbean is not bound to follow a previous decision of its own if it is satisfied that it was given *per incuriam*. In this case, the trial judge exercised his discretion to recall his original judgment as having been made *per incuriam*. However, this does not at all times affect the doctrine of precedent as illustrated in the cases of *R v Northumberland Compensation Appeal Tribunal ex p Shaw*[50] and *Cassell v Broome*.[51]

Similarly, courts are not bound to follow *obiter* statements. As we have noted, these may or may not have legal accuracy and may even become the basis for a future *ratio decidendi*. In the interim, however, they cannot be treated as authoritative.[52]

Precedents based on assumptions of law

Where a precedent has been arrived at without argument of the relevant legal precepts and the legal proposition incorporated into the *ratio decidendi* was merely assumed to be correct, the resulting precedent is not binding. The leading case, even in the UK, is the Privy Council decision from Jamaica, *Baker v The Queen*.[53] The question before the Privy Council was whether the exemption of capital punishment for juveniles applied to persons who had not attained 18 years at the date of the commission of the murder, or whether the relevant date was the time of sentencing (at which

---

48   [1972] AC 944, p 1026.
49   (1982) 30 WIR 88, relying on the English decision of *Young v Bristol Aeroplane Co Ltd* [1944] KB 718.
50   [1951] 1 All ER 268.
51   [1972] AC 1027.
52   This approach was followed in by the Grand Court of the Cayman Islands in a case which concerned offshore banking, *Re BCCI* [11994–95] CILR 56.
53   [1975] AC 774 (Privy Council) (Jamaica).

time the person was 18 years or over). An existing Privy Council precedent answered the question in favour of the former but the interpretation of the law had been merely adopted and not argued before the court. The Privy Council determined that the Court of Appeal was not bound to this precedent. It noted the practice of the Privy Council (the Board) not to raise for argument new points of law and inferred that the interpretation of the law had been merely assumed and not decided. The Court explained why such a precedent could not be binding:

> A consequence of this practice is that in its opinions delivered on an appeal the Board may have assumed without itself deciding, that a proposition of law which was not disputed by the parties in the court from which the appeal is brought is correct. The proposition of law so assumed to be correct may be incorporated, whether expressly or by implication, in the *ratio decidendi* of a particular appeal; but because it does not bear the authority of an opinion reached by the Board itself it does not create a precedent for use in the decision of other cases.[54]

It appears that such cases without argument may be ignored even by first instance judges and even when they originate from final courts.[55]

Distinguishing precedent

Flexibility and the need for change may also be achieved by the possibility of distinguishing decisions. The process of distinguishing is perhaps the principal means which judges employ to evade judicial authorities which they consider inappropriate or unsound, thus enabling the doctrine of precedent to be flexible and adaptable. A precedent, whether persuasive or binding, need not be applied if it can be distinguished on its facts. To distinguish a precedent, a court must point to a material difference in the facts of the precedent and the current case. The judge in the later case is expected to justify why the distinction in the material facts is such as to depart from the precedent to permit the application of a different rule of law. In the process, the court will be assisted by counsel.

The process of distinguishing precedents as a principal means to effect change in the law is not without its critics. Gilmore argues, for example, that:

> Our use of precedent has become self-defeatingly narrow. We chop logic, we split hairs, we distinguish the indistinguishable. And as we do so, the course of the judicial decision following our impossible refinements becomes capricious and unpredictable. If you sharpen the point of a pencil too fine, the point – or the pencil – will disappear. So with our use of precedent.[56]

Reversing a decision

A precedent which has been overruled must be distinguished from a decision which has merely been reversed. In the latter, only the particular case in issue is affected, and the body of law or legal principle remains unchanged. In contrast, where a precedent

---

54   *Ibid*, at p 788.
55   See, eg, *Re Hetherington Deceased* (1990) Ch 1, on the question whether trusts established for saying masses for the dead were charitable trusts.
56   *Op cit*, Gilmore, fn 45.

has been overruled, the rule of law or legal principle which formed the decision has been affected and will continue to impact on future cases.

First impression decisions

Change in the common law can also occur where there is an absence of a precedent on a particular legal issue. In such circumstances the judge must create a precedent in accordance with general principles. Such cases are described as cases of first impression. In strict theory, these run counter to the *raison d'être* of the doctrine of precedent, for here, the judge is indeed required to create law rather than to apply it. Judges coming to the issue later in the day are not required to follow the decision. A simple example of this is found in a case from the OECS Court of Appeal, in a matter from Grenada, *AG of Grenada v The Grenada Bar Association,*[57] where the Court had to consider the powers of appointment for public servants laid down under the Constitution. Chief Justice Byron refused to follow an earlier first impression case from his colleague judge in a similar case from St Lucia, saying: 'The rules of *stare decisis* do not require that any first instance decision is binding, and we are at liberty to consider the question afresh and rule on its corrections.'[58]

THE DECLARATORY PRECEDENT AND THE OVERRULING OF PRECEDENT – NEW DEVELOPMENTS

Certainly, a precedent which has been overruled is not an authority, binding or otherwise. However, as we have seen, the process of overruling principles of law is approached with caution by the courts, since this would undermine the characteristic of certainty within the law and would also disturb contractual arrangements and financial agreements. Hence, it is only where a principle is manifestly wrong or has become irrelevant, spent and untenable that it will be overruled.[59]

The attitude toward the overruling of decisions is intricately bound up with the declaratory theory of the common law. This theory posits that the rules of the common law have existed from time immemorial, hence the common law cannot be changed. Rather, certain rules are restated for accuracy. Consequently, the judge's function is not to create or change the common law, but solely to find the correct statement of law and declare it. The theory proceeds upon the separation of powers principle. The practical effect of this theory is that where a decision is overruled by a higher court, it is decreed to be based on a misunderstanding of the law. The earlier incorrect legal principle is deemed never to have existed. The logical consequence is that judicial overruling operates retrospectively, as opposed to the overruling by statute which operates prospectively.

---

57   Civil Appeal No. 8 of 1999, decided 21 February 2000 (ECSC, Grenada).
58   *Ibid,* p 9.
59   See, eg, *Miliangos v George Frank (Textiles) Ltd* [1976] AC 443, where the House of Lords overruled its previous judgment that the judgment debts must be given in sterling.

Challenges to the declaratory theory – creating new legal rules

The notion that judges do not create law, but merely declare it, can be exposed as somewhat of a legal fiction, or at least, a misinterpretation of the judge's role. We explore the question whether judges make law in more depth later in this chapter.[60] Here, it suffices to note that indeed, the declaratory theory as a fundamental tenet of the English common law has been vigorously challenged. This was evident, for example, in the case of *Jones v SOS for Social Services*.[61]

There is thus authority for the view that the declaratory theory has been undermined to a great extent and that the more modern attitude toward the judge's role is that it is partly declaratory and partly innovative. Indeed, many argue that even the application of existing law to new circumstances, something which common law judges do routinely, is not clearly distinguishable from the creation of a new rule of law.[62] Justice Wit, in the newly constituted Caribbean Court of Justice (CCJ), in the landmark case of *AG and Others v Joseph and Boyce*,[63] had this to say:

> There is worldwide acceptance that the development of unwritten or common law is not simply the discovery of law and the making of declarations as to 'what it is and always has been', but that it is a form of creating law.

As we noted earlier, the power to overrule decisions prospectively has always been recognised in the USA. It should be obvious that if we accept the strict application of the declaratory theory, the potential for change would be seriously curtailed. It has an even more limiting effect in the Commonwealth Caribbean as there would be little basis for establishing an indigenous jurisprudence in the region.[64]

We noted earlier that the highest court in the hierarchy will bind all other courts and will consider themselves bound by their earlier decisions. However, the strict application of the latter rule in the landmark *London Street Tramcars*[65] case was discredited to some extent in 1966. In that year, the House of Lords in England, in a Practice Statement or Practice Direction made by their Lordships, declared that they would in future depart from their own decisions when it appeared right to do so. The Practice Direction stated that their Lordships 'recognise that the rigid adherence to precedent may lead to injustices in a particular case and also unduly restrict the proper development of the law'.[66] This statement advanced the earlier *dicta* in the case of *Scruttons Ltd v Midland Silicones Ltd*[67] where, although it was felt that the rule in *London Street Tramcars* was too rigid, their Lordships considered themselves bound by such a rule until it was altered.

---

60   See p 159.
61   [1972] AC 944, p 1026.
62   See, eg, Cross, R and Harris, JW *Precedent in English Law*, 1991, Oxford: Clarendon Press, 4th edn, p 29. The authors believe that the declaratory theory is beneficial in giving judges reasons not to follow a case of which it strongly disapproves. *Ibid*, p 35.
63   CCJ Appeal No CV 2 of 2005, decided 8 November 2006; Judgment of Mr Justice Wit, p 29, para 41.
64   See the discussion on 'The Caribbean Perspective – Difficulties in the Operation of Precedent', below, and Chapter 5 ('The Reception or Imposition of English Law and Its Significance to Commonwealth Caribbean Jurisdictions').
65   [1898] AC 375.
66   Practice Direction (Judicial Precedent) [1966] 1 WLR 1234, House of Lords. Indeed, the rule of binding precedent is of relatively recent origin, a product of the 20th century. *Young v Bristol Aeroplane Co Ltd* [1944] KB 718.
67   [1962] AC 446.

The important Practice Direction is regarded as having the force of law. The effects of this change in the law can be seen in subsequent cases such as *Jones v SOS for Social Services*,[68] *Miliangos v George Frank Textiles*[69] and more recently, in *Murphy v Brentwood District Council*.[70] The latter involved the question of liability for negligence.

The implications of the new direction of overruling precedent is equally important for the Commonwealth Caribbean, both because the Privy Council and Caribbean Court of Justice (CCJ), the two final courts in the region, will follow it and because it represents an important philosophical change for all superior courts in the region. The new principle was approved in *AG of St Kitts and Nevis v Reynolds:*[71]

> Neither their Lordship's Board nor the House of Lords is now bound by its own decisions, and it is for them, in the very exceptional cases in which this Board or the House of Lords has plainly erred in the past, to correct those errors.[72]

While, as discussed below, the Privy Council is not bound to precedent, it too has been influenced by the more liberal attitude toward the overruling of precedent and has been less conservative in its approach. Vivid examples are seen in the now famous case of *Pratt and Morgan*[73] and in the line of death row cases, discussed further in the following section. In *Pratt*, the Privy Council departed from its own precedent in *Riley*[74] and agreed that undue delay in hanging prisoners on death row could constitute cruel and inhumane punishment as prohibited under s 17 of the Constitution of Jamaica.

Notwithstanding, the power to overrule decisions, such a power is still only to be exercised sparingly.[75] In particular, where the court is asked to deviate from precedent in cases which involve questions of policy or highly controversial issues, it will not be moved easily.

Persistent overruling

Usually, when a final court of appeal overrules a past decision, this guarantees a certain finality to the question at hand and it is not expected that the older decision will be revived at a later sitting.[76] For example, in *Rees v Darlington Memorial Hospital NHS Trust*,[77] the House of Lords was invited to overturn its earlier precedent of some four years on the question of whether a disabled woman was entitled to costs attributed to her disability of bringing up a healthy child in a case where that child had

---

68 [1972] AC 944, p 1026.
69 *Above*, fn 59.
70 (1990) 2 All ER 908. See also *British Railways Board v Herrington* [1972] AC 877, where the House of Lords refused to follow a previous legal principle relating to the duty of care owed by an occupier or land to the trespassers.
71 (1979) 43 WIR 108, p 123, (Privy Council) St Kitts and Nevis.
72 But note that ordinary practice directions from the English courts will not bind Caribbean courts. See *Mohammed v Home Construction Ltd* (1988) 43 WIR 380, (Trinidad and Tobago). An English practice direction on civil procedure could not have effect unless it had been adopted in the jurisdiction.
73 (1993) 43 WIR 340.
74 [1982] 3 All ER 469 (Privy Council); [1983] 1 AC 719.
75 See, eg, *Knuller v DPP* [1973] AC 435, p 455.
76 Cross and Harris note, for example, that there has been no case where this has occurred. *Above*, fn 18, at p 112.
77 [2004] 4 LRC 102

been born as a result of negligence on the part of the hospital in a failed sterilisation. The House of Lords said:

> It would reflect no credit on the administration of the law if a line of English authority were disapproved in 1999 and reinstated in 2003, with no reason for a change beyond a change in the balance of judicial opinion.[78]

In other words, this was a vote for stability and consistency.

To overrule and then revive decisions at 'whim' would certainly import a high degree of unpredictability into a legal system valued for its constancy. Yet, this kind of inconsistency has been the experience in the Commonwealth Caribbean in recent times. In a line of cases on questions involving the death penalty, such as whether undue delay or its mandatory nature violates the constitutional guarantee of cruel and inhuman punishment, or whether death row prisoners were entitled to stays of execution while awaiting the outcomes of their applications to international bodies, there has been extraordinary vacillation by the Privy Council.[79]

Theoretically, this unpredictability can be partly explained by the fact that these cases spring from different jurisdictions. However, the more likely explanation is the deep philosophical, ideological and policy issues at play, giving fuel to the notion that there are no 'right answers' in law for such hard questions, particularly where they involve the Constitution. It also underscores the notion that such difficult issues are best handled by persons within the society and not by judges disconnected by culture, geographical distance and social reality.

CIRCUMSTANCES IN WHICH FINAL COURTS SHOULD OVERRULE

The mere fact that the final court views a past decision as being wrongly decided is not usually sufficient to bring about an overruling of precedent.[80] The decision must cause or produce injustice in a particular case. As the 1966 Practice Direction itself notes, the courts must be persuaded that the identified error and injustice, if not rectified, would 'unduly restrict' the proper development of the law. Even then, the courts will examine whether the appropriate and desirable development in the law is best left to statutory intervention by Parliament. Lord Hoffman, in a powerful dissenting opinion in the Privy Council judgment of *Lewis v AG of Jamaica*[81] recognised this. He said: 'The fact that the Board has the power to depart from earlier decisions does not mean that there are no principles which should guide it in deciding whether to do so.' He went on to indicate that the judgment of the court in deciding whether to overrule a previous decision was:

> customarily informed by a series of prudential and pragmatic considerations designed to test the consistency of overruling a prior decision with the ideal of the rule of law, such as whether the previous rule is intolerable because not in practice workable, or whether . . . 'related principles of law have developed' as to have left the old rule no

---

78   *Ibid*, at p 111. The Court relied on *Knuller v DPP, above*, fn 75.
79   See, eg, *Roodal v The State of Trinidad and Tobago*, (2003) 64 WIR 270 (Privy Council, Trinidad and Tobago); *Lambert Watson v The Queen* [2005] 1 AC 472. These cases are discussed in more detail below and in Chapter 12 ('International Law as a Source of Law').
80   Lord Wilberforce in *The Hannah Blumenthal* (1983) AC 854 at pp 911–913.
81   *Above*, fn 8 at p 89.

more than a remnant of 'abandoned doctrine', or whether facts have changed 'or come to be seen so differently, as to have robbed the old rule of significant application or justification'.[82]

The 1966 Practice Direction recognised that overruling was to be the exception rather than the norm. Lord Gardiner emphasised: 'Their Lordships regard the use of precedent as an indispensable foundation upon which to decide what is the law'. In particular, the courts will 'bear in mind the danger of disturbing retrospectively the basis on which contracts, settlements of property and fiscal arrangements have been entered into and also the especial need for certainty as to the criminal law'.[83]

The House of Lords, in particular, appears to be adamant that a decision should not be overruled where no new significant rationales have been advanced for this course or no change in the circumstances surrounding the case. Certainly, the House of Lords is careful to prevent litigants merely exploiting the fact that other judges may simply come to new decisions. In *Blumenthal*, for example, Lord Wilberforce warned that:

> Nothing could be more undesirable . . . than to permit litigants, after a decision has been given by this House with all appearance of finality, to return to this House in the hope that a differently constituted committee might be persuaded to take the view which its predecessors rejected . . . It requires more than doubts as to the correctness of such opinion to justify departing from it.[84]

In other words, courts recognise that there is room for two 'eminently possible views' and a mere 'doctrinal disposition to come out differently' from a previous court should not be entertained.[85]

Further, it appears that final courts will generally exercise restraint in disturbing established precedent where there is evidence that Parliament, by refusing to enact legislation to correct a criticised precedent, prefers the status quo,[86] thus expressing comity with the legislature.

Courts will also heed the extent to which a changed precedent will upset long-standing social arrangements based on existing precedents. Similarly, where the issue is not one of fundamental importance, or is merely of academic interest, there is less impetus for final courts to overrule precedent.

Nevertheless, it cannot be said that there is evenness or even hard and fast rules in relation to the elements which final courts will take into account when deciding whether to overrule, or not to overrule, a particular precedent. Until recently, in the Commonwealth Caribbean, one could discern a pattern of timidity or perhaps thoughtful conservatism on the part of the Privy Council in overruling precedents, but arguably, the opposite is now true.

Notwithstanding the discussion above, it should be reiterated that final courts are *not* strictly bound to precedent. Yet, since the Privy Council and presumably, the new CCJ, will continue to accept precedents in many cases almost unquestionably, it

---

82 Lord Hoffman, *ibid*, at pp 89–90. Lord Hoffman was himself quoting from the US case *Planned Parenthood of Southeastern Pennsylvania v Casey* (1992) 505 US 833 at 854.

83 [1966] 1 WLR 1234. This is reiterated in *Cassell v Broome* [1972] 1 AC 1027 at 1054 (HL).

84 *Ibid*, at pp 911–12.

85 From the Joint Opinion of Justices O'Connor, Kennedy and Souter in *Planned Parenthood of South Eastern Pennsylvania v Casey* 505 US 833 (1992) at p 864, endorsed by Lord Hoffmann in *Lewis, above*, fn 8 at p 74.

86 *La Pintada* [1985] AC 104 at 130.

provides a logical basis for determining in what circumstances Commonwealth Caribbean final courts will accept their freedom to depart from past decisions, whether their own, or of the still authoritative House of Lords.

The propulsion toward overruling precedents may also depend on the particular area of law with which the law is concerned. While every litigant considers his or her matter before the court to be important, there are some issues which are deserving of closer scrutiny by a court with the authority to overrule precedent. Matters of life and death, personal liberty come to mind, as opposed to, for example, matters less related to basic notions of survival. Lord Steyn's remarks in his dissenting judgment in *Fisher v Minister of Public Safety and Immigration et al*[87] are instructive:

> ... the innate capacity of different areas of law to develop varies. Thus the law of conveyancing is singularly impervious to change. But constitutional law governing the unnecessary and avoidable prolongation of the agony of a man sentenced to die by hanging is at the other extreme. The law governing such cases is in transition. This is amply demonstrated by the jurisprudence of the Privy Council over the last 20 years.[88]
> ... In Pratt's case the Privy Council ... departed from the earlier decisions of the Privy Council and held that prolonged and unacceptable delay, pragmatically set at periods in excess of five years, might be unconstitutional and in important subsequent decisions the Privy Council ruled that the five-year period is not a rigid yardstick but a norm from which the courts may depart if it is appropriate to do so in the circumstances of a case ...[89] After a long struggle effect was given to the constitutional guarantee of human rights enshrined in article 17(1). But there are important unresolved questions. Now for the first time the important issue must be squarely faced whether prolonged and unacceptable pre-sentence delay may be taken into account to tilt the balance.

We now know that since Lord Steyn's remarks, even further fine-tuning of the constitutional impact of the provisions on cruel and inhuman punishment has taken place. In the landmark but highly controversial case of *Lewis v AG of Jamaica*,[90] the Privy Council reversed its recent decision on the question of whether there was a right not to be executed before international human rights commissions had reported on death penalty petitions and whether the exercise of the prerogative of mercy was reviewable. In so doing, the Privy Council overturned *de Freitas v Benny*[91] and *Reckley v Minister of Public Safety and Immigration (No 2)*.[92] The Privy Council gave its views on overruling, particularly in cases which involved the death penalty:

---

87 [1998] AC 673 (Privy Council, The Bahamas) at pp 686–687.
88 He further noted: 'In 1976, and again in 1979, in unanimous judgments the Privy Council held that a condemned man could not complain about delay of his execution caused by his resort to appellate proceedings: *de Freitas v Benny* [1976] AC 239; *Abbott v AG of Trinidad and Tobago* [1979] 1 WLR 1342. In 1983 cases involving delays of between six and seven years in the execution of condemned men in Jamaica came before the Privy Council: *Riley v AG of Jamaica* [1983] 1 AC 719. The majority observed that it could hardly lie in the applicant's mouth to complain 'about delay caused by appellate proceedings (p 724F). The ruling of the majority was in absolute terms: whatever the reasons for or length of delay in executing a sentence of death lawfully imposed, the delay can afford no ground for holding the execution to be a contravention of section 17(1)' (p 726H). Lord Scarman and Lord Brightman dissented from the 'austere legalism' of the majority. That dissent helped to keep alive the idea that under a constitutional guarantee against inhuman or degrading treatment or punishment prolonged and unnecessary delay may render it unlawful to execute the condemned man. Ten years later the issue again came before the Privy Council in *Pratt v AG for Jamaica* [1994] 2 AC 1.
89 See *Guerra v Baptiste* [1996] AC 397 and *Henfield v AG of The Bahamas* [1997] AC 413.
90 *Above*, fn 8 at p 75.
91 [1976] AC 239.
92 [1996] AC 527.

Their Lordships are compelled to consider whether they should follow these two cases. They should do so unless they are satisfied that the principle laid down was wrong, not least since the opinion in *Reckley No 2* was given as recently as 1996. The need for legal certainty demands that they should be very reluctant to depart from recent fully reasoned discussions unless there are strong grounds to do so. But no less should they be prepared to do so when a man's life is at stake . . . if they are satisfied that the earlier cases adopted a wrong approach. In such a case, rigid adherence to a rule of *stare decisis* is not justified.[93]

Yet, we may ask, is the roller-coaster ride on the question of the unconstitutionality of circumstances surrounding the death penalty justified? Interestingly, while often overruling has the effect of making the law more relevant to society and more in keeping with public sentiment, in the chain of cases on the death penalty, the Privy Council decisions, while perhaps more internationally palatable and up to date, have arguably made the law more out of sync with public values in Commonwealth Caribbean jurisdictions. The decisions may also be seen to be out of touch with the needs of the administration of justice at the current time.

Finding the balance – the priority for judicial development

Caribbean judicial views on precedent appear to have taken a drastic about turn in the death penalty cases, from a position of excessive conservatism and rigidity to one of extreme fluidity. The newly constituted CCJ seemed to have gone along with this new faith when it endorsed the overruled precedent in *Lewis*, albeit with different reasoning. It is as yet too early to determine whether this new dispensation is to be confined to such emotive subject areas or whether one can identify a more innovative approach to precedent.

Certainly, Lord Hoffman's caution in *Lewis* is not only legitimate, but also more consistent with the orthodox principles on overruling, that precedent should not be overruled where no new reasons for the change have been identified by the court and the only rationale is a belief that the precedent is simply wrong.[94] In *Planned Parenthood*,[95] the well-known abortion case, the court complained that 'no judicial system could do society's work if it eyed every issue afresh in every case that raised it'.[96]

But equally, refusing to review carefully a decision believed to be wrong is failing to do the work our legal system demands of judges The ultimate purpose of the judicial function is to find truth and justice. This should not be sacrificed easily to institutional norms which place emphasis on predictability. Predictability is good, but justice is better. There is certainly a baseline which can effect an appropriate balance between the two.

At this juncture of our legal development, and considering that we have had little input into the current image of our law, it is perhaps more important to give greater weight in finding that balance to mature, serious review of long held precedents, although this may, in the short term, encourage some instability in the legal system.

93   *Above*, fn 8 at p 75, relying on *R v Secretary of State for the Home Department, ex p Khawa* [1984] AC 74, *Pratt and Morgan, above*, fn 83.
94   See, eg, JW Harris 'Towards Principles of Overruling – When Should a Final Court of Appeal Second Guess?' (1990) 10 OJLS 135, at 159–160.
95   *Above*, fn 82.
96   *Ibid*, p 854.

Luckhoo Ch, of the Guyana Court of Appeal, formulated an appropriate principle in *Seepersaud v Port Mourant Ltd*:[97]

> ... if this court is satisfied that a previous decision of the court was wrong, then ... the court is at liberty to revise its previous stand. To hold otherwise, would be to stultify the growth and development of the law, particularly where it is incumbent on the court, as I believe it is on this court, to develop the jurisprudence of an independent country, even though it might do so along principles that have long been accepted and applied.

This approach deserves commendation.

RULES OF PRECEDENT FOR COURTS OF APPEAL

In the Commonwealth Caribbean, Courts of Appeal are bound to follow the decisions of either the Privy Council, or where they have submitted to the appellate jurisdiction of the newly constituted CCJ, that court. Courts of Appeal have sometimes challenged this rule of rigid hierarchy in favour of more autonomy. Such initiatives have produced much tension, particularly in the UK. For example, the House of Lords has had occasion to remind Courts of Appeal of their judicial responsibility in this regard. In *Cassell and Co Ltd v Broome*,[98] Lord Halisham told a rebellious Court of Appeal:

> [In] the hierarchical system of courts which exists in this country it is necessary for each lower tier, including the Court of Appeal, to accept loyally the decisions of the higher tiers.[99]

There is a tentative view that Courts of Appeal have authority to refuse to follow obsolete decisions of final appellate courts under the principle of obsolescence.[100] But final courts have declared that even in such cases, the duty to overrule falls to them and not to lower Courts of Appeal.[101]

Earlier Court of Appeal decisions

In general, Courts of Appeal are bound by their own earlier decisions.[102] However, there are three exceptional circumstances where such decisions are not binding. First, a Court of Appeal may choose between two conflicting authorities. The decision which is not followed is deemed to be overruled. Secondly, a Court of Appeal is bound to refuse to follow its own decision where, although not expressly overruled, it conflicts with a decision of a higher court. In the Commonwealth Caribbean, this would mean a decision from the Privy Council or the CCJ, as the case may be. Finally, as explained earlier, a Court of Appeal is not bound to follow a decision if it has been reached *per incuriam*.

---

97 GY 1972 CA 12, at p 6; Civ Appeal No 21 of 1971, decided 1974, (Court of Appeal, Guyana), p 6.
98 [1972] AC 1027.
99 *Ibid*, p 1054.
100 See, eg, *Pittalis v Grant* (1989) QB 605.
101 See, eg, *Milliangos v George Frank (Textiles) Ltd* [1976] AC 433, at 459 and *Cassel, above*, n 98 at p 1054.
102 [1944] KB 718; [1946] AC 163. See also *Fareel v Alexander* [1977] AC 59. This rule appears to be accepted in the Commonwealth as a whole.

Well-known attempts have been made, notably by Lord Denning, to promulgate a rule that a Court of Appeal has the liberty to depart from its own earlier decisions as the circumstances warrant, as is the case with the House of Lords. In *Gallie v Lee*,[103] Lord Denning stated:

> I do not think we are bound by prior decisions of our own . . . we are not fettered as it was once thought; it was a self-imposed limitation, and we who imposed it can also remove it. The House of Lords have done it. So why should we not do it likewise.[104]

Denning's view has, however, met with considerable opposition,[105] even in the Commonwealth Caribbean. Apart from the strict circumstances outlined above, our Courts of Appeal will usually consider themselves bound by their own previous decisions in civil cases. This was confirmed in *Wigley v Bellot*[106] and *Vieira v Winchester*.[107] In *AG of St Kitts and Nevis v Reynolds*,[108] the court was of the view that it was:

> most important in the public interest, that the Court of Appeal should be bound by its own decisions on questions of law, save for the three exceptions specified in *Young v Bristol Aeroplane Ltd*.

The responsibility for correcting any defective judgments which come from the Court of Appeal therefore lies in final appellate courts and not later sittings of the Court of Appeal:

> the Court of Appeal should . . . leave it to the final appellate tribunal to correct any error in law which may have crept into any previous decision of the Court of Appeal . . . it is for them [their Lordships] . . . alone to correct the errors.[109]

This may create an incongruous and sometimes unjust situation, particularly when one considers that access to the final courts in the region are not as frequent as may be desirable. The result is that what is agreed to be an inappropriate precedent could remain alive for lengthy periods of time simply because the final court has not had the opportunity to correct it!

However, in exceptional circumstances, at least one Court of Appeal in the region will itself correct its error, even in a civil case. The Guyanese Court of Appeal has taken a more radical approach than its counterparts in this regard. This, however, may be explained by the fact that until recently, the Guyana Court of Appeal was the court of final decision in Guyana. In *Munisar v Bookers Demerara Sugar Estates Ltd*,[110] the Guyanese Court of Appeal did so in an employment law case. It justified this departure from established principle on the grounds that the previous decision was 'productive of injustice'.[111] Again, in *The State v Gobin and Griffith*,[112] the Court, while noting the distinction between the rules of precedent for the civil and criminal jurisdictions of Courts of Appeal, discussed below, did not rule out a departure from previous decisions in civil cases:

---

103   As established in the landmark case of *Young v Bristol Aeroplane Co Ltd* [1969] 2 Ch 17.
104   *Ibid*, p 21.
105   See *Cassell v Broome, above*, fn 98.
106   (1965) 9 WIR 193.
107   (1966) 10 WIR 400.
108   (1979) 43 WIR 108, p 123, (Privy Council, St Christopher and Nevis).
109   *Williams v R* (1974) 26 WIR 541.
110   (1979) 26 WIR 337.
111   *Ibid*, p 383, *per* Luckhoo JA.
112   (1976) 23 WIR 256.

Our court will exercise judicial review whenever there is to be determined, some broad issue of justice, public policy or question of legal principle.[113]

Deviation for criminal jurisdiction

A distinction should be made between the civil and criminal jurisdictions of a Court of Appeal with respect to the operation of the doctrine of precedent. The Criminal Division of a Court of Appeal may not always be bound by decisions emanating from the respective division of the Court. Primarily, the Court will not consider itself bound by its previous decision in a criminal matter where this would cause injustice to the appellant. The rationale for this rule is that criminal matters involve the liberty of the subject. The Court should have the discretion to decide in such serious circumstances.[114] The rule has also been extended to the criminal jurisdiction of Supreme Courts in the first instance, as illustrated in the case of *R v Greater Manchester Coroner.*[115]

The English rule that there is a distinction between civil and criminal decisions is accepted and followed in the region. This means that Caribbean Courts of Appeal will not bind themselves to their previous decisions in criminal cases, whether these decisions are from pre-independence courts or Courts of Appeal from other jurisdictions.[116]

> Although in civil matters a Court of Appeal, subject to certain exceptions, proceeds on the basis that it is bound by its own decisions, the same rule does not apply to criminal appeals.[117]

In *The State v Gobin and Griffith,*[118] the Guyanese Court of Appeal explained the rule clearly:

> [T]he principle underlying *stare decisis* in the Guyanese Court of Appeal is not the same for criminal as for civil cases. In criminal cases it is less rigid. The jurisdiction of the court to overrule previously decided cases is a continuing one . . . in a criminal case or matter which is plainly wrong and manifestly unjust, will overrule it [the precedent] without hesitation.[119]

Previous Privy Council Decisions where appeals to Privy Council have been abolished

With the abolition of appeals to the Privy Council, Courts of Appeal now have an additional question to resolve. How are they to treat with past decisions of the Privy Council? Are they at liberty to deviate from these precedents now that the jurisdiction of the Privy Council has been abolished? This question was relevant to the Guyana Court of Appeal when Guyana became the first country in the region to abolish

---

113   *Ibid*, p 304.
114   See *R v Gould* [1968] 2 QB 65.
115   *Ex p Tal* [1984] 3 All ER 240.
116   *Williams v R* (1974) 26 WIR 541.
117   *Ibid*, p 548, *per* Lord Rees JA. See also *Johnson v R* (1966) 10 WIR 402.
118   (1976) 23 WIR 256.
119   *Ibid*, at 304.

appeals to the Privy Council. The question is just as relevant for those countries which have accepted the jurisdiction of the CCJ, discussed below.

No doubt abolition gives a certain latitude to Caribbean judges. Guyana's Court of Appeal, upon its abolition of appeals to the Privy Council and its assumption as the final court, addressed the matter squarely in *Glen v Sampson*.[120] The Court was searching for a general principle on the question whether the Court of Appeal could not merely decline to follow Privy Council Appeals, but overrule the decisions of former courts of coordinate jurisdiction:

> [W]ith the Privy Council no longer at the summit in hierarchy of authority, are we not now possessed, for that very reason, of an authority that is ultimate and superior to that formerly held by our immediate predecessor . . . It seems to me there is no alternative in our present situation but for us to refuse to follow even those of the Privy Council if they conflict with later decisions of our Court of Appeal. There being no higher authority to look up to, we cannot permit matters to remain at large and conflicting and competing precedents to militate against certainty and development in the law.

The landmark CCJ case of *Joseph and Boyce* has now answered this question decidedly. According to the CCJ, such precedents 'continue to be binding . . . notwithstanding the replacement of the JCPC, until and unless they are overruled by this court'.[121]

RULES OF PRECEDENT FOR THE PRIVY COUNCIL

It is now settled that the Privy Council will not consider itself bound by its previous decisions. This was illustrated in the case of *Nkambule v R*,[122] where the Privy Council refused to follow a previous decision on innovative constitutional grounds. Recently, in *Fisher v* Minister of Public Safety and Immigration *et al*,[123] Lord Steyn, in a dissenting judgment which was to find favour with later courts, reminded the Privy Council: 'there is no binding authority compelling the Privy Council as a matter of precedent to decide the narrow question one way or other. Indeed, as recently as October 1996 the Privy Council expressly left this question open for subsequent decision.'[124]

However, except for the adventurous approach to death row cases, discussed below, evidence has shown that the Privy Council is reluctant to disturb its previous decisions. In practice, it will only review a decision if a new point of law has arisen, or it has reviewed its reasoning on a previous point of law. The fact that this settled practice has been disturbed appears to have to do with the area of law involved, constitutional law, which involved difficult policy issues. Thus, this may not be a radical departure from the norm in general.

Courts of Appeal, High Courts or Supreme Courts and all other lower courts must follow the decisions of the Privy Council, at least those from their own jurisdiction,

---

120   Civ Appeal No 9 of 1971, Court of Appeal, Guyana, p 9.

121   *Above*, fn 23, p 9, para 18, rejecting the arguments raised in *Bradshaw v AG* [1995] 1 WLR 936 (PC); (1995) 46 WIR 62 (PC).

122   [1950] AC 379.

123   [1998] AC 673 (Privy Council, The Bahamas).

124   *Ibid*, 687. The case concerned the well-known scenario of the possibility of a violation of cruel and inhuman punishment where undue delay occurs on death row. See also, *Eaton Baker v R* (1975) 23 WIR 463.

and treat them as binding.[125] Where there are two conflicting Privy Council decisions, the lower court is entitled to 'choose to follow whichever decision it found more convincing.'[126] The same principle applies with respect to the CCJ. This might occur, as in the Cayman case of *Smith*,[127] where the previous decision has been determined to be 'bad law' by other decisions of the Privy Council and a different approach taken, even if the earlier decision was not expressly overruled.

Where Privy Council precedent conflicts with House of Lord precedents

There is authority for the view that lower courts may refuse to follow a Privy Council precedent where that precedent conflicts with a precedent from the House of Lords. This was treated as an absolute rule by Carey J in the Jamaican case of *Jamaica Carpet Mills*:

> An appellate court in respect of which the Privy Council is the court of last resort may decline to follow a decision of that body which is in conflict with a later decision of the House of Lords where the following preconditions exist: (i) a point of positive law (that is, the common law) has been settled by the decision; (ii) the House of Lords has adverted to and indicated wherein lay the error of the earlier decision; and (iii) if the matter were to come up before the Privy Council, it would be bound to respect the later decision of some of its members sitting in another place.[128]

However, as the discussion on the relationship between Commonwealth Caribbean courts and English courts below[129] demonstrates, this rule is suspect.

Further, the rule is not absolute. Reasons peculiar to the jurisdiction, such as differences in statute, local circumstances and custom will militate against its acceptance.[130]

The CCJ and precedent

Until the CCJ outlines its own policy on binding precedent, the question is an open one. Nonetheless, its expected that it will operate along similar lines to the Privy Council and allow itself the greatest flexibility in coming to a decision. The issue of precedent is pertinent not only with respect to the CCJ's own precedents but how it will deal with past precedents of the Privy Council and even of the House of Lords.

Happily, the CCJ has already answered at least one of these questions and in so doing, staked out a noble objective of the court. In *AG v Joseph and Boyce*,[131] de la Bastide (the President of the court) and Saunders, in a joint judgment, found:

> The main purpose in establishing this court is to promote the development of a Caribbean jurisprudence, a goal which Caribbean courts are best equipped to pursue. In

---

125 Subject to the discussion below, p 145, about the uncertainty of the Caribbean approach to the hierarchy of courts.
126 *Smith v Commr of Police* [1980] CILR 126, 129.
127 *Ibid.*
128 (1986) 45 WIR 278, p 293, per Carey J.
129 *Below*, p 153.
130 *Ibid.*
131 *Above*, fn 23.

the promotion of such a jurisprudence, we shall naturally consider very carefully and respectfully the opinions of final courts of other Commonwealth Caribbean countries and particularly, the judgments of the JCPC which determine the law for those Caribbean States that accept the Judicial Committee as their final appellate court.

While the Justices did not speak directly to the impact of Privy Council precedents to countries which assumed CCJ jurisdiction, except in relation to matters before the court while the Privy Council was still the final court, the message was clear. This is, therefore, a firm indication that the CCJ does not consider itself bound to precedents from the Privy Council or any other court.

Questions also need to be raised with respect to the issue of precedent as it obtains to the original jurisdiction of the CCJ, that is, issues of treaty law, particularly as this is a jurisdiction which does not spring from the common law tradition which enshrines the doctrine of precedent. However, we will return to these and other question on the CCJ in a following chapter.[132]

Implications where highest court not bound to precedent

An intriguing point which has not been aired concerns the implications for *stare decisis* in legal systems where the highest court in the hierarchy is not bound to precedent. We often proceed along the same thought-lines as in the UK, forgetting that in the UK system, the House of Lords, unlike the Privy Council, has in fact, been traditionally bound to its previous decisions. It seems more than a little incongruous that, in such a unique arrangement, the rules of *stare decisis* should be so precisely followed in the legal system as a whole. Does such a system presuppose that there is greater inherent flexibility in our court systems with regard to precedent? Should our Courts of Appeal, for example, have greater freedom to depart from even the Privy Council or soon to be CCJ decisions, or, at least, their own decisions? As always, the argument against such moves comes down in favour of certainty.

Yet, it is clear that there are two distinct arms under the doctrine of *stare decisis* as conceived in the UK: (1) that each lower court follows the decisions of courts higher in the hierarchy; and (2) that final courts are, with few exceptions, strictly bound to their past decisions. These two pillars lay the foundation for the doctrine of *stare decisis* and in the Commonwealth Caribbean, where only one pillar is easily discernible, it seems that the doctrine is less rigid or strong. The source of authority for the *stare decisis* principle is pertinent to the issue. On the one hand, *stare decisis* can be viewed as a fundamental rule of law in the common law legal tradition. On the other, it is a rule of established practice or usage, a question of judicial comity. Viewed as a practice, it appears more easily amenable to change, such as where judges come together to change the practice, as occurred in the 1966 Practice Direction. Yet, the House of Lords has been reluctant to accept this description, fearing that it lends support to the claim by some Court of Appeal judges that they too can create new Practice Directions on precedent for Courts of Appeal.[133] Yet, if it is a rule of law, on what basis does the Privy Council ignore it and can legal systems with the Privy Council or like courts at the helm truly be said to be participating in the doctrine of *stare decisis* as expressed

---

132 Chapter 17 ('The Caribbean Court of Justice').
133 See *Young v Bristol Aeroplane, above*, fn 103, for a discussion of this issue.

under English law? Further, the House of Lords can create new Practice Directions even when not sitting to discharge its judicial functions.[134] Does this diminish its rule-making power?

DECISIONS OF HIGH COURTS

Strictly speaking, a decision from one High Court is not binding on another High Court judge. These are first instance decisions. This rule is followed in the Commonwealth Caribbean in the interest of consistency in the law. A decision of the High Court is binding on inferior courts, such as magistrates' courts and tribunals. However, since decisions from High Courts do not have binding authority, they are not reliable precedents. A decision from another High Court judge will, however, usually be persuasive as High Court judges appear reluctant to depart from judgments from their brothers and sisters.

The rule also needs to be considered where there are conflicting High Court decisions. What should happen in such circumstances? In *Minister of Pensions v Higham*, [135] Lord Denning stated that where there are conflicting decisions of courts of co-ordinate jurisdiction, the later decision was to be preferred if it was reached after full consideration of earlier decisions. This approach commended itself to Douglas CJ of the Barbados Supreme Court in the case of *Nurse v Nurse*. [136] In that case, his Lordship was faced with conflicting *dicta* of two Australian high court judges. Applying the principle in *Higham*, he held that where the court was faced with conflicting *dicta*, the latter *dictum* should be followed in the interests of certainty.

MAGISTRATES' COURTS AND *STARE DECISIS*

The decisions of magistrates' courts are not significant in the doctrine of precedent. One important reason is that such decisions are rarely reported in law reports. This makes it difficult to locate the judicial precedent. Even if decisions were reported, they would not be binding on any court, as magistrates' courts are the lowest in the hierarchy. Magistrates' courts do not bind themselves to their own decisions, but they are expected to be judicially consistent.

It goes without saying that magistrates are expected to follow strictly precedents from higher courts. It is a rare instance indeed when this principle is violated. However, there was just such a occurrence in the colourful case of *McClean et al v R*,[137] a case from the Cayman Islands. The magistrate in that case, in refusing to follow a Court of Appeal decision, is reported to have said: 'this court will not take cognizance of any judgment that was given in that *Gibson* case. They will have to give it again and again as far as this court is concerned; over and over again. So it is out.' This elicited a strong response from the Grand Court:

[T]his court is not easily taken aback, but that comment, and the attitude behind it, is

---

134   See Viscount Dilhorne's remarks on practice at (1979) AC 264, 336.
135   [1948] 2 KB 153.
136   (1984) 38 WIR 59 (HC, Barbados).
137   KY 1990 GC 25, pp 6–7.

most surprising. Judicial discipline demands that each court in the judicial hierarchy accepts and applies the law as interpreted by the court above it . . . It is not for this court or the summary court to refuse to apply a decision of the Court of Appeal. To do so makes a nonsense of our system of judicial precedent.

CONSTITUTIONAL LAW DECISIONS

Decisions on questions of constitutional law seem to stand out as an exception to a rigid adherence to the doctrine of binding precedent. This has to do with the nature of a Constitution as a living instrument. This has been demonstrated clearly in the judicial phenomenon relating to the death penalty and beginning with *Pratt & Morgan* and beyond, discussed below. The authority for this proposition and relevant examples are explored in more detail in other chapters.[138] Here, it suffices to note the words of Lord Wright:

> [G]enerally speaking, a rigid method of precedent is inappropriate to the construction of a Constitution which has to be applied to changing conditions of national life and public policy.[139]

Lord Steyn was also aware of this when he compared precedents from different areas of law and their susceptibility to being overruled in the *Fisher* case, discussed above.[140]

Yet, while this is undoubtedly true, the exception applies more squarely to appellate courts which have more freedom to depart from their own previous decisions. It leaves undisturbed the rule that lower courts are bound to decisions of courts above them in the judicial hierarchy.

THE CARIBBEAN PERSPECTIVE – DIFFICULTIES WITH HIERARCHY IN THE OPERATION OF PRECEDENT

While, in theory, the legal systems of the Commonwealth Caribbean may adhere to the strict theory on the doctrine of judicial precedent, the doctrine may not always operate in the way in which it was intended. This is due to the peculiarities in the region's legal systems which relate both to structure and outlook.

A complex hierarchical structure of courts

An important practical difficulty with respect to the operation of the doctrine of precedent in the region relates to the concept of the hierarchy of courts. The emphasis placed on a hierarchical structure of courts assumes that there is an identifiable and uncontested line of authority existing between the courts in the hierarchy. In the Commonwealth Caribbean, the nature of this relationship of authority is not always clear.

Although we do not have a problem with a multiplicity of courts within the

---

138 Chapter 7 ('The Written Constitution as a Legal Source') and Chapter 14 ('The Rules of Statutory Interpretation').

139 Lord Wright 'Precedents' 8 CLJ 118 at 135.

140 *Above*, fn 87.

hierarchy, there are other problems. There is a fairly simple structure *within* the hierarchy, but a complex system of courts when one considers the region as a whole. For example, there is a psychological nexus between all courts in the region because of the fact that, with the exception of Guyana, and more recently, Barbados, all the jurisdictions share the Privy Council as their final Court of Appeal.[141] This nexus is reinforced by political, sociological and economic similarities and a notion, however ill defined, of a single CARICOM community and identity. While this exerts an unifying influence on the legal system, it creates a confusion in the operation of precedent, as discussed below.

In addition, due to the maze of courts existing and previously existing under colonialism in the region, it is not easy to reconcile the status of decisions emanating from courts in the hierarchy. The CCJ will not automatically resolve these difficulties. Consequently, the following discussion will still be pertinent.

Thus, the question of which courts are to bind which in the hierarchy of courts does not evoke a simple response in the Commonwealth Caribbean. For example, are modern courts bound by pre-independence courts? Further, how should we place decisions emanating from existing sub-regional courts and previous regional courts, such as the Eastern Caribbean Supreme Court[142] or the defunct Federal Supreme Court respectively?

The complexity of the above questions is increased when one considers the inadequate system of law reporting in the region.

Pre-independence courts

The status of pre-independence courts presents the least difficulty. Most writers and judges agree that these, even if from the same jurisdiction, are persuasive rather than binding.[143] This approach was followed in *Hanover Agencies v Income Tax Commission,*[144] which is still the defining authority. The rationale of this rule is based on the different constitutional status of the two courts and the principle of 'judicial comity'.[145] The *Hanover* case was decided during the initial period after independence, when Commonwealth Caribbean judges were perhaps as yet unaccustomed to their new found freedom. It discussed the status of the newly constituted independence Court of Appeal of Jamaica. In particular, the court considered whether the decisions of the pre-independence Court of Appeal were binding on the new Court of Appeal. It was stated therein:

> I am satisfied that this court is not bound by the decisions of the former Court of Appeal. This court was established by s 103 of the Constitution . . . as a superior court of record, and although by s 8 of the Judicature (Appellate Jurisdiction) Law 1962, the jurisdiction and powers of the former Court of Appeal were vested in this court, the

---

141   When the full reach of the appellate jurisdiction of the CCJ is assumed, a similar situation will ensue.

142   Organisation of the Eastern Caribbean States. These share a subregional court, discussed in Chapter 15 ('The Court System of the Commonwealth Caribbean').

143   See, eg, Burgess, A, 'Judicial precedent in the West Indies' (1978) 7 Anglo-Am LR 113.

144   (1964) 7 WIR 300.

145   *Ibid.* The concept of 'judicial comity' refers to the respect which courts of equal status accord each other. It was used, for example, in the Cayman Islands case of *Re BCCI* [1994–95] CILR 56.

court is separate and distinct . . . This court, however, will always regard the decisions of the former Court of Appeal with the greatest of respect and as being of strong persuasive authority.[146]

Again, in *Glen v Sampson*,[147] the now independent Court of Appeal of Guyana said: 'there is no alternative but for us to *overrule* former judgments of the British Caribbean Court of Appeal, and refuse to follow even those of the Privy Council, if they conflict with later decisions of our Court of Appeal.'[148]

Decisions from other Caribbean Courts of Appeal

With regard to post-independence courts, it is well established that decisions of a Court of Appeal in a West Indian jurisdiction other than its own are of persuasive and not binding authority. This was confirmed in the case of *Aziz Ahamad v Raghubar*.[149] Indeed, Burgess suggests that the 'overwhelming weight of the authorities . . . seem to show that these precedents are of a persuasive nature only'.[150]

Sub-regional courts

The status of decisions from sub-regional courts, such as the OECS Court of Appeal, may be more problematic. These may be treated as either a single court sitting in several jurisdictions, or as a separate Court of Appeal for each jurisdiction. If one takes the latter approach, then, consistent with the above rule on courts from other jurisdictions, decisions from the court which do not come from the particular jurisdiction should merely be persuasive. In contrast, in the former scenario the decisions should be treated as binding.

The OECS court differs from the Privy Council in that it was deliberately and formally constituted as a regional court. This provides good argument that decisions should be treated as binding even on courts in another OECS jurisdiction.

Some help may be gleaned from *dicta* which discussed similar subregional courts which are now inoperative. In *Wigley v Bellot*,[151] for example, the Court of Appeal of the Windward and Leeward Islands, then a sub-regional court, felt that it was bound, in a St Kitts case, to follow a precedent from St Vincent, enunciated by the same court. The court in this case relied on the *dicta* in *Young v Bristol Aeroplane*[152] on the doctrine of *stare decisis*, that the Court of Appeal must follow its own decisions.

In practice, the status of such decisions do not seem to present difficulty. The OECS Court of Appeal simply treats them as binding. The question is perhaps only of concern for academic clarity.

---

146   (1964) 7 WIR 300, pp 306–07, *per* Waddington JA.
147   (1972) 19 WIR 237.
148   *Ibid*, 244, *per* Crane JA. Note that Guyana had already abolished appeals to the Privy Council.
149   (1967) 12 WIR 352.
150   *Op cit*, Burgess, fn 143, p 113. He justifies this assertion on the basis of cases such as *White v Morris* (1965) 12 WIR 421 and *Ahamad v Ragubar*, (1967) 12 WIR 352.
151   (1965) 9 WIR 193.
152   *Above*, fn 49.

DECISIONS OF THE REGIONAL FINAL COURTS – THE PRIVY COUNCIL AND THE CCJ: REGIONAL OR DOMESTIC?

The status of decisions emanating from the Judicial Committee of the Privy Council or the Caribbean Court of Justice appear to be the most difficult to reconcile. The Privy Council still holds the dominant position in the hierarchy of courts in most of the jurisdictions in the Commonwealth Caribbean. Different conclusions may be drawn with respect to Privy Council decisions depending on whether such decisions emanate from the particular jurisdiction deciding the instant case, or whether the relevant precedents come from another jurisdiction. Similar questions arise with respect to the CCJ. Further, the position of Guyana and Barbados, which have abolished recourse to the Privy Council as the final appellate authority, will necessarily ensure a different perspective to the issue.

We have already seen that the Privy Council is not bound to precedent, but in practice will bind itself to its own decisions. The question remains, how is the Privy Council, which is a *de facto* regional court, to treat its own decisions when sitting in a different jurisdiction from that which the precedent originated? It appears that precedents of the Privy Council originating from one Commonwealth Caribbean jurisdiction will usually bind other jurisdictions in the region. However, there is support for the view that a Court of Appeal could refuse to follow such Privy Council precedents from another jurisdiction if the decision is felt to be wrong.

Where Privy Council precedents originate from a separate jurisdiction, even if the two systems are similar or identical, it is difficult to reconcile the position that courts are bound by such precedents. It seems to smack of 'judicial imperialism'[153] and may be nothing more than a hangover from colonial rule. In the case of *Bakshuwen v Bakshuwen*,[154] on a question of Mohammedan law, the Privy Council bound an African court to a Privy Council precedent originating in India. The *dictum* in the case of *Robins v National Trust*,[155] and the resulting statement that 'colonial courts' are bound by House of Lords' judgments, have often been used as justification for the practice. Yet, the *dictum* in *Robins* is wide, vague and out of context with notions of independence. Notwithstanding, the decision of *R v Singh*,[156] a Jamaican case, clearly supports the proposition that Privy Council precedents may bind other courts which share its jurisdiction even if they are geographically outside of the region where the court believes that the previous 'decision [is] conclusive upon the point under consideration'.[157]

Jamaica Carpet Mills v First Valley Bank[158] also answers the particular question of whether Privy Council decisions from one jurisdiction should bind another jurisdiction. Relying on the cases of *R v Commr of Police ex p Cephas (No 2)*[159] and *Bakshuwen v Bakshuwen*,[160] the court confirmed that decisions from the Privy Council could bind

---

153   The term 'judicial imperialism' was used by White, D, in 'Jettison the Privy Council – you t'ink it easy?', 1976, unpublished, University of the West Indies. She was speaking there of the reluctance of the region to abandon appeals to the Privy Council.
154   [1952] AC 1.
155   [1927] AC 515.
156   (1963) 5 WIR 61.
157   *Ibid*, p 63, *per* Lewis JA.
158   (1986) 45 WIR 278.
159   (1976) 24 WIR 500.
160   *Above*, fn 154.

all of the courts which shared its jurisdiction. The court in *ex p Cephas*, in considering whether a Privy Council judgment from Nigeria could be binding, said:

> That judgment is binding on this court because although it was given in a case coming from another territory the issue of law in both cases is the same.[161]

The justification for judicial policy which seeks to unify the jurisprudence of all courts which participate in the jurisdiction of the Privy Council seems to be the desire to promote uniformity of legal principle within the common law world. This approach is exemplified in the case of *Robins v National Trust Co*,[162] where it was posited that the House of Lords should exert a controlling influence on colonial courts. Even in the absence of the colonial context, the desire for consistency within the common law appears to be undiminished.[163]

However, even if one were to concede that the trend toward uniformity was justifiable during the period of colonialism, the changes brought by political independence should produce a different result. Notwithstanding the aims and objectives of independence with respect to the jurisdiction of post-independence courts, the existence of the final appellate court having its geographical and juris-prudential location in England has caused much difficulty, often undermining the creativity of such courts.

There is one situation which can be philosophically justified. Where there are two conflicting Privy Council decisions, and the decision which is a more accurate reflec-tion of the law is the one which emanates from another jurisdiction, it should be followed. This is to ensure credibility within the law and the doctrine of precedent This approach was followed in the Cayman Islands case of *Smith v Commr of Police*.[164]

A Privy Council decision from another jurisdiction is sufficient to allow a Court of Appeal to depart from its own previous decision. This is a deviation from the rule that a Court of Appeal should not so depart, discussed above, p 138. There was such an occurrence in *Williams v R*.[165] There, the issue of the existence of a doctrine of excessive force was considered. The problems facing the operation of precedent in the West Indies were clear. The Trinidad and Tobago Court of Appeal was faced with four conflicting precedents: its own previous West Indian decision of *Johnson v R*,[166] a Privy Council precedent from Jamaica, English precedents, and precedents from other common law jurisdictions. When the court considered the vexed question of which was the legitimate authority, Rees JA accepted that the Jamaican Privy Council decision overruled *Johnson v R* and was the correct one.

Privy Council decisions from other jurisdictions binding in practice

Yet, to argue that Privy Council decisions originating from other countries should not be binding might be an exercise in academic abstraction. In practice, it is rare indeed

---

161   *Above*, fn 159, p 502.

162   *Above*, fn 155.

163   See the discussions below on the declaratory theory and the circumstances in which final courts should overrule decisions, 'Decisions from the House of Lords and other English courts – the desire for consistency in the common law'.

164   [1980–83] CILR 126. See also, *Eaton Baker v R* (1975) 23 WIR 463.

165   (1974) 26 WIR 541.

166   (1966) 10 WIR 402.

to find a West Indian court deviating from a Privy Council precedent, whatever its origin. Instead West Indian courts seem to console themselves by pointing out that they can, should, or might do so, but they rarely take the plunge. Consider the statement of Sir Alistair Blair-Kerr J in the Bermudan case of *Waler v R*,[167] which examined whether a Privy Council precedent from Trinidad and Tobago,[168] on the status of confessions challenged as involuntary, was binding:

> [T]he time may come when this court will have to decide if it is bound by the decision in the *Seeraj Adjodha* case . . . Meantime, the *safest course* . . . is to follow the *Seeraj Adjodha* decision [emphasis supplied].

In Guyana, of course, there was no intellectual difficulty, as that country had abolished appeals to the Privy Council. In *Persaud v Plantation Versailles*,[169] the Guyanese Court of Appeal noted that 'the doctrine of *stare decisis*, in so far as that court is concerned, is a dead letter with us.' With Guyana's acceptance of the final appellate jurisdiction of the CCJ, however, this issue comes alive again.

Yet, in Guyana, while the constitutional link with the Privy Council had been severed, it is naive to believe that the symbiotic relationship with the Privy Council had been similarly aborted. In *The State v Evans*,[170] the Guyanese Court of Appeal, while boasting of its jurisdictional freedom to decide cases differently from the House of Lords and the Privy Council, which it saw as its 'constitutional duty,' conceded that:

> . . . it will be predisposed to accept, and normally will accept a judgment of the House of Lords on a point of English common law as correct as our law.[171]

The issue of whether courts are bound to follow Privy Council decisions where they come from other jurisdictions in the Commonwealth Caribbean was dramatically revisited in the landmark Privy Council decision of *Pratt and Morgan v AG of Jamaica*.[172] The Privy Council held that undue delay on death row constituted cruel and inhuman punishment and was therefore a violation of a convicted murderer's constitutional rights.

Before *Pratt and Morgan*, courts from other Commonwealth Caribbean jurisdictions had considered themselves bound to the earlier authority on the issue, *Riley v AG of Jamaica*,[173] a Jamaican precedent. In *Richards v AG*,[174] for example, the Court of Appeal of St Kitts felt unable to go against the Privy Council ruling, although it had been a controversial and much criticised decision.

All Commonwealth Caribbean courts examining subsequent undue delay cases

---

167   (1984) 42 WIR 84, p 100.
168   *Adjodha v The State* (1981) 32 WIR 360.
169   (1979) 17 WIR 107, p 132, *per* Crane JA.
170   (1975) 23 WIR 189.
171   *Ibid*, pp 206–207, *per* Haynes JA.
172   (1993) 43 WIR 340.
173   [1982] 3 All ER 469, Privy Council; (1982) 35 WIR 279; This held that undue delay on death row could not constitute cruel and inhuman punishment as defined under s 17 of the Constitution.
174   (1992) 44 WIR 141.

have felt bound to follow *Pratt and Morgan* despite the great dislocation in the system of justice it has caused and the outcry against its effects.[175]

As we have seen, the *Pratt and Morgan* decision has spawned ancillary constitutional questions of what should be considered cruel and inhuman punishment with respect to capital punishment. For example, prison conditions and the mandatory nature of the death penalty were also vigorously examined by the courts. In the latter line of the cases, even recent Privy Council decisions were challenged and overruled. It seems, however, that the convoluted histories of these constitutional questions had less to do with whether the Privy Council was bound to its previous decision in a case from a different jurisdiction and more to do with attempting to find appropriate answers to hard questions of law.[176]

The *Pratt and Morgan* line of cases also illustrates dramatically the timid stance taken by Commonwealth Caribbean judges with respect to Privy Council decisions and their own role in defining their destinies, and re-emphasises the traditional dilemma posed by Privy Council decisions.

Authority for refusing Privy Council precedents from other jurisdictions

Yet, the position taken by the Commonwealth Caribbean and other Commonwealth courts on the question of Privy Council precedents from other jurisdictions is not absolutely uniform. Note the bold and thus far, unchallenged position taken by the Royal Court of Jersey in *Qatar v Sheikh Khalifa*.[177] Here, Sir Phillip Bailhache, quoting from the earlier case of *Hall v AG*,[178] said:

> The decisions of the Privy Council, in so far as they decide the law of Jersey, are of course binding on all Jersey courts. But a decision of the Privy Council which decides the law of Hong Kong, New Zealand or any other country is not binding. Such decisions are persuasive but the degree of persuasiveness will depend on the similarity of the point of issue between the law of Jersey and the law of the country from which the appeal is being brought.

The Court continued:

> We would respectfully add that the degree of persuasiveness may also depend upon social and policy considerations particular to this jurisdiction.[179]

On the question of whether the landmark decision of *Reyes v R*[180] deeming the mandatory death penalty unconstitutional should be applied to other Commonwealth Caribbean decisions, the Privy Council has also been prepared to deviate from existing Privy Council precedents from other jurisdictions where social and other

---

175   Even the Privy Council recognised the devastating effects the decision had on the legal systems of the region. See, eg, *Henfield and Farrington v AG of The Bahamas* (1996) 49 WIR 1, discussed in Chapter 16 ('The Privy Council'). The only challenge to the ruling thus far comes from the Belizean Court of Appeal in *Harris v AG of Belize*, where the Court pointed out that 'each jurisdiction would have to be considered in light of its own peculiar circumstances'.

176   For further discussion on this development, see Chapter 12 ('International Law as a Source of Law'), and above.

177   (1999) 2 ITELR 143 at 151.

178   [1996] JLR 129, 148.

179   *Ibid*.

180   (2002) 60 WIR 42 (PC).

circumstances differ. This deviation was partly as a result of different legal elements pertinent to the issue, but also because of the subjective subject matter at stake. This encouraged the overruling of precedents.[181]

Given the few instances where cases actually reach the Privy Council, it would seem that there are many opportunities for an intrepid judge to artfully refuse to follow Privy Council decisions from other jurisdictions.

It is evident that the practice of binding courts to decisions from other countries is inconsistent with the strict application of the doctrine of precedent and its corresponding requirement of a hierarchy of courts. A decision of the Privy Council or the CCJ on an appeal from a separate jurisdiction cannot be said to be that of a court operating *within* the jurisdiction. Strictly speaking, in a region which is not politically united, a 'regional' appellate court should act as a separate court in each jurisdiction. The questions of independence and statehood are again brought to the fore. Indeed, in *Persaud*,[182] Crane JA saw the abolition of the Privy Council as the final court of appeal in Guyana as a step in the right direction in the development of a Commonwealth Caribbean jurisprudence. He also felt that decisions of the Privy Council were only persuasive in Guyana, at least those delivered after the abolition date, and that all Privy Council decisions, including those from other countries decided before abolition, should be considered as persuasive only.

The CCJ and precedents from other jurisdictions

The CCJ will not be plagued with familiar problems of colonialism or judicial imperialism. Yet, the theoretical difficulty presented by the operation of the doctrine of binding precedent in the context of a regional final Court of Appeal serving independent legal systems has not been resolved with the establishment of a CCJ. We are unlikely to see departures from the status quo. Decisions from the CCJ will probably transcend narrow nationalist borders and bind Caribbean neighbours on grounds of convenience, consistency and uniformity.

Interestingly, as there is a judge from the Netherlands on the CCJ, even decisions from Suriname, based on civil law, might infiltrate the CCJ and ultimately, other Commonwealth Caribbean courts. We have already begun to see evidence of this with the judgment of *AG v Joseph and Boyce*,[183] where Justice de Wit, the justice from the Netherlands sitting on the CCJ, gave a judgment concerning the impact of

---

181 For example, there were differences identified in the saving law provisions of the various Constitutions. See, eg, *Lambert Watson v The Queen* [2005] 1 AC 472, where their Lordships explained this anomaly: 'The Board's task has been to construe the supreme law clauses and existing law clauses as it finds them ... In *Matthews* and in *Boyce and Joseph* the laws in question are existing laws. In the present case the law in question is not' (para 52). Counsel argued that the social conditions in Jamaica were different from those in Belize, St Lucia and St Kitts and therefore the question of the mandatory death penalty should be decided differently. Their Lordships accepted the difference in social conditions but these were not sufficient. In *R v Hughes* (2002) 60 156 (PC) it was noted that neither in that appeal nor in *Reyes* were their Lordships told of any legal or social differences between Belize and St Lucia which would cause the Board to adopt a different approach to the matter in that case (para 23). In *Watson* there was a clear implication that the Privy Council accepts that, in appropriate cases, such precedents are not binding.

182 (1970) 17 WIR 107.

183 *Above*, fn 23.

international law on domestic legal systems very much couched in the language and philosophy of a civilist lawyer schooled in the monist tradition.[184]

A homogeneous jurisprudence

The question of whether Privy Council or CCJ decisions from other Commonwealth Caribbean jurisdictions are binding is perhaps a moot point in practice. Even if a Court of Appeal refuses to follow such a precedent, the Privy Council or CCJ, at the appellate sitting, if it occurs, is not likely to uphold the negation of what is, in substance if not in theory, the same court. While it may be theoretically correct, it may not be realistic to expect any other than the current practice. It is perhaps inevitable that the decisions of any regional court will filter through to all Commonwealth Caribbean jurisdictions.

The new arrangement with the CCJ gives the current practice of a relatively homogeneous jurisprudence some legitimacy.[185] Still, an underlying and somewhat intriguing question remains. Do we want a homogeneous Commonwealth Caribbean law? In a region which still clings to the fallacy of insularity and illusions of self-sufficiency, it is a question not unrelated to the debate on political and economic regional unity.

DECISIONS FROM THE HOUSE OF LORDS AND OTHER ENGLISH COURTS – THE DESIRE FOR CONSISTENCY IN THE COMMON LAW

Status of decisions from the UK House of Lords

A question raised earlier now merits further consideration. What is the status of decisions from English courts, in particular the House of Lords, in the Commonwealth Caribbean legal system?

This assumes particular significance within the context of the doctrine of the reception of law. Under the reception of law theory, English law forms an integral part of law in the Commonwealth Caribbean. The underlying question is this: at what point do sovereign, independent States cease to receive English law? This was discussed in an earlier chapter.[186] To some extent, also, we are repeating ideas previously raised in our discussion of the declaratory theory.[187]

In the present context, we must ask: to what extent should a sovereign nation with its own values, ideals, local policy and local circumstances allow itself to be influenced by a foreign jurisprudence? In response to this question, one can see some distinction between decisions of the common law itself and decisions on the interpretation of statute law.

The idea of a sovereign legal system dependent upon an independent system of

---

184   For further discussion, see Chapter 12 ('International Law as a Source of Law').
185   Since there has been a concerted regional effort to create a 'regional' court.
186   See Chapter 5 ('The Reception or Imposition of English Law and its Significance to Commonwealth Caribbean Jurisdictions').
187   See above p 131.

precedent is challenged where the hierarchical system of courts is distorted. In the region, the Privy Council has often violated the philosophy underlying the doctrine of precedent in its practice of adopting decisions of the House of Lords as binding precedent, then proceeding to bind Commonwealth Caribbean courts to such precedent. This approach has been achieved directly and indirectly. In the former technique, the Privy Council uses English decisions to form the basis of its own judgments. It then becomes binding on Commonwealth Caribbean courts. The Privy Council has also acknowledged ostensibly House of Lords' decisions as binding, thus presuming a nexus between itself and the House of Lords. Such practices are understandable given the often common overlapping membership of the Privy Council and the Appellate Committee of the House of Lords, remarked upon in *de Lasala v de Lasala*.[188]

The approach of the Privy Council to English precedents has no real juristic justification under the doctrine of *stare decisis* since the House of Lords is not a court within the hierarchy of courts in the Commonwealth Caribbean. Consequently, precedents emanating from the House of Lords can have no legitimate status as binding precedent.

This is perhaps the reason why the Privy Council's practice of binding itself to House of Lords decisions is by no means uniform. As confirmed in *Frankland v R*,[189] the Privy Council retains the freedom to identify a particular legal rule laid down by the House of Lords as being erroneously propounded as the correct rule under the common law which, accordingly should not be followed.

Not surprisingly, given the general practice by the Privy Council, lower Commonwealth Caribbean courts have sometimes treated House of Lords decisions as directly binding. This was demonstrated in the case of *King v R*,[190] a Jamaican case, where the Court of Appeal treated the English decision of *Karuma*[191] as binding.

Commonwealth Caribbean courts may follow a decision of the UK House of Lords even where this conflicts with a Privy Council decision. This is particularly the case where the House of Lords decision is the later decision. Such an approach treats House of Lords rulings as more authoritative both in the UK and in the Commonwealth Caribbean. However, given that the Privy Council tends to flow with the tide of reasoning of the House of Lords, it may be conceptually justifiable. The phenomenon was illustrated in the case of *Jamaica Carpet Mills*.[192]

In *Jamaica Carpet Mills*, a case prompted by the devastating effects of consecutive devaluations of the Jamaican dollar, the Court of Appeal of Jamaica considered the date of payment for a foreign debt. The court decided the case in accordance with the landmark decision of the House of Lords, *Milliangos v George Frank (Textiles) Ltd*,[193] which it viewed as being the authoritative precedent on the question, and a point of 'common law'. In doing so, the Court felt justified in refusing to follow corresponding, but conflicting decisions of the Privy Council.

Commonwealth Caribbean courts have, however, been prepared to concede that House of Lords decisions are only binding to the extent that they promulgate a point

188   [1979] 2 All ER 1146 at 1153.
189   (1987) AC 576.
190   (1968) 12 WIR 268.
191   [1951] AC 197.
192   (1986) 45 WIR 278. Discussed above, p 148.
193   [1975] 3 All ER 801.

of the common law of general application. Where local circumstances are different, they will not be binding.[194]

Further, as we will see in our following discussions, some courts have taken a different approach to the accepted authority of decisions from UK courts, relying on the 'local circumstances' rule' and a different view to the doctrine of reception, to legitimise their stance.

CODIFIED COMMON LAW

Where West Indian law embodies or incorporates parts of English common law in statute, sometimes even in identical legislation, the status of English precedent is even more uncertain. Should the courts copy the English interpretation of such legislation as expressed in case law?

Caribbean statutes based on English law are often interpreted as if corresponding English decisions are binding. Some *dicta* suggest that at least with respect to statutes *in pari materia*, that is, identical statutes, English decisions are binding. This was the argument made in *Village Cay Marina v Acland and Others*:[195]

> It must be therefore that the English law, except where provisions in that law are unenforceable and could have no effect in the Virgin Islands or where the rules of court here provide something that modifies that English law, prevails here and must be used and followed.[196]

In contrast, when the issue was addressed in *Jaganath v R*,[197] it was suggested that English decisions are merely persuasive. This was a discussion of the application of the doctrine of *mens rea* to St Lucia.

In *R v Barbar*,[198] the Jamaican Court of Appeal rejected the argument in *Bakshuwen*[199] that Privy Council interpretations of identical statutes should be binding on another jurisdiction. The court was of the view that:

> ... the true position is that where a colonial legislature passes a law *in pari materia* with an English Act the colonial appellate court is not bound to follow decisions of the English appellate courts construing the English enactment but such decisions are of course entitled to great respect.[200]

This was also accepted as the correct principle in *Jamaica Carpet Mills*.[201] It is notable that the *Barbar* decision was expressed with reference to colonial legislation. There is even less justification for binding authority where legislation identical to English Acts is passed in the post-independence period.[202]

---

194   See *Jamaica Carpet Mills*, *above*, fn 158, pp 292–293, *per* Carey J, relying particularly on the New Zealand case of *Corbett v Social Security Commission* [1962] NZLR 878.
195   Unreported, No 198 of 1992, decided 23 March 2001 (High Court, BVI).
196   *Ibid*, p 5. However, this is *dicta* from a dependent territory and not a sovereign State and may possibly be distinguished on that ground. See also *Trimble v Hill* [1879] 5 App Cas 342, Privy Council.
197   (1968) 11 WIR 315.
198   (1973) 21 WIR 343.
199   [1952] AC 1.
200   (1973) 21 WIR 343, 350.
201   *Above*, fn 158.
202   As still occurs. See, eg, the Administrative Justice Acts of Barbados and St Lucia, replicas of Ord 53 of the English civil law procedure.

The better view is that such English decisions should be used merely as guides to statutory interpretation, as held in the case of *Chettiar v Mahatmee*.[203] This view is supported when one considers the subjectivity of the process of statutory interpretation, discussed below.[204] The interpretation given to a statute by the English courts, or other jurisdiction from which legislation is borrowed,[205] may not necessarily reflect the intention of Parliament. Similarly, even if the legislature in a Commonwealth Caribbean country uses words identical to those in a foreign statute, it is not necessarily the case that the intention is the same.

Local circumstances rule and precedent

We should consider also that the status of statutes *in pari materia* is limited by two rules: first, the 'local circumstances rule', which States that such statutes should apply only in so far as local conditions permit and are consistent with their interpretation. The 'local circumstances rule', as defined by Blackstone, is well established and recognised by the courts of law.[206] It is a fundamental aspect of the reception of law doctrine, discussed previously.[207] This rule was illustrated in the innovative case of *AB v Social Welfare Officer*.[208] Here, the phenomena of matrifocality and extended families in the Commonwealth Caribbean were recognised as justifications for deviating from English *dicta* which limited the ability of grandmothers to adopt children.

Secondly, statutes *in parti materia* may be distinguished on grounds of local policy.

PRECEDENT AND THE RECEPTION OF LAW AS DECLARED IN THE CARIBBEAN

Commonwealth Caribbean countries received the English common law and the nature of that reception has implications for the application of the doctrine of precedent. If one accepts the declaratory theory of the common law, that is, that the legal principles of the common law already exist and are merely declared, the logical conclusion is that these existing and immutable legal principles are already contained with the body of law received from, or imposed by, the former colonisers. Further, one could take a broad view of reception to mean that the law as identified by England is continuously being received.

---

203 [1950] AC 481.
204 See Chapter 14 ('The Rules of Statutory Interpretation').
205 See, eg, *Proverbs v Proverbs* (2002) 61 WIR 91, where the Barbados Court of Appeal followed precedents from Australia instead of case law from the UK, on the basis that the Barbados Family Law Act was almost identical to the Australian statute. The Court also suggested that English judges had distorted the meanings to be attached to their corresponding statute through erroneous statutory interpretation.
206 Tucker (ed) *Blackstone's Commentaries* (1803) 1969, New York: Kelley, p 107: '. . . colonists carry with them only so much of the English law as is applicable to the conditions of an infant colony . . . The artificial requirements and distinctions incident to the property of a great and commercial people, the laws of police and revenue . . . and a multitude of other provisions are neither necessary nor convenient for them.'
207 See Chapter 5 ('The Reception or Imposition of the Common Law and its Relevance to Commonwealth Caribbean Jurisdictions') and Chapter 14 ('The Rules of Statutory Interpretation').
208 (1961) 3 WIR 420.

Such views greatly undermine the potential for flexibility and creativity in the law. This is because they assume that once a legal principle is declared, it binds all jurisdictions which belong to the common law world. This would mean, further following the strict theory of judicial precedent, that decisions from the House of Lords in England, the highest court in England, and presumably the most authoritative court in the English common law system, of which we are a part, should always bind Commonwealth Caribbean courts. Such a view explains the practice, discussed above, where both Commonwealth Caribbean courts and the Privy Council itself, treat House of Lords decisions as authoritative. The unfortunate consequence of this position is that Commonwealth Caribbean judges will have no authority to overrule precedent, shape West Indian law, nor contribute to the development of the common law. Not surprisingly, this view has met with resistance from Commonwealth Caribbean academics and some judges.

Yet, if we are to examine the case law, we find that criticism of the declaratory theory or an all-embracing reception of English law, is not truly reflected in Commonwealth Caribbean decisions. With few exceptions, the traditional approach in practice is to treat decisions from England as containing unchangeable rules which automatically apply in the Commonwealth Caribbean. The case law illustrates that Commonwealth Caribbean courts tend to treat all English cases, even decisions from inferior or lower English courts, in this way, that is, as declaring common law principles. This is a mechanical approach and greatly undermines the potential for creating a unique jurisprudence in the region.

One of the most instructive examples is the case of *Collymore v AG*,[209] which concerned the right to strike. Here, Wooding, J, in examining the issue, chose to bind himself to the position as expressed under English case law, which had never protected such a right. He essentially ignored the new, independent Constitution of Trinidad and Tobago and its provisions which had sought to protect freedom of association. Wooding could find no right to strike because it had never existed under the common law. Apart from the constitutional implications of this decision,[210] Wooding's judgment betrays a rigid adherence to the belief that correct principles of law are only those which could be located under expositions from English courts.

In *Johnson v R*,[211] Wooding was just as reactionary. When confronted with the much criticised House of Lords case of *DPP v Smith*,[212] he felt that:

> . . . since any decision of the House of Lords must be regarded as the prevailing law and, in so far as it interprets it, the common law of England, we must, whatever our own view, accept its judgment in *Smith* as declaratory of the law here.[213]

Nor is the attitude confined to judges schooled in a pre-independence jurisprudence. The more recent decision of *Jamaica Carpet Mills Ltd v First Valley Bank*,[214] is just as deferential to the House of Lords. The Jamaica Court of Appeal accepted the proposition outlined in *Tai Hing Cotton Mill Ltd v Liu Chong Hing Bank Ltd*,[215] that 'the

---

209   (1967) 12 WIR 5.
210   See the discussion in Chapter 7 ('(The Written Constitution as a Legal Source').
211   [1966] 10 WIR 402.
212   [1961] AC 290.
213   *Above*, fn 211, p 405. On the assumption that the common law was part of the law of Trinidad and Tobago.
214   *Above*, fn 158.
215   [1985] 2 All ER 947.

authority for the determination of English law [the common law] . . . is the responsibility of the House of Lords in its judicial capacity'.[216] Commonwealth Caribbean courts, including the Privy Council, could not deviate from the expositions of the common law as laid down by the House of Lords.

This approach is not confined to the Commonwealth Caribbean. It has also had juristic appeal in other Commonwealth jurisdictions such as New Zealand, which have retained the Privy Council as the final court. Indeed, the jurisprudence from New Zealand and Australia has been instrumental in defining the Commonwealth Caribbean approach. In *Jamaica Carpet Mills*, for example, the court relied on the New Zealand decisions of *Archer v Cutler* and *Hart v O'Connor*[217] to formulate its rule.

In fact, the early *dicta* of *Robins v National Trust Co Ltd*,[218] which had stated that the House of Lords was the supreme tribunal to settle English law, and *Rookes v Barnard*,[219] a similar decision, are still in use in Commonwealth Caribbean and other Commonwealth courts. In *Douglas v Bowen*,[220] the Jamaican court specifically relied on *Rookes* in finding that the House of Lords' determination on the award of exemplary damages was binding:

> It cannot be said . . . that in Jamaica the common law relating to the award of damages, inherited as it was from England in 1664, has been shown to have developed in any way different from the way it has in England.[221]

Still, the restrictive and conservative stance taken by ex-colonial courts is not to be viewed as unique. We saw earlier that the process of judicial reasoning itself, depending as it does on judicial precedent and the limitations imposed by judges themselves, presumes an inherent rigidity in the common law. It is to be expected that courts newer to the doctrine of precedent will be even more timid in seizing their freedom.

Indeed, Weeramantry[222] has pointed out that in Australia, when judges were faced with golden opportunities to create law in circumstances where there were no binding precedents available, they have often still looked to English precedent. In one such case, *MLC v Evatt*,[223] instead of the court treating the case as one of first impression, thus giving itself complete freedom, it analysed English decisions in detail 'on an implicit assumption that the principle that emerged from them would automatically be the right principle for Australia'.[224]

Similarly, in *Public Service Board of NSW v Osmond*,[225] in a decision reminiscent of Wooding's failure to look at the existence of a right to strike from a new perspective,[226] the Court of Appeal of Australia rejected the lower court's initiative in developing a

---

216   (1986) 45 WIR 278, at 288.
217   [1980] 1 NZLR 386 and [1985] 2 All ER 880, respectively. In the latter, the New Zealand court found that the English law on the contractual capacity of a mentally disabled person was binding in New Zealand. It was a settled principle of the common law, from which even the Privy Council could not depart.
218   [1927] AC 515.
219   [1964] 1 All ER 367.
220   (1974) 22 WIR 333.
221   *Ibid*, p 338.
222   Weeramantry, CG, 'Judicial Reasoning in the Common Law', Ninth Commonwealth Law Conference, 1990, New Zealand: Commerce Clearing House, p 84.
223   (1968) 122 CLR 628.
224   *Ibid*.
225   (1986) 63 ALR 559.
226   In *Collymore v AG, above*, fn 209.

requirement for reasons under natural justice. It merely observed: 'There is no general rule of the common law requiring reasons.' Weeramantry subsequently complained:

> The common law would still permit a person who sees a two-year-old child on a railway track in the path of an approaching train to pass by without intervening. Few other legal systems would. Common law judges, relying on precedent, are content, unless statute interferes, to confirm such anachronisms.[227]

As demonstrated earlier, the Privy Council has been an important vehicle in perpetuating this uniformity in the common law by treating House of Lords decisions as the appropriate instruments for proclaiming common law principles. The Privy Council reaffirmed this in *Hart v O'Connor*,[228] a New Zealand case, denying that it had the power to depart from earlier decisions and in effect, denying that country's right to its own development of the common law.

CAN CARIBBEAN JUDGES MAKE LAW?

The well-known adage that 'judges do not make law' is, of course, a fundamental tenet of the separation of powers doctrine and the declaratory theory. Whilst a legal fiction, it explains the philosophy behind the rigid adherence to judicial precedent, even in the face of the obvious unsuitability of the existing legal principle to the circumstance or even the particular jurisdiction. Yet, the declaratory theory is no longer authoritative and many distinguished jurists and writers have acknowledged and even boasted, that judges do, in fact, make law.[229]

For example, Lord Wright asks:

> If judges do not make law, how is it that a legal system evolved in the days of the feudal system is adequate to do duty in the nuclear age? Evidently there has been law making somewhere along the line.[230]

Many jurists have questioned whether judicial reasoning, which depends on a supposedly logical structure of an insulated judgment proceeding step by step from a proposition which existing case law has yielded, is appropriate in a modern context. Lord Radcliffe, for example, has observed:

> . . . if the law is to stand for the future, as it has stood in the past, as a sustaining pillar of society, it must find some point of reference more universal than its own internal logic.[231]

Until we resolve this question, 'the judicial mind remains a prisoner of the ancient fiction that the judges do not make law'.[232]

In the Commonwealth Caribbean, an eminent justice from the CCJ, Justice Adrian Saunders, has joined the debate, stating candidly: 'Judges do make law'. He identified at least three circumstances in which he believed judges created law. First, he explained that it is not always the case that principles of the common law cover the

---

227   *Op cit*, Weeramantry, fn 222, p 87.
228   [1985] AC 1000.
229   See Cross, *op cit*, fn 18, p 35.
230   Wright (Lord), *Legal Essays and Addresses*, 1939, London: Butterworths, p xvi.
231   Radcliffe (Lord), *The Law and its Compass*, 1961, London: Faber & Faber, p 40.
232   *Above*, fn 15.

issue before you. In such a case, the judge must formulate new law. We should note that this is, of course, the example of first impression cases which are traditionally accepted as creating law.

Secondly, Justice Saunders noted that at times the principles that one may extract from the common law 'are only appropriate if these principles are modified'. Thirdly, he continued, there are instances when common law principles, if applied to relevant interests will yield answers contrary to public policy. Thus, in these refined circumstances, judges must make law. However, we reiterate that only judges of final courts can do so.[233]

The question remains, however, even if we accept in principle that judges can make law, do we accept that Commonwealth Caribbean judges have just as much authority as their English brothers and sisters to do so? In *Meespierson (Bahamas) Ltd v Grupo Torras SA,*[234] a case important to the offshore financial sector of the region, Gonsalves-Sabola P confirmed the tendency of Commonwealth Caribbean judges to err on the side of excessive conservatism and orthodoxy. He had to decide the question whether he should follow the traditional rule that courts have no jurisdiction to grant a free-standing mareva injunction in the absence of a substantive claim against the defendants in the jurisdiction. He was invited to follow the more adventurous stand taken by his judicial counterparts in Jersey, in the case of *Solvalub Ltd v Match Investments Ltd,*[235] where the Jersey judge adopted the dissent in the landmark case on the question. Rather than taking that route. Gonsalves-Sabola had this to say:

> The Jersey Court of Appeal approved the dissenting opinion of Lord Nicholls . . . founded on comity and the need to protect the reputation of Jersey as an important financial centre . . . I do not regard these Channel Island decisions . . . as persuasive authority. I do not perceive a public policy in The Bahamas, standing as a sovereign State, which drives the Bahamian judge to be creative to the extent of making a serendipitous discovery of a common law principle equivalent to the provisions of s 25 of the Civil Jurisdiction and Judgments Act 1982[236] . . . with appropriate self-reproach I acknowledge communion with the late Lord Denning's 'timorous souls' of The Siskina fame who would not take 'fresh courage' and exercise what was seen as the judge's inherent jurisdiction to lay down the practice and procedure of the courts instead of waiting for the Rules Committee to act, if not Parliament itself. That was really an invitation to preempt . . . Parliament . . . and justifying the judicial activism involved as being required by justice or the comity of nations.[237]

Apart from distancing himself from judicial activism, Gonsalves-Sabola appears to accept unquestioningly, the binding nature of the precedent set by the UK House of Lords in *The Siskina*[238] as laying down the appropriate rule for mareva injunctions. In so doing, he was unable to discern even a public policy or local circumstances in the Bahamas and its unique offshore sector, which could justify the deviation from such precedent.

---

233 Law Lecture, Law Faculty, University of the West-Indies, Cave Hill, Barbados, 17 November 2006. See also Justice Wit's remarks in *Boyce*, op cit, fn 63.
234 (1999) 2 ITELR 29.
235 (1997–98) 1 OFLR 152.
236 That statue had changed the common law principle on the point.
237 *Above*, fn 234, p 38.
238 [1979] AC 210.

At the other end of the scale sits *Lewis,* where the dissenting judge openly accused his judicial brothers of judicial activism.[239]

The restrictive interpretation of precedent established by English courts is fuelled by the fact that some Commonwealth countries have very wide reception clauses,[240] which have been interpreted to mean that, in the absence of statute, a court must apply the common law of England, at least, as existed as at the date of the reception clause.[241] Seldom have the courts relied on the local circumstances exceptions found in statutes for authority to 'mould' the common law. Indeed, as noted in *Musa,* where there is a wide reception clause specifically incorporated into domestic law, as is the case in Belize, there is more authority to strictly apply the common law as found in England.[242]

MOULDING THE COMMON LAW AMIDST LOCAL CIRCUMSTANCES

Yet, the impact of English precedent is not to be regarded as a closed debate. An alternative approach is to examine the constitutional status of independent West-Indian courts as addressed in the post-independence case of *Persaud v Plantation Versailles.*[243] There, the role of the West Indian judge was viewed in a more dynamic way:

> [W]e judges will no longer consider ourselves hidebound by English decisions, but with mature judgment in appropriate cases will strike out and mould the common law ... to suit the needs of our ever changing society.

The *Persaud* approach emphasises not the date or relevance of reception, but independence and the advent of written Constitutions. It suggests that these latter events allow us the opportunity to develop an indigenous jurisprudence.

Surprisingly, on this issue, courts in the dependent territories of the Commonwealth Caribbean have often been more pragmatic than their counterparts in independent Commonwealth Caribbean countries. For example, the Bermudan courts have followed the *Persaud* principle. In *Crockwell v Haley et al,*[244] the Bermudan Court of Appeal refused to follow a House of Lords decision on the question of the assessment of damages. The court declared that the decision was merely persuasive, as the circumstances in Bermuda were different, in particular, the fact that Bermuda residents paid no income tax. Yet, this decision may not be as radical as it first appears. It relied, in essence, on the local circumstances rule which, we have seen, has always been an acceptable exception to binding precedent.

Similarly, in *National Trust for Cayman Islands v Planning Appeals Tribunal, Central Planning Authority and Humphreys (Cayman) Ltd,*[245] the Grand Court of the Cayman

---

239   *Above,* fn 8.
240   See Chapter 5 ('The Reception or Imposition of English Law and its Significance to Caribbean Jurisdictions').
241   See, eg, *Musa v The Speaker of the House of Representatives et al,* Unreported, Nos 455 and 456, decided 22 January 1998, Supreme Court, Belize.
242   *Ibid,* pp 33–34.
243   *Above,* fn 169, p 118.
244   Unreported, No 23 of 1992, decided 29 June 1995, CA, Bermuda.
245   [2002] CILR 59.

Islands declared, correctly, that decisions from the English Court of Appeal were only persuasive in the Cayman Islands. It further reiterated that on questions of the common law, even decisions of the House of Lords, while strong authority, were only of great persuasive authority on the Privy Council. Principles of the common law as expressed in the English courts were not applicable where local circumstances were different. The Court was deciding the question whether conditional fees violated public policy in the Cayman Islands and saw it as a 'singular opportunity to move the common law forward in this instance.'[246] The Court recognised very clearly the different public policy considerations that arose in the Cayman Islands.[247]

It is certainly the case that domestic conditions will sometimes be very different from those in the UK, thereby making proclaimed rules of the common law an uneasy fit. Good examples include prevailing social and cultural norms and matters informed by economic circumstances.

If we accept that Commonwealth courts should on occasion depart from established principles of the common law as laid down by English courts, under what circumstances should this occur? This question was fully explored in the Australian case of *Australian Consolidated Press Ltd v Uren*.[248] The Australian High Court, from which the appeal came, had to decide whether to follow the movement in the common law on the instances where awards for exemplary damages were suitable, as laid down in the case of *Rookes v Barnard*.[249] It declined to do so. It was uncontested that the issue of exemplary damages had been well settled in Australia pre-*Rookes v Barnard*. The Privy Council upheld the decision, recognising that there were instances when the common law did not need to develop uniformly and acknowledging indirectly, that other Commonwealth courts have the authority to reject common law precedents laid down by the House of Lords. This is the divergent, as opposed to the unitary approach to the common law. Lord Morris of Borth-y-Gest said:

> There are doubtless advantages if within the parts of the Commonwealth . . . where the law was built upon a common foundation development proceeds along similar lines. But development may gain its impetus from any one and not from one only of those parts. The law may be influenced from any direction. The gain that uniformity of approach may yield is however far less marked in some branches of the law than in others. In trade between countries and nations the sphere where common acceptance of view is desirable may be wide . . . But in matters which may considerably be of domestic or internal significance the need for uniformity is not compelling.[250]

The Court was persuaded by the fact that the law in Australia was already well settled. Further, it found that that law had not been founded on 'faulty reasoning' nor misconceptions. The Court also recognised that there is room in the law to accommodate divergent policy rationales.

The *Uren* decision further underscores a point often missed by Caribbean jurists. This is that Commonwealth Caribbean courts have a responsibility too to help develop the common law and that the evolution of the common law is not a one-sided

---

246   *Ibid*, p 65.
247   Following *de Lasala v de Lasala* [1980] AC 546.
248   [1969] 1 AC 590 (Privy Council).
249   [1964] AC 1129 (House of Lords).
250   *Ibid*, 641.

process. Yet, the Privy Council itself has openly acknowledged this possibility, saying, in the case of *Invercargill City Council v Hamilton:*[251]

> The ability of the common law to adapt itself to the differing circumstances of the countries in which it has taken root, is not a weakness, but one of its greatest strengths. Were it not so, the common law would not have flourished as it has, with all the common law countries learning from each other.

A rare example of the divergent approach is the Trinidad and Tobago case of *Abbott v The Queen.*[252] The issue in that case was whether duress was available as a defence to someone alleged to have committed murder as a principal in the first degree, as stated in the House of Lords precedent of *Lynch v DPP for Norther Ireland.*[253] The court held that, on issues of the common law, courts in jurisdictions from which appeals lie to the Privy Council need not regard themselves as bound by decisions of the House of Lords.[254]

The ability of the common law to adapt itself to the changing norms of other societies is one reason for its very survival. As stated in *Cassell and Co v Broome:*[255]

> The common law would not have survived in any of those countries which have adopted it, if it did not reflect the changing norms of the particular society of which it is the basic legal system. It has survived because the common law assumes a power in judges to adapt its rules to the changing needs of contemporary society.

Lord Bingham of Cornhill agrees that the future of the common law will 'not be uniform but variegated' as judges from different parts of the common law contribute to the 'ever-developing jurisprudence of the common law world'.[256]

Still, instances of decisions where judges have commented on the inapplicability of binding precedents from English courts are few and far between. In effect, the practice in Commonwealth Caribbean courts has been to surrender their judicial sovereignty to English courts.

Clearly though, the evolution of a country's jurisprudence depends much on the maturity of its legal system and political consciousness. This has been ably demonstrated in other Commonwealth countries such as Australia, India and even the US, which have strayed bravely from the path of English precedent as time went on.

An indigenous jurisprudence from a Caribbean Court of Justice

How would a unified CCJ instead of the Privy Council affect the development of an indigenous jurisprudence and the doctrine of precedent? Would such a court produce uniformity in decisions or take into account the differing socio-economic conditions of each country? Would the court be original in its thinking, or would it merely rubber-stamp English jurisprudence? If the latter approach is taken, the court may not justify its establishment. We have already been given some indication of the court's

---

251 [1996] AC 624, 640.

252 [1977] AC 755.

253 [1975] AC 653.

254 See also *De La Sala v De Lasala* [1980] AC 653.

255 [1972] AC 1027, *per Lord Diplock.*

256 Sir Gerard Brennan, 'Address on Retirement' 21 May 1998, p 10, quoted in 'The Common Law: Past, Present and Future' by the Right Honourable Lord Bingham of Cornhill, [1999] CLB 18, at p 28.

good intentions in the *Boyce* case, discussed above.[257] However, only time will tell whether these intentions translate merely into window dressing or whether real change in legal policy and direction is effected. The advent of this new indigenous court will at least give the opportunity to formulate law and legal policy which is more reflective of West Indian reality. We will return to this question in our discussion on the Caribbean Court of Justice.[258]

CONCLUSION – A DIRECTION FOR CARIBBEAN PRECEDENT

In examining the operation of doctrine of precedent in the Commonwealth Caribbean, we have seen that the historical conjuncture of the region cannot be isolated. Hence, continuing modes of the reception of the English common law are central to the question of the potential for the development of an indigenous jurisprudence. Similarly, the retention of colonial attitudes of dependency on British legal thought is important to the issue.

As the discussion illuminates, the answers to the questions concerning the operation of the doctrine of judicial precedent in the Commonwealth Caribbean are still not clear cut. In the final analysis, it would seem that only a few courts will respect the legal sovereignty and identity of independent jurisdictions and will not attempt to impose an alien jurisprudence upon them.

Judicial interpretation and precedent should function within the modern context, as a tool for social engineering, to address creatively the political, social and economic needs of our own societies. To ensure this, our courts should deviate from the anglicised version of the law and a mechanical approach to cases, as seen above.

An approach to judicial precedent which does not attempt to allow the law to reflect social reality and an individual society's notions of legal morality and accuracy is not the way forward. This can hardly be justified and upheld in a society which claims that it is seeking to establish and assert its independence and a Caribbean-flavoured jurisprudence. We saw earlier that the common law grew out of English custom and practice. The doctrine of judicial precedent is the chief means by which this custom is perpetuated as legal rules. It is questionable to what extent such rules should be applicable outside of their own social context.

The stance adopted by Denning on the application of precedent to our society is to be preferred. He agrees that the common law must not be copied wholesale or without proper regard to local circumstances:

> The common law cannot be applied in a foreign land without considerable qualification. Just as with an English oak . . . you cannot transplant it . . . and expect it to retain its tough character.[259]

This approach favours the adoption of persuasive precedent rather than a rigid adherence to binding legal principles. The retention of procedural mechanisms, such as the doctrine of binding judicial precedent, buffered with psychological postures which perpetuate the Englishness of our law needs to be re-examined if we are ever to

---

257   *Above*, fn 23.
258   Chapter 17 ('The Caribbean Court of Justice').
259   In *Nyali Ltd v AG* [1956] QB 1, 16.

hope to fashion law according to our own likeness. In the words of de la Bastide, then Chief Justice of Trinidad and Tobago, and now the first President of the newly constituted CCJ, in the case of *Bushell v Port Authority of Trinidad and Tobago and Others*:[260]

> It may be that we are too prone in jurisprudential and constitutional matters to transport from England and transplant in Trinidad and Tobago conventions, concepts and constructs without critically examining whether the soil conditions in which they have grown and flourished in their native land are, or can be, replicated in this country.

The historical evolution of our law and legal tradition makes it imperative for our judges to start their reasoning with English precedents, but in view of the ultimate goal of justice in the law, there is no parallel imperative to adopt the English position in all cases. Indeed, one wonders whether there could come a time when West Indian jurists could speak in similar vein to their Australian counterparts, one of whom described the common law as:

> . . . the law created and developed at first by English judges and in more recent times, chiefly by Australian judges.[261]

---

260 (1998) 56 WIR 460, at 462. de la Bastide was examining the question whether estate police were public servants and recognised that the Trinidad and Tobago Constitution, as well as other social arrangements, differed from those of the UK.

261 Brennan, *above,* fn 256 at p 29.

CHAPTER 9

EQUITY AS A SOURCE OF LAW

INTRODUCTION – THE DUAL STRUCTURE OF THE COMMON LAW

We saw earlier that the common law grew out of the customs and practices of the English, as promulgated in the ancient common law courts. Yet, when we speak of the common law as a legal tradition, we are not only referring to the body of law defined by the common law courts. We must also include a body of law which developed in separate and different English courts. This body of law is known as 'equity', or equitable principles. In lay persons' language, equity means fairness, justice, or what is morally just, but in a legal sense, it is a much more specific concept. Still, it embraces such notions, as it is a system which was inspired by ideas of justice. It is commonly said that the law of equity is based on rules of conscience. Today, however, equity is simply a branch of the law standing apart from the common law. It may be defined as those principles of English law which were developed and applied in the chancery, admiralty and ecclesiastical courts.

Equity, is, therefore, a separate and distinct body of English law which grew up alongside, but not together with, the common law. While equity is part of the common law tradition, it is not part of the common law. Initially, this may seem confusing. What it means is that the common law tradition has a dual structure. This duality is unique and embodies both the substance and the application of the law. One part of the common law is made up of the common law rules, while the other comprises the rules of equity. Maine has described it thus:

> The next instrumentality by which the adaptation of law to social wants is carried on I call equity, meaning by that word any body of rules existing by the side of the original civil law; founded on distinct principles and claiming incidentally to supersede the civil law in virtue of a superior sanctity inherent in those principles.[1]

We may notice that the use of the term 'common law' connotes several different things. First, it may mean that belonging to the 'English' law or legal tradition as described in Chapter 3 ('Legal traditions – types of legal systems in the Commonwealth Caribbean'). Secondly, it may refer to that source of law which is not legislation or other legal sources within the English legal tradition, but which comes from case law or precedent. Finally, we may use the term 'common law' to mean that which is not equity, that is, the law developed by the ancient common law courts as distinct from that developed by the Courts of Chancery.

While equitable rules are also 'law', we make a theoretical distinction between 'equitable' rules, rights and remedies and 'legal' rules, rights, and remedies. The latter is confined to those developed by the common law courts as distinct from the Courts of Chancery.

Equity is an important legal subject which is a separate and wide area of law. In

---

1 Maine, HS, *Ancient Law*, 1888, New York: Henry Helt, p 27.

this section, we look briefly at its nature and content. We are more concerned, however, with its place within the law and legal system as a source of law.[2]

THE HISTORICAL JUSTIFICATION FOR AND DEVELOPMENT OF EQUITY

Equity evolved so as to correct the often rigid and inflexible rules of common law, which could prevent justice. While the common law developed on an ad hoc basis, and was designed to be a flexible system of law capable of providing innovative solutions to problems as they arose, it did not retain its original character. As the doctrine of *stare decisis* developed, it encouraged rigidity within the law, as we discussed in Chapter 8.[3] The convenience of such a doctrine was not limited to judicial precedents, but extended to procedural matters. The common law devised strict legal procedures, which also had the effect of promoting rigidity.

In addition, the lack of creativity meant that many litigants were left without a legal remedy for their problems, as the law was confined to the judicial precedents and procedures identified by the common law courts. The common law had become immutable and sometimes irrelevant to its society. What was designed to promote uniformity and avoid chaos created immobility and inefficiency within the law. These problems provided the impetus for the creation of equity. Where the common law could not remedy its own restrictions, equity stepped in.

A good illustration of the problem existed within the systems of writs and forms of action. Forms of action included a writ and particular rules of pleasing and proof, a specific form of judgment and a method of executing judgment.[4] By the end of the 13th century the kinds of available writs and their forms of action had become inflexible. Under the common law, these systems of writs and forms of action were mandatory. No action could be brought in the royal courts without a writ (which was then a letter in the name of the King commanding someone to do what was specified in the writ). There were, for example, 'writs of right' commencing an action of land and 'writs of trespass' for injury to person or property. Litigants had to try to fit their circumstances into the writ in order to bring their cases before the common law courts. If they could not, they could obtain no redress.

Similarly, because of the increasing complexity of social and commercial life and the resulting variety of litigation before the courts, there was a need for new remedies. The only remedy available under the common law was damages, which is payment in money as compensation for a wrong. This was not always a satisfactory solution. In some instances a plaintiff did not want monetary compensation. Instead, he or she wanted the defendant to return something, such as land, or to evict the defendant from the land. This propelled the advent of new equitable remedies, discussed below.

---

2   For a good account of one branch of this subject, the trust, particularly as it relates to the Commonwealth Caribbean, see Kodilinye, G, *Commonwealth Caribbean Law of Trusts: Text, Cases and Materials*, 1996, London: Cavendish Publishing.

3   'The common law and the doctrine of judicial precedent'.

4   These forms of action were abolished by the UK Judicature Acts of 1873–75. Nowadays, an action in the High Court is usually begun by a writ of summons, commanding one to appear in court to answer a particular claim.

THE COURT OF CHANCERY

The Court of Chancery was originally simply the 'sessions' of the Chancellor, who was the King's Chief Minister. He was usually a member of the King's clergy. The famous Thomas Moore was one such Chancellor. The Court of Chancery only became a separate and distinct court in the 15th century.

The matters which were brought to the King through the Chancellor were those in which no suitable redress or remedy could be found under the common law as had developed by that time. Where the common law could not give a remedy or enforce a remedy, informal petitions were addressed to the Council, which ordered specific relief in the interest of justice. These petitions were then passed to the Lord Chancellor.

The Chancellor acted on the conscience of the parties. He issued writs of attendance and gave relief. He was given wide discretion and authority to decide cases as he saw fit, in the interest of justice and fairness. These Chancellors were very creative and built up a body of principles, called equitable principles, which sought to correct the deficiencies of the common law. Thus, this special Court of Chancery existed in order for the Prerogative to exercise his power to correct injustices within the legal system. In theory, the 'fountain of justice' was the King. At that time, the monarch was believed to be infallible, as he was God's representative.

THE NATURE AND CONTENT OF EQUITY

Since equity exists to correct the deficiencies of the common law, it may grant remedies even if no strict legal right exists. In practical terms, for example, equity will give effect to the intention of the parties, notwithstanding the absence of some formality.[5] For example, a mere agreement to create a formal lease is enough to create a legal obligation due to the maxim, 'equity looks on that as done which ought to be done'.[6] Similarly, if a contract is signed or put into writing, as is required for it to be strictly 'legal', equity will uphold it if an intention to create a legal obligation exists.[7]

One of the essential differences between equity and the common law is that whereas common law remedies are available 'as of right', regardless of the plaintiff's conduct once there is an infringement of his legal right, equity is a discretionary remedy. Thus an equitable remedy is only granted if the court decides that the plaintiff deserves it. As a result, even if there is a wrong but the plaintiff's conduct was inappropriate, he receives no remedy. Likewise, if damages, which is a 'legal' remedy, for a wrong are sufficient, the court may not award an equitable remedy.

Even though equitable remedies are discretionary, this does not mean that such discretion is to be exercised arbitrarily. Rather, the discretion is exercised according to fixed and settled rules, such as in the circumstance where enforcing a contract would cause hardship, as illustrated in the case of *Shiloh Spinners Ltd v Harding*.[8]

---

5   See *op cit*, Kodilinye, fn 2, Chapter 2.
6   See, eg, the Cayman Islands case of *Levy v Levy* (1952–79) CILR 5. If there are documents which provide evidence of binding arrangements, a court of equity is bound to enforce them as such.
7   See, eg, *Walcott v Barclays Bank DCO* (1974) 26 WIR 554.
8   [1973] AC 691.

A good description of the nature of equity is found in the ancient case of *Dudley v Dudley*:

> Now equity is no part of the law, but a moral virtue, which qualifies, moderates, and reforms the rigour, hardness and edge of the law, and is an universal truth; it does also assist the law where it is defective and weak ... Equity therefore does not destroy the law, nor create it, but assists it.[9]

'Maxims of equity'

The nature of equity is further expressed by examining the 'maxims of equity'. These are sayings which have developed that illustrate the way in which the body of law that is equity will be applied. The more popular of these legal maxims are:

(a) 'Equity does not suffer wrong to be without remedy.' This maxim expresses the ability of equity to create a new remedy where none exists under the common law.

(b) 'Equity does not assist a volunteer.' For example, a decree of specific performance to compel a person to do something will not be granted to a person who has given no consideration for it.

(c) 'He who comes to equity must come with clean hands.' This is perhaps one of the best known of the maxims and explains that a person who expects a remedy in equity must himself have a clear conscience and must have done no wrong with respect to the matter before the court.[10] The requirement of clean hands was discussed in the landmark case of *Hubbard v Vosper*,[11] where the plaintiff sought an injunction to restrain breach of copyright and confidence in a book critical of the cult of Scientology. The plaintiff was found to have been protecting their secrets by deplorable means and was not therefore deserving of a remedy in equity. Similarly, in *Duchess of Argyll v Duke of Argyll*,[12] the plaintiff, now divorced from the defendant, obtained an injunction to prevent the publication of articles about the marriage. He contended unsuccessfully that the plaintiff should fail because she had an immoral attitude towards the marriage while it lasted. However, this was not sufficient to refute an action in equity since 'uncleanliness' must be in relation to the relief sought.

(d) 'Equity looks to the intent and not to the form.' The doctrines of part performance and estoppel may be traced to this maxim.

(e) 'Equity acts *in personam* rather than *in rem*.' In accordance with this maxim, the right of a beneficiary will be viewed essentially as a personal right rather than a right in the property itself and cannot, therefore, be assigned.[13]

(f) 'He who seeks equity must do equity.' This is similar to the requirement for 'clean hands'. It means that a person applying for an equitable remedy must be prepared

---

9 (1705) Prec Ch 241, p 244; [1705] 24 ER 118.

10 See, also, the Caribbean cases of *Boustany v Pigott* (1993) 42 WIR 175, where the court held that it could infer unconscionable conduct; *Sheik Mohammed Adam v Mohammed Mursalin* (1989) 43 WIR 257; *Hawley v Edwards* (1984) 33 WIR 127; and *Cayman Arms Ltd v English Shoppe Ltd* [1990–91] CILR 299.

11 [1972] 2 QB 84.

12 [1967] Ch 302.

13 See, eg, *Moss and Pearce v Integro Trust (BVI) Ltd* [1997–98] 1 OFLR 427, a case from the British Virgin Islands which reaffirms this principle even with respect to offshore financial matters.

to act in an equitable manner himself. As explained in *Hawley v Edwards*,[14] while this maxim goes hand in hand with the maxim on 'clean hands', the difference is that the requirement to 'do equity' looks to the future and not to the past, as the requirement to come with 'clean hands' does.[15] Consequently, the respondents, in a case of specific performance, should have been prepared to do equity and pay interest on the purchase money for the property of which they had deprived the appellant. It is also illustrated in the case of *Chappell v Times Newspapers Ltd*,[16] where the Court of Appeal refused an injunction to restrain breach of contract where the plaintiff was unwilling to perform his part of the contract.

New rights and remedies

The effect of equity is manifested mainly in the areas of property and contract law. One of its chief contributions is the concept of equitable property, such as the 'trust'. The trust is peculiar to common law systems. It arises where property is conveyed to T (the trustee) in circumstances where equity will compel him to administer it for the benefit of B (beneficiary). The trust is also instrumental in succession law where property is involved, such as in the drafting of wills.

Some examples of new rights created by equity include the rights of a beneficiary under a will or a trust, the existence of an equitable interest and the equity of redemption which relates to mortgages. For example, in *Construction Services Ltd v Daito Kogyo Co*,[17] two companies entered into a consortium agreement to negotiate a contract. The court found that the deviation from the consortium agreement by the defendant for its sole benefit without the consent of the plaintiff company was a breach of a fiduciary relationship tantamount to a trustee deriving a benefit from a trust.

New remedies arising from equity include the injunction, one particular type of which, the Mareva injunction, is discussed below, p 174. This prevents some foreseeable wrong from occurring, such as a nuisance; specific performance, which seeks to compel someone to perform an obligation existing under either a contract or trust; rectification, which is a remedy available to correct a mistake even where a contract is under seal where it does not reflect the true intention of the parties; and restitution, which commands the defendant to place the plaintiff in his original position before the wrong occurred.

To illustrate: in *Errington v Errington*,[18] the concept of the contractual licence was discussed. The father bought a house in his own name for his son and daughter-in-law. He paid one-third of the purchase price and the daughter-in-law and son paid the future instalments on the understanding that they would inherit it. The father died leaving the house to his widow, and the son then departed from the matrimonial home. It was held that the daughter-in-law still had a right to the property grounded in equity.

---

14   (1984) 33 WIR 127.
15   *Ibid*, p 131.
16   [1975] 1 WLR 482.
17   (1994) 49 WIR 310.
18   [1952] 1 All ER 149.

THE MODERN EXPRESSION OF EQUITY

The original Court of Chancery was not a slave to procedure like the common law courts. The Chancellor was able to create new rights and remedies as justice required, thus giving birth to the maxim 'equity varies as the length of the Chancellor's foot'. By around 1690, however, most of the rules and principles of equity had become as firmly established as those of the common law. Thus, although equitable principles were originally concerned with correcting the inflexibility of the common law, today the rules of equity are just as rigid as the common law. They have developed into a relatively fixed body of laws. Even the circumstances in which the court will exercise its equitable discretion are now fairly well defined, as seen in the maxims of equity, discussed above, p 169.

Today, equity is no longer viewed as being merely corrective of the common law, but as having an independent existence, as stated in the 18th century case of *Gee v Pritchard*:[19]

> The doctrines of this court ought to be as well settled, and made as uniform almost, as those of the common law ... Nothing would inflict on me greater pain, in quitting this place, than the recollection that I had done anything to justify the reproach that the equity of this court varies like the Chancellor's foot.

Thus, the court of equity had become not a court of conscience, but a court of law. In a contemporary context, the rules of equity do not reflect its original flexible character. Some judges have failed to treat equity as the dynamic tool that it is, thus robbing it of its potential to find creative legal solutions. For example, in *Re Diplock*,[20] it was said:

> ... [If] a claim in equity exists it must be shown to have an ancestry founded in history and in the practice and precedents of the courts administering equity jurisdiction. It is not sufficient that because we may think that the 'justice' of the present case requires it, we should invent such a jurisdiction for the first time.

THE ROLE OF THE LEGISLATURE IN CREATING EQUITABLE PRINCIPLES AND OFFSHORE DEVELOPMENTS

Not all defects of the common law have been remedied by judicial creativity. It is sometimes left up to Parliament and the legislature to create the necessary changes in the law. This role is particularly important because of the timidity of judges in fully exploiting the creative potential in the law. Today, legislation sometimes intervenes to create or extend equitable jurisdiction where the court holds that none exists or it is restricted.

For example, since the UK Judicature Acts,[21] the use of the injunction as an equitable remedy has widened, particularly in the areas of tort, labour law and administrative law. Injunctions have also helped to develop new rights, such as the law of restrictive covenants in property law.

---

19 (1818) 2 Swan Ch 402, p 414; [1818] 36 ER.
20 [1948] Ch 465, pp 481–82.
21 UK Judicature Acts 1873–75.

An interesting legislative development is found in St Lucia. Because of the hybrid legal tradition there, equity was introduced by way of legislation and its development has been unorthodox.[22]

NEW DEVELOPMENTS BY THE COURTS

Very few new equitable rights or remedies have been created since the 19th century. Yet, although modern courts have not been as innovative as their ancient counterparts in creating new equitable principles, there are exceptions. Some judges, notably Lord Denning, have tried to keep the spirit of equity alive. In *Re Vandervell's Trusts No 2*, Lord Denning said:[23]

> Every unjust decision is a reproach to the law or to the judge who administers it. If the law should be in danger of doing injustice, then equity should be called in to remedy it.

Because of this new found spirit of inventiveness, some important developments in equity have occurred in contemporary times. The most outstanding perhaps are the creation of the doctrine of equitable estoppel and those of the equitable remedies of the Mareva injunction and the Anton Piller order. These may legitimately be regarded as more dynamic aspects of equity.

The doctrine of equitable estoppel operates whenever, in the particular circumstances, it would be unconscionable for a party to be permitted to deny that which, knowingly or unknowingly, he has allowed or encouraged another to assume to his detriment.[24]

In *Bacchus and Another v Ali Khan and Others*,[25] the Guyanese Court of Appeal considered the doctrine of equitable estoppel in relation to an insurance policy. The insurance company, pursuant to a 'conflict of litigation clause', handled litigation concerning an accident by the insured. Judgment was given against the insurance company. For the appeal, the insured appointed new counsel to act on their behalf. The company applied for the restoration of the appeals.

The court held that the insured, by accepting the 'conduct of litigation' clause, had extinguished his right to change solicitors without the company's consent. The defendants, having taken advantage of the 'conduct of litigation' clause, had raised an equity which estopped them from interfering with the conduct of the proceedings. Gonsalves-Salboa JA further explained:

> The categories of circumstances attracting the application of an estoppel are not closed . . . 'of all doctrines equitable estoppel is surely one of the most flexible'.[26]

---

22   See Chapter 4 ('The Hybrid Legal Tradition') and Chapter 5 ('The Reception or Imposition of English Law and its Significance to Caribbean Jurisdictions').

23   [1974] Ch 269, p 322.

24   See *Taylors Fashions Ltd v Liverpool Victoria Trustees Co Ltd* [1981] 1 All ER 897, p 915, *per* Oliver J.

25   (1982) 34 WIR 135.

26   *Ibid*, pp 176–77, *per* Gonsalves-Salboa JA, relying on *Amalgamated Investment and Property Co Ltd v Texas Commerce International Bank Ltd* [1981] 1 All ER 923. See, also, *Guyana and Trinidad Insurance Company v Rentokil* (1983) 40 WIR 171.

The remedies of the Mareva injunction and the Anton Piller order were created to assist the court in law enforcement efforts. They are extensions of the injunction. The Anton Piller order, taken from the case of *Anton Piller v Manufacturing Processes Ltd*,[27] is a form of the mandatory injunction or order for discovery. It allows entry into premises relevant to an action to inspect and remove documents, placing them in custody. This is only done in exceptional circumstances where, in the interests of justice, it is essential that the plaintiff should inspect, and where, if the defendant were forewarned, there is a danger that vital evidence would be destroyed or taken out of the jurisdiction.

Similarly, the Mareva injunction, named after the case of *Mareva Compania Naviera SA v International Bulkearners SA*[28] is a type of interlocutory injunction created in 1975. It is an order restraining the defendant from removing assets from the jurisdiction while trial is pending, where there is a real risk that he may do so. This is to ensure that the plaintiff will not be left without a judgment which he cannot enforce.

OFFSHORE LEGISLATIVE DEVELOPMENTS

The offshore trust in equity

Offshore financial jurisdictions (sometimes called 'international financial jurisdictions') in the Commonwealth Caribbean have been particularly innovative in developing equitable principles. These are found, for example, in the innovative trust law and corresponding jurisprudence which have been created by such countries to address the needs of offshore investors. Extensive changes to traditional trust law principles have been made under offshore legislation. As the trust is a key institution under equity, this is a significant development within the legal system. The offshore trust has, for example, redesigned the rule against perpetuities, characteristic of the onshore trust. Under this rule the trust could not continue in perpetuity. Many offshore jurisdictions have accordingly increased the maximum specified perpetuity period or have abolished the rule against perpetuities entirely.[29]

Similarly, they have created purpose trusts which do away altogether with the rule that trusts must contain identifiable beneficiaries.[30] More recently, legislation has been enacted in the British Virgin Islands to allow trustees to escape the onerous commercial duties imposed on them by the common law.[31] These changes have been made in the name of commercial efficiency.[32]

---

27 [1976] Ch 55.

28 [1975] 2 Lloyd's Rep 509.

29 See, eg, the Belize Trusts Act 2000 (Rev) of Belize, the Banks and Trust Companies Law 1995 of the Cayman Islands and the International Trusts Act 2002 of St Lucia. Legislation in the UK has also made changes to the trust. See, eg, the Variation of Trusts Act 1958. This extends the concept of the trust. However, such changes are not as far-reaching as offshore responses to the trust.

30 See, eg, the Special Trusts (Alternative Regime) Law 1997 of the Cayman Islands.

31 See the Virgin Islands Special Trusts Act 2003 of the British Virgin Islands.

32 For in-depth reading of the special legislative trust regime and related jurisprudence created by offshore financial jurisdictions in the Commonwealth, see Rose-Marie Antoine, *Trusts and Related Tax Issues in Offshore Financial Law*, Oxford University Press, 2005.

Such countries have not been as emboldened to be creative with respect to the divergent development of equity through case-law.[33]

OFFSHORE JURISPRUDENCE AND THE MAREVA INJUNCTION

Like the trust, the Mareva injunction and the Anton Pillar order have particular significance for those Caribbean jurisdictions which are offshore financial centres. Offshore legislation is often deliberately designed to avoid onshore laws and judgments which can undermine offshore investment and offshore structures. For example, offshore law might provide that jurisdiction over offshore companies and trusts is vested solely in the offshore country or that certain judgments will not be enforced.[34] Further, offshore companies and trusts may contain 'flight' clauses which enable them to relocate to another jurisdiction if their assets are threatened by onshore creditors or claimants. This is compounded by the fact that offshore investment is also protected by strict confidentiality laws.[35] What this means in practice is that if an offshore investor is being prosecuted, for example, for money laundering or financial fraud, he may have great opportunity to resist the enforcement of any adverse judgments made against him onshore. Consequently, those pursuing him may not be able to obtain access to his assets. Even if a judgment can be enforced against him, he may be able to move his assets before enforcement or seizure is effected.

Recognising the potential for such criminal abuse in offshore financial investment, courts in Caribbean offshore financial centres have been willing to assist onshore countries in preventing perpetrators from benefiting from their crimes. The use of the new equitable remedies of the Mareva injunction and the Anton Piller order have proved most useful in this regard. For example, in the Bahamas, one of the leading offshore financial centres in the region, in the case of *Banco Ambrosiano Holdings v Calvin*,[36] the Supreme Court of the Bahamas showed its willingness to award the Mareva in appropriate circumstances. The court found that where there was a *prima facie* case of wrong doing by a defendant:

> . . . there was no merit in allowing judicial timidity in granting or maintaining the injunction where is a real risk of assets being withdrawn from the jurisdiction . . . It would be judicial irresponsibility to turn a blind eye to the evidence of fraud.

Here, the assets were placed in an offshore trust which contained a 'flight clause'.[37] Similarly, in *Private Trust Corp v Grupo Torras SA*,[38] the Bahamian Court of Appeal

---

33 See, eg, the discussion in Chapter 5 ('The Reception of English Law and its Significance to Caribbean Jurisdictions'), in particular, the cases of *Bridge Trust Co Ltd and Slatter v AG and Others* (1996) CILR 52 (Grand Court, Cayman Islands) and *AG (Bahamas) v Royal Trust Co (No 2)* (1983) 36 WIR 1 (CA, the Bahamas), where the Cayman Islands and Bahamian courts, respectively, considered whether to develop their own path in relation to trusts but declined to do so. Cf *Grupo Mexicana de Desorollo SA v Allison Bond Fund Inc* 119 Sup Sl 1961 (1999).

34 See, eg, the Belize Trusts Act, *above*, fn 29.

35 See, eg, the Confidential Relationships (Preservation) Act 1993 of the Cayman Islands (rev'd 1999).

36 Unreported No 237 of 1987, S Ct the Bahamas.

37 *Ibid*, p 11.

38 [1997–98] 1 OFLR 443.

upheld a Mareva injunction to restrain the assets of an offshore trust incorporated in the Bahamas. This was to enforce a judgment of an English court which had imposed a worldwide Mareva against the settlor of the trust. The court found that the terms of the trust – in particular, the existence of a 'flight clause' which could be put into operation at the request of the settlor – justified the injunction.

In fact, offshore courts have noted that these new remedies are of more significance in offshore countries than in onshore ones. In *Kilderkin Investments Ltd v Player*,[39] an injunction brought by a Canadian receiver to identify, preserve and recover assets of the defendants located within the Cayman Islands was successful. The action was for alleged fraud and breach of trust. The court found that the risk of the removal of assets by defendants in offshore jurisdictions was even greater than in the UK. There was a strong suggestion that it would more easily grant the injunction:

> ... in applications for a Mareva injunction in this jurisdiction ... different considerations may arise from those in England. Where considerable sums of money are involved and the persons concerned have no strong ties to the Islands, or a company is involved which can easily fold or be stripped of its assets, the temptation to remove assets from the jurisdiction to escape the effects of a judgment of this court must be great. That temptation gives rise to a risk. *Risk* may be *inferred from circumstances* here *which might not give rise to the same inference in England* [emphasis added].[40]

These new developments are a significant reminder of the innovative potential of equity and its role in looking to the true aim of the law, that is, to promote justice, rather than being weighed down by legal technicality. As stated by Lord Denning: '... the courts have discovered the new equity. It is fair and just and flexible, but not as variable as the Chancellor's foot. It is a great achievement'.[41]

The courts in Caribbean offshore financial jurisdictions have not been content with meekly applying orthodox equitable principles of the Mareva injunction and related restraint orders. In some cases, they have also been prepared to stretch existing equitable principles. This occurred, for example, with respect to the use of the worldwide Mareva. In sync with an innovative line of decisions coming from offshore jurisdictions elsewhere, the courts have expanded the scope of worldwide Marevas by asserting extra-territorial jurisdiction to award such Marevas by virtue of deviating from the traditional rule that application for interlocutory orders must originate from a substantive action over which the court has jurisdiction in the first instance.[42] This is demonstrated for example, in *Grupo Torras SA v Meespierson (Bahamas) Ltd*.[43]

---

39 [1980–83] CILR 403.
40 *Ibid*, p 408.
41 Denning, A, *Landmarks in the Law*, 1984, London: Butterworths.
42 *Re The Siskina* [1979] AC 210.
43 (1998–99) 2 OFLR 553 (SC, The Bahamas), overturned by the Court of Appeal (1999) 2 ITELR 29. This is in accordance with *Solvalub Ltd v Match Investments Ltd* [1997–98] 1 OFLR 152 (CA, Jersey). See also *Walsh v Deloitte & Touche*, [2001] UKPC 58, although arguably an *obiter* judgment. Not all Caribbean courts have gone along with this judicial activism however. In Belize, for example, in *Securities & Exchange Commission v Banner Fund International* (1996) 54 WIR 123, the Supreme Court of Belize refused to upset precedent and follow the trend.

THE RELATIONSHIP BETWEEN THE COMMON LAW AND EQUITY

Equity, of course, if one examines its historical background and operation, is not a self-sufficient system or source of law. It presupposes the existence of the common law. If we abolished equity we would still have a coherent system of the common law, but not vice versa.

Originally the Chancery Court had an exclusive jurisdiction in equity where the common law had no remedy or relief. In addition, the court of equity had a concurrent jurisdiction where the common law recognised the right but offered no remedy. For example, where there was a threatened commission of a tort, it could grant an injunction to refrain someone from committing a nuisance. The Court of Chancery had an auxiliary jurisdiction where the common law recognised a legal obligation and gave a remedy but was unable to enforce the remedy.

Because of the nature of equity it was inevitable that it would conflict with the common law. Between 1873–75, the UK Judicature Acts abolished the conflict between common law courts and the Court of Chancery (equity) by abolishing these courts and transferring their jurisdiction to the new Supreme Court of Judicature. The effect of the creation of a Supreme Court was that the administration of the common law and equity were fused, but not the substantive body of law or rules of equity and the common law themselves:

> . . . the two streams have met and now run in the same channel, but their waters do not mix.[44]

For example, an award of damages is still a legal common law remedy and available as of right, whereas equitable remedies are still discretionary.

Where there is conflict between the rules of the common law and equity, the rules of equity prevail. It should be remembered that when one is relying on an equitable right or remedy, all the maxims of equity still apply.

The general effect of the Judicature Act was to convert the 'exclusive' and separate jurisdiction of equity into a concurrent jurisdiction and to abolish its auxiliary jurisdiction. There is therefore no need to go to a separate court if one wishes to obtain an equitable remedy. This is as true in the Commonwealth Caribbean as it is in the UK. Still, equity continues to perform the same function, complementing and supplementing the common law in accordance with moral notions of justice and fairness. It is the common law's 'safety valve'.

---

44 *Op cit*, Denning, fn 41.

CHAPTER 10

CUSTOM AS A SOURCE OF LAW

Both custom and convention may be sources of law. These are legally distinct concepts but they share certain important characteristics. They both arise out of the social *mores* and practices of a people. Similarly, they both depend on an additional process before they can be appropriately viewed as legal sources. This missing link is the judicial process. The courts must declare customs and conventions as law and not mere social practice. As such, custom and convention cannot be considered as entirely independent sources of law.

CUSTOM

In most societies, customs evolve over time to become law. Laws which evolve from customs are more likely to reflect the social reality of which they are a part. Arguably, in the Commonwealth Caribbean, our laws have never reflected our customs. For all practical purposes, modern day Caribbean society is an imported society. Colonisation and slavery, through the plantation system, saw to it that the customs which were brought by the African slaves and the Asian indentured labourers did not survive meaningfully. Similarly, the customs of the original peoples, the Amerindians, were lost. Our legal systems and their laws were shaped by the plantocracy. We have already seen how the doctrine of reception gave birth to these laws.[1]

However, if we are serious about the indigenisation of our law and legal systems, we must extract the principles that govern our social existence and give such principles expression in law. This is not to suggest, however, that all our customs are legally desirable.

In any event, for the notion of custom to have any relevance to our society, we need to fashion new rules to govern customary law. As we shall see, the rules governing custom in English law are woefully inappropriate to our historical, sociological and even geographical circumstances. Often, this has made it difficult for custom to be expressed as law. Yet, while custom may be a rare source of law in the Commonwealth Caribbean, this infrequency in no way should diminish its importance to the legal landscape, particularly to a society serious about self-definition.

THE COMMON LAW RULES OF CUSTOM

Custom may be viewed as both an historical and legal source of law in the Commonwealth Caribbean since, in one sense, it is the principal source of all English law, as it formed the basis of the common law which has been transplanted to the region. Today, however, English law makes a distinction between custom and the common law. Where the common law exists, then custom is in abeyance. The common law is law that applies to the entire realm. In contrast, in modern times, when English lawyers speak of custom, they really mean local custom which becomes a source of

---

1   See Chapter 5 ('The Reception of English Law and its Significance to Caribbean Jurisdictions').

law. When we speak of custom as a legal source, we are concerned with the rules of law which apply in a particular locality and form a body of law distinct from the common law. In the Commonwealth Caribbean, custom is of particular importance in the areas of land law or property law and family law.[2]

The South African case of *Alexkor v Richtersveld Community*[3] helpfully describes the essential character of legal custom or indigenous law:

> . . . it is important to bear in mind that, unlike common law, indigenous law is not written. It is a system of law that was known to the community, practised and passed on from generation to generation. It is a system of law that has its own values and norms. Throughout its history it has evolved and developed to meet the changing needs of the community.

Custom has two fundamental characteristics:

(a) first, it must be an exception to the common law;

(b) secondly, it must be confined to a particular locality. Traditionally, this locality was a parish, borough or county.

Given these two characteristics, we can appreciate that local custom is not a source of law which is relied upon often.

Unlike the rules of the common law, customary rules of law are not judicially noticed or given recognition until settled by judicial decision. The party who pleads a customary right must prove its existence. That party must convince the court that the custom satisfies certain tests, initiated, in the main, by Blackstone.[4] The tests are as follows:

(a) *Antiquity*

The local custom must have existed from time immemorial. A somewhat arbitrary date to reflect this notion of 'time immemorial' was fixed by the UK Statute of Westminster I, 1275. The relevant date is 1189. In most instances, it would be difficult to prove a custom that existed since 1189. In practice, the courts accept the alleged custom if it was in existence for a very long time. Often, the court may rely on the evidence of the oldest available local inhabitant of the area as a witness to the customary practice. Consider *Simpson v Wells*.[5] The appellant was charged with obstructing a public footpath by setting up a refreshment stall. He claimed that he had a customary right by the Statute Sessions. It was shown that the Statute Sessions were first authorised in the 14th century by the Statute of Labourers. Consequently, the alleged right could not have existed from 1189.

(b) *Continuance*

The custom must have existed continuously, that is, since 1189, or the accepted date without interruption. Any proved interruption defeats the claim. However, non-usage of the right does not defeat it.

(c) *Peaceable enjoyment*

The custom must have existed peaceably, by common consent or without oppos-

---

2   Custom is also an important source of law in labour law. However, this is not the same kind of custom discussed in this section.

3   [2004] 4 LRC 38 (Constitutional Court, SA), at p 40.

4   See Tucker, SG (ed), *Blackstone's Commentaries* (1803) Vol 1, 1969, New York: Kelley, pp 76–78.

5   (1872) LR 7 QB 214.

ition. It must also have come into force with consensus. It could not have been forced, nor evolved in secret or by licence.[6]

(d) *Mandatory*

The custom must be obligatory or mandatory. Whatever rights are given must be given as of right. For example, if the giver allows the receiver to have a passage through his land (a right of way), it cannot be at his whim. This is true of all rules of law.

(e) *Certainty and clarity*

The custom must be certain and clear in all respects. It must, for example, be capable of being defined precisely. This includes the locality to which it applies, the people to whom rights are granted and the extent and content of those rights.

(f) *Consistency*

Customs must not be contradictory; they must be consistent with one another. Thus if one custom contradicts another, the procedure is to deny the other. For example, a right to public access cannot exist alongside a right to undisturbed access. As Blackstone[7] says, one man cannot claim a custom to have windows overlooking another's garden and the other claim a right to obstruct or prevent those windows.

(g) *Reasonableness*

The custom cannot be unreasonable. If it can be shown that it was unreasonable in 1189, then the claim would fail. Custom may survive if it conflicts with the more general rules of the common law, yet if it is repugnant to a fundamental principle of the common law it will not be regarded as reasonable. In *Wolstanton Ltd v Newcastle*,[8] the Lord of the Manor of Newcastle claimed a customary right to take minerals from a tenant's land without paying compensation. This was held to be unreasonable and could not be upheld.[9]

These are demanding requirements. Not surprisingly, claims to local custom in modern times are rare. This is particularly so in the Commonwealth Caribbean.

THE APPLICATION OF CUSTOM IN THE CARIBBEAN

Overcoming restrictive rules on custom

Is there a basis for elevating custom and traditional practices in the Commonwealth Caribbean to law? The customs of at least two important groups in the society may substantiate such an initiative. These are the customs and social practices of people of African heritage, who have inherited some of the customs of their ancestors, particularly in relation to land, and those of the original peoples, the Amerindians. In the case of the former, this describes the majority of the populations in the Commonwealth

---

6   See *Caplan v DuBoulay* No 29 of 1999, dec'd 31 May 2001 (HC, St Lucia).
7   *Op cit*, Blackstone, fn 4, p 78.
8   [1940] 3 All ER 101.
9   See, also *Egerton v Harding* [1974] 3 All ER 689 and *New Windsor Corporation v Mellor* [1974] 2 All ER 510.

Caribbean. First, however, one must overcome the obstacles to the judicial recognition of custom.

The above tests for judicial recognition of a custom do not apply neatly to the Commonwealth Caribbean. First, and most important, the date of 1189 which establishes the test of antiquity cannot be employed. If customs are to be recognised in the region a different date of antiquity or other test needs to be established. In the isolated instances where Commonwealth Caribbean courts have considered the date of antiquity, they have acknowledged that the 'newness' of the conquered territories of the region must modify the date. In *Eden and Eden v R*,[10] for example, the appellants contended that there was a local custom around North Sound in the Cayman Islands to the effect that title to swamp or cliff land was shared equally between the owners of the land at the opposite ends of the feature. The Crown's right to customary title was also contested on the basis that it had been overridden by s 17(1) of the Land Adjudication Law 1971.

The court held that although a local custom could not derogate from a 'good documentary title' within the meaning of the Land Adjudication Law 1971, it could have significance in relation to title acquired by 'open and peaceful possession', but only to a limited extent. More important, the court found that the date of antiquity in the Cayman Islands 'might be from a date in the second half of the 19th century, when the law and custom applicable to land tenure had become reasonably settled and accepted amongst the communities in the various localities, and have continued without interruption since that immemorial origin'.[11]

The test for locality is just as limited in the Commonwealth Caribbean. If we consider the small sizes of our jurisdictions in the region, what is the cut off point for a 'locality'? Could a village of 100 people be sufficient?

Accordingly, it is exceedingly rare to find a case which makes reference to custom. Passing reference was made by Corbin JA in his dissenting judgment in *Sabga v Solomon*.[12] His Lordship was prepared to apply the custom of banks in respect of certified cheques to uphold the validity of a cheque.[13]

Custom under the St Lucia Civil Code

Interestingly, the St Lucia Civil Code expressly sanctions resort to custom if the Civil Code is obscure or silent on the point in issue. Attempts have been made in a few cases to invoke custom. In *Cazaubon v Barnard Peter and Co*,[14] it was argued that 'there was a custom existent in the island which required a month's notice to terminate the contract of a clerk'. However, Carrington CJ rejected the argument for a lack of evidence. In a later case, *Clarke v Cadet*,[15] Benett CJ rejected on evidential grounds an attempt to show that local usage was helpful in determining whether the cutting of certain fruit trees constituted waste under the Civil Code. Both cases dramatise the reluctance of the courts to sanction custom and local usage.

---

10   [1952–79] CILR 406.
11   *Ibid*, pp 415–16.
12   (1962) 5 WIR 66.
13   *Ibid*, pp 78–79D.
14   (1883) St L G 216.
15   (1902) St L G 921.

In the important case of *Caplan v DuBoulay*,[16] the substance of the law on custom was examined in relation to St Lucia's civil law tradition. The plaintiffs claimed customary rights of usage and enjoyment to the Queen's Chain by virtue of the fact that they were the owners of the hinterland to the Queen's Chain. This, they argued, gave them actual possession. Barrow CJ (Ag) made a number of important observations about the claim to customary law in this regard. He first noted that the law pertaining to the Queen's Chain in St Lucia was 'rooted in Ancient French Law' and therefore the English common law on the issue was not applicable. This was full recognition of the civil law aspects of St Lucia's legal tradition, including customary law. He went further to observe that the fact that two neighbouring islands, St Vincent and Tobago, had laws which made statements on the issue was not significant because of the 'different histories of the respective territories', St Lucia alone being a jurisdiction of significant civil law traditions.

While the court accepted that the owners of the property had long enjoyed the use of the Queen's Chain, it found that this usage had always been subject to permission from the Crown. Discounting the value of a practice growing up based on 'implied permission' by the Crown, the court found that no customary rights could be said to exist.

The judgment appears to rely implicitly on the rule of peaceable enjoyment alluded to earlier, that the alleged custom must be by way of consensus and could not be derived by way of a licence. That the enjoyment relied on permission by the Crown was viewed as something akin to a licence, with the court persuaded by the argument that the Crown retained the right to deny permission at any time. The fact that the holder of a permission or licence chooses not to deny it for a lengthy period, even over centuries, does not, it appears, terminate the right to deny.

The defeat of custom in this case, however, seems unduly harsh and is perhaps better contained to rights of usage which involve the State. It is doubtful whether a private owner who had allowed a usage such as a right of way for nearly 200 years without contesting such usage could so easily defeat a claim to customary rights.

The court also had difficulty locating the certainty and consistency requirements of legal custom in its quest to ascertain what limits, if any, had been placed on the usage.

In addition, the cases discussed above demonstrate the high evidential burden which is attached to proving legal custom and even identifying customary practices.

CUSTOM AND LAND OWNERSHIP

A convincing thesis is made by Professor Marshall for the incorporation of local land law custom into West Indian law. He argues that this 'pure or diluted Englishness of West Indian land law enables us to pinpoint its main characteristics of which the most obvious and perhaps the most important is that it has few points of reference of its own'.[17] Our land law fails to take into account the realities of the socio-economic situation. It is odd, he continues, 'that in an area where the vast majority of people are

---

16 *Above*, fn 6.
17 Marshall, OR, 'West Indian Land Law: Prospectus and Reform' (1971) 20 Social and Economic Studies 1, Barbados: UWI, p 4.

of African or Asian descent, the law relating to land holding and succession should reflect so little of the Caribbean social reality and family structure'.[18]

For example, there are fundamental differences between English notions of land alienation and those from the West Indies. These differences are not reflected in the law. English rules refrain from imposing conditions against alienation while the reverse is true in West Indian societies.

While the law is silent on these differences, sociological studies in the Caribbean give evidence of clear customs of land ownership which could easily be transposed into the legal system. For example, the system of land ownership reflects adherence to the concept of village land and family land which are not regarded as freely alienable. In Guyana, Raymond Smith's study[19] records definite feelings in village communities that rights over village lands should be retained by the village communities and not be alienated to outsiders. His study also demonstrates some of the methods adopted to ensure compliance with the unwritten law of the village. For example, when a village woman marries an outsider, her family conveys land to her rather than to her husband so as to avoid the risk of the land being alienated without her knowledge and that of her family.

In Guyana, a more accurate picture is that there are different legal customs relating to land. James[20] explains further that in Guyana, there is a distinction to be made between forms of land ownership originating from the Afro-Guyanese customs and those of the Amerindians. The Afro-Guyanese custom of land ownership, originally from Africa, more particularly, West Africa, is a form of collective ownership of land by the family, which James describes as 'children property', whereas the Amerindian form of land ownership is collective ownership by the entire community, called 'native title'.[21] The children property found in Guyana is akin to forms of customary ownership identified in other Commonwealth Caribbean jurisdictions such as in the Bahamas, where it is called 'generation property' and in Jamaica, 'family property', discussed below.

These Afro-centric forms of land holding are all based on notions of ancestral land. Yet, because of our history, the concept of 'ancestral land' in the West Indies, of necessity has a more recent identity and can be traced back only as far as emancipation in 1833. Consequently, whilst 'the generation for purposes of ownership of family property might look back to time immemorial in West Africa . . . ours dates only to 1833 when Afro-Guyanese were accorded legal personality and could then own landed property.'[22]

Similarly, in Edith Clarke's work,[23] she relies on the oral tradition to depict the customary system of land tenure in Jamaica, where a distinction is drawn between 'family land' and bought land. Family land in its primary sense is land inherited from

18   *Ibid*, Marshall.
19   Smith, R, 'Land tenure in three villages in British Guiana' (1955) 4 Social and Economic Studies 64, ISER, UWI.
20   RW James, 'Land Tenure: Tradition and Change' (2001) 2 Carib LR 163.
21   The concept of 'native title' is not peculiar to Guyana, but is attributed generally to customary title held by indigenous peoples. See the discussion below, p 190.
22   James, *op cit*, fn 20, p 165. This observation applies equally to other Commonwealth Caribbean countries.
23   Clarke, E, 'Land tenure and the family in four communities of Jamaica' (1953) 1 Social and Economic Studies 43. See, also, Clarke, E, *My Mother Who Fathered Me*, 1957, Kingston: Randell, Chapter 2.

an ancestor who acquired it by gift from the slave owner at the time of emancipation, as distinct from bought land, which is land acquired by purchase subsequent to emancipation.[24] Family land belongs to all the family and is held in trust by one member for the family: it is inalienable and is transmissible to all the family. Moreover, any member of the family has rights of use over the land which are not lost through non-exercise, for however long a period. Family land may be sold by agreement between members of the family who are *sui juris*, but this is regarded as a 'wrong thing to do'.[25]

In contrast, bought land is not immediately subject to any restrictions and the owner has the right to dispose of it by sale, gift or will as he or she pleases. 'Any such action is resented, however, as cutting across the natural expectation of the family to inherit, and so there is a constant impetus to the creation of family land in the secondary sense outlined above.'[26] In fact, it would seem that once bought land has been inherited by all the family, the principle of inalienability is automatically invoked.

This description displays fundamental differences to the common law in the attitudes and use of land. These differences are derived only from custom but are nevertheless significant and authoritative. Without their recognition by the legal system, anomalies within the law are created.

The customary system of land ownership in the Commonwealth Caribbean is reminiscent of that operating in Nigeria.[27] Yet there is an important difference. In Nigeria, the customary rules form part of the law of the land, while in the West Indies they 'remain on the periphery of legal knowledge and social awareness'.[28]

Yet, such attitudes toward land ownership are not static. As our societies modernise, they tend to deviate from traditional norms which may be considered to be noncommercial. The diminution of community family values also helps to undermine them. At the same time, there may be attempts to strengthen the traditional notions of community land ownership based on custom. It is noteworthy that in countries of small size, with increasing pressures on the availability of land, these customary values assume more prevalence.

West Indian chattel houses

Some issues remain topical. For example, Caribbean academics and jurists have argued that customary rules governing the ownership of 'chattel houses' should inform the law on fixtures and chattels as derived from English property law.[29] Presently, English law would regard these houses as fixtures (belonging to the owner of the land), despite the obvious intention of their builders and the owners of the land upon which they rest to regard them as movable lodgings, and as such, the property

---

24 It also has a secondary meaning in that it can include land which was originally bought land but which has been subjected by its owner to a sort of customary entail.

25 *Op cit*, Clarke, 1953, fn 23, p 45.

26 *Ibid*, Clarke, 1953, p 45.

27 For an account of this system see Kasunmu, J and James, J, in their monograph, *Alienation of Family Property in Southern Nigeria*, 1966, Idaban: Idaban UP.

28 *Op cit*, Marshall, fn 17, p 5.

29 See, eg, Liverpool, NJO, 'Towards Reforms in Commonwealth Caribbean Real Property Law' in Alexis, F, White, D and Menon, PK (eds), *Commonwealth Caribbean Legal Essays*, 1982, Cave Hill, Barbados: UWI.

of the builder. This results in great injustice. This was the substance of Wooding CJ's *obiter* statement in *Mitchell v Cowie*,[30] a case from Trinidad and Tobago, where he warned that, in the future, the courts might need to consider whether common real property laws could be subject to any special rights of removal to allow such chattel houses to be removed from the land. However, Wooding was careful to rely strictly on the common law test of what constitutes a chattel as that affixed to the land, based on an objective test.

Liverpool remarks that 'a poor man with no home and land' could not contemplate leaving these houses behind and that 'it is a matter of everyday occurrence that such houses are removed either in whole or in part to their new location'.[31]

The issue was revisited, this time by the Bahamian Court of Appeal, in the case of *O'Brien Loans Ltd v Missick*.[32] The Court found it inappropriate to rely on the strict English interpretation of a chattel as espoused by Wooding in *Mitchell v Cowie*. Instead, it gave judicial recognition to the West Indian way of life in forming a relevant test. Finding that the issue in the West Indies required a more 'subjective approach' than the objective test earlier relied on, Hogan P of the Court of Appeal said:

> If this case was to be determined by a strict application of the view he [Wooding] had expressed and in the environment of England, I think it would be very difficult to resist the appellant's claim [that it was a fixture] ... the concept of a chattel house has however, been a feature of countries in this part of the world ... to a much greater extent than in England and I believe it would be wrong to ignore that aspect in determining this appeal.[33]

Georges JA put the matter even more boldly. Noting the West Indian custom to become 'yearly tenants of plots of land on which they build houses' and the absence of any intention by such tenants to 'benefit the landlord by adding value to the land', he deemed the English test unfit for the West Indian social reality, as it was impossible to distinguish between the use of the house as a chattel and the better enjoyment of the land as the English test required. Consequently, the object and purpose test propounded in the English authorities should yield to a determination on the circumstances of the case as to whether there was an intention to retain the movability of the house as a chattel.[34] The court also explained that the custom of the removal of chattel houses from one side to another used to be a 'fairly common occurrence in some of the islands of the West Indies. The houses were small, constructed of wood and built so as to be removed when the tenant of the land moved to another plot of land'.[35]

The inherent tensions between customary rules and the common law inevitably produce conflict. Clarke bears witness to this when she writes:

> Disagreements between members of the family over family land are in Jamaica one of the most common causes of litigation and invariably the reason is the attempt of one or more members to establish an individual right by exploiting the conflict between the

30 (1964) 7 WIR 118 (CA, Trinidad &Tobago).
31 *Above*, fn 29 Liverpool, p 202.
32 (1977) 1 BLR 49.
33 *Ibid*, p 55.
34 *Ibid*, p 59.
35 *Ibid*, p 60.

unwritten traditional system which is current in one segment of the society and the legal code which is applicable to the whole society.[36]

Succession

Tensions between the written common law and customary practices are also apparent in the law on succession and in its philosophy. The legitimacy of birth is the premise upon which the English common law proceeds on questions of inheritance and succession. It also adopts the principle of primogeniture. Under this principle, males are given priority over females and seniority is a decisive factor in settling succession.

These English notions of legitimacy and primogeniture do not accord with the traditional or customary patterns of succession of the Commonwealth Caribbean and some other common law countries. As discussed above, it is a West African value system which has been embodied in land law custom. Because of this, under the customary system of inheritance and land ownership in the Commonwealth Caribbean, there is no discrimination between legitimate and illegitimate children. Further, there is no sex discrimination, daughters being equally eligible with sons.

Family law issues

Under West Indian custom, quite apart from succession matters, no distinction is made between illegitimate and legitimate children. This is believed to be an offshoot from West African traditions, where illegitimacy is virtually unknown. It is perhaps due to the legitimacy and acceptance accorded to polygamy in such societies. Accordingly, children may be legitimate by virtue of acknowledgement or recognition by their fathers which customary constraints impel them to make.[37] According respect to custom, practices and traditions in the Commonwealth Caribbean will afford a similar result. Sociologists accept that concubinage and births out of wedlock are social and cultural facts in West Indian society.[38]

The existence of custom is even more complex in those ex-colonial countries which belong to the 'Old World', countries in Africa and Asia. Crabbe speaks of the need to appreciate 'the difficulties that now face countries which had their own systems of jurisprudence before the advent of colonial rule. Austin, Holmes, Kelsen and Pound[39] did not even seem to know of the experience of what is termed customary law. And if they did, they did not regard the customary law as law.'[40] While Crabbe focuses primarily on African customs, he acknowledges the similarity between African and Commonwealth Caribbean mores. As seen earlier, these customs have, to an extent, been transplanted to West Indian societies.

For example, in *Katekwe v Mhondoro Muchabaiwa*,[41] the Supreme Court of

---

36 *Op cit*, Clarke, 1953, fn 23, p 44.
37 See Rheddock, R, *Feminism and Feminist Thought: An Historical Overview*, 1986, Trinidad: UWI.
38 *Ibid*, Rheddock. See also Mohammed, P, 'The Caribbean Family Revisited', in Mohammed, P and Shepherd, C (eds) *Gender in Caribbean Development*, 1988, St Augustine: UWI.
39 These are all noted legal philosophers.
40 The Hon Mr Justice VCRAC Crabbe, Former Professor of Law, UWI, 'Custom and the Statute Law' [1991] Stat LR 90, p 92.
41 Unreported Sup Ct Civil Appeal No 87 of 1984, Zimbabwe.

Zimbabwe had to examine the inconsistencies between customary law and a post-independent statute on the question of the status of women in a case of the seduction of an 18-year-old female. Under the new Act, she was a 'woman', as the age of majority had been changed from 21 to 18 years. In contrast, under the customary law, she was still a minor. Accordingly, the customary law did not recognise her right to sue independently. Instead, it gave to her father or guardian the authority to sue on her behalf.

The Court had to consider whether it was Parliament's intention to abolish the anomaly created by the exclusion of African women from attaining majority status because customary law deemed them perpetual minors. Considering that the new Act, unlike the previous enactment, had expressly been extended to apply to customary law, it found that Parliament did have such an intention. It intended to create an equal status between men and women and to ignore custom.[42]

REFORMS BASED ON CUSTOM

Incorporating established West Indian customs into the law will give a more just and realistic picture of West Indian society. The legislatures of the region and, to a lesser extent, the judiciary, have begun to acknowledge this. Several countries in the region have changed the law by legislation to abolish the legal concept and effects of 'illegitimate' or 'bastard' children. In Jamaica, for example, the Status of Children Act provides that 'the relationship between every person and his father and mother shall be determined irrespective of whether the father and mother are or have been married to each other . . . The rule of construction whereby in any instrument words of relationship signify only legitimate relationship . . . is hereby abolished.'[43]

Similarly, the practice of 'squatting' on unoccupied land, perhaps a hangover from generations of deprivation by a landless, dispossessed people, is now given some legitimacy in certain Caribbean legal systems. Typically, in the region, laws on squatting are lenient. For example, in Grenada, after 12 years of undisturbed 'squatting', a squatter is entitled to title of the land. The common law notion of property ownership is perhaps not as justifiable in such a context.

Settled land use and occupation have traditionally given rise to property rights in other circumstances and may be supported by statute. In the case of *AG for British Honduras v Bristowe*,[44] the Privy Council held that settlers of the land had acquired property rights against the Crown on the basis of their occupancy and use of the land for a period of more than 60 years. At that time, the Nellum Tempus Act 1861 prevented the acquisition of title by the Crown over land that had been possessed for periods over 60 years.

On occasion, case law may be just as innovative. In an intriguing judgment from

---

42   The case is criticised by Crabbe, *op cit*, p 40.
43   Law No 36 of 1976, s 3(1) and (2). The original philosophy behind the rejection of illegitimate children by the law seems to have been this: 'A promiscuous intercourse and an uncertain parentage, if they were universal, would soon dissolve the frame of the Constitution, from the infinity of claims and contested rights of succession. For this reason, the begetting of an illegitimate child is reputed a violation of the social compacts'. Long, E, *History of Jamaica*, 1774, London: Lowndes, repr in *Slaves, Free Men, Citizens: West Indian Perspectives* 1973, USA: Anchor, p 81.
44   (1880) 6 App Cas 143 (PC, British Honduras). British Honduras is now Belize.

Trinidad and Tobago, the case of *Lett v R*,[45] the Court of Appeal refrained, at least, from denying the relevance of customary norms. The appellant was convicted of murdering another woman during a quarrel. Her defence was provocation, on the basis that the woman had called her an old 'mule', meaning a barren woman in dialect. The appellant also contended that the victim was a 'socouyant' who sucked the baby out of her womb every time she became pregnant.[46] While the Court did not refer directly to custom, it was of the opinion that such a situation could have grounded a defence in provocation and had been rightly left the jury. There was, therefore, an implicit acceptance of the relevance of customary mores in the law, in this case to contradict well-established common law rules that words do not ground the defence of provocation.

In Commonwealth countries other than the Caribbean, a more proactive approach to customary law may be discerned. The judicial practice in respect of custom is to recognise it to the extent that it does not conflict with fundamental precepts of the common law, or even 'modern' notions of law. We can draw this conclusion even from the Zimbabwean case of *Katekwe*, considered above. The underlying policy of the court seemed to have been that the inequality of women as evidenced under customary law conflicted with modern, 'civilised' notions of law as expressed under the common law.

DIFFICULTIES IDENTIFYING CUSTOM THROUGH ORAL TRADITIONS

Despite some successes, custom continues to be too rarely identified by the courts or Legislature in the Commonwealth Caribbean. It appears that indigenous norms and values which form the basis of custom succumb easily to English and other external influences and ideals of what law should be.

Our customs are inevitably gleaned from evidence through our oral tradition. This may be inaccessible or unreliable. Only in rare instances are customs and practices documented since the region is not noted for historical record-keeping. Even where written accounts have been made, such recorded history may be coloured or distorted, either deliberately or through misunderstanding. In fact, recounts of some West Indian history by early writers who were mere observers of West Indian society, have been treated with suspicion by later indigenous historians. Indeed, Eric Williams, renowned West Indian historian, complained that 'Imperialist historians openly set out to despise the West Indian capacity', and called on the Trinidad peoples to reject the histories written by those who 'sought only to justify the indefensible'.[47] Thus, the description of customs in those periods as described by these early historians may be inaccurate or even dubious and conflicting accounts may ensue, making it even more difficult for a court to identify. This is a phenomenon well recognised in relation to the historical accounts of slavery, one which contemporary West Indian historians have set about correcting.

---

45   (1963) 6 WIR 92.

46   *Ibid.* A 'socouyant' is a figure in Trinidad mythology. She is a beautiful woman who appears at night and sucks the blood out of her victims.

47   'A Lecture on *Intellectual Decolonisation*' 29 April 1964, Howard University, Washington, DC, p 13, Eric Williams Memorial Collection, St Augustine: UWI, No 638.

One South African case, *Alexkor Ltd & Anor v Richtersveld*,[48] describes this self-same dilemma in adjudicating on the evidence of South African custom. The case gives some helpful advice as to how courts should locate and view legal custom:

> In applying indigenous law, it is important to bear in mind that, unlike common law, indigenous law is not written ... indigenous law may be established by reference to writers on indigenous law and other authorities and sources, and may include the evidence of witnesses if necessary. Caution must be exercised when dealing with text-books and old authorities because of the tendency to view indigenous law through the prism of legal conceptions that are foreign to it. In the course of establishing indigenous law, courts may also be confronted with conflicting views on what indigenous law on a subject provides. The dangers of looking at indigenous law through a common law prism are obvious. The two systems of law developed in different situations, under different cultures and in response to different conditions.[49]

THE INDIGENOUS PEOPLES AND CUSTOM

Indigenous peoples in the region, the Amerindians and Mayas, are often referred to as 'Caribs and Arawaks'. Archaeologists however explain that as generic names, these are inaccurate. For example, the indigenous peoples of Jamaica and other parts of the region are Tainos, who are defined by Rouse as 'the ethnic group that inhabited the Bahamian Archipelago, most of the Greater Antilles, and the northern part of the Lesser Antilles prior to and during the time of Columbus'.[50]

If we were to acknowledge the fact that these indigenous peoples, who lived here when the territories were rediscovered, were a people with established laws and customs, we could include any remaining practices of theirs in our judicial recognition of legal custom. Yet, because of historical prejudice against these indigenous peoples, the lack of adequate historical verification and the possible incompatibility with the English common law, this is an exceedingly difficult exercise. Consequently, any customs to be verified are biased towards those which can be identified from the date of the reception of law during the colonial period. An important exception is with respect to land use and title.

Yet, the Amerindians and Mayas were not without their authoritative customs and legal processes. Anthropologists have noted, for example, that amongst the Amerindians 'crimes were punished by the injured party or his relatives, the *lex*

---

48   [2004] 4 LRC 38 (Constit Ct).

49   *Ibid*, pp 40–41. See also *Members of the Yorta Yorta Aboriginal Community v Victoria & Others* [2003] 3 LRC 185 (HCA Australia) at p 205, where Gleeson CJ noted that 'any analysis of the traditional laws and customs of societies having no well-developed written language by using analytical tools developed in connection with very differently organised societies is fraught with evidential difficulty'.

50   Irving Rouse, *The Tainos: Rise and Decline of the People who Greeted Columbus*, 1992, New Haven: Yale University Press, p 185. Since the name 'Arawak', or sometimes 'Amerindian', is often used in the existing literature, in this book we sometimes use the more general terms 'Amerindian' or 'indigenous peoples' to describe peoples who originally inhabited the region, to avoid confusion and pay tribute to the original reports. It is acknowledged, however, that the Arawaks and Tainos were distinct ethnic groups, the Arawaks being the peoples who lived in the northern part of the Guianas; Rouse, *ibid*, p 173. The Arawaks are believed to have inhabited the Guiana Coast, South Eastern Trinidad, centuries after Columbus's arrival, around 1894 and are included as one of five Indian nations that existed in Trinidad. Jane, C, *The Four Voyages of Columbus*, 1988, NY: Douer. See also Lesley-Gail Atkinson (ed) *The Earliest Inhabitants – The Dynamics of the Jamaican Taino*, 2006, Kingston, Jamaica: UWI Press.

talionis being rigidly observed'.[51] There was apparently 'no such thing as public punishments'.[52] In the case of adultery, public action was taken by the Orinoco Carib. The 'Carib is the only nation which has a punishment fixed for adulterers, who are put to death by the whole village populace in the public place'.[53]

Early case law recorded the conflict between Amerindian custom and the common law. In *The Fiscal v Billy William*,[54] the judgment of the Court of Criminal Justice of Demerara and Essequibo to sentence the appellant Amerindian to death for slaying his wife for adultery was considered by the Court of Appeal. While the Court rejected the view that Amerindians comprised a free nation existing beyond the jurisdiction of the English courts, it acknowledged the customs of the Amerindian peoples. Yet, the existence of these customs presented difficulty to the Court as it considered that it was unjust to impose the common law in such circumstances. In his despatch to Governor D'Urban, Lord Goderich said:

> When this convict inflicted a deadly wound on his wife, he seems to have been actuated by a wide opinion of justice, and to have conformed to the traditionary maxims of his tribe . . . he had been taught to believe himself the proper judge and avenger of such guilt. I entirely concur . . . in thinking it impossible to punish a homicide committed under such circumstances in the same manner as wilful murder is punished on a member of a Christian . . . community.[55]

Although Lord Goderich's first impulse was to set the convict free, he decided to banish him instead. This sentence was a further acknowledgement of Amerindian custom as the Court recognised that if the appellant had been set free, his wife's family would have slain him in revenge.

Similar difficulties were encountered in other colonial territories with indigenous populations. In *R v William*, it was noted: 'Although dwelling among us . . . they [the indigenous peoples] are still essentially a distinct people, governed by their own customs and petty chiefs'.[56]

These cases represent a measure of judicial recognition of Amerindian custom. It cannot be said that this recognition was given the certainty and clarity of law as required by the rules of custom. Still, it represented limited acknowledgement that the customs and practices of the indigenous peoples were authoritative and binding in their own communities sufficient to change the shape and application of the common law as applied to them. This, after all, is the substance of customary law, although it supports our earlier argument that the rules of custom must be modified if they are to be meaningful in Commonwealth Caribbean societies.

Yet, such recognition was short lived. After emancipation, as a matter of policy, in general, the laws of the State were applied equally to all persons and any

---

51 Roth, WE, 'An Introductory Study of the Arts, Crafts and Customs of the Guiana Indians (1916–17)', (1924) 38 Bureau of Amerindian Ethnology, Washington, p 557.
52 *Ibid*, pp 557–58.
53 Gumilla, J, 'Historia Natura'(1791) 1 Civil y Geografica de las Naciones Situadas en las Riveras del Rio Orinoco, Barcelona, p 132, cited in Shahabuddeen, M, *The Legal System of Guyana*, 1973, Georgetown: Guyana Printers, p 226.
54 Report from the Select Committee on Aborigines (British Settlements), PP 1837 (425) vii, 1, p 83.
55 *Ibid*.
56 Governor Wodehouse to Labouchère, CO No 49, 19 April 1856, cited by Hall, HL, *The Colonial Office, A History*, 1937, London: Longmans, Greene, p 143.

special acknowledgement of the customs of the indigenous peoples was almost forgotten.[57]

Today, it is perhaps more accurate to say that, rather than the law attempting to assimilate the indigenous peoples fully, or, on the other hand, acknowledge their customs, it adopts a relatively detached stance. As we will see, custom, as it relates to property rights of the indigenous peoples, is treated differently because of new legal developments. In other respects, however, although there is *de jure* jurisdiction over these indigenous peoples, accounts of oral history demonstrate that the law will not often intervene, at least in relation to well-defined indigenous communities.[58] This approach accords with fairly recent international law developments toward the self-determination of indigenous peoples.

Shahabuddeen writes, for example: 'So the existence of jurisdiction did not itself settle the difficult and sometimes delicate question of its exercise'.[59] The result is that the indigenous peoples of the region have a certain margin of leeway under the law. In the case of Guyana, this may also be because of geographical circumstance. By and large, the Amerindians of Guyana are found deep in the hinterland of the country in areas not easily accessible by the authorities. In Belize and Dominica, the indigenous peoples live in a specially reserved areas. Similarly, the Maroons, the indigenous peoples of Jamaica, live in a particular district. Alternatively, we may argue that the attitude of the law is simply one of neglect.

PROPERTY RIGHTS OF INDIGENOUS PEOPLES – LINKING CUSTOM WITH COMITY

The recognition of native title

Special mention must be made of 'native title' or 'indigenous title'[60] to land occupied and used by the indigenous peoples of the region and indeed, the world. This is a form of property title which is derived from a recognition of and respect for the customs of indigenous populations as they relate to land. The full legal recognition of such title is a relatively recent phenomenon and is part of a broader movement to rectify some of the historical injustices meted out to the original peoples by those who conquered their lands.

Under the common law, 'native title' is now an accepted concept. However, 'native title' is also recognised in civil law countries. Further, international law has contributed greatly to the legitimacy of the doctrine of 'native title', seeing it as an aspect of human rights and self-determination.[61]

Under the common law approach, we will expect to see the familiar rules of legal

---

57   Initially, laws except the criminal law had been applied. After emancipation, the Act made the application of the law all-encompassing. Note however, our discussion in Chapter 1 ('Introduction to Law and Legal Systems in the Commonwealth Caribbean') and the provision made for reservations of indigenous peoples in Guyana and Dominica.

58   See earlier mention of the interview with the Amerindian Chief of Dominica, Chief Corrie, in Chapter 1.

59   *Op cit.* Shahabuddeen, fn 53, p 229.

60   Sometimes called 'aboriginal title'.

61   James Anaya 'Indigenous Peoples' Participatory Rights in Relation to Decisions About Natural Resource Extraction: The More Fundamental Issue of what Rights Indigenous Peoples have in Lands and Resources', (2005) 22 Ariz J Int'l & Comp Law 7.

custom, as discussed above, being employed. However, there are some significantly different nuances which remain to be noted, in particular, the source of the customs at issue and the flexibility allowed because of the particular historical circumstance.

In identifying the existence of native title under the common law, Anaya asserts that:

> Courts in common law countries that have developed from colonial settlement patterns, including Australia, Canada and the United States . . . a body of doctrine that specifically upholds 'original' or 'aboriginal' rights of the indigenous or native peoples . . . Within this body of common law doctrine, aboriginal rights to lands exist by virtue of historical patterns of use or occupancy and may rise to the level of a legal entitlement in the nature of exclusive ownership, referred to as 'native' or 'aboriginal title'.[62]

The recognition of native title brings with it entitlements to free-standing rights to fish, hunt, gather, or to otherwise use resources or have access to lands.[63]

Native title has its origins in the characteristic customs of land use and occupation by indigenous peoples. It is recognised that the rights which attach to native title are collective rights, to be held and enjoyed by the particular indigenous population as a whole. The underlying customs and mores which give rise to native title are also identified as being cultural and even spiritual in nature, given the particular attitudes of indigenous peoples to land.

In a defining case on native title under the common law, *Mabo v Queensland (No 2)*,[64] Justice Brennan of the High Court of Australia gave a helpful explanation about the origins and nature of native title. He said:

> Native title has its origin in and is given its content by the traditional laws acknowledged by and the traditional customs observed by the Indigenous inhabitants of a territory. The nature and incidents of native title must be ascertained as a matter of fact by reference to those laws and customs.[65]

In *Mabo v Queensland*,[66] Justice Brennan affirmed that native title and aboriginal rights in general flow, not only from customs as is recognised under the common law, but also from international law.[67] These international law rights are buttressed by several Conventions, such as the International Covenant on Civil and Political Rights, the International Labour Organisation Convention (No 169) on Indigenous and Tribal peoples in Independent Countries and the American Convention on Human Rights.

In addition, indigenous rights to lands are now accepted as customary international law, not merely domestic custom, as noted by the Inter-American Court on Human Rights in *Awas Tingni*.[68] The Court accepted the view of the Inter-American Commission that given the gradual emergence of an international consensus on the rights of indigenous peoples to their traditional lands, such rights are now a matter of

---

62   James Anaya 'Maya Aboriginal Land and Resource Rights and the Conflict Over Logging in Southern Belize', [1998] 1 Yale H R Dev & Dev L J 17, at p 23.
63   As explained eg in *Antoine v Washington* 420 US 194 (1975), *R v Adams* [1996] 110 CCC (3d) 97 (Can).
64   (1992) 175 CLR 1 (Australia).
65   *Ibid*, at p 58.
66   (1988) 166 CLR (Australia).
67   *Ibid*, p 42.
68   *Case of the Mayagna (Sumo) Awas Tingni Community v Nicaragua*, Inter-Am Ct HR (Ser C) No 79 (2001) (judgment on merits and reparations of 31 August 2001). Abridged version reprinted in 19 Ariz J Int'l & Comp Law 395.

customary international law. These rights were separate and distinct from the rights located under domestic law. Thus, the international right to property, as articulated under Article 21 of the American Convention on Human Rights, encompassed the communal property regimes of indigenous peoples as defined by their own customs and traditions. Accordingly, 'possession of the land should suffice for indigenous communities lacking real title to property of the land to obtain official recognition of that property'.[69]

Native title may be protected under statute or even treaty, but it is noteworthy that it may exist independently of such legislative instruments, being viewed in the nature of custom which is to be judicially acknowledged. For example, in Guyana, under the Amerindian Amendment Act 1976, certain lands were formally identified and demarcated and the Amerindian community was given title over them. Section 8 of the Act states:

> all the rights, titles and interests of the State in and over the lands situated within the boundaries of any district, area or village shall without further assurance be deemed to be transferred to and vested in the respective (Amerindian) Council for and on behalf of the Amerindian Community.[70]

The particular lands are identified in the Schedule of the Act. However, full ownership and control of the lands remain uncertain and proposals have been made to strengthen the law by including further provisions in the Constitution.[71]

Assertions to native title by the Mayas and the Maroons

By contrast, in Belize, the ownership and control of lands occupied by the indigenous peoples, the Mayas, have been contentious. In a landmark case, *Toledo Maya Cultural Council v AG of Belize*,[72] the Mayas of the Toledo district asserted rights over lands and resources in that district in response to grants from the Belize government giving logging concessions to private companies over 480,000 acres in the Toledo district. The Maya asserted these rights in the absence of any government grant or specific act of recognition, seeking a declaration that they 'hold rights to occupy, hunt, fish and otherwise use' the contested lands and that such rights 'in accordance with the common law and relevant international law, arise from and are commensurate with the customary land tenure patterns of the Toledo Maya'.[73] They also asserted a violation of their rights to property and equality under the Belize Constitution.

Unfortunately, no judgment ensued from the Supreme Court in the *Toledo* Case.

While the Supreme Court of Belize deprived us of a full exploration of the issue of domestic customary land title in the Commonwealth Caribbean, we may extrapolate the correct legal position from other common law countries which have similar legal

---

69   *Ibid, 19 Ariz J Int'l & Comp Law* at p 438. Nicaragua was ordered to demarcate the land, giving title to the Tingni Community and taking into account its customary law, values, customs and mores.

70   Traditional rights of usage of the Guyanese indigenous peoples over their lands have been recognised by successive treaties with the Dutch and English, for example, under the Articles of Capitulation 1803.

71   See RW James, *above*, fn 20, p 175.

72   No 510 of 1996, Sup Ct, Belize.

73   *Ibid* pp 1–2, Notice of Originating Motion.

systems and experiences with indigenous land usages, such as Australia, New Zealand, Canada and South Africa.

The acknowledgement of native title and property rights over lands and natural resources originating from customary land tenure patterns of indigenous peoples also recognise the cultural and even spiritual elements of such land practices.[74]

More recently, the Maroons of Jamaica have asserted a claim to native title, in circumstances similar to those in the *Toledo* case. The assertion by the Maroons that they are indigenous peoples entitled to native title may appear surprising, given that the Maroons are identified as peoples of African ancestral roots, who refused to succumb to the evils of slavery, escaping to the Jamaican mountains and successfully battling the Europeans to retain their freedom. As such, they were not in Jamaica at the time of the European conquest. It is undisputed, however, that they have settled in the Cockpit country for centuries, maintaining their own customs. They have also been declared indigenous peoples by UNESCO. Their recognition as indigenous peoples comes in part because they intermixed with members of the Taino population, the native peoples of Jamaica.[75]

Maroon communities, called Bush Negroes, also exist in Suriname, living in the interior of the country. They have largely 'been left to their own criminal jurisdiction for minor offences'.[76]

Identifying the group

Since native rights are collective rights, the court must first identify the group asserting title as an indigenous community. This requires that the community be identified as one existing from antiquity, practising the mores and customs of the ancestral group. There must be, in essence, the existence of a 'culturally distinctive community or society with historical origins that predate the effective exercise of sovereignty by the State or its colonial precursor'.[77] Further, that community must be practising 'customary land tenure or resource that can be identified as a part of the cultural life of the community.'[78]

In Belize, for example, there is documented evidence from archaeologists that the Mayas occupied and used the land in the Toledo district from ancient times, extending as far back as at least 400AD, and this land use and occupation continued without interruption. The evidence also shows that there are ancestral links between the people who occupy the Toledo district today and the indigenous peoples of that period, establishing 'cultural continuity'.[79]

---

74 Note, however, that rights to mining and mineral resources appear to be less identifiable. See, eg, the limits in the ILO Convention.

75 Two peace treaties were signed between the Maroons and the British in 1739 and 1740, and lands were granted to the Maroons under these treaties. See Carey, B, *The Maroon Story*, 1977, Jamaica: Agouti Press.

76 Munneke, H and Dekker, A 'Suriname' in Kritzer, H (ed) *Legal Systems of the World*, 2002, USA: ABC-CLIO Inc.

77 Anaya 1998, *above*, fn 62, p 30.

78 *Ibid*, p 31.

79 See Richard M Leventhal, 'Maya Occupation and Continuity in Toledo' 1–10 (24 February 1997) unpublished manuscript, appended to the Affidavit of Richard M Leventhal, in the case of *Toledo Maya County Council v AG of Belize*, No 510 of 1996 (Sup Ct, Belize).

The Mayas of the Toledo district in Belize perpetuated their land tenure and resource use customs in a separate part of the country, the Toledo District. They also maintained patterns of authority and regulation over these customs, for example, in the use of the Alcalde, the authority figure of the community. Consequently, well-defined rules and mechanisms of control that regulate land and resource use within and among villages may be identified. Such a structure has been described as one of the defining characteristics of contemporary Maya culture in Toledo.[80] The centrality of customary land tenure and resource use to Maya survival and cultures is high-lighted by the affidavits from Maya individuals. These affidavits provide first-hand accounts of Maya agricultural, hunting, fishing and gathering practices, and uses of forests and woods.[81]

While the existence of this culturally distinct group was contested by the Belize State, as seen below, the Inter-American Commission accepted the evidence that the Maya were indeed the indigenous peoples of Belize and that they had maintained their customs and culture.

Consistency in indigenous custom

It is well established that indigenous customs may give rise to native title even if these customs have been adapted to meet contemporary needs, or those of the State, provided that they retain their indigenous character. In *Members of the Yorta Yorta Aboriginal Community v Victoria & Others*,[82] the Yorta Yorta tribe appealed a decision on the basis that the trial judge had employed a 'frozen in time approach', not making proper allowance for appropriate adaptations of their indigenous customs. Gleeson CJ reiterated the established principle that although there was a requirement that the traditional customs be those which existed at the time of conquest,

> demonstrating some change to, or adaptation of, traditional law or custom . . . will not *necessarily* be fatal to a native title claim . . . The key question is whether the law and custom can still be seen to be traditional law and traditional custom. Is the change or adaptation of such a kind that it can no longer be said that the rights or interests asserted are possessed under the . . . traditional customs observed . . .?[83]

Continuity in indigenous custom

The rule on continuity has been similarly modified. Consequently, while, according to the rules of custom and international law, the criteria of continuity and consistency must be fulfilled, the courts have ruled that in establishing continuity in the customs and usage attached to native title, there is no need to prove 'an unbroken chain of continuity' between present and prior occupation. This is an acknowledgement of the circumstances of colonial conquest when the indigenous peoples were often forced to move from the land, at least temporarily. To do otherwise would be 'perpetuating the historical injustice suffered by aboriginal peoples at the hands of colonisers who

---

80   Anaya 1998, p 36, relying on affidavits from archaeological experts attached to the *Toledo Maya County Council v AG of Belize* Case, No 510 of 1996 (Sup Ct, Belize).
81   *Ibid.*
82   [2003] LRC 3LRC 185 (HCA Australia).
83   *Ibid*, p 213.

failed to respect' the rights of indigenous peoples.[84] The fact that the nature of the occupation has changed, or been interrupted would not ordinarily preclude a claim to native title, as long as a substantial connection between the indigenous people and the land endures.[85] What is required is that there be 'substantial maintenance of the connection' between the people and the land.[86] This substantial claim was established with respect to the Maya people of Belize, despite periods when they were forced to evacuate the district by the Spanish. For centuries the Maya's system of land use consisted of migratory patterns. Even after forcible removal by the Spanish, they never abandoned their lands. 'The historical record shows that the Maya consistently have resisted efforts by the Spanish and the British to remove them or encroach upon their lands and that, to the extent possible, they have returned to the lands from which they or their kin have been ousted.'[87]

The rule of custom that the relevant practice must have existed since time immemorial is therefore fulfilled, but taking account of historical realities. The courts have actually used the phrase 'time immemorial', as seen, for example, in cases before the US Supreme Court.[88]

How distinguished?

It has been held that indigenous rights and interests may be defeated where they conflict with fundamental tenets of the common law. In *Yorta Yorta v Victoria*,[89] for example, the High Court of Appeal of Australia noted that the reference to the *recognition* of indigenous rights and interests serves to emphasise that the common law may refuse to recognise such rights and interests where they are 'antithetical to fundamental tenets of the common law'. The point is also made in the case of *Wik Peoples v State of Queensland and Others*.[90] In *Wik*, the High Court of Australia noted:

> Those [customary] rights are then measured against the rights conferred on the grantees ... If inconsistency is held to exist between the rights and interests conferred by native title, rights and interests must yield to that extent, to the rights of the grantees.[91]

However, as discussed below, under international law, the threshold for extinguishing indigenous rights because of conflict with competing legal traditions is higher, given the treatment of indigenous rights as customary international law and inalienable rights.

---

84   *Delgamakwu v British Columbia* (1997) 153 DLR (4th) 193.
85   *Ibid.*
86   *Mabo v Queensland, above*, fn 64, at 257–258. See also *Members of the Yorta Yorta Aboriginal Community v Victoria & Others, above*, fn 82.
87   Anaya 1998, *above*, fn 62, p 38.
88   See, eg *Oneida v Oneida Indian Nation* 470 US 226, 234 (1984).
89   *Above*, fn 82, p 211.
90   (1997) CLB 201, 205; (1996) 141 ALR 129, at p 133.
91   *Ibid.* The case concerned the recognition of native or customary title to land in the face of a statute which did not explicitly recognise such title and impliedly abolished it. In finding that the statute should not be construed as necessarily extinguishing native title, the court made specific acknowledgement of customary rights and law: 'Whether there was extinguishment can only be determined by reference to such particular rights and interests as may be asserted and established in relation to the land ... This cannot be done by some general statement. It must focus specifically on the traditions, customs and practices of the particular Aboriginal group claiming the right'. *Ibid*, at p 205. See also, *Thayorre People v State of Queensland and Others* (1996) 141 129, HC.

International law aspects

Because of the failure of the Supreme Court of Belize to adequately adjudicate on the Toledo Maya Community case, the Maya subsequently took the matter to the Inter-American Commission of Human Rights.[92] The Commission concluded that the State had violated the property rights guaranteed in Article XXIII of the American Declaration, to the detriment of the Mayan community, by failing to adopt effective measures recognising the right to communal land ownership of lands that have been traditionally occupied by these indigenous peoples, as well as by failing to delineate and establish titles by other means, and by failing to implement the required mechanisms to clarify and protect the legal status of the lands on which these indigenous people are entitled to exercise their rights.

The Commission also found that the State had violated the Mayan people's right to property guaranteed under Article XXIII of the American Declaration, to the detriment of the Mayan people and in the absence of their informed consent, by granting logging and oil concessions to third parties for the exploitation of resources located within lands that should have been delineated and titled, or protected by other means.

In addition, the Commission found violations of the Mayan people's right to equal protection under the law, right to non-discrimination and right to judicial protection. Accordingly, the Commission recommended that the State of Belize:

1. Adopt in domestic law, and through fully informed consultations with the Maya people, the legislative, administrative, and any other measures necessary to delimit, demarcate and title or otherwise clarify and protect the territory in which the Maya people have a communal property right, in accordance with their customary land practices . . .

2. Carry out the measures to delimit . . . and title . . . lands of the Maya people . . . abstain from any acts that might lead the agents of the State, or third parties acting with its acquiescence or its tolerance, to affect the existence, value, use or enjoyment of the property located in the geographic area occupied and used by the Maya people . . .

3. Repair the environmental damage caused by the logging concessions granted by the State over territory traditionally occupied and used by the Maya people.[93]

CUSTOM OR COMITY?

While both domestic law and international law have located the rights of indigenous peoples firmly in customary law, it is arguable that there are philosophical differences between the traditional principles of custom and the circumstances of indigenous rights. The English rules of custom grew up *within* a legal system and speak to practices which deviate from the more widely spread norms. Yet, these deviant practices are insular and can still be clearly identified as part of the legal system.

---

92 Report No 40/04, Case 12.053, Merits, Mayan Indigenous Communities from the Toledo District, Belize, 12 October 2004.
93 *Ibid.*

In the case of indigenous peoples, those practices with which we are concerned originated from an entirely separate and different legal tradition, but found their way into a competing legal system through conquest. In this transplantation process, although the legal tradition was replaced formally, these practices or customs were not, and they survived as marginal mores within the new legal tradition. The source of the law being affirmed is not internal but external.

Giving recognition to these indigenous practices is not, therefore, merely recognising a local custom. Rather, it is giving recognition and respect to a competing legal tradition. In this sense, therefore, it is more in the nature of comity, the principle of private international law, which requires that respect be given to the laws and legal traditions of another country.

Courts have not used the language of comity, but they have recognised and made explicit reference to the legal systems of the indigenous peoples. In *Delgamuukw v British Columbia*,[94] for example, Lamer CJ, examined the source of native title and said:

> Aboriginal title arises from the prior occupation ... by original peoples. That prior occupation is relevant ... because aboriginal title originates in part from pre-existing systems of aboriginal law. The law of aboriginal title does not, however, only seek to determine the historic rights of aboriginal peoples to land; it also seeks to afford legal protection to prior occupation in the present day.[95]

Similarly, in *Members of the Yorta Yorta Aboriginal Community v Victoria & Others*,[96] Gleeson CJ emphasised that:

> recognition [of native title] by the common law is a requirement that emphasises the fact that there is an intersection between legal systems and that the intersection occurred at the time of sovereignty. The native title and interests ... are those which existed at sovereignty, survived that fundamental change in legal regime, and now, by resort to the processes of the new legal order, can be enforced and protected.

Gleeson CJ made the point to underscore that native title does not originate in the common law.[97] Rather, common law methods are employed to identify and protect it.

It has been noted too that because these indigenous customs originated outside of the dominant legal systems imported by settler societies, aboriginal rights generally are held to be inalienable, except to the sovereign that asserts authority over the corresponding territory.[98]

Similar arguments may be raised with respect to customs transported from Africa. However, although Africa clearly had established legal systems before the imperialist powers invaded the continent, the legal systems of Africa have not been given express recognition by the courts as have those of the indigenous peoples.

This is another reason why the rules of custom as identified by the common law can be seen to be somewhat alien and even inappropriate to the experiences of the Commonwealth Caribbean and other parts of the Commonwealth, all previously conquered territories.

---

94   (1997) 153 DLR (4th) 193 (Can).

95   *Ibid*, 246–247.

96   *Above*, fn 82, pp 211–212.

97   He said: 'To speak of the "common law requirements" of native title is to invite a fundamental error. Native title is not a creature of the common law.' *Ibid*, p 211.

98   See *United States v Santa Fe Pac RR Co* 314 US 339, 353–354 (1941); *Mabo v Queensland (No 2)*, *above*, fn 66 at 58–60. See Anaya 1998, *above*, fn 62, p 25.

With the dawn of the 21st century and the resolve of the indigenous peoples of the hemisphere to achieve self-governance, or, at least, some measure of self-determination, we may see more evidence of indigenous customs written into the law in the future.[99]

COLLECTIVE RIGHTS AND WEST INDIAN CUSTOM

It may be observed that many of the customs identified in the region underscore notions of collective rights and interests as opposed to individual rights, such collective rights being located squarely in values of community. This is perhaps most obvious with respect to the land ownership issues discussed above which were clearly disparate from individualistic notions of landholding known to English and Western law.

Such ideas of community, manifested in ideas of collective responsibilities and interests, may be seen also in other forms of property and social interaction, largely untapped by the law. For example, a unique custom of 'banking' money, complete with its own unique loan functions, is found in the region. Known by various names such as the 'sou sou' in Trinidad and Tobago and the 'turn' elsewhere in the region, it is executed by a group of persons pooling their monies, and an administrator distributing the sum of the pool at various intervals to each individual member in turn. This is a form of capital which enables poor persons, often unable to obtain loans in formal financial institutions, to secure enough funds for a particular purpose. Similarly, the phenomenon whereby community members get together to carry out a particular task, such as helping to build a house or till the land, is further evidence of community-based custom.

If we are to conceive of custom as creating rights, the collective ethos of so much of West Indian custom may prove a further obstacle in the elevation of custom in our legal system. In Commonwealth Caribbean countries, we have become accustomed to a system of rights which prioritises the individual over the collective given that our Constitutions are based on notions of civil and political rights which are individualistic in character. It has proven difficult in the past to interpret our Constitutions with a more liberal conception of rights in the collective, such as, for example, economic and cultural rights. The infamous case of *Collymore v AG*[100] which sounded the death knell of the right to strike, an important collective right for trade unions, is but one example. It will require a significant step forward to re-think the value of collective rights and afford more legitimacy to customs based on notions of community. Yet, given the psyche of our West Indian societies, it will be a step well taken.

THE INSULARITY OF THE COMMON LAW AND THE IMPACT ON CUSTOM

The argument on the use of customs in West Indian law is related to the broader points on the failure of the common law in general, and the Commonwealth

---

99   See Chapter 1 for a discussion of the Amerindian Treaty which has these objectives.
100   (1967) 12 WIR 5.

Caribbean common law in particular, to consider the social norms and needs of the society at large.

The common law can be fairly criticised as being insular, narrow-minded, imperialist and even racist.[101] It has often refused to accept, within its process of judicial reasoning, that social, cultural and anthropological perspectives may legitimately inform the law in certain circumstances. With the recent exception of the indigenous peoples, nowhere is this more apparent than in the attitude of the common law to the customs and laws of its conquered peoples of other lands, peoples who, today, we accept had strong legal processes and customs of their own. Yet, even while legal scholars may accept this sociological fact, they fail often to reflect that understanding in the legal thought processes of the common law.

Cottran and Rubin[102] argue that sophisticated legal concepts underpin the administration of justice in the traditional African societies. These can illuminate modern legal thinking. They give as an example the notion of ownership as subject to the superior rights of the social group. Such notions of ownership have built in attitudes which can be helpful in global problems. For example, the underlying principle of a trusteeship of land, in place of the concept of absolute ownership, could alleviate environmental pollution. Land is an inheritance to be preserved for future owners.

RW James further complains that certain concepts which we have accepted as being European actually have roots in African law and custom. He makes reference to the concept of corporate personality in traditional land law as being African and not borrowed from English law.[103]

From the indigenous peoples we have seen too the spiritual relationship with land and notions of collective responsibility that attach to it. These are values that are now being learnt by peoples all over the world concerned about care-taking the environment and the creatures that inhabit the earth. Yet, our common law has been slow to identify and acknowledge these value systems as legal customs of the particular groups that make up our plural societies.

From our discussion it is evident that the existing rules of customary law are inadequate to address the needs of West Indian society. An alternative and simpler means of elevating established West Indian customs to a source of law would be via the Constitution. This would not be an unheard of step. It is the route taken in countries like Papua New Guinea and Ghana. In Ghana, the 'common law' is listed as a source of law under the Constitution. However, this 'common law' is defined to include customary law, 'the rules of law which by custom is applicable to particular communities of Ghana'.[104] In Papua New Guinea, custom is similarly enshrined in the Constitution as a source of law.[105] Interestingly, Papua New Guinea has chosen to deviate from the traditional English rules of customary law. For instance, it gives

---

101   A point occasionally acknowledged by the courts. For example, in rejecting the theory of 'terra nullius' (uninhabited lands), which operated to deny indigenous peoples title and rights over land, Justice Brennan of the High Court of Australia in *Mabo v Queensland* fn 64, *above*, pp 41–42, described the theory as 'unjust and discriminatory' and asserted that it 'it is imperative in today's world that the common law should neither be nor be seen to be frozen in an age of racial discrimination.'

102   Cottran, E and Rubin, N *Readings in African Law*, 1970, London: Cass.

103   *Above*, fn 20, p 167.

104   The Constitution of Ghana, 1969, Chapter 1.

105   See the Constitution of Papua New Guinea, Schedule 2.

recognition of indigenous practices priority over antiquity. 'Custom', as defined by the Constitution:

> ... means the customs and usages of indigenous inhabitants of the country existing in relation to the matter in question at the time, when, and the place in relation to which the matter arises, regardless or not the custom or usage has existed from time immemorial.[106]

This emphasis was given judicial recognition in *Re Sannga Deceased*:[107]

> Custom ... develops from time to time ... The customs of our people ... are capable of meeting modern developments.

To the extent that customary practices can be located in West Indian society, they should likewise form a legitimate basis of the law. To borrow the words of Justice Bernard Narokobi:[108]

> My heart bleeds and longs for the day when our ... norms, customs, sanctions, perceptions and methods of dispute settlement will be given their fullest significance.[109]

---

106   *Ibid*, Schedule 1.
107   (1983) PNGLR 142, 157.
108   Judge of the National Court of Papua New Guinea and Principal Legal Advisor, cited in Kapi, M, 'The Underlying Law in Papua New Guinea', Ninth Commonwealth Law Conference, 1990, New Zealand Commerce Clearing House, p 129.
109   *Ibid*.

CHAPTER 11

CONVENTION AS A LEGAL SOURCE

The subject of Convention is more appropriately an aspect of constitutional juris-prudence. In fact, it has formed the basis of much scholarly constitutional discussion and debate, both within and outside the region.[1] It is discussed here briefly, as it has some significance as a source of law.

In the Commonwealth Caribbean, Conventions have particular importance in relation to certain political and constitutional procedures, such as the exercise of sovereign power. Unlike custom, convention is not limited to any particular location but, instead, to a particular activity or sphere.

The main controversy on Conventions surrounds their enforceability. Conven-tions existed primarily as non-justiciable practices in the UK and were transplanted into Commonwealth Caribbean legal systems. Today, many of them exist as codified legal principles enshrined in the Independence Constitutions. Does this change their original non-enforceable character? The short, but perhaps simplistic answer is yes, at least for most such Conventions. The importance of certain expressed political Conven-tions for us in the region, therefore, is that they now have constitutional authority, as they have been written into the Constitutions. Thus, they no longer depend on judicial recognition for legal force. Rather, they have been transformed into 'hard law' and are enforceable. We can no longer conclude, as does Hart, with respect to such trans-formed Conventions, that 'convention is not law because the courts do not recognise them as imposing a legal duty'.[2]

Yet, there are some written Conventions which are more contentious. While they may be enshrined in the Constitutions, they are difficult, if not impossible to enforce. Certainly, if we consider the doctrine of the reception of English law in relation to our discussion of Convention, there is authority for the view that certain parliamentary Conventions were not meant to be enforceable in Commonwealth Caribbean jurisdic-tions. These Conventions, such as parliamentary privilege, were meant to apply exclusively to the Houses of Parliament in England. They were born out of a particu-lar social circumstance which was not suited to the colonies and should not have been received as part of the common law. This view commended itself, for example, to the Guyanese courts in *Jagan v Gajraj*,[3] which held that the privileges, immunities and powers of the British Parliament are not automatically received by a colonial legis-lature. As such, the Speaker of the Assembly had no power to commit for breach of privilege.[4]

Examples of these difficult Conventions are that the Governor General or President[5] must assent to legislation before it is passed and that the Prime Minister

---

1   See, eg, DeMerieux, M, 'The Codification of Constitutional Conventions in the Commonwealth Caribbean' (1982) 32 ICLQ 263.

2   Hart, HLA, *The Concept of Law*, 1994, Oxford: Clarendon, p 118.

3   (1963) 5 WIR 333, p 340.

4   See, also, *Kelly v Carson* (1842) 4 Moo PCC 63 from Jamaica on the question of the power to commit contempt in Parliament.

5   The ceremonial Head of State. In countries which have named themselves Republics, such as Trinidad and Tobago, the office which used to be that of the Governor General, is now that of a President.

must consult with the Governor General on matters of State (the latter being a convention which is rarely practised). Similarly, in relation to the Convention that the President appoints senators on the advice of the Prime Minister, can the President refuse to appoint senators chosen by the Prime Minister? These Conventions call into question the very character of governance in West Indian States, where the fountain of power lies not in the ceremonial Head of State, but in the elected leader, the Prime Minister (or President, in Guyana).

The subject of political Convention caught the attention of the Trinidad and Tobago legal and political commentators in dramatic fashion. The controversies surrounded the then President, the ceremonial Head of State, who determined that he had certain Executive-type powers.

The Trinidad examples are complex and involved the refusal of the President, the Head of State, a non-executive office, to act upon the advice of the Prime Minister to revoke the appointment of two senators and replace them with two new senators and further to appoint as senators, seven persons who were defeated in the recently concluded December 2000 elections. The practice had been that the President would automatically accept the advice of the Prime Minister in such matters, but President Robinson refused to do so, allegedly in the public interest, drawing upon what he referred to as his right to advise, counsel and warn the Prime Minister in relation to the general discharge of his duties.[6]

Unfortunately, the constitutional dilemmas presented by the Trinidad and Tobago presidency on the issue of Convention were never answered with judicial authority, as the matters did not come before the courts. Nevertheless, it is doubtful whether a court, appraised of the fundamental principles of constitutional governance, would have held that an expansion of presidential power in such fashion was justifiable. To do so would render the system unworkable and dislocate the accountability of government served by democratic elections.

The issue is complicated by the fact that some functions allocated to Governors General or other ceremonial Heads of State are made expressly non-justiciable and therefore cannot be inquired into by the Court. One example is section 32(5) of the Constitution of Barbados[7] which reads: 'Where the Governor-General is directed to exercise any function in accordance with the recommendation or advice of, or with the concurrence of, or after consultation with, any person or authority, the question whether he has so exercised that function shall not be enquired into in any court'. Such ousting provisions make it imperative for the nature and extent of political Conventions to be determined precisely.

As we have seen, both conventions and custom evolve from the established usage and practices of a people. They must be recognised by the legal system before they are deemed to be law. Yet, there is an important philosophical difference between the two. While Convention represents almost exclusively another aspect of English social practice, custom in the Commonwealth Caribbean may, if allowed, reflect the

---

6   For political commentary on these scenarios see Ghany H, 'Constitutional Interpretation and Presidential Powers: The Case of Trinidad and Tobago', 2001, unpublished mimeo; and Ghany, H, 'Parliamentary Crisis and the Removal of the Speaker: The Case of Trinidad and Tobago' (1997) 3 J Legis Stud 112. Certain new consultative powers had been given to the President under the new Trinidad and Tobago Constitution of 1976, such as the appointment of the Chief Justice after consultation with the Prime Minister, but this was not one of them.
7   The Barbados Independence Order 1966, SI No 1455.

indigenous practices of the region. It is perhaps ironic that it is Convention rather than custom which has been enshrined in our written Constitutions.

Yet, in the political arena, there is an increasing enthusiasm for treating convention as hard law. This perhaps reflects, not so much the suitability of these English grounded practices to our legal systems, but rather the lack of adequate and consciously formulated mechanisms to drive our constitutional democracies. With the several initiatives toward constitutional reform, it is expected that such political Conventions will be reviewed by a people more accustomed to political power and constitutional governance and better placed to appreciate and rectify their deficiencies. In the interim, the status of Convention as a source of law remains in transition.

CHAPTER 12

INTERNATIONAL LAW AS A SOURCE OF LAW

THE NATURE AND STATUS OF INTERNATIONAL LAW

We do not traditionally consider international law as a separate and distinct source of law. However, this is a myopic view, which can now be legitimately challenged. It is becoming increasingly clear that, in modern times, the body of rules and principles which constitute international law exerts a great influence on municipal legal systems. It is a dynamic, norm-building legal source. The influence of international law may be seen as a direct source of law within the municipal or domestic system, or as an indirect source of law. In both instances, it is an important legal source.

In the Commonwealth Caribbean, for reasons which will be discussed further, international law as a legal source is particularly significant with respect to constitutional and human rights law.

International law is itself derived from three sources: (a) treaties or international agreements; (b) international customary law; and (c) opinions and decisions of international courts or tribunals. International courts may also look at the teachings of highly qualified publications as a secondary or auxiliary source. International agreements or treaties may be interpreted by international or regional courts or other international bodies or committees which are given the authority to do so under the particular international legal instruments.[1] These interpretations form part of the body of international legal norms and principles.

National or domestic legal systems adopt rules of international law as part of their legal systems by way of agreement, that is, Conventions and treaties, or by way of accepting practice, which practice may then develop into binding international custom. All legal systems are influenced by such international declarations, protocols, agreements or Conventions. These establish or declare certain legal principles believed to be desirable for all nations. Examples are the UN Declaration on Human Rights, the United Nations International Covenant on Civil and Political Rights[2] (hereinafter the UN Covenant), including the latter's Optional Protocol, the UN Covenant on Economic, Social and Cultural Rights, International Labour Organisation Conventions which govern industrial relations and the United Nations Convention on the Rights of the Child.[3] Such Conventions and declarations attempt to bind Party States to desirable standards of behaviour as enshrined under the various instruments. Obligations arising out of regional legal instruments can also be discussed under the umbrella of international law.

If we consider that international law is of sufficient authority to ground legal rules within the municipal State, this begs the question, what is the substance of international law? Is it really law as we know it? We may view international law as a

---

1   The United Nations Human Rights Committee (UNHRC) considered below, p 209, is one such body. Similarly, the World Trade Organisation (WTO) and the International Labour Organisation (ILO) have their own committees. The ILO's judicial body is the Committee on Freedom of Association.

2   999 UNTS 171, 6 ILM, 1966.

3   All the countries in the region have ratified these Conventions.

branch of ethics rather than law, a kind of international morality. Certainly, international law is treated as if it is of a legal character, that is, with respect to its language, form and *modus operandi*, but many of its principles originated from legal philosophers within the civil law tradition. It may simply be the philosophical underpinning of other laws. Why, then, do we need to consider it as a separate, legal source?

If one argues that the only essential conditions for the creation of law are the existence of a political continuity and the recognition by its members of settled rules binding upon them, then international law satisfies these. Harris, for example, views international law as a 'system of customary law upon which has been erected . superstructure of conventional or treaty-made law'.[4]

Perhaps the best evidence of international law as law, is that every State recognises that it does exist and that it is under obligation to observe it. It is true that there are violations of international rules or principles but, similarly, there are violations of municipal law. It can therefore be adequately described as a source of law within the legal system based upon this element of acceptance. As we saw earlier in this book, law may be based on some form of acceptance or consensus within a society. In this instance, the society is the international community.[5]

Incorporation of treaties

Nonetheless, the rules of international law are complex and the status of international law in the domestic legal system is sometimes uncertain. For example, in a domestic or municipal jurisdiction, mere ratification of a treaty or international instrument does not necessarily mean that that instrument has become legally binding in the strict sense. It may be considered of persuasive effect only. It is often necessary to carry out a process called 'incorporation' before an international rule becomes legally valid within the particular jurisdiction. It thereby becomes domestic law and has binding effect in the same way as any other domestic law. We may observe that, with incorporation, the true and original source or origin of the law is international law and not indigenous legislation. The legal norms are derived from international opinion or practice.

The question of the enforceability of international custom is less controversial, albeit difficult to establish. Oppenheim notes, for example, that, as regards the UK, all rules of customary international law which either are universally recognised or have, at any rate, received the assent of the court, are 'per se the law of the land'.[6] The English common law and, by extension, our common law have, however, been more hostile with regard to unincorporated treaties. This is perhaps curious if we consider that it is the latter which has the State's express and formal consent.

Legal rules are thus posited through the existence of treaties, treaty obligations and international custom. This promotes conformity by national States. Brierley[7]

---

4   Harris, L, *Legal Philosophies*, 1980, London: Butterworths, p 588.
5   See the section on the 'The contemporary functions of law' in Chapter 2 ('The Historical Function of Law in the WI – Creating a Future From a Troubled Past').
6   Jennings, R and Watts, A (eds), *Oppenheims's International Law*, 1992, London: Longman, p 56.
7   Brierley, J, *The Law of Nations – An Introduction to the International Law of Peace*, 6th edn, 1963, Oxford: OUP.

contends that although the lay person sees only the breaches of treaties, in the form of wars and other international conflicts, this is the exception rather than the rule. Indeed, hundreds of decisions handed down by international courts imposing damages have been honoured by defendant States. Further, the extent to which international legal norms have been incorporated into municipal law means that such norms can now be directly enforced by governments and domestic courts. This leads to the conclusion that international law is also observed as municipal law. We may say that there is a 'law habit' in international relations. In the words of Brierley, the instances in which judgments of international tribunals have been flouted are so rare that the headline reader may well place them in the 'man bites dog' category. Treaties may not compel obligations in the sense of a contractual obligation but, at minimum, there is an obligation, even if diplomatic in nature, reinforced by a 'sense' of law.

We reiterate that a system of law may not depend on sanctions for its authority, but its acceptance by the community.

DECISIONS FROM INTERNATIONAL COURTS AND BODIES

We may examine the effect of decisions and opinions emanating from international courts, and indeed, the very existence of such courts, to see whether international law may be accurately described as a source of law. Such decisions may be considered sources of law in the same way as judicial precedents are legal sources within a common law legal tradition. These decisions address violations of particular treaties and international instruments, often giving interpretations of such instruments, thereby building up a system of international case law. Further, a country, after a particular negative international decision, may change its law to prevent international embarrassment. This illustrates the indirect effect of international law as a legal source. Of course, such decisions can only be considered persuasive precedents. However, they do determine the internationally accepted boundaries of conduct and may be binding on States or, at the very least, highly persuasive and greatly influential.

Such decisions come not only from international courts, but also from tribunals established by international organisations. These may have their own treaties or international agreements which individual countries have signed. Such bodies perform a judicial function, although they are not, in all instances, courts. They examine the extent to which Member States are in conformity with the relevant international instruments. The effect of such decisions may have a significant impact on the legal system.

Agreements concerning international trade are particularly topical and influential. One recent example of great significance is the ruling from the World Trade Organisation (WTO) that the preferential quota system for bananas exported from ACP countries, including the Caribbean, to Europe violates fundamental precepts of the WTO's free trade agreement. This ruling is treated as binding by European States.

International adjudicating bodies which allow individuals to petition them for relief will normally require that local remedies must be exhausted before they are admitted. This means that the petitioner must bring his case before the local courts in the first instance and obtain a judgment. There are exceptions to this rule. One notable exception is where the remedy under the domestic law is not available or effective.

International decisions and human rights

By far the most significant impact of these international judicial precedents is in the area of human rights. This is also true outside of the region. The two most important international human rights bodies in this regard are the European Court of Human Rights (the European Court) and the United Nations Human Rights Committee (UNHRC). In the UK, for example, the decisions of the European Court have been highly influential in English constitutional law jurisprudence. Because of this region's relationship with the UK, this is also an important development for us in the Commonwealth Caribbean, not least because the English judges of the Privy Council have been considerably influenced by this jurisprudence and have allowed it to filter through to our law. The credentials of international law as a legal source in the human rights arena cannot be doubted in this area today.[8]

In the famous *Sunday Times* case,[9] for example, the UK was pressed to reform its law on freedom of expression and freedom of the press, to bring it in line with the standard of international law. This case concerned the Thalidomide baby tragedy, where several parents sued the manufacturers of the drug Thalidomide, which had resulted in their giving birth to deformed babies. While negotiations to settle the claims were still pending, *The Sunday Times* planned the publication of an article which reviewed the evidence on the question of negligence. The Attorney General obtained an injunction to prevent publication, on the basis that it was a contempt of court. *The Sunday Times* argued that the restriction, although 'prescribed by law' was not 'necessary' in a democratic society within the meaning of Article 10 of the European Convention on Human Rights. Accordingly, it was not justified and constituted an infringement of fundamental rights to freedom of the press and free speech. The European Court agreed, concluding that the interference did not correspond to a social need sufficiently pressing to outweigh the public interest in freedom of expression within the meaning of the Convention. It was not, therefore, a legitimate restriction of fundamental rights. The tests used by the European Court for imposing restrictions on fundamental human rights were much more liberal than that of the English Court, the latter being much more willing to impose restraints on such rights. This international court ruling has produced a significant change in English constitutional jurisprudence and has also influenced Commonwealth Caribbean public law. It demonstrates the power of international law and decision-making as a legal source.

In more recent litigation, the UK has been forced to rethink its law on part-time female employment in view of the landmark decisions of the European Court in cases like *R v SOS for Employment ex p Equal Opportunities Commission*.[10] In that case, the House of Lords found that that parts of the Employees' Protection (Consolidation) Act 1978 were incompatible with the European Convention, in that it gave part-time employees fewer labour rights in areas such as redundancy benefits. The decision was framed in feminist jurisprudence, as the Court recognised that, as most part-time employees were women, the practice resulted in inequality and discrimination.

The impact of human rights decisions on law and legal systems is particularly significant in the Commonwealth Caribbean. This is so for two reasons. First, there is

---

8   See the discussion on the 'death row phenomenon' below, 209 and in Chapter 8 ('The Common Law and the Doctrine of Judicial Precedent').

9   (1979) 2 EHRR 245.

10 [1993] 1 WLR 872; [1994] Croner's Employment Digest 58.

nexus between international human rights rulings and Commonwealth Caribbean law because of the similarity between Commonwealth Caribbean Constitutions and international human rights instruments. This, coupled with the Privy Council's new-found justification for expanding human rights jurisprudence, has resulted in osmosis beneficial to the development of international human rights standards in the region. Secondly, several Commonwealth Caribbean countries are signatories to the Optional Protocol on Human Rights, discussed below, p 209.

Thus, if we wish to underscore international law as an indirect source of law, we need only look to our own Constitutions in the Commonwealth Caribbean and their respective Bills of Rights provisions. Indeed, there is what may be described as a symbiotic relationship between international human rights instruments, in particular, the European Convention on Human Rights, and Commonwealth Caribbean Con-stitutions. The European Convention is itself based on the UN Declaration on Human Rights. This implies an acceptance of internationally accepted human rights standards as promulgated by such Conventions as the UN Declaration on Human Rights and the European Convention on Human Rights and interpreted by their relevant adjudication bodies. This factor has impacted on Caribbean human rights jurisprudence which has looked to the interpretation of the European Convention, for assistance with interpreting Commonwealth Caribbean Constitutions. Barnett notes, for example, that:

> [t]he most systematic and significant adoption by Caribbean legal systems of inter-national human rights norms has been through the mechanism of the Bill of Rights guarantees of written Constitutions.[11]

Even the courts have recognised the extent to which Constitutions have been shaped by such norms. In the landmark case on the manner in which these written Constitutions are to be interpreted, *Minister of Home Affairs v Fisher*,[12] the court noted that West Indian Constitutions were influenced by the European Convention and the Universal Declaration on Human Rights. Again, in the case of *Fisher v AG of the Bahamas*,[13] Lord Steyn, in arguing for an even more expansive interpretation of the *Pratt and Morgan* principle said:

> It is necessary to bear in mind the genesis of Art 17(1). It was taken from Art 3 of the European Convention for the Protection of Human Rights and Fundamental Freedoms (1953), which served as a model for the Constitutions for most of the Caribbean countries.

He then went on to consider how the European Court had interpreted Article 3 of the European Convention.[14]

There is no indication that the heavy influence of European human rights juris-prudence and, by extension, international human rights norms, will be curtailed. The effect of this is that there is now a well developed body of international human rights case law of particular relevance to Commonwealth Caribbean jurisdictions. It is dif-ficult to ignore this important jurisprudence. In fact, recent events have demonstrated

---

11 Barnett, L, 'Caribbean judicial approach to constitutional and conventions human rights provisions', seminar on Human Rights and the Machinery of Justice, 1993, Inter-American Institute of Human Rights, p 6.
12 [1980] AC 319, PC Bermuda; (1979) 44 WIR 107. See the judgment of Lord Wilberforce.
13 Privy Council Appeal No 53 of 1997, decided 12 December 1997, PC, the Bahamas, p 18.
14 *Ibid*, pp 19–21.

that this body of case law has been, and will continue to be instrumental in shaping Commonwealth Caribbean constitutional law. This influence is particularly evident in the emerging jurisprudence on the death row cases.

INDIVIDUAL RIGHTS TO PETITION INTERNATIONAL BODIES

The United Nations International Covenant on Civil and Political Rights contains an Optional Protocol. Under this protocol, States Parties can choose to have human rights applications determined by a special committee set up under the Convention: its supervisory arm, the UNHRC. A similar mechanism exists under the American Convention on Human Rights. What is different about these applications is that they encompass the individual right of petition, that is, individual citizens of a party State and not merely the State itself have *locus standi* to come before the relevant international body or committee. This is an unusual jurisdiction in international law, which is normally concerned about relations between States.

Bodies such as the UNHRC will consider communications from individuals to determine whether there has been a breach of the UN Covenant. The Optional Protocol, for example, has been an important jurisprudential source for the evaluation and evolution of human rights. These include, among others, the right to liberty and security of the individual,[15] the right to privacy,[16] the right of the family to protection,[17] and equality before the law.[18]

However, the UNHRC and other such bodies are not courts. Their findings are not binding on States Parties. Indeed, they do not even give decisions, merely opinions which are inherently persuasive. Their ultimate strength is not judicial precedent, sanctions or other coercion. Rather, it is persuasion, custom, consensus-building and the construction or creation of norms by the interpretation of the UN Covenant which States will hold to be sacred and consequently will accept. This acceptance may merely be attributable to a fear of 'embarrassment'. Still, such bodies and, in particular, the UNHRC appear to wield enormous influence and their jurisprudence is substantial and important. This is perhaps not surprising when one considers the current status of international decisions or opinions as a source of law, discussed above, p 207.[19]

There is absolutely no doubt, for example, that the Optional Protocol has been instrumental in formulating the *Pratt and Morgan* principle on cruel and inhumane punishment arising out of undue delay to implement the death penalty, now so well known in the region.[20] Long before the Privy Council decision in *Pratt and Morgan*,

---

15   Under Article 9. See *Vuolanne v Finland*, Report of the Human Rights Committee, UN GAOR, UN Doc No 265/87.

16   Under Article 17. *Cziffra v Mauritius*, Report of the Human Rights Committee, UN GAOR, UN Doc No 5/78.

17   Article 23. *Cziffra v Mauritius*, Report of the Human Rights Committee, UN GAOR, UN Doc No 35/78.

18   Article 26. *De Vries v The Netherlands*, Report of the Human Rights Committee, UN GAOR, UN Doc No 182/84.

19   As at 1989, there were over 371 applications before the UNHRC. *Op cit*, Lallah J, 'The domestic application of international human rights norms,' in Ninth Commonwealth Law Conference, 1990, New Zealand Commerce Clearing House, p 394.

20   From the case *Pratt and Morgan v AG of Jamaica* (1993) 43 WIR 340; [1993] 4 All ER 769, PC Jamaica.

developments were taking place at the UNHRC on the rights to counsel, a fair trial, against undue delay and cruel and inhumane punishment, with specific reference to the Commonwealth Caribbean. As early as 1989, in an application by the same defendants as to whether their rights under the UN Covenant had been violated, *Pratt and Morgan v Jamaica*, the UNHRC found that undue delay on death row while awaiting appeals could constitute cruel and inhumane punishment.[21] This relied on an earlier judgment of the UNHRC from Norway.[22]

The case of *Robinson v Jamaica*[23] is also notable. Here, the UN Human Rights Committee addressed the question whether there was a right to counsel for an accused facing the death penalty. The UNHRC disagreed with both the Jamaica Court of Appeal and the Privy Council holding that such a right must be viewed as a fundamental human right, again imposing higher standards for the observance of human rights than the national jurisdiction.

Indeed, in 1992, before the Optional Protocol was a familiar feature in the Caribbean human rights arena, this writer wrote of the potential influence which this international source of law could have on Caribbean human rights jurisprudence:

> . . . can any State ignore the dynamic jurisprudential trend emerging from the UNHRC? The lessons from the history of the cases, from their journey from Caribbean courts to the UNHRC, sound a warning to those who insist on ignoring the full potential of written Bills of Rights.[24]

At the time, other academics perhaps scoffed at the idea that such a body could be so instrumental to Caribbean law and could so greatly influence the Privy Council, particularly as the issue of undue delay had previously been unsuccessfully litigated before the Privy Council.[25] History, however, has confirmed this view. It is a dramatic example of international law as a legal source.

WITHDRAWAL FROM THE IAHRC AND THE UNHRC

In 1998, Jamaica withdrew the right of individual petition to the UNHRC, while Trinidad and Tobago rescinded the Inter-American Convention, and consequently, its court and commission.[26] Trinidad and Tobago later re-acceded to the American Convention, but with a wide reservation precluding the UNHRC from hearing any cases relating to the death penalty. These withdrawal decisions were motivated solely by the desire of those governments to deny death-row inmates further opportunity to delay implementation of the death penalty. Because of the successful recourse by

---

21   Comm Nos 210/1986 and 225/1987, Report of the Human Rights Committee, UN GAOR, 44th Sess, Supp No 40, p 222, UN Doc A/44/40 (1989). The UNHRC also found that the fact that the accused had not been notified of the date of execution until 45 minutes before it was due to take place was a violation of the UN Covenant. For further comment on this opinion and related views of the UNHRC, see Antoine, R-M B, 'The Judicial Committee of the Privy Council B an inadequate remedy for death row prisoners' (1992) 41 ICLQ 179.

22   *OF v Norway*, UNHRC Judgment No 271/1978.

23   UNHRC Comm 128/1987.

24   Antoine, R-M B, 'International law and the right of legal representation in capital offence cases – a comparative approach' (1992) 12 OJLS 293.

25   In *Riley v AG of Jamaica* [1982] 2 WLR 557, PC, Jamaica.

26   See *News and Developments* 'Trinidad and Tobago withdraws from International Human Rights Treaties' [1997] 11 *InterRights Bulletin* 183.

death row prisoners to these two international bodies, there was the perception that they were obstructing the cause of popular justice in those countries. There is a danger that other Commonwealth countries will follow suit.[27]

The *Pratt and Morgan* ruling, discussed above, unleashed considerable unease among Commonwealth Caribbean governments, burdened with increased crime levels. Now, with the opting out of the Optional Protocol and the Inter-American Convention, these States are asserting their sovereign right not only to hang, but to hang in their own time.

Conflict between international law and domestic concerns

The move to abolish the individual right to petition is a rejection of what is seen as too radical and utopian a human rights jurisprudence coming from these international human rights bodies on the subject of the death penalty. It is a jurisprudence, the governments believe, which interferes with their political and judicial sovereignty to determine their own legal norms and policies. It is also, ultimately, a rejection of international legal norms and policy in favour of nationalist concerns, and under-scores the traditional conflict between these two strains of law. It is ironic that the reason that the Optional Protocol itself faced such antagonism is because of its effi-cient and progressive approach in relation to human rights complaints from member States, many of them emanating from the Commonwealth Caribbean. This is an unfortunate step. As is clear from the description of the Optional Protocol above, it does not exist solely to serve the interests of prisoners on death row, as the current propaganda seems to suggest.

At this juncture, Commonwealth Caribbean jurisprudence on this issue seems to be at a crossroads. On the one hand, the courts and constitutional jurisprudence seem to be steadily moving towards an acceptance of international legal norms within the municipal legal framework. On the other, the West Indian public appears to be a clamouring for a different kind of justice, one which inevitably involves a significant deviation from accepted international values.

Legal policy and the political will are not often so divergent. Yet, given the pro-pensity of Caribbean courts to define the law with reference to the English common law and given the UK's current 'love affair' with European-style human rights,[28] we suggest the courts' steady progression towards a more generous interpretation of the written Constitutions to bring them more in line with international human rights norms will likely win the day.[29] Indeed, recent cases have shown an enthusiasm for further expanding judicial interpretation of the constitutional provisions on cruel and inhuman punishment.[30] Despite the Executive's attempts to abort the influence of international law on the legal system, Commonwealth Caribbean judges are not likely to ignore international law jurisprudence in the future, even if outside of the relevant international law instruments. This is particularly so in view of the relationship with the European Convention, discussed above, p 208.

---

27 Barbados preferred to amend its Constitution to attempt to dilute the effect of the *Pratt and Morgan* line of decisions. See Chapter 7 ('The Written Constitution as a Legal Source').

28 See the discussion in Chapter 1 on the UK's determination to incorporate the European Con-vention and to enforce its international obligations on human rights.

29 See Chapter 7 ('The Written Constitution as a Legal Source').

30 See *Peters v Marksman* (1997) 2 Carib LB 91, and *Hobbs et al* [1994] CLB 45.

Paradoxically, the authoritative position of such international bodies and international law is also demonstrated with the opting-out of these international bodies. This move is evidence that Commonwealth Caribbean States do not find it easy to 'disobey' the decisions of these bodies. Instead, they prefer to remove themselves from the purview of their moral and legal authority.

WHAT IS INTERNATIONAL CUSTOM?

Where a practice develops among States in such a uniform and constant manner that it becomes accepted by the international community, it is called 'international custom'. Such custom, as we have seen, is treated as binding on all States and becomes part of the law of all nations. It does not, therefore, depend on a treaty or other international instrument for its validity. While there is consensus that international custom is binding, its defect as a source of law is that it is difficult to prove. The following cases illustrate its nature and existence.

In *Colombia v Peru*,[31] known as 'the asylum case', after an unsuccessful rebellion in Peru, a warrant was issued for one of the leaders of the rebellion. He was granted asylum by Colombia in one of its Peruvian embassies. Colombia asked Peru for safe conduct to allow him out of the country, but Peru refused. Colombia then brought a case against Peru, claiming that as the State granting asylum, it was competent to qualify the offence (that is, to decide whether the offence was political or not, which would have determined the asylum issue). Colombia relied partly on an alleged regional custom peculiar to Latin American States. The International Court of Justice held that the party relying on such custom must prove that it was established in such a way as to make it binding on the other party. The claim was unsuccessful, since the evidence disclosed much uncertainty and contradiction in the exercise of diplomatic asylum.

In the *North Sea Continental* case,[32] the International Court of Justice considered the question of the rules of international law applicable to the delimitation of the continental shelf. In particular, the Court had to determine whether the 'equidistance principle', which had come into being partly on the basis of State practice after the Geneva Convention, was a rule of customary international law binding on all States. It was held that Article 6 of the Geneva Convention was a norm creating a provision that had generated a rule, which, while only conventional or contractual in origin, has since passed into the general corpus of international law, and is now accepted as such by the *opinio juris*, so as to have become binding even for countries which have never, and do not, become parties to the Convention. A new rule of international custom had been created.

In the subject area of labour law, Ruth Ben Israel[33] has argued that while international legal instruments such as the UN Covenant do not contain explicit references to a right to strike, the right can be located as part of international legal custom. All countries protect the freedom of workers to withhold their labour by striking. It is implicit in the notion, expressly protected in national Constitutions and international

---

31   (1950) ICJ 266.
32   *Germany v Denmark* (1969) ICJ 3.
33   Ben Israel, R, *International Labour Standards: The Case of the Freedom To Strike: A Study Prepared for the ILO*, 1988, Deventer, Antwerp, London, New York: Kluwer.

human rights instruments, of the protection against slavery. This finds juristic justification, for example, in the case of *UAW-AFL Local v Werb*.[34]

This is a controversial point, particularly in the Commonwealth Caribbean, as the now famous case of *Collymore v AG*[35] held that there was no constitutional right to strike in Trinidad and Tobago as this could not be derived from the freedom of association. The *dictum* has been followed in other Commonwealth countries, including those in the Commonwealth Caribbean. Still, the judgment has been severely criticised.[36] It is, further, an old judgment. Recent judicial developments have moved closer to Ben Israel's argument. One good example is the Scandinavian case of NHO-ARD[37] which accepted that a right to strike was implicit under Convention No 87 of the ILO on Freedom of Association. This Convention promulgated a right which was accepted by all nations. As with Caribbean Constitutions, the right to strike under the Convention is not explicit but the freedom of association is protected.

It is clear, therefore, that once a practice has been elevated to the status of international custom, it becomes binding on all States and is a legitimate source of law.

INTERNATIONAL LAW, MUNICIPAL LAW AND THE CONSTITUTION

There is much judicial and other authority for the rule that a State cannot rely upon its municipal law to avoid its international obligations. This gives force to the argument that international law is a valid source of law in any jurisdiction. The Draft Declaration on Rights and Duties of States 1949,[38] under Article 13, gives justification to this thesis:

> Every State has the duty to carry out in good faith its obligations arising from treaties and other sources of international law, and may not invoke provisions in its Constitutions or its laws as an excuse for failure to perform this duty.

The *Exchange of Greek and Turkish Populations* case substantiates this view.[39]

Yet, domestic courts are reluctant to conform to this view, particularly if constitutional norms will be violated. This is not without intellectual or jurisprudential justification. As we saw in our earlier discussion on the Constitution, it represents the ethos of a people. It is the legal expression of their accepted values and beliefs. Where, as in the Commonwealth Caribbean, a people have chosen to redefine their identity through independence and independent Constitutions, the Constitution is an even more significant expression of identity. No two societies are identical. Why should a people sacrifice their hard-won deals to a faceless, uniform, international 'Constitution' which may not accurately reflect their social norms and values?

---

34   336 US 245 (1949).
35   (1967) 12 WIR 5.
36   See, eg, Okpaluba, C, *Essays in Law and Trade Unionism*, 1975, Trinidad: Key Caribbean, pp 48–56.
37   (1990) 10 ILLR 63.
38   [1949] YBILC 286.
39   Advisory opinion. PCIJ Rep, Series B, No 10, 20 (1925).

The difficulty is vividly expressed by writers in Australia:

> There is something amiss with a polity that to achieve its aims, enters treaties with undemocratic committees of the United Nations – to overrule the processes by which it itself is governed. This was not the intention of those who drafted the Constitution; nor is it the wish of Australians today – misuse of the external affairs power is a big threat to our Federal structure.[40]

Further:

> I . . . find it ironic that so many contemporary Australians determined to protect us from the non-existent threat of English tyranny, fall over each other in a scramble to surrender Australian sovereignty to a rag, tag and bobtail of unrepresentative United Nations committees, accountable to nobody.[41]

A counter argument is this. International legal norms which member States are expected to obey are only those which all international communities have declared to be acceptable. Member States have also expressed their approval by ratification. Why should they now refuse to conform? Yet this argument is weaker in relation to international custom. There, individual countries have not expressly accepted the international norms.

However, despite the expanding reach of international law, there is no clear principle which dictates that the Constitution must be subservient to international law. We will return to this in our discussion of the justiciability of international norms and the death penalty.

REGIONAL LAW

Legal obligations and influences also arise out of regional treaties and agreements. Their effects as sources of law are similar to those from international treaties and instruments. In the Commonwealth Caribbean, the two most significant regional instruments are the CARICOM Treaty[42] and the Inter-American Convention on Human Rights. In addition to treaties, there is the OECS sub-regional grouping, which performs a similar function to CARICOM for the countries of the Eastern Caribbean.

The CARICOM Treaty

The CARICOM Treaty was the result of initiatives towards economic and political integration within the Commonwealth Caribbean community and established the regional entity known as the Caribbean Community and Common Market (CARICOM). Recently, Caribbean countries outside the Commonwealth have been accepted, at least partially, under the Treaty. These include Suriname and Haiti.

---

40 John Hyde, in *The Australian*, 2 September 1994, cited in [1992] CLB 651, p 652, *per* Kirby J.
41 *Ibid*.
42 The Treaty of Chaguaramas 1973 as revised in the Revised Treaty of Chaguaramus Establishing the Caribbean Community including the CARICOM Single Market and Economy', 5 July 2001, Nassau, the Bahamas. This establishes the constitutional framework of CARICOM. See the discussion on the interpretation and application of this treaty and the Revised Treaty of Chaguaramus in Chapter 17 ('The Caribbean Court of Justice').

The Treaty is presently focused on economic and trade matters and not political integration. Political and economic integration are usually accompanied by laws and legal practices which define the parameters of cooperation. CARICOM is no exception. In many instances CARICOM agreements are incorporated into municipal law. A recent example is the agreement to allow certain qualified CARICOM nationals to work anywhere in the region without a work permit.[43]

The Organisation of American States

Beyond CARICOM, the countries of the region belong to the regional organisation called the Organisation of American States, the OAS. This has particular significance for human rights because of the existence of the Inter-American Convention on Human Rights, which is the human rights instrument particularly applicable to the region. To some extent, we have already explored the importance of this in our discussion on international and regional human rights bodies. The Inter-American Convention on Human Rights has established an adjudicating body, the Inter-American Human Rights Commission, (the IAHRC), to determine breaches of the Convention. Currently, as with the UNHRC, the most popular use of this body is as an avenue of appeal by convicted persons on death row, as seen in the *Roosevelt Edwards* case.[44]

A distinguishing feature of the Inter-American Convention is its applicability to the States of the American region, even where these States have not ratified the Convention. This was confirmed in the decision of the Privy Council in *Fisher v AG of the Bahamas*.[45] Their Lordships noted new information from the Government's counsel that under the regulations made pursuant to the Statute of the Inter-American Commission on Human Rights, provision is made for a procedure applicable in the case of complaints of violations of human rights imputable to States which are not Parties to the American Convention on Human Rights.[46] This is by virtue of the Charter of the Organisation of American States/American Convention on Human Rights.[47]

THE ENFORCEABILITY AND JUSTICIABILITY OF INTERNATIONAL LAW

In general, international law allows States some measure of freedom to determine how they will implement a ratified treaty. The methods may be through direct incorporation of the rights and obligations enshrined in the treaty by way of enacting similar domestic legislation, the reform of existing laws to give effect to the treaty, or

---

43   See, eg, the Immigration (Amendment) Act 1996 of Barbados, which implements this.

44   No 7604 Res 1/84 Int-Am CHR 54 (1984) OEA Ser L/V/11 63 Doc 10 Rev 1 (1985).

45   Privy Council Appeal No 53 of 1997, decided 12 December 1997, PC, the Bahamas.

46   See *ibid*, p 14. The consequence of this finding is that the time to be considered as undue delay must be extended to make room for this additional procedure. To this end, earlier decisions which had put the relevant time as three and a half years in the Bahamas were decided *per incuriam*.

47   This point is particularly noteworthy in view of the fact that, as noted previously, one country in the region, Trinidad and Tobago, initially withdrew from the Inter-American Convention. Yet because of the IACHR's legal effect outside the parameters of the Conventions, that country could still be violating the legal values inherent in the Convention.

self-executing operation of the treaty, such as the reflection of treaty obligations in judicial precedent. This choice does not mean that Party States to a treaty do not have obligations toward it.

> ... Whether States are Parties to particular instruments or not, they are still answerable to the various international mechanisms for any failure in implementation and it is immaterial, for the purpose of the State's responsibility, whether the failure is that of the legislative, the executive or the judicial arm of the State.[48]

Apart from incorporation of the Treaty into domestic law, the extent to which States have obligations towards international law which are enforceable and justiciable is a controversial issue. However, as seen below, the argument toward enforceability and justiciability is on stronger ground in the sphere of international human rights.

The current trend in common law courts is that they are now more willing to treat international notions of human rights and international human rights opinions as justiciable and enforceable. This provides a further source for international human rights, which will merge with and become part of domestic law. The modern view on the effect of treaties seems to be that international norms are justiciable, at least in so far as domestic law does not specifically contradict them.

With respect to certain treaties, they may require a method of enforcing relevant obligations. For example, Article 2 of the UN Covenant demands that States Parties create a system of enforcement. This may mean that, although there might be doubt as to whether a State has violated a treaty obligation in a particular instance, such as where the international rule is found not to be part of the domestic law, there would be no doubt that the State has violated its obligation to procure a method of enforcing such an obligation. Treaty obligations should, therefore, be viewed as imposing legal obligations, regardless of whether a State has incorporated that treaty.

Several cases have demonstrated that the courts can rely on principles found in international law treaties on deciding questions of law which are vague or unclear, or where there is no relevant common law rule on the point. Indeed, some judges advocate that a court has a duty to do so. Certainly, at the very least, a treaty may be regarded as representing legislative policy and thus assist in revolving the issue of statutory interpretation.[49]

> The judiciary has as much responsibility as the other arms of the State to ensure, in the exercise of its functions, the greatest possible consistency between national jurisprudence and the international jurisprudence which is now evolving ... Increasingly, judges at the highest jurisdictional level are no longer content to refer to jurisprudence evolved by their counterparts in other national jurisdictions, but also refer to the jurisprudence evolved by international bodies.[50]

---

48 *Op cit*, fn 19.
49 See *R v SOS of the Home Dept ex p Brind* [1991] 1 AC 696, pp 733, 787–89; *Rantzen v Mirror Group Newspaper Ltd* [1994] QB 670, CA. Some cases suggest that international norms should only be considered where there is an ambiguity in the domestic law; see *Derbyshire v Times Newspapers* [1992] 3 WLR 49, pp 49–50. But this may be too narrow a view. Higgins suggests that international treaties must be considered even where domestic law is clear. Higgins, R, 'The relationship between international and regional human rights norms and domestic law' [1992] CLB 268.
50 *Op cit*, Lallah, fn 19, p 397.

To his credit, Lord Denning had long recognised the inevitability of the influences of Treaty law. In *Bulmer v Bollinger*,[51] commenting on the influence of the EU Treaty on English law, he said:

> The Treaty is like an incoming tide. It flows into the estuaries and up the rivers. It cannot be held back.

It should be noted, however, that notwithstanding these legal developments, common law legal systems such as ours are still careful to define themselves as adhering to the dualist doctrine. This doctrine stipulates that international law and domestic law exist in two separate spheres and that international law is not directly enforced in the domestic legal system unless incorporated by statute or is an aspect of customary law. It may be observed that there is an exceedingly thin line between the dualist doctrine and the legal trend which admits that international law can create binding obligations by whatever mechanisms in certain circumstances. Such refined distinctions led at least one Commonwealth Caribbean jurist to question whether this is just a legal farce.[52]

It is clear, therefore, that while Commonwealth Caribbean legal systems conform to the common law dualist approach to international law that it does not supersede domestic law unless incorporated, the courts are more and more adopting unilaterally, treaty obligations and values, without benefit of the legislative process. As this jurisprudence has been significant to Commonwealth Caribbean legal systems, and indeed, has posed challenges for the sovereignty of our legal systems, we explore them in some detail below. Indeed, several English cases have affirmed the modern principle that treaties can create enforceable obligations in appropriate circumstances, particularly in the area of human rights.[53] In other common law jurisdictions, the trend toward justiciability is the same. In *Tavita v Minister of Immigration*,[54] the Court of Appeal of New Zealand rejected the Crown's argument that it was entitled to ignore international instruments. It said:

> That is an unattractive argument, apparently implying that New Zealand's adherence to the international instruments has been at least partly window dressing . . . The law as to the bearing on domestic law of international rights and instruments declaring them is undergoing evolution.[55]

The Court felt that there was a 'duty of the judiciary to interpret and apply national Constitutions, ordinary legislation and the common law in the light of the universality of human rights'.[56] Similarly, in Australia, in the case of *Mabo v Queensland*,[57] the court said: '. . . international law is a legitimate and important influence on the development of the common law, especially when international law declares the existence of universal human rights.'

---

51 [1974] Ch 401; [1974] 2 All ER 1221.
52 See Justice Wit's remarks in the case of *AG et al v Joseph and Boyce*, CCJ Appeal, No CV 2 of 2005, decided 21 June 2006 (Barbados), considered in detail below.
53 See *Marshall v Southampton* [1986] 1 CMLR 688; [1986] 2 All ER 584, *Van Duyn v Home Office* [1975] Ch 358; [1974] 3 All ER 56; on the question of freedom of movement, *Marleasing SA v La Commercial Internacional de Alimentacion SA* [1992] 1 ECR 4135. At the very least, national courts should, as far as possible, interpret domestic law so that it conforms with treaty norms unless there is a specific contradiction.
54 [1994] 2 NZLR 257.
55 *Ibid*, p 266.
56 *Ibid*.
57 (1992) 175 CLR 1.

In the Commonwealth Caribbean, this view has found favour with some courts. For example, in *Peters v Marksman*,[58] the High Court of St Vincent and the Grenadines expressly declared the justiciability and enforceability of international law. It found that flogging with the cat-o'-nine-tails in St Vincent violated Article 1 of the UN Declaration on the Prevention of Crime and the Treatment of Offenders, which was part of the law of St Vincent.[59]

Further, Certain Commonwealth Caribbean courts have rejected corporal punishment, grounding their reasoning in the universal norms shared by civilised nations. In *Hobbs et al v R*,[60] for example, the Court of Appeal of Barbados looked to international norms and the evolving standards of civilisation in making its decision that the cat-o'-nine-tails was unlawful. The Court said:

> Punishments which are incompatible with the evolving standards of decency that mark the progress of a maturing society . . . are repugnant . . . What might not have been regarded as inhuman or degrading decades ago may be revolting to the new sensitivities which emerge as civilisation advances.

Similarly, notions of gender equality, absent or weak in domestic legislation and even in Constitutions, have benefited from the courts' awareness of international ideals and their willingness to adopt them. This was the case, for example, in a case on sexual harassment from Trinidad and Tobago, where the Industrial Court looked toward ILO Conventions and international standards of appropriate conduct at the workplace to come to its decision that a co-worker who had sexually harassed another, should have been dismissed as his actions went against good industrial relations practice.[61]

However, the most pronounced jurisprudence highlighting the increased influence of international law on the domestic system has been in relation to death penalty cases, initiated in *Pratt and Morgan*.[62] These seemingly radical decisions on the death penalty were in line with human rights jurisprudence from international courts and bodies. Increasingly, Commonwealth Caribbean courts, whether local courts or the Privy Council sitting as a Caribbean court, are being influenced by normative standards laid down by notions of international consensus of what are human rights and democratic ideals.

The Supreme Court of Belize took a more conservative position in *Re Admission to Practice of Fitzgerald*,[63] in considering the effect of a non-incorporated, but ratified treaty in Belize. It emphasised that it was not binding on municipal courts.[64] Nevertheless, the Court found that such treaties could be relied upon to interpret municipal law, as there was a presumption that Parliament does not intend to pass law in conflict with its treaty obligations.[65]

The interrelationship between international human rights norms and domestic

---

58 (1997) 2 Carib LB 91.

59 *Ibid*, p 92.

60 [1994] CLB 45.

61 See, eg, *Bank Employees Union v Republic Bank Ltd* (Unreported) No. 17 of 1995, decided 25 March 1996, (Industrial Court) Trinidad and Tobago.

62 *Pratt and Morgan, above*, fn 20.

63 (1997) 2 Carib LB 99.

64 This was the Agreement Establishing the Council of Legal Education, ratified by Belize in 1993.

65 (1997) 2 Carib LB 99, p 100.

law is also well developed in the USA.[66] In other countries, in particular those which belong to the civil law tradition, such as Norway, Sweden and Denmark, when treaties are ratified, they are expressly treated as a source of law, thereby adhering to the monist doctrine.[67]

However, international law has severe shortcomings, especially with regard to the question of enforcement. How do we punish States? We cannot imprison governments. Other sanctions are extremely limited and sometimes ineffective. In addition, States are often reluctant to impose sanctions on other countries, particularly if they are friendly or powerful nations. We saw this in relation to the refusal by many countries to impose sanctions on South Africa for its adherence to the system of apartheid. Consequently, the enforcement of international law is usually left to negotiation and diplomacy, which often are not as effective as we may desire.

INCONSISTENT APPROACHES, INTERNATIONALISM VERSUS LEGISLATIVE SUPREMACY

As we saw earlier, there is a distinct effort to embrace universal legal standards, particularly where human rights are involved. Nevertheless, this regional trend toward internationalism, however marked, cannot be regarded as consistent. Some courts, in particular the Privy Council, appear to be redirecting their decisions away from perhaps more abstract ideas of international law and practice to more concrete expressions of legislative will. Thus far, these have been more pronounced in relation to non-capital punishment cases.[68] They demonstrate a willingness to turn away from a liberal internationalist trend, preferring instead to give effect to the intention of the legislature, even where that intent seemingly violates accepted international values about human rights. This allows domestic law to once again trump over international law and constitutional jurisprudence to be more predictable, albeit more conservative. This is not an undesirable approach, as it allows constitutional change to be what it is supposed to be, the rational, reflective expressions of the ideals of the peoples in any particular society as laid down by their representative legislature. In contrast, ignoring the legislative will creates the danger of making law the unpredictable 'plaything' of judges influenced by norms which do not always represent that society.

On the question of corporal punishment, for example, the Privy Council, in the case of *Pinder v R*[69] upheld a judgment of the Court of Appeal of the Bahamas and agreed that a law which reintroduced corporal punishment into the Bahamas was *intra vires* the Constitution. This result was achieved despite the fact that the courts clearly viewed corporal punishment as inhumane and degrading punishment, when assessed from the perspective of civilised societies as recognised in the international sphere. Whilst agreeing that Constitutions should be interpreted purposively, the Privy Council stated:

> If the Court indulges itself by straining the language of the Constitution to accord with its own subjective moral values then ... instead of embodying only relatively

---

66   See *Filartiga v Peria-Irak*, 630 2d 876 (2d Cir 1980).

67   *Op cit*, Higgins, fn 49, p 1273.

68   Perhaps underscoring the suspicion that the death penalty cases are really a means to an end, the desire to abolish the death penalty.

69   [2002] UKPC 46.

fundamental rules of right, as generally understood by all English-speaking communities, [the Court] would become the partisan of a particular set of ethical or economical opinions.[70]

A Constitution is an exercise in balancing the rights of the individual against the democratic rights of the majority. On the one hand, the fundamental rights and free-doms of the individual must be entrenched against future legislative action if they are to be properly protected; on the other hand, the powers of the legislature must not be unduly circumscribed if the democratic process is to be allowed its proper scope. The balance is drawn by the Constitution. The judicial task is to interpret the Constitution in order to determine where the balance is drawn; not to substitute the judges' views where it should be drawn.[71]

The approach taken in the case of *Sharma v AG*,[72] where the Trinidad and Tobago Court of Appeal refused to adjudicate on a the treaty facilitating the establishment of the CCJ, is also evidence of the conservative approach to unincorporated treaty law.

More important perhaps, is the Privy Council's apparent reversal of its position on the mandatory nature of the death penalty in *Boyce and Another v The Queen*.[73] The Court found that a law decreeing the mandatory death penalty for murder in Barbados was an 'existing law' and remained constitutional whether or not it was inhuman or degrading punishment. The law was also constitutional despite the fact that it was inconsistent with various human rights treaties to which Barbados was a party. Surprisingly, the Privy Council in the *Boyce* case also expressly stated that its earlier decision in the case of *Roodal v State of Trinidad and Tobago*,[74] which had declared the mandatory death penalty unconstitutional, had been wrongly decided and should not be followed.

Unincorporated treaties revisited – distinction between *Boyce* and earlier cases

Since the Privy Council judgment in *Boyce*,[75] the issue of the status of unincorporated treaties in domestic law has been raised as a direct issue before the courts, affording us an opportunity to re-examine and fully assess it. This discourse was addressed by the Barbadian Court of Appeal in *Joseph and Boyce v AG of Barbados*,[76] a matter which ended in the CCJ, which Barbados had by then accepted as its final court of appeal. The substance of the matter was whether the Barbados Privy Council (BPC), the body which had the authority to consider petitions for mercy, was compelled to await the

---

70   Quoting from Holmes J in his first opinion for the Supreme Court of the United States (*Otis v Parker* (1903) 606, 609).

71   *Pinder, above,* fn 69 at 51.

72   [2005] 1 LRC 148 (Trinidad and Tobago).

73   [2004] UKPC 32.

74   [2004] 2WLR 652 (PC, Trinidad and Tobago). The issue was considered within the context of a saving law clause in the Constitution which purported to save the mandatory nature of the death penalty, as it had been in existence before the advent of the Constitution. The majority of the Privy Council looked to international law for inspiration, finding that on 'its true construc-tion', and taking into account the international obligations of Trinidad and Tobago, that is, their ratification of the American Convention on Human Rights, the relevant provisions provided a discretionary rather than a mandatory death sentence for the offence of murder.

75   *Above,* fn 73.

76   *Above,* fn 52.

outcome of a petition by a person on death row to the IACHR, before coming to its decision. Barbados had ratified but not incorporated the relevant treaty which provided for an individual right to petition, the American Convention on Human Rights, into domestic law.[77]

In *Boyce*, the Court of Appeal relied on the earlier Privy Council decision of *Lewis*, and held that the BPC was in fact obliged to await the outcome of a petition to the IACHR. The question had been raised in the controversial *Lewis* case with respect to proceedings of the Jamaican Privy Council, (JPC) the body equivalent to the BPC. The Privy Council in *Lewis* based its decision on the notion that due process, which it found to be a constitutionally protected concept, required that the JPC could not proceed without considering the report from the international body. The net result was that the Jamaican proceedings had been *ultra vires* the Constitution and the sentences of Lewis et al had to be commuted.

The *Lewis* decision is therefore the authoritative precedent on the question for those countries which have not yet accepted the jurisdiction of the CCJ. Nonetheless, it is a contentious and troubling decision and can also be faulted for not laying down clear principles for taking the positions that it did. Not surprisingly, the *Lewis* precedent has been used to derive principles which go beyond the scope of its mandate, such as the notion that international law from unincorporated treaties is now directly enforceable in domestic law in the monist tradition.[78] This view of these cases betrays a very superficial reading of the relevant case law and is based on a flawed assumption. The airing of the issue before the CCJ is therefore to be welcomed as it provides another opportunity, not only to clarify the meaning of *Lewis* but also to identify appropriate legal principles on the issue.

The implications of *Boyce* for the enforceability of international law

The *Boyce* decision is indeed a landmark one and the CCJ, unlike the Privy Council, confronted the legal challenges which these cases posed head on. However, the decision is not without its own difficulty and many misconceptions will continue to arise about what the CCJ actually ruled and the correct legal principles which are to apply in such cases.[79]

It is hoped that the unclear aspects of the judgment would be rectified in later

---

77   A collateral issue was the reviewability of the exercise of the prerogative of mercy, another constitutional law trend. The *Lewis* line of cases and now *Boyce* (CCJ) hold that this prerogative power can be reviewed to ensure that procedural fairness obtains.

78   On the dubious assumption that international law treaties are now directly enforceable, one writer asserts that citizens of Barbados are entitled to direct protection against discrimination on the grounds of HIV/AIDS, enforceable by the courts, as a result of various international human rights Conventions that Barbados has ratified! See Cummins, H Phd Thesis 'the Employment Contract and HIV/AIDS', Barbados: UWI, 2006.

79   It is clear that *Boyce* was a hard case, not only because of the issues raised, but because of the situations of the appellants. These were not the main culprits in the murder case. The persons who had actually initiated the crime had pleaded guilty and negotiated life sentences instead of death. Boyce and company went to trial and ended up ironically, not only with a guilty verdict, but a sentence harsher than those who had been the ringleaders in the murder. There was a sense that this was unjust and it is possible that there was a sympathy element before the courts in trying their utmost to find a solution to the legal conundrum. Barbados had in fact amended its Constitution to ensure that the death penalty was a mandatory sentence and to counter precedents which suggested otherwise. See the Constitutional Amendment Act No 14 of 2002. The constitutionality of this amendment was upheld in *Boyce* (PC), *above*, fn 73.

judgments. Unfortunately, judges do not usually have the opportunity to explain to those who read their judgments what they actually meant! In our legal system which is characterised by judicial precedent, the law evolves not by what judges mean to say but what was actually said or not said. The judgment is therefore only the sum of how readers interpret it and further, how judges and lawyers distinguish it.

Despite ambiguities in the judgment, the CCJ's answer to the question of unincorporated treaties and their impact on the death penalty is to be preferred to the Privy Council's response in *Lewis*.[80]

In *Boyce*, the CCJ answered the question with reference to the doctrine of legitimate expectation, a doctrine born out of judicial review in administrative law. It is nonetheless questionable to what extent this doctrine is applicable to such treaty rights, particularly when they concern persons on death row?

The courts in the death row cases were, of course, faced with several serious dilemmas. Perhaps the most difficult was presented by the now well-known *Pratt and Morgan* principle on undue delay and inhuman punishment. Governments, in attempting to avoid the international treaty process were trying to avoid the problem of undue delay in administering justice identified in *Pratt*. They could do this only by preventing the lengthy process of petitions to international bodies, a process which they could not expedite as they had no control over it. In some cases, this was done by issuing written instructions as to the relevant time period before capital punishment would issue, as occurred in the *Lewis* case. The CCJ held that a petitioner had a right to time enough for his petition to be heard and later considered by the Mercy Committee.

The *Pratt* decision also had ramifications for the very existence and legitimacy of the CCJ as a final court of appeal in the region. On the one hand, many jurists, including the distinguished President of the CCJ, while still Chief Justice of the Trinidad and Tobago Supreme Court, had made it quite clear that the *Pratt and Morgan* line of decisions was inappropriate and that the Privy Council was out of touch with Caribbean realities.[81] On the other hand, the CCJ came into being surrounded by accusations that its purpose was to be a 'hanging court'. Had it given its first important decision and permitted a hanging, this would have made the accusation a self-evident truth.[82] However, perhaps in attempting to prevent this, the CCJ, effected an uneasy compromise and may have lost, not only some of its independence, but an opportunity to truly clarify the distorted jurisprudence that surrounds human rights and treaty obligations. Yet, it may be unfair or unwise to expect a court which is still attempting to justify its very existence to hold in favour of an argument that in fact undermines its *raison d'être*.

Due process and legitimate expectation – new rights or new routes?

While several cases had considered the effect of the right to petition under unincorporated treaties where death row appeals were involved, the approach to

---

80   *Lewis v AG of Jamaica* [2001] AC 50 (PC).
81   See de la Bastide CJ's comments in Chapter 16 ('The Privy Council').
82   Indeed, the *de la Bastide/Saunders* judgment demonstrates quite clearly that the CCJ was aware of these reservations when they admitted that there was a lot of 'speculation' surrounding the approach the CJJ would take to death penalty cases. *Above*, 52, p 8.

these cases had been inconsistent, to say the least. In *Fisher,*[83] for example, it was held that there was no legitimate expectation to a hearing before the international body before the local committee could decide the question of mercy and effect the death penalty, since express instructions were issued by the Government which ran counter to any expectation. In *Briggs,*[84] the court preferred to take the due process route in similar vein to *Lewis*. In *Higgs,*[85] the court said yes to the legitimate expectation but only a procedural one which could be overridden by notice.[86] It is easy to agree with the de la Bastide/Saunders judgment in *Boyce* that 'this branch of law is in an unsettled state and is still evolving. Novel and difficult questions of law are involved here.'[87]

Consequently, the CCJ had to contend, in particular, with the live Privy Council precedent in *Lewis*, to the effect that the local Mercy Committee in Jamaica, before making a decision on a pardon, had to await the report of the international body when a person on Death Row petitioned the international body to hear its case.

In truth, what these cases purport to do, is to lay down guidelines for procedural rights in accordance with notions of due process, natural justice or legitimate expectation where a country has ratified the relevant human rights Convention and an application is duly made to the relevant international human rights body. In the case of death row inmates, the courts have said that the applicant is entitled at least to have any Report from these bodies considered by the local mercy committee.[88] The cases lay down no change in the law relating generally to the non-enforcement of substantive rights in a ratified treaty where that treaty has not been incorporated directly into domestic law.

Indeed, the case law makes it clear that due process or 'protection of the law' or natural justice already exists under the Constitution and so, we are not talking about any new right derived from international law.

In *Lewis,* therefore, the question of the enforceability of treaty provisions was incidental to the context of natural justice which mandated consideration of international human rights norms set out in ratified treaties:

> In considering what natural justice requires, it is relevant to have regard to international human rights norms set out in treaties to which the State is a party, whether or not those are independently enforceable in domestic law.[89]

Lord Millett in *Lewis* also said:

> The due process clause must therefore be broadly interpreted ... The content of the clause is not immutably fixed at that date [the date at which the Constitution came into force].

The genesis of the procedural rights, therefore, if we are to accept the majority view in

---

83   *Above*, fn 13.
84   (1999) 55 WIR 460; [2000] 2 AC 40.
85   (1999) 55 WIR 10; [2002] 2 AC 228.
86   This seems to be what concerned the CCJ, the fact that procedural legitimate expectations could be easily overridden.
87   *Boyce*, CCJ, *above*, fn 52, p 47.
88   *Lewis, above*, fn 80, and *Boyce, above*, fn 52.
89   *Ibid, Lewis*, p 24, *per* Lord Slynn.

Lewis, stems not from the treaty but from constitutional due process or protection of the law.[90]

It would appear that such broad internationalist values are already secured within the internal mechanisms of the State. Such values appear to have an evolutionary character, even capable of keeping pace with changing norms which exist outside of the domestic legal system.[91]

Yet, Hoffman's dissent in *Lewis* is instructive. It hinges on the fundamental principle of the separation of powers doctrine which clothes the dualist doctrine. Law-making power is given to the Legislature, not to the Executive. Accordingly, the signing of a treaty by the Executive cannot promulgate law. Lord Hoffman laments, somewhat poetically:

> The majority have found in the ancient concept of due process of law a philosopher's stone, undetected by generations of judges, which can covert the base metal of executive action into the gold of legislative power. It does not, however, explain how the trick is done.[92]

There are, therefore, several reasons for viewing the Privy Council's majority judgment in *Lewis* as a weak one, a conclusion which the CCJ itself came to.[93]

The *Teoh* precedent on legitimate expectations to treaty rights

In *Boyce,*[94] the CCJ was attracted to the Australian precedent of *Teoh*[95] in which the court found that while unincorporated treaties were not directly enforceable, citizens had a legitimate expectation to the procedures established by such treaties. It is clear however, that the *Teoh* decision cannot be read to mean a reversal or abolition of the dualist tradition.

All that the doctrine of legitimate expectation does with respect to treaties, is to give rise to procedural expectations, that a particular (fair) procedure will be followed, in this instance, a hearing of the issue before the relevant international body.[96] It was clear that it was only the entitlement to the actual hearing before the international body that was being protected and a subsequent consideration of any report

---

90 *Lewis* however conceded that the recommendations of the Commission were not binding on the Governor General in the exercise of the prerogative of mercy, but given the terms of the treaty which the government ratified, the Mercy Committee should await a ruling from the international body. The court took pains to remind us that unincorporated treaties, though they create 'obligations for the State under international law, does not . . . create rights for individuals enforceable in domestic courts.' Page 32.

91 This view certainly conflicts with that of Lord Hoffman who said: 'Human rights in their practical and important sense are therefore national, not universal.' 'Why We Need a Caribbean Court of Justice', Speech by the Rt Hon Lord Leonard Hoffman, Annual Dinner of the Law Association of Trinidad and Tobago, 10 October 2003, Trinidad and Tobago.

92 *Lewis, above,* fn 80.

93 The CCJ noted: 'It seems to us that the effect which the majority gave to the treaty i.e. expansion of the domestic criminal justice system so as to include the proceedings before the Commission, was inconsistent with their protestations of support for the strict dualist doctrine of the unincorporated treaty. In the result [the reasoning was] . . . unsupported by legal principle.' *Above,* fn 52, p 36, para 76.

94 *Above,* fn 52.

95 [1995] 3 LRC 1.

96 The CCJ perhaps confused the question of whether such an expectation was substantive or procedural, yet this does not take away from the essence of the argument.

which that body made by the local mercy committee. In such cases, therefore, the fairness of the hearing is simply a duty to *consider* the rights enshrined in the treaty before making a determination.

Nonetheless, even if we accept the legitimate expectation doctrine in relation to these cases, the pertinent question must be how and when can such expectations be defeated? Can a legitimate expectation defeat a specific law or legal rule, or even expressed notice contra to the expectation? Earlier death penalty cases had not been persuaded by the legitimate expectation argument.[97] Even if a legitimate expectation existed, a notice by the State stating that it would not delay after a stated time period could make the expectation ineffective. In *Fisher*,[98] for example, the written instructions issued were sufficient to thwart any legitimate expectations that may have arisen.

In *Boyce*, we are allowing a legitimate expectation to defeat specific legal rules. The fact is that as a result of *Pratt* and its progeny, there is a specific legal rule in Caribbean constitutional law which mandates that States must complete the procedures for justice in relation to capital punishment efficiently, and execute convicted persons if needs be, before a specific time period, usually five years. The court should have considered the existence of this specific legal rule. This was a legal rule capable of defeating the legitimate expectation. There is, further, a conflict, not only with ordinary law but with the Constitution. Permitting the legitimate expectation in such circumstances, offends the principle that notwithstanding the influence of international law in certain circumstances, in the face of a conflict with domestic law, international law does not apply and, at any rate, can never override constitutional principles. Indeed, this was a point conceded and even emphasised by Justice Wit in *Boyce* (CCJ).[99]

Danger of a broad interpretation of the *Boyce* principle

The CCJ did warn that the *Boyce* 'decision should not be seen as opening up avenues for the wholesale domestic enforcement of unincorporated treaties.' Despite this proviso, however, the breadth of the legitimate expectation principle, which can and has already been applied to other treaties, makes it a dangerous avenue for expansion. This is especially the case because of the reliance on substantive, instead of procedural legitimate expectation.

The fine distinctions drawn in *Boyce* and other cases create a danger that they will be interpreted to mean that Commonwealth Caribbean States now have directly enforceable Treaty obligations which citizens can claim by pursuing remedies before international bodies such as the various Human Rights Commissions and Committees. This would mean that we could now be defined as monist States, no longer conforming to the dualist doctrine of international law.

While the CCJ did not say this, or at least, mean to say this, the judgment does not go far enough in dispelling that opinion, already being aired after the Privy Council's decision in *Lewis* and the Court of Appeal's decision in *Boyce*. Indeed, even prominent

---

97   See *Fisher v Minister of Public Safety and Immigration (No 2)* (1998) 53 WIR 27.
98   *Ibid.*
99   *Above*, fn 52.

international law academics such as Vascianne have suggested that such international law rights are now essentially part of domestic law, although wondering whether they are to be limited to death penalty cases.[100] The legitimate expectation principle is, however, elastic enough to go beyond death penalty cases.[101]

Yet, although the CCJ's decision could have been more forceful on the point, it is somewhat unfair to ascribe such a view to them. The CCJ was well aware that the application of the doctrine of legitimate expectation could not be equated to a finding that ratified treaties create directly enforceable rights in domestic law as a result of any legitimate expectation created by the ratification of the treaty. Indeed, the CCJ affirmed the principle of the non-enforceability of unincorporated treaties. The duty of the BPC was merely to consider the Report but its recommendations were not binding.

Reiterate the traditional position

Our best course of action is to accept that these cases, both from the CCJ and the Privy Council, do not promote a deviation from the traditional principle that international law is not directly enforceable, as embodied in the dualist doctrine. This would be a face-value approach, as it is indeed the one element of consensus to be discerned from the varied approaches to the question of individual petitions and other influences from non-incorporated treaties.

Such a face-value approach allows us to take a broad perspective to these cases, reconciling them according to their particular interpretations of what may be termed 'sub-rules' such as legitimate expectation or due process, but leaving the fundamental principles of the dualist doctrine undisturbed. Thus, we may not agree with the particular applications of the due process or legitimate expectation theories, as discussed above, but we can agree that such principles have relevance to the questions asked in these cases.

Certainly, at minimum, all of the judges concerned are emphatic that substantive rights encompassed in the various treaties are not now automatically secured to the citizens of the Commonwealth Caribbean as a result of some new embrace of the monist doctrine. Their several statements of caution should assure us of their commitment to the dualist doctrine.

Indeed, Justice Wit, in *Boyce,* saw the fine distinctions made in the *Lewis* and *Boyce* line of cases as evidence of a hypocritical approach. Coming from a judge schooled in the civilist tradition it is not surprising. Wit complained:

> Intriguingly, the courts, although never having relinquished their relevance for the doctrine that unincorporated treaties cannot create rights, gradually devised methods to escape the dire consequences of rigid orthodoxy. These methods invariably led them to accept concepts that seem to be at variance with the official doctrine.[102]

It may well be that the courts are in fact seeking to maintain a legal fiction, but it is one which, for the time being, they are not prepared to relinquish. Justice Wit's view is

---

100   See CCJ Conference of 2 March 2007, Trinidad and Tobago. See also Cummins, above.
101   See *Naidike and Naidike v AG of Trinidad and Tobago* (2004) 65 WIR 372 (PC, Trinidad and Tobago) and *Teoh, above,* fn 95 respectively.
102   *Boyce, above,* Judgment of Justice Wit, p 21.

evidence of a jurisprudential and philosophical clash of two legal systems, the civil law, entrenched in monism, and the common law, embedded in dualism. Yet, in some ways, the two systems are closer than realised, as treaties are automatically brought to Parliament in civil law legal systems, so that here too, it is Parliament and not the Executive, which creates legal rules.[103]

It is demonstrable that all of these various positions on the treaty petition process are still well within the accepted parameters as to when international law can be said to have force in a domestic legal system. For example, it is well established, as we have seen, that references to treaties may be made when interpreting provisions and Constitutions, where domestic law is unclear or unambiguous.

It may be helpful to quote exactly what was said in the relevant cases. In *Lewis v AG of Jamaica*,[104] for example, Lord Slynn in the majority judgment revealed his true thinking:

> It is now well established that found domestic legislation should as far as possible be interpreted so as to conform to the State's obligation under such a treaty (*Matadeen v Pointu* [1999] 1 AC 98, 1149-H).[105]

In truth, therefore, the dualist doctrine is applied in these cases, at least in principle. They actually confirm the traditional view, that there is a presumption that Parliament intends to legislate in conformity with treaties and treaty provisions will apply where there is an ambiguity.[106] As we have demonstrated, the difficulty is in the application of this principle.

The concern with these judgments is that they rely substantially on distorted legal principles, or at best, legal rules stretched beyond recognition to fit a particular construct. Distorted legal principle will have more averse consequences in the long run. Governments, for example, will continue to want to opt out of optional protocols which secure the individual right to petition international human rights bodies.[107] States will also be more cautious about signing treaties which they are not ready to implement.

The net result of *Boyce* and related case law

In sum, we can draw a number of conclusions from the proper interpretation of *Boyce* and other cases of its genre:

(1) Commonwealth Caribbean States still conform to the dualist system. Thus, international treaties are not directly enforceable in Commonwealth Caribbean legal systems.

(2) Such treaties have an impact on the domestic legal system and cannot be ignored.

---

103   In order to avoid such legal conflicts in the future we may well see a more conscious effort by the Executive to bring treaties to Parliament as a matter of course. One can only hope that such a move will result in more and not less adoption of important treaties.

104   *Lewis et al v AG of Jamaica*, (2000) 57 WIR 275 (PC, Jamaica).

105   *Lewis, ibid*, p 22.

106   See, eg, *Boyce, above*, fn 52, p 26.

107   See Antoine, R-M B, 'Opting out of the Optional Protocol: The UNHRC on death row – is this humane?' (1998) 3 Carib LB 30.

They are to be heeded where there is no domestic legal conflict with their provisions.[108]

(3) There are no entitlements to substantive rights found in treaties, that is, the actual rights enshrined in those treaties.

(4) There is an entitlement to procedural rights to access the treaty, in particular a right to be heard by treaty bodies with respect to those treaties where the State has ratified provisions allowing the individual right to petition. This is derived from a legitimate expectation to a fair procedure or, under the Privy Council approach, as part of the due process or protection of the law provisions found in our Constitutions.

(5) Local appellate processes, including non-judicial processes such as those hearing petitions for mercy must *consider* any reports emanating from these international human rights bodies.

(6) Reports from international human rights bodies are neither determinative nor binding on local authorities.

CONCLUSION

We can now legitimately claim that international law is a source of law in the Commonwealth Caribbean, at least in relation to human rights issues. The route may be indirect, through the Privy Council and more recently, the CCJ, which have bound themselves to certain human rights norms. Alternatively, it may be direct, for example, through the opinions of international bodies such as the UNHRC, the reflection of international human rights instruments in written Commonwealth Caribbean Constitutions or the changing status of the enforceability of international human rights norms.

---

108   The CCJ erred on the factual aspect of this point but stated the principle correctly.

CHAPTER 13

LEGISLATION AS A SOURCE OF LAW

THE IMPORTANCE OF LEGISLATION

Legislation is an important source of law in the Commonwealth Caribbean. In fact, in a modern context, there is a tendency for legislation to become even more important. This is because more codification is taking place in the Commonwealth Caribbean and elsewhere in the common law world. This is further evidence of the merging of the common law and civil law legal traditions, discussed above, Chapter 2. Weeramantry states emphatically that 'in the next century ... statutes will unquestionably be the major source of law'.[1]

It should be noted that the Constitution is, strictly speaking, part of the legislative process in the Commonwealth Caribbean, although considered as a separate source of law. Because of its supreme place in the legal system and its significance to other sources of law, it is discussed separately.[2] However, while legislation may be the legal source of the future we should note that it is not a modern legal form, but one deeply rooted in the past. Today, legislation is synonymous with the civil law tradition and the civilisation of Rome and Greece. However, long before these Western civilisations we had the laws of Manu. The Code of Manu has been described as being:

> ... written in verse and divided into 12 chapters. In most parts, the rules are so clearly and concisely stated that nothing can be gained by attempting to summarise or condense.[3]

Just as ancient are the Codes of Hammurabi, the 'completest and most perfect monument of Babylonian law'.[4]

THE NATURE AND ROLE OF LEGISLATION

Both common law and legislation embody legal rules which derive authority from legitimate authorities and institutions of the State. In the case of common law, the appropriate institution is the court while with legislation it is Parliament. There are important differences between these two sources of law. One substantial difference is that legislation emanates from the deliberate law making function of the State.[5] It is that deliberateness which is to be emphasised. Another difference is the directness of the legislative process.

Fuller argues, for example, that there are two main points of difference between

---

1 Weeramantry, CG, 'Judicial Reasoning in the Common Law', Ninth Commonwealth Law Conference, 1990, New Zealand Commerce Clearing House, p 91.
2 See Chapter 6 ('The Written Constitution as a Source of Law').
3 Allen, S, *The Evolution of Governments and Laws*, 1916, p 1005, cited in Crabbe, VCRAC, 'Has Parliament an intention?', in Kodiliyne, G and Menon, PK (eds), *Commonwealth Caribbean Legal Studies*, 1992, London: Butterworths, p 47.
4 *Encyclopedia Britannica*, Vol 11, 1968, London: McHenry, p 41.
5 See, eg, Akzin, A, 'Legislation: Nature and Functions' (1968) 9 International Encyclopaedia of Social Sciences 221.

legislation and custom. First, legislation is deliberately made, whereas 'custom, having no author, simply grows or develops through time'. The second is that 'custom expresses itself not in a succession of words, but in a course of conduct'.[6]

In the Commonwealth Caribbean, the authority to make law through legislation is given to Parliament. This authority is conferred by the Constitution. Parliament is also given the power to confer or delegate such law-making power on other authorities or functionaries. This is the subject of delegated legislation, discussed below, p 234.

Accordingly, all the Constitutions of the Commonwealth Caribbean have a provision almost identical to the following: 'Subject to the provisions of this Constitution, Parliament may make laws for the peace, order and good government . . .'.[7] The authority to make legislation is also derived from the 'separation of powers' doctrine.

The pattern in modern common law legal systems appears to be that principles of law are born out of the common law and equity but the detail of such law is embodied in a statute. The jurisdiction of the courts is also statutorily defined. The common law itself can, therefore, be seen as an area of great development of codification.

How does legislation differ from the common law and equity? Why is it convenient to change the focus of the law to legislation? The answer lies in the fact that because the common law and equity are based on the doctrine of precedent, they are inherently limited. As we saw in Chapter 7, they can only create or develop new principles by building on the old and by manipulating case law.[8] However, legislation is creative and dynamic. It can embody radical and new principles of law. It is not necessary to formulate legislation by referring to already existing principles. Further, one can categorically repeal existing law, that is, abolish it totally and quickly, unlike the common law and equity. Legislation is therefore an efficient agency of law reform, perhaps the best tool for law reform. 'The capital fact in the mechanism of modern States is the energy of legislation.'[9] For this reason it may be more convenient for Commonwealth Caribbean jurisdictions to turn to legislation rather than the common law and precedent to develop a more Caribbean law.

Crabbe, reflecting on the role of legislation draftspersons when creating new legislation, remarks that legislation 'is an instrument of change and innovation in any country'.[10] Certainly, in ex-colonial societies like the Commonwealth Caribbean, this role assumes greater importance and an additional dimension. Legislation must be used to reverse the alienation of English laws and customs to allow the law to reflect the goals and aspirations of West Indian society.

> Not all colonial statutes [or precedents] are necessarily good for the respective countries. The policies that informed them may be diametrically opposed to the present aspirations and development of the people. It is necessary to . . . dig out the weeds, to nurture the institutions in the light of present day circumstances, to sustain the substance that would enhance the development of the law. Progress is the realisation of utopias.[11]

---

6   Fuller, R, *Anatomy of the Law*, 1971, Harmondsworth: Penguin p 64.
7   The Constitution of Dominica, s 41. See, also, the Constitution of the Bahamas, s 52, the Barbados Constitution, s 35, and the Constitution of Trinidad and Tobago, s 53.
8   See Chapter 8 ('The Common Law and the Doctrine of Judicial Precedent').
9   Pound, R, *Social Control Through Law*, 1968, Hamden: Archow, p 383.
10 The Hon Mr Justice VRAC Crabbe, Former Professor of Law, Faculty of Law, and Director of the Legislative Drafting Programme, UWI, 'Custom and the statute law' [1991] Stat LR 90, p 91.
11 *Ibid.*

We see too that legislation is different from other sources in that it is its own legal source. In contrast, the common law and equity, for example, we can only ascertain legal rules by reference to other legal sources, such as precedents. Legislation looks inward to itself and does not need to refer to other legal sources. Instead, we must simply interpret the statute under the rules of statutory interpretation. We will see later that it is not always easy to find the true intention of a statute and we may have to look at case law and precedent to interpret and determine legislation. In this sense, we can say that, in practice, legislation may feed on case law.

FUNCTIONS OF LEGISLATION

What are the functions of legislation? Broadly speaking, they are to carry out law reform, and create, alter or revoke law in order to fulfil the intention of the legislative body and ultimately the people. As we will see, an important function of legislation is to fill in the gaps found in other sources of law such as the common law or equity. However, a more detailed description of the functions of legislation may be given. These functions are:

(a) *Revision*

The revision of substantive rules of the common law may occur when the law has become stale or incapable of adaptation, or when an unpopular decision is made by the courts. Revision can overcome the restrictive way the doctrine of precedent works, thereby creating change.

It should be remembered that law is supposed to be a vibrant social tool for progress. The common law and precedent are not always efficient in this role, as the common law judge is powerless to effect change, even where public opinion is in favour of such change. The judge cannot create law but can only illuminate on the need for law reform. For example in a spate of child pornography in the schools of the region in circumstances where there was no law or penalty adequate to deal with the enormity of the crime, judges were forced to set limits on sentencing, irrespective of any desire to punish criminals convicted of such crimes. This propelled the legislature to devise new criminal offences and sentences for such crimes.

(b) *Consolidation of enactments*

Where a certain area of law has developed piecemeal, legislation may be passed to clarify and simplify the status of the law. Consolidation does not, however, alter the substance of law but merely its form. There are three ways to effect consolidation:

• pure consolidation or re-enactment;
• by making corrections and minor improvements;
• by making amendments.

(c) *Codification*

Codification is similar to consolidation, except that the latter only refers to statutes already existing, whereas codification can make case law into statute. It serves essentially the same function as consolidation, that is, to simplify and clarify the law. Where areas of law are consolidated and codified, we call this a code. A good example is the current initiative in labour law in the Commonwealth Caribbean toward codes. This seeks to bring together all the diverse statutes on labour law into a coherent, modern and unified piece of legislation.[12] We may view the code as an elevated type of legislation.

(d) *Collection of revenue or monetary control*

There are certain specific statutes which have the sole function of regulating fiscal concerns or the collection of revenue. This is an important function of legislation. Examples are statutes which implement Value Added Tax (VAT) or Customs duty.

(e) *Implementation of treaties – incorporation*

When a country enters into an international treaty, it undertakes to implement laws in conformity with such a treaty. Such a process usually requires the enforcement of relevant treaty obligations. After the signing or ratification of the treaty, a country may wish to ensure that it is enforceable under local law.[13] At this juncture, legislation which mirrors the treaty or parts of it must be passed locally. This is usually undertaken via a statute under a process called 'incorporation'. The function here is to harmonise and standardise international law and include it within the legal framework of domestic law. The treaty then becomes part of the municipal or domestic law. Countries which sign treaties are under a duty to legislate so as to enforce the treaty.[14] For example, several countries in the region have incorporated international money laundering agreements into their domestic law.[15]

(f) *Social legislation*

The use of the legislative function to create 'social legislation' is concerned with the day-to-day administration of the country rather than creating criminal offences or rights and duties of individuals. Usually, Parliament tends to delegate such legislation to subordinate bodies and these are given the power to make regulations for this purpose. An example is immigration regulations. Social legislation is, therefore, usually part of the administration function of the State.

(g) *Public policy*

Legislation may also be enacted in the public interest to outline a particular policy of the State, satisfying the demands of the public for such a law or the State's intention to move in a new direction.

(h) *Response to pressure groups*

Any change in the law may be a response to pressure groups within the society. Legislation is the most efficient means of effecting such changes and demonstrating a sensitivity to the concerns of these peer groups. Good examples are environmental legislation and human rights law.

---

12   As a result of recommendations under the CARICOM Harmonisation of Labour Law Report, 1992, CARICOM, a Declaration of Principles on Labour Law is already in place, but this, although an example of a code, is not binding. Antigua and Bermuda already has a Labour Code 1975. The Parliament of St Lucia passed a comprehensive Labour Code in 2006, but it remains to be brought into force. These Labour Codes, however, also encompassed law revision, effecting substantive changes to Labour Law.

13   See the discussion on the problems of the enforceability of international law in Chapter 12 ('International Law as a Source of Law').

14   Decisions of the international courts which interpret the treaty are also to be followed by local courts.

15   See, eg, the Money Laundering (Prevention) (Amd) Act 2001, of Dominica.

TYPES OF LEGISLATION

There are three main forms of legislation, Acts of Parliament, delegated legislation and autonomic legislation. Acts of Parliament are also called statutes. In the pre-independence context, these were called Ordinances.[16] In addition, there is a special form of legislation known as Orders in Council.

ORDERS IN COUNCIL FROM THE PREROGATIVE

Orders in Council are made under the Prerogative[17] with the advice of the Privy Council. The Prerogative is the residue of the special common law power given to the Crown or Head of State. The power to make Orders in Council is a limited power. Such instruments are not, therefore, viable alternatives to Acts of Parliament. Their main application is in relation to the armed forces, states of emergency and the Civil Service. The exercise of the prerogative power is normally subject to less judicial scrutiny than other types of legislation, although this is changing in the region.[18] In *Council of Civil Service Unions v Minister for the Civil Service*,[19] regulations were made pursuant to the prerogative power denying civil servants in the security forces the right to strike. These were upheld. The courts were hesitant to intervene into the realm of national security.

While most countries in the region are still subject to the Crown, the fact of independence means that the Queen of England has very little influence on these countries. It is to be expected, therefore, that the use of the prerogative power in this manner is almost unheard of. One situation where it could legitimately have been used and about which it was discussed, was at the time of the Grenada invasion by the US in 1983. This occurred after a coup in which the Prime Minister was assassinated. The US intervened and claimed that it did so in order to restore public order and at the request of the Governor General. Britain, however, was reportedly affronted at this step, as such a request should have been made only by the Queen, or alternatively, a request by the Governor General to the Queen, for Britain's assistance. It was also the Crown which would have had the authority to make general security arrangements, including Orders in Council.

Orders in Council made under the prerogative power must be distinguished from Orders in Council made under the delegated law function, discussed below, p 234. Where Orders in Council are made under a statutory power, they are statutory instruments. The latter does not differ in substance to other types of subsidiary legislation, although they are usually regarded as its 'most solemn and dignified form'.[20]

---

16   The concept of an Ordinance is still important in the Caribbean. Some of these laws enacted during colonialism still exist on the statute books.

17   In most Commonwealth Caribbean countries, the Head of State is still the Queen of England. Certain countries, such as Trinidad and Tobago and Guyana, are now Republics. This means that the Queen as Head of State has been replaced. In Trinidad and Tobago, for example, there is a President.

18   See, eg, *Hochoy v NUGE* (1964) 7 WIR 174.

19   [1985] AC 374.

20   Miers, D and Page, A, *Legislation*, 1990, London: Sweet & Maxwell.

ACTS OF PARLIAMENT

Acts of Parliament are created by the legislative arm of Parliament as part of its inherent law-making function under the 'separation of powers' doctrine. There are two kinds of parliamentary statute:

(a) private Acts – private legislation is that proposed by a corporation, company or private organisation. It will affect only the proposer or sponsor of the Act;

(b) public Acts – public Acts of Parliament are those statutes with which we are more familiar. A public statute is proposed by the people through its representatives in Parliament. It will affect the entire nation.

Public legislation also includes statutes which are passed in conformity with international treaties or agreements.

Statutes or Acts of Parliament usually have a 'long title' and a 'short title'. The long title is the official name. It is essentially a synopsis of the legislation's content and aims. Following the title is the 'date of assent' by the Head of State. The 'date of assent' need not be the date on which the statute came into force. A separate date may be given from which time the statute has effect. The 'words of enactment' are the words 'be it enacted . . . ' which are found in statutes. Before enactment, the legislation is called a 'Bill'. The procedure for elevating a Bill to an Act, thereby conferring on it the authority of law, is as follows.

Where public legislation is proposed, it must be discussed by both the Upper and Lower Houses of Parliament, the Upper House comprising the non-elected body, the Senate. After the Bill is drafted, it is introduced in either the Lower or Upper House of Parliament to be endorsed and then to be passed in the other House. There is a first reading, second reading and third reading of the Bill. The first reading is actually only an announcement of the title of the Bill. At the second reading the Bill is debated.[21] In practice, a Bill is more often introduced in the Lower House. Any Member of Parliament may introduce a Bill, but this is usually done by government. After an Act is passed it must be assented to by the Head of State, after which a date is set for it to come into force. The date on which the Act will come into force may be chosen by a functionary such as the Minister in whose portfolio the subject matter falls. Alternatively, the Head of State may choose the date at which the Act comes into force.

DELEGATED OR SUBSIDIARY LEGISLATION

Delegated or subsidiary legislation is the type of legislation with which administrative lawyers are concerned. It is the body of legal rules created by subordinate or statutory bodies which have specific power to do so because Parliament has delegated that power to them. Delegated authorities are given wide discretion to formulate the details of such legislation. However, the authority for creating the substance of the legislation remains vested in Parliament. We view delegated legislation as a more indirect source of law.

---

21   After the second reading, there is usually a committee stage whereupon the clauses of the Bill are debated, but not its general principles. Amendments may be made. At the third reading, the Bill may be passed. There is usually very little debate at this stage.

There are important differences between Acts of Parliament or statute and delegated legislation. They are both legal sources. Both have force of law and legal authority. However, because delegated authorities do not have the authority to formulate legal policy, delegated legislation is subject to more scrutiny by Parliament and the courts. This is correct legal principle because it is, ultimately, Parliament's responsibility to create law. When Parliament delegates the power to make subsidiary legislation to a statutory body, it does not intend that body to have complete authority. The main types of delegated legislation are bylaws and regulations or orders.

Regulations or orders

Regulations, also called 'rules' or 'orders' are created by government departments and are the most popular form of delegated legislation. They are often statutory instruments and are normally cited by calendar year and number, for example, SI 1998/10, and by a short title.

Bylaws

Bylaws are rules made by a governmental authority subordinate to Parliament, such as a local authority or independent statutory corporation, for the regulation, administration or management of a certain district, undertaking, property, etc. They are binding only on the persons who come within this restricted scope. They are statutory instruments only if the enabling or parent Act authorising them to be made declares them to be.

FUNCTIONS OF DELEGATED LEGISLATION

There are several reasons for the creation of delegated legislation. Most of these have to do with administrative efficiency. Dicey argues, for example, that:

> ... the cumbersomeness and prolixity of ... statute law ... is due in no small measure to futile endeavours of Parliament to work out the details of large legislative changes. The substance and form of the law would probably be a good deal improved if the executive could work out the detailed application of general principles embodied in Acts of Parliament.[22]

Speed and efficiency

Parliament may not be able to wait for their deliberations to be complete before implementing the details of a statute. The process of approving new legislation in Parliament is a lengthy one. It must also allow for parliamentary debate, which may further slow down the process. Delegated legislation, in contrast, is speedy.

---

22 Dicey, A, *Introduction to the Study of the Law of the Constitution*, 10th edn, 1959, London: Macmillan.

Technicality

Another reason for the creation of a delegative function in the making of legislation is that the subject matter of delegated legislation may be very technical, and best left to experts.

Special knowledge

The process of creating legislation might also require specific or local knowledge from experts or people in a particular location. Discussion with specific groups such as farmers or bankers may be needed. This is best left to experts rather than politicians.

Flexibility

Because delegated legislation is able to avoid the lengthy parliamentary approval process, it is not as cumbersome to change as Acts of Parliament. It can be revoked or amended easily.

Bulk

Legislation may require details which are too numerous to place in an Act of Parliament. Acts of Parliament are primarily geared toward the public's consumption, whereas delegated legislation is most often utilised by bureaucrats and subsidiary bodies. It is, therefore, more sensible to put the details of the law in the latter. For example, where Parliament creates legislation on occupational health and safety, scientific details about harmful chemicals are more conveniently placed in delegated legislation.

Future developments

With delegated legislation, the process of adding details as necessary to the provisions of the law is facilitated. This makes it easier to cater for future developments which need to be reflected in the law.

AUTONOMIC LEGISLATION

Autonomic legislation is a special type of delegated legislation. The major difference between autonomic legislation and other forms of delegated legislation is that, in the case of the former, an autonomous body has an independent power to legislate for its own members and, in limited cases, for members of the public. This power is usually conferred by Parliament, but this is not always the case. However, in all cases, the power is sanctioned by Parliament. Examples of autonomous legislative bodies are the Bar Councils, the respective Chambers of Commerce[23] and churches. Autonomic

---

23   Such as the Barbados Chamber of Commerce and Industry recognised under Cap 376 B.

legislation is also subject to judicial control under modern principles of administrative law.

A good example of such legislation is seen in the Privy Council decision of *Gatherer v Gomez*.[24] In that case, Parliament enacted the Anglican Church Act[25] to settle, *inter alia*, the relationship between church and State. By s 24, the Diocesan Synod established under the Act was empowered to make rules, Ordinances, canons and regulations as it thought fit for the general management, discipline and good government of the church. The Privy Council struck down a regulation which was used to retire Reverend Gatherer at the age of 65 on the ground that it was not published in the Gazette in accordance with s 16(1) of the Interpretation Act.

CONTROLLING THE LEGISLATIVE PROCESS

Both Acts of Parliament and delegated legislation and its control must be subject to controlling mechanisms to ensure that the law making function is not abused. Acts of Parliament and delegated legislation are subject to both parliamentary and judicial controls. However, the controlling mechanisms for delegated legislation are more numerous and stringent.

Controlling Acts of Parliament

In the case of Acts of Parliament, there is an important difference between the UK and Commonwealth Caribbean jurisdictions. Contrary to the UK position, which conforms to the doctrine of parliamentary sovereignty, Acts of Parliament are not unlimited in jurisdiction in the Commonwealth Caribbean, but must be measured against the Constitution, which is supreme.[26] This means that in the Commonwealth Caribbean, unlike the UK, Acts of Parliament are subject to judicial scrutiny under the principle of judicial review.[27] This doctrine allows legislation to be examined by the courts to see whether it is *intra vires* or in accordance with the principles of the Constitution.

The parliamentary process through which Acts of Parliament are debated is also an important mechanism for control. There, proposed statutes may be amended or rejected altogether. Ordinary citizens, through their participation in public debate, also have a role to play in this process.

PARLIAMENTARY CONTROL OF DELEGATED LEGISLATION

There must be proper supervision and scrutiny of delegated legislation by Parliament. The rationale behind this type of control is that the mandate for legislative making authority is given to Parliament. Members of Parliament are the ones elected to represent the people, and care should be taken not to violate this government of the people, namely representative government.

---

24 (1992) 41 WIR 68.
25 Cap 375.
26 See the discussion in Chapter 7 ('The Written Constitution as a Legal Source').
27 *Ibid.*

Types of Parliamentary control include:

(a) laying – this means merely presenting the document to Parliament, with no discussion or explicit approval of it. Instead, approval is implied;

(b) laying, subject to affirmative resolution – in this process, after the laying of the legislation before Parliament, an affirmative vote must be obtained in order for the legislation to be passed;

(c) laying, subject to a negative resolution – in this situation, the legislation must be laid before Parliament and if, after a certain number of days, there is no objection to it, it is passed. It must be laid within a stated period (for example, 40 days) after it is created, or else it becomes void;

(d) publication – the legislation must be published for it to become law. It will usually be published in the *Government Gazette*.[28]

As we will see, these requirements may also be subject to judicial control.

JUDICIAL CONTROL OF DELEGATED LEGISLATION

Delegated and subsidiary legislation provide the source of decision-making power for administrative bodies. Administrative decision-making power is discretionary. When such bodies act outside the scope of this power, the courts may review their actions with a view to providing a remedy to those members of the public who have been affected. The act of wrongdoing is described as *ultra vires*, while the review process is called judicial review. The court is able to carry out this inquiry because of its inherent supervisory jurisdiction to supervise subordinate decision-making bodies. This is supported by its function to uphold the rule of law and the ideals of justice.

The process of judicial review of administrative action is increasingly important in the Commonwealth Caribbean. One reason for this importance is the added support for the judicial review process found under Commonwealth Caribbean Constitutions. Similarly, the principle of natural justice, a pillar of administrative law and the judicial review function, is enshrined in Commonwealth Caribbean Constitutions.

To add support to the judicial review process, two jurisdictions in the Commonwealth Caribbean have enacted ordinary legislation codifying the principles of judicial review. These are Barbados and St Lucia, under their respective Administrative Justice Acts.[29] These statutes codify and often clarify the common law principles of administrative law which have developed radically in recent years. They further provide distinct and separate mechanisms for judicial review procedures without excluding the processes and remedies available under the dynamic common law jurisprudence in this area.[30]

The Court of Appeal may control the delegated legislative process at two separate stages, called pre-emergent control and post-emergent control. Pre-emergent control concerns the examination of the procedures expected to be carried out before the legislation comes into effect. Under pre-emergent control the court examines whether

---

28   See *Gatherer v Gomez* (1992) 41 WIR 68.
29   See, eg, the Administrative Justice Act 1980 of Barbados.
30   For example, the doctrine of legitimate expectation has been further developed under the common law, in particular, its substantive aspects, since the promulgation of these statutes.

any set 'conditions precedent' (preconditions), such as laying or consultation, which have been laid down by Parliament have been satisfied. In post-emergent control, the court is concerned with inquiring into the validity of the regulations after they come into effect. The court will test whether it is acceptable to and in conformity with the parent statute. The concern of post-emergent control is that power conferred by Parliament is not abused.

The use of judicial mechanisms to control delegated legislation under the principle of judicial review is the subject of administrative law. We can separate this judicial process into procedural *ultra vires* and substantive *ultra vires*.

Procedural *ultra vires*

Procedural *ultra vires* concerns the examination of the process used to create the legislation to determine whether it was appropriate. If there were preliminary procedures which were not followed, the court may find that the legislation was not legitimately effected and is *ultra vires*. Often, these questions arise at the pre-emergent control stage.

It is not always that a failure to follow such procedural requirements or preconditions would be fatal to the exercise of delegated power. Some preconditions are mandatory, and others are merely directory. Where they are directory, the regulations will not be void. Courts have been inconsistent with regard to whether these preconditions are mandatory or not. The exception is where the procedural requirement springs from the Constitution, such as a requirement to consult, as seen in *Re Alva Bain*.[31] Similarly, in *Kelshall v Pitt*,[32] the minister had the authority declare a state of emergency. However, before he could do so, he was required to put a review tribunal in place, as required under the Constitution. He exercised the power to make the regulations without fulfilling this condition precedent. The regulations were held to be *ultra vires* and of no effect, since he had failed to put a review tribunal in place.

The jurisprudence surrounding the issue of mandatory and direct requirements or conditions has been considerably advanced in recent years and subject to sometimes surprising interpretations by the courts. These are discussed in Chapter 14 ('The Rules of Statutory Interpretation'). Suffice it to say that the distinction between the two forms is no longer as clear. Further, formulae of words used are not necessarily determinative. Words which are apparently coercive in character, for example, may not be mandatory.

The courts will examine the parent Act to find these preconditions. Common examples are the requirements for consultation and laying as seen in *Biggs v COP*,[33] the case of the infamous train robber. In that case, the minister had power under the Extradition Act to make regulations. However, the regulations had to be laid in Parliament within a specific time. Biggs, a convicted robber, went free because the regulations were held to be invalid due to the non-fulfillment of this precondition which was viewed as mandatory.[34] Similarly, in *AG v Barker*,[35] the requirement that

---

31 Unreported Suit No 3260 of 1987, H Ct, Trinidad and Tobago.
32 (1971) 19 WIR 136.
33 (1982) 6 WILJ 121.
34 See, also, *Lau v Percy* (1960) 3 WIR 47. A notice of refusal was mandatory. Consequently, where no notice was given, the regulations were of no effect.
35 (1984) 38 WIR 48.

regulations under the Education Act which purported to set out the conditions for the qualifying examinations for admission to secondary schools were subject to the affirmative resolution procedure. This was a mandatory requirement, the violation of which was sufficient to invalidate the 1982 Education Regulations.

In contrast, in *Springer v Doorley*,[36] three months after they had been read, the regulations had not been approved by both Houses of Parliament as required. The court held that the provision of laying was only directory. The regulations could therefore stand.

The requirement as to publication is usually strict. Thus, in *Kelshall v Pitt*[37] and *Gatherer v Gomez*,[38] the regulations were legal only where published, as required by the parent Act.

Where Parliament requires that the minister or other relevant delegated body can only exercise power after consultation with other bodies, this will usually be mandatory. In *Port Louis Corporation v AG*,[39] the intention of government was to change the boundaries of Port Louis, but the minister was required to consult the relevant local authority. The local authority requested an extension of time before expressing its views. The minister refused. It was held that the regulations were *ultra vires*. By refusing to allow the extra time, the requirement had not been met. Consultation was a mandatory requirement and not a mere formality.

Substantive *ultra vires*

In contrast to procedural *ultra vires*, in substantive *ultra vires*, the court is concerned with the content of the subsidiary legislation as measured against the parent Act. Consequently, the courts will examine the actions of tribunals and the purview of delegated legislation to ensure that they are not *ultra vires* the original legislative function and purpose as embodied in the parent Act. Since it is the parent Act or enabling statute which gives the authority to make subsidiary legislation, its terms must be respected. Delegated legislation can only be valid if it is within the legislative powers conferred on it by Parliament.

Where, for example, a functionary creates legislation completely outside the subject matter of the power delegated, or goes beyond the boundaries of that power, there is a breach of *ultra vires* in a substantive sense. Subsidiary legislation must be confined to the limits of the parent Act. For example, if Parliament gives authority to regulate children's playgrounds, the delegated authority may not regulate for playgrounds and parks, otherwise it will be *ultra vires* or outside of the jurisdiction granted. A striking example of this was seen in *AG v Barker and Another*.[40] The issue was whether the Minister of Education had the power to intervene into the conduct of the admission and/or transfer of students to secondary schools pursuant to the rules governing the competition. It was held that the functions of the Minister of Education as set out under the Education Act 1981 did not empower him to determine the qualifying mark

---

36   (1950) LRBG 10.
37   (1971) 19 WIR 127, p 136.
38   (1992) 41 WIR 68.
39   [1965] AC 1111.
40   (1984) 38 WIR 48.

of a pupil in the secondary schools' entrance exam. Accordingly, reg 25(93) of the Education Regulations 1982, by purporting to give the minister such power, was *ultra vires* the Act and invalid.

In *Bonadie v Kingston Board*,[41] the Ordinance empowered the Board to make laws for regulating the period when elections to the Board should take place, but did not authorise the Board to make a bylaw to determine disputed elections. The bylaw was therefore *ultra vires* and invalid, since it went beyond the power or jurisdiction of the parent Act.[42]

The actual exercise of the delegated power by the relevant authority may also be found to be *ultra vires* the parent Act, the delegated legislation or fundamental precepts of law. This is a wide and complex subject under administrative law. The courts have devised intricate rules to control this power. For example, a delegated authority cannot exercise the discretion he is given to decide matters arbitrarily, unfairly, irrationally or unreasonably, nor must he take irrelevant considerations into account. Whilst this topic is beyond this book, a recent example which touches on another of our areas of concern will suffice. In *Mohammed v Morraine and Another*,[43] the court considered whether the refusal of a School Board to allow a student to attend classes in Muslim dress violated the Regulations under the Education Act of Trinidad and Tobago. The court found that it did, as the Board had applied the Regulations inflexibly and had not taken into account the 'psychological effect' of the refusal, which was a relevant consideration. It had also taken into account irrelevant considerations, such as the question of school tradition.

Injustice and unconstitutionality

Subsidiary legislation will also be declared *ultra vires* if it goes against certain fundamental presumptions in law. Examples are where it is partial or unequal in its operations, or is manifestly unjust. Further, delegated legislation may not contravene public policy, nor should it be retroactive.[44]

Just as with Acts of Parliament, delegated legislation cannot violate the principles of the Constitution. In the *Mohammed* case, examined above, the court did not find that the Education Regulations violated the constitutional protection of equality under the law. Similarly, in *Belize Broadcasting Authority v Courtenay*,[45] reg 10 of the Broadcasting Regulations of Belize set out the matters to be considered by the Broadcasting Authority before it could give its consent to the televising of political broadcasts. The Court of Appeal found that this did not give the Authority arbitrary powers of censorship and was not a hindrance of the right to freedom of expression as protected under the Constitution of Belize. Accordingly, it was not *ultra vires* the Constitution.

---

41 (1963) 5 WIR 272.

42 See *Francis v Pilotage Authority* (1969) 14 WIR 196. Here, the essential question was whether the delegate authority had the power to abolish compulsory pilotage.

43 (1995) 49 WIR 371. This case was also discussed in Chapter 3 ('Legal Traditions – Types of Legal Systems in the Commonwealth Caribbean').

44 See the famous case of *Congreve v Home Office* [1976] QB 629 (the *TV Licensing* case). The Home Office sought to make new regulations concerning the licensing of televisions retroactive to prevent television owners from benefiting before the regulations came into effect. This was held to be *ultra vires*.

45 (1986) 38 WIR 79.

Thus delegated or subsidiary legislation must pass a threefold test:

(a) it must conform to the intention, purpose and jurisdiction of the parent Act;

(b) in its creation, the appropriate procedural safeguards must be adhered to; and

(c) it must not violate constitutional norms nor other legal norms such as public policy reasonableness, rationality or justice.

CRITICISMS OF DELEGATED LEGISLATION

There are several criticisms which can be levelled against delegated legislation. First, it may be viewed as undemocratic. It is not created by those we elected. This further underlines the difficulty of creating checks and balances in the delegative process. Unlike Acts of Parliament, we cannot affect the end result by voting Members of Parliament out of office if we do not like it! Secondly, delegated authorities often subdelegate their functions to others. This can cause further problems.

In addition, there is so much subsidiary legislation that it is difficult to keep track of it, especially for ordinary citizens. Even Parliament itself may not be fully aware of the content of delegated legislation. Another important defect is that the controls against its abuse may not always be efficient. The most important control of delegated legislation is the process of judicial review. Yet judicial review procedures may not be even carried out. If citizens do not challenge such delegated legislation, these controls are not effective. Commonwealth Caribbean societies do not have a strong tradition of challenging government and government-associated procedures and decisions before the courts. While this is changing slowly, it is currently a significant self-imposed defect.

Even if delegated legislation and administrative decisions are challenged before the courts, this is not a certain process. Judicial review is a relatively new and dynamic area of law. Its rules are not always well defined or consistent. For example, delegated authorities are typically given wide discretion. They may, for example, be given power to make regulations as they 'see fit'. Previously, the restrictions which courts could place on such powers were quite limited. While modern courts are now more aggressive in challenging subordinate bodies, administrative law is a technical subject. Is this the best way to control such laws?[46]

---

46 For a discussion of the judicial review process in the Commonwealth Caribbean, see Fiadjoe, A, *Commonwealth Caribbean Public Law*, 2nd edn, 1999, London: Cavendish Publishing.

CHAPTER 14

STATUTORY INTERPRETATION

INTRODUCTION

As a source of law, case law can be legitimately criticised as lacking certainty. This is, of course, because it depends solely upon the reasoning of a judge, albeit within the context of judicial precedent. Not surprisingly, the judicial mind is often unpredictable, and different judges may come to varying conclusions about a particular set of circumstances. Ultimately, this makes it difficult to determine the outcome of a case. The process of distinguishing judicial precedent might be even more imprecise and subjective.

Legislation, or 'hard law' may, therefore, be viewed as a more certain and reliable source of law than precedent. The society, through its representatives, the legislature and Parliament, decides the status of the law and simply writes it down in a statute. Yet, this may be a simplistic view. The meaning and effectiveness of a statute is only apparent when judges have interpreted it. This may be a difficult exercise. As we will see from the following discussion, the process of interpreting legislation or statutes may introduce even more unpredictability into the process of law making than does judicial precedent.

As Zander explains, 'statutory interpretation is a particular form of a general problem – the understanding of meaning, or more broadly still, communication'.[1] Several factors may cause doubt in the language used in statutes. These include:

(a) ellipsis – the drafter may refrain from using certain words which are regarded as implied;

(b) the drafter may use a broad term and leave it to the reader to ascertain to which situations it applies;

(c) ambiguous words may be used deliberately. In some cases, for example, these may be in the situation where the subject matter is politically or socially contentious. It is then left to a legal challenge to choose a meaning;

(d) unforeseeable developments may change the original meaning of the statute;

(e) there may be inadequate or inappropriate wording which could be the result of a printing error or poor drafting.

To resolve the problems of interpretation, the courts have created rules of statutory interpretation. These refer to the main methods or fundamental mechanisms which courts employ in their quest to derive the meaning of a statute. Traditionally, three rules were employed by the courts. However, in recent times, other rules and approaches have emerged which complement or, in some cases, threaten to subsume the earlier three rules. In addition to these 'rules of interpretation', courts have other tools or aids to assist them in interpreting legislation. These are also discussed in this chapter, following our exposition of the main rules or approaches.

These rules of statutory interpretation have been adopted wholesale in the Commonwealth Caribbean and we should not, therefore, expect to find more than

---

1   Zander, M, *The Law Making Process*, 4th edn, 1994, London: Butterworths, p 105.

minor deviations from English precedents and jurists in our case law. The one exception is our approach to interpreting the Constitution, largely because in the UK, from which our rules on statutory interpretation are derived, there is no written Constitution.

The rules or approaches may be listed as follows:

(a) the literal rule;
(b) the golden rule;
(c) the mischief rule;
(d) the rule of purposive construction;
(e) the policy approach; and
(f) the unified contextual approach.

It is not always easy to tell which of these rules the courts will apply. Further, the modern rules or approaches seem to overlap, in substance if not in tautology. For example, the so-called 'policy approach' can be discussed under the 'rule of purposive construction.'[2]

Commonwealth Caribbean countries also have Interpretation Acts, in which are found principles to guide judges in the interpretation of all other statutes.[3] Limited assistance may be derived from these statutes, as they are primarily concerned with minor guidelines to interpretation, such as the rules that the singular includes the plural and 'he' includes 'she'.[4] In an important case from Barbados, *CO Williams Construction Ltd* v *Blackman and Another*,[5] concerning the question whether the courts could review Cabinet decisions, the Interpretation Act was relied upon to conclude in the affirmative. It was found that the provision in the Interpretation Act that words in the singular included the plural sufficed to enable the word 'Minister' to be read as including the Cabinet in relation to the exercise of a power or duty conferred or imposed by enactment.

While the Interpretation Acts do not envelop fundamental approaches to statutory construction, they are nonetheless important as an initial step to interpreting statutes. The point is well made by Blackman, J in the case of *The Public Counsel v The Fair Trading Commission*.[6] In seeking to find the meaning of 'costs' in the Fair Trading Commission Act Cap 326 B of Barbados, Justice Blackman appropriately sought assistance from the Interpretation Act, Cap 1 saying: 'The approach I adopt in interpreting the Act is that where a word or term is not defined within the specific piece of legislation it is obligatory to first look within the Interpretation Act for assistance.'[7]

Intriguingly, even the Interpretation Acts, which are designed to assist in the interpretation of all other statutes, may be subjects of statutory interpretation themselves. This problem arose with regard to the Interpretation Act 1962 of Trinidad and Tobago in the case of *Grant v Jack*.[8]

---

2 This is the approach taken here.
3 See, eg, the Interpretation Act of Jamaica, Vol 11, *Laws of Jamaica* and the Interpretation and General Clauses Act of Guyana, Chap 2:01.
4 See, eg, s 6 of the Guyana Act, which reads: '. . . unless the context otherwise requires, words in the masculine include the feminine . . . Month means calendar month.'
5 (1994) 45 WIR 94.
6 No 373 of 2006, decided 28 September 2006 (HC, Barbados).
7 *Ibid*, p 15.
8 (1971) 18 WIR 123.

Seeking Parliament's intention

The grounding principle in the exercise of statutory interpretation is that it is Parliament's intention, and not the will of judges, which is to be given expression. Judges do not make law; they merely find it. They cannot substitute their meaning for that of Parliament's. Yet, while judges often say that in interpreting statutes they seek to discover the intention of Parliament, this is not always evident, nor even accurate. What the courts are seeking, said Lord Reid in *Black-Clawson International Ltd v Papierwerke Waldhof-Aschaffenburg AG*, is 'the meaning of the words which Parliament used. [Judges] are seeking not what Parliament meant, but the true meaning of what they said'.[9]

In practice, statutory interpretation may not be as efficient an exercise as the rules suggest. In the first place, the notion of the 'intention' of Parliament is itself misleading and contentious. Crabbe describes it as a:

> ... myth encouraged by the doctrine of separation of powers. It is mere dogma ... To begin with, Parliament never had an intention to introduce legislation. Others had ... Parliament did not ... write what is called its Act. Parliamentary counsel did.[10]

Consequently, seeking Parliament's intention may not be very helpful in ascertaining the meaning and object of a statute. This is not mere hair-splitting. As we will discover, almost all of the rules of statutory interpretation exclude the views and discussions of those who really know what the legislation was about or intended. Consider that there is a considerable amount of background work involved in preparing legislation. Government departments and committees make recommendations proposing new legislation, studies are commissioned, conferences held, consultations made and public debate aired. Yet, by and large, the legal exercise of statutory interpretation ignores this legislative process and concerns itself almost exclusively with the legislative end product, the statute as printed in the Act of Parliament. Crabbe further complains: 'Experience has taught us that Parliament has no mind. And if Parliament has no mind, how can it have an intention?'[11]

THE RULES CONSIDERED

The literal rule

The literal rule puts forward the simple approach that the will and intention of Parliament is best discovered by following the literal or natural meaning of the words in the statute. In *Jalousie v The Labour Commissioner and Attorney General of St Lucia*,[12] Edwards J adopted *in toto* the early statement of the rule made by Tendal CJ in the *Sussex Peerage* case:[13]

---

9   [1975] AC 591, p 613.
10 The Hon Justice VCRAC Crabbe, Former Director, Legislative Drafting Programme, University of the West-Indies, 'Has Parliament an intention?' in Kodilyne, G and Menon, PK (eds), *Commonwealth Caribbean Legal Studies*, 1992, London: Butterworths, p 7.
11 *Ibid*, p 50.
12 No 2004/1998, decided 26 July 2006 (HC, St Lucia) at p 6.
13 (1844) 11 Cl and Fin 85, p 143.

If the words of the statute are in themselves precise and unambiguous, then no more can be necessary than to expound those words in their natural and ordinary sense. The words themselves alone do, in such cases, best declare the intention of the lawgiver.

The collateral rule here is that the courts will be cautious about presuming Parliament's intention and will find that, had Parliament intended a certain result, it would have said so clearly, in plain language. A simple example will suffice. In *Brown v Brown et al*,[14] the Supreme Court of The Bahamas, contemplating s 33 of the Matrimonial Causes Act, Ch 125, found that, taken in its entirety, it contemplated that orders could be made for the benefit of children of a marriage who were past 18 years but remained dependent adults and that if Parliament had intended that no order for maintenance could be made unless the application was made before the child's 18th birthday, 'it would have said so in clear and explicit language.'

The reliance placed on the literal and natural meaning of words used in a statute means that judges are not required, nor expected, to look elsewhere for assistance in interpreting the statute. The words, of themselves, are sufficient and independent. The background to the legislation, its policy objectives, other sections within the statute, and other potentially useful indices of meaning, are all excluded. However, the rule allows the court, in situations of doubt, to have recourse to the Preamble to the Act, which is viewed as a 'key to open the minds of the makers of the Act.'[15]

Unfortunately, the intention of Parliament can sometimes be overshadowed by the priority given to literalism. Despite this, the court will find in favour of clarity, in the sense of a predictable literal meaning, rather than attempting to decipher, by other means, what Parliament truly intended. So, for example, in *Alexandra Resort and Villas Ltd v Registrar of Time Share*,[16] in interpreting s 10(1)(a) of the Time Sharing Ordinance, on the question of the amount of the funds to be paid into an escrow fund. Ground, CJ refused to examine legislation from other countries for assistance. Although accepting that 'nowadays, legislation is to be interpreted purposively', he felt that this did not enable him to 'go behind the clear words of the statute.'[17]

Initially, at least, the literal rule applied even where a literal meaning led to an apparent absurdity. This was a highly detached position taken by the courts. The proposition was put most succinctly by Lord Esher in *R v Judges of the City of London Court*:[18]

If the words of an Act are clear, you must follow them, even though they lead to a manifest absurdity. The court has nothing to do with the question whether the legislature has committed an absurdity.

The literal rule has been generously applied in several Commonwealth Caribbean cases. A graphic illustration of the rule and its weaknesses may be found in the case of *Baptiste v Alleyne*.[19] The accused was found *outside* a house, with his hand through a window choking a female occupant. He was charged with the offence of being 'found *in* any building with intent . . .', and was convicted. He appealed against the

---

14 BS 2004 SC 25 (The Bahamas).
15 *Sussex Peerage, above*, n.13, p 143.
16 TC 2002 SC 8 (Turks and Caicos).
17 *Ibid*, para 5.
18 [1892] 1 QB 273, p 290.
19 (1970) 16 WIR 437.

conviction. The Court of Appeal found that if a person is to be convicted of such an offence, there must be clear and unmistakable evidence that he has been, as the section said, 'found in' the building. De la Bastide, JA, for the Court of Appeal, said:

> There was no such evidence in the instant case, for on a full and reasonable interpretation of the evidence which was that the appellant was standing on the ground outside of a window with both hands inside the house, he cannot in this court's view be said to have been 'found in the building' on a literal meaning or ordinary interpretation of the words of s 29(d) of the Larceny Ordinance.

The Court of Appeal allowed the appeal, quashing the conviction. The decision in *Baptiste* is consistent with a correct interpretation of the literal rule. However, the layperson might be forgiven for concluding that the end result was surprising. Was that what Parliament really intended?

The danger of following closely the literal meaning of the words of a statute without paying enough attention to its purpose is also demonstrated in the case of *Evon Smith v R*.[20] The case concerned the interpretation of s 2 of the Offences Against the Person (Amendment) Act 1992, in particular, the offences of capital murder and murder. It was decided against the backdrop of recent rulings by the Privy Council in Jamaica (and elsewhere in the region) that the mandatory death penalty was unconstitutional. Accordingly, the court had to decide whether the offence committed when the appellant broke into a dwelling house and killed his girlfriend warranted the death penalty as a capital murder offence or not.

The relevant provision defined 'capital offences' as 2(d) 'any murder committed by a person in the course or furtherance of . . . (ii) burglary or housebreaking; (iii) arson in relation to a dwelling house'. The appellant broke into his girlfriend's house and chopped her to death, but did not steal or commit any other felony. The majority judgment did not treat this as amounting to capital murder but merely murder, on the ground that the Act required a duality of purpose on the part of the murderer to kill and to do something else, steal, commit arson. If there was only one criminal purpose, to kill, it was not capital murder. The majority found that if the Legislature had intended that every person who kills after breaking into his victim's home was guilty of capital murder, it would have said so clearly. Instead, it restricted the categories of capital murder with 'absolute clarity'.

However, the dissenting judgment by Lord Hoffman and Lord Hutton seems to get to the heart of the matter more successfully. It points out that the purpose of s 2(1)(d) was to protect citizens from being murdered in their own homes by intruders who break in at night. Further, the section attempted to deter such murders:

> We consider that the Legislature could not have intended that an intruder who broke into a house, which he believed to be unoccupied, for the purpose of stealing . . . then, coming upon the occupier, killed him . . . should be guilty of capital murder, but that a person who broke into a house with the express purpose of killing the occupant and did so should not be guilty of capital murder . . . it is difficult to see why the Legislature would think that the intruder who breaks in with the express purpose of killing the occupier should be regarded as less heinous.

In *R v Ramsonhai and Duke*,[21] the unpredictability of the literal rule was again highlighted. This was a case from Guyana. Here there was an appeal against

---

20 [2005] UKPC 43 (Jamaica).
21 (1961) 3 WIR 535.

conviction for the offence of 'conspiracy with another to prosecute any person for an alleged offence knowing that person to be innocent'. A police officer prosecuted a person on the false allegation of the two appellants.

At first instance, the trial judge directed the jury that if they believed the evidence, 'it would amount to agreeing to prosecute or agreeing to cause the man Mohammed Ali to be prosecuted.' On appeal, the now defunct Federal Supreme Court held that:

> the words 'to prosecute' in s 330 are to be construed in their strict sense and are not to be extended to include a conspiracy between two or more persons to cause another person to be prosecuted . . .[22]

Even where words in their literal and natural meaning would cause hardship, or where it is undesirable, the court has no authority to deviate from the clear meaning of the statute. This was illustrated in the case of *Hope v Smith*.[23] Here, the court construed the meaning of the phrase 'any summary offence' found under s 104 of the Summary Courts Ordinance, which gave the police power to arrest offenders under the statute and place them in custody. The court found that the phrase was not confined to property offences. While this construction resulted in hardship to the appellant:

> . . . where the language of an enactment is clear and unambiguous, it is not the function of the courts to relieve against any harshness which it may or may not be thought to occasion. That is a matter for Parliament to consider. And, if Parliament thinks that any hardship which any legislation may cause can be avoided by the judicious exercise of discretion by those to whom is committed the duty administering it, the courts must decline to assume a corrective power which they do not at all possess.[24]

However, this excessively narrow reading of the literal rule can no longer be considered legitimate with the advent of the more recent rules of statutory interpretation, considered below. At minimum, a more holistic and contextual approach may be employed in the use of the literal rule.

The literal rule was thus restated by Sir Vincent Floissac in *Savarin v William*,[25] giving the rule more latitude and credibility by utilising a contextual approach. Floissac stated:

> I start with the basic principle that the interpretation of every word or phrase of a statutory provision is derived from the legitimate intention in regard to the meaning which that word of phrase should bear. That legislative intention is an inference drawn from the primary meaning of the word or phrase with such modifications to that meaning as may be necessary to make it concordant with the statutory context.[26]

We should note, however, that this more liberal reading of the literal rule is still confined to context within the statute.

---

22 (1961) 3 WIR 535. See, also, *The State v P Sharma and L Williams* (1977) 25 WIR 166, which upheld the earlier decision in *R v Ramsonhai and Duke, above*, fn 21.

23 (1963) 6 WIR 464. On the specific point of undesirability, see *Ramoutar v Maharaj*, No 1557 of 1995, decided 27 June 2001 (HC, Trinidad and Tobago).

24 *Ibid*, p 467. Cf *Peters v Marksman (Superintendent of Prisons) and the AG* (1997) 2 Carib LB 91 where, in lamenting the failure of the Legislature to reform penal law to allow sentences more humane than the cat-o'-nine-tails, the court said: 'If the legislature chooses not to act, the court will not sit silently by while the basic right of citizens to be treated as human beings is denied.' At p 93.

25 (1995) 51 WIR 75 at 77, Civil App No 7 of 2001, para 10 (CA, Antigua & Barbuda).

26 *Savarain, ibid*, at p 6, para 21.

Defects of the literal rule

The cases above illustrate that the literal interpretation of words used in a statute do not always evoke the intention of Parliament and, as such, may be inadequate as a means to interpret statutes. The defects of the literal rule have been noted by many writers and jurists. Some of the several deficiencies may be stated in this way:[27]

(a) The most important flaw in the literal rule is the assumption that words have plain, ordinary meanings apart from their context. This is based on a false premise, as demonstrated in the case law.

(b) Judges who apply the rule often speak of using the dictionary meaning of a word. However, dictionaries usually provide alternative meanings and these are often ignored. Where there is more than one meaning to a word, it still requires interpretation, which may be a subjective process.

(c) Similarly, the plain meaning approach cannot be used for general words, which are obviously capable of bearing several meanings. In the Bahamian case of *Betts and Others v COP*,[28] for example, Gonsalves-Sabola, CJ identified several meanings for the word 'found' when he had to ascribe meaning to s 28(5) of the Dangerous Drugs Act, which outlawed being found in possession of narcotics. In the Chief Justice's judgment the word included not only being apprehended at a place, but also being seen or discovered. Thus, the fact that the police saw the plaintiff dropping bales of hemp from an aircraft was sufficient to ground the offence.

(d) Curiously, while judges often say the meaning of a particular word is plain, they then proceed to disagree as to its interpretation. For example in *London and NE Railway Co v Berrinan*[29] and *Ellerman Lines v Mannay*,[30] all the judges said the meaning of the relevant words were plain, but different views were given as to their meaning.[31] Again, in *Newbury District Council v Secretary of State for the Environment*,[32] all five judges gave different meanings to the word 'repository', although agreeing that it had a clear and natural meaning.

(e) The plain meaning theory is useful outside the court room, but not in it, where two parties seek to give the rule definition and deliberately encourage alternative uses of statutory words. A judge then has to choose his preferred interpretation.

(f) The literal approach is based on a narrow concentration on the actual words used to the exclusion of the surrounding circumstances that might explain what the words were actually intended to mean. It avoids, to its detriment, the use of other statutory interpretative aids, such as Parliamentary debates, the long title of the Act, etc.

(g) The emphasis placed on the literal meaning of the words of a statute assumes a perfection of draftsmanship which is unrealistic.

(h) One may argue that the literal approach is lazy. Judges do not truly try to understand the statute, as they need not bother whether interpretation makes

---

27 See Zander, *above*, fn 1, pp 120–126.
28 BS 1991 SC 36.
29 [1946] AC 278.
30 [1935] AC 126.
31 See, also, *Nathan v Barnet LBC* [1979] 1 WLR 67.
32 [1980] 2 WLR 379.

sense in the particular context. This hardly leads to a correct interpretation of Parliament's intention.

Despite the recognised defects of the literal rule, it remains the primary rule of statutory construction. However, today there is a more enlightened approach to the literal rule, one considerably influenced by the other rules of interpretation, discussed below. In interpreting a statute, judges will first consider the natural, plain or literal meaning of the words used therein. Parliament is presumed to have used the words intended to give effect to the statute's true meaning. Judges will also seek to give the most benevolent interpretation to the meanings of the words. They recognise too that words have different shades of meaning. A good illustration of this is found in the case of *Betts,* discussed earlier.[33] In this case, the court held that the word 'found' could be interpreted in more than one way, either narrowly or expansively. A more expansive interpretation to mean merely being 'seen', where the offence of being found in possession of drugs, was appropriate. The law would 'offend against commonsense if it fails to allow a purposive construction of the word "found" in the particular statutory context in which it appears.'

Gonsalves-Sabola CJ affirmed that an 'intention to produce an unreasonable result is not to be imputed to a statute if there is some other construction available.' Here, the rigid, selective, literal interpretation was to be avoided. Thus, not only are 'artificial or anomalous constructions to be avoided...[but] where two possible constructions present themselves, the more reasonable one is to be chosen.'[34]

It is only if the literal approach produces difficulty that other rules of statutory interpretation are employed.

Perhaps a more modern expression of the literal rule is this. In interpreting a statute, judges must give to words used in a statute their literal meaning, but must not do so to the exclusion of other relevant factors. Such factors may include the contentious nature of the words used and the context of their use.

The golden rule

The golden rule proceeds upon the assumption that Parliament does not intend an absurd or ineffective result. To avoid such a result, words will be implied into a statute if they are absolutely necessary. The first recorded use of the phrase 'golden rule' seems to have been by Jervis CJ in *Mattison v Hart.*[35] The rule was restated in *Grey v Pearson,*[36] by Parke B (later to become Lord Wensleydale). It is this latter dictum which was to become the focal point for the development and application of the rule. Lord Wensleydale said:

> I have been long and deeply impressed with the wisdom of the rule, now, I believe, universally adopted . . . that in construing . . . statutes, and all written instruments, the grammatical and ordinary sense of the words is to be adhered to, unless that would lead to some absurdity, or some repugnance or inconsistency with the rest of the instrument, in which case the grammatical and ordinary sense of the words may be modified, so as to avoid that absurdity and inconsistency, but no farther.

---

33   *Above,* fn 28.
34   *Ibid,* p 40, quoting from Maxwell, *Interpretation of Statutes,* 12th edn, p 203.
35   (1854) 14 CB 357, p 385.
36   [1857] 6 HC Cas 61, p 106.

The rationale of the rule is that the legislature could not possibly have intended what its words signify, and that the modifications thus made are mere corrections of careless language which give the true meaning and object of the Act. Where the main object and intention of a statute are clear, it must not be reduced to a nullity by the drafter's unskillfulness or ignorance of the law, except in a case of necessity, or the absolute intractability of the language used. Nevertheless, the courts are very reluctant to substitute words in a statute, or to add words to it, and it has been said that they will only do so where there is a 'repugnancy to good sense'.[37]

The rule may thus be expressed as a rule of commonsense, treated as such in *Barnes v Jarvis*,[38] where Lord Goddard, CJ said: 'A certain amount of commonsense must be applied in construing statutes'. This commonsense approach was followed in the case of *Ramoutar v Maharaj*.[39] In this case, the court had to decide the meaning of taking 'steps' in relation to trials under the Rules of Court. The court found that it would not be 'in accord with a commonsense approach, and would lead to an absurd result' to hold that the plaintiff was required to take steps specifically against the first and second defendants as opposed to taking steps to further the action, in order to prevent the matter from being out of time. In this case, the plaintiff had furthered such action by taking steps against a third defendant and indeed, could not have proceeded against the first and second defendants until this step had been taken.

The rule allows the court to alter the structure of a sentence, give unusual meanings to particular words, alter their collation, or reject them altogether.[40]

There are several cases applying the golden rule in the Commonwealth Caribbean.[41] An excellent illustration of the rule is provided in *Davis v R*.[42] The appellant parked his car at the airport. He was charged and convicted by a magistrate for an offence which prohibited 'parking a vehicle elsewhere than in the place provided for that purpose and in the manner required by an authorised officer'. On appeal, it was submitted by counsel for the appellant that the provision yielded an absurd meaning. The Court of Appeal agreed.

The Court found that a literal interpretation of the regulation made 'nonsense' of it. The intention of the statute maker could only have been to require that all persons park in authorised parking places, and that when they do park there, to park in a manner that was in accordance with directions. Two offences had been created, one of parking in the wrong place, and the other of parking in the wrong manner. For example, motorists must park so that they do not block the entrance or exit, or prevent the removal of another car already parked there. Accordingly, the Court introduced the words 'elsewhere than' to qualify the words 'in the manner required' so that the

---

37 *Ibid*, p 106.
38 [1953] 1 WLR 649, at p 652.
39 *Above*, fn 23, pp 19–20.
40 See Maxwell, R. *Maxwell on the Interpretation of Statutes*, 11th edn, 1980, London: Sweet & Maxwell, p 228.
41 The rule is of ancient pedigree in the region. For example, in *Arbuckle v Subransingh* (1909) 1 T and T Sup Ct R 364, Lucie-Smith CJ also used the rule because there are 'cases which shew that the court will interpolate words into a section of an Act of Parliament when the literal language of the Act leads to a manifest contradiction of the apparent purpose of the enactment or to some absurdity, hardship or injustice, presumably not intended, under the influence of an irresistible conviction that the legislature could not possibly have intended what its words signify and that the modification thus made is a mere correction of careless language and really gives the true intention.'
42 (1962) 4 WIR 375.

regulation could read intelligibly and sensibly and the object of the Act preserved. It held that the appellant was charged with a breach of the first portion of the regulation – 'parking elsewhere than in a place provided' – and was clearly proved to have committed that offence.[43]

Courts, are however, reluctant to add to, or imply words into a statute, and rightly so. Edwards J, in the *Jalousie* case[44] explained:

> The other relevant rule of English statutory interpretation, allows a judge to read in words which he/she considers to be necessarily implied by words which are already in the statute. The judge has a limited power to add to, alter or ignore statutory words in order to prevent a provision from being unintelligent, absurd, totally unreasonable, unworkable or totally irreconcilable with the rest of the statute.

He continued:

> The line between judicial legislation, which our law does not permit, and judicial inter- pretation in a way best designed to give effect to the intention of Parliament is not an easy one to draw ... before our courts can imply words into a statute the statutory intention must be plain and the insertion not too big or too much at variance with the language used by the legislature.[45]

In like vein, the golden rule contemplates that a court can ignore grammatical errors within a statute if the words are clear. This occurred in *Enmore Estates Ltd v Darsan*.[46] In that case, there was an error of grammar in the Workmen's Compensa- tion Ordinance of Guyana, which the Privy Council ignored correctly in construing the statute.

Similarly, in *Lewis v St Hilaire et al*,[47] the Privy Council, in a case from St Vincent, employed the golden rule to confirm that the appellant's matter had been rightfully struck out by the lower court for want of prosecution. While there were no express words in the Court's procedural rules which linked them to the requirement that a matter be 'ripe for hearing' before it could be struck out, the Court found that words of qualification could be implied to establish such a link. This was on the ground of 'necessity' as, without it, the Court's rules 'would have no scope for independent operation and would be unable to fulfil the public interest in dealing with the mis- chief of delays in civil litigation.'[48]

Judicial authorities therefore establish that the judicial interpreter may deal with careless and inaccurate words and phrases in the same spirit as a critic deals with an obscure or corrupt text. If he is satisfied, from the context or history of the statute, or from the injustice, inconvenience, or absurdity of the consequences to which it would lead, that the language used does not ruly express the intention, he or she may amend it accordingly.[49]

---

43 *Ibid*. The court also referred to the speech of Lord Dunedin in *Whitney v IRC* [1926] AC 37, p 52, where he said: 'A statute is designed to be workable, and the interpretation thereof by a court should be to secure that object unless crucial omission or clear direction makes that end unattainable . . .'

44 *Above*, fn 12, para 25.

45 *Ibid*, para 26.

46 (1970) 15 WIR 192.

47 (1996) 1 Carib L B 119, PC.

48 *Ibid*, p 120.

49 *Ibid*.

Criticisms of the golden rule

The golden rule should not be viewed as a significant departure from the literal rule. Essentially, it suggests that the judge must follow the literal approach and the golden rule will only be resorted to where the judge is prepared to hold that the result of the literal meaning is manifestly absurd or unreasonable. Priority is, therefore, still afforded to the literal meaning of words. We have seen too, from the cases, that the rule contemplates only that errors or omissions were made in the language and does not attempt in a fundamental way, to go behind the words used or which should have been used in the statute. This is, therefore, a limited exercise of judicial power. Indeed, in the final analysis, the golden rule is applied in very few cases.

In addition, absurdity is a concept no less vague and indefinite than 'plain meaning'. It is difficult to reconcile the cases based on a finding of 'absurdity'.

Consequently, the application of the golden rule is erratic. As Zander puts it, 'one can never know whether a particular conclusion will be so offensive to the particular judge to qualify as an absurdity and if so, whether the court will feel moved to apply the golden rather than the literal rule'.[50]

There is also the danger, in allowing judges to decide whether a meaning is 'absurd', that we are giving them too much room to manoeuvre. They are perhaps being allowed the freedom to deviate from Parliament's intention in accordance with their own subjective evaluation of what is absurd. We should recall that the cardinal principle is that judges do not make law, they only interpret it. The golden rule, like the literal rule, still avoids the utilisation of other aids, such as parliamentary debates, to discover Parliament's true intention. At the same time, it allows changes to Parliament's words.

The mischief rule

The mischief rule is perhaps the oldest known rule of statutory interpretation. It attempts to look at what defect, wrong or 'mischief' Parliament was trying to correct when it enacted the particular statute. The classic statement of the mischief rule is that given by the Barons of the Court of Exchequer in the *Heydon* case:[51]

> That for the sure and true interpretation of all statutes in general (be they penal or beneficial, restrictive or enlarging of the common law), four things are to be discerned and considered.

These four things are:

(a) What was the status of the law before the Act was passed?

(b) What was the defect or 'mischief' for which the law had not provided?

(c) What remedy did Parliament propose to cure the defect?

(d) The reason of the remedy.

---

50 *Op cit*, Zander, fn 1, pp 112–13. See, eg, *The Altrincham Electric Supply Co Ltd v Sale UDC* (1936) 154 LTR 379, in which the arbitrator, the trial judge and a majority of the House of Lords applied the literal rule, and the Court of Appeal and a minority of the House of Lords applied the other rule.

51 (1584) 3 Co Rep 7a.

The judge's duty is to interpret the legislation so as to suppress the mischief and advance the remedy 'and to add force and life to the cure and remedy, according to the true intent of the makers of the Act, *"pro bono publico"'*.[52]

Despite its archaic language, the rule has stood the test of time. However, the modern approach to the mischief rule is to use it in a broader sense, to allow the court to look at the background of the statute. This may be viewed as part of the purposive approach, discussed below, p 256. In fact, the court in the *Heydon* case did permit such a broad view, but subsequent emphases on literalism had narrowed its context. In explaining the reborn mischief rule in the landmark case of *Black Clawson*,[53] Lord Reid said:

> The word 'mischief' is traditional. I would expand it this way. In addition to reading the Act you look at the facts presumed to be known to Parliament . . . and you consider whether there is disclosed some unsatisfactory state of affairs which Parliament can properly be supposed to have intended to remedy by the Act.[54]

The broad view of the rule has been accepted in Commonwealth Caribbean courts. For example, it was expounded by Lucie-Smith CJ in *Bailey v Daniel*[55] where the four elements identified in the *Heydon* case were reiterated. The court confirmed that the first and elementary rule of construction remained the literal rule, but found that it could deviate from it where adequate grounds are found, either in the history or cause of the enactment or its context, or in the consequences which would result from the literal interpretation, for concluding that that interpretation does not give the real intention of the legislature. Further, the court found that:

> . . . the true meaning [of a statute] is to be found, not merely from the words of the Act, but from the cause and necessity of its being made, which are to be ascertained not only from a comparison of its several parts, but also from extraneous circumstances.

In *Guyana Labour Union v McKenzie*,[56] Gonzales-Sabola, JA looked at a Report on the legislation, taking comfort from Lord Reid's judgment in *Black-Clawson*:[57]

> The general rule in construing any document is that one should put oneself in the shoes of the maker or makers and take into account relevant facts known to them when the document was made.

Similarly, in *Bata Shoe Co Guyana Ltd et al v Commissioner of Inland Revenue et al and the Guyana Unit Trust Management Co*,[58] the Court of Appeal of Trinidad and Tobago looked at a report of a legislative committee to find the mischief.[59]

The implications of the mischief rule

In general, the mischief rule may be regarded as being more embracing and encompassing than the other rules of interpretation because it goes beyond the mere

---

52 *Ibid.*
53 *Above*, fn 9.
54 *Ibid*, p 614.
55 (1910) 1 T and T Sup Ct R 379.
56 GY 1981 CA 11.
57 [1975] 1 All ER 810 at 814.
58 TT 1976 CA 53.
59 Relying again on *Black-Clawson, above,* fn 9 and *Letang v Cooper* [1964] 2 All ER 933, *per* Lord Denning.

language of the statute. It recognises at least, that often, language cannot be clearly understood in the absence of its context. In this sense, the rule embodies a 'rather more satisfactory approach' than the other two rules.[60] Nonetheless, the rule is not without difficulty.

The rule invites the question: where is the court to look to identify the mischief? In *Black Clawson*,[61] Lord Diplock noted that, when the rule was first propounded, the mischief was identified by examining the Preamble and other words of the statute. 'It was a rule of construction of the actual words appearing in the statute and nothing else.' Yet, the Preamble and other words in the statute may not be useful indicators of the intention of Parliament, at least with respect to the interpretation of a particular statutory provision.

The broad view of the mischief rule, although useful, may not be as liberal as it first appears. Lord Diplock in *Black Clawson*, while advocating a broader approach, did not clarify how far the court is allowed to look. In practice, the rule remains rather inward looking and there were limits placed on the 'extraneous' factors which could be used to discern Parliament's intention.[62]

Nevertheless, the mischief rule does not appear to be as incestuous as either the golden rule or the literal rule. It allows a more realistic appraisal of the meaning of statutory words by permitting a more holistic perspective of the Act. In fact, as will be seen further, the rule has provided support for those who argue for a purposive approach to interpretation.

CONTEMPORARY APPROACHES

Difficulties and inconsistencies with the three main rules of statutory interpretation have led to alternative approaches to interpretation. In general, proponents of these new approaches argue that too much emphasis is placed on literalism and the words contained *within* the statute and not enough on the context and aims of the Act.[63] While there is consensus that this is the right approach, there is still a considerable amount of debate about the extent of the judiciary's freedom in this exercise, bearing in mind that the law making function remains exclusive to the legislature.

The unified contextual approach

Increasingly, the courts are being urged to adopt a unified contextual approach to interpretation. Under this approach greater prominence is given to the context of words used in a statute. That approach has been promoted by Sir Rupert Cross.[64] The contextual approach is really an amalgam of the other rules. It suggests that courts make a progressive analysis of the status. The essential components of the approach are as follows: the judge must first give effect to the ordinary or, where appropriate,

---

60 As described by the UK Law Commission, 1969.

61 *Above*, fn 9.

62 For example, Hansard or notes of parliamentary proceedings could not be used until the advent of cases such as *Pepper v Hart*, discussed below.

63 See, eg, the UK Law Commission Report 1969.

64 Bell, J and Engle, G (eds), *Cross on Statutory Interpretation*, 3rd edn, 1995, London: Butterworths, pp 50–59.

the technical meaning of words. However, he must determine the extent of words with reference to the general context of the statute. The leading authority is *AG v Prince Ernest Augustus of Hanover*.[65] In that case, Viscount Simmonds defined the context to include 'not only other acting provisions of the same statute, but its Preamble, the existing state of the law other statutes *in pari materia* and the mischief which can by other legitimate means, discern what the statute was intended to remedy'.[66] The defect of the statute is also to be considered as part of the context.[67]

If the judge finds that the primary meaning of the words produces injustice, absurdity, anomaly, or contradiction, then he may move on to consider other possibilities. For example, he may choose a secondary meaning.[68] There is a presumption that Parliament does not intend the absurdity.

A judge may also include words necessarily implied by the words in the statute or exclude or alter words. However, such an exercise should be rare and should only be resorted to if the words are unworkable or totally irreconcilable with the rest of the statute, or to avoid an absurdity. As Lord Scarman said in *Stack v Frank Jones (Tipton) Ltd*:[69]

> If the words used by Parliament are plain, there is no room for the 'anomalies' test, unless the consequences are so absurd that, without going outside the statute, one can see that Parliament must have made a drafting mistake. If words 'have been inadvertently used', it is legitimate for the court to substitute what is apt to avoid the intention of the legislature being defeated ... If a study of the statute as a whole leads inexorably to the conclusion that Parliament had erred in its choice of words, for example, used 'and' when 'or' was clearly intended, the courts can, and must, eliminate the error by interpretation. But, mere 'manifest absurdity' is not enough; it must be an error (of commission or omission) which in its context defeats the intention of the Act.

We should note that, even here, the judges are still not looking primarily outside of the statute for its meaning.

In applying the above rules, the judge may resort to certain aids to construction and presumptions.

The purposive approach

Lord Denning, one of the most creative judges of the contemporary courts, has championed a purposive approach to interpretation. This approach seeks to promote the general legislative purpose underlying the provision in issue.[70] It suggests that the court can use a wide variety of aids to find this purpose. In *Magor and St Mellons v Newport Corporation*,[71] Lord Denning said:

---

65   [1957] AC 436.
66   See, also, Lord Normand, *ibid*, p. 465 and Lord Sommervell, *ibid*, pp 473–74.
67   *Mansell v Olins* [1975] AC 373.
68   See *Barnard v Gorman* [1941] AC 378; *Richard Thomas and Baldwin's Ltd v Cummings* [1955] AC 321.
69   [1978] 1 WLR 231.
70   *Notham v London Borough of Barnet* [1978] 1 WLR 220, p 228.
71   [1950] 2 All ER 1226, p 1236, CA.

> We do not sit here to pull the language of Parliament to pieces and make nonsense of it
> ... We sit here to find out the intention of Parliament and carry it out, and we do this
> better by filling in the gaps and making sense of the enactment ...

However, in *ex p Nilish Shah*,[72] Lord Scarman put forward a narrower test for the purposive approach. He was of the opinion that a purposive construction may only be adopted if judges 'can find in the statute read as a whole or in material to which they are permitted by law to refer as aids to interpretation an expression of Parliament's purpose or policy'. In other words, a broader contextual approach may be adopted. In *Universal Caribbean Establishment v Harrison*,[73] for example, the Court of Appeal, in construing s 7(1) of the Industrial Court Act on the jurisdiction of the Antigua Industrial Court, said: 'speculation as to Parliament's intention is not permissible, but the policy which dictated the statute may be taken into account. Of course, one must bear in mind the oft repeated danger involved, as opinions as to what the policy is, may differ greatly.'[74]

The purposive approach, in emphasising that words are to be read with context, further assumes that contexts may change. Consequently, an 'updating construction' should be employed, allowing the statute to be read as 'always speaking'. This point was made in the Bermudan case of *Re First Virginia Reinsurance Ltd*,[75] where the Companies Act 1981 of Bermuda had to be interpreted with respect to its insolvency provisions. The court accepted that the statute had been based on the Companies Act 1948 of the UK which itself had been interpreted by the courts. This interpretation, as evidenced by the UK case law, was however, rejected by the Bermudan court, as being outdated and irrelevant. The court observed:

> The *Re Galway* case, decided early in the 1700's within an archaic mid-19th century
> statutory framework, can have little bearing on interpreting in the early 21st century,
> the scope of director's powers under a late 20th century statute.[76]

Further, Kawaley, J advised:

> In my view, the Companies Act 1981 must be construed not just according to its terms,
> but also in the wider commercial context of Bermuda today. This Act is one to which an
> updating construction must be given, allowing it to be read as 'always speaking'.[77]

Another way of limiting Denning's purposive approach is to use it together with the literal rule. In *Suffolk County Council v Mason*,[78] for example, it was found that both approaches yield the same result. Some judges have adopted a purposive approach where a literal approach would lead to absurdity or defeat the object of the Act.[79]

Other judges have roundly criticised Lord Denning's approach. Lord Simonds, for example, has described 'filling in the gap' as a 'naked usurpation of the judicial function under the guise of interpretation'.[80]

---

72 [1983] 2 AC 309, p 348.
73 (1997) 56 WIR 241.
74 *Ibid*, p 243.
75 (2005) 66 WIR 133 (Supreme Court, Bermuda).
76 *Ibid*, p 141.
77 *Ibid*, p 146.
78 [1979] AC 705.
79 See, eg, *R v Ayres* [1984] 2 WLR 257.
80 *Magor and St Mellons v Newport Corporation* [1952] AC 189, 191, HL.

In *Fraser v Greenaway*,[81] the Court of Appeal of the Eastern Caribbean States seemed to accept the widest version of the rule. The court considered the words of the Land Surveyors Act 1975, which had repealed the earlier Act of 1879. The new Act provided that surveyors licensed under the old law 'shall be deemed to have been licensed' under the new Act. In litigation to determine whether the appellant was so licensed, the court, because of the 'chronic ambiguity' of the words 'shall be deemed', found it necessary to rely on a purposive approach:

> I prefer to be guided by the fundamental rule that the interpretation of a statutory word . . . is the ascertainment of the meaning which the Legislature intended that the word or phrase should bear . . . Section 32 of the new law cries out for a purposive construction.[82]

Further, the court felt that the:

> statutory content comprises every other word or phrase used in the statute and all relevant circumstances which may be regarded as indications of the Legislative intention . . .[83]

In fact, literalism only became fashionable in the 19th century. The courts are now witnessing a greater emphasis on purpose. As early as 1569, for example, the court in *Stowell v Lourch*[84] said:

> . . . everything which is within the intent of the makers of the Act, although it be not within the letter, is as strongly within the Act as that which is within the letter and the intent also.

What is important then, is the spirit and not the letter of the law.

The purposive approach, despite its critics, appears to be the most accepted approach to statutory interpretation today. Further, developments in the other rules, such as the relaxation of the rule against the use of Parliamentary debates, discussed below, p 270, and the reformulation of the mischief rule, point to a more purposive construction of statute. Even the UK Law Commission of 1975 accepted that judges placed too much emphasis on literalism to the detriment of legislative purpose. They, in effect, approved of Denning's formulation.

The Constitution and the purposive approach

The purposive approach is particularly important when interpreting Constitutions in the Commonwealth Caribbean. This has been noted exhaustively in constitutional jurisprudence. Indeed, we can argue that the extent to which a purposive approach is employed in construing written Constitutions in the region represents the most significant departure from English rules of statutory interpretation. We may also ask whether the purposive approach to interpreting Constitutions is identical to the purposive approach to interpreting ordinary statutes. We examine this approach further in a following section of this chapter.

---

81   (1991) 41 WIR 136.
82   *Ibid*, pp 138–39.
83   *Ibid*.
84   (1569) 1 Plowden 353; 75 ER 536.

The policy approach

The purposive approach can also include what Griffiths views as making political choices or conforming to a particular policy.[85] This means that where there is an ambiguity within the statute, judges will choose the interpretation that best suits their view or policy.

This is brought out in an interesting case from Australia which is also useful to the issue of customary law.[86] In *Wik Peoples v State of Queensland and Others*,[87] the High Court considered whether the Land Act necessarily extinguished all incidents of native or customary title accruing to the Wik peoples, an Aborigine tribe. In finding that it did not, the court was mindful of Parliament's policy to afford rights to Aborigines. Although this was not specifically expressed in the statute, the court relied on the history of land tenureship, disposal of Crown land and the customs of the Aborigines to come to its conclusion. It said:

> Essentially, the function of the court is to give effect to the purpose of the Queensland Parliament in adopting the exceptional course found ...[88]

RULES OF LANGUAGE AND PRESUMPTIONS

In addition to the primary rules of interpretation as described above, the courts have developed a number of 'rules of language'. Unlike the rules of construction discussed above, these are not legal rules and 'simply refer to the way in which people [lawyers] speak in certain contexts'.[89] Of the several rules of language the following may be singled out.

Ejusdem generis

This rule says that general words which follow two or more particular words in an Act must be confined to a meaning of the same class (*ejusdem generis*) as the particular words. The intention is to cover a wide range of similar circumstances by first creating a genus, category or class that is two or more examples, followed by a general expression which has the effect of extending the operation of the statute to all particular circumstances which are within the genus created. In this way, the statute does not need to list all the relevant examples. The rule is best explained by illustrations.

In the landmark case of *Powell v Kempton Park Racecourrse Co*,[90] for example, a section of the Betting Act prohibited the keeping of a 'house, office, room, or other place' for betting with persons resorting thereto. At issue was whether 'Tattersall's Ring' at a racecourse was an 'other place' within the meaning of the Act. The House of

---

85   Griffiths, JAG, *Politics of the Judiciary*, 1986, London: Fontana.
86   See the discussion in Chapter 10 ('Custom as a Source of Law').
87   [1997] CLB 201.
88   *Ibid*, p 207.
89   Bell and Engle, cited in Cross, *op cit*, fn 64, p 89.
90   [1899] AC 143. See also *Gairy v Lloyd et al* (1962) 4 WIR 413, p 417C.

Lords held that it was not, since the words 'house, office and room' created a genus of indoor places. A racecourse, being outdoors, did not fall within the genus.[91]

Similarly, the Sunday Observance Act 1677 provided that 'no tradesman, work-man, artisan, labourer or other person whatsoever shall do business or work of their ordinary calling' on 'the Lord's Day'. In several cases, the provision was held to apply to other persons with occupations of a *similar* kind to those specified. It did not include, for example, a coach proprietor,[92] or a farmer.[93]

A clear category must first be identified for the rule to take effect. This point is illustrated in *Nicholas v The Special Constable Force Association et al*,[94] on a question as to whether 'special constables' were entitled to the same privileges of accommodation and housing as the Jamaica Constabulary Force. The relevant Act stated that 'special' constables were to enjoy all the 'powers, authorities, privileges . . . as the Jamaica Constabulary Force' while on duty. However, Ellis, J found that the structure of the section fractured any presumed category of words, thereby prohibiting the application of the *ejusdem generis* rule.

No genus or class was identified in the case of *AG of the Cayman Islands v Wahr-Hansen*.[95] In this case, the Privy Council rejected the argument made by the Attorney General that the words 'any organisation or institutions operating for the public good' coming immediately after a phrase contained in a trust agreement that the trustees could distribute income to 'any one or more religious, charitable or educational insti-tution or institutions' were subject to the *ejusdem generis* rule. The court held that on a literal construction, the trusts and powers found in the same group were not charit-able and should not, therefore, be given a restricted meaning. Rather, the wording of the entire clause demonstrated an intention to establish general welfare trusts and not merely those with strictly charitable purposes.

It is also clear from the *Wahr-Hansen* case, that the *ejusdem generis* rule is not divorced from the more general rules of statutory interpretation, such as the literal rule. Indeed, it should be reiterated that the *ejusdem generis* rule is merely a rule of language and not a rule of law. As such, it cannot override the rules of interpretation and must be subservient to them. This point is made in the case of *Jacques v Attorney General of the Commonwealth of Dominica*.[96]

In the *Jacques* case, the court examined s 6(1) of the Carnival Order Act 1998, as amended, which proclaimed that 'on the Carnival days any person who uses any apparatus, device, instrument, musical instrument or radio by means of which sounds may be mechanically or electronically produced or reproduced, before 4.00 a.m. and after 8.00 p.m. . . . commits an offence'. The applicant was apprehended for playing his sound system, which produced sounds electronically, on the stated days and contended that s 6(1) had to be interpreted to mean musical instruments from which sounds are mechanically produced, and not sounds electronically produced, according to the *ejusdem generis* rule. However, the court, although fully cognisant of the *ejusdem* rule, affirmed that it applied only unless it is reasonably clear from the

---

91   See also *R v Hussain* (1965) 8 WIR 65, p 88.
92   *Sandeman v Beach* (1827) 5 LJ (OS)KB 298.
93   *R v Clearwater* (1864) 4 B & S 927.
94   JM 1997 SC 11 (Jamaica).
95   (2000) 56 WIR 174 (PC).
96   DM 2000 HC 5.

context or the general scope and purview of the Act that Parliament intended that they should be given a broader significance. In other words, the broad purpose of the statute was to be given priority over the restrictive *ejusdem* rule of language. Thus, the court found that electronically produced sounds came within the mischief contemplated by the Act, overriding the *ejusdem generis* rule.[97]

Expressio unius est exclusio alterius

Another important rule of language seeks to exclude by implication that which is not specifically mentioned in the description of a class of things. Maxwell defines this rule as follows:

> . . . where a statute uses two words or expressions, one of which generally includes the other, the more general term is taken in a sense excluding the less general one: otherwise there would have been little point in using the latter as well as the former.[98]

The rule is illustrated clearly in the case of *Harricrete Ltd v The Anti-Dumping Authority et al.*[99] The subject of inquiry in this case was the meaning of s 8(3) of the Tax Appeal Board Act of Trinidad and Tobago, in particular, the ambit of its powers to address appeals arising from grievances under the Anti-Dumping Act. The court found that the Board had powers only to simply dismiss or allow appeals, as these were the only remedies mentioned in the provision. To 'allow' an appeal could not, for example, include to vacate, nullify, annul or quash such an appeal. The court came to its decision by confirming that s 8(3), by listing the remedies available and expressing two things, impliedly excluded any other in accordance with the 'expressio' rule.

Noscitur a sociis

This rule states that words derive colour and meaning from those which surround them. For example, in *Pengelly v Bell Punch Co Ltd*,[100] the word 'floors' in the phrase 'floors, steps, stairs, passages and gangways' which were required to be kept free from construction, was held not to apply to part of a factory floor used for storage rather than passage.

Mandatory versus directory

Certain words used in a statute may raise the question whether they impose strict requirements or whether they allow latitude.

The words 'shall' and 'may' have often fallen into contention in this manner. It used to be thought that the terms 'mandatory requirement' and 'directory requirement' appropriately described the nature of the obligations contained in the usage of such words. However, recent cases have been at pains to discredit this approach.

The issue has been aired most often in the context of judicial review cases, where a

---

97   *Ibid*, p 8.
98   *Op cit*, Maxwell, fn 34, p 1.
99   (Unreported), No 1254 of 2000, decided 31 May 2001 (High Court, Trinidad and Tobago).
100 [1964] 1 WLR 1055. The rule was followed in *Munro v Commr of Income Tax* (1966) 9 WIR 409.

decision-maker has been given authority to do or not do something, usually involving procedural requirements. The courts have now explained that the true nature of such words, is not so much whether they are *prima facie* obligatory or discretionary, as once thought, but rather the effect or consequences of the act or omission.

The approach was explained in the case of *Charles Herbert v Trinidad and Tobago Judicial Services Commission and Authority*,[101] which inquired into the discretionary powers granted under reg 90(1) of the Public Service Commission Regulations of Trinidad and Tobago, in particular, breach of the time limit provisions.

The Privy Council held that the question of whether the time limit provisions were mandatory or directory was one that should be avoided. The more appropriate question was whether the framers of the regulation intended that time limits be complied with and whether that intention was clearly stated. Further, it should be asked whether a failure to comply with the time limit would deprive the Public Service Commission of its jurisdiction, rendering its decisions null and void. The answers to those questions could come only from examining the overall regulatory scheme and the purpose and policy of the time limit. In the instant case, the fact that the time limits seemed to be designed primarily to expedite the procedure, that is, a mechanism for convenience, made it unlikely that their breach was intended to lead to the frustration of that ultimate purpose. Further, their breach resulted in no material prejudice or unfairness to the proceedings or to fundamental rights. Consequently, their breach was not prejudicial to the Commission's decision.

In *Belvedere Insurance Ltd v Caliban Holdings Ltd*,[102] Maxwell, JA adopted the *dicta* of Millett, LJ in *Petch v Guernsey (Inspector of Taxes)*:[103]

> The principles upon which this question should be decided are well established. The court must attempt to discern the legislative intention . . . Further . . . in each case you must look to the subject matter, consider the importance of the provision to the general subject intended to be secured by the Act.[104]

PRESUMPTIONS OF STATUTORY INTERPRETATION

In addition to the rules discussed above, the courts, when faced with doubtful cases, may apply certain presumptions. These serve as first principles imposed on the statute to be interpreted. The main presumptions are as follows:

(a) *The presumption against changes in the common law*

The courts will contain the abrogation of the common law in its interpretation of statute to only what is necessary to give effect to the intention of the Act.[105] Put another way, statute must clearly express its intention to override a principle of the common law before a change to the common law will be upheld. In *Re The*

---

101   (2002) 61 WIR 471.

102   (Unreported) Civ App No 15 of 2000, decided 5 June 2001 (CA, Bermuda).

103   [1994] 3 All ER 731.

104   *Belvedere, above*, fn 102, pp 5–6. See also *Marcoplos v Silver Sands Lodge Condominium Management Co* BS 2004 SC 5 (The Bahamas), where the word 'shall' was treated as mandatory so as to avoid an unjust result when the object of the Act was considered. It was the effect of the word which was considered.

105   See *Black-Clawson, above*, fn 9, p 614.

Matter of a Reference by the DPP Under Section 18 of the Criminal Appeal Act, Chapter 113 A,[106] the Court of Appeal of Barbados utilised this presumption, albeit without making any express reference to it, in its interpretation of the Criminal Appeal Act. It found that s 102 of the Act did not exclude the application of the well-established common law Turnbull guidelines on identification evidence. While the Act did not mention the Turnbull guidelines, they were not specifically excluded. Accordingly, since the Act was silent on the application of the guidelines, they should be regarded as included.

(b) *The presumption against ousting the jurisdiction of the courts*

The court will presume that the jurisdiction of the courts will not be ousted or avoided except by the plain and express words of a statute. However, case law illustrates that even where words ousting the jurisdiction of the court (ouster clauses) are clearly expressed in legislation, the courts have resisted them. Often, where a statute seeks to oust the jurisdiction of the courts, the courts will devise ways and means to circumvent the ouster. This is an important subject of administrative law. In general, courts have jealously guarded their jurisdiction to supervise administrative bodies, even in the face of such 'ousters'. They will not easily interpret legislation to infer the abortion of that power.[107]

One such route of defeating the ouster is illustrated in *Griffith v Barbados Cricket Association.*[108] Despite the presence of a statutory ouster attempting to preclude the court from reviewing decisions of the Cricket Association, the court found that, as the dispute related to a matter of natural justice, this was an inherent part of its jurisdiction and it could determine the mater. Further, the fact that the Act prohibited the Association from making laws 'repugnant to the laws of Barbados' invited the court's jurisdiction, as it was the final arbiter on such matters of law.[109]

A rare exception to this trend of rejecting ordinary statutory ouster clauses is seen in the case of *Caroni (1975) Ltd v Association of Technical, Administrative and Supervisory Staff,*[110] where the then Chief Justice de la Bastide upheld the ouster contained in the Industrial Relations Act 1972, finding the words of the ouster clause to be 'very explicit'. He cautioned:

> However reluctant this court may be to accept that its jurisdiction has been ousted by an Act of Parliament . . . the intention of Parliament is too clear in this instance to be deflected by any presumption of law or canon of construction. It is clearly the duty of this court to give effect to it. We must not be tempted to do otherwise by pictures painted of the gross injustices which may be perpetuated if we recognise and accept the restriction which Parliament has imposed on our right to interfere.[111]

The distinction in this case and other ouster clause cases may be in the fact that the jurisdiction barred from the court was not one originally vested in any court, but a

---

106 (Unreported) No 1 of 2001, decided 26 February 2002, CA, Barbados.
107 See, eg, *Thomas v AG of Trinidad* [1982] AC 113; *Re Alva Bain*, (Unreported) No 325 of 1987, 30 July 1987, H Ct, Trinidad and Tobago.
108 (1989) 41 WIR 48.
109 Similarly, where it is a human rights issue. See *Barnwell v AG* (1993) 49 WIR 88, which even defeated a constitutional ouster in litigation concerning a removal of a judge from office.
110 (2002) 67 WIR 223 (CA, Trinidad and Tobago).
111 *Ibid*, p 225.

new jurisdiction to determine whether a dismissal of a worker was 'harsh and oppressive' which owed its origins entirely to statute. Chief Justice de la Bastide fully recognised that this was a new jurisdiction.

In the Commonwealth Caribbean the trend toward ignoring or rejecting ousters seems to be contained to statutory ousters. The rule against ousting the jurisdiction of the court should therefore be treated differently where the ouster clause is contained in the Constitution. In such cases, the ouster clause is usually respected and upheld since the Constitution is the supreme law.

(c) *The presumption against altering existing rights*

Statutes which have the effect of encroaching existing rights, whether personal, or property rights, are to be interpreted strictly, preserving, as far as possible, those rights. The court will presume that Parliament will not alter such rights unless specifically expressed.[112] The word 'rights' under this rule is to be construed widely and includes, for example, the right of a person to 'bring, defend, conduct and compromise legal proceedings without an unwarranted obstruction' which is viewed as a basic right of citizenship.[113]

(d) *The presumption that persons should not be penalised except under clear law*

Under this rule, if words in a penal statute are ambiguous and there are two reasonable interpretations, the more lenient one will be applied to an accused. The rule dictates that there should be legal certainty before persons may be sanctioned, thus giving those affected by the new law the opportunity to know the law and understand the penalties which may be levied against them. The presumption has been particularly useful in tax avoidance cases. The presumption was reaffirmed in the case of *Ramoutar v Maharaj*.[114]

The rule is particularly important where the liberty of the individual is at stake and where there is doubt, the courts will adopt a construction favouring the liberty of the individual. In *Naidike and Naidike v AG*,[115] for example, s 15 of the Immigration Act of Trinidad and Tobago gave police and immigration officers a power of arrest over persons believed to be illegally 'resident' in Trinidad and Tobago. Naidike applied to renew his work-permit but was refused. He was then arrested. The issue was whether the arrest was lawful. The court found that the scope of s 15 was uncertain since it was unclear whether the power of arrest arose only in respect of persons against whom a deportation order had been made. Accordingly, that uncertainty had to be resolved in favour of the liberty of the individual. The Privy Council reiterated that the 'governing principle is that a person's physical liberty should not be curtailed or interfered with except under clear authority of law.'[116] The court also explained that there were limits placed on this general rule as identified in *Wills v Bowley*.[117] The presumption could be rebutted, for example, where issues such as the maintenance of public order was at stake or, generally, in the public interest. In such circumstances, powers conferred

---

112 *Lilleyman v LRC* (1964) 13 WIR 224.
113 *Ramoutar, above,* fn 23, p 18, citing FAR Bennion, *Statutory Interpretation,* 3rd edn 1997, p 659.
114 *Ramoutar, ibid.*
115 (2004) 65 WIR 372 (PC, Trinidad and Tobago).
116 *Ibid,* p 391.
117 [1983] 1 AC 57.

by Parliament should 'not lightly be rendered ineffective'.[118] The Privy Council went on to find that nothing in the *Naidike* case suggested that the public interest or democratic process would be served by applying the wide, rather than the narrow interpretation to s 15.

The general principle was put eloquently in the case of *R v IRC, ex p Rossminister Ltd:*[119]

> ... [While] the courts may look critically at legislation which impairs the rights of citizens and should resolve any doubt in interpreting in their favour, it is no part of their duty, or power, to restrict or impede the working of legislation, even of unpopular legislation; to do so would be to weaken rather than to advance the democratic process.

(e) *The presumption against the retroactive operation of statutes*

This is a firmly established rule.[120] Its rationale is to prevent the harsh and chaotic operation of law. For example, if penal statutes were made retroactive, a convict could find himself or herself serving an additional sentence for something for which he or she had been sentenced years before! Similarly, it would wreak havoc on property law and the law of contract. It is therefore presumed that Parliament does not intend to alter the law applicable to past events so as to alter the rights and obligations of the parties in a manner which is unfair to them unless a contrary intent is clearly demonstrated.[121]

(f) *The presumption that ordinary statutes do not bind or affect the Crown*

This operates unless reference is made to the Crown expressly or by necessary implication.[122]

(g) *The presumption toward fairness and justice*

It is to be presumed that Parliament intends to further the ends of justice. Thus, where there are two conflicting constructions of an enactment, the court will 'strive to avoid adopting a construction that leads to injustice'.[123]

(h) *The presumption of constitutionality*

Parliament is presumed to make laws which are in conformity with the Constitution. This presumption is of special importance in the region. The approach to interpreting Constitutions, which is one different to the interpretation of ordinary statute, is considered separately below.

(i) *The presumption that a later statute repeals the former*

Where two statutes conflict, the later statute is presumed to have repealed the former.[124] This presumption was rebutted appropriately, in the Cayman Islands case of *Cruz-Martinez v Cupidon*[125] in order to avoid a 'nonsensical' meaning to the statute in issue. The court, employing a purposive interpretation to the question of whether the correct limitation provision under the conflicting statutes was one

---

118 *Naidike, above,* fn 115, p 391.
119 [1980] AC 952, at pp 997–98.
120 See, eg, *Hoyte v Liberation Press* (1975) 22 WIR 175.
121 *Wilson v First Country Trust Ltd (No 2)* [2004] 1 AC 816 (HL), p 831.
122 See the various Interpretation Acts which make this clear.
123 *Bank of Jamaica v Industrial Disputes Tribunal,* (Unreported) No 116 of 2001, decided 12 June 2001 (Supreme Court, Jamaica).
124 See *Paradise Island Ltd v AG* (1986) 39 WIR 8.
125 [1999] CILR 177.

year or three years, found that the later statute incorporated the provision which changed the limitation period in error, as the draftsman was under the impression that it was giving effect to current UK law. The actual mischief intended to be remedied was the change from the unjust one-year limitation period to three years. Allowing a later statute which reinstated the one-year period went against the purpose of the Act and the intention of Parliament and therefore, the later statute's provision was not be accepted.

(j) *The presumption where provisions within a statute conflict*

In *Owens Banks Ltd v Cauche*,[126] the Privy Council, per Lord Ackner, put paid to the notion that there is a presumption that where there is an irreconcilable inconsistency between two provisions of the same statute, the later provision prevails. The correct principle, according to the Law Lord, is that 'where such an inconsistency exists, the courts must determine, as a matter of construction, which is the leading provision and which one must give way to the other.'[127] It was Lord Ackner's clarification which was accepted by Sir Vincent Floissac, CJ, in the case of *Parker v Nike*.[128]

(k) *The presumption against contradicting ratified international treaties where they do not conflict with domestic law*

This is not traditionally listed as a presumption of statutory interpretation but rather a rule of international law. Nonetheless, given the importance of international law to the domestic legal system in recent times, the propensity of the courts to act in conformity with international law obligations and the pronouncements that they have made on the subject, it can now be legitimately included amongst the presumptions applied by the courts.[129]

AIDS TO INTERPRETATION

A judge may consult a wide range of material when he seeks to give meaning to the words in a statute. These materials are referred to as 'aids to interpretation.' Some of these aids may be found within the statute. These are referred to as 'internal aids'. Others may be found outside of the statute. These, in turn, are described as 'external aids'.

Internal aids

Although specific rules attach to the various aids to interpretation discussed below, we should reiterate that in the more modern formulation of the literal rule, which relies on a contextual reading of the statute, all of the internal aids listed here will be regarded as being incorporated into the literal rule. Sir Vincent Floissac explains this usage of the literal rule in the case of *Savarin v William:*[130]

---

126   (1989) 36 WIR 221.
127   *Ibid*, p 226.
128   (1996) 54 WIR 135.
129   See a full discussion of the impact of international law in Chapter 12 ('International Law as a Source of Law').
130   *Above*, fn 25, para 10.

That legislative intention is an inference drawn from the primary meaning of the word or phrase . . . In this regard the statutory context comprises every other word or phrase used in the statute and all implications therefrom.

The long title

It has long been established that the long title could be used as an aid to interpretation.[131] In *Black Clawson*,[132] Lord Simon said that the long title was part of the context and should be read as 'the plainest of all guides' to the general objectives of a statute. Yet, he cautioned that 'it will not always help as to particular provisions.'

A good example of the use of the long title may be seen in *Fisher v Raven*.[133] In that case, the House of Lords had to determine the meaning of 'obtained credit' in a provision of the UK Debtors Act 1869. Relying on the Act's long title for assistance, the court held that the term was confined to obtaining credit in respect of the payment or repayment of money only and did not extend to cover the receipt of money on a promise to render services or deliver goods in the future. The long title described the statute as: 'An Act for the abolition of the imprisonment for debt, for the punishment of fraudulent debtors.' The long title was, therefore, read to support the view that the Act only dealt with debtors in the ordinary sense of the word.

In contrast, in *Ward v Halmad*,[134] the court disregarded the long title of an Act and widened its applicability to cover cases not mentioned by the long title.

As we have noted, the usage of the long title and other parts of the statute are sometimes subsumed under the broad meaning of the literal rule so as to find the literal meaning. Modern courts have advocated the use of the title and other parts of the statute. In *Liberty Club v AG of Grenada*,[135] for example, in answering a question on the recognition of trade unions, the Court of Appeal relied on the long title, pointing to its usefulness as an aid of interpretation while still employing a literal approach.[136] Byron JA pronounced:

> This title clearly indicates the intention of the legislature to provide for the compulsory recognition of trade unions that represent a majority . . . An interpretation of s 3(1) and 4(2) to require that a union be certified as the bargaining agent . . . gives effect to the purpose declared in the long title, and would accord with the statutory context.[137]

This dictum was followed in *Jalousie*.[138] Edwards J reminded the court that: 'The settled rules of interpretation permit the court to refer to the long title of the Act.'[139]

In general, the long title is a minor aid to construction. It should be noted, too, that the long title should not be confused with the Preamble.

---

131 See *Fielding v Morley Corporation* [1899] 1 Ch 134.
132 *Above*, fn 9, p 647.
133 [1964] AC 210,
134 [1964] 2 QB 580.
135 (1996) 52 WIR 172 (CA, Grenada).
136 The long title read: 'An Act to provide for compulsory recognition, by employers of trade unions that present a majority of workers.'
137 *Above*, fn 135, pp 175–76.
138 *Above*, fn 12, paras 9 and 41.
139 *Ibid*, para 12.

The Preamble

The Preamble is that part of the statute which precedes the enacting words and sets out the reason for the statute's being. It is generally in the Preamble's recitals that the mischief to be remedied and the scope of the Act are described. However, modern statutes very rarely contain a Preamble. Even where one is included, it is usually too brief to be of assistance.

Nevertheless, it is well established that resort to the Preamble is permissible. In *AG v Prince of Hanover*,[140] Lord Normand summarised the position with respect to the use of the Preamble:

> It is therefore clearly permissible to have recourse to it as an aid to construing the enacting provisions. The Preamble is not, however, of the same weight, as an aid to construction of a section of the Act, as are other relevant enacting words to be found elsewhere in the Act or even in related Acts. There may be no exact correspondence between Preamble and enactment, and the enactment may go beyond, or it may fall short of the indications that may be gathered from the Preamble. Again, the Preamble cannot be of much or any assistance in construing provisions which embody qualifications or exceptions from the operation of the general purpose of the Act. It is only when it conveys a clear and definite meaning in comparison with relatively obscure or indefinite enacting words that the Preamble may legitimately prevail.

In addition, the Preamble cannot prevail over clear enacting words.

The short title

The short title, said Lord Moulton in *Vacher and Sons Ltd v London Society of Compositors*,[141] is a 'statutory nickname' solely 'for the purpose of facility of reference.' Therefore, it can hardly be used to resolve doubt. The short title of an Act does not always reflect the content of the Act accurately. Some judges have, however, questioned whether it should always be ignored.[142]

Headings

Headings are not strictly part of a statute. Notwithstanding, they are sometimes treated as an aid to construction as part of the context. The formal position was enunciated by Lord Reid in *DPP v Shildkamp*.[143] He questioned to what extent it is permissible to give weight to punctuation, cross-headings and side notes to sections in the Act. He found that in theory, these should be disregarded because they are not the product of anything done in Parliament.

However, it may be more realistic to accept the Act as printed as being the product of the whole legislative process, and to give due weight to everything found in the printed Act. Yet, in many cases the provision before the court may never have been mentioned in debate in either House, and it may be that its wording was never closely

---

140   [1957] AC 436, *per* Lord Normand.
141   [1913] AC 107, p 117.
142   As in *Re Booker* [1915] 1 KB 21, p 40.
143   [1971] AC 1, p 10.

scrutinised by any Member in debate in either House. However, it is not very mean-ingful to say that the words of the Act represent the intention of Parliament but that punctuation, cross-headings and side notes do not. Of these, Lord Reid gave the greatest weight to headings.

> When the court construing the Act is reading it through to understand it, it must read the cross-headings as well as the body of the Act and that will always be a useful pointer as to the intention of Parliament in enacting the immediately following sections. Whether the cross-heading is no more that a pointer or label or is helpful in assisting to construe or even in some cases to control the meaning or ambit of those sections must necessarily depend on the circumstances of each case.[144]

While a heading may be used to resolve a doubt where the enacted words are ambiguous, it cannot be used to alter the meaning of enacted words which are clear. It should be noted too, that headings or side-notes may actually be misleading in that they may not be accurate reflections of what is contained in the body of the statute. This point is well illustrated in a New Zealand case, *R v Panine*.[145] The case inquired into whether 'unlawful entry' was an essential element of the offence of aggravated burglary under the Crimes Act 1961, despite a heading to that effect. The court noted that the 'title of the section alone, whether or not technically accurate in covering the elements of the offending identified, cannot alter the correct construction of this sub-section'. Rather, the actual language used in the section of the statute and its legislative history overrrode the potential effect of a recourse to headings.

Marginal or side notes

Marginal notes are inserted for facility of reference. It is possible for a marginal note to bear no relation to the content of a provision. For that reason, early cases did not treat side notes as a legitimate aid of interpretation. That view has changed. In *Stephens v Cruchfield RDC*,[146] Lord Clifford observed:

> While the marginal note to a section cannot control the language used in the section, it is at least permissible to approach a consideration of its general purpose and the mischief at which it is aimed with the note in mind.[147]

The present position as enunciated in *Shildkamp* is that a court may look at marginal notes in cases of ambiguity. The use of marginal notes is also part of the contextual approach, discussed above. In *R v Montila*,[148] it was said that marginal notes are 'as much part of the contextual scene' as explanatory notes and 'such materials' were admissible 'aids to construction'. However, in practice, side notes usually carry little weight and cannot displace the plain meaning of an enactment.

Special significance of marginal notes in the Caribbean

Despite the general rule on marginal notes, in Commonwealth Caribbean jurisdictions, marginal or side notes may have special significance and should, accordingly,

---

144 *Ibid.*
145 [2003] 2 NZLR 63.
146 [1960] 2 QB 373, p 383.
147 [1971] AC 1, p 10.
148 [2004] 1 WLR 3141 at pp 3150–51.

be treated with more respect by the courts. This point was made in *AG v Wood*,[149] a surprisingly liberal judgment of the Grand Court of the Cayman Islands. The Court considered whether there was a contradiction between the provisions of the Judicature Law and the Criminal Procedure Code on the question of a time limit for the prosecution of certain summary offences.

In coming to its decision, the Court made specific use of the marginal notes. It was conscious that it was deviating from established English rules of statutory interpretation, yet it felt justified in doing so because:

> Unlike the Parliament at Westminster, the Legislative Assembly of these islands in common with many legislatures in dependent territories does from time to time pass upon, enact and amend the marginal notes to sections of a law and it follows that the courts are entitled in suitable cases to have regard to these notes as an aid to interpretation.

Punctuation

Until recently, the punctuation found in a statute was ignored. Indeed, it was fashionable to draft legislation and legal documents without punctuation. The modern position is that punctuation will be considered to the same extent as non-enacting words, although it may be altered or ignored where necessary to give effect to the purpose of the statute.[150] Punctuation is especially relevant in the contextual approach. In *Douglas v The Police*,[151] the court found it necessary to pay attention to commas in the statute, as punctuation marks were held to be 'among the components of the statutory context'. Thus, the use of punctuation does not 'transcend judicial statutory interpretation'.[152]

External aids

Law Commission reports and parliamentary debates

Law Commission reports are helpful in determining the pre-existing state of the law. However, the recommendations contained in these reports cannot be regarded as evidence of parliamentary intention, as Parliament may not have accepted the recommendations or acted upon them. One cannot, therefore, interpret the words of a statute in accordance with such reports. These propositions find support in the *Black Clawson* case.[153]

The more important question, however, is whether the court can use the actual discussions about the Act as an external aid, particularly parliamentary debates and reports. This is a topical issue and an area of considerable development.

Traditionally, the courts have prohibited the use of parliamentary debates. This is sometimes called the exclusionary rule. Various reasons have been offered

---

149 [1988–89] CILR 128 at pp 132–33.
150 See, eg, *Hanlon v Law* Society [1981] AC 124, p 198; Inland *Revenue Commrs v Henchy* [1960] AC 748, p 765.
151 (1992) 43 WIR 175.
152 *Ibid*, p 178.
153 *Above*, fn 9.

by the House of Lords to justify this position. In *Beswich v Beswich*,[154] Lord Reid explained:

> For purely practical reasons we do not permit debates in either House to be cited: it would add greatly to the time and expense involved in preparing cases involving the construction of a statute if counsel were expected to read all the debates in Hansard, and it would often be impracticable for counsel to get access to at least the older reports of debates in select committees of the House of Commons; moreover, in a very large proportion of cases such a search, even if practicable, would throw no light on the question before the court . . .

The *dictum* of Lord Scarman in *Davies v Johnson*[155] gives another explanation of the rule. His Lordship explained that what is said in Parliament:

> . . . is an unreliable guide to the meaning of what is enacted . . . The cut and thrust of debate and the pressures of Executive responsibility are not always conducive to a clear and unbiased explanation of the meaning of statutory language.

We can outline the reasons given by the courts for ignoring parliamentary debates and reports. These are:

(a) time and expense;

(b) impracticality;

(c) lack of access to parliamentary materials;

(d) unreliability of the discussion.

The above reasons are based on purely administrative or technological matters, rather than substantive or philosophical objections. This is with the exception of the last, unreliability. These rationales also fail to place emphasis on the context of an Act, an emphasis which we saw previously was regarded as the modern approach. They therefore seem out of sync with a contemporary approach to statutory interpretation, which adopts more liberal means in an attempt to secure the true intention of Parliament, and which, as we know, is the ultimate aim of statutory interpretation.

One important rationale for the exclusionary rule, however, is that it preserves the constitutional functions of the courts in relation to the Executive. Courts have a constitutional function to interpret law and be mediators between the State and the private citizen. In *Black Clawson*, Lord Reid felt it would be a degradation of the judicial function if courts were to be merely a reflecting mirror.[156]

In addition, as noted in *Davies v Johnson*,[157] courts need to promote legal certainty. Citizens should have access to justice which is defined by identifiable sources. Parliamentary debates are neither reliable nor clear.

Not surprisingly, the courts are moving away from an isolationist approach to statutory interpretation, even with regard to the use of external aids. This is a recent initiative. The landmark case is *Pepper v Hart*.[158] In this revolutionary case, the House of Lords had to interpret the Finance Act and its implications for the taxation of

---

154 [1968] AC 58, pp 73–74.

155 [1979] AC 264, p 350.

156 *Above*, fn 9, p 629.

157 [1979] AC 264.

158 [1993] 1 All ER 42.

schools. The Lords held that the rule prohibiting the courts' referral to parliamentary material as an aid to statutory interpretation should be relaxed. They therefore overruled previous precedent on the question.

The *Pepper* case followed an earlier decision which allowed the courts to look at parliamentary material in interpreting subsidiary legislation.[159] However, *Pepper v Hart* contains certain provisos. The rule may only be relaxed where:

(a) there would be no breach of parliamentary privilege;
(b) the legislation was so obscure that the literal meaning led to an absurdity;
(c) the parliamentary material to be relied on is primarily ministerial statements, or statements from another promoter of the statute;
(d) the parliamentary material is clear.

Despite the conditions laid down for the relaxation of the rule, the decision is a landslide victory for the prioritisation of context or purpose of statutes. It deviates substantially from insular, legalistic and narrowly technical ways of looking at legislation and reaffirms the purposive approach, discussed above, p 256. Consider, for example, what Lord Griffiths had to say:

> The days have long passed when the courts adopted a strict constructionist view of interpretation which required them to adopt the literal meaning of language. The courts now adopt a purposive approach which seeks to give effect to the true purpose of the legislation.

He further questioned why the courts should cut themselves off from the one source by which they could find an authoritative statement of Parliament's intention.

The decision in *Pepper v Hart* is also in keeping with developments in other common law jurisdictions. These seemed to have exerted considerable influences on the court.[160] This, together with the abolition of the rule with respect to subsidiary legislation, encouraged the court to 'flow with the tide of modernism'.

The court also found that it was 'artificial' to allow the examination of parliamentary material for finding the 'mischief' but to prevent the court from looking at such material to 'remedy' that mischief. These fine distinctions between looking for the mischief and looking for the remedy were technical and inappropriate. The court adopted a pragmatic approach, in that it accepted the inevitability of errors and uncertainties in a modern context where so much legislation was being created. Parliament had never intended such ambiguities. It is perhaps ironic that the courts should now adopt a practical approach when the reason for the rule in the first place was based on practicalities.

The courts should not 'blind' themselves to a clear indication of intent. Indeed, the exclusionary rule was viewed as a self-imposed limitation. In addition, the attitude toward the rule was inconsistent. The *Pepper v Hart* decision is, therefore, a welcome one. As Stone argues:

> ... on what basis is it explicable that lawyers can regard with equanimity cases in which judges may pronounce *ex cathedra* that so and so could not have been in the legislator's

---

159   *Pickstone v Freeman* [1988] 2 All ER 80.
160   For example, the rule was already overruled in Australia and New Zealand. See, eg, the dictum of Lord Oliver in *Pepper*.

minds when the parliamentary debates ready to hand (but judicially unopened) might show that that was precisely what was in their minds?[161]

Pepper v Hart also rejects the 'practical difficulties' rationale on which the exclusionary rule was based. The court noted that parliamentary materials could be readily available. Indeed, New Zealand and Australia had not faced such a problem. While the cost of securing parliamentary materials is expensive, it is not prohibitive. Further, a court would not be overwhelmed with parliamentary material, as the rule would only be relaxed in limited cases and this could be strictly controlled.

> The courts should not deny themselves the light which parliamentary materials may shed on the meaning of the words Parliament has used and thereby risk subjecting the individual to a law which Parliament never intended to erect.[162]

The rule in *Pepper v Hart* now appears to be mainstream in the Commonwealth Caribbean despite the obstacle of parliamentary privilege. The Barbadian case of *The Public Counsel v The Fair Trading Commission*,[163] demonstrates how easily the hurdle of privilege can be overcome, allowing easy access to parliamentary debates and speeches. In this case, counsel simply obtained permission from the Speaker of the House of Assembly to use the extracts from Hansard of the debates in Parliament which related to the creation of the Fair Trading Commission and the mechanism for hearings to the Commission, the issue at hand.[164] Indeed, Blackman, J noted how helpful these debates were to his deliberations.

The implications of Pepper v Hart

The objection to parliamentary material on the basis of unavailability and lack of access is not a sound one in today's context. Indeed, the advance of computer and data technology can easily solve such problems at a relatively low cost.

Nevertheless, *Pepper* is not without difficulty. While it is a welcome initiative, which moves closer to the content of a statute, one can sympathise with the concerns expressed in *Davies*[165] on the unreliability of parliamentary information in the heat of debate.

Further, the observation in *Pepper v Hart*, that the rule will only be relaxed where parliamentary statements are clear, is ambiguous. How will the courts determine when a statement of intention is clear? Where there are conflicting or vague statements, does this not involve a subjective analysis of the statement which returns us to the familiar problems of the other rules of interpretation?

On the other hand, it is clear that the exclusionary rule was 'judge-made' and self-imposed. In fact, in the 17th and 19th centuries, the courts were free to look at the parliamentary history of legislation.[166] Still, the case has far-reaching implications which will most probably go far beyond its original limits. This is because the ultimate basis of the decision is the legitimacy of the principle of purposive

---

161 Stone, J, *Precedent and Law: Dynamics of Common Law Growth*, 1985, London: Butterworths, p 351.
162 *Above*, fn 158, *per* Lord Browne-Wilkinson.
163 *Above*, fn 6.
164 *Ibid*, pp 28–31.
165 [1979] AC 264.
166 See, eg, *Ash v Ashby* (1678) 3 Swans 663.

construction or the contextual approach. It addresses much more than the desirability or otherwise of using parliamentary material. It is, in fact, a strong statement in favour of placing words in their proper context, by whatever means necessary.

What, then, is to prevent lawyers from attempting to expand the new rule further in the interest of context, beyond, for example, ministerial statements as presently allowed under Pepper? This may well be a good development, but it is not without its own danger. Too wide a net may capture contexts alien to Parliament's true intention.

We may also consider what will be the effect of the modern trend to broadcast parliamentary debates. What are the implications for this new transparency? It is somewhat absurd that information which is actually in the public domain should be ignored. We could question too whether the *Pepper* decision does violation to the 'separation of constitutional functions' principle. This issue was raised in *Pepper*, but not answered. Perhaps we can answer the question by saying that, after having accessed the words of Parliament, it is still left up to the courts to interpret them, to give them life. The use of parliamentary material is just another guide like any other. The courts do not abdicate their role by following this route. The implication is that the *Pepper* approach would not violate the constitutional function.

A possible retreat from *Pepper v Hart*

Since 2000, after an initial enthusiastic welcome by the courts, the path-breaking and authoritative decision of *Pepper v Hart* has been considerably eroded by the developments in certain English courts, in particular, the House of Lords. This followed a full seven years of honeymoon bliss for the precedent where the courts fully embraced the principle. Indeed, the courts even expanded *Pepper v Hart*, referring to parliamentary material even where the conditions laid down in *Pepper v Hart* were not met and where the language of the statute seemed clear. For example, in *Holden and Co v Crown Prosecution Service (No 2)*,[167] Lord Bridge said: 'our new freedom to refer to Hansard solves the mystery.'

The genesis of these decisions which threaten to result in the demise of the *Pepper v Hart* principle, if not a clear overruling of its precedent, comes originally not from an equally authoritative precedent, but instead from a lecture given by Lord Steyn.[168] Misgivings over the *Pepper v Hart* ruling were, of course, not absent before Lord Steyn's lecture. However, these came mainly from academic writers who were still attached to the traditional reservations toward reversing the exclusionary rule on parliamentary debates. Lord Steyn's speech however, coming as it is from a House of Lords judge, lends a more pronounced credibility to such concerns, not least because the views expressed by Lord Steyn have now found their way into the courts.[169]

While the traditional justifications for the exclusionary rule are many, Lord Steyn based his objections to *Pepper v Hart* and consequent loyalty to the exclusionary rule on two main propositions. First, Lord Steyn rejected outright the notion that Parliament could have an intention which could be identified by heeding Parliamentary

---

167 [1994] 1 AC 22 at 37.

168 The Oxford Hart Lecture, May 2000, consequently published: Lord Steyn, '*Pepper v Hart* – A Re-examination' (2001) 21 OJLS 59.

169 Note that Lord Millet also criticised the *Pepper v Hart* decision extra-judicially. See Lord Millet, 'Construing Statutes' (1999) 20 SLR 107 at 110.

speeches. Secondly, and more importantly, he relied on the argument that the use of parliamentary material to interpret statutes was a violation of the separation of powers constitutional principle, 'shifting legislative power from Parliament to the Executive' because it treated 'statements of Ministers as Acts of Parliament', as 'canonical', as 'a trump-card', and even 'as a source of law'. This deprived the courts of their discretion to apply and interpret law.[170] Lord Steyn further suggested that these important constitutional arguments had not been addressed in *Pepper* and consequently the decision could not be regarded as good law.

As we have seen, these are not new arguments in support of the exclusionary rule that seeks to exclude parliamentary material, and indeed, it is untrue that such arguments were not addressed in *Pepper v Hart*. In fact, they were comprehensively examined and rejected. Nevertheless, Lord Steyn did not reject *Pepper v Hart* altogether or suggest that it should be overruled. Rather, he maintained that it should be restricted to its facts. *Pepper v Hart* had been a tax case where taxpayers had relied on what the Minister responsible for the new tax law had said in Parliament about the meaning of the statute. As such, Lord Steyn felt that it would be unfair to permit the Executive to go back on these 'categorical assurances' and the Executive was estopped from so doing. Lord Steyn advocated that apart from these estoppel situations, resort to *Hansard* should only be had in order to ascertain the 'mischief' Parliament sought to rectify – the traditional premise for accessing parliamentary material.

Lord Steyn's whittling down of *Pepper v Hart* is reflected in cases before the House of Lords, most notably *R v SOS for the Environment, Transport and the Regions, ex p Spath Holme Ltd*.[171] Such cases have pronounced on the difficulties attached to *Pepper v Hart* and generally found that the requirements outlined in that case were not met, in particular the third criterion that ministerial statements be clear and conclusive. The narrow approach outlined by Lord Steyn thus appears to be gaining ground. Even more than this, questions on the constitutionality of the *Pepper v Hart* decision have come to the fore. For example, in *Spath Holme*,[172] Lord Hope alluded to it, as did Lord Hoffman in the *Robin* case.[173]

Lord Steyn himself transformed his extra-judicial views on *Pepper v Hart* into precedent when he applied his estoppel argument in the case of *R v A (No 2)*,[174] specifically referring to his Hart lecture, also reiterated in *Spath Holme*. Lord Steyn further expanded on his narrow view of *Pepper v Hart* in a subsequent lecture, viewing the appropriate rule as based on 'an estoppel, a legitimate expectation principle of fairness, or whatever else'.[175]

What has been described as the 'retreat' from *Pepper v Hart*[176] is by no means consistent. The Court of Appeal and Lord Phillips MR in particular, have been very supportive of the *Pepper v Hart* decision, refusing to follow the Steyn principles. Lord

---

170 Steyn, *above*, fn 168, pp 64, 68 and 70.

171 [2001] 2 AC 349 at pp 398–99, *per* Lord Nicholls. See also *Robin v Secretary of State for National Insurance* [2002] UKHL 32 at 40, *per* Lord Hoffman; *P (A Minor) v National Association of School Masters* [2003] 2 AC 663 at 678 *per* Lord Hoffman.

172 *Above*, fn 171, 407–408.

173 *Ibid*.

174 [2001] UKHL 25; [2002] 1 AC 45; [2001] 3 All ER 1.

175 Lord Steyn 'The Intractable Problem of the Interpretation of Legal Texts' (2003) 25 Sydney LR at 15, 16.

176 By S Vogenauer, in an excellent article entitled 'A Retreat from *Pepper v Hart*? A Reply to Lord Steyn', [2005] 25 OJLS 629.

Nicholls too, in the House of Lords, has remained loyal to *Pepper v Hart*.[177] In *R (Quintavalle) v Human Fertilization and Embryology Authority*,[178] he felt that it was appropriate to utilise the Minister's 'express statement to Parliament upon the very issue of construction under consideration' on the question of the banning of a form of scientific research in relation to embryos.[179] It was felt that the words of the statute were not sufficient to ascertain Parliament's true intention and resort had to be had to parliamentary material, thus ignoring the narrow principle advocated by Lord Steyn.

Lord Steyn's objections to *Pepper v Hart* are not only not new, but can also be rebuffed. The notion of Parliament's intention is not to suggest that this intention is a tangible thing but rather a hypothetical construct or expression to mean the true meaning of the text of the statute.[180]

The constitutional objection also seems baseless if one considers, as noted earlier, that the court merely uses parliamentary material as an aid to construction and retains the discretion to determine the legal meaning of the words used. Further, the line between permitting parliamentary material to ascertain the 'mischief' Parliament attempted to rectify (the traditional approach under the exclusionary rule) and using parliamentary material to discern Parliament's intention, or the objective of the Act, is one that is very difficult to distinguish.

It has also been pointed out that the *Pepper v Hart* precedent is being effectively overruled. This, of course, is being done without the benefit of an open and full judicial discussion on the matter. In contrast, *Pepper v Hart* was arrived at unanimously and after extensive argument.[181] At the very least, more cogent reasons need to be advanced for this retreat from *Pepper v Hart*.

Other external aids

Other external aids include dictionaries, judicial precedent, statutes *in pari materia*, and statutory instruments. There is no contention surrounding the usage of dictionaries in statutory interpretation. In fact, the literal or plain meaning approach relies heavily on this aid. In the case of statutory instruments, the question is whether a Regulation may be used in interpreting an Act. The answer is contained in several propositions formulated in *Harlow v Law Society*.[182] These are:

(a) Subordinate legislation may be used in order to construe the parent Act, but only where power is given to amend the Act by Regulations or where the meaning of the Act is ambiguous.

(b) Regulations made under the Act provide a parliamentary or administrative *contemporanea expositio* of the Act but do not decide or control its meaning; to allow this would be to substitute the rule making authority for the judges as interpreter and would disregard the possibility that the Regulation relied on was misconceived or *ultra vires*.

---

177   See *Wilson v First Country Trust* [2004] 1 AC 816.
178   [2004] QB 168 at 186.
179   See also *R (Jackson) v AG* [2005] EWHC 94.
180   As we have already seen above p 245. See also Vogenauer, *above*, fn 176, pp 644–46.
181   *Vogenauer, ibid*, p 633.
182   [1981] AC 124, pp 193–94.

(c) Regulations which are consistent with a certain interpretation of the Act tend to confirm that interpretation.

(d) Where the Act provides a framework built on by contemporaneously prepared regulations, the latter may be a reliable guide to the meaning of the former.

(e) The Regulations are a clear guide, and may be decisive, where they are made in pursuance of a power to modify the Act, particularly if they come into operation on the same day as the Act which they modify.

(f) Clear guidance may also be obtained from Regulations which are to have effect as if enacted in the parent Act.

Pari materia statutes as aids

In the Caribbean, the interpretation given to statutes *in pari materia* (identical statutes) is not only commonplace, but may also be said to have special significance. This is because many statutes stemmed from the colonial legal practice whereby UK statutes were applied, often wholesale, to the dependent territories (subject to the local circumstances rule, discussed below). Even after independence, it is the practice to 'borrow' legislation from other Commonwealth countries. Where legislation was modelled on UK legislation in colonial times, previous interpretations of the statute are regarded as binding. At the very least, the treatment of *in pari materia* statutes is always regarded as highly authoritative.

Using later statutes to assist in interpretation

In rare cases, a statute enacted after the one in contention, is used as an aid in interpretation. This usage was explained in the case of *Guischard Crawford et al.*[183] Judge Dean-Armorer stated:

> The rules of statutory interpretation do not generally permit later legislation to be used in construction except in limited cases . . . Maxwell on the *Interpretation of Statutes* (12th edition) writes at p 70: 'For the later statute to become relevant there must be something obscure or ambiguous . . . in the earlier one . . . some phrase fairly and equally open to diverse meanings . . . If such an ambiguity can be found it becomes permissible to look at later statutes', not perhaps to construe earlier statutes but to see the meaning which Parliament puts on the self-same phrase in a similar context . . .

THE MODERN APPROACH TO STATUTORY INTERPRETATION

Pepper v Hart, discussed above, p 270 is perhaps just the latest in a long line of cases signalling the movement away from a literal, artificial, technical approach to statutory interpretation to one grounded in its true context and social reality. This is, after all, the true significance of *Pepper v Hart*. The traditional rule which sought to exclude parliamentary material is clearly not in keeping with the purposive approach and is now to be replaced.

---

183   TT 2004 HC 57 (High Court, Trinidad and Tobago).

Let us return to the question of Parliament's intention. Little by little, courts seem to be moving away from self-imposed limitations in their attempt to discover Parliament's intention. The most important characteristic of modern statutory interpretation is flexibility. This flexibility is manifested in both form and substance. There is flexibility in form, in the sense that courts are willing to use a variety of rules in a single case and are not confined to a single rigid rule. Flexibility in substance is seen in their drive to examine many more indices of Parliament's intention.

Judges have not yet taken the quantum leap towards accepting all of the various legislative processes, such as public debates, committee reports, and so on as legitimate aids in the court room. Yet, the modern approach is at least prepared to acknowledge the existence of these.

What judges are realising is that the finding of legislative intent must rely also on sources outside the Act, such as the sponsors and lobbyists of the particular statute. All that Parliament, through its drafter, has done, is to give its approval, as the legal arm of government, to an intention conceived, nurtured and brought forward by others. 'They that "made" law were not the Members of Parliament. Some Members of Parliament were, most probably, dragooned into saying "aye".'[184]

In effect, the courts are willing to allow themselves more information concerning the social context of the problem with which they are faced. As Lord Simon declared as far back as *Black Clawson*,[185] 'Why should the court deny itself any part of the light and insist on groping for a meaning in darkness or half-light?'

Indeed, are judges ever entirely divorced from these social contexts? Do they really bring a totally insular and objective view to the exercise of statutory interpretation? Do they even, as they say, avoid looking at external aids? As Mason J of the Australian High Court confessed at the Interpretation Symposium of 1983:[186]

> . . . competent judges and counsel always look at *Hansard*. Only naive solicitors could think otherwise . . . It is better that [judges'] curiosity should be satisfied publicly rather than privately.

SPECIAL APPROACHES TO STATUTORY INTERPRETATION IN THE COMMONWEALTH CARIBBEAN

While Commonwealth Caribbean jurisdictions conform largely to the well-established rules of statutory interpretation applied in the UK and throughout the Commonwealth, there are a number of points of variance to note. Three particular approaches unique to pre-colonial, now independent, or in some cases, still dependent territories, are to be noted:

(1) The local circumstances rule – which applies particularly in the context where identical legislation is transplanted to colonial or ex-colonial territories.

(2) The existence of written Constitutions containing comprehensive Bills of Rights which came about upon the advent of independence and which introduced special rules for interpreting Constitutions.

---

184   *Op cit*, Crabbe, fn 10, p 53.
185   *Above*, fn 9, p 646.
186   (1983) AGPS 81, p 83.

(3) The rules applicable to legislation received directly from the UK where the territory is still dependent.

The local circumstances rule

We have already met the 'local circumstances rule' in previous chapters,[187] but here its importance as a rule of statutory interpretation remains to be noted.

The rule attempts to address situations where legislation, identical or *in pari materia*[188] to that found in the UK is introduced into the jurisdiction. Such transplantation may have taken place either during colonialism or post-independence. The question arises in both circumstances whether interpretations of such parent legislation are authoritative.[189]

The local circumstances rule provides an exception to the general reception of law doctrine and allows the court to deviate from previous UK statutory interpretation where local conditions which are different to those which obtain in the UK exist in the jurisdiction at hand. The general principle under the reception of law doctrine is as stated in the Canadian case of *Pollock v Manitoba*,[190] by the Manitoba Court of Appeal, where it was declared:

> A statute must be interpreted in the context of the common law in which it was enacted. In Manitoba, that included the common law and the statutory law of England as it was on July 15, 1870, the date of reception of the law of England in the province.

In *Carrerras Group Ltd v Stamp Commissioner*,[191] for example, the Privy Council had to consider whether the meanings attached to the Transfer Tax Act of Jamaica, a statute identical in wording to the Finance Act 1965 (UK), upon which it was modelled, was the same as put forward by the English courts. The case was important, as the UK interpretations had formed the basis for considerable developments in revenue law, developments which had reverberated throughout the Commonwealth.[192] Notwithstanding, the Privy Council found that the interpretations of the two statutes could not be the same for tax purposes. It found that the Jamaican legislation, although it used the same language as the UK Act, was concerned with 'a different kind of tax' and that accepting the English interpretation would create an irrational system of taxation for Jamaica, which could not have been the intention of the legislature. The Court made an important pronouncement on the local circumstances rule:

---

187   See, eg, Chapter 5 ('The Reception or Imposition of Law and its Significance to the Commonwealth Caribbean').

188   The case of *AG of Dominica v Theodore*, (1999) 57 WIR 129, (CA, Dominica), at p 133, explains what is meant by statutes *'in pari materia'*: '(1) Acts which have a collective title or a single subject matter; (ii) Acts which are required to be construed as one, again a recognition of a single subject matter; (iii) Acts which have short titles that are identical; and (iv) other Acts which deal with the same subject matter on the same lines'; relying on Francis Bennion, *Statutory Interpretation*, (3rd edn. 1997) *per* Satrohan Singh, JA.

189   Identical legislation from other countries may also be introduced but as there is no question of such legislative interpretations being binding, a special rule is not necessary.

190   272 DLR (4th) 142; 2006 DLR LEXIS 322.

191   (2004) 64 WIR 228.

192   The *Ramsay* doctrine on composite steps in a transaction and consequent tax liability, from the case of *WT Ramsay Ltd v IRC* [1982] AC 300.

Their Lordships do not accept that meanings can be transposed in this way from the legislation of one country to that of another.[193]

The Court further noted the differences in the rationales of each tax scheme. Similarly, in *Re First Virginia Reinsurance Ltd*,[194] a Bermudan court was cognisant of the fact that over time, local circumstances may change, bringing the statute out of step with its parent Act and necessitating an updated approach.

SPECIAL APPROACHES TO INTERPRETING CONSTITUTIONS

The Constitution is a form of legislation, albeit a special type and it is to be expected that the general rules of interpreting statutes will apply to Constitutions. This is true to a large extent. For example, the plain language rule applies, as Lord Millett noted in the case of *Pinder v R*,[195] when he considered that to interpret the words 'any law' to protect only pre-existing law, that is, law existing before the advent of the Constitution, was 'an impossible construction of the plain words of Article 17(2) of the Constitution.'[196]

However, the courts have carved out special rules of construction which apply to Constitutions. These rules or approaches are in keeping with the special character of the Constitution which mandate a sensitivity to the underlying values, ideals and philosophy of that instrument. These rules may be listed as:

(i)   the application of presumptions;

(ii) the need for a purposive approach to construction;

(iii) the need to treat with saving or existing law provisions;

(iv) the recognition of influences of international law on the Bill of Rights; and

(v)   the special treatment afforded provisions found solely in the Preamble.

The presumption that legislation is *intra vires* the Constitution

A presumption of constitutionality attaches to Commonwealth Caribbean Constitutions. This presupposes that Parliament does not act arbitrarily or overreach its powers or boundaries beyond what is acceptable as good constitutional governance. As such, legislation which is promulgated is presumed to be constitutional. Indeed, this is a foundational rule of statutory interpretation in Commonwealth Caribbean jurisprudence.

The existence of this presumption in favour of the constitutionality of statutes does not mean that legislation cannot be found to be *ultra vires* the Constitution and be declared null and void. Rather, the courts will proceed cautiously where legislation is challenged on constitutional grounds and the threshold for challenging legislation as unconstitutional is accordingly high.

The presumption of constitutionality is twofold. It can mean either that the legislation does not *prima facie* violate or hinder the right or hinder enjoyment of the right

---

193   *Above*, fn 191, p 232.
194   *Above*, fn 64.
195   (2002) 61 WIR 13 (Privy Council, The Bahamas).
196   *Ibid*, at p 20.

in issue or that it falls within the constitutionally permitted limitation laid down by the Constitution.

In countries other than Trinidad and Tobago, the presumption is that the legislation is reasonably required for the goals stated.

We should note that the presumption of constitutionality relates mainly to legislation. With respect to the common law, different rules may apply, and in some countries, the Constitution itself may recognise this and allow for rectification. For example, in South Africa, as seen in the *Thebus*[197] case, the Constitution provides avenues for developing the (unconstitutional) common law to bring it in line with constitutional values. This may be similar to the existence of modifying saving law clauses in our Constitutions, discussed below, but ours are not so explicit.

The presumption was infamously used to uphold a controversial statutory provision in St Lucia. This was in the case of *Girard v St Lucia Teachers' Union*.[198] The applicant contested her dismissal from the Teaching Service. She had been dismissed pursuant to the Teaching Service Commission Regulations, which required a female teacher to be dismissed when she became pregnant for the second time while unmarried. The applicant contended that this was a violation of her constitutional rights of equality and freedom from discrimination and that the Regulations were *ultra vires* the St Lucia Constitution. In failing to find a constitutional violation, the court noted that, because of the presumption of constitutionality, the burden of proof of showing that a parliamentary statute was unconstitutional was on the person alleging unconstitutionality.

A number of other cases have highlighted this presumption of constitutionality. For example, in *Faustin v AG of Trinidad and Tobago*,[199] Kelsick JA said:

> Nullification of enactments and confusion of public business are not lightly to be introduced. Unless, therefore, it becomes clear beyond reasonable doubt that the legislation in question transgresses the limits laid down by the organic law of the Constitution, it must be allowed to stand as the true expression of the national will.[200]

In older cases this presumption was interpreted broadly, granting much leeway to Parliament and imposing a 'heavy burden' on a litigant, as demonstrated in *Ramesh Diprajkumar Mootoo v AG*.[201] However, recent developments demonstrate that the presumption may be less onerous than first supposed and there has been a more restrictive view of the presumption. In *Observer Publications Ltd v Matthews and Others*,[202] a case from Antigua and Barbuda on freedom of expression, Lord Cooke of the Privy Council explained away the *Mottoo* point of view in this manner:

> This is true, in as much as the courts will strive, in pursuance of such provisions as are found in ss 2 and 19 of the Constitution ... to read down legislation if sufficiently precise implications may be articulated, so as to make it conform to the Constitution.[203]

---

197 *Thebus and Another v S* (2003) 10 BCLR 1100 (CC).
198 (Unreported) Civil Suit No 371 of 1985, decided 17 December 1986, H Ct, St Lucia. The judgment was affirmed in *AG v Girard and the St Lucia Teachers' Union*, Civil Appeals Nos 12 and 13 of 25 January 1986; digested in (1991) 1 Carib LR 90.
199 (1978) 30 WIR 351.
200 See also *St Luce v AG and Another* (1975) 22 WIR 536, pp 540–41A and the discussion in Chapter 7 ('The Written Constitution as a Legal Source').
201 (1979) 30 WIR 411 at p 415.
202 (2001) 58 WIR 188.
203 *Ibid*, p 205.

How does one rebut the presumption of constitutionality?

In *Hinds v R*,[204] it was said:

> . . . in order to rebut the presumption their Lordships would have to be satisfied that no reasonable member of the Parliament who understood correctly the meaning of the relevant provisions of the Constitution could have supposed that [the law enacted] was reasonably required for the protection of any of the interests referred to, or in other words, that Parliament was either acting in bad faith, or had misinterpreted the provision of the Constitution under which it purported to act.

This is a high threshold indeed, particularly when one considers that 'bad faith' requires some kind of intention and malice and is a burdensome test for rebuttal, going beyond even the rational connection test put forward by the self-same courts.

The Privy Council in *Hinds* further explained that Parliament only had to determine *prima facie* what was reasonably required, but that what was reasonably required 'involves considerations of public policy which lie outside the field of the judicial power and may have to be made in the light of information available to Government of a kind that cannot effectively be adduced in evidence by means of the judicial process.'[205]

This is a surely a 'cop out', and may be seen to be more appropriate, if at all, only to those cases which fall within the realm of national security. Certainly, Parliament does not have a monopoly in understanding public morality, public health or even the nature of democracy itself!

In *AG v Caterpillar Americas Co*,[206] the means of rebutting the presumption was outlined in this manner:

> the court will not be astute to attribute to a Legislature motives or purposes or objects which are beyond its powers. It must be shown affirmatively by the party challenging a statute, which is, on the face of it *intra vires*, that it was enacted as part of a plan to effect indirectly something which the Legislature had no power to achieve directly.

An explanation of how the presumption is to be rebutted is found also in *AG v Antigua Times Ltd*,[207] which asked whether, in hard cases (where it was not immediately clear that the legislation was reasonably required), evidence should be brought before the court demonstrating that the Act was reasonably required. In such circumstances, the burden of proof, as it were, would shift to the State to demonstrate the Act's justification, once it is determined *prima facie* that the statute violates rights. The Privy Council said:

> Their Lordships think that the proper approach to the question is to presume, until the contrary appears or is shown that all Acts passed by the Parliament of Antigua were reasonably required.[208]

More recent cases have explored the presumption further and constructed clearer tests for rebutting the presumption. Where Constitutions enshrine the provision that

---

204   [1977] AC 195, at p 224.
205   *Ibid.*
206   (2000) 62 WIR 135 at p 148.
207   [1976] AC 16.
208   *Ibid.*

abrogations of rights be 'justifiable' in a free and democratic society, these cases have put forward a two-step test for demonstrating constitutionality, requiring legislation to satisfy both the 'reasonableness' requirement and the requirement that it be justified in a free and democratic society.

It may be observed too, that the new approach to the presumption of constitutionality also places different weights to the attached burdens of proof and the requirements to displace the burden have been considerably relaxed. In *Observer Publications*, the Privy Council explained it in this way:

> The onus upon those supporting the restriction is to show that it is reasonably required. If the latter onus is discharged, the burden shifts to the complainant to show that the provision or the thing done is not reasonably justifiable in a democratic society.[209]

It is notable that, some countries, such as Canada, have rejected this presumption altogether.

The presumption of constitutionality is therefore not an insuperable obstacle in the path of the complainant. Rather, the 'presumption is an aid to the construction of the actual legislative words in resolving any ambiguities or obscurities'.[210]

The purposive construction of Constitutions

It is now well-established that Commonwealth Caribbean Constitutions are to be interpreted purposively, bringing to life the important aims, objectives and values of the Constitution as a living social instrument.

In the landmark case of *Minister of Home Affairs v Fisher*,[211] the interpretation of the word 'child' was in issue. The Privy Council noted that, while in ordinary Acts of Parliament there was an assumption that the word meant 'legitimate child', this was not the case in construing a Constitution. These independent Constitution were drafted in a 'broad and ample style which lays down principles of width and generosity' to give effect to international standards of human rights. The interpretation of such Constitutions called for a 'generous interpretation avoiding . . . the austerity of tabulated legalism suitable to give the full measure of fundamental rights and freedoms referred to'. Their Lordships also emphasised that Constitution should be interpreted with 'less rigidity . . . than other Acts'.

Even more important is the finding that the Constitution could be treated as '*sui generis*, calling for principles of interpretation of its own, suitable to its character . . . without necessary acceptance of all of the presumptions that are relevant to legislation of private law.'[212] The result was that the word 'child' could be interpreted differently, to include 'illegitimate child'.

While the purposive approach is unquestioned, the meaning to be attached to 'purposive' can perhaps be inquired into in the face of what may be seen to be

---

209 *Above*, fn 202, p 189. See also, *Cable and Wireless (Dominica) Ltd v Mappin* (2000) 57 WIR 141 at p 152.
210 *Ibid, Observer Publications*.
211 [1980] AC 319, PC Bermuda, (1979) 44 WIR 107.
212 (1979) 44 WIR 107, pp 112–13.

excessively liberal interpretations of our Constitutions in recent times. This phenomenon is explored more comprehensively in two earlier chapters,[213] examining closely the death penalty cases which have been responsible for some of the most dynamic evolutions of Commonwealth Caribbean jurisprudence.

Yet, liberal interpretations of Caribbean Constitutions are not confined to death penalty cases. Provisions relating to freedom of expression have enjoyed similar generosity. The student of Commonwealth Caribbean constitutional law can be forgiven for asking, as we did in a previous chapter,[214] whether a 'purposive' construction means more than envisioning aims and objectives and also encompasses the notion that the Constitution is so elastic as to be able to accommodate radically changed ideas and values without the need for constitutional amendment, in essence, mere judicial activism.

It is perhaps just such a sentiment that the Privy Council shared in the *Pinder* case, when it refused to outlaw corporal punishment which had been saved by the Constitution although it ran counter to universal standards.[215]

Saving law or existing law clauses

The phenomenon of the saving law or existing law clauses found in some Commonwealth Caribbean Constitutions has already been discussed in Chapter 7. Here, we note that in the exercise of statutory construction, the court must be aware of the existence and meaning of such clauses as often, they give a more restrictive meaning to the issue at hand. Thus, it is not sufficient for the court to apply the plain meaning, or even a purposive interpretation of the words in a provision of the Constitution affected by a saving law clause. Rather, the provision in issue must be interpreted in conjunction with the saving law clauses.

The distinction to be made between partial or special saving law clauses and full or general saving law clauses is also important. In addition, the Constitution itself often allows severability of offending legislation so as to bring it into conformity with the Constitution. Such clauses are, therefore, instrumental tools in interpreting Commonwealth Caribbean Constitutions.[216]

A collateral provision to be found in some Constitutions must also be considered. There is a type of savings law clause which is a transition provision that allows the court to construe the existing law with such modification as is necessary to bring it into conformity with the Constitution. These are sometimes called 'modification clauses'. The effect of this is that the offending law is not made null and void but is allowed to survive, with amendments.

---

213   Chapter 12 ('International Law as a Source of Law') and Chapter 7 ('The Written Constitution as a Legal Source').

214   Chapter 7 ('The Written Constitution as a Legal Source').

215   *Pinder v R, above,* fn 195, discussed in Chapter 12 ('International Law as a Source of Law'). See also *Reyes v R* [2002] 2 WLR 1034 'The court has no licence to read its own predilections and moral values into the Constitution.'

216   We should note that existing law clauses found in the various Constitution are not identical. Some are partial existing law clauses. This is one reason for the different results from various constitutional challenges from several jurisdictions on whether the death penalty is mandatory.

Such a provision was considered in the case of *AG of Dominica v Theodore*.[217] The issue here was whether an existing law, the *Road's Ordinance 1961*, which allowed the State to acquire private land without compensation could stand in the face of a provision in the Constitution which mandated compensation. The court utilised s 6(2) of the Constitution, which allowed it to construe the Roads Ordinance 'with such modifications, adaptations, qualifications and exceptions as may be necessary to bring them into conformity with the Constitution' and thereby made the law constitutional by deleting the words 'without compensation' and substituting it with 'with compensation'. Similarly, in *Beasejour Estates Ltd v AG of Grenada*,[218] the court made its observation while relying on the principle in the landmark case of *AG of St Kitts v Reynolds*.[219] It said:

> [the] Reynolds case thus exemplifies the fundamental difference between ordinary statutory interpretation and constitutional construction (i.e. construction decreed by a 'Westminsterial' Constitution for the purpose of saving or validating existing laws which were in force immediately before the Constitution). In the case of ordinary statutory interpretation . . . we are concerned with the intention of . . . Parliament. In the case of constitutional construction of existing laws, we are concerned with the common intention of Her Majesty in Council and of the Parliament which requested the Constitution. Because of this fundamental difference . . . it is possible under the constitutional construction of the words of an existing law to ascribe to those words a meaning which they could not be held to bear under their ordinary statutory interpretation. That is why . . . Lordships in *Reynolds* case had no difficulty in constructing the 1959 Order and the 1967 Regulations with such generosity.[220]

The courts have been increasingly predisposed to treat the saving law clause as being subservient to more modern views of a rights based approach to the law, in particular, the Bills of Rights. This was more fully discussed in an earlier chapter.[221]

International law influences on the Constitution as an aid to interpretation

The influence of international human rights norms on Commonwealth Caribbean jurisprudence, particularly in relation to human rights is again to be noted here, although fully aired in a previous chapter.[222] Many courts have made several pronouncements about the need to heed such norms when interpreting Constitutions. In contrast, other judges have commented that this is too zealous an approach.

Provisions found in the Preamble

Human rights provisions may be located only in the Preamble or introductory clause to the Bill of Rights of Commonwealth Caribbean Constitutions, and not in the bodies

---

217   (1999) 57 WIR 129.
218   GD 1993 CA 12.
219   [1979] 3 All ER 136, *per* Lord Salmon.
220   *Beausejour Estates, above*, fn 218, p 17.
221   Chapter 7 ('The Written Constitution as a Legal Source').
222   Chapter 12 ('International Law as a Source of Law'). See, for example, *Roodal v The State*, (2003) 64 WIR 270 (Privy Council, T&T) on the question of the mandatory death penalty.

of those instruments.[223] The most striking example is the non-discrimination provision relating to sex. Such a construct has led to important constitutional challenges as to how such constitutional provisions are to be interpreted, in particular, whether such preamble provisions are justiciable, or whether merely declaratory.

The rationale for this debate lies in the relationship of the Preamble to the redress clause which gives authority for a person who believes that his or her rights have been violated to apply to the High Court for redress. Where the redress clause does not specifically include the Preamble in its listing of the human rights provisions for which redress may be sought, courts have held that the Preamble rights are not justiciable except in so far as they are also detailed in the body of the Constitution. This interpretation does not hold for the procedural fairness provision, expressed as due process or protection of law in the Preamble, as such provisions are seen to be inherent in the rule of law and already secured under the common law.[224]

The issue was aired in the *Girard* case, discussed above.[225] There, the St Lucian court held that a provision which existed only in the Preamble, in this case, protection from discrimination on the ground of sex, was not justiciable. It appears, however, that some Commonwealth courts are willing to challenge such assumptions.[226] In *R v Financial Services Commission (Gibraltar)*,[227] a case involving the right to privacy in relation to information on companies, a Gibraltar court, in examining the Constitution of Gibraltar, reviewed Antigua's Constitution, which it viewed as similar. It found that rights in the Preamble were justiciable.

---

223 Exceptions are the Constitutions of Trinidad and Toabago, Guyana and to an extent Antigua and Barbuda, because the Preamble and redress clauses are differently worded.
224 See the discussion in Chapter 7 ('The Written Constitution as a Legal Source').
225 *Above*, fn 198.
226 See the Belize case of *Selgado v AG et al* BZ 2004 SC 7.
227 [2003] 4 LRC 133.

PART III

THE ADMINISTRATION OF JUSTICE IN THE COMMONWEALTH CARIBBEAN

CHAPTER 15

THE COURT SYSTEM OF THE COMMONWEALTH CARIBBEAN

The legal system in any jurisdiction depends on a well-ordered, efficient system of courts to administer justice. It is only where such a system exists and where the said courts are able to dispense justice with integrity that we can say that the legal system has validity and sustainability.

Both the structure and the character of the court system are important and these are, therefore, the subjects of inquiry in this chapter. A certain coherence to the court systems and administration of justice in the region may be noted although they are by no means homogenous.

Since the legal tradition prominent in the Commonwealth Caribbean is that of the common law tradition, which originated in England, the court system of the territories is also influenced by this tradition. The courts in the region, therefore, are modelled on those of England. The power to create and regulate such court systems, however, is no longer derived from the former colonising power, but from the written Constitutions and other local statutory instruments to be found in the territories which have gained independence.[1] This power was reaffirmed in the case of *Hinds v R*.[2]

The court system is organised according to a three-tier structure corresponding to the rank which the particular court is accorded in the judicial system. The higher the court in the hierarchy, the more authoritative. For most countries in the region, the court which sits at the top of the hierarchy of courts is the Judicial Committee of the Privy Council, based in England, often called simply 'the Privy Council'. This judicial body is the final Court of Appeal for those jurisdictions. For a few countries which have now discontinued appeals to the Privy Council, the newly constituted Caribbean Court of Justice is the final Court of Appeal.[3]

Three types of courts can be identified in the Commonwealth Caribbean: inferior courts; superior courts, or courts of record; and the Privy Council or Caribbean Court of Justice, the superior courts placing second in the hierarchy. In addition, in Jamaica can be found a different type of court falling between superior and inferior courts, namely an intermediate court.

Also falling outside of the rigid hierarchical structure outlined above are the specialised courts which are to be found in the region. Such specialised courts may be either inferior, intermediate or superior courts, but by virtue of their specialised roles and jurisdictions, they must be placed outside of the boundaries of the ordinary courts.[4] Regional and international courts also have an important bearing on the judicial system of any jurisdiction. In the Commonwealth Caribbean, there are two such regional courts, one of which is the Caribbean Court of Justice, above, and the

---

1 See Chapter 1. Most of the territories of the Commonwealth Caribbean have now attained independence from Britain, the exceptions including Montserrat, Anguilla, Bermuda, the Cayman Islands and the British Virgin Islands.
2 [1976] All ER 353.
3 The Privy Council and the Caribbean Court of Justice are discussed in detail in Chapter 16 ('The Privy Council').
4 See Chapter 18 ('Specialised Courts, Tribunals and Functions').

other, a regional Supreme Court which sits immediately below the Privy Council, the Eastern Caribbean Supreme Court.

INFERIOR COURTS

Stipendiary magistrates and circuit magistrates

At the lowest end of the court system lie the inferior courts or courts of summary jurisdiction which, as the term suggests, deal with the lesser judicial matters. Inferior courts have no appellate jurisdiction and comprise magistrates' courts and petty sessional courts, the latter manned by justices of the peace. These petty sessional courts have largely criminal jurisdiction. They are empowered, for example, to issue summonses and warrants of arrest and may also grant bail for persons under arrest. Justices of the peace and magistrates have jurisdiction to conduct preliminary examinations of persons charged with indictable offences to ascertain whether such persons should be committed for trial before a jury in the High Court.[5] They also have a summary criminal jurisdiction to deal with minor offences, where such jurisdiction is conferred upon them by statute. In most jurisdictions, summary jurisdiction over juveniles and maintenanance of children is the domain of magistrates or the justices of the peace.[6] Other quasi-judicial matters may also be handled by these justices, for example, applications for liquor licences. Appeals from the petty sessions go to the High Court. Justices of the peace are laypersons granted power to issue warrants, administer oaths and maintain the peace.

The seriousness of the jurisdiction to issue search warrants was explored in *Comissiong v AG, COP et al.*[7] The Barbados Court of Appeal explained that the purpose of the requirement that a warrant be issued by a magistrate or a justice of the peace is to 'interpose the protection of a judicial decision between the citizen and the power of the State'.[8] Quoting from the case of *AG of Jamaica v Williams,*[9] the Court continued:

> ... the function of the justice is to satisfy himself that the prescribed circumstances exist. This is a duty of high constitutional importance. The law relies upon the independent scrutiny of the judiciary to protect the citizen against the excesses which would inevitably flow from allowing an executive officer to decide for himself whether the conditions under which he is permitted to enter upon private property have been met.

Also included among courts of inferior jurisdiction are coroners' courts. The function of these courts is to investigate the causes and circumstances surrounding suspicious or unnatural death. The coroner or chief officer of this court is usually a magistrate and sits with a petty jury. The type of inquiry which this courts holds is called an inquest. At the inquest, witnesses attend, and the verdict is termed an 'inquisition'.

By far the most popular of the inferior courts in terms of number are the

---

5 See, eg, the Barbados Magistrates' Jurisdiction and Procedure Act, s 25(1).
6 Note the case of Jamaica, which has a separate Family Court to deal with questions of child maintenance. See Chapter 18 ('Specialised Courts, Tribunals and Functions').
7 (Unreported) Civ Appeal No 16 of 1998, dec'd 16 April 2000 (CA, Barbados).
8 *Ibid*, p 2.
9 [1997] 3 WLR 389 (PC, Jamaica), at p 395.

magistrates' courts, which are run by stipendiary or circuit magistrates. There are essential differences between inferior courts and superior courts in jurisdiction and in the procedure followed. This procedure is labelled 'summary' in the inferior courts and is generally quicker than that of the superior courts, the main reason being the absence of a jury.

The jurisdiction of inferior courts is severely limited, either by placing a monetary limit determined by statute to the type of offence which may be heard, or by restricting the jurisdiction to particular types of offences. The jurisdiction of magistrates' courts is conferred by statute and magisterial authority must be confined within the parameters of the statute'.[10] It is diverse and voluminous.

Statutory limits are fixed in relation to the fines which magistrates may impose as well as to the quantum of damages and costs which they may award. Appeals from magistrates normally go to the Court of Appeal in the particular jurisdiction. In Barbados, however, such appeals go to a special division of the High Court called the Divisional Court.[11]

Inferior courts are also differentiated from superior courts by their geographical jurisdiction. Such courts are normally located in various parts of the particular country, as opposed to superior courts, which are usually centralised. For example, in Barbados, magisterial jurisdiction is divided into six geographical districts hosting approximately 12 courts.[12]

The phenomenon of travelling magistrates, known as circuit judges, may be noted in the Bahamas. These magistrates are a function of the geographical structure of the Bahamas, a large group of islands clustered together to make up one nation-state. The circuit magistrates travel around the Family Islands to hear matters. In addition, there are magistrates confined to specific geographically defined districts, as in other countries in the region. Further, there are Commissioners' Courts in the Family Islands (known also as Local Government and Administrators) made up of laypersons who hear minor matters.

In a case from the Bahamas, *Johnson (Oscar) v R*,[13] it was established that although the jurisdiction of a magistrate is limited to his district,[14] upon the true construction of s 12(2) of the Magistrates Act, the jurisdiction of stipendiary and circuit magistrates is not limited to the district to which he has been assigned but is exercisable individually and collectively in all districts in the Bahamas.[15]

Unlike superior courts, inferior courts have a dual function, that is, an investigative function and a trial function, in criminal matters.[16] As regards the trial function, the magistrates are mainly responsible for trying summary offences, that is, offences

---

10   *Noel v Noel* (Unreported) Civil Appeal No 4 of 1998, dec'd 23 November 1998 (CA, Antigua & Barbuda).

11   Magistrates' Jurisdiction and Procedure Act (Cap 116) (1971 Rev), s 131.

12   Magistrates' Court Act 1996.

13   (1990) 56 WIR 23 (CA, The Bahamas).

14   Under the Magistrates Act, Cap 42. s 3(2) (d).

15   The relevant provision under s 12(2) of the Magistrates Act, Cap 42 of the Bahamas reads: 'Any person appointed to be a stipendiary and circuit magistrate shall be *ex officio* a magistrate for the whole of the Bahamas and shall have in each and every district all the powers, duties and liabilities conferred or imposed upon a magistrate by any law, but may be assigned by the Chief Justice to a particular district ... Notwithstanding any such assignment a stipendiary and circuit magistrate so assigned may exercise jurisdiction in any other district or districts.'

16   Resident magistrates' courts, which are found in Jamaica and are intermediate courts, but can assume an inferior jurisdiction, also have an investigative function.

required to be tried summarily by the statue creating the offence. The investigative function comes from the criminal jurisdiction of the magistrates' courts which requires such courts to hold a preliminary inquiry into an indictable matter to determine whether there is enough evidence for the matter to be sent to trial in the High Court. This is the investigative function.

As regards civil matters, the jurisdiction of inferior courts, apart from being limited by monetary value, is also limited by the nature of the civil offence. Specific types of civil matters are clearly excluded. In the main, such exclusions relate to certain categories of tort, for example, libel and slander, malicious prosecution, probate matters, seduction and in some cases title to land.

Inferior courts are also differentiated on the basis of the type of remedy they can grant, which is strictly limited, and by their geographical jurisdiction. Such courts are normally located in various parts of any particular country, as opposed to superior courts, which are usually centralised. Inferior courts sit without a jury.

Resident magistrates' courts

Resident magistrates' courts are perhaps best described as intermediate courts, since they fall between inferior courts and superior courts in relation to their jurisdiction. Such courts are to be found in Jamaica, where resident magistrates are located in each parish. These courts are similar to the county courts of England. The resident magistrate is the judicial officer who mans the court. He is assisted by a clerk of court and a bailiff, the former who is a legally qualified person, an *ex officio* justice of the peace and the court administrator and prosecutor, in cases where the resident magistrate assumes jurisdiction over indictable offences. The jurisdiction of the resident magistrates' court is far wider than that of the stipendiary magistrates. This jurisdiction includes a number of indictable offences, as well as civil jurisdiction in excess of the statutory monetary limits of the jurisdiction of the ordinary magistrates' courts of the other territories.

Interestingly, resident magistrates have a special jurisdiction in relation to redundancy matters under s 17 of the Employment (Termination) Redundancy Payments Act 1974 of Jamaica, which provides: 'Notwithstanding any provision in any enactment limiting the jurisdiction of Resident Magistrates in relation to claims arising from contract, a Resident Magistrate shall have jurisdiction in any action arising from a contract of employment to which this Act applies, or from any claim in respect of redundancy payment in which the amount claimed does not exceed seven thousand dollars.'

Hybrid offences

Recently, legislative change has enabled inferior courts to try indictable cases in certain limited circumstances. In such situations, an accused is given a choice as to whether he wishes to have his case tried before the High Court before a jury, or summarily, before a magistrate. Offences which may be so tried are called 'hybrid offences'.[17] Where a case is tried summarily in this way, the penalties, if the accused is

---

17   This is a new category of offence. See, eg, in Barbados, Magistrates' Jurisdiction and Procedure Act 1971, s 46(1).

found guilty, will be less harsh since they will conform to the usual summary penalties.[18]

In *Kwame Apata v Roberts (No 2)*,[19] it was established by the Court of Appeal of Guyana that where a 'hybrid offence' has been tried summarily, the person who has been tried retains the right to appeal to the Court of Appeal.

A magistrate has a discretion to decide whether an accused will be allowed to proceed summarily with respect to a 'hybrid' offence. For example, as held in *Chadee v Santana*,[20] if the accused seeks to retract his consent to summary trial and the magistrate is satisfied that the accused is deliberately delaying his trial, the magistrate may take this into account in considering a request for the mode of trial. In such circumstances he may refuse the request.

However, the final authority as to how to proceed, whether summarily or by way of indictment, rests with the Director of Public Prosecutions (DPP). In *DPP v Sullivan & Others*,[21] the DPP initially gave his consent for the defendant to be tried summarily, but later changed his mind indicating by way of a written direction to the magistrate, that the case should be tried by way of indictment. The magistrate declined to follow the written direction from the DPP and the DPP moved the court to order the magistrate to show why he should not cause further proceedings in the case to be conducted as a preliminary inquiry.

SUPERIOR COURTS OF RECORD

Jurisdiction of superior courts

Superior courts or Courts of Record themselves consist of two tiers, comprising a High Court or Supreme Court and a Court of Appeal with such jurisdiction, powers and authority as are conferred on these courts by the Constitutions or any other law.[22] Collectively, the court is often called the Supreme Court. The High Court is usually the trial court or the Court of First Instance, while the Court of Appeal carries out the appellate function of the Supreme Court. Nomenclature is not necessarily important in describing the superior court function of the region, since, in some of the countries, for example, Belize and the Bahamas, the High Court is called the Supreme Court and there is an additional Court of Appeal.

In the Commonwealth Caribbean the jurisdiction of the Supreme Court is grounded in the Constitution, unlike inferior courts where ordinary statute establishes magistrates' courts and jurisdiction. Ordinary legislation supplements the jurisdiction of the superior courts and gives it detail. Since the Constitution grants

---

18   See, eg, the Summary Jurisdiction (Proceedings) Act 2000, cap 99, of Belize, ss 79–80, which makes provision for indictable offences to be tried summarily and where an election for summary trial is made, for the procedure to be the same as for other summary trials.

19   (1988) 31 WIR 219.

20   (1987) 42 WIR 365.

21   (1996) 54 WIR 256 (CA, Guyana).

22   See, eg, the Barbados Constitution, s 80(1) supplemented by the Supreme Court of Judicature Act, Cap 117 A, and the Trinidad and Tobago Constitution, s 99. Courts of Court Martial will also have superior, independent jurisdiction.

jurisdiction to superior courts, their jurisdiction cannot be taken away otherwise than by the Constitution. This point is highlighted in the case of *Re Niles (No 2)*.[23]

Similarly, the powers of the Court of Appeal cannot be enlarged without the appropriate constitutional procedure where such enlargement results in the narrowing of citizens's rights. In *The State v Boyce (Brad)*,[24] for example, statute purported to give the Director of Public Prosecutions a right of appeal in criminal proceedings after an acquittal. This not only violated the due process rights of an accused but also violated the constitutional provisions for amending the jurisdiction of the Court of Appeal.[25]

The High Court or Court of First Instance of superior jurisdiction is primarily a court of original jurisdiction (to try a matter in the first instance). However, it may have an appellate jurisdiction also. This court has appellate jurisdiction over summary matters arising from inferior courts such as petty sessional courts, and in certain instances, over administrative tribunals on a point of law. As noted previously, in Barbados, a special situation exists whereby appeals from magistrates' courts go to a special division of the High Court called the Divisional Court.[26]

The original jurisdiction of the High Court operates for both criminal and civil cases. The court has unlimited jurisdiction in civil and criminal cases. As regards damages, no limit is placed on the amount which the court may award, although in practice, certain well established principles are adhered to in assessing the quantum of damages. The jurisdiction of the various High Courts or Superior Courts is roughly equivalent to that of the High Court of England, as noted in *Re Crutchfield*.[27] This is, however, not necessarily the case for the Courts of Appeal. The civil jurisdiction of the High Court covers all actions and proceedings in equity, the common law, divorce and matrimonial causes, probate, bankruptcy and admiralty matters. It is normal, however, for proceedings over which the inferior courts have jurisdiction – generally matters involving small sums of money or relatively unimportant questions of law – to be resolved in those courts, reserving the more important civil cases for the High Court.[28]

The High Court, or superior Court of First Instance, has criminal jurisdiction over all treasons, felonies and misdemeanours.[29] Generally, the criminal jurisdiction of this court is exercised only for the more serious offences which are tried on indictment, leaving the lesser offences to be tried summarily in the inferior courts or intermediate

---

23 (2003) 66 WIR 64: ' "There shall be a Court of Appeal for Jamaica" . . . the words that follow . . . "which shall have such jurisdiction and powers as may be conferred upon it by this Constitution or any other law," do not entitle Parliament by an ordinary law to deprive the Court of Appeal of a significant part of such appellate jurisdiction . . .' at p 87, affirming the *dictum* of Lord Diplock in *Hinds, Hutchinson, Martin and Thomas v R* (1975) 24 WIR 326 at p 337. See also the discussion in Chapter 7 ('The Written Constitution as a Legal Source').

24 (2005) 65 WIR 283 (CA, Trinidad and Tobago).

25 Note that the court does not have the power to prohibit the reporting of trial proceedings, thereby violating freedom of expression, freedom of the press and the like. See *Independent Publishing Co Ltd v Attorney General and Another* (2004) 65 WIR 338 (PC, Trinidad and Tobago).

26 See Magistrates' Jurisdiction and Procedure Act (Cap 116) (1971 Rev), s 131.

27 BZ 1998 CA 4.

28 The Court of First Instance may be divided into Divisions of specialist jurisdiction. For example, in Barbados, there are three divisions of the High Court: the Civil Division, the Family Division and the Criminal Division.

29 The court sits in its criminal jurisdiction at specific periods, called 'Assizes'.

courts. In cases where a criminal offence is created by statute, there is a presumption that such offence is triable by the High Court in the absence of any express provision to the contrary. Appeals from the High Court go to the Court of Appeal, although in Trinidad and Tobago it is possible via special provision to allow certain cases to go directly to the Judicial Committee of the Privy Council without exhausting the remedy available at the Court of Appeal.

All the Constitutions of the Commonwealth Caribbean provide for judicial review by the courts where a citizen contends that his fundamental rights have been abrogated.[30] The citizen may make such application for redress via the High Court or Supreme Court. This is a very important jurisdiction. In fact, such courts can be viewed as the 'guardians' of the Constitution. A constitutional motion to the Privy Council or the Caribbean Court of Justice is also available to a person who seeks redress for alleged violation of fundamental rights as secured under the Constitution, where application for redress has failed before the Supreme Court.

Courts of Appeal have appellate jurisdiction only. These courts do not sit with a jury, because they are not concerned with reviewing the evidence or facts of a case. Rather, they adjudicate on matters of law. An uneven number of judges constitute a Court of Appeal, usually three. They hear appeals from magistrates' courts and the High Court or superior Court of First Instance or from specialised courts such as certain matters from the Family Court in St Vincent. Appeals are as of right only in exceptional cases such as an alleged violation of constitutional rights. Other cases require leave to appeal. Criminal appeals are limited to the following:

(a) against conviction on any ground which involves a question of law alone;

(b) with leave of the Court of Appeal or upon the certificate of the trial judge that it is a fit case for appeal;

(c) with leave of the Court of Appeal against sentence, where that sentence is not one fixed by law.

The Court of Appeal also has jurisdiction to hear appeals from the decisions of special courts, such as the Industrial Court of Trinidad and Tobago and certain statutory quasi-judicial bodies.

It has been made clear in *Re Niles (No 2)*[31] that Courts of Appeal have residual power to revisit and, where appropriate, re-open an appeal regardless of whether the original order of the court has been entered. However, this power is to be exercised only in exceptional situations where, for example, procedural unfairness has been demonstrated.

The superior courts have jurisdiction in electoral cases. Cases involving electoral disputes are confined to the High Court and Court of Appeal. Similarly, matters concerning the determination of questions of membership of the legislature (be it Senate or House of Assembly) are to be determined by the High Court. In some countries the decision of the High Court is final on this matter.[32] In others, for

---

30 See, eg, the Barbados Constitution, s 24, and the St Lucia Constitution, s 16. See, also, the jurisprudence on this in Chapter 7 ('The written Constitution as a legal source').

31 *Above*, fn 23 at pp 71–72.

32 Barbados, Belize, Jamaica.

example, in the OECS States,[33] an appeal may be launched as of right to the Court of Appeal, but no appeal shall be from any decision of the Court of Appeal.[34] The Bahamas has an unusual formula for hearing disputes. A special court, styled an 'election court,' is to be created.[35]

The superior court also has an inherent supervisory jurisdiction over statutory bodies and statutory powers. This is the subject of Administrative Law which is concerned with the judicial review of the decisions from such bodies by the superior courts. This, however, is not an appellate function. Rather, the judicial review function inquires only into *how* such decisions were made. In some cases, for example, the court may refer a matter back to the administrative authority for it to make the decision in accordance with the law. The difference between a review and an appeal was explained in *Re Niles*,[36] holding that a power to hear matters on the disciplining of attorneys was a power of judicial review and not an appeal.

The Supreme Court of Judicature Acts in the region, apart from describing the functions and jurisdictions of the various superior courts, also lay down the procedure and operational details of these courts, and give power to create court regulations or rules.

THE EASTERN CARIBBEAN SUPREME COURT

The Constitutions of the region may also make provisions for the sharing of appellate jurisdiction. For example, those countries which belong to the Organisation of Eastern Caribbean States (OECS) share a unified Supreme Court, the Eastern Caribbean Supreme Court (ECSC). The countries include Antigua, Dominica, Grenada, St Lucia, St Vincent, St Christopher and Nevis, Montserrat, Anguilla and the British Virgin Islands. The provisions governing the court systems are to be found in the West Indies Associated States Supreme Court Order.[37] The Order establishes a Supreme Court comprising a Court of Appeal and a High Court, both headed by a Chief Justice, whilst the High Court comprises a number of *puisne* judges.[38] Three judges sit in the Court of Appeal, which is headquartered in St Lucia. However, it is an itinerant court and the judges travel throughout the jurisdictions comprising the Member States, in order to hear matters. The High Court is manned by a resident judge. This means that while there is a single Court of Appeal, there are several High Courts which make up the jurisdiction of the Eastern Caribbean Supreme Court. The Order also establishes and sets out the jurisdiction and powers of the court, procedural matters relating to

---

33   See below, p 221.

34   Eg, St Vincent, s 36(1)(6)(8); Antigua, s 44(1)(6)(8). It is clear these courts are conceived of as superior courts of record.

35   Section 51 of the Bahamas Act, which reads:

> 51–(1) An Election Court, consisting of two Justices of the Supreme Court appointed by the Chief Justice or, if for any reason two such Justices are not available, one such Justice and the Chief Magistrate or a Stipendiary and Circuit Magistrate appointed by the Chief Justice, shall have jurisdiction to hear and determine any question whether: (a) any person has been validly elected as a member of the House of Assembly . . .

> An appeal lies to the Court of Appeal whose decision is final.

36   *Above*, fn 23. See also *R v IDT ex p Jamaica Civil Service Association*, (Unreported), Suit No M 36 of 2001, decided 12 April 2002 (SC, Jamaica), at pp 6–7.

37   SI 1967/223.

38   Section 4.

officers of the court and matters incidental thereto. The Order has been incorporated into the laws of the various territories by special legislation.[39] In addition, there is provision for the court in the Schedules of the Constitutions of Member States.

The jurisdiction and powers of this regional court are to be determined by the provisions of the Constitution, and any other law of the State invoking this shared jurisdiction. For instance, in the St Lucian Act,[40] the High Court has 'original jurisdiction in all civil causes and matters' except matters assigned to district courts, and the Court of Appeal has jurisdiction in relation to appeals from the High Court in criminal and civil matters, as well as appeals from magistrates' courts.

Section 3 of the Act provides that 'the process of the Supreme Court shall run throughout the States, and any judgment of the court shall have full force and effect and may be executed and enforced in any of the States'. Provision is also made for the expenses of the court. Subject to other agreements by the member governments, the cost of the court 'shall be borne by governments of the States, in equal proportions' from the States' consolidated funds.[41] There is provision for the establishment of a Judicial and Legal Services Commission.[42] Noteworthy is s 18(2)(a), which provides for the designation of two chairpersons from Member States, who will sit on this Commission for a period of three years. At the end of this tenure, another two chairpersons from different States are chosen by the Prime Minister or Chief Minister. This cyclical arrangement is to ensure that each Member State is represented and included in the operation of the court.

GRENADA'S REVOLUTIONARY EXPERIMENT WITH A FINAL SUPREME COURT

Of great historical interest is the judicature experiment of Grenada during its People's Revolution of 1979–83. The People's Revolutionary Government, which took power in a revolutionary, but bloodless coup, disengaged Grenada from both the regional ECSC and the Privy Council. This was partly achieved indirectly, by the suspension of the Westminster Constitution at the beginning of the Revolution, as the Constitution incorporated the Courts Order 1969 which had established the regional court. Further, the People's Law No 14 1979 proclaimed that the Courts Order 1967 'shall no longer apply to Grenada'. The Courts Act 1971, which had regulated the regional court in Grenada, was also repealed.[43]

In place of the regional court and the Privy Council, Grenada established a Supreme Court, consisting of a High Court and Court of Appeal, which had final appellate jurisdiction.[44]

Intriguingly, after the fall of the Revolution in 1983, the legality of the Revolutionary

---

39   See, eg, in St Lucia by Act No 17 of 1969; St Vincent Act No 8 of 1970; Antigua and Barbuda, Act No 26 of 1969 and in St Christopher and Nevis, Act No 17 of 1975.

40   No 17 of 1969, s 7.

41   *Ibid*, s 15.

42   *Ibid*, s 18.

43   People's Law No 4 1979. Appeals to the Privy Council were abolished under the Privy Council (Abolition of Appeals) Law 1979, People's Law No 84 1979.

44   See the Establishment of the Supreme Court of Grenada Law 1979, People's Law of 1979.

Supreme Court was questioned by the very persons who had established it, the former government leaders of the Revolution.[45]

The challengers to the court's legality claimed that the Supreme Court was unconstitutional and that the only court competent to try them was the regional Supreme Court, as established under the original Constitution. In effect, this was a challenge to the legitimacy of the act of suspending the Constitution and the Revolution itself.

In historic litigation which considered these complex jurisprudential issues,[46] the Revolutionary Court was held to be legitimate on the basis of the doctrine of necessity. Grenada subsequently returned to the OECS regional system and to the Privy Council in 1991.[47]

THE ALCALDE COURTS IN BELIZE

A special feature of the administration of justice in the region is found in Belize, that is, the existence of the Alcalde Courts. In truth, Alcalde 'courts' are not part of the judiciary but fall under the Executive and are therefore not courts in the strict sense. They nevertheless, perform important adjudicative functions. The Alcade's jurisdiction is summary in nature and encompasses both minor civil and minor criminal jurisdiction. However, it is limited to the indigenous (Maya) community in Belize. The positions of Alcade and Deputy Alcade are elected ones.[48]

THE JUDICIARY

To ensure the proper functioning of the administration of justice and, in particular, the court system, it is essential that judges be independent. This is an appropriate subject of constitutional law, but we consider it briefly here within the context of the proper functioning of the court system. The Canadian case of *Valente v R*[49] is very instructive. The court pronounced on the importance of the concept of judicial independence. It noted that:

> Judicial independence involves both individual and institutional relationships: the individual independence of a judge as reflected in such matters as security of tenure and the institutional independence of the court as reflected in its institutional or administrative relationships to the executive and legislative branches of government.[50]

The court in the *Valente* case further held that independence connotes a status or

---

45   The Revolution came to a violent end in 1983 when, after an internal power struggle, one faction of the revolutionary government assassinated the popular revolutionary leader, Maurice Bishop, and several other persons. The key members of this rebel faction were subsequently tried and convicted for the murders. It was during this trial that they contested the legality of the Supreme Court as a means of challenging the validity of their trials.

46   *Mitchell v DPP* [1985] LRC (Const) 127, H Ct Grenada; [1986] LRC (Const) 35, CA Grenada and (1985) 32 WIR 241, PC.

47   See the Constitutional Judicature (Restoration) Act 1991, Act No 19 of 1991, ss 4 and 5 respectively.

48   See Chapter 10 ('Custom as a Source of Law'), for further discussion of the Mayas in Belize.

49   [1985] 2 SCR 673.

50   [1985] 2 SCR 673, p 674.

relationship to others, in particular, to the executive branch of government, which is hinged on objective conditions or guarantees.[51]

The judges of the aforementioned case expounded further, and set out the 'essential conditions' for the independence of the judiciary, namely:

(a) security of tenure;

(b) financial security – that is, security of salary or other remuneration and, where appropriate, security of pension;

(c) institutional independence of the tribunal with respect to matters of administration, which bear directly on the exercise of judicial function. In other words, the degree to which the judiciary should have control over the administration of the courts.

The distinguished West Indian jurist, the Rt Hon Mr Justice PT Georges, upon his appointment in 1999 as the sole independent Inquirer to examine the question of the independence of the judiciary in Trinidad and Tobago, had this to say in seeking to clarify the purpose of the safeguards put in place for securing the independence of the judiciary:

> The safeguards are not intended for the benefit of the persons holding the office of judge. Rather, they are intended to ensure that the Supreme Court, the institution ultimately charged with the protection of the Fundamental Human Rights and Freedoms of all persons in Trinidad & Tobago, can fearlessly enforce those rights when called upon to do so.[52]

He further explained that one of the rights to be so protected was the right of the individual to equality before the law, and that underlying this right is the concept of the rule of law. He continued:

> A free and democratic society cannot exist without the rule of law. Essentially, therefore, the independence of the Judiciary must be the cornerstone of such a society.[53]

This concept of the independence of the judiciary is well embedded in our Commonwealth Caribbean Constitutions via the 'separation of powers' doctrine. Along with the independence of the judiciary, we need also to consider the jurisdiction of the judiciary, which is critical to the doctrine of the separation of powers.

It is necessary to emphasise two aspects of jurisdiction under the separation of powers doctrine:

(a) in general, protection of the courts' monopoly of judicial power; and

(b) in particular, the protection of the jurisdiction of specified courts.

The general doctrine that the courts have a monopoly of judicial power was held to be part of the constitutional law of Jamaica and, by extension, the constitutional law of the Commonwealth Caribbean in the instrumental case of *Hinds v R*.[54] That case decided the point that unless the Constitution provides otherwise, a judicial power cannot be exercised by a body other than the court.

---

51   *Ibid.*

52   *The Report of the Rt Hon Mr Justice PT Georges on the Independence of the Judiciary*, reproduced in Carib L B 28, at p 30.

53   *Ibid.*

54   [1976] 1 All ER 353.

In addition, a court is only lawfully established according to the provision of the Constitution or relevant statute. The mere fact that a judge acts in an official capacity does not necessarily mean that he is exercising his judicial 'court' function. This point was recently illustrated in *Williams et al v The Queen*.[55] Under the Offences Against the Person (Amendment) Act 1992, provision was made for a single judge of the Court of Appeal to classify murder offences into capital murder and non-capital murder and for three judges to review the classification. It was held by the Privy Council that, where judges were acting in such a capacity, they could not be regarded as a 'Court of Jamaica' within the meaning of s 110(5) of the Constitution.

The second aspect, that is, the particular jurisdiction of certain courts, has already been dealt with above, p 293.

The requirements relating to the appointment, tenure and removal of judges and the structure of the judiciary are provided for in the respective Constitutions. This accords their status the highest possible respect and authority.

For example, in some Constitutions, it is provided that the judiciary is headed by a Chief Justice, who is President of the Court of Appeal. The judiciary also comprises such number of other Justices of Appeal and puisne judges as prescribed by Parliament.[56] The Jamaica Constitution establishes a Supreme Court headed by a Chief Justice and other senior *puisne* judges.[57] The Constitution also establishes a Court of Appeal, requiring a President, Chief Justice, three other judges and such other judges as may be prescribed by Parliament.[58] The President of the Court of Appeal is responsible for the arrangement of the work of the court and shall preside whenever he is sitting in that court.[59]

Belize adopted the Jamaican approach. The Constitution established a Supreme Court of Judicature and a Court of Appeal.[60] The Justices of the Supreme Court shall be the Chief Justice and such number of other justices as described by Parliament.[61] The Court of Appeal comprises a President and such number of other justices as may be prescribed by the National Assembly.[62]

The model found in Guyana is interesting. Its Court of Appeal comprises a Chancellor, who is President of the Court of Appeal, the Chief Justice and such other number of Judges of Appeal described by Parliament.[63]

In most countries appointment of *puisne* judges is made by an independent judicial services commission as established under the various Constitutions. There are different methods for selecting a Chief Justice, such as in Barbados, by the

---

55   (1997) 2 Carib LB 75, PC Jamaica.
56   Trinidad and Tobago Constitution, s 100(1); Bahamas, s 101(1).
57   Jamaican Constitution, s 97(1)(2).
58   See Jamaican Constitution, s 103(1), (2).
59   *Ibid*, s 103(1), (2).
60   Belize Constitution.
61   *Ibid*, s 95(2).
62   *Ibid*, s 100(2).
63   Guyana Constitution, Art 124. See, also, the Constitution of the Bahamas, ss 93(1) and 98, which establish a Supreme Court and a Court of Appeal respectively, and which make provision for the appointment of the corresponding judicial personnel. The justices of the Supreme Court comprise a Chief Justice and such other of other justices as may be prescribed by Parliament. The Court of Appeal comprises: (a) a President; (b) the Chief Justice, by virtue of his office as head of the judiciary. The Chief Justice shall not sit in the Court of Appeal unless invited so to sit by the President of the Court; and (c) such number of other justices of appeal as Parliament may describe.

Governor General, on the advice of the Prime Minister, after consultation with the Leader of the Opposition.

Under the various Supreme Court of Judicature Acts or corresponding legislation, the required qualifications for such judges are also provided for. Usually, one such prerequisite is that they must be a legal advocate of not less than 10 years' standing.

The role of judges in the Commonwealth Caribbean should also include their function as interpreters of the Constitution, guardians of the rights and freedoms embodied in these Constitutions, adjudications of questions about the validity of legislation and catalysts in creating an indigenous jurisprudence.

Provisions relating to tenure and removal of judges are particularly detailed in an attempt to immunise judges from political or other arbitrary interference or caprice, thereby conferring on them security of tenure and independence. Such protection is also given a constitutional foundation. Thus, judges may only be removed for inability to discharge the functions of office, for example, due to infirmity, misconduct, or corruption. Further, the power to remove judges is vested not in one person's discretion, but in a Judicial Committee or comparable body which has the power to make recommendations as to removal. However, such power of removal can only be exercised after an investigation of the charge by a tribunal of two or more persons.

In *Barnwell v AG and Another*,[64] the Court of Appeal struck down a decision to remove a High Court judge from office for alleged misconduct. The Chairman of the Judicial Services Commission, and not the entire Commission as required by the Constitution, had made the decision. As such, it was *ultra vires* the Constitution. The Commission could not adopt the decision of the Chairman as its own.

A number of other attempts to remove or discipline judges have found their way into the courts. In *Meerabux v Attorney General of Belize*,[65] for example, the issue was the composition of the body, the Advisory Council, established to hear matters relating to the removal and discipline of judges in Belize. The Supreme Court was of the view that the Advisory Council did not meet the established standards accepted in the Commonwealth, the Latimer Guidelines on independence and impartiality for the Judiciary. Justice Blackman, although refusing to grant the declaration that the Applicant judge had been deprived of his constitutional right to the protection of the law, noted that former requirements such as that members of the Council should be attorneys, had been dispensed with. He made a call for better methods to secure the independence of the judiciary through a more careful scrutiny of provisions relating to bodies granted powers to impact on the tenure of judges. He said:

> I urge the Belize Parliament to actively revisit the mechanisms that are in place for the disciplinary review of senior office holders, as home-spun creations are not necessarily appropriate in a modern, developing, progressive . . . society. The seminal observation by Kennard JA in *Barnwell*[66] . . . at page 159 on the implications for fairness and impartiality, when one lives in a small society should not be disregarded.[67]

Noteworthy is the recent Commission of Inquiry in St Lucia, where two ex-Prime Ministers who were before the Commission asserted that a retired OECS judge had

---

64   (1993) 49 WIR 88.
65   BZ 2002 SC 3, upheld in BZ 2002 CA 5.
66   *Above*, fn 71.
67   *Above*, fn 65 at p 28. See also *Rees et al v Crane* (1994) 1 All ER 833 at p 837(j) to 838(f).

been an *employee* of the OECS governments while in office. This is not entirely correct as politicians should not be viewed as the employers of judges. In fact, Heads of Government of the OECS have the authority to appoint judges to the Eastern Caribbean Supreme Court after selections by the relevant Commission. Otherwise, this would be contradictory to the notion of judicial independence.[68]

Judges with political backgrounds

Some thought should be given to the situation, increasingly apparent in Commonwealth Caribbean jurisdictions, where a person who was formerly the holder of a political office, or was in some way directly involved in partisan politics is appointed a judge. In such situations, is judicial independence impaired? This is the case, for example, in Barbados, where there was a change to the Constitution to accommodate such judicial appointments. In 1974 changes were made with regard to the appointment of judges, diminishing the role of the independent Judicial and Legal Services Commission and placing more autonomy in the hands of the Executive.[69] For example, the former Attorney General was able to be appointed as Chief Justice.

These circumstances were questioned in the Jamaican case of *Panton and Another v Minister of Finance and Another (No 2)*,[70] where the appellants challenged the validity of a hearing before the Court of Appeal to determine whether the Financial Institutions Act 1992 was *ultra vires* the Constitution. The appellants alleged that their right to an independent and impartial trial had been infringed since the President of the Court of Appeal had been the Attorney General when the Act had been presented to the Governor General for his assent and had signed the certificate to the effect that the Act was 'not contrary to the Constitution.' Further, the President had been the legal advisor to the Government responsible for promulgating the Act. Accordingly, the appellants argued, the President of the Court of Appeal was biased.

The Privy Council disagreed. In dicta which surely has important implications for the administration of justice and its relationship with the political realities of the day, the Privy Council, although confirming the principle of judicial independence, recognised that 'the purity of principle may require to give way to the exigencies and realities of life.'[71]

This abstract principle was to be distinguished from the cases where a judge who had previously held political office or been involved directly in the political process had 'introduced the Bill, or campaigned for it . . . or adopted it as a particular cause which he was determined to promote . . .'.[72] Mere membership or involvement in partisan politics was not, however, sufficient to impute judicial bias.

Perhaps unwittingly, the Privy Council highlighted a phenomenon which may be viewed as one of necessity in small, developing countries such as ours in which there is a relatively small pool of excellence to choose from. Often, the characteristic necessary for judicial selection and eminence are the same qualities desired in political

---

68   See the case of *Lewis v AG of St Lucia*, unreported Civil Appeal No 12 of 1997 and *Compton v AG of St Lucia, above*, fn 75.
69   The Constitution Commission of Barbados has recommended the reversal of the 1974 changes.
70   (2001) 59 WIR 418 (PC, Jamaica).
71   *Ibid*, at p 427. Indeed, in 'extreme cases the doctrine of necessity may require a judge to determine an issue even although he would otherwise be disqualified.' *Ibid*.
72   *Ibid*, p 426.

office. Persons of such character may be invited to serve the country through the formal political process at a much earlier age than they would or could be appointed to the Bench. To deprive the community of the wisdom and experience of such persons may be shortsighted. Indeed, the Privy Council also observed that judges who come with such experience may indeed be better off.[73]

Thus, a career in politics, or even close association with Cabinet members or a mere association with a particular government or political policy is not necessarily detrimental:

> In countries where it is recognised and accepted that judges may well have behind them a history of political affiliation or partisan interest it has also to be recognized that such historical associations can be put aside in the interest of performing a judicial duty with independence and impartiality.[74]

Finally, on this point, it should be observed that the position taken by the Privy Council in the *Panton* case and others discussed in *Panton* is quite different from that taken in the case of *Compton v AG*.[75] In the latter case, the impartiality of a Commissioner was questioned merely because the Commissioner had been a former Court of Appeal judge and Compton, the then Prime Minister, had been one of a number of Prime Ministers with authority to appoint her, or in that case, extend her tenure. This was sufficient to preclude the appointment of the said Commissioner on the ground, not of actual bias, of which there was none, but on the maxim, 'justice must be seen to be done.'

It seems curious, to say the least, that the standards of potential bias should be more restrictively applied in a Commission of Inquiry, which is not a judicial process, than in a court of law established under the Constitution!

PROBLEMS ADMINISTERING JUSTICE

Surprisingly, problems with the court system in the Commonwealth Caribbean have been noted since the late 19th century. An early Chief Justice in the 1880s, Sir John Gorrie, had this to say:

> The present system of weak magistrates on small salaries with large powers is the very worst which could be devised.[76]

At the time of Gorrie, CJ's comment, magistrates were lay persons, 'untrained . . . invariably local landowners, merchants or professional men with close ties to the island elites'.[77]

Today, the problem of untrained magistrates has been alleviated, though not entirely solved in all countries of the region. However, magistrates and judges face

---

73   *Ibid*, p 428, para 17.
74   *Ibid*, p 428.
75   *Compton v AG of St Lucia*, unreported Civ App No 14 of 1997, decided 9 February 1998, CA, St Lucia.
76   Words of John Gorrie, CJ, Leewards 1883–1888, CO 152/159 Attached to C 3840: memo by Chief Justice 4/8/84, documented in Bridget Brereton *Law, Justice and Empire: The Colonial Career of John Gorrie 1829–1892*, 1997, Jamaica: UWI Press, p 201.
77   *Ibid*.

other problems, which impair their ability to function efficiently and fairly within the legal system no less.

Lack of resources and delay – the impact of underdevelopment

The problem of delay in the administration of justice in the Commonwealth Caribbean has been identified as 'the single most consistent complaint in every legal system' in the region.[78] This issue has not been merely documented, but judicially noticed. Indeed, it was such a problem that spurred the line of cases on cruel and inhuman punishment as a result of undue delay on death row.[79] A telling point is that these judgments betray the dollars and cents implications of Caribbean justice. The slowness of the judicial system is due mainly to a lack of financial resources which can expedite proceedings and appeals and, in some cases, the paucity of legal representation. Such problems really point to the impact of underdevelopment on the legal system. It is such underdevelopment due to a lack of financial resources which holds the administration of justice to ransom.

This lack of resources permeates every level of the legal system. Delroy Chuck laments, for example, that there is a lack of research facilities for judges at the courts, once again, pointing to the expenses of maintaining adequate libraries. This is exacerbated by inadequate physical work structures, not conducive to productivity.

To compound this matter, judges lack independent financial resources, which may have an impact, not just on their power to define their work circumstances, but also on their independence. Often, they must depend on a government department for funding. Indeed, this was the subject of contention in Trinidad and Tobago, when the then Chief Justice objected to the phenomenon as an abrogation of the constitutional requirement of judicial independence.[80]

There is also concern, one shared by other countries outside of the region, that due to the relatively poor financial remuneration for judicial officers, the Bench and magistracy are unable to attract the finest minds. It is usually far more lucrative for attorneys to practice privately and they often only consider the Bench at the end of a distinguished career. At that point, one may argue that their best mettle has been spent.

Legal representation and legal aid

A significant problem in the administration of justice in the region is the lack of adequate legal aid. Where it is available, it is often only for the most serious offences, such as murder. An exception may exist, such as in Barbados, for legal aid for juveniles. In a legal system where contingency fee arrangements in which attorneys are

---

78 Delroy Chuck 'What Improvements Would I like To See in the Judicial System over the Next Ten Years', February 1991, *Caribbean Justice Improvement Seminar*, Ocho Rios, Jamaica, p 9.

79 Beginning with the well-known case of *Pratt and Morgan v Attorney General of Jamaica* (1993) 43 WIR 340 (PC), discussed in other chapters. See, eg, Chapter 7 ('The Written Constitution as a Legal Source'), Chapter 8 ('The Common Law and the Doctrine of Judicial Precedent').

80 See *The Report of the Rt Hon PT Georges, above*, fn 52.

paid a percentage of winning costs are not accepted in the system[81] and where there are high levels of poverty, this is a serious deficiency.

Where legal representation is available, studies have demonstrated that it is often inefficient. This has had devastating implications for persons accused of murder.[82]

Access to the courts

Clearly, a lack of access to legal representation can impact negatively on the citizen's access to the courts. Such deficiencies are clearly related to the issue of the personal finance of potential litigants. Justice is expensive and is generally only available to the relative few who can afford to pay for it. In the case of the highest echelons of the judicial system, the Privy Council, those who manage to access the courts right up to a court of appeal may lack the financial resources to go further and approach the English-based Privy Council. This problem is addressed in a following chapter.[83]

Apart from issues of cost, arrangements for the access to such courts may be inherently discriminatory. For example, in Barbados, in family matters, married persons have access to a superior court, the High Court, while those in common law unions, although recognised by the law, must seek redress before the magistrates' courts.

How one is able to approach a court may, of course, also be determined by issues of class and more indirectly, race, as class and race are often linked in the region. This, for example, influences juvenile justice.[84]

To ensure the independence and impartiality of judges, salaries and allowances are expected to be generous. Judges are also privileged from criminal and civil actions for anything said or done while acting within their jurisdiction, even if seemingly without just cause.[85]

Despite these aforementioned safeguards built into the Constitution and other legislation to maintain the independence of the judiciary, the politics of size and lack of human and financial resources may undermine the achievement of this goal. It is often perceived that in small societies such as ours, it is difficult for judges to achieve the social distance necessary for impartiality and fairness. Professor Patchett observes that:

> The difficulties of the judge in such mini-States are often adverted to. It is not possible to remain anonymous or even easy to avoid the public eye. Not only are the personal characteristics of a judge likely to be well known in the community, but sometimes there is an unhealthy interest in them. The judge cannot easily hold himself apart from close contacts with those who may appear before him. Were it possible to confine his

---

81 This has however, been successfully challenged in the Cayman Islands. See *National Trust for Cayman Islands v Planning Appeals Tribunal, Central Planning Authority and Humphreys (Cayman) Ltd* [2002] CILR 59 (Grand Court, Cayman Islands).

82 See Antoine, R-M B, 'Equal Access to Justice' in G Kodilyne and P K Menon (eds) *Commonwealth Caribbean Legal Studies*, 1992, London: Butterworths, 333.

83 See Chapter 16 ('The Privy Council').

84 See Chapter 18 ('Specialised Courts, Tribunals and Functions').

85 In the Commonwealth Caribbean, the age of retirement for judges ranges between 62 and 65 years, which is much earlier than in England, where it is 75 years.

friendships to the legal profession alone (which it is not), his association with the persons actively involved in political life, would, in fact, be guaranteed.[86]

This is perhaps exacerbated in pluralistic societies, divided along multi-racial, ethnic or rigid class lines. Yet, in defence, it may be said that these constraints may be over-emphasised, for few societies may be said to be truly homogeneous. The concept of objectivity, born out of total isolation, is perhaps elusive in all legal communities.

However, it is apparent that the efficiency of the system of administration of justice in the region suffers as a result of insufficient qualified personnel and finances, the latter of which results in extremely poor conditions of work.

A further problem which could affect the efficient functioning of the judiciary is the relative lack of specialised decisions and courts. This means that the judge in the Commonwealth Caribbean is expected to adjudicate upon wide and varied areas of law in a system where there is understaffing and, unlike some other countries, no additional aid for researching cases.

---

86 Patchett, KW, 'Legal problems of the mini-State: the Caribbean experience' [1974–77] Cambrian L Rev 57.

CHAPTER 16

THE PRIVY COUNCIL

CARIBBEAN CROSSROADS – FROM THE PRIVY COUNCIL TO A REGIONAL SUPREME COURT

Status of the Privy Council and power to abolish appeals

At the apex of the court system in most of the jurisdictions in the Commonwealth Caribbean lies the Judicial Committee of the Privy Council (the Privy Council), which presently serves as the final Court of Appeal for all of the countries of the region, with the exception of the Republic of Guyana and Barbados.[1] The Privy Council is based in Britain and became established as the final court for the respective countries during colonialism.

The region finally created its own Court of Appeal with the establishment of the Caribbean Court of Justice (CCJ) in April 2005. However, at the time of going to press, not all countries had accepted this appellate jurisdiction, most having chosen to retain the appellate jurisdiction of the Judicial Committee of the Privy Council (the Privy Council). Only Barbados and Guyana have thus far accepted the CCJ as the final appellate court. In contrast, the original jurisdiction of the CCJ extends to all CARICOM countries. The CCJ is discussed fully in the following chapter.

The reasons advanced for keeping the Privy Council's appellate jurisdiction and declining that of the CCJ are many. At the top of the list are fears that the CCJ will not dispense impartial justice, that it will be too costly, that the region will not be able to choose judges based on merit, that those judges will not be competent enough to make the right decisions, and that the larger countries in the region will dominate the court. At the outset, one may observe the preponderance of reasons that seem connected to points made earlier in this book about insecurity and dependency which plague us as a people in our moves toward development.[2] Yet, the CCJ represents so much to Caribbean peoples.

As there is still a considerable amount of opposition to the abolition of Privy Council appeals from many Caribbean citizens, including some of the legal community, the following discussion on the merits and demerits of the Privy Council's jurisdiction remains relevant. Indeed, the Bahamas has already stated that it is unable to make a commitment to participation in the court at the present time.

Unfortunately, some of the opposition to the CCJ may be attributed to partisan politics. For instance, on the one hand, while in office as the Prime Minister of Trinidad and Tobago, Basdeo Panday, promoting the CCJ, stated that the ability of that country to give effect to the Agreement and act as the headquarter country of the court will ultimately depend on the agreement of the Opposition, which, in fact, had

---

1   In Guyana, the Privy Council's jurisdiction was abolished under the Judicial Committee of the Privy Council (Termination of Appeals) Act 1970. Grenada abolished appeals to the Privy Council during the 'Grenada Revolution', but this was of temporary effect only. See the earlier discussion on Grenada's experiment with its own final appellate court in Chapter 15.

2   See, eg, Chapter 1 ('Introduction to Law and Legal Systems in the Commonwealth Caribbean') and Chapter 8 ('The Common Law and the Doctrine of Judicial Precedent').

been hostile to the idea.[3] Yet, when Panday's party became the Opposition, it refused to agree to Trinidad and Tobago's accession to the appellate jurisdiction of the very CCJ which they had championed!

The net effect of these developments is that there now exists two separate and distinct final courts of appeal in the region: the traditional Privy Council, inherited from colonial times and the home-grown CCJ, a product of independence and self-determination. We can, therefore, best describe this moment in our legal history as a period of transition, when the region as a whole is at a crossroads, moving along the path to legal independence, but at a slow and sometimes uncertain pace, with some vehicles still in 'park' mode.

In the interim period, before the Caribbean Court of Justice becomes a full reality for all Commonwealth Caribbean States, the Privy Council remains an important subject for the region as a whole. In this book, therefore, we discuss both courts, the Privy Council and the CCJ, as well as the question of the desirability of abolishing final appeals to the Privy Council. The latter is by no means a novel discussion, but one still of great relevance to the majority of Commonwealth Caribbean States.

Although most of the countries of the region have attained independence from Great Britain, much of the former jurisdiction of the Privy Council over the ex-colonies has been retained. However, the nature of this jurisdiction has changed.

The issue of the impact which independence had over the jurisdiction of the Privy Council was addressed in the case of *Ibralebbe v R*,[4] a case from Ceylon, which shared a similar colonial experience with the Commonwealth Caribbean and, consequently, a similar Privy Council jurisdiction. In this case, it was argued that the Ceylon Independence Act 1947 had had the effect of abolishing the right of Privy Council appeal previously enjoyed under British rule, since the continuance of that right was 'inconsistent with the status of Ceylon as an independent political body'.[5] Relying on the combined effect of the imperial and Ceylonese laws and Regulations concerning Privy Council appeals, as well as the argument that the Privy Council was an independent court exercising a jurisdiction founded on the Prerogative, the Privy Council held that the Privy Council appeal was part of the judicial system of Ceylon, and a part of the structure of original and appellate courts. When a territory having constitutional power to do so, as Ceylon now had, decided to abrogate the appeal to the Judicial Committee, it effected an amendment of its own judicial structure.[6]

The continuance of appeals to the Privy Council in no way impaired independence and sovereignty, since the Parliament of Ceylon, under its constitutional power, as an independent nation, may at any time modify or terminate appeals to the Privy Council.[7]

There is a provision made for eminent judges from the Commonwealth Caribbean to sit on the Privy Council. Still, this power is rarely exercised and few appointments of West Indian judges are made to the Privy Council.

---

3   15 July 1998, CANA News Agency.
4   [1964] AC 900.
5   *Ibid*, p 912.
6   *Ibid*.
7   *Ibid*, p 925.

METHOD OF ABOLISHING APPEALS

The issue to be determined is whether the region might be more adequately served by a regional Court of Appeal, rather than a court comprising mainly English judges sitting in England, as the Privy Council. This has been the subject of numerous debates, articles, public lectures and discussion and will be discussed further below.[8] An initial question in the debate concerns whether, and in what circumstances, Commonwealth Caribbean States have authority to abolish appeals to the Privy Council.

The fact that an independent Commonwealth territory has the power to abolish appeals to the Privy Council was reaffirmed in the Grenadian case of *Mitchell v R*.[9] Here, the Privy Council was asked to address the issue of the constitutionality of the Grenadian Court of Appeal, the court which purported to replace the Privy Council as the final Court of Appeal in that jurisdiction under the People's Laws of the People's Revolutionary Government regime. The Privy Council held that it no longer had jurisdiction to hear appeals from Grenada, since the right to appeal had been legitimately abolished by the government in power.

What is undisputed is that the Constitutions of various countries in the Commonwealth Caribbean provide a clear right to abolish appeals to the Privy Council, as has been done in Grenada, the Republic of Guyana and more recently in Barbados by legislation. The methods of doing so, however, vary, ranging from a relatively simple legislative procedure in the Bahamas,[10] to complex requirements in the OECS States which often require a referendum.[11] In the middle ground, the other countries require that there be a majority parliamentary vote before appeals to the Privy Council can be abolished. The exact majority varies from country to country. In Trinidad and Tobago, for example, a vote of not less than two-thirds of all the Members of the Senate and three-fourths of all the Members of the House of Representatives is required.[12]

A number of salient points are discernible from the above statements with regard to the jurisdiction and status of the Privy Council. First, it is clear that the legal status of the Privy Council as the final appellate court was transferred and not aborted during independence. Secondly, the *raison d'être* for the Privy Council is no longer grounded in that court being a court whose function is to promote uniformity in the common law throughout the former Empire. Before independence, the judicial systems of the Commonwealth were part of the British Empire and the Privy Council was an essential element of the system. Pre-independence Commonwealth courts were therefore justified in applying English municipal law in deciding cases, as illustrated in *Robins v National Trust Co.*[13] Now, however, the binding authority of Privy Council decisions rests solely on the fact that the Privy Council is the highest court

---

8   See, eg, de la Bastide, J, 'The Case for a Caribbean Court of Appeal', Fourth Anthony Bland Memorial Lecture, Faculty of Law, UWI, in [1995] 5 Carib LR 401; White, D, 'Jettison the Privy Council – you t'ink it easy?', 1976, unpublished, University of the West Indies.

9   (1985) 32 WIR 241, PC.

10   Under the Constitutions of the Bahamas, s 105(3), 'Parliament may by law' provide for the Privy Council's functions to 'be exercised by any other court established for the purpose'.

11   See, eg, the Constitutions of Dominica, s 42; St Christopher, s 39; See too s 41 of the Saint Lucia Constitution Order 1978 which is even more complex.

12   See the Trinidad and Tobago Constitution, s 54(3).

13   [1927] AC 515. See the discussion in Chapter 8 ('The Common Law and the Doctrine of Judicial Precedent').

of each individual independent territory's judicial system. The authority for this assertion is founded on the specific retention of the Privy Council as the final appellate court found in the Constitutions of the Commonwealth Caribbean and other legislative provisions which ground this avenue of appeal.[14]

ASSUMPTION OF APPELLATE JURISDICTION

While the Privy Council is the final Court of Appeal for most jurisdictions in the region, this description of the court is perhaps misleading when one considers the actual jurisdiction and policies of the Privy Council. Its jurisdiction is severely limited, and it only functions as a Court of Appeal in a very restricted sense.

Under the common law, there is no right of appeal in all cases. Rather, an appeal must be specially conferred. Consequently, early appeals to the Privy Council were entertained as a matter of grace. Later, it became the practice to include a right of appeal to the Privy Council in colonial territories, with or without leave of the Colonial Court. Thus, two forms of appeal to the Privy Council developed and are still evident in contemporary Commonwealth Caribbean legal systems, namely, those brought as of right, and those brought with leave. Leave is required from the local Court of Appeal or from the Privy Council, the latter either where there was no provision made for an appeal, or where the local court has refused leave.

The grounds for appeal to the Privy Council are laid out under the respective Constitutions.[15] The usual jurisdiction of the Privy Council with regard to appeals from Commonwealth Caribbean countries is as follows. Appeals are available 'as of right' in civil judgments, where the amount in dispute is of the prescribed statutory value, or exceeds the stated statutory limits, or where the claim involves property of a prescribed value or upwards. Appeals are also available 'as of right' in civil or criminal matters which involve a question of constitutional interpretation. In *Tiger Air Inc v Summrall*,[16] it was held that this civil jurisdiction extended to interlocutory judgments of the Court of Appeal and not only to final judgments, provided that the prescribed statutory monetary values were met. Appeals of decisions in proceedings for dissolution or nullity of marriage may also lie as of right.[17]

It should be noted that even where a right of appeal to the Privy Council exists, leave must first be obtained by the Court of Appeal. This point was noted in *Electrolec Services Ltd v Issa Nicholas (Grenada) Ltd.*[18] The Privy Council explained that under the Judicial Committee (General Appellate Jurisdiction) Rules Order 1982 (The Judicial Committee Rules), notwithstanding that the case may be one in which an appeal lies as of right, the leave of the Court of Appeal must be obtained. Such leave is not, however, a matter of discretion for that court.[19] The Court of Appeal has the power, however, to prescribe certain conditions where authorised by statute, such as, in this

---

14   See, also, the West Indies Associated States (Appeals to the Privy Council) Order 1967, which provides for appeals to the Privy Council from decisions of the regional Court of Appeal.

15   See, eg, the Constitutions of Dominica, s 106; Jamaica, s 110; Belize, s 104; Barbados, ss 87(2) and 88; St Lucia, s 108; Trinidad and Tobago, ss 54, 109; and St Christopher and Nevis, s 99.

16   (1982) 32 WIR 65.

17   See, eg, the Constitutions of St Christopher and Nevis, s 99; and Dominica, s 106.

18   [1997] UKPC 50 (Grenada).

19   Para 5.

case, to require security for the payment of such costs that the Privy Council may order the appellant to pay. The Court of Appeal will satisfy that the case is one in which the right of appeal exists.

Although not expressed in the Constitution, it has also been established, by the case of *Sundry Workers v Antigua Hotel and Tourist Association*,[20] that a right of appeal lies from the Industrial Court to the Privy Council.[21]

Appeals lie at the discretion of the local court in civil proceedings where the question is 'one of great general public importance or otherwise ought to be submitted to Her Majesty in Council for decision'.[22]

The Legislature may enlarge or restrict the Court of Appeal conditions for appeal to the Privy Council, but the Court of Appeal cannot exercise its inherent power to grant or deny leave to impose further conditions restricting the right to appeal granted by the Constitution.[23]

In addition to these two basic categories of appeal, there is provision for appeal by special leave of the Privy Council. This is by virtue of the Sovereign's Prerogative in either civil or criminal cases, or where leave has been refused.

The concept of special leave was explored, intriguingly, by one of the first cases to come before the CCJ, *Griffith v Guyana Revenue Authority and Attorney General of Guyana*.[24] The concept is reproduced exactly in relation to the CCJ's jurisdiction. The case confirms that special leave is purely a matter of grace. The CCJ granted special leave in this case.

Further, the court's discretion will usually be exercised to grant special leave if there is a realistic possibility of a miscarriage of justice if leave is not given for a full hearing.

In very exceptional cases, the Privy Council will accept jurisdiction to hear a second appeal, the first being entertained and dismissed. This is distinguishable from the instance where a first petition for leave has been dismissed, which requires less exceptional circumstances. Hearing an appeal for a second time operates against the interests of the public that there should be a limit or finality to legal proceedings, but may be nonetheless required in the interests of justice.[25]

Certain matters are given priority with regard to the jurisdiction of the Privy Council. For example, it is notable that the Constitutions of the Commonwealth Caribbean entrench a right to appeal to the Privy Council in constitutional motions alleging the violation of fundamental constitutional rights or freedoms. Conversely, the Constitutions specify that no right of appeal lies with respect to certain matters,

20   (1993) 42 WIR 145 (Antigua).

21   There are two industrial courts in the region, in Trinidad and Tobago and Antigua. See the discussion in Chapter 7 ('The Written Constitution as a Legal Source') and Chapter 18 ('Specialised Courts, Tribunals and Functions').

22   See, eg, the Constitutions of Jamaica, s 110; Barbados, s 88; St Christopher, s 99; and Dominica, s 106.

23   See *Crawford and Others v Financial Institutions Services Ltd* (2003) 63 WIR 169 (PC, Jamaica).

24   CCJ App No 1 of 2006. See the discussion in Chapter 17 ('The Caribbean Court of Justice').

25   See *Ramdeen v The State* (2000) 56 WIR 185 (PC Trinidad and Tobago), where the petitioner, who had been convicted of murder and whose appeal had been heard and denied by the Privy Council, sought new leave to appeal upon the availability of new evidence. The Privy Council referred the question, which it viewed as very important, to a hearing by the full Board of five members of the Judicial Committee, the hearing of a new appeal to follow if leave should be granted.

for example, those relating to electoral disputes. This was confirmed in *Russell et al v AG*.[26]

The legislatures of all the jurisdictions have the authority to prescribe additional rights of appeal.[27]

Self-limits on jurisdiction

It should be noted, however, that the Privy Council has often itself limited the exercise of its appellate jurisdiction, even where the criteria set out above appear to have been satisfied. For example, in criminal cases, the Privy Council exercises its discretion to grant leave to appeal sparingly. It will not act as a court of criminal appeal unless it can be shown that some serious miscarriage of justice has occurred, either by a violation of *due process* of law, or by a violation of the principles of natural justice or other serious injustice. This rule was clearly established in the leading case of *Re Dillet*[28] and reiterated in *Baughman v R*,[29] when the Privy Council dismissed an appeal in a murder case, finding no demonstration of an error of law. All that the appellant had shown was that there might be room for more than one view as to the strength of the prosecution's case. This was inadequate as a ground of appeal to the Privy Council, as it was not the function of that court to act as a second tier Court of Appeal to review the evidence.[30]

In *Harracksingh v AG*, the Privy Council explained: 'It is axiomatic that even where a case on paper would support a decision either way, the trial judge's decision ought not to be disturbed unless it can be demonstrated that it is affected by material inconsistencies and inaccuracies or he may be shown to have failed to appreciate the weight . . . of circumstances admitted or proved . . .' Thus, with regard to criminal appeals, leave to appeal cannot be granted where the grounds suggested could not sustain the appeal itself. Therefore, misdirection in itself, or even some irregularity will not necessarily be sufficient to ground an appeal.[31] There must be something which, in the particular case, deprives the accused of the substance of a fair trial and the protection of the law, or which, in general, tends to divert the due and orderly administration of the law into a new course, which may be 'drawn into an evil precedent in future'.[32] This was illustrated in the case of *Senevirante v R*[33] where there was a misdirection to the jury in a murder trial.

It will, however, exercise jurisdiction where there is 'some clear departure from the requirements of justice', as stated in *Riel v R*.[34] Further, as ruled in *Esnouf*

---

26 (1997) 2 Carib LB 1.
27 Note that the Privy Council, and presumably the CCJ, also have power to grant interim relief, springing from the inherent power of a superior court to supervise and protect its own procedures. See *Belize Alliance of Conservation Non-Governmental Organizations v Department of the Environment and Another* [2004] 1 LRC 630 (PC Belize).
28 (1887) 12 AC 459, PC.
29 (1999) 56 WIR 199.
30 (2004) 64 WIR 362 (PC, Trinidad and Tobago) at p 368.
31 See the case of *Ex p Macrea* [1893] AC 346 on this point.
32 *R v Bertrand* (1867) LR 1, PC, 520, reaffirmed in *Wallace and Fuller v R* [1996] UK PC 43, para 18. The Board will not repeat the process performed by the appellate court. The power of review of the Board is exercised on a much narrower basis.
33 [1936] 3 All ER 36.
34 (1885) 10 AC 675.

v AG of Jersey,[35] the Privy Council will not grant special leave except where questions of great and general importance are likely to occur often, and where there is no other remedy to alter such circumstances. Consequently, in 1989, in the case of *Reid v R,*[36] after several years of lobbying with regard to the misuse of identification evidence in Jamaican capital offence cases, the Privy Council was finally convinced that the issue was important and frequent enough to be addressed.

New evidence and damages

Even where it can be established that some substantial injustice did occur, the Privy Council will not grant leave to consider points of law or evidence not previously raised in the courts below. It confirmed this judicially in *Eaton Baker and Another v R:*[37]

> . . . it is important to bear in mind that the normal practice is not to allow the parties to raise for the first time . . . a point of law which has not been argued in the court from which the appeal is brought.

The Privy Council has consistently stated that it does not consider itself competent to review facts or the evidence, since it does not have the benefit of the presence of witnesses, nor is it *au fait* with the prevailing surrounding circumstances as are the local courts. It reaffirmed this in *John and Others v DPP for Dominica.*[38]

Another aspect of this approach to be tentative with respect to local conditions is seen in the award of damages. As stated in several cases, such as *France and Another v Simmonds*[39] and *Selvanayagan v University of the West-Indies,*[40] the Privy Council will not usually disturb an assessment of damages by the local court.

In *Gleaner Co Ltd v Abrahams,*[41] a case concerned with the quantum of damages awarded, the Privy Council emphasised that the amount was dependent on local factors which the Court of Appeal was best placed to assess, even where the Court of Appeal had not explained how it arrived at the reduced amount. More surprisingly, the Privy Council further stated that whether or not guidance as to the amount of awards for defamation should be sought from awards in personal injury cases was a question of policy to be fashioned by judicial opinion in Jamaica and the Privy Council would not take a view on the matter.[42]

Civil appeals

In civil cases, the issue must be one of sufficient importance. In *Etoile Commerciale SA v Owens Bank Ltd (No 2),*[43] for example, the Privy Council considered that clarification

---

36   [1989] 3 All ER 340; (1989) 37 WIR 346.
35   (1883) 8 AC 304, p 308.
37   (1975) 23 WIR 463, p 471.
38   (1985) 32 WIR 230. See, also, *Hannays v Baldeosingh* (1989) 41 WIR 388.
39   (1990) 38 WIR 172.
40   (1983) 34 WIR 267. See also *Panday v Gordon* [2005] UKPC 36.
41   (2003) 63 WIR 197 (PC, Jamaica).
42   Similarly, it will decline jurisdiction in relation to submissions as to the quantum of estimates of value or such matters as the practice of valuers within the jurisdiction in disputes relating to the compulsory acquisition of land. *Blakes Estate Ltd v Government of Montserrat* (2005) 67 WIR 83 (PC, Montserrat).
43   (1993) 45 WIR 136.

of the law on the circumstances under which a foreign judgement could be resisted was sufficiently important, in an offshore jurisdiction where several international companies operated, to grant leave.[44] However, the question of a point of law of public importance is interpreted restrictively. Leave will not normally be granted unless, for example, the appeal will raise serious issues with respect to personal status, such as slander.

As regards property cases, the value of the property must be considerable for the Privy Council to consider granting leave in cases where there is no 'right to appeal', as illustrated in the case of *Akar v AG of Sierra Leone*.[45]

While the Privy Council may have jurisdiction as of right in divorce cases,[46] it has itself narrowly curtailed this jurisdiction. For example, as established in *Johnson v Johnson*,[47] it will only be prepared to entertain an appeal relating to the distribution of the matrimonial assets in 'exceptional circumstances'. It has found the detailed investigation of the figures involved 'wholly unsuitable for the appellate function of the Board'. It is concerned instead with the 'correction of egregious errors of law and substantive miscarriages of justice' in divorce proceedings.[48]

Constitutional matters

With respect to constitutional issues, however, the jurisdiction of the Privy Council is more generous, as there is no strict requirement for leave to appeal. Thus, the individual challenging the abrogation of his fundamental rights has address via the High Court, as provided for under Commonwealth Caribbean Constitutions, and a right to final appeal to the Privy Council, providing that all local remedies to redress such rights have been exhausted. However, in *Walker and Richards v R*,[49] the Privy Council insisted that it could not act as a Court of First Instance, even in constitutional matters, when it was invited to do so in a death row case.[50]

Limited access to appeals

It is apparent, therefore, that the Privy Council does not automatically operate as a full appellate court, whatever its stated jurisdiction, nor is it an easily accessible court. Further, the limited boundaries of its jurisdiction mean that petitions for leave may be dismissed, not because they have no substantive merit, but because they fall outside the narrow bounds of the jurisdiction. The actual statistics of the number of cases determined by the Privy Council support this view. For example, in the ten years between 1983 and 1993, the Privy Council determined only 163 cases from the entire Commonwealth Caribbean. It gave a mere 87 cases out of 292 special leave to proceed.[51]

---

44   This brought it under the St Vincent Constitution, s 99.
45   [1969] 3 All ER 384.
46   See, eg, the Constitutions of Grenada, s 104; and Dominica, s 106.
47   (1992) 41 WIR 91.
48   *Ibid*, p 92.
49   (1993) 43 WIR 363.
50   See, also, *Taylor v R* (1995) 46 WIR 318 and *Bell v DPP* (1980) 32 WIR 317.
51   *Op cit*, de la Bastide, fn 8, p 403.

This limited jurisdiction of the Privy Council and the tendency of the court to shy away from assuming jurisdiction mean that the remedy of the appeal to that body is, in effect, an extraordinary remedy. In practice, it further curtails its jurisdiction to hear and determine appeals by binding itself to precedent although, in strict theory, it is not required to do so.[52] Indeed, this writer has argued elsewhere that appeals to the Privy Council can be considered as extraordinary and ineffective remedies in certain cases and need not always be exhausted before taking a case to an international adjudicating body.[53]

REPLACING THE PRIVY COUNCIL WITH A CARIBBEAN COURT OF JUSTICE

While the retention of the Privy Council as the final Court of Appeal is a debate which has occupied the attention of many Caribbean jurists, judges, practitioners and the public at large, de la Bastide says, cryptically, that it is 'almost impossible to win the argument'.[54] It is certainly legitimate to question whether the Privy Council has contributed meaningfully to the development of an indigenous jurisprudence or even the development of the legal system in general. This question is particularly topical, as the Caribbean Court of Justice will replace, at least partially, appeals to the Privy Council. The issue assumes political, economic, nationalistic and even emotional overtones and is inextricably bound up with the issues of independence and sovereignty. To address this question adequately one must examine carefully both the jurisdiction and the policies of the Privy Council. However, for a book of this nature we must be conscious of the fact that this discussion, however interesting, may soon be obsolete, except as a historical note.

The issue has been given further impetus due to the emphases given to topics such as economic and political integration for Caribbean peoples, the dangers of EU integration for the region and the need to reverse the unpopular Privy Council decision that undue delay on death row was cruel and inhuman punishment. Once again, therefore, we ask whether the time has come for the total abolition of appeals to the Privy Council and replace such an avenue with an indigenous final Court of Appeal, the CCJ?

The arguments for retention had, and still have, popular support and were underscored by the 1974 Trinidad and Tobago Constitutions Commission. The Commission found that:

> ... the overwhelming view of the organisations and individuals represented to us in favour of retaining such appeals. That too is what the lawyers want.[55]

Just as many arguments may be put forward supporting the abolition of appeals to the Privy Council. Further, with the desire to hang prisoners on death row, and

---

52 See the discussion in Chapter 8 ('The Common Law and the Operation of the Doctrine of Judicial Precedent in the Commonwealth Caribbean').
53 See Antoine, R-M B, 'The Judicial Committee of the Privy Council: an inadequate remedy' (1992) 41 ICLQ 179.
54 *Op cit*, de la Bastide, fn 8, p 5.
55 The Report of the Trinidad and Tobago Constitutional Commission (the Wooding Report) 1974, p 6.

what is perceived as the Privy Council's obstacle to that ambition, there is now more popular support for abolition by John Public.

Sovereignty and nationhood

Many arguments have been advanced over the years. Sovereignty, of course, continues to be a key dynamic in the debate. Telford Georges put it eloquently when he said:

> an independent country should assume the responsibility for providing a court of its own choosing for the final determination of legal disputes ... It is a compromise of sovereignty to leave that decision to a court which is part of the former colonial hierarchy, a court in the appointment of whose members we have absolutely no say.[56]

He continued:

> In real life anyone who behaved that way would evoke pity and exasperation, like the grown man who demonstrates his independence by continuing to live free at home.[57]

Modern day retentionists have underplayed concerns about sovereignty, dismissing them as emotive, despite the fact that this is a defining political and legal principle of any nation-state and a principle which surely grants validity to the very legal system. Anthony agrees that the sovereignty argument is compelling and insists that the:

> need for the nations of the Caribbean to assert the constitutional legitimacy of our own civilisation, is more fundamental than a mere emotive claim to a theoretical sovereignty, without practical significance, or persuasive symbolism. It is in my view, simply a hard statement of principle, which should not admit to compromise at this point in our history.[58]

Douglas Mendes, a well-respected legal practitioner, also supports the sovereignty point. He states bluntly that the sovereignty argument is the 'only argument that is logical and it is the only argument that is needed in support of the proposition of our final Court of Appeal.'[59]

The appropriate role for the Privy Council

Perhaps the most damning indictment against the Privy Council is its failure to adapt to its role as a final appellate court reflecting the needs and mores of its adopted countries. This is so particularly in relation to its use of precedent. We have already aired many of our concerns with respect to the failure to create an indigenous jurisprudence for the region and these concerns are relevant here also. The observations by Justice Saunders and President de la Bastide of the CCJ in *AG et al v Joseph and Boyce*,

---

56   The Rt Hon Telford Georges, 'Feature Address to The Symposium on a Caribbean Court of Justice Report', Barbados, 28 November 1998, p 13, hereinafter the CCJ Symposium Report.

57   *Ibid.*

58   Kenny D Anthony, 'Reshaping Caribbean Jurisprudence: Prospects and Possibilities of the Caribbean Court of Justice – An Address to the Grenada Bar Association by the Hon Kenny D Anthony, Prime Minister of Saint Lucia and Lead Prime Minister for the CCJ', Grenada, May 2003, p 4.

59   Douglas Mendes, CCJ Symposium Report, *above*, fn 56, p 27.

CCJ Appeal,[60] that the CCJ is mindful of its role in this regard is to be welcomed. Hopefully, this will not be mere rhetoric.[61]

The liberation of Caribbean jurisprudence from restrictive attitudes to precedent may also be accomplished at another level with the abolition of appeals to the Privy Council. Caribbean Courts of Appeal will be less self-conscious and timid in their approach to decision-making, mindful of the fact that no longer do they have a British Privy Council as an overseer, eager to impose centuries-old British doctrine and legal philosophy contained in English precedent, no matter the circumstances,

Whether the deliberate subservience of Caribbean law has been conscious or unconscious, there is little doubt that there will no longer be the need to receive approval from a Privy Council steeped in orthodoxy at worst, and an alien creativity, at best.

> Unquestionably, the existence of a right of appeal to the Judicial Committee of the Privy Council affects the confidence of our Courts. At times, our Courts appear to be always looking over their shoulders across the vast ocean of sea towards the Privy Council for applause and approbation. This subjugation or subservience of judicial thought and independence cannot be justified in independent and sovereign States.[62]

We saw in our earlier discussion on precedent that the Privy Council does not always act as if it is a court of superior authority on Commonwealth Caribbean law, but often undermines its own authority. For example, as noted earlier, although the Privy Council is not bound to follow the *rationes decidendi* of its previous decisions, but has power to overrule them, it will exercise this power only in very rare circumstances.[63] As discussed below, on those occasions where it has overruled precedent with alacrity, it has seemed to be because of the excessive and arguably, inappropriate influence of precedents from international courts and not because of a sensitivity to evolving Caribbean norms.[64] The contentious practice of the Privy Council to bind itself to precedents originating from the House of Lords in England is also evidence of its failure as an authoritative court.

The only justification for the Privy Council in an independent context can be its ability to determine appeals in accordance with the needs and expectations of its new clients. It must adhere to an evolutionary theory of the common law, acknowledging that the changing norms of a particular society impact upon the law, thus creating a change in legal principle. This is the essence of the 'local circumstances rule'. In such a situation, a legal principle as espoused by the House of Lords may not be the correct statement of the law and a local court may deviate from such precedent. This approach is based on the assumption of the divergent conception of the common law, where local circumstances can produce change, as opposed to the unitary concept.

---

60 No CV 2 of 2005, decided 8 November 2006.
61 See above, Chapter 8 ('The Common Law and the Doctrine of Precedent').
62 Justice A Saunders of the Caribbean Court of Justice, 'Strengths and weaknesses of a regional appellate court and recommendations for enhancing such court's effectiveness', quoting at p 7 Prime Minister Kenny Anthony of St Lucia 'Reflections on the Perception of Justice in the Commonwealth Caribbean', 2002. Address delivered in Jamaica.
63 See the discussion in Chapter 8 ('The Common Law and the Doctrine of Judicial Precedent'). For example, this was illustrated in *Eaton Baker and Another v R* (1975) 23 WIR 463. The issue here was whether an earlier Privy Council decision, that there was no jurisdiction in the courts of Jamaica to pass a death sentence upon a person under 18, was binding. In this case, the Privy Council did not bind itself.
64 See Chapter 12 ('International Law as a Source of Law').

The divergent approach to the common law has been upheld in the Trinidad and Tobago case of *Abbot v The Queen*,[65] following cases like *De Lasala v De Lasala*[66] and *Australia Consolidated Press Ltd v Uren*.[67]

It is the expectation that the common law would adapt to the different circumstances which it meets. This provides the rationale for the originality of the Privy Council and its deviation from judicial precedent when assuming appellate jurisdiction over the unique jurisdictions that make up the Commonwealth Caribbean. There is an implicit assumption that the Privy Council is equipped to determine and assess social norms and reflect them in legal policy.

However, the jurisprudence of the Privy Council does not prove this. The Privy Council has exhibited a tendency to be swayed by international decisions and opinions, even in opposition to local sentiments. This is seen in the line of cases involving capital punishment. Essentially, these decisions are merely a reflection of similar precedents emanating from the UN Human Rights Committee and the European Court on Human Rights.[68] Whatever the correctness of these decisions, judging from the furore raised, it is doubtful whether the Privy Council correctly assessed the prevailing norms of West Indian society on this issue. It seemed to rely more on its own distaste for capital punishment. These rulings preclude Caribbean courts from hanging prisoners awaiting capital punishment, whether because the punishment is mandatory, a petition to an international body has been denied, or because of delay. Indeed, as the backlog of criminal cases makes it almost inevitable that prisoners will spend a long time on death row, which will constitute 'undue delay', few persons on death row will suffer the death penalty.

One consequence of the death row decisions is that the Privy Council's attitude on this matter has provided the impetus for renewed initiatives towards a regional Court of Appeal to replace appeals to the Privy Council. Indeed, it appeared to have realised the devastating consequences of its decisions only with hindsight. In *Henfield and Farrington v AG of the Bahamas*,[69] for example, the Privy Council commented: 'Their Lordships are conscious that the conclusion which they have reached . . . may cause some concern among those responsible for the administration of justice . . . They are very much aware of the problems in certain countries in the Caribbean which have given rise to unacceptable delays in execution, which in their turn have inevitably led to the establishment of the principle in *Pratt*.'[70]

The death row issue has even produced conflict between the Privy Council and the Court of Appeal. In one case, in Trinidad and Tobago, the condemned was actually hanged 12 minutes before news was communicated that the Privy Council had rushed through a stay of execution. The Chief Justice of Trinidad and Tobago explained that this was a genuine 'mix up' and that the Privy Council's criticism of the Court of Appeal on this matter was an 'unnecessary affront to the local court of appeal'.[71] Nevertheless, it reveals the tensions between the Privy Council's position

---

65 [1977] AC 755.
66 [1980] AC 546.
67 [1969] 1 AC 590. See Chapter 8 ('The Common Law and the Doctrine of Judicial Precedent').
68 See the discussion of this in Chapter 8 ('The Common Law and the Doctrine of Judicial Precedent') and Chapter 12 ('International Law as a Source of Law').
69 (1996) 49 WIR 1.
70 *Ibid*, p 15.
71 *Op cit*, de la Bastide, fn 8, p 417.

on capital punishment and that of the majority in the Commonwealth Caribbean. Still, given the respect paid to English decisions in general, there is no guarantee that a regional Court of Appeal would decide such issues much differently and indeed, the first death penalty case before the CCJ, *Boyce*,[72] although pains were taken to point out that the death penalty was a lawful penalty, seems to support this view.

On a related note, the Privy Council's decision in the litigation concerning the attempted *coup* by the Muslimeen group in Trinidad and Tobago in July 1990 also suggests that it is not in touch with social realities in the Commonwealth Caribbean.[73] During the coup, in which an indeterminate number of persons were killed, the members of the Muslim rebel group held the then Prime Minister and other Members of Parliament hostage. They made a 'bargain' with the Prime Minister that they would release the hostages if they would be pardoned for their actions during the coup. The Privy Council upheld the validity of the pardon. This is a much criticised decision, even to the extent that the Privy Council has been accused of encouraging the 'making of deals with terrorists'.[74]

The limited jurisdiction of Privy Council, as carved out by itself, discussed above, further makes questionable the role of the Privy Council as an appropriate final Court of Appeal for the region. One can legitimately ask whether the Privy Council is an effective avenue of appeal. It is thus important to consider what kinds of cases will go to the CCJ in view of the fact that, at present, the appellate jurisdiction of the Privy Council is severely limited. Is there a need to expand the present appellate jurisdiction of the court functioning as the final appellate authority in the region? It is not clear that these questions have been satisfactorily resolved by the present arrangements for the CCJ.

Arguments on dependency

Some of the old arguments advocating retention of the Privy Council highlight the vulnerability of the West Indian psyche, a reluctance to think for ourselves and define our destinies. White claims that such arguments have a common basis, in that they reveal a 'dependency psychology rooted in slavery and indenture'.[75]

Indeed, many of the reasons given by the Commission in their Minority Report do indeed seem to suggest a reluctance on the part of the Commission to assume the responsibility of independence. They include that:

> . . . it would be an extravagance to cut ourselves off from the source of our law and from the contemporary evolution of a legal system whose relevance and value to our affairs we consider to be unquestionable. The Privy Council gives us the opportunity to benefit from, and contribute to, a common pool of case law and to keep in touch with a variety of similar legal systems.[76]

The argument put forward, that the abolition of the Privy Council will result in us

---

72   *Above*, fn 60.

73   *Phillip and Others v DPP* [1992] 1 AC 545.

74   *Op cit*, de la Bastide, fn 8, p 419.

75   Dorcas White, 'Jettison the Privy Council – you t'ink it easy', unpublished mimeo, UWI, Cave Hill, Barbados, 1976, p 401.

76   *Op cit*, the Wooding Report, fn 55.

cutting ourselves off from the source of English law and depriving ourselves from contributing to the English common law, is decidedly misplaced, for it is certain that the jurisprudence of the region will continue to be influenced by English legal trends. Further, in the increasingly communicative world, legal systems commonly draw from each other without the necessity of a common court at the head of the hierarchy. Indeed, there is no evidence that the legal systems of Grenada and Guyana, both of which abolished appeals to the Privy Council, have been compromised in any way. Rather, some may argue that such abolition enhanced the creativity of the judges with regard to the making of precedent. We have already seen that Commonwealth Caribbean jurisprudence has helped to develop the human rights law of Britain. There is no reason to believe that this will cease.

With regard to the Minority Report's complaint about a desire to break with colonialism, what, we may well ask, is wrong with seeking to distance ourselves from our 'colonial past'? Delinking from the Privy Council may be regarded as a final act of constitutional repatriation of our legal system.

Perhaps one may find favour instead with the view of the Majority Report of the Commission, which favoured abolition and which saw abolition within the context of attempting to determine our own destiny.

Cost of justice

The sentiment that independence should not have a price tag is a legitimate one.[77] Yet, the issue of the cost of maintaining the CCJ has always been an important deterrent to its establishment. In a region still regarded as developing and where problems of devaluation, recession and stringent financial policy are constantly apparent, the question of financing a court of this magnitude cannot be trivialised. Whilst funds have been sourced to start the court and a trust fund established, the long-term financing of the CCJ may still be problematic. This is exacerbated by the fact that there may be insufficient cases to keep such a court busy enough to justify its cost and existence:

> ... the Privy Council costs us nothing, since it is supported by the British taxpayer. To stand aloof from the Privy Council at this stage in favour of a local jurisprudence is, in our view, an attempt to rationalise a political desire to remove ourselves from what was our colonial past.

Yet, in truth, maintaining the colonial link is not as cheap as is often thought. For the individual petitioner, the cost of going to the Privy Council is extremely high and often prohibitive. It is, perhaps, one reason for the low turnover of Privy Council Appeals.

The question of cost is not limited to the funding of the CCJ. A grave defect in our legal system is the relatively poor access to justice. Justice is expensive at every level, mainly because of the absence of contingency fees as found in the US and the glaring absence of adequate legal aid for many matters. This is compounded, of course, by the relatively high levels of poverty in the region, where litigation is perhaps viewed as a

---

77 See, eg, Dorcas White's argument, *above*, fn 75. However, it should be noted that the CCJ will be funded by external monies.

luxury.[78] It is particularly costly where appeals have to be brought to the Privy Council, not the least because the rules of the court dictate that British counsel must be retained.

Indeed, the Majority Report attacked the 'freeness' point – what one author has described as the 'freeness mentality'.[79]

> ... the argument based on the absence of cost ... leads us to consider whether independence becomes meaningless when we are offered dependence without charge.[80]

Competence of Caribbean peoples – a leap to enlightenment

The dependency and insecurity questions are not unrelated to question marks surrounding the competence of our people to serve as judges on a final Court of Appeal. Retentionists argue that the Privy Council is far more likely to be continuously staffed with high-quality judges. The assertion is made that the judges of the Privy Council are men of judicial eminence, which means that we secure for ourselves the same wisdom and learning as the British themselves enjoy.

On this note, the popular argument that judges of the Privy Council, trained in the common law tradition, are unable to comprehend written Constitutions is perhaps unfounded. This is particularly the case when one considers that the Privy Council has often demonstrated a willingness to give more liberal and purposive interpretations to Caribbean Constitutions, in particular, Bills of Rights, than their Caribbean counterparts.

There is disagreement among other writers on this point, many of whom are attempting to ascertain whether the Privy Council can give good guidance on 'rights' issues now that Britain has incorporated the European Convention on Human Rights. On the one hand, Zander[81] is very generous in his appraisal of the Privy Council's record on human rights. On the other, Ewing and Gearty disagree with Zander and find the Privy Council's adjudication on human rights to be sorely lacking. They complain that there is little to support the view that the Privy Council has shown a strong concern for fundamental rights and a willingness to defy legislative or governmental authority in the name of high principles of constitutionality.[82] The truth may be found somewhere in the middle.

Several cases belie the argument that the Privy Council is incapable of interpreting our written Constitutions, such as *Thornhill v AG*,[83] where the need for a purposive construction of the Constitution was stressed, and *AG v Ryan*,[84] which upheld the existence of the principles of natural justice within the Constitution of the Bahamas,

---

78 A recent view expressed by the Chief Magistrate of St Vincent and the Magistrate for the Family Court there is that legal aid should be available even for family court and divorce matters, as many couples stay together simply because they cannot afford a divorce. *First OECS Law Fair*, 17 September, 2004, Kingstown, St Vincent. Legal aid, where granted, such as in murder cases, has largely been viewed as inadequate.

79 *Op cit*, White, fn 75.

80 *Op cit*, the Wooding Report, fn 55.

81 Zander, M, *A Bill of Rights*, 1975, London: Barry Rose.

82 Ewing and Gearty, *Freedom under Thatcher – Civil Liberties in Modern Britain*, Oxford, 1990, pp 271–73.

83 [1981] AC 61.

84 [1980] AC 718.

in a case where citizenship was refused without adherence to such principles. Further, in the *Liyange* case,[85] the prosecution and punishment for participation in a Ceylonese coup, pursuant to retroactive legislation, was held by the Privy Council to violate the judicial function enshrined in that country's Constitution.

Indeed, the judgments of the Privy Council on human rights matters have become increasingly liberal and sophisticated in terms of constitutional jurisprudence. This may be as a result of the influence of the interplay between English law and the European Human Rights Convention jurisprudence. It is paradoxical and even ironic that it is at this juncture, when the Privy Council is even more generous about our human rights than we may be ourselves, that we choose to divorce ourselves from its jurisdiction.

On the other hand, because the judges of the Privy Council are trained in the British tradition of parliamentary sovereignty, they are presumed not to have the kind of legal reasoning required to interpret written Constitutions. As illustrated above, the Privy Council has demonstrated that it can interpret written Constitutions, but there have been several cases where the argument can be shown to have some element of legitimacy. Thus, it is certain that, just as there are *dicta* supporting the ability and willingness of the Privy Council to interpret Commonwealth Caribbean Constitutions purposively, there are conflicting *dicta* illustrating that court's stubborn adherence to rigid common law principles.[86] At best, one may conclude that the approach of the Privy Council to written Commonwealth Caribbean Constitutions has been riddled with inconsistency.

Indeed, the UK has a poor record with regard to human rights at the European Court of Human Rights, and the argument has been advanced that one reason for this deficiency is because of the absence of a Bill of Rights.[87]

One may also point to the lack of familiarity with the practicalities of West Indian life, for example, the adequacy of damages as related to economic conditions, sociological peculiarities such as matrifocal societies and the prevalence of common law marriages and children born out of wedlock. There are clear differences in socio-cultural make up between the UK and the Commonwealth Caribbean which it is unrealistic to expect a foreign court to be familiar with. This places a greater duty on Caribbean counsel to bring to their arguments such nuances to 'educate' the court on the uniqueness of West Indian life.

Finally, on this question, it is clear that the argument that the region is incapable of producing judges of a sufficiently high quality is one premised solely on dependency and lack of confidence in our own worth and a belief that anything foreign is superior. Indeed, the evidence is that our judges are sound. Between 1983 and 1993, 63 per cent of their decisions were upheld by the Privy Council.[88] This negative vision of our judicial acumen further illustrates a reluctance to invest in the future, despite the apparent financial limitations.

Kenny Anthony, speaking at the inauguration of the CCJ,[89] encapsulated this in

---

85   [1966] 1 All ER 650.
86   See the discussion in Chapter 7 ('The Written Constitution as a Legal Source').
87   See, eg, Zander, M, *A Bill of Rights*, 1975, London: Barry Rose.
88   In addition, many decisions of the Privy Council which have overturned lower courts, have been severely criticised by the English counterparts of that court. See Ewing, *above*, fn 82.
89   'Leap to Enlightenment'. Address by Dr The Hon Kenny D Anthony Prime Minister of St Lucia and Lead Prime Minister on the Establishment of the CCJ at the Inauguration of the Caribbean Court of Justice, POS, Trinidad and Tobago, 16 April 2005, p 7.

one word: 'confidence'. He reminded the Caribbean peoples that the region's legal profession and judicial system had a 'glorious past, among the strongest in the Commonwealth, for three-quarters of a century.'[90] He recalled the distinguished contribution that the region's legal practitioners, whom he described as 'professionals of choice' have made elsewhere in the Commonwealth and internationally. This includes sitting as Chief Justices in many parts of Africa, a judge at the International Court of Justice in the Hague, the Chairperson of the International Tribunal on the Law of the Sea in Hamburg, one of the first judges on the International Criminal Court, Chairmanship of the Inter-American Juridical Tribunal. Indeed, he remarked, in 'per capita terms I doubt if any other community in the world has served the world-wide cause of justice more comprehensively and more consistently than has the Caribbean.'[91]

Consequently: 'The Caribbean is not a fledgling State approaching tentatively the threshold of the rule of law.'[92] Establishing a CCJ is not a leap into the dark, to be feared, but a 'leap to enlightenment' to be embraced.[93]

Our unrecognised contribution to the Privy Council's jurisprudence

A point which is often overlooked is one that is positive for Caribbean jurisprudence. This is that Caribbean legal practitioners and Caribbean judges are often those who create the defining precedents in our jurisprudence although they seldom get the credit. Statistics show that a large percentage of Caribbean Court of Appeal decisions are actually approved by the Privy Council and the reasoning therein merely adopted.[94]

Yet, it is the Privy Council judgments that we cite approvingly and the justices of that court which get the credit for these outstanding jurisprudential creations. This is particularly the case in constitutional jurisprudence. Because of their relative unfamiliarity with written Constitutions, English judicial personnel may be less *au fait* with constitutional matters than our jurists. The fear that our judicial personnel is incapable of forming intellectually adequate arguments is, therefore, grossly inaccurate.

Thus, Commonwealth Caribbean practitioners and judges have themselves contributed to the collective wisdom of the Privy Council and indirectly to the corpus of the common law. This is especially so in relation to constitutional law matters, with which English judges were previously unfamiliar. Indeed, the Privy Council itself has acknowledged the learning and reasoning of local judges in some of our landmark decisions. A fine example is the affirmation of Georges J in *Thornhill v AG*.[95] The influence on the Privy Council is not limited to the Commonwealth Caribbean courts. Other Commonwealth courts have contributed too. Consider, for example, the reliance of the British courts on Australian legal policy and precedents in the landmark

---

90   *Ibid*, p 3.
91   *Ibid*, p 5.
92   *Ibid*.
93   *Ibid*, p 7.
94   According to Former Chief Justice of Trinidad and Tobago, Michael de la Bastide, now the President of the CCJ. See 'The Case for a Caribbean Court of Appeal', *op cit*, fn 8.
95   [1981] AC 61, PC, Trinidad and Tobago. The Rt. Hon. Telford Georges, recognised as a leading jurist, former Privy Councillor and Chief Justice in more than one country.

decision of *Pepper v Hart*[96] on statutory interpretation. Wooding J's judgment on the question of a right to strike in *Collymore v AG*[97] is another example of a Caribbean point of view, albeit controversial, which has been exported all over the Commonwealth.[98]

There are still some practical difficulties to be faced in the establishment of a Caribbean Court of Justice. For example, do we have adequate case reporting facilities to ground good decisions? Additionally, there may not be a sufficient amount and variety of litigation to provide an adequate system of precedent. The CCJ aims to overcome these difficulties by making judgments available online.

Impartiality

It is argued too that the Privy Council is removed from and uninfluenced by the pressures of our local, social and political forces. Political distance is therefore equated to impartiality. The latter argument has proved to be one of the most popular arguments to a people fearful of political interference in a society which they view as politically partisan and sometimes corrupt.

Apart from considerations of political and social distance, we may also consider the potential danger of corruption of judges, who will now have more legal authority. As elsewhere, there have been instances where judges in the region have been convicted for bribery. One contributing factor to the potential for corruption, if indeed the danger is greater than elsewhere, could be the inability of the fragile economies of the region to maintain adequate salaries for judges.

In the Agreement Establishing the Caribbean Supreme Court (the Agreement). political leaders have a say only in the appointment of the President of the court under a majority vote. All other judges of the court are appointed by an independent regional Judicial and Legal Services Commission.[99] The one regional court in existence, the OECS Court, suggests that, in practice, such regional arrangements have worked well although they may not be entirely immune from political and parochial influences with respect to the appointment of its judges. In that scheme, the regional political leaders have a veto over the appointment of judges of the court. In fact, at times, it is difficult to secure the appointment of a Chief Justice. The CCJ Agreement, as we will see in the following chapter, is an even more insulated one.

In a case in St Lucia with clear political overtones, at least a suspicion of political influence was evident. Two ex-Prime Ministers of St Lucia were before a retired judge of the OECS who was the Commissioner inquiring into alleged wrongdoing during their respective administrations. They sought judicial review on the basis that she would be biased, because while she had been a judge, she had been refused an extension of tenure during the time when one former Prime Minister was her 'employer' and the other responsible for the appointment while acting as the OECS Director. The claims betrayed the attitude of the former Prime Ministers that the judges of the court were subject to political influence.[100]

---

96   [1993] 1 All ER 42. See Chapter 12 ('The Rules of Statutory Interpretation').
97   (1967) 12 WIR 5.
98   See, eg, *The Alberta Reference Case* (1987) DLR (4th) 161.
99   Discussed below, Chapter 17 ('The Caribbean Court of Justice').
100 *Lewis v AG of St Lucia*, unreported, Civil Appeal No 12 of 1997 and *Compton v AG of St Lucia*, unreported, Civil Appeal No 14 of 1997; related litigation, decided 9 February 1998, ECSC, St Lucia.

Yet, political appointment of judges is no stranger to legitimate legal systems, as is demonstrated in the UK and the US. We do not often question the ability of judges in those legal systems to give politically neutral judgments.

Closely linked to the fear of political partisanship is the issue of potential impartiality due to pre-trial prejudice. Thus, the questions relating to the politics of size may affect the operation of the court. Is the region too small to expect true justice, for example, is a fair trial possible in circumstances where the case has been heavily criticised and discussed throughout the region?

The issue of the impartiality of judges is certainly an important one. However, although political distance may be desirable on the one hand, it can also be a disadvantage. For example, if a government wishes to conduct a political or social experiment, such as collective land ownership or socialism, as occurred in Grenada, the English court might be too removed from the political sentiment of the time. The question of the political will of the people and their political mandate will then assume greater importance. Since the Privy Council will tend to be alienated from the political feelings and sympathies of the people, it is unrealistic to expect that court to adjudicate on such matters appropriately. The point is not far-fetched, for on the question of Zimbabwe's independence, the Privy Council, in *Madzimbamuto v Burke*, [101] felt that Britain had the right to revoke independence, within the context of Zimbabwe's struggle for political freedom. Yet, in contrast, nearer to home, the conservative Privy Council, in effect, conceded that the political regime under the socialist People's Revolutionary Army had achieved legitimacy.[102]

It may also be naïve to think that the Privy Council is apolitical with regard to larger issues, and that judges trained in what is arguably a conservative, capitalistic and imperialist tradition would not bring such thinking to bear on cases before them in a manner which may not necessarily be in the interests of the region. One may see judicial conflicts, for example, where multinational concerns are involved, such as companies usually being owned by European and North American interests. Again, the existence of Caribbean offshore financial laws and policies, which sometimes directly threaten the economic interests of the capital-intensive 'onshore' countries such as the UK, poses intriguing questions in this regard.

The wider issue is that, in some cases, a final Court of Appeal such as the Privy Council will be called upon to examine what are, in truth, questions of policy. Such questions are best left to those within the particular society. This is perhaps best brought out in the two controversial Privy Council decisions of *Pratt and Morgan v AG of Jamaica*,[103] *Phillips and others v DPP*,[104] discussed above, p 318. What the judges are about here is a not a search for some uniquely correct common law solution to a problem, but rather the balancing of important considerations that are in competition. It is not so much whether the Privy Council gave the right answer to these questions, but whether they ought to be answering them at all.[105] This, perhaps, is the grounding argument for establishing a regional Supreme Court.

---

101   [1969] AC 645, p 743.

102   It should be noted that the Privy Council avoided the actual issue by declining jurisdiction to hear appeals from Grenada, which had abolished the avenue of appeal to the Privy Council under the PRG regime, discussed in the case of *Mitchell v DPP* (1985) 32 WIR 241, PC.

103   (1993) 43 WIR 340.

104   [1992] 1 AC 545; (1991) 40 WIR 410.

105   *Op cit*, de la Bastide, fn 8.

... the decisions which a final Court of Appeal is called upon to make ... are sometimes not very different from those made by a democratically elected Parliament ... In making such decisions, one is not unearthing some universal verity, but determining what is best for a particular society in the circumstances existing at a certain point in its history. I would have thought that it was essential for the decision makes in such cases to have an intimate knowledge, acquired at first hand, of the society for whom the decision is made.[106]

A hypocritical jurisprudence?

There is also the question of hypocritical political expediency, that is, that if we abolish the Privy Council in the name of independence, we will continue to cite the same Privy Council judges, the same English decisions and statutes, but will not allow the men in person to continue to sit on the appeals. This political convenience is viewed as hypocritical. Our discussion on judicial precedent perhaps justifies this view.[107]

Other questions relating to precedent still remain to be answered. Should the court be a regional court in every sense of the word and bind jurisdiction regardless of which part of the region the precedent originated, or shall only decisions from the particular country be binding? There would appear to be no theoretical justification for the latter.

Composition of the court and final concerns

Difficult questions relating to the composition and location of the Caribbean Court of Justice have now been addressed. There is no express provision for judges to be chosen on the basis of quotas assessed by nationality. In the first composition of the court, there are two judges, including the President of the Court, from Trinidad and Tobago, two judges from Guyana, one from St Vincent, while the remaining judges are from outside of CARICOM. These appear to be selected on the basis of merit only and it is to be hoped that the selection of judges will continue to proceed harmoniously. Experiences with the establishment of other regional institutions, such as CARICOM and the University of the West Indies, have illustrated that these are often contentious issues. The sceptics among us will certainly ask whether integration on any scale can work in the Commonwealth Caribbean. This has some validity, particularly when one considers the failed attempt at political federation. It may be questioned whether the West Indies is too pluralistic and cosmopolitan a society to be able to function within a regional final court which is located within the society itself. Georges remarks, in an apt analogy to cricket, that whenever we have to 'pick a team' we seem to encounter difficulty.[108]

Anthony notes the erroneous assumption that justice is served merely by having access to the Privy Council. This is reminiscent of the complaint of the most distinguished jurist Telford Georges that 'there is a tendency to confuse finality with infallibility'.[109]

---

106   *Op cit*, de la Bastide, fn 8, p 429.
107   See Chapter 8 ('The Common Law and the Doctrine of Judicial Precedent').
108   The Rt Hon Mr T Georges, Lecture, 4 October 1996, Cave Hill, UWI.
109   CCJ Symposium Report, *above*, fn 56, p 10.

We also have the positive example of an integrated court in the OECS Court of Appeal and a Guyana final Court of Appeal since that country abolished appeals to the Privy Council many years ago. One cannot easily discern any particular political biases in these courts. They should serve therefore as reassurances to Caribbean peoples since they have operated efficiently, and largely without stains of bias or incompetence. Further, an independent Legal Commission has been established to ensure impartiality and competence in judicial selection for the CCJ.

CHAPTER 17

THE RENEWED INITIATIVE TOWARDS A CARIBBEAN COURT OF JUSTICE

It is difficult to examine the subject of this chapter, the Caribbean Court of Justice (CCJ), without close reference to the several issues discussed in the previous chapter, 'The Privy Council', as the two courts are so inextricably intertwined, the very existence of the one being determinative of the other. It is the perceived disadvantages of the Privy Council that propels a Caribbean final Court of Appeal into being. As such, this chapter should be read with the previous chapter, since the discussion in the latter is essential to the examination of the issues involving the CCJ.

On 16 April 2005 the long-standing efforts of the region to create their own final Court of Appeal came to fruition with the inauguration of the CCJ.[1] However, not all of the countries of the region have joined the momentum toward sovereign and independent justice by putting an end to final appeals to the Privy Council. Some, like Jamaica, while their governments have supported the idea, have been plagued with much opposition to the cutting of ties with the apparent fountain of justice that is the Privy Council, based in England. Indeed, the opposition in Jamaica led to a successful, albeit criticised, court challenge that the legislation purporting to facilitate the accession to the CCJ had not been passed in accordance with the procedures laid down under the Constitution.[2] It should be noted, however, that all of the independent Commonwealth Caribbean countries will participate in the original jurisdiction of the CCJ, discussed further below, even when they have put the court's appellate jurisdiction on hold.

The relevant treaty instrument is the Agreement Establishing the Caribbean Supreme Court (the Agreement). The court will act as the final Court of Appeal for all Commonwealth Caribbean States which have acceded to the appellate jurisdiction of the court under the Agreement, currently only Barbados and Guyana. This jurisdiction will replace that of the Privy Council.

While other countries have agreed in principle to accept the CCJ as their final Court of Appeal, its eventual reality is collateral to the abolition of appeals to the Privy Council. This itself is constrained by the constitutional limitations of abolishing appeals to the Privy Council, discussed in the previous chapter and political tensions that still exist over the question, notably in Jamaica and Trinidad and Tobago. If Caribbean governments do not achieve the requisite parliamentary majorities or public approval in their respective jurisdictions, the CCJ will not fulfil its true mandate as a regional Court of Appeal.

As we have seen, the considerable opposition to the CCJ as a final Court of Appeal for all countries in the region has not been an obstacle to its establishment. This is largely because the Provisional Agreement establishing the CCJ required a minimum

---

1 The political leaders of CARICOM agreed to establish the much anticipated regional Supreme Court. In July 1998 at the 19th meeting of the Conference of Heads of Government of the Caribbean Community in St Lucia.

2 See *Independence Jamaica Council for Human Rights (1998) Ltd v Others v Marshall-Burnett and Another* (2005) 65 WIR 268 (PC, Jamaica). See also *Sharma v AG* [2005] 1 LRC 148, in which a similar but unsuccessful action was mounted, this time contesting the validity of the Commission appointed to select members of the court, discussed further below.

of only three Contracting Parties before it entered into force.[3] Thus, as anticipated, we have seen the establishment of the court before unanimous agreement by CARICOM. It will also be difficult for a Contracting Party to leave the court. A notification period of three years is required.

Rationale for establishing the CCJ

The earlier edition of this book commented on the timing of the move towards establishing the CCJ, albeit acknowledging that initiatives and discussion on the issue were by no means novel and despite advocating the need for such a court.

While the long-standing intention and commitment toward a final Court of Appeal cannot be questioned seriously,[4] it is reasonable to argue that the initiative which finally provided the impetus for the CCJ was coloured by additional and extraneous considerations, in particular, the implications of the *Pratt and Morgan* judgment.[5] Nonetheless, it is a matter of historical record that the Ramphael Commission, in its report 'Time For Action,'[6] had asserted, a full year before *Pratt and Morgan*:

> The case for a Caribbean Supreme Court, with both a general appellate jurisdiction and an original one, is now overwhelming and indeed it is fundamental to the process of integration.

There is at least a suspicion, however, that this initiative was not propelled solely by rational arguments and policy such as those discussed in the previous chapter. Instead, the common denominator of this new renewed thrust toward judicial 'freedom' and other such initiatives, was to enable Caribbean governments and judges to hang prisoners on death row. To put it another way, it was to enable States to fulfil their constitutional mandate of effecting the death penalty, which they believed was being frustrated by Privy Council decisions. Apart from moving toward the CCJ with renewed vigour, the move toward the CCJ was also accompanied by collateral initiatives. Some States attempted to prevent petitions to international human rights bodies by death row prisoners by issuing time limits governing such petitions.[7] In addition, the somewhat draconian measure was taken, in the cases of Trinidad and Tobago and Jamaica, of withdrawing from the Optional Protocols to international human rights instruments which allowed petitions to international human rights bodies such as the Inter-American Human Rights Commission and the United Nations Human Rights Committee.[8] Effecting the death penalty was certainly viewed as important. There is certainly little doubt, therefore, that the Privy Council's high-handed approach to constitutional interpretation with regard to the death penalty and its failure to appreciate the principles by which Caribbean peoples wish to live, have acted as catalysts to the institution of the CCJ, although the process was not initiated by that

---

3   Provisional Article XIX.
4   For a historical account of the initiative toward a Caribbean Court of Appeal, see Rawlins, H 'The Caribbean Court of Justice, A History and Analysis of the Debate', 2000, Guyana: CARICOM .
5   *Pratt and Morgan v AG of Jamaica* (1993) 43 WIR 340 (Privy Council).
6   An Overview of the Report of the West Indian Commission (Time For Action), 1992, Barbados: West Indian Commission Secretariat.
7   See the discussion in Chapter 12 ('International Law as a Source of Law').
8   See Antoine, R-M B, 'Opting out of the Optional Protocol: The UNHRC on Death Row – Is This Humane?' (1998) 3 Carib LB 30.

phenomenon.[9] This is but another example of the way in which international forces have plunged us along a path which some maintain that we are not yet ready for.

We should be clear. This thrust came not only from Caribbean politicians but from the Caribbean public at large, who wished to see justice done.

The initiative towards a Caribbean Court of Justice, in view of our discussion in the previous chapter, is to be welcomed as a step in the right direction. Yet, as argued elsewhere, these initiatives can also be viewed as doing the 'right thing for the wrong reasons'. It is unfortunate that the impetus for this long-sought goal should be seen to be for an objective which is now considered by many, whether in the region or outside it, to be evidence of a barbaric society.[10] The combined effect of these initiatives, even if coincidental – the deviation from these international human rights bodies and the abolition of appeals to the Privy Council – appears dubious and even detrimental to legal development.

Already, the initiative has encountered some difficulties at the local level. There is some concern that the proposed changes should be effected only with dialogue with the Privy Council itself. In Trinidad and Tobago, the proposal seems now to have been 'watered down' to an intention to abolish appeals only in relation to certain criminal matters, at least in the near future. A Trinidad and Tobago Bill to amend the Constitution proposed that the decisions of the Court of Appeal in constitutional matters arising out of a criminal matter be final and un-appealable. It also sought to impose a requirement that leave of the court be obtained before redress for alleged constitutional violations can be pursued.

In this book we have explored in much detail several implications of the *Pratt and Morgan* decision.[11] One view put forward as the rationale for the decision is that the Privy Council sought to bind us to the UK's own policy of abolishing the death penalty. The fallacy of this policy has already been explored in relation to the question of international norms and values which are clearly evident in the judgement.[12] But was there also, as some assert, an imperialistic element such as to warrant the almost instantaneous actions of abolishing the appeals to the Privy Council and seeking to remove other 'outside' influences, such as the Optional Protocol?

This is perhaps not a question that can be answered conclusively. There have clearly been instances of judicial imperialism in the past.[13] But should we be more concerned about the remedy we have sought? The excessive and voluntary reliance of Commonwealth judges on English precedent, in particular, from the House of Lords in England, which is not a court within the hierarchy of Commonwealth Caribbean courts, as is the Privy Council, has been well documented.[14] Caribbean judges and legislatures have not had difficulty in the past with binding themselves to such precedents and courts. Isn't this also judicial imperialism? This phenomenon has been

---

9   Beginning with the landmark decision of *Pratt and Morgan v AG of Jamaica* (1993) 43 WIR 340 (Privy Council), which held that undue delay on death row constituted cruel and inhuman punishment which violated Commonwealth Caribbean Constitutions.

10   *Op cit*, Antoine, fn 8.

11   See eg, Chapter 7 ('The Written Constitution as a Legal Source').

12   See Chapter 12 ('International Law as a Source of Law').

13   See Dorcas White's criticism of the case of *Robins v National Trust* [1927] AC 515, that it was an instance of judicial imperialism. The decision was to the effect that the English courts could exert a controlling influence on colonial courts. Dorcas White, 'Jettison the Privy Council – you t'ink it easy', unpublished mimeo, UWI, Cave-Hill, Barbados, 1976

14   *Ibid*, White. See, also, Chapter 8 ('The Common Law and the Doctrine of Judicial Precedent').

accompanied by a call for Caribbean judges to be more independent and indigenous in their thinking and to 'strike out and mould the common law' in their own likeness.[15]

Does the renewed initiative toward the CCJ mean that this would be a reality? Cynics might be forgiven for thinking that even without the 'interference' of external bodies such as the Privy Council, Caribbean jurisprudence might not look very different in the 21st century, that the distinct influence of the ex-colonial masters as illustrated by excessive reliance on House of Lords judgments and European human rights jurisprudence will still be evident. If this is correct, why the uproar over sovereignty concerns? Would we, as some suggest, lose the opportunity for these courts and bodies outside the region at least to consider more intimately Caribbean judicial thought when they consider appeals? This has long been seen by the Privy Council and even the UNHRC as a valuable instrument in helping to shape their own judgments and the consequent jurisprudence. In this way, Caribbean ideals and opinions are included in the development of legal thought. Such an argument does not undermine the value of establishing a regional Court of Justice. It merely questions the rationale of doing so on the basis that Privy Council judges are out of touch with Caribbean reality and imperialistic. However, as we saw in out discussion on the merits and demerits of abolishing appeals to the Privy Council in our previous chapter, the judgments of a final Caribbean court will be easily accessible to courts outside of the region.

While the Caribbean Court of Justice of the future cannot be accused of being an 'imperialistic court', it can be attacked if it is too easily influenced by foreign or colonial values. The difficulty of containing criticisms on the basis of the sovereignty of individual contracting States will also remain. There may well be decisions which some may see as eroding the sovereignty of individual Member States. Sovereignty concerns were the genesis of the collapse of the West Indian Federation in the 1960s.

It is also dangerous to assume that Caribbean judges, even those in the future Caribbean Court of Justice, isolated from the 'corrupting' influence of both the UNHRC and the Privy Council, will reject the *Pratt and Morgan* principle. Indeed, this would be a contradiction of the evolution which is evident from an examination both of Commonwealth Caribbean constitutional interpretation. Even in *Riley*,[16] there was a dissent by Lords Scarman and Brightman to the majority view that undue delay could not constitute cruel and inhuman punishment under the Constitution. Indeed, one distinguished jurist, Aubrey Fraser, was moved to note that 'it may not be rash to hope that, before long, it [the dissent] would prevail'.[17] It is Caribbean courts which have passed stays of execution and certain Caribbean writers have pointed to the constitutional inconsistencies surrounding the attempt to enforce the death penalty. Will a Caribbean Court of Justice decide differently? Have we advanced the law and legal systems on this issue any further with this move?

Perhaps the real question should be whether the Legislature should abolish the death penalty itself instead of forcing the courts to devise ingenious ways to thwart it? The focus on the CCJ distracts from this very real question which should be occupying the minds of Caribbean peoples and governments. Certainly it distracts from the very legitimate issue of establishing an indigenous Caribbean final Court of Appeal.

---

15   *Persaud v Plantation Versailles* (1971) 17 WIR 107, p 112.
16   [1983] AC 719, p 727.
17   Editorial comment (1982) 1 WILJ 1.

In general, the institution of the CCJ brings with it high expectations of the West Indian peoples, not just in relation to good judicial development, but to the formation of a West Indian legal identity. It is expected too that the court will enhance sovereignty and access to justice. In sum, the Caribbean expects the CCJ to be a panacea for the many evils identified as resulting from having, what is essentially a foreign court perched at the helm of West Indian justice.[18] It is with such ideals in mind that we examine the structure, jurisdiction and jurisprudence of the CCJ.

The Constitution of the Caribbean Court of Justice

The Caribbean Court of Justice is comprised of a President and not less than five judges, but no more than nine judges at a sitting, being an uneven number. The Heads of Government have authority to increase the number of judges which can sit in the court.[19]

The seat of the court will be in the territory of a contracting party, presently, Trinidad and Tobago, as determined by a qualified majority of the contracting parties from time to time. However, it will also have authority to sit, as circumstances warrant, in the territory of any other contracting party. It may also sit in two divisions where it is constituted of at least ten members.[20]

Aside from the President of the court, the appointment, removal and discipline of judges, and the determination of their terms and conditions of service, fall under the purview of a specially established regional Judicial and Legal Services Commission. The President can only be appointed or removed by the qualified majority of three-quarters of the Contracting Parties in conjunction with the recommendation of the Legal Services Commission. Persons qualify for appointment as judges of the court if they have served as judges of a court of unlimited jurisdiction in the Commonwealth for a minimum of 15 years or have distinguished themselves in practice for a similar period of years.[21]

Funding arrangements for the CCJ

The troubling issue of funding for the CCJ and the resultant concern about the cost of establishing the CCJ has been addressed by the creation of a special trust fund to finance the CCJ in the amount of US$100 million. The strategy is for independent and sustainable financing of the court. As noted in the CCJ's First Annual Report:

> The trust fund is capitalized in an adequate amount so as to enable the expenditures of the court to be financed by income from the Fund. In this way, the expenditures of the court including the remuneration of the judges would not be dependent on the disposition of governments. Significant capital expenses have been assumed by the

---

18 See Chapter 16 ('The Privy Council'), for a discussion of the deficiencies of the Privy Council as a final court.
19 Article IV, 1 and 3.
20 Article III, 2.
21 See Article IV (10). Article V lays down the establishment of the regional Judicial and Legal Services Commission which consists of a variety of persons, including representatives from the Law Associations, the Dean of the Faculty of Law and the Secretary General of CARICOM.

host Government in that the building of the CCJ is being provided by Trinidad and Tobago.[22]

The trust fund is administered by an independent Board of Trustees made up of members drawn from across the region, including eminent financial professionals.

Appointment of judges

To allay fears of judicial partiality, the appointment of CCJ judges has been insulated from the political process by the establishment of a Regional Judicial and Legal Services Commission (RJLSC)[23] which has the responsibility for the appointment and removal of judges to the CCJ. The RJLSC is made up of distinguished persons from across the region including persons nominated by the Law Faculty of the University of the West Indies, the various Bar Associations, the Director General of the OECS and the Secretary General of CARICOM. It is chaired by the President of the CCJ.

The governments of the region only have a voice in the selection of the President of the CCJ and not the other justices of the court. Even here, however, political distance has been maintained. The RJLSC is responsible for the actual selection of nominees to the post of President. While Heads of Government must approve the appointment, they cannot substitute a nominee but must await a fresh selection by the RJSLC.

Judges of the CCJ may only be removed by an affirmation of a tribunal established specifically for such purpose.

THE JURISDICTION OF THE CARIBBEAN COURT OF JUSTICE

Differences in jurisdiction

The most significant departure of the Caribbean Court of Justice from the jurisdiction of the Privy Council is that it has a dual jurisdiction, that is, both appellate jurisdiction and original jurisdiction.

APPELLATE JURISDICTION

A potentially important difference in practice, if not in theory, of the Caribbean Court of Justice from the Privy Council, is that it has 'all of the jurisdiction and powers possessed in relation to that case by the Court of Appeal of the contracting party from which the appeal was brought'.[24] As noted earlier, the Privy Council does not, in practice, act in an ordinary appellate capacity as it has limited its jurisdiction in this regard. If the Caribbean Court of Justice takes a more expansive view of its appellate jurisdiction, this will be a considerable achievement. However, it is not apparent that

---

22 See The Revised Agreement Establishing the Caribbean Court of Justice Trust Fund. Note, however, that Article XXVIII of the Agreement requires the expenses of the court and the Commission to be borne by the Contracting Parties.

23 Article V.

24 Article XXV(6).

this is the deliberate intention of the drafters of the Agreement. Indeed, with respect both to jurisdiction and procedure, the CCJ borrows heavily from the Privy Council and may similarly fetter its own jurisdiction.

The division of jurisdiction with respect to the category of appeals evident in the Privy Council's jurisdiction has been maintained. Thus, appeals are divided into those as of right, those with leave and those with special leave. The nature and substance of the stated jurisdiction of the Caribbean Court of Justice are also similar to that of the present jurisdiction of the Privy Council. In so doing, the Caribbean community has arguably denied itself the opportunity of redressing some of the defects of the existing jurisdiction of the Privy Council, discussed in the previous chapter. Many litigants will continue to be deprived of access to redress by a court higher than the Court of Appeal in their respective jurisdictions.

Yet, there is sufficient room for flexibility in relation to accessing the court, but this is a function of the discretion of the judges who sit on the court. It is hoped that they will take a wide view of their jurisdiction and allow greater access to the region's final Court of Appeal than did the Privy Council. More specifically, appeals will lie as of right from decisions of Courts of Appeal in the Contracting Parties in:

(a) final decisions in civil proceedings where the matter on appeal is of the value of not less than $25,000 Eastern Caribbean currency or where the appeal involves property of the same value;

(b) final decisions in proceedings for dissolution or nullity of marriage;

(c) final decisions in any civil or other proceedings which involve a question of the interpretation of the Constitution of the Contracting Party;

(d) final decisions given in the exercise of the jurisdiction conferred upon a superior court of a Contracting Party relating to redress for contravention of the provisions of the Constitution of a Contracting party for the protection of fundamental rights;

(e) final decisions given in the exercise of the jurisdiction conferred on a superior court of a Contracting Party relating to the determination of any question for which a right of access to the superior court of a Contracting Party is expressly provided by its Constitution;

(f) such other cases as may be prescribed by any law of the Contracting Party.[25]

Appeals lie with leave from the Court of Appeal of the relevant contracting party in civil proceedings which involve a question of great or general importance.[26] Appeals will lie with special leave of the Caribbean Court of Justice from any decision of the Court of Appeal of a contracting party in either criminal or civil matters.[27]

Our earlier discussion demonstrates that the rules on special leave are not different to what is familiar from the Privy Council and thus far the CCJ has interpreted these rules in like manner to the Privy Council. This was demonstrated In *Griffith v Guyana Revenue Authority and Attorney General of Guyana*,[28] one of the first cases to come before the CCJ, concerning the status of employment in the Public Service. This

---

25   Article XXV(2).
26   Article XXV(3).
27   Article X, 1, 2 and 3.
28   CCJ App No 1 of 2006.

was a constitutional matter and so there was an appeal as of right to the CCJ. However, the appellant was required by rule 10 of the CCJ rules to obtain leave to appeal from the Court of Appeal within 30 days of the date of the Court of Appeal judgment. The appellants failed to do so, claiming that as the CCJ was new, he was unaware of the procedure. He requested instead, special leave to proceed. The CCJ affirmed the correct procedure, viewing the Court of Appeal leave mechanism as 'little more than a gate keeping exercise'[29] since the Court of Appeal had no discretion to withhold leave in 'as of right' cases on the ground of merit.

In *Griffiths*[30] Nelson JJA explained that special leave was not defined in the CCJ Act but referred to describe leave in contradistinction to leave to appeal obtained or obtainable from the court whose decision is the subject of the appeal.[31] He accepted that special leave did not refer to appeals as of right, such as constitutional cases, but to civil and criminal cases which do not lie as of right or where leave cannot be obtained. He further identified another avenue for special leave, that is, in the exercise of the final court's inherent jurisdiction when the Court of Appeal has wrongly refused leave or where no application for leave has been made to the Court of Appeal.[32] Special leave is purely a matter of grace. The CCJ granted special leave in this case.

Again, in *Cadogan v The Queen*,[33] the CCJ said: 'The grant of special leave is, of course, a matter of discretion. However, if there is a realistic possibility of a miscarriage of justice if leave is not given for a full hearing, then leave will be given.' Special leave is, however, only available in relation to Court of Appeal appeals. As such, it is not available for an appeal against the order of habeas corpus by a judge, which order could not be appealed to the Court of Appeal.[34]

While the source of jurisdiction of the Caribbean Court of Justice is the Agreement, Contracting Parties have liberty to expand this jurisdiction in certain limited respects. Specifically, they may extend the stated appellate jurisdiction to allow other categories of appeals both as of right and by leave in 'such other cases as may be described by law of the Contracting Party'.[35]

The CCJ and precedent

We have already explored exhaustively the issue of judicial precedent and its peculiar problems in the region in an earlier chapter,[36] and more specifically, the CCJ's relationship with precedent. Only a few new points need to be aired here, while reiterating some important principles.

---

29 Para 19, *per* Nelson JJA.
30 *Above*, fn 28.
31 *Ibid*, at para 18.
32 *Ibid*, para 23.
33 CCJ Appeal No AL 6 of 2006 (Barbados), para 2.
34 See *AG of Christopher and Nevis v Rodionov* (2004) 65 WIR 115 (PC, St Christopher and Nevis).
35 See, eg, provisional Arts X 1 (d) and X 2 (b).
36 See Chapter 8 ('The Common Law and the Doctrine of Judicial Precedent').

Stare decisis and the CCJ's appellate jurisdiction

At least one writer has advocated that the CCJ is to be bound by its decisions under the doctrine of *stare decisis* with respect to its appellate jurisdiction.[37] While the CCJ must apply the doctrine of *stare decisis* to its original jurisdiction, there appears to be no justification for the view that the doctrine applies with respect to appeals. Pollard bases his assertion on the clause contained under Article 111 to the effect that: 'The decisions of the Court shall be final'. He contends that similar words were used by Lord Halisbury to locate the *stare decisis* doctrine in the case of *London Tramways Co Ltd*. The words attributed to Lord Halisbury are: 'a decision of this House upon a question of law is conclusive.' Pollard suggests that the words used in the Agreement are 'ominously reminiscent' of the *London Tramcars* formula and therefore 'it may be persuasively argued that the intention of the drafters was to accord determinations of the CCJ the same status as decisions of the House of Lords prior to 1966'.[38]

This argument is difficult to concede. While such words may have been the jurisprudential origin of binding precedent, it has long been established that final courts of appeal have the power to overrule decisions. More importantly, it is incontestable that the Privy Council has never been ruled by the doctrine.[39] With regard to its appellate jurisdiction, the CCJ has not deviated in any way from that of the Privy Council and it is implausible that it should choose to do so in this regard, particularly as flexibility in decisions in the interest of justice has been a much sought after goal in Caribbean jurisprudence. Moreover, in *Boyce*, Justice Saunders and President de la Bastide underscored the CCJ's role in creating an indigenous jurisprudence. This is surely an indication of a flexible attitude to precedent.[40] A more likely reading of the finality provision in the Article is that finality must refer to the fact that no further appeals lie from the CCJ to any other court and nothing more.

The CCJ's attitude to Privy Council and other precedents

As the CCJ is an entirely new court with an independent and final jurisdiction, it cannot be bound to previous decisions from other courts, even authoritative courts such as the Privy Council. This rule should obtain even where the previous Privy Council decision emanates from the very same jurisdiction from which the matter being heard originates.

The observation made in *Boyce*, that the CCJ will 'consider very carefully and respectfully the opinions of the JCPC in matters from States which still accept the Privy Council as their final court,'[41] seems to support this view. Whilst it made no reference to Privy Council precedents from States which *now* accept the CCJ's jurisdiction, since Privy Council judgements in practice bound the entire region before the advent of the CCJ, the implication here is that *all* Privy Council precedents are merely persuasive and not binding. Moreover, regardless of whether the CCJ pronounced

---

37   D Pollard, *The Caribbean Court of Justice, Closing the Circle of Independence*, 2004, Kingston, Jamaica: The Caribbean Law Publishing Co.

38   *Ibid*, p 73.

39   See, eg, *AG of St Kitts & Nevis v Reynolds* (1979) 43 WIR 108 (PC, St Kitts & Nevis).

40   *AG et al v Joseph and Boyce*, No CV 2 of 2005, decided 8 November 2006. See also Chapter 8 ('The Common Law and the Doctrine of Judicial Precedent').

41   *Ibid*.

authoritatively on the question, its conduct demonstrated clearly that it did not consider itself so bound, as it proceeded to deviate from the Privy Council precedent in *Lewis*.[42]

But perhaps the most meaningful and certainly the most courageous sentiment expressed on the subject of the effect of the abolition of Privy Council appeals is that of Crane J, in the Guyanese case of *Persaud v Plantation Versailles*,[43] who said:

> It seems to me it is only the natural consequence of its abolition as the final Court of Appeal for Guyana that the Privy Council should lose its place as a binding force in the hierarchy of authority. *Ipso jure* its pronouncements have ceased to be authoritative.

The CCJ must promote the divergent approach to the common law. Certainly, it is not only expected, but it is the duty of the CCJ to conform to the divergent, and not the unitary concept of the common law that the common law must develop along different paths in different countries.[44] Indeed, the delinking from the Privy Council will considerably dilute the unitary concept of the common law, as the Privy Council was a key instrument in enforcing this concept.[45]

The CCJ has a mandate to liberate the region from inhibiting Privy Council precedents and even House of Lords judgments which impact negatively on our legal systems, while still permitting such precedents to be carefully considered by our courts. Ultimately, in similar vein to the assumption of its new role by the final courts of Canada, Australia and the like,[46] the CCJ must be viewed as the final and ultimate authority on the law of the countries accepting its jurisdiction. Rand, J, of the newly constituted Supreme Court of Canada after the Privy Council was abolished, put it even more directly when he said:

> The powers of this court in the exercise of its jurisdiction are no less in scope than those formerly exercised in relation to Canada by the Judicial Committee.[47]

Closing the circle of independence means more than simply establishing a CCJ. Rather, that court must assert its own judicial independence and define an appropriate legal philosophy for Caribbean peoples, a true appreciation of the common law tradition, which is inherently cosmopolitan and adaptable, and of which we are a part. The occasion not only expects adherence to this divergent approach, but indeed, demands it.

It goes without saying that despite the CCJ's flexible approach to precedent, such flexibility does not extend to lower courts in the hierarchy, and CCJ decisions will now bind such lower courts. This is the case even where, or especially where, the lower court is confronted with two conflicting decisions, one from the Privy Council and the other from the CCJ.

Some consideration should be given to the instance where the lower court matter

---

42   See the discussion of these cases in Chapter 12 ('International Law as a Source of Law'). See also Chapter 8 ('The Common Law and the Doctrine of Judicial Precedent').

43   (1970) 17 WIR 107 at 132. Guyana had just abolished appeals to the Privy Council.

44   See Chapter 8 ('The Common Law and the Doctrine of Judicial Precedent') for a discussion of these concepts.

45   Although the Privy Council has on occasion promoted a divergent view, such as in the case of *Australian Consolidated Press Ltd v Uren* [1969] AC 1129 on the question of punitive damages.

46   See *Viro v The Queen* (1978) 141 CLR 88.

47   *Reference re Farm Products Marketing Act (Ontario)* (1957) 7 DLR 2d 257.

commenced before its country accepted the appellate jurisdiction of the CCJ, but this is an interim matter only.

Overruling by the CCJ

As yet, the CCJ has given no indication as to the circumstances in which it will overrule its own decisions, whether it will take a conservative or more liberal approach to the question. It is difficult to see how conservatism in this regard will serve the CCJ's stated goal of creating a Caribbean jurisprudence, which it described as one of the main reasons for establishing the court.[48] Of course, overruling Privy Council decisions which are essentially English in outlook cannot be seen in the same light as overruling its own decisions. Nonetheless, the reasons for retaining precedents, either from the Privy Council or the CCJ's own previous decisions are essentially the same, the need for certainly and predictability. The CCJ has another issue to consider, that is, the need to ensure that it does not present itself as a court unsure of itself, willing to overturn its decisions at every turn while it searches for its own internal philosophy and notions of judicial truth.

Nonetheless, the CCJ will have to decide, perhaps sooner rather than later, whether certainty is to be sacrificed to creativity in its noble quest. Caribbean jurisprudence has been framed in a conservative, reactionary mode since its inception and the results, while stable and predictable for the most part, can hardly be said to be inspiring, or in some cases, even particularly relevant.

At this juncture, the CCJ seems to be imbued with a pioneering spirit, and this surely augurs well for Commonwealth Caribbean legal systems. It can, however, be pioneering and innovative with regard to Caribbean legal thought as it is at present, without taking a liberal view of overruling.

The Australian Court which replaced the Privy Council jurisdiction, for example, did not take an enthusiastic view of overruling, at least initially. Gibbs J in *Viro v The Queen*,[49] stated that the court 'will not differ from a decision any more readily than we will depart from one of our own decisions.' Notwithstanding, the *Viro* court was aware of its social responsibility affirming that Privy Council decisions were not binding and affirming the duty to 'assess the needs of Australian society.' Moreover, the Australian social context differs radically from our own and the tool of social engineering can be seen to be most needed in societies such as ours, which have been socially traumatised by slavery and colonialism, modes with distinct racist overtones.[50]

THE CCJ'S ORIGINAL JURISDICTION

The original jurisdiction of the CCJ is a much welcomed and important aspect of the court. However, this is a severely limited jurisdiction, restricted to the interpretation and application of the Treaty establishing CARICOM and laying down its sphere of

---

48   See *Boyce, above*, fn 40.
49   (1978) 141 CLR 88.
50   Note that social engineering is now a formal concept in the Guyanese courts. They understood this need particularly when they broke away from the Privy Council. See Chapter 2 ('The Historical Function of Law in the WI – Creating a Future from a Troubled Past').

operation.[51] All of the independent Commonwealth Caribbean countries will participate in this original jurisdiction,[52] even those which have not accepted the appellate jurisdiction of the CCJ.[53]

In the Commonwealth Caribbean, the goal of socio-economic development is closely aligned with that of economic unification and regional integration. These make it imperative that there be a clear and credible means of adjudicating the inevitable disputes that emerge with trade regimes and inter-governmental economic policies. Hitherto, an effective mechanism for this purpose had been lacking in CARICOM, despite the CARICOM Treaty[54] which attempted to define and regulate trade and economic regimes for the region, a main focus of which is the Caribbean Single Market and Economy (CSME). The CCJ, with its original jurisdiction to interpret and adjudicate on the CARICOM Treaty and related issues, will fill this glaring gap in Caribbean jurisprudence.

While other mechanisms for dispute resolution under the CARICOM Treaty already exist, these are deficient largely because they emphasise political and not legally binding solutions. Some writers argue that they were initiated as a compromise out of concern for the loss of sovereignty.[55] The CARICOM Conference is given authority to make legally binding decisions but these must be unanimous and are clothed in political and not legal authority because the Conference is made up of Member States which may have national interests in the outcome of the dispute. The element of impartiality is therefore lacking. So too, are the adjudicative tools necessary for the resolution of disputes which are essentially legal in nature, and more particularly, may straddle difficult questions of international law and transnational commerce.

Power to enforce decisions in international law

In addition, decisions of the Conference, existing within the sphere of international law, may arguably need to be ratified and incorporated into domestic law before they become binding and enforceable.[56] This point is raised incidentally in *Sharma v AG*,[57] where a member of the Opposition in Trinidad and Tobago applied for judicial review

51 The Treaty of Chaguaramus, as revised 2001. The original treaty was revised to make way for the Caribbean Single Market and Economy (CSME) and to cement the establishment of the CCJ.

52 The Conference is the meeting of the Heads of Government of CARICOM.

53 Increasingly, matters related to trade and competition are emerging. They too, have impacted significantly on the minds of the man and woman on the Caribbean street. The most recent, and perhaps the most volatile example, is the fishing impasse between Trinidad and Tobago and Barbados. In that scenario, Barbados fisher-folk illegally entered Tobagonian waters on a consistent basis, following migratory flying fish which had left Barbadian waters for more favourable Tobagonian waters. The issue expanded when Barbados, rather belatedly, claimed that the waters themselves were in dispute. Consequently, a maritime boundary dispute ensued.

54 Revised Treaty of Chaguaramus Establishing the Caribbean Community including the CARICOM Single Market and Economy, 5 July 2001, Nassau, The Bahamas.

55 See K A Brown 'Unity for Survival' in *N Lacasse & L Perret, Free Trade in the Americas (A Hemispheric Approach)*, Montreal: Wilson & Lafleur, 1994, pp 335–68. D Berry, 'Original Jurisdiction of the CCJ Over the CARICOM Treaty' in Rawlins, Berry and Antoine, 'Caribbean Justice For All – The Case For a Caribbean Regional Court', 2000 (3) Contemporary Legal Issues, p 46.

56 K A Brown, *ibid*.

57 [2005] 1 LRC 148 .

challenging the decision of the Executive to participate in a Commission established under the CCJ Treaty. At the time, Trinidad and Tobago had ratified the Agreement but had not incorporated it into law. The appellant argued that the Commission was illegal and void, in that the Executive had no power to participate in establishing the Commission or the court and that the use of public expenditure toward the CCJ was unconstitutional and illegal since the Agreement was not part of the law of Trinidad and Tobago.

The Court of Appeal dismissed the appeal, finding that the issues raised were not justiciable by the municipal courts because the 'CCJ Agreement 2001 was an international treaty to which the government was a party'. Treaty-making was solely the purview of the presidential Prerogative. Further, 'since treaties only operated on the plane of international law, they had no domestic legal effect, therefore, municipal courts could not adjudicate upon or enforce rights or obligations arising out of treaties. Until the Agreement was incorporated, it operated entirely on the ethereal international law plane . . .'.[58]

The existence of a court which has a domestic presence within the legal system will overcome these contentious issues of enforceability in the domestic legal sphere, as opposed to the international sphere. Thus, in contrast to other mechanisms for resolving disputes, the decisions of the CCJ are directly enforceable under domestic law.

Carnegie points out however, that even with the existence of the CCJ jurisdiction, other international law dispute resolution procedures, some of which go beyond CARICOM and are binding, are retained.[59] Such mechanisms include the Competition Commission under chapter 8 of the Revised Treaty of Chaguaramus, the WTO Dispute Settlement procedures and the supervisory role of COTED in relation to subsidies, dumping and anti-competitive practices.[60] These create 'conflicts of conflict resolution jurisdiction' and will impact on the operations of the CCJ, although he argues that the CCJ procedure should be prioritised.

Whatever the alternative mechanisms available, it is clear that the CCJ provides an authoritative, recognisable and deliberate avenue for identifying legal obligations under the Treaty and for providing legally binding and directly enforceable dispute resolution under the Treaty.

Since the decisions of the CCJ are not subject to appeal, it acts as a final court even in respect to its original jurisdiction.

Relationship with domestic courts

While the CCJ is now the authority to pronounce upon matters relating to the Treaty, the Agreement recognises that domestic courts may, from time to time, be faced with matters which overlap with, or impact upon Treaty matters. Accordingly, provision is

---

58   *Ibid*, at pp 158–59, *per* Nelson JA.

59   ANR Carnegie 'International Law and the Original Jurisdiction of the Caribbean Court of Justice: Conflicts of Conflict Resolution Jurisdiction'. 2006, UWI, (unpublished mimeo). He makes the point also that there is no hierarchy with respect to conflicting international conflict resolution jurisdictions which makes it difficult to determine whether the CCJ is to be subservient to these other mechanisms.

60   By virtue of Article 30 of the Agreement and the words of the Treaty's preamble: 'Affirming that the employment of internationally accepted modes of disputes settlement in the Community will facilitate achievement of the objectives of the Treaty'. Carnegie, *ibid*, p 5.

made in the Agreement for domestic courts to refer questions of law relating to the Treaty to the CCJ where they are essential for determining the domestic matter. Article XIV states:

> Where a national court or tribunal of a Contracting Party is seized of an issue whose resolution involves a question concerning the interpretation or application of the Treaty, the court or tribunal concerned shall, if it considers that a decision is necessary to enable it to deliver judgment, refer the question to the Court for determination before delivering judgment.

Nature of the CCJ's original jurisdiction

The original jurisdiction of the CCJ is comprehensive, compulsory and exclusive. Article XVI of the Agreement specifically expresses the compulsory nature of the CCJ's original jurisdiction, thus Contracting Parties cannot make reservations to the effect that they will not accept the CCJ's original jurisdiction.

Two categories of this original jurisdiction may be identified: (a) Advisory Jurisdiction and (b) Contentious Jurisdiction.

Advisory jurisdiction is granted under Article XIII of the Agreement: 'The Court shall have exclusive jurisdiction to deliver advisory opinions concerning the interpretation and application of the Treaty. Such opinions are to be invoked only at the request of Contracting Parties.' Since these are not judgments of the court, they are not precedents, nor do they create legally enforceable obligations. They are, however, authoritative statements of the law and may be relied upon as indications of future judgments and resulting legal obligations which attach.

With regard to the CCJ's contentious jurisdiction, more immediately important to dispute solving, Article XII provides as follows:

1. Subject to the Treaty, the Court shall have exclusive jurisdiction to hear and deliver judgment on:
    (a) disputes between Contracting Parties to the Agreement;
    (b) disputes between any Contracting Parties to this Agreement and the Community;
    (c) referrals from national courts[61] or tribunals of Contracting Parties to this Agreement;
    (d) applications by nationals in accordance with Article XX1V, concerning the interpretation and application of the Treaty.

Exclusive original jurisdiction

The exclusive nature of the original jurisdiction of the CCJ is to be underscored. However, the question of exclusivity is somewhat troubling to some. There is a suggestion that domestic courts may have jurisdiction in relation to private disputes. For example, Berry says: '. . . technically the CCJ is not given *exclusive* jurisdiction over all Treaty-related disputes, since national courts can look at private disputes that may

---

61   This includes the Eastern Caribbean Supreme Court (a regional court), by virtue of Article XII(2).

implicate the CARICOM Treaty or Annex: Articles IX(A)(c) and IX(c).'[62] However, this conclusion is questionable and may run counter to the intent and spirit of the Treaty. Although the Agreement acknowledges that questions of Treaty law may come before domestic courts, it does not abdicate its exclusive jurisdiction in deciding such questions, but rather, expects domestic courts to refer these matters. It should be noted that although referral is at the discretion of the court or tribunal under Article XIV, that once such a question is identified as concerning the Treaty, the court cannot proceed to pronounce on the question, since this jurisdiction is reserved for the CCJ by the use of the word 'shall'. The clear intent here is exclusivity to the CCJ.

An interesting question has been raised as to whether the Privy Council in those countries where it still has jurisdiction, can proceed to adjudicate on questions relating to the Treaty in domestic matters which touch on the Treaty.[63] Certainly, the Privy Council, as any other court, may do so unwittingly, by not realising that the matter involves the application or interpretation of the Treaty, and therefore must be referred. Apart from this, there would appear to be no justification for the Privy Council unilaterally assuming jurisdiction to decide such questions as it is a matter which properly relates to the original and not appellate jurisdiction of the CCJ, which original jurisdiction is compulsory for contracting parties.

It is suggested, however, that the Privy Council, or any domestic court, ironically, can in fact make pronouncements on a Treaty-related question where such a question is *not* necessary to determine the matter at hand. This is because it is only in situations of necessity that the referral procedure is to be invoked. The important point to note here, however, is that such pronouncements must be treated as *obiter* since they are not necessary to decide the question. Such a situation will in no way disturb the authority of the CCJ on questions concerning the Treaty.

In contrast, with respect to broad questions of international law which the CCJ must apply,[64] as distinct from specific questions within the context of regional law relating to the Treaty, the CCJ cannot pretend to have exclusivity. It is here that Carnegie's lament about the lack of hierarchical norms with respect to international dispute solving is most pertinent.[65] It is plausible and even likely that conflicting dicta on principles of international law may ensue from the CCJ and various other domestic courts.

Stare decisis

Somewhat surprisingly for a body immersed in international law, the doctrine of *stare decisis* applies to judgments of the CCJ when exercising its original

---

62 See Berry, *above*, fn 55 at p 56. This refers to the provision allowing the courts to refer disputes but to an earlier version of the Agreement. See also p 57.

63 Pollard, eg, suggests that : 'Omission by Member States to oust the jurisdiction of the Judicial Committee of the Privy Council could lead to a ludicrous situation where that institution could have a determinative role in respect of issues concerning the interpretation and application of the Treaty and on which the Caribbean Court of Justice has ruled. Indeed, this is the position as it exists today and which, in the present submission, is juridically feasible but politically unacceptable.' Duke E Pollard, *The Caribbean Court of Justice – Closing the Circle of Independence*, 2004, Jamaica: Caribbean Law Publishing Company, p 101.

64 Under Article XVII. However, the CCJ may move beyond the rules of international law where equity demands it and cannot refuse to determine a case if there is no applicable principle of international law on the basis of the *non liquet* rule.

65 See above, fn 59.

jurisdiction.[66] As we have learnt, strict adherence to the *stare decisis* doctrine is not a characteristic feature of final courts, nor is it for international adjudicatory bodies. Further, the doctrine has been responsible for many of the ills of Caribbean jurisprudence.[67] McDonald warns that the 'rules that have been developed around the doctrine of precedent will have to be applied creatively in the context of the CCJ. From the appellate jurisdiction perspective, it is much easier for judicial reticence to be the order the day.'[68]

There is, however, provision made for the revision of judgments when new facts are discovered.

Access to the courts by individuals

In keeping with modern trends in international law, ordinary citizens of CARICOM are given access to the CCJ with respect to its original jurisdiction.[69] This, however, is not an individual *right* of petition but can be invoked only upon the discretion of the contracting State Party upon special leave. Such *locus standi* is dependent upon the individual demonstrating prejudice, a direct benefit or right, upon agreement by the contracting party that the individual espouse the claim on its behalf or in the interest of justice.[70]

Under Article XVIII, provision is also made for the intervention of third parties to a dispute where such a third party demonstrates a substantial interest.

Practical difficulties of the CCJ's operation

In this infant state of the CCJ, there are still some practical issues which impact on the Court's jurisdiction to be ironed out. One important issue identified by the Registrar and the CCJ is the right of audience of attorneys admitted to practice within CARICOM from countries which are Contracting Parties to the Agreement, but outside of the Schedule to the Council of Legal Education Act. These include attorneys from Suriname, for example.[71]

THE FUTURE OF CARIBBEAN LEGAL SYSTEMS UNDER THE CARIBBEAN COURT OF JUSTICE

It remains to be seen whether the Caribbean Court of Justice will be more pioneering with respect to its approach to deciding cases. Our earlier discussion on the failure of

---

66   Article XXII: 'Judgments of the Court shall be legally binding precedents.'
67   See the discussion in Chapter 8 ('The Common Law and the Doctrine of Judicial Precedent').
68   Sheldon McDonald *The Caribbean Court of Justice – Enhancing the Law of International Organizations*, 2005, Jamaica: The Caribbean Law Publishing Company, p 45.
69   See Chapter 12 ('International Law as a Source of Law') for a discussion of the prevalence of the individual right of petition to international bodies with respect to international human rights instruments, particularly, as they impact on death row prisoners.
70   Article XXIV.
71   Registrar and Chief Marshall of the CCJ, 2005–2006 Annual Report of the CCJ, Trinidad and Tobago, p 5. The CLEA is the body which grants accreditation for legal practitioners in the region.

the Privy Council to do so is not confined to that Court.[72] The Caribbean Court of Justice will face similar challenges, despite the assertion in the Preamble to the Agreement that the Court 'will have a determinative role in the further development of Caribbean jurisprudence through the judicial process'. With respect to its appellate function an examination of the nature, status and jurisdiction of the anticipated Caribbean Court of Justice reveals that it is to be a carbon copy of the Privy Council in all respects except for the complexion of its judges. In view of our discussion above, cynics might well ask whether Caribbean governments should return to the drawing board if they want meaningful change. Yet, the success of the CCJ lies not so much in the formal expressions of its jurisdiction or status. Rather, such success and the consequent reward for Caribbean peoples reside first, in the very existence of such a court and secondly, in the attitude and conduct of the judges who man this powerful instrument of judicial and legal development. There is every hope that the first slate of judges carefully chosen to steer the court in its initial steps, appreciate this and are well equipped and able to fulfil its mandate. Such judges can inspire confidence in the new court. Will the new court, under its present terms of reference, be an opportunity, or an opportunity lost?

Certainly, a Caribbean Court of Justice, confidently appraised of its true role, would also have tremendous symbolic value, enhance national and regional pride, indicate a desire for genuine change and the will to shape our own future instead of being a society of 'mimic men'.

---

72 See Chapter 16 ('The Privy Council').

CHAPTER 18

SPECIALISED COURTS, TRIBUNALS AND FUNCTIONS

THE CONCEPT OF SPECIALISED FUNCTIONS

We use the term 'specialised court' in a somewhat loose way, since it may refer to something which is not a separate court at all. For example, we may have a specialised jurisdiction within an ordinary court, such as a magistrates' court, which may deal with juvenile matters. If we wish to describe a specialised court, tribunal, jurisdiction or function, it may be seen as one authorised by law to take cognisance of certain special and specified causes and matters. It has a limited jurisdiction which concerns only those types of cases.

The concept of specialised courts and tribunals emerged as a response to the need for adjudicating bodies which would give separate attention and expertise to certain matters that could not be properly addressed in ordinary courts of law. There are a number of reasons why the ordinary courts may be considered inadequate to address these matters. It may be for expediency. For example, there may be an overwhelming bulk of legal matters to be determined in a particular subject area. Another reason is that the nature of certain matters may go beyond the boundaries of the strictly legal or could be highly technical and specific. There may also be a need to simplify certain procedures. These may warrant a special body to address them. Alternatively, such bodies could be established simply to highlight the importance and uniqueness of a particular area of law. A specialised court or jurisdiction may also be set up to integrate related matters which are dealt with in various other places. The special function of these courts is usually supported by the use of specialised or expert personnel in the related field.

Any particular jurisdiction may have specialised courts and tribunals in the form of industrial courts and tribunals, family courts, Juvenile Courts, divorce courts, administrative courts, revenue courts, and income tax appeal boards or tribunals and even Public Service Commissions. The list is not exhaustive. In small jurisdictions, specialisation of the judicial function may be less appropriate or practical. For example, in the Commonwealth Caribbean, the limitations of size may mean that not enough family-related problems reach the ordinary courts in order to justify the creation of a separate family court. This seems to be the view of the Chief Justice of at least one jurisdiction.[1] Consequently, matters which are deemed to require special attention do not necessarily require a separate court or tribunal. Such matters may be handled by a special division of the High Court. One example is the division created to handle divorce proceedings.[2]

---

1   That of Barbados. Sir D Williams, as posited in a lecture entitled 'A light arising', 1990, Faculty of Law, UWI. Yet, smaller jurisdictions such as St Vincent and the Grenadines, have seen fit to implement family courts. See below.
2   As in Barbados.

THE STATUS OF SPECIALISED COURTS

A specialised court may be either a Superior Court of Record, as, for example, the Industrial Court of Trinidad and Tobago, from which appeals go directly to the Court of Appeal, or an inferior court, as illustrated by the various Juvenile Courts in the region. Alternatively, it may be an intermediate court, such as the Family Court of Jamaica.

Whatever its status, such courts will have the usual powers granted to ordinary courts of law corresponding to the particular jurisdiction they have been given. All the specialised courts, tribunals and functions have original jurisdiction. This means that they can try matters coming before them at first instance, with the right of an appeal reserved to the appropriate court in the hierarchy.

Specialised tribunals, on the other hand, are not vested with judicial powers akin to that of a court. Instead, their jurisdiction is best described as quasi-judicial and is part of the administrative legal process.[3] Thus, the ordinary courts of law have an inherent supervisory jurisdiction to review decisions emanating from such tribunals on a point of law. This process is called judicial review of administration action. Persons who sit on specialised tribunals need not be qualified legal personnel. They are merely given a discretion to make decisions on particular matters.

INDUSTRIAL COURTS

All the countries in the region have some special mechanism with which to determine industrial relations matters. These are either industrial courts or industrial tribunals. Industrial tribunals may be either separate quasi-judicial bodies as in Jamaica, Dominica and Belize, or a division under the Ministry of Labour. In the latter instance, the body is purely administrative.[4]

The year 1965 brought with it a new sphere of industrial relations in Trinidad and Tobago as it saw the introduction of compulsory arbitration for labour disputes matters. This was to replace the voluntary approach to industrial relations characteristic of the British common law which had hitherto prevailed, and which still does in several Commonwealth Caribbean countries.[5]

This new approach was instituted by the Industrial Stabilisation Act 1965, later replaced by the Industrial Relations Act 1972. The Act attempted to arrest the deterioration in the industrial relations climate, manifested by a high level of strike activity.

It sought to do this by undermining industrial conflict, in particular strike action. An essential feature of the new system was the creation of an industrial court, the first of its kind in the Commonwealth Caribbean.[6] The rationale behind the establishment of the industrial court was the belief that the ordinary courts of law had proved inadequate in handling labour relations matters. This is borne out on examination of

---

3   Hence, such bodies are the appropriate subjects of the field of administrative law.
4   As in Barbados.
5   Eg, in Barbados, Guyana and St Lucia.
6   Established under the Industrial Relations Act 1972. See the discussion in Chapter 21 ('Alternative Dispute Mechanisms').

the legal history of trade unions and industrial relations matters in the region and elsewhere. For example, it has been widely observed that ordinary courts of law proved to be no friend of the unions and the labour element, as illustrated by the evolution of the common law with respect to labour relations.[7] Historically, courts regarded combinations or associations of workers as being in restraint of trade or criminal conspiracy. More recently, workers' actions have been viewed as tortious acts by the courts of law.[8] The ordinary courts have constantly refused to recognise collective labour activities as valid, thus ensuring that the labour movement and the courts were at cross-purposes.

Indeed, Ewing, writing on the inadequacies of the common law and the ordinary courts to address the problems of labour, says:

> British policy makers have historically responded to the common law problems by providing an immunity to defendants for known tort-based actions. This, however, has proved ineffective partly because of the amoebic capacity of the common law to move in new and unforeseen directions, and partly because of the restrictive approach to construction adapted by Her Majesty's judges.[9]

It was believed that a special court, as well as a special type of law and legal procedure, should be designed for the important area of labour relations to alleviate such political and ideological biases and anti-labour judicial attitudes.

With such justifications for their establishment, it is not surprising that industrial courts have a unique orientation. For example, they are characterised by the 'principles and practices of good industrial relations', a concept peculiar to the area of labour relations and unknown to other areas of law.[10] They are expected to take into consideration the principles of equity and 'good conscience' in examining the substantial merits of a case.[11] In addition, legal techniques are not prioritised in such courts. Rather, the requirements of human relations which are essential to industrial relations, such as negotiation, take precedence.

This is not surprising, for specialised courts tend to take on the character of their sphere of reference. The field of labour relations is based on human relations through negotiation, and the reliance on this instead of legal technicalities is appropriate.

Chief Justice de la Bastide, in describing the rationale and operation of the Industrial Court of Trinidad and Tobago in the case of *Caroni 1975 Ltd v Association of Technical, Administrative and Supervisory Staff*,[12] had this to say:

> What distinguished a dismissal that is harsh and oppressive from one that is not, is a matter which the Act clearly regards as grounded not in law, but in industrial relations practice . . . The policy of the statute is obviously to entrust that function only to judges of the Industrial Court who come equipped with experience of, and familiarity with, industrial relations practice. This is a qualification which judges of the Supreme Court do not necessarily or even ordinarily have.

---

7   See, eg, the celebrated writings of Kahn-Freund, O, *Labour and the Law*, 6th edn, 1997, London: Stevens; and Wedderburn, KW, *The Worker and the Law*, 3rd edn, 1986, Harmondsworth: Penguin.

8   See, eg, *Joseph v Allied WAWU*, unreported, Suit No 258 of 1990, H Ct, Dominica.

9   Ewing, KD, 'Rights and immunities in British labour law' [1988] Comp Lab LJ 35.

10 See, eg, the Industrial Relations Act 1972, s 10(3), of Trinidad and Tobago, which enshrines this concept.

11 *Ibid.*

12 (2002) 67 WIR 223 (CA, Trinidad and Tobago) at pp 224–25.

There are two industrial courts in the region, in Antigua and Barbuda and in Trinidad and Tobago. These are discussed separately. These industrial courts are different from ordinary courts of law not only in terms of policy and focus but also in relation to jurisdiction, procedure and personnel.

THE INDUSTRIAL COURT OF TRINIDAD AND TOBAGO

Status and appeals

The court in Trinidad and Tobago is a High Court or Supreme Court of Record which has jurisdiction to try all labour law matters.[13] Appeals from the court go directly to the Court of Appeal, but the right of appeal is limited in Trinidad and Tobago. In fact, the IRA 1972 further specifies: 'The decisions of the court on any matter before it under subsection (2) shall be binding on the parties thereto and is final.'[14] Accordingly, appeals will only be heard on limited grounds, for example, where they raise questions of lack of jurisdiction or natural justice. The Industrial Court is not, however, to be treated like an administrative tribunal over which courts have inherent supervisory jurisdiction. Consequently, in *Caribbean Ispat Ltd v Steel Workers Union of Trinidad and Tobago*,[15] de la Bastide refused an appeal based merely on an alleged error of law made by the Industrial Court.

The question of appeals was also visited in the case of *Caroni (1975) Ltd*,[16] in this instance, with respect to decisions on the dismissal of workers, regulated by s 10 of the IRA. The section provided:

> **10(6)** The opinion of the [Industrial Court] as to whether a worker has been dismissed in circumstances that are harsh and oppressive or not in accordance with the principles of good industrial relations practice ... shall not be challenged, appealed against, reviewed, quashed or called into question in any account whatever.

The Court of Appeal, in examining this provision in conjunction with s 18(2) above, was clear that it ousted the jurisdiction of the Court of Appeal to hear the appeal. Indeed, the court found that 'the intention of Parliament is too clear in this instance to be deflected by any presumption of law or canon of construction. It is clearly the duty of this court to give effect to it.'[17]

The Court found further that it was impossible to enumerate all of the circumstances in which an appeal would lie to the Court of Appeal against a decision of the Industrial Court. Rather, it would have to be determined on a case-by-case basis.[18] However, breach of natural justice and procedural irregularity were identified as appropriate circumstances for appeals. In *Sundry Workers v Antigua Hotel and Tourist Association*,[19] it was decided that although not expressly provided for under the

---

13   Industrial Relations Act 1972, s 7.
14   Section 16.
15   (1998) 55 WIR 479 (CA, Trinidad and Tobago).
16   *Above*, fn 12.
17   *Ibid*, p 225.
18   *Ibid*, p 226.
19   (1992) 42 WIR 145.

Constitution, an appeal lies 'as of right' from a decision of the Court of Appeal determining an appeal from a judge of the industrial court.[20]

Personnel

The persons who sit on such a court are not all required to be legal persons. Indeed, the court attempts to draw from as wide a cross-section of persons involved in industrial relations matters as possible. For example, an attorney of considerable experience, qualified to be a High Court judge, can head the court in the form of a President. The Vice President of the court must be similarly qualified. Other persons who sit on the court include economists, accountants and persons experienced in industrial relations, such as trade unionists.[21]

Jurisdiction

The court's jurisdiction involves the hearing and determination of all proceedings related to industrial relations matters referred to it by the relevant person, usually the minister.[22] In the case of industrial disputes, the court only assumes jurisdiction after attempts at voluntary conciliation have broken down and legislative conciliatory machinery has been exhausted. Exceptions to this rule include disputes in the 'essential services' such as electricity services and disputes contrary to the public interest. These may be referred directly to the court. The court is also responsible for the registration of collective agreements and matters incidental thereto.

The court may make all such suggestions and do all such things as appear to it to be right and proper for reconciling the parties. With this rather informal jurisdiction, outlined above, one sees the court's deviation from legal technicality. This is part of its function under the principle of good industrial relations.

Since the court is a Superior Court of Record, in the exercise of its jurisdiction, it has all such powers, rights and privileges as are exercised in a High Court of Justice in dealing with and adjudicating upon any action brought before it.

The court may take into consideration such facts as it considers relevant and material, even if such facts would not be otherwise admissible in another court of law. This laxity is with the proviso that the parties are informed of the substance of these facts and are given the opportunity of adducing evidence in regard thereto, in accordance with the principles of natural justice.

The Industrial Court in Trinidad and Tobago may also guided by certain unique considerations in adjudication. These include the necessity to maintain a high level of domestic capital accumulation with a view to increasing the rate of economic growth, employment, opportunity, productivity, inflation, balance of trade and Trinidad and Tobago's financial competitiveness on the world market. Under the previous legislation, the Industrial Stabilisation Act 1965, these considerations were mandatory, but this is no longer the case.

---

20 See the discussion on the Privy Council appeals in Chapter 16. This ruling would obtain to both industrial courts.
21 See the Industrial Relations Act, s 4.
22 *Ibid*, s 7.

The Industrial Court also has wide powers with regard to remedies. Apart from an award of damages, it can also order reinstatement for dismissed workers or exemplary compensation. The latter is with respect to situations where dismissal is found to be harsh or oppressive, unreasonable, unjust and not in accordance with good industrial relations practices.

The dismissal of workers is a good example of the type of dispute commonly referred to the Industrial Court. In fact, the court has special jurisdiction in relation to dismissals.[23] This is with regard to the award of the remedy of reinstatement and/or award of exemplary compensation. These were not remedies available under the common law for industrial relations matters. Further, the court has power to inquire into the circumstances of dismissal to ascertain whether it was lawful, that is, in accordance with the common law principles of dismissal and natural justice. A special feature of the Industrial Court is that individual persons do not usually have *locus standi* with respect to its jurisdiction. This means that individuals cannot come before the court to litigate a matter concerning them. The appropriate party is the union, the worker's representative.[24]

THE INDUSTRIAL COURT OF ANTIGUA

The Industrial Court of Antigua and Barbuda was established by the Industrial Court Act No 4 of 1976. The concept of a specialised court for labour or industrial law matters was not new to Antigua and Barbuda, for the court was to some extent an improved version of the 1967 model.[25] That court suffered an early death, however, as it was abolished in 1972. The rebirth of the court in 1976 brought with it a more expansive jurisdiction.

The jurisdiction of the court is similar to that of Trinidad and Tobago. Thus, the court can hear and determine trade disputes and complaints, issue injunctions in respect of strikes and lockouts, and regulate the power of unions to strike once proceedings relating to a trade dispute are pending before it. The functions and procedure of the Industrial Court of Antigua are similar to those of Trinidad and Tobago. For example, the court sits in two divisions and is presided over by a President and 'such number of other members as may be determined . . . from time to time'.[26] The wide powers given to the Trinidad and Tobago Industrial Court with respect to remedies are also duplicated.

In the case of *Universal Caribbean Estates v Harrison*,[27] the contentious question whether the Industrial Court had jurisdiction over dismissal complaints brought by individuals and unconnected with a trade dispute was answered in the affirmative.

Perhaps the most radical, and certainly the most controversial change made by the new Industrial Court Act was s 17(4) which read:

Subject to sub-s (1) the hearing of any proceeding before the court and an order or

23　Industrial Relations Act, s 10.
24　*Ibid*, s 84(1).
25　The latter court had been created by the Trade Disputes (Arbitration and Settlement) Ordinance No 13 of 1967.
26　Section 4 (b) No 6 of 1985 Industrial Court (Amendment) Act.
27　(1997) 56 WIR 241 (CA, Antigua and Barbuda).

award of any finding or decision of the court in any matter, including an order for award:

(a) shall not be challenged, appealed against, reviewed, quashed or called into question in any court on any account whatsoever;

(b) shall not be subject to prohibition, mandamus or injunction in any court or on any account whatsoever.

The above ouster clause sought to give the court powers suitable to a Superior Court of Record. However, unlike its counterpart in Trinidad and Tobago, the Industrial Court of Antigua and Barbuda is an inferior court, not a Superior Court of Record with inherent supervisory jurisdiction. This means that its decisions are subject to appeal. Consequently, s 17, which sought to exclude the supervisory jurisdiction of superior Courts of Record, was struck out after litigation in the case of *Farrell v AG*.[28]

EFFECTIVENESS OF THE INDUSTRIAL COURTS

Both the Industrial Courts of Trinidad and Tobago and of Antigua have produced a considerable jurisprudence. In this regard, they have contributed significantly to the development of the law in industrial relations matters and have made relief in such matters more accessible.

However, this has produced its own difficulty. In both countries, there is a huge backlog of cases awaiting determination before the respective courts. Indeed, in *Jorsingh v AG of Trinidad and Tobago*,[29] the failure of the Industrial Court of Trinidad and Tobago to deliver a judgment after six and a half years was sufficient to constitute a violation of the appellant's constitutional rights. The appellant had been unlawfully dismissed and had applied to the court for redress, in particular, the award of damages. The Court of Appeal found that his right to equality before the law under s 4 of the Constitution had been infringed. Accordingly, he was entitled to be compensated for the loss suffered as a result of the judgment having not been given within a reasonable time.

Another problem faced by the courts is their focus on unionised employees rather than simply all workers. Because of this *locus standi* requirement, large numbers of workers are, in effect, precluded from the court's jurisdiction. In addition, the court's powers to award reinstatement, although lauded as a significant achievement, is not often utilised.

THE FAMILY COURT

The year 1975 saw the heralding of a new dawn in family relations for the legal system of Jamaica, with the passing of the Judicature (Family Court) Act.[30] This provided for a single court with jurisdictional powers over all legal proceedings related to family life, except that of divorce. This phenomenon can truly be described as a landmark in West Indian legal history, being the first of its kind in the region. The idea

---

28   (1979) 27 WIR 377.

29   (1997) 2 Carib LB 94.

30   As revised 1995. This Act established the Family Court as a Court of Record.

has not yet been successfully transplanted to the Caribbean as a whole. As recently as 1990, one government, that of Trinidad and Tobago, was still toying with the idea of setting up of such a court.[31] It has, however, found root in Belize, St Vincent and St Lucia.[32]

Family Courts do not conform to a universal definition because of the divergent nature of the problems which concern the family in different societies. The jurisdiction of such courts varies depending on the priority given to the court and the nature of the problem. Some courts may take the form of a court of summary jurisdiction, while others may be placed on a par with a superior Court of Record. For instance, if it is felt that certain family matters need to be afforded more respect, a country may choose a superior court. An example might be the provision of child maintenance. Other countries may not create a special court for such purposes, but instead make provision for incorporating what may be termed 'family court approaches' into their general court system. Whatever the method, it is characterised by conciliation and protection.

In addition, the type of jurisdiction given to Family Courts may vary. For example, in the region, in some jurisdictions which have established Family Courts, these have subsumed the jurisdiction of the Juvenile Courts (discussed below). They are therefore Family/Juvenile Courts. This is the case in St Vincent and St Lucia, for example.[33]

The need for such a court in Jamaica grew out of the recognition of the inadequacy of the law to deal with the realities of family life such as concubinage and illegitimacy. As Patchett notes, our law:

> . . . makes no concessions to the Negro family structure . . . it insists upon principles out of touch with social facts and customarily ignored.[34]

Although certain jurisdictions have made some attempt to make the jurisprudence more indigenous and reflective of the West Indian family's needs, such as the abolition of the concept of illegitimacy, the above statement on the position of the law as it relates to the societies in which we live is still largely true.[35]

Further, the legal procedures by which family matters were dealt with were fragmented. There was no court with unified authority over family matters. This often resulted in chaos. There was also a need for a policy focused on prevention through guidance and counselling to help family units *before* their problems developed into irremediable breakdown. This was to be achieved by the incorporation of legal and social services, an indispensable feature of the family court system.

In St Lucia, for example, through the network of social services, including counselling services associated with the court, the court is able to make referrals to the

---

31   That country's Cabinet-appointed Committee on Family Services included among its recommendations the setting up of such a court in its goal of the establishment of machinery for effectively protecting the rights of children.

32   See, eg, in Belize, the Family Court Act 1988, Cap 83A, 1990 Rev, and in St Vincent, the Family Court Act 1992. See also the Family Court Act, No 4 of 1995 of St Lucia.

33   See, eg, s 4 of the St Lucia Family Court Act which lists the Children and Young Persons Act No 11 of 1972 among its jurisdiction.

34   Patchett, KW, 'Some aspects of marriage and divorce in the West Indies' (1959) 8 ICLQ 632.

35   See, eg, *In the Estate of B* [1999] CILR 460, where the Succession Act 1995 of the Cayman Islands was interpreted so as to deny illegitimate children a share in their father's estate. Note too, the anomaly with respect to the access to the courts in Barbados with respect to such matters. Although common law unions are recognised by law, married persons are granted access to the High Court, a court of superior jurisdiction with greater status, while those in common law unions must proceed to magistrates' courts. See also the discussion in Chapter 10 ('Custom as a Source of Law').

appropriate human service division, thereby acting as a type of screening vehicle. On the other hand, Dalphinis-King[36] points to the need for an even more cohesive approach to social services. This complaint on the fragmented social institutions dealing with such matters, is also echoed in Barbados.[37]

The aim of the creation of the family court was, therefore, an attempt to fill the gaps and inadequacies of the legal system as it relates to family matters.

> It was regarded as the human approach . . . The measure, if effective, will be a giant step forward . . . an attempt for the State to heal social wounds, beginning at the fundamental level by helping to keep together the straining fabric of family and home life.[38]

The Family Court has an obvious sociological thrust. Its main aim can be viewed as the prevention of the breakdown of the family unit and generally, to protect the welfare of the members of the family, especially children. Where such attempt at prevention of family breakdown fails, it seeks to improve the general administration of family laws and speedy rehabilitation of those who seek the court's assistance. There is a greater underlying aim, that is, an increase in the stability of the country as a whole.

In St Lucia, the constituents of the court have benefited from voluntary counselling programmes. An encouraging phenomenon in the field of domestic violence is the willingness of increasing numbers of males to present themselves for counselling on such matters.[39] In a region where domestic violence is a serious problem, this is an important function, particularly its rehabilitative aspects.

Apart from domestic violence issues, these courts appear to play a significant role in child maintenance matters, a common problem. This may be related to the relatively high levels of poverty in the region.

It is clear however, that the Family Court is not a panacea for all social problems falling within its jurisdiction. For example, a large measure of the cases that fall under the jurisdiction of the Family Court is linked to broader social problems. Apart from obvious issues such as drug abuse, poverty, and even gender inequities, mental health issues exacerbate and sometimes cause the problems of domestic violence,[40] lack of child maintenance and the like. Such problems are incapable of being solved solely, if at all, through family courts, or even ordinary courts, while counselling and other preventative functions can make a dent in these issues of social malaise.

Personnel and procedure

The Family Court aims to present a relaxed and informal atmosphere in keeping with its sociological emphasis. Indeed, the human approach is exemplified in Jamaica, where the court is located away from other courts of law and even includes a waiting

---

36   Rumelia Dalphinis-King, Director of the Family Court of St Lucia, 'Family Court Perspective of Socialisation and Youth Crime', Paper presented to the *First OECS Conference on Youth Crime and Violence*,' 11–12 October 2006.

37   Joey Harper, Director of the Child Care Board, Barbados, Public Lecture, 24 October 2001, UWI, Cave-Hill, Barbados.

38   Cumper, G, 'The Family Court: Jamaica', in Workshop on Social Legislation Relating to the Family and Child in the Caribbean, 22–26 September 1975, unpublished conference papers, Trinidad.

39   Dalphinis-King, *above*, fn 36.

40   Leading often to juvenile delinquency as discussed below. A high percentage of young persons are both offenders and victims.

area equipped with cribs for babies. In addition, to facilitate the process, provision is made for courts to be held in areas other than ordinary places of sitting.[41]

There is a co-ordination between the legal and social services which forms the support base of the court. This is especially important for preventative work. Persons may even visit the court for assistance before contemplating family related litigation, such as divorce. Examples of support services and social agencies which play an active role in the court's operations are: the Child Care and Protection Division of the Government, the Adoption Board, the Legal Aid Clinic, Family and Marriage Counselling Departments and the Probation Department.[42]

In Belize, under s 4(2)(c) of the Family Court Act, a prerequisite for appointment as a judge is that the person 'by reason of his training, experience and disposition' is a suitable person to deal with family matters.[43]

Special training is given to family court personnel in order to help them understand the roles and functions of this co-ordinated unit. Therefore, non-legal staff are trained in legal procedure and legal staff are given a sociological orientation.[44] The non-legal staff is headed by the court co-ordinator who functions as an administrator. This function includes the screening of incoming cases and their assessment. In Belize, this co-ordinator is appointed by the Public Service Commission.[45]

The court in Jamaica is equivalent in status to a resident magistrates' court and thus the two judges have the same standing as that of the resident magistrates.[46] In St Vincent and Belize, the court is equivalent in status to a magistrates' court.[47]

The court relies on a thorough, investigative and questioning approach in its operation. It also aims for a progressive attitude with a view towards the reform of outdated and even irrelevant laws and policies. Hearings may be in closed session at the discretion of the judge. The procedures of the magistrates' court apply to the family court with any necessary adaptations. In the case of St Vincent, under s 11(1) there is provision for restriction of publication, printing or broadcasting of names and addresses or any particulars relating to proceedings concerning (a) maintenance or domestic matters; (b) juveniles; (c) victims of sexual offences. This is done in an effort to ensure that the proceedings and findings of the court are not disclosed to the general public. The Acts make provision for the court to be held in places other than ordinary places of sitting.[48]

Jurisdiction

Under s 3(1) of the Judicature (Family Court) Act 1975 of Jamaica, the Family Court is a Court of Record which 'shall have such jurisdiction and power as may be conferred

---

41   See, eg, of the Belize Act, s 24.
42   See, eg, the Belize Family Court Act, s 20, which provides for an association between the Family Court and social welfare agencies. In St Lucia, see s 5 of the Family Court Act.
43   See, also, of Belize Act, s 5.
44   St Vincent provides for non-judicial officers of the court under s 7(1). The Belize Act makes similar provision under ss 6(2) and 4(7). Under the Belize Act, s 8, the judge must ensure that such persons receive legal training.
45   See the Belize Act, s 19(1).
46   See the Jamaica Act, s 5(1), (2), (3) and (4).
47   See the respective Family Court Acts, s 4.
48   See the respective Family Court (in the region) Acts, s 6.

upon it by virtue of this Act or any other law'.[49] The jurisdiction of the court is therefore not entrenched, the intention being to leave scope for change in the jurisdiction of the court.[50]

The court also has an express jurisdiction to deal with such matters or causes arising out of specific Acts such as the Affiliation Act, the Children (Adoption of) Act, and the Children (Guardianship and Custody) Act.[51] There is no specific description of the functions of the court or its exact jurisdiction in the Act. This is in keeping with the trend of establishing family courts by enactment of simple statutes.

It is difficult to ascertain whether the family courts in the region are functioning well and obtaining their objectives. One could argue that the Jamaican court has learnt from the mistakes of its counterparts in other jurisdictions, such as Canada, the USA and the UK. There, it was believed that the low status and priority accorded to such courts undermined their effectiveness. Hence, the Jamaican court has been afforded a high enough status and power for it to function effectively and gain respect. But, in St Lucia and St Vincent, the status of the court is that of an inferior court. Note too that in St Lucia, aspects of family law are contained in the Civil Code, as a result of St Lucia's civil law influences.[52] However, staffing and proper facilities appear to be problematic. Further, the concept of 'specialised' tends to have the disadvantage that it creates connotations of an extra-legal character. The Family Court has suffered somewhat from this stigma. Its sphere of reference, the socio-economic unit of the family, tends to exacerbate the image. In St Lucia, there are already complaints that attorneys do not take the court seriously.[53]

It is now left to the other Caribbean jurisdictions to examine the Jamaican experience and learn any lessons that may be forthcoming.

JUVENILE COURTS

Moore and Wilkinson[54] define a Juvenile Court as a 'court of summary jurisdiction constituted for the purpose for hearing any charge against a child or young person or for the purpose of exercising of any jurisdiction conferred on any Juvenile Courts'.[55] Nevertheless there is no golden rule that a Juvenile Court must be of summary jurisdiction, although this is the tendency in the Commonwealth Caribbean.

As was noted earlier, in certain jurisdictions, the Juvenile Court jurisdiction is now incorporated under the Family Court.[56] Where this occurs, the jurisdiction of the court as a whole is much broader than a typical Juvenile Court. Nonetheless, the juvenile jurisdiction of such Family Courts will be largely the same as Juvenile Courts in other countries of the region.

---

49 See, also, the St Vincent Act, under s 3(1).

50 See, also, the provisions for expansion of jurisdiction under the St Vincent Act, s 3(2).

51 See the schedules of the aforementioned Acts for the exact jurisdiction in this area in each of the three territories.

52 See Chapter 4 ('The Hybrid Legal Systems of St Lucia and Guyana').

53 See Dalphinis-King, *above*, fn 36.

54 Moore, T and Wilkinson, T, *The Juvenile Court: A Guide to Law and Practice*, 1994, Chichester: Barry Rose.

55 *Ibid*, pp 10–11.

56 See, eg, St Vincent and the Grenadines and St Lucia.

One should note further that a Juvenile Court may not be a separate court in a physical sense. Rather, it could be an ordinary magistrates' court sitting in its capacity as a Juvenile Court. Any magistrates' court may be deemed a Juvenile Court for such a purpose.[57] When such a court exercises its jurisdiction over juveniles in this manner, it sits in an exclusive jurisdiction to determine matters relating to juveniles only. Such other special rules and procedures will thereby be applied to the particular sitting of the court.

The underlying philosophy of such courts is that persons who qualify as juveniles should be viewed not as criminals, but as young persons to be guided and helped. The court attempts to have regard to the welfare of such persons. Indeed, the Juvenile Court is not only concerned with protecting the deviant child or offender, but also the abandoned child on the streets and the child who is simply 'in need of care'.[58] This jurisdiction is sometimes described as jurisdiction for 'status offences'. These are offences which will not normally be considered as 'offences' if committed by adults, although vagrancy is still an offence in many jurisdictions. This jurisdiction presents its own difficulty, as we will see below.

In the Commonwealth Caribbean, the concepts of family law and juvenile delinquency were borrowed, not surprisingly from England. Such special legislative provisions for juveniles are common in the region, although individual provisions vary minutely from country to country. It is useful to trace the evolution of the law as it relates to the treatment of juveniles.

The treatment of juveniles has changed radically from previous times. In the 19th century, there was no substantial body of law relating specifically to liability, treatment or welfare of children in the UK. Juveniles were treated in the same way as adults under the law. Thus punishment was fixed by the law, with little attention paid to the age of the offender. Hence, children could be goaled or even hanged.[59] It was only after the Industrial Revolution and its resultant social reforms that the idea of a system designed specifically for children's needs emerged. The first Juvenile Court was created in the UK in 1908.

The establishment of Juvenile Courts in the Commonwealth Caribbean sought to impose such reform in the law which would bring about an improvement in the welfare of juveniles within the court system. For example, the enactment of the Juvenile Act in Jamaica sought to repeal the existing piecemeal legislation relating to children and young persons and to provide in its place a modern and comprehensive law dealing with juveniles. The law was welcomed by one writer as 'the new legislation ... designed to set up for the first time special Juvenile Courts with institutions attached to them to stem the rising tide of juvenile delinquency in the colony ... one of the most important pieces of legislation our colony has yet enacted'.[60]

Juvenile courts work hand in hand with certain social institutions, such as the

---

57   See, eg, in the Bahamas, under the Magistrates' Court Act, Cap 42, where the Chief Magistrate has power to establish a Juvenile Court in any magisterial district. See also the new concept of a Children's Court in Jamaica, under the Child Care and Protection Act 2004.

58   See s 8 of the new Child Care and Protection Act of Jamaica 2004. This Act replaces the Juvenile Offenders Act of Jamaica, Cap 10:03.

59   Charles Dickens' famous novel, *Oliver Twist*, dramatises the cruel treatment of children in those times.

60   Henriques, CGK, *Juvenile Delinquency and the Law*, 1958, London: Eyre and Spottiswoode.

Probation Office and the Social Welfare Department. In many jurisdictions, police officers are also given special training as to how to deal with juveniles. Policy guidelines inform these practices. For example, juveniles are not arrested at schools, there may be permission needed from doctors for searches and only female officers may be allowed to interview juveniles. They may also initiate social programmes aimed at preventing juvenile delinquency.[61]

All such courts in the region may be criticised, in that the persons who try these cases are not specialists as they should be, hence undermining the effectiveness of the system.

The impact of the Convention on the Rights of the Child

The administration of the justice system in relation to juveniles must now be examined in relation to the standards set by the United Nations Convention on the Rights of the Child (CRC), the United Nations Standard Minimum Rules for the Administration of Juvenile Justice (the Beijing Rules)[62] and the United Nations Guidelines for the Prevention of Juvenile Delinquency (the Riyadh Guidelines).[63] All Commonwealth Caribbean countries have ratified the CRC, and while not directly enforceable in law, it poses obligations, at minimum, for States to implement its provisions. It will also be persuasive as standard setting for courts.

In *Naidike v AG of Trinidad and Tobago*,[64] in an immigration decision in the Privy Council relied expressly on the CRC in coming to its conclusion that Naidike had been unlawfully detained. The court had to consider the impact of the work-permit decision on Naidike's young child. Baroness Hale of Richmond found that such a case involved the respect for family life in relation to a child under s 4(1) of the Constitution of the Trinidad and Tobago. Consequently, the decision-maker had to balance the reason for deportation against the impact upon family members as required under Arts 3 and 9 of the CRC. The court quoted Article 3.1 of the Convention: 'In all actions concerning children, whether undertaken by public or private social welfare institutions, court of law, administrative authorities or legislative bodies, the best interests of the child shall be a primary consideration'.[65]

Who is a juvenile?

The common law tends to classify a juvenile as a person under the age of 17, although various jurisdictions may legislate otherwise. Further classification can be made between a young person and a child. For example, a young person may be described as above a certain age, usually 14 years, but still a minor, being below the age of 16, 17 or 18 years as the law determines. For example, in Trinidad and Tobago, a 'child' means a person under the age of 14 years whilst a 'young person' means a person

---

61   See, eg, the Drug Abuse Resistance Education (DARE) in St Lucia, and the Juvenile Liaison Scheme in Barbados.
62   Gen Ass Resln 44/33.
63   Gen Ass Resln 45.
64   (2004) 65 WIR 372 (PC, Trinidad and Tobago).
65   *Ibid*, at p 396.

who is 14 years or upward and under the age of 16 years.[66] Since these terms are inter-changeable, we refer in this book to 'juveniles' meaning persons who are minors in the eyes of the law and deserving of special treatment in the administration of justice.

Age of criminal responsibility

There is also an age declared by law to be beyond the age of criminal responsibility (the *doli incapax* rule). In the case of Jamaica, s 62 of the Child Care and Protection Act 2004 deems this to be 12 years, an increase from the previous eight years, while in Guyana, the age limit is ten years.[67]

In view of the increasing rates of violent acts being committed by very young persons in the region, together with the ages of criminal responsibility, which, in many cases, are below that stipulated by the CRC and Beijing Rules, it is instructive to examine how the issue has been dealt with from a human rights perspective, in particular how the age of criminal responsibility is inextricably tied to the more general question of a fair trial.

The issue was highlighted in two highly publicised cases which originated in the UK and ended up before the European Court of Human Rights. These are *V v UK*[68] and *T v UK* which arose out of the same incident.[69] Two boys, who were ten years at the time of the offence of abducting and murdering a toddler, and 11 years upon conviction, were sentenced to detention during Her Majesty's pleasure. In the UK, the age of criminal responsibility is ten years. V complained by virtue of his publicised trial in an adult Crown Court and the punitive nature of his sentence: that his rights not to be subjected to inhumane and degrading punishment under Article 3 of the CRC had been violated; that he had been discriminated against because a person under the age of 10 would not have been held criminally responsible under Article 14 and that his rights to liberty under Article 5 and to a fair trial under Article 6 had been violated. Of these, for our purposes, Arts 5 and 6 are most important. Indeed, the Court did find that there had been violation of these rights. It is notable that our Constitutions have similar provisions.

In examining the question of any violation of Article 6, whether V's right to a fair trial, specifically his right as an accused to participate effectively in his criminal trial had been violated, the Court found that the age of an accused was pertinent to the issue. In so doing, it also considered the impact of the CRC and the Beijing Rules. While the Court conceded that, as yet, there were no clear standards among Member States to the CRC on the minimum age of criminal responsibility and therefore the age of responsibility attributed to V was not in of itself a breach of the Convention, it found that it was essential that where a young child was charged with a grave offence attracting high levels of media and public interest, it is necessary to conduct the hearing in such a way as to reduce as far as possible his or her feelings of intimidation and inhibition.

---

66   Under the Children's Act, Chap 46:01 (Rev Laws of Trinidad and Tobago), s 2. In Antigua, a juvenile is defined as being 16 years and under, while in St Lucia, under the Children and Young Persons Act 1972, a child is a person under 12 and a juvenile under 16.

67   Under the Juveniles Offenders Act 1973, s 2. Barbados has also increased its age in light of the CRC. In St Lucia also, the age of criminal responsibility is 12 years, under the Children and Young Persons Act 1972.

68   (1999) 30 EHRR 121.

69   *Ibid.*

The Court agreed with the UK that there was a public interest in the open administration of justice. However, in the circumstances of this case, where there was an open trial and even V's name had been publicised, and there was evidence that V had not been able to comprehend fully the proceedings, had been in a state of trauma, and been unable to talk of the circumstances of the offence in any meaningful way, V's right to participate effectively had been impaired. Accordingly, there was a violation of Article 6 of the Convention.

Jurisdiction over juveniles

Persons falling under the jurisdiction of the Juvenile Court can be classified into three main groupings:

(a) juvenile offenders – that is, those who have committed criminal offences;

(b) juveniles in need of care and protection; and

(c) juveniles deemed to be beyond control.

Such persons are required by law to be brought before the Juvenile Court. With regard to (b) and (c), as we have established, juveniles coming before the court for these purposes are regarded as having 'committed' status offences.

With respect to children 'beyond control', the court generally has a jurisdiction to bring the parents and guardians before the court for treatment also.

The term 'in need of care and protection' is deemed to have a wide interpretation. It includes:

(a) children against whom certain offences have been committed. Frequent examples are sexual abuse or physical abuse;

(b) children who have been associating with persons who have committed such offences, hence creating a potential danger of abuse; and

(c) children, who, having no parent or guardian, or inadequate parents or guardians, are falling into bad association, influence, or who are exposed to moral danger.

The Juvenile Court may, if it deems necessary, take steps for removing such juveniles from undesirable surroundings and for seeing that proper provision is made for education and training.

This wide and generous jurisdiction is seen, for example, under the Juvenile's Offenders Act of Guyana where it is provided that:

> . . . any person may bring before the Juvenile Court any person apparently under the age of 17 years who:
>
> (a) is found begging or receiving alms;
>
> (b) is found wandering and not having any home or usual place of abode or visible means of subsistence or . . . having no parent or guardian; or
>
> (c) is found destitute . . . ; or
>
> (d) frequents the company of any reputed . . . thief, or reputed prostitute.[70]

In addition, welfare institutions, such as the Child Care Board of Barbados, have

---

70 Cap 10:03, Law 44 of 1948, Rev 1973, s 17. See also, s 11 of the Children's Act, Cap 46 (Rev) of Trinidad and Tobago, where a juvenile may be taken to a 'place of safety' and detained there until he or she can be brought before a magistrate under s 44.

jurisdiction to remove juveniles in danger of abuse and neglect from their parental homes or other environments and provide mechanisms whereby such juveniles can be fostered or placed in a more protective environment. This would usually entail intervention by the court, for example, an application to the High Court.[71]

The treatment for all the various categories of juveniles is largely the same.

How does the law protect the deviant child, the child on the streets or the child in need of care? The rationale behind much of the legislation on juveniles is to decrease the number of potential juvenile offenders. Juvenile crime is on the increase throughout the region. For example, in Jamaica and Trinidad and Tobago, there is an increasing number of youth gangs and a high rate of robbery and violence. However, much of the court's work is to do with children in need of care and protection, rather than offenders. This is due perhaps to the prevailing social conditions, for example, poverty and low levels of parental responsibility.

Consequently, in Jamaica, an advisory council was established, whose duty was to advise and report to the relevant ministry, matters affecting the application of juvenile law. Several public and social organisations have representation on the council.

From our exposition on the wide jurisdiction of Juvenile Courts, we see that the aims of such courts are to help rehabilitate, not to punish. There is, therefore, a preventive function as well as a correctional function in the law dealing with juveniles. This is a radical improvement on the common law, which originally only contemplated punishment.

Constitution and procedure

Juvenile courts in the Commonwealth Caribbean are headed by a magistrate or, in the case of Jamaica, a resident magistrate as chairperson, and two justices of the peace, one of whom is usually a woman. There is an underlying policy to appoint as magistrates in the Juvenile Court persons who are specially suited to deal with such cases, for example, persons who are *au fait* with the social background of the kind of child who frequently appears before such a court. Other aspects of the court's jurisdiction take cognisance of the juvenile's social circumstances. For instance, the court must inquire into the juvenile's background so as to enable it better to adjudicate in his interest. Details concerning the juvenile's home environment, medical history and school relations, will be relevant. In Dominica and St Christopher and Nevis, provision is made for two welfare officers, called 'assessors', to sit with the magistrate.[72]

Juvenile courts are deemed to have all the powers of the magistrates' or resident magistrates' courts. In Jamaica, the court sits in different parishes as often as necessary to exercise its jurisdiction, usually once per week, and may convene in a separate building from the ordinary courts of law. The rationale behind the latter provision is in order to emphasise the difference between Juvenile Court and the ordinary courts of law. It also highlights the law's concern in protecting, rather than punishing juveniles. In Trinidad and Tobago, the magistrate who adjudicates juvenile cases must sit

---

71 See, eg, s 5 of the Child Care Board Act, Cap 381 of Barbados.
72 See the Children and Young Persons Act, Cap 37 of Dominica and the Juvenile Act, Cap 39 of St Christopher and Nevis.

elsewhere than where he or she sits for ordinary matters. However where a juvenile is fined jointly with an adult, he may be tried by an ordinary court. This is particularly the case if the juvenile is being tried for a serious offence.

Juvenile offenders

The law relating to juveniles lays down certain special procedures for arraigning and trying juveniles who commit offences. There are important procedures before, during and after trial. For example, if it is not possible for a child to be taken to a magistrate, police officers have the discretion not to release the juvenile if they view releasing the juvenile as being contrary to justice or exposing him or her to negative influences.[73]

Every attempt is made to keep the juvenile away from the usual harshness of the court proceedings. For example, throughout the Commonwealth Caribbean, legislation provides that, upon arrest, children are to be kept separate from other adult prisoners. They should not, therefore, be kept in a prison cell awaiting arrest, or be allowed to come into contact with hardened criminals, who may have a bad influence on them.[74] To this end, the law further provides that the juvenile should be brought before the court speedily and be granted bail.[75] In some cases, where the juvenile is charged jointly with an adult, he may be fined.

Before appearance in court, notice is usually served on the probation office in order that information may be gathered as regards the child's home, school record, age, health and character.

Except for the most serious of indictable offences, such as manslaughter and murder, all cases concerning juveniles are tried summarily.[76] Generally, procedure in Juvenile Courts is informal, based more on an attempt to assist the juvenile rather than an adversarial approach.

Privacy and assistance

When a juvenile is being tried by a court of summary jurisdiction, the general procedure of the court changes, as the court must ensure that the juvenile understands what is happening. In specific cases, where the charge is against another young person, if the court sees it fit, the juvenile is given a choice of trial. This choice may also be made in relation to indictable offences (other that manslaughter and murder). The juvenile may be assisted by his parents or guardians and the court ensures that the difference between the two types of trial is understood by the juvenile.[77]

The court is required to explain to a juvenile before its jurisdiction, in as simple a language as possible, the reason for his or her attendance at court. There is a statutory duty placed on the court to ascertain a juvenile's defence so as to assist him or her or

---

73   See, eg, ss 11, 73 and 74 of the Children's Act, Cap 46 (Rev) of Trinidad and Tobago.

74   In Trinidad and Tobago, eg, under ss 73 and 74 of the Children's Act, Cap 46 (Rev), the Commissioner of Police has a duty to provide separate facilities for the detention of juveniles and to make them available to all magisterial districts. See, also, the Antigua Act, s 15.

75   See, eg, the Juvenile Offenders Act of Barbados, s 3(3) and (5).

76   See, eg, the Trinidad Summary Courts Ordinance, Cap 3, No 4, s 96 (1) and (2).

77   See, eg, the Trinidad and Tobago Summary Courts Ordinance Ch 3, s 96(3). There are also provisions under the Police Powers Act, s 2, and specified offences which enable the court procedure to change in a trial for a specified offence.

the parent or guardian in putting the necessary questions to witnesses. For example, under s 23(1) of the Children and Young Persons Act of St Lucia, this is expressly outlined.[78]

Only certain authorised persons are allowed in the Juvenile Court while it is in session. These are persons directly concerned with the case. Others must receive special permission from the court before they may attend. This is to protect the child from harmful publicity.[79] Parents or guardians and the probation or welfare officer are, however, required to be present. Publications of the court's proceedings must also receive special permission.

On this subject, a case from the UK is worthy of note. In *Re S (a child) (identification: restriction on publication)*,[80] the House of Lords, in applying the Human Rights Act of the UK to the question of privacy for Juvenile Court proceedings held that this must be balanced against the right to freedom of expression under Article 8 of the European Convention on Human Rights. There was a public interest to be served in information gathering about such trials where the juvenile was not concerned in a criminal trial. In this case, the publicity sought was to be able to publish the names and photographs of the parents of a child who had been murdered by his mother and the name and photograph of the dead child. The court agreed that this could promote informed debate about criminal justice and thereby promote the rule of law.

In any event, the anonymity or confidentiality rule may not operate efficiently in the Commonwealth Caribbean and juvenile records often find their way into the system. For example, in Barbados, s 3 of the Juvenile Offenders Act provides for anonymity for juveniles. Similarly, the Sexual Offences Act provides for such proceedings to be held in camera. In practice, however, juvenile convictions can come to the notice of the courts, for example, by oral testimony. Further there are no requirements that juvenile records be sealed, expunged nor kept separate from adult records, a situation noted by the Penal Reform Committee.[81]

We will discover, from our discussion below, that many of the procedures laid down for the protection of juveniles are observed more in the breach.

Evidence from children and the oath

Certain rules of criminal procedure are peculiar to juveniles. For example, a child may not be allowed to take the oath and give sworn evidence, since he or she may be considered incompetent to give evidence due to immaturity. The general rule is that children may give sworn evidence if they appear, on examination by the court, to be able to appreciate the nature and consequences of an oath. As was said in *R v Brasier*,[82] a child must be able to 'entertain of the danger and impiety of falsehood'. The child need not be aware of the existence of God, but must merely satisfy the judge that he or she appreciates the solemnity of the occasion and the duty, when on oath, to tell the truth. He must, therefore, understand the nature of truth, as discussed in *R v Hayes*.[83]

---

78   See also, s 99 of the Summary Courts Act, Cap 4.20 of Trinidad and Tobago.
79   See, eg, s 87(4) and s 100 of the Children's Act, Cap 46 (Rev) of Trinidad and Tobago.
80   [2006] 4 All ER 683 (HL).
81   *Report of the Committee on Penal Reform (Barbados) 1980* of Barbados, p 51.
82   (1979) 1 Leach, 199.
83   [1977] 2 All ER 288.

Because of the potential unreliability of the evidence of children, an accused cannot be convicted on the evidence of a child, unless such evidence is corroborated by some other material evidence implicating the accused. A child who purposely gives false evidence or testimony may be tried summarily, for perjury. The unsworn evidence of another child is not sufficient for the purposes of corroboration,[84] although the sworn evidence of another child may be adequate for the purposes of corroboration, as discussed in the case of *DPP v Hester*.[85]

Sentencing options

Several options for sentencing are open to the court. Juvenile offenders may be placed under the care of a probation officer or child care officer. Such officer is required to visit the juvenile at home regularly to supervise his or her conduct. Also available is a probation order, which requires the offender to visit the probation office for help and advice if the juvenile is over 14 years of age. Failure to comply with the order may result in a return to the court for resentencing. The juvenile may also be fined.

Interestingly, the parents of a juvenile offender can also be fined for failing to exercise proper control. This is of course an unusual jurisdiction, as the parent himself is not the offender.[86] The court can also make an order requiring the parent to enter into a cognisance for the good behaviour of the juvenile.

Juveniles may be placed in the care of a fit person or an orphanage if it is deemed necessary to remove them from their surroundings.

The court may make an order, such as the Approved School Order, which gives a designated 'reform' school the authority to keep the juvenile for three years or other period for detention up to 16 years of age. However, this is not normally done for juveniles under ten years of age. In extreme cases, where a juvenile is deemed too unruly for a reform school, he or she is sent to prison.[87]

Juveniles may also be fined, usually an unrealistic option, or whipped.[88] However, corporal punishment, although still on the statute books of several countries in the region, is an unusual penalty and has been declared unconstitutional in some jurisdictions. It also violates the CRC.[89] Few countries provide for community service orders

---

84 See s 19 of the Children's Act, Cap 46 of Trinidad and Tobago and s 17(2) of the Perjury Ordinance, Cap 4, No 15, of Trinidad and Tobago, the latter of which exempts a child giving such unsworn testimony from committing perjury.

85 [1973] AC 296; [1972] 3 All ER 1056. Note too that an accused may be 'convicted' on the uncorroborated evidence of a child provided that the court warns the jury of the danger of convicting the accused person on that uncorroborated evidence. See, eg, s 19(6) of the Trinidad and Tobago's Children's Act, Cap 46. However, a child may be convicted of perjury if he or she lies on the evidence. Section 19(7), *ibid*.

86 See, eg, the Barbados Act, *above*, fn 75, s 16.

87 See the Barbados Act, s 16.

88 See the Magistrates' Code of Procedure Act of Antigua, s 99. The whipping instrument is a rod of tamarind. See also s 1304 of the Criminal Code of St Lucia. title 97.

89 See, eg, recent rulings in the region prohibiting the use of the cat-o'-nine-tails as cruel and inhumane punishment and elsewhere, the whipping of juveniles. But cf *Pinder v R* (2002) 61 WIR 13 (PC, the Bahamas). See too Chapter 12 ('International Law as a Source of Law'). See also Article 37 of the CRC, which declares that no child 'shall be subjected to torture or other cruel, inhuman or degrading treatment or punishment'. Rule 17.3 of the Beijing Rules also specifically outlaws corporal punishment for children.

for juveniles or alternative sentencing.[90] A juvenile under 17 years, or, in some jurisdictions, 18 years, who attends, or attended, a certified industrial school, and is convicted of an offence for which an adult could be imprisoned without the choice of a fine, may be sent to an industrial reform school for a duration of one to five years. This punishment may vary, but he or she may not be imprisoned. Juveniles of similar ages may be transferred from a prison to an industrial school.[91] Because juveniles are rarely detained, penalties are usually monetary. When a conviction is recorded, it is seldom considered a felony conviction. Juveniles should only be imprisoned in exceptional circumstances.[92] When and if a juvenile is imprisoned, he is never supposed to be subjected to hard labour.[93] In instances where a juvenile under 18 years commits an offence punishable by death, such sentence may not be pronounced against him or her, and instead the juvenile is detained during her Majesty's pleasure.[94]

However, in practice, juveniles who have been arrested often face sentencing as adults if they are over 18 years by the time the trial has concluded. Courts have had to consider the effect of delayed sentences on such juveniles turned adults. In *R v Wright*,[95] for example, the court had to consider whether the defendant, who had committed the offence of wounding with intent while he was 17, was liable to imprisonment because he had turned 18 at the date of conviction. The court decided against such sentence, which it also deemed to be unconstitutional. Similarly, in *Ramkissoon v R*,[96] the court, on ascertaining that the offender was a juvenile at the time of the commission of the offence, changed his sentence. A contrasting result was obtained in *Gordon v The Queen*.[97] The latter decision may, however, not be considered good law in the light of later cases and the provisions of the CRC, which expressly outlaws such harsh sentences for juveniles. In a landmark decision from Jamaica, *Baker v The Queen*,[98] the important question was whether the exemption of capital punishment for juveniles applied to the time of commission of the offence, to persons who had not attained 18 years at the date of the commission of the murder, or whether the relevant date was the time of sentencing. The Privy Council refused to follow an existing Privy Council precedent which had answered the question in favour of the former.

Since the decision of *DPP v Mollison*,[99] the question of the detention of juveniles at 'Her Majesty's Pleasure' has been revisited. The Privy Council determined that 'Her Majesty's Pleasure' must be construed as 'the Court's pleasure', in order to avoid unconstitutionality. In *Mollison*, the practice had been to leave the discretion conferred under s 29 of the Juveniles Act 1951 to detain juveniles, to the Governor General, Her Majesty's representative. The Privy Council found, however, that this

---

90   For example, in St Lucia, the relevant Act does not allow for such community service for juveniles.
91   See, eg, ss 58–59 of the Magistrates' Code of Procedure Act of Antigua and Barbuda and s 59 of the Trinidad and Tobago Children's Act, Cap 46.
92   See, eg, *R v Wright* (1972) 18 WIR 302.
93   The Children's Act, Cap 46 of Trinidad and Tobago, s 79.
94   See *ibid*, s 80.
95   (1972) 18 WIR 302.
96   (1962) 5 WIR 250 (CA, Trinidad and Tobago).
97   (1969) 15 WIR 359.
98   (1975) AC 774 (PC, Jamaica).
99   (2003) 64 WIR 140 (PC, Jamaica).

practice infringed the constitutional principle of the separation of powers which required that judicial authority to determine a sentence was reserved to a court and could not be conferred on an executive officer.[100] Further, such a fundamental constitutional principle was not overridden by the saving law doctrine which preserved existing law.[101]

In fact, the USA is one of the few countries in the world which allows juveniles to be hanged. It is the main reason why that country refuses to ratify the CRC.

In need of care and protection

As we saw earlier, Juvenile Courts are expected to perform a 'guardian-like' role in relation to children who come before the courts for 'status offences' or generally, children in need of care and protection. In Trinidad, for example, if juveniles are found begging, they may be sent to an orphanage. Likewise, juveniles may be sent there if deemed destitute, for example, where their parents are in prison; if they have no home nor apparent means of subsistence; if they seem to be cared for by unfit parents or guardians;[102] or if they are frequently being subjected to negative influences from criminals, prostitutes or other such persons.[103] If the juvenile is 14 or 15, however, he or she may be sent to a relative or other fit adult who can adequately care for him or her.[104]

As discussed further below, juveniles who are brought before the courts for 'status offences' and are simply in need of protection, are often treated in the same manner as juvenile offenders with respect to the 'solution' obtained. They are therefore likely to end up in a special facility for juvenile offenders.

Juveniles beyond control may be placed under a supervision order or in the care of a fit person. Further, the parent of such a child is obliged to enter into a recognisance to exercise proper care of such juvenile in the future.

Legal aid for juveniles

Few countries in the region provide for legal aid to juveniles, and this exacerbates the inefficiencies of juvenile justice, as discussed below. In those countries that do provide such aid, it is usually only for capital offences, or, as in Barbados, for indictable offences. Further problems abound. One human rights organisation has noted, for example, that even where legal aid is available, juveniles are not informed of these facilities despite statutory provisions that make it mandatory for juveniles to be advised of this right.[105]

In a rare case challenging this weakness in the system, *Corbin v COP*,[106] Chief Justice Sir Denys Williams quashed a conviction of a 13-year-old boy who had been

---

100 See Chapter 7 ('The Constitution as a Legal Source'), for a discussion of this principle.
101 See also *Browne v R* (1999) 54 WIR 2213 (PC, St Christopher and Nevis).
102 For example, if the parent or guardian fails to provide adequate food, clothing, medicine, rest or lodging for him. See the Children and Young Persons Act of St Lucia, s 5(2).
103 See the Children's Act, Cap 46 of Trinidad and Tobago, ss 9 and 11.
104 See the Juveniles Act of Antigua, ss 4 and 7.
105 See the *Caribbean Rights Report*, 2000, Barbados.
106 No 19 of 1999 (CA, Barbados).

charged with assault. Alluding to s 17 of the Community Legal Services Act Cap 112A, which provides for the grant of legal aid in all indictable offences to minors, the Chief Justice determined that this right existed even where the minor elected, as in this case, to be tried summarily since the core offence remained an indictable one.[107] The Chief Justice further located the right within the constitutional context of the right to be given adequate facilities for the preparation of his defence (right to a fair trial) under s 18(2) of the Constitution.

In Trinidad and Tobago, where there is also provision for legal aid to minors, the Court of Appeal has gone a step further in its observations on the need for juveniles to be given assistance in the courts. In *Leith v The State*,[108] the appellant, a young person who had been below the age of 16 at the time of the offences for which he was charged, rape and assault, claimed that his lawyer had misrepresented his intentions as to the plea by pleading guilty when he had instructed counsel to 'fight' his case, in other words, to defend him on a 'not guilty' plea. He further contended that counsel had advised him that if he pleaded guilty he would receive only a three-year sentence, as he was only then 16 years. He had, he argued, rejected this advice. Instead, the guilty pleas had been entered and he had been sentenced to 15 years.

While the court did not quash the convictions, Sharma JA noted that it is 'highly desirable (perhaps necessary) that when young persons are charged, if statements are to be taken from them, some responsible and independent person should be present to witness the taking of the statement as young persons need to have assistance and advice.'[109]

New developments in the control of juveniles

More recent trends in the UK have moved towards the care and control of juveniles outside the court system but, as yet, the Caribbean has not followed this new approach in any formal way. To some extent, the Education (Amendment) Act 1996 of Barbados and Education Acts in the OECS are attempting to go in this direction, as teachers will also have jurisdiction over students with respect to offences.

The Barbados Act, for example, is an attempt to impose stringent forms of social control on juveniles who are seen as being susceptible to modern societal ills such as drug abuse.[110] Under the Act, provision is made for a school teacher or principal to have search and arrest powers which are akin to those of police officers with respect to pupils at school. For example, under s 64A of the Act, where a teacher has 'reasonable grounds for believing that a pupil has in his possession any intoxicating liquor, controlled drug . . . gun . . . the teacher may search the pupil's person and the pupil's property'.

During the exercise of such powers, the school teacher has the same privileges and immunities as those conferred on a police officer by law.[111] Where pupils are

---

107 Relying on *Hastings and Folkestone Glassworks Ltd v Kelson* [1949] 1 KB 214, at p 220: 'An indictable offence . . . is none the less "indictable" because if the prosecution chose, it could proceed in respect of it summarily.'
108 (2001) 61 WIR 435.
109 *Ibid.*
110 Both Bermuda and the British Virgin Islands have instituted Drug Courts.
111 Education (Amendment) Act 1996 of Barbados, s 64A(9).

convicted under these new provisions of the Act, they may be ordered to undergo counselling and rehabilitation, in addition to any other penalty imposed. The normal jurisdiction under the Juvenile Offenders Act and the relevant penalties apply to the Education Act.

PROBLEMS WITH JUVENILE JUSTICE – THEORY VERSUS REALITY

As we have seen, all countries in the region have legislation relating to juveniles which include laudable content and noble objectives as to how juveniles should be treated before the law and the rationales for juvenile justice. Such legislation is augmented by the provisions of the CRC which all of the countries in the region have ratified.[112] Nonetheless, when one examines the actual operation of juvenile justice in the Commonwealth Caribbean, as has been done by country studies pioneered by UNICEF,[113] serious deficiencies are revealed, exposing a clear dichotomy between theory and reality.

In some instances, such deficiencies are due to the now familiar problem of a lack of financial resources. In others, however, it has more to do with social norms which militate against a more humanitarian and rights centred approach to juvenile justice, as expected under the CRC. In sum, while the CRC stresses rights, the approach of our juvenile justice system often speaks the language of 'spare the rod and spoil the child'. In large measure, they fail to fulfil the objectives of preventative, protective, rehabilitative rights systems.

Protection goals and the problem with status offences

One of the most serious problems in the juvenile justice system is the way in which the aim of protecting juveniles in need of care has been hijacked by the system. This is so both for children who are abused, abandoned or ill-treated in some way, and other juveniles who commit status offences. Indeed, the very concept of a 'status offence' betrays a philosophical approach which is inappropriate to the ideals of caring, protecting and rehabilitating juveniles. Recall that such offences are not offences ordinarily recognisable under the law for adults. Rather, these are juveniles who, because of the vulnerable position that they find themselves in, their negative status, are brought before the courts. Studies have demonstrated a clear link between such status offences and issues of poverty.[114] So, for example, juveniles found wandering the street, associating with criminals, sexually abused and exploited, probably because they have no stable homes, may find themselves before the courts. Because of a lack of appreciation for the differing circumstances of such juveniles who are not

---

112   And by extension the United Nations Standard Minimum Rules for the Administration of Juvenile Justice (the Beijing Rules) Gen Ass Resln 44/33 and the United Nations Guidelines for the Prevention of Juvenile Delinquency (the Riyadh Guidelines) Gen Ass Resln 45/112.

113   See 'A Study on Juvenile Justice in the Caribbean–Country Reports' presented to the Regional Symposium on Juvenile Justice in the Caribbean (Symposium Report), 19–21 September 2000, UNICEF, Trinidad and Tobago. See also an earlier study of six countries in the region: Antoine, R-M B, 'UNICEF Ratification on the Convention on the Rights of the Child in the Commonwealth Caribbean', 1992, Barbados.

114   See the Symposium Report, *ibid*.

accused of any crime, or because of a lack of resources, such juveniles are often treated in the same way as juvenile offenders. Consequently, they are placed in juvenile 'homes', in effect, deprived of their very liberty. This not only raises serious ethical issues, but is of constitutional interest, as discussed below.

Indeed, in the Barbados UNICEF study, juveniles removed from negative sexual influences complained that although they were the victims, they were made to feel like criminals.[115] Notably, in many cases, the adults who perpetuated such offences against juveniles were not arrested, in some cases due to cultural norms which underplayed such offences.

It has also been observed that more children are entering the criminal justice system as a result of an increasing tendency by adults to use juveniles to facilitate crime. Such crimes include drug offences and sexual offences.[116]

Problems with sentencing options

Punitive rather than rehabilitative forms of sentencing were more often employed in the juvenile justice system. This is in part due to the lack of foster homes and child care options available to the court. In addition, formal sentencing options are limited, in particular non-custodial sentences and court avoidance procedures. For example, as seen above, community service orders were not available in all jurisdictions, forcing recourse to juvenile homes, which are not far removed from prison facilities in terms of lack of facilities, recreational and educational opportunities, harsh discipline and lack of freedom of movement. Thompson-Ahye complains, for example, that: '[t]he reality is that all of these [juvenile] institutions suffer from lack of resources of all kinds. They lack human resources in terms of quantity and quality; equipment, plant and machinery and tools . . . They lack basic toiletries . . . Some juveniles had no beds . . .'[117]

Where more rehabilitative forms of sentencing were available, they were often under-utilised. On the other hand, reports from the Family and Juvenile Courts suggest that in some cases, parents and guardians approached the court to put their children in these institutions, as they were unable to control them.[118]

Public perception

The public perception of juvenile offenders and other juveniles who appeared before Juvenile Courts, also helped to undermine the very aims of juvenile justice to prevent, protect and rehabilitate. Many of the UNICEF country studies noted that juvenile crime was perceived as a serious problem in society and the solution was seen to be harsh punishment.[119] In fact, juvenile detentions were on the increase. In Belize, for example, the number of juveniles currently serving time in prison has 'quadrupled

---

115   Antoine, R-M B, 'Juvenile Justice in Barbados, Country Report', UNICEF, 2000, Barbados.
116   See the Symposium Report, *above*, fn 113.
117   See Thompson-Ahye, H, 'Juvenile Justice in the Caribbean – Trinidad and Tobago, Country Report' 2000, UNICEF, Trinidad and Tobago, pp 47–48.
118   Symposium Report, *above*, fn 113.
119   See Cuffy, V, 'St Vincent Report on Juvenile Justice 2000, UNICEF, St Vincent', Antoine, *above*, fn 115.

within the last decade'.[120] However, it is unclear whether this was not partly due to the failure of preventative systems in the first place and the too ready resort to detention solutions such as juvenile institutions and prisons.

Dalphinis-King, speaking on juveniles, also notes that an 'examination of statistical data from the Family Court over the past nine years illustrates a growth of anti-social behaviours, particularly violent behaviours.'[121]

Juvenile delinquency – a legal and sociological concept

Since the juvenile justice system extends to juveniles who have not committed legal offences, the understanding of the term 'juvenile delinquency' is sometimes blurred. In strict legal terms, a juvenile delinquent is one who has committed a legal offence and is thus liable to punishment. However, since juveniles who are in need of care and protection also come before the court, there is a perception that such persons are also delinquents, particularly since they often end up in juvenile detention facilities due to inadequate foster care. Such a juvenile will become stigmatised as a juvenile delinquent. The notion of juvenile delinquency thus has both legal and sociological meanings.

Perhaps more alarming is the link that has been established between juveniles who are detained in juvenile homes and adult offences. Many juveniles who have spent time in these detention facilities find their way back into the justice system as adult offenders.[122] This includes not only repeat offenders, but also juveniles who were sent to 'stay' in these institutions when found in need of care and protection. The result is that the justice system not only fails such juveniles at the initial level but also has a negative influence on them.

Psychological and mental problems and the lack of remedial measures

One aspect of juvenile justice which is seldom raised is the link between juvenile deviancy and psychological factors. Information from juvenile institutions reveals that there is a noticeable prevalence of juveniles being sent to such institutions who may be described as academically sub-standard, mentally challenged and even suffering from forms of mental illness. Many children were actually undiagnosed dyslexics. These problems are thought to have directly impacted on their eventual delinquency or social deviancy.[123]

A UN study on disabilities seems to confirm this observation and may also help to explain the relatively higher number of boys than girls entering the justice system. The study reveals that 'significantly more boys were identified as disabled as compared to girls' and that the 'most common disability identified in the survey was

---

120   Hancok, F, 'Juvenile Justice in Belize, Country Report', 2000, UNICEF, Belize.
121   Rumelia Dalphinis-King, Director of the Family Court in St Lucia 'Family Court Perspective of Socialisation and Youth Crime', Paper presented to the First OECS Conference on Youth Crime and Violence, 11–12 October 2006.
122   See Symposium Report, *above*, fn 113.
123   Interviews with Dodds, the Barbados Reform School, as documented in the Barbados Country Report, Antoine, *above*, fn 115 reveal such relationships.

difficulty in learning.'[124] For these juveniles who are really persons with special needs, the juvenile system was totally inadequate.

A link between poor parenting, domestic violence and juvenile deviancy has also been identified. In St Lucia, for example, a study revealed that '15% of adolescent girls and 17% of boys reported being physically abused'.[125]

Constitutional issues

As noted above, in practice, juveniles in need of care or juveniles who commit status offences may be sent to juvenile institutions for prolonged periods. Constitutional implications arise from such situations. First, such juveniles have been deprived of their liberty and freedom of movement without due process, since they have not been charged with any crime and accorded a punishment of deprivation of their liberty under the law. This contravenes the various Constitutions. Juveniles who try to escape from those institutions can be sent to prison, thus compounding the injustice.

With respect to juveniles who were sent to reform schools because they committed crimes, one may ask whether the punishment fulfils constitutional requirements of proportionality. Such offenders may find that for relatively minor offences, they are deprived of their liberty and indeed, their education and other entitlements, for a very long time.

The very trial process may be questioned in relation to possible constitutional violations. Rights such as the right to be informed of the charge, not to be compelled to confess guilt, legal representation and other rights associated with the right to a fair trial are often compromised in juvenile trials. The 'Synthesis of Juvenile Studies Report', after examining several country studies on juvenile justice in the region noted that: 'as can be gleaned from the findings in the various country studies on juvenile justice is that ever single country fails in its duty to ensure due process to its juveniles and that the poor and the dispossessed . . . fare the worst.'[126] This is particularly the case as juvenile offenders (at least those who reach the courts), have been observed to fall most often in the lower income brackets of society and can ill afford adequate legal representation.

This violates both the spirit and letter of international guidelines and Conventions which require a rehabilitative rather than a punitive approach. They are also inherently discriminatory, as adults do not suffer the same fate except under archaic vagrancy laws against wandering, enacted during the slavery era.[127] On the other hand, it is incontestable that such care and protection provisions aim to be in the best interests of the child, albeit paternalistic. In developing countries without strong welfare policies and relatively high levels of poverty, there are few alternatives to care without a heavy-handed approach by the State.

---

124 Brain Toole, 'The Challenge of Children with Disabilities in the Caribbean.' Paper presented to the UNICEF Symposium: Rights of the Child and the Caribbean Experience, 15 March 2000, Barbados.

125 Dalphinis-King, *above*, fn 121 at p 4.

126 Thompson-Ahye, H (ed) 'Juvenile Justice in the Caribbean – A Rights Approach to Children in the Juvenile Justice System – Synthesis of Juvenile Justice Studies' UNICEF, 2000, Trinidad and Tobago, (the 'Synthesis Report'), p 23.

127 See, eg, Vagrancy Acts, discussed in Chapter 2 ('The Historical Function of Law in the West Indies – Creating a Future from a Troubled Past').

Due process and in particular, the right to a fair trial is also violated because of the lack of special child advocates for juvenile accused and the tendency of the courts to rely on probation officers who speak for juveniles. This prevented the full participation of the juveniles as required by Article 4 of the CRC.[128]

Ironically, a situation is created whereby juveniles accused of breaking the law may be afforded due process safeguards while those who have committed no offence have no such safeguard, precisely because they are not being tried for any offence.

Locating the juvenile

The different age groupings within the concept of a juvenile may also be problematic. Some juveniles below the age of 18 but above 16 years may fail to be protected adequately, or at all, by the system of juvenile justice. For example, in Barbados, as elsewhere, juveniles over the age of 16 are tried in ordinary courts and not Juvenile Courts as they are not covered under the provisions of the Juvenile Offenders Act except under s 3(2), where, in the opinion of the Juvenile Court, it serves justice to do so.

Most of the pertinent legal provisions on juvenile justice relate specifically to persons under 16 years. This includes, for example, special protections in trial proceedings, pre-trial publicity and confidentiality. Further, accommodation at juvenile institutions may be secured only to juveniles under the age of 16.

Perhaps more significant in the Caribbean, are social attitudes and perceptions as to who is really a juvenile deserving of protection. These social values and mores, often negative toward young persons, and sometimes children, are manifested in the treatment of our juveniles in the justice system.

Adequate facilities

The lack of suitable facilities at police stations often results in juveniles being kept in cells with adult offenders as there may be no separate remand facilities. This violates legislation, discussed above, which mandates that juveniles be kept separate from negative influences in such situations. It also offends rule 17 of the Riyadh Guidelines, which require that juveniles awaiting trial are to be presumed innocent and treated as such. The Guidelines also require that juveniles be given custodial sentences only as a last resort. Paradoxically, however, in the case of remands, this is often the first resort due to a lack of a separate care facility. Similarly, typically, there are no separate facilities for girls. Even more problematic are the lack of adequate foster facilities and the poor physical state of juvenile institutions. All of these problems, which can be traced to a lack of financial resources, have a significant impact on the system of juvenile justice.

Thompson-Ahye notes, for example, that in many of the States in the region: 'there are no remand facilities for juveniles who, if they are not freed on bail are remanded in police stations, where they "rest" on benches in full view of the general populace and adult detainees'.[129]

---

128   See Thompson-Ahye, H, Synthesis Report, *above*, fn 126, p 26.
129   This is the position, for example, in Anguilla, Antigua and Barbuda, St Vincent and Turks and Caicos Islands, above, Synthesis Report, *ibid*, p 32.

Class and gender concerns

Persons from lower income brackets and girls or young women also appear to suffer further injustices within the justice system. With respect to class differences, low income and poverty are seen to be particularly significant. Poverty as a catalyst for deviant or undesirable behaviour is reflected throughout the juvenile justice system. As early as 1877, the relationship between class or income and juvenile deviancy was observed. The youths coming into contact with the juvenile justice system were observed to be 'half-starved and uneducated . . . grew up stealing and begging . . . and eventually graduated to adult criminal activities.'[130] In fact, the need to curtail juvenile poverty and vagrancy was an important rationale in the establishment of the juvenile justice system in the Commonwealth Caribbean.

The correlation between poverty, class and juvenile justice is also exacerbated by the fact that legal aid is not usually efficient or even available, and richer juveniles are able to avoid punishment. Further, the negative perception attached to juveniles, particularly those from certain backgrounds, also impacts on whether alleged offenders even reach the courts, or when they do, the kind of sentence they would receive. Anecdotal evidence suggests that magistrates endeavour to avoid sending juveniles who belong to 'prestige' schools or to 'good homes' to Reform Schools, whereas the same concerns do not attach to less well-placed juveniles.[131]

Class overtones often spill over into the safeguards expected in the trial process. Apart from the legal aid issue, 'the public perception of due process and the juvenile is that the entitlement varies in direct relation to the class and status of the juvenile's family. To street children, due process is a pipe dream, to the children of the wealthy and prominent members of the society, if they are arrested at all, due process is their right and entitlement. Thus it sometimes happened that the children of the poor and dispossessed, may be assisting the police with enquiries . . . may be questioned in the absence of their parents, may be beaten into a confession and may have no access to legal representation . . .'[132]

In the case of girls, the link with poverty is often more acute. For example, girls are often more vulnerable than boys to social practices linked to sexual exploitation. Girls who are victims of such practices complain that they are treated worse than the adult offenders. In fact, adults associated with such practices are often not arrested whilst young girls are brought before the courts. Studies suggest that this is some-times due to the difficulty of gathering evidence. In some cases, parents are involved in these negative practices, either directly, or by using their children for financial gain in exchange for sexual favours, and refuse to testify.[133]

Similarly, a clear trend with distinct gender overtones may be discerned in relation to 'wandering' offences. In Barbados, for example, in 1990, there were 18 cases of wandering, while in 1995, this had increased to 36 cases. The term 'wandering' is really a euphemism for sexual offences in these cases, as the police explained that when they found girls cohabiting with adults or engaging in sexual offences, such as

---

130 The Report of the Committee on Poor Relief 1877, Barbados.
131 See Symposium Report, *above*, fn 113.
132 Synthesis Country Report, fn 126, p 24.
133 See Antoine, Barbados Country Report, 2002, *above*, fn 115 reporting on Police Interviews. This is corroborated by other Country Studies. See Symposium Report, *above*, fn 113.

prostitution, they would charge them with the lesser 'offence' of wandering, to protect them.[134]

Girls are often doubly discriminated against. On the one hand, they are more likely to be brought before the courts for sexual behaviour in instances when a boy would not. Further, once such sexual behaviour or potential behaviour is acknowledged by the justice system, they are stigmatised. More discriminatory treatment could be meted out in juvenile institution. For example, at Summervale, the Barbados institution for girls, there are stricter rules than for Dodds, the institution for males, because of a fear that the girls would 'get pregnant'.[135]

These myriad problems significantly affect the administration of justice to juveniles in the Commonwealth Caribbean, and the subject is ripe for reform.

THE GUN COURT

This court was established by the Gun Court Act in 1974 to deal with the offence of illegal possession of firearms and other offences involving a firearm where possession of the firearm by the accused was illegal. The court could sit in three divisions:

(a) a Resident Magistrates' division;

(b) a Full Court division (presided over by three resident magistrates); and

(c) a circuit court division presided over by a Supreme Court judge.

The Act also provided that all trials should be held in camera and that for certain specified offences, a mandatory sentence of detention with hard labour should be imposed, from which the detainee could be discharged only at the direction of the Governor General acting in accordance with the advice of a Review Board (a non-judicial body) established by the Act. In *Hindus v R*,[136] the Privy Council held that the Act was inconsistent with the Constitution of Jamaica to the extent that (a) it conferred jurisdiction on the Full Court division, to try offences which lie outside the jurisdiction of the lower judiciary in Jamaica, and (b) it provided for the determination of the sentence in an individual case by a non-judicial body. By the application of the doctrine of severance, however, the court survived with its two other jurisdictions.

As result of this decision, the Act was subsequently amended by the Gun Court (Amendment) Act of 1976. The Full Court division was replaced by a High Court division consisting of a Supreme Court judge sitting without a jury; and the provision allowing for discharge by the Review Board was replaced by compulsory sentence of imprisonment of hard labour for life.

---

134   Antoine, *ibid*, para 1.14.

135   Increases in the number of girls entering the juvenile justice system appear to be true for the entire region. See, eg, King, *above*, fn 121, p 9, noting the trend for St Lucia.

136   [1976] All ER 353.

REVENUE COURTS

Jamaica

A Revenue Court was established in 1972 to replace both the Income Tax Appeal Board and the jurisdiction of a judge in chambers to hear appeals from that Board. It is a Superior Court of Record which deals with questions relating to taxes, duties and other impositions due to the Government – a modern day Court of Exchequer.

Trinidad and Tobago

The Income Tax Appeal Board adjudicates on appeals from the Board of Inland Revenue. It consists of a Chairman, a Vice Chairman and such other members as may be appointed. Both the Chairman and Vice Chairman must be barristers at law of more than 10 years' standing, and the other members are chosen from among persons who are knowledgeable or experienced in law, commerce, finance, industry; accounting, taxation or the valuation of property.

All appeals against assessment are heard in camera unless the Board, on the application of the appellant, directs otherwise. Provision is made for the jurisdiction of the Board to be exercised by the Chairman or Vice Chairman and two other members, but this composition may be varied if the parties consent, or in matters of practice and procedure.

CHAPTER 19

THE JURY SYSTEM

THE NATURE AND COMPOSITION OF THE JURY

The jury system of a trial is an essential element of the democratic process. It attempts to secure fairness in the justice system. Traditionally, the jury system has been viewed as a cornerstone of the administration of justice under the common law tradition. However, the use of the system of trial by jury is on the decline. Today, its use differs, depending on whether (a) it is a civil or criminal matter, and (b) in criminal matters, whether it is a summary or an indictable offence.

The modern jury is composed of a maximum of 12 members. Typically, in murder and treason, the jury consists of 12 members, while in other criminal trials it may be nine.[1] In civil matters, the jury often consists of nine members.

Before this century, the jury system was widely believed to be one of the chief safeguards of rights against the abuse of judicial power. Trial by jury was felt to be an essential and inviolable right, a security blanket to ensure the liberties of citizens as against the State. As noted by Lord Camden:

> Trial by jury is indeed the foundation of our free Constitution; take that away and the whole fabric will soon moulder into dust.[2]

The notion of the jury system as an essential feature of the democratic process is not a contemporary one. Interestingly, the original jury were the King's judges, and there was no concept of the independence of the judiciary as we know it today.

Essentially, the jury's purpose is to be the sole judges of the facts as opposed to the law. In contemporary times, we believe that, to be judges of fact, one must come to the court ignorant of the facts. Impartiality in adjudicating is therefore based on ignorance of the facts. Strangely, however, the original method used by the ancient jury was just the opposite. Indeed, in Henry II's time, the jury were drawn from the persons in the neighbourhood who were taken to have knowledge of all the relevant facts. This concept, peculiar to modern minds, was later changed to that of:

> . . . a body whose duty is to hearken to the evidence and return a verdict accordingly, excluding from their minds all that they have not heard in open court.[3]

Thus, the ideal for the modern jury is complete obscurity. To this end, if any juror has knowledge of the facts, he must state this publicly. The need for impartiality is demonstrated in the case of *Howe v R*.[4] Here, one of the jurors had been present at a previous conviction of the accused. This was sufficient grounds to establish bias.[5]

---

1 See, eg, of the Jury Act 1990 of Grenada, s 21, which follows this format.
2 As quoted in Jackson, M, *The Machinery of Justice in England*, 7th edn, 1977, Cambridge: CUP.
3 Devlin, P (Sir), *Trial by Jury*, 1956, London; Stevens, p 2.
4 (1972) 19 WIR 517.
5 See, also, *R v Kray* (1969) 53 Cr App R 412 and *R v Liverpool City Justices ex p Topping* [1983] 1 WLR 119. See the discussion on the discharge of the jury and pre-trial publicity, *below*, p 380.

THE SPECIAL JURY

Apart from the common jury, outlined above, there is, in some Caribbean jurisdictions, such as Barbados, what is known as a 'special jury'.[6] This jury usually consists of persons with special qualifications, whether professional or trade, which relate to the matter being tried. The special jury may be used at the discretion of the judge for certain important or complicated civil cases where it is felt that specialised or technical knowledge on the part of jurors is essential for the efficient dispensing of justice.

In the case of the special jury system outlined above, strong reasons must be given before the court exercises its discretion. This was confirmed in the case of *Police Commissioner v Hinds*.[7] This is perhaps why it is seldom employed, although given the complex matters involving finance, telecommunications and the like, and given that judges may not have such expertise, the need for it may have increased.

The 'special jury' is not a modern invention. Of historical note are the special juries of medieval times, such as juries composed of the cooks and fishmongers who sat in respect of charges of selling bad food.[8]

THE RIGHT TO TRIAL BY JURY

Despite the importance of jury trials to the administration of justice and the democratic process, there is no right to trial by jury in all cases. In the Caribbean, as elsewhere, trial by jury seems to be diminishing in importance, at least for certain types of offences. There are several reasons for this decline. Two of the most important are the rapid growth in the volume of litigation and a general appreciation that juries are both unpredictable and fallible.

In determining whether trial by jury is available for an offence, the first important question is whether the offence is of a civil or criminal nature. If it is a criminal matter, it must then depend on whether it is a summary or indictable offence. As a general rule, trial by jury is only available for indictable offences.

The Bahamas and Bermuda are the only countries in the Commonwealth Caribbean which have enshrined a constitutional right to trial by jury. This is with respect to criminal cases triable in the Supreme Court.[9] This was discussed in *Commissioner of Police v Davis*.[10] The case concerned an attempt to try and punish drug-related offences through the magistrates' courts, but using penalties similar to those found in the Supreme Court. The court found that this was an unconstitutional attempt to oust trial by jury. It was seen in effect, as a transfer of the Superior Court's jurisdiction. In contrast, in *R v Stone*,[11] a case similar in substance to Davis, the Jamaica Court of Appeal disagreed that trial without a jury in the newly constituted gun court violated a constitutional right, as trial by jury in criminal cases was not expressly or impliedly

---

6 See, also, the Jury Act of Trinidad and Tobago (Chap 6:53) 1980 (rev), ss 8(1) and 29.
7 (1959) 2 WIR 305, Barbados.
8 See 'Ordinance of the Staples', 27 Edw 3, st 2, c 8 (1353) and 28 Edw 3, c 13 (1354).
9 Under the Constitution of the Bahamas, s 20(2)(g), and the Bermuda Constitution Order, s 6(2)(g).
10   (1993) 43 WIR 1.
11   (1977) 25 WIR 458.

entrenched in any of the provisions of the Constitution.[12] Trial by jury is also constitutionally protected in the USA.

Jury trials have undergone further scrutiny in the region. In *Re Eric Darien, A Juror*,[13] the applicant was summoned for jury service in the Jamaica Circuit Court. He asked to be excused from serving on the ground that his conscience did not permit him 'to take part in judging a person'. He was refused exemption on the basis that that was not a legitimate ground for exception under the Jury Law. He then contended that his objections fell within those provisions of the Constitution of Jamaica designed to protect him in the enjoyment of his freedom of conscience, and should be upheld on that ground.

The Supreme Court of Jamaica, while conceding that jury service may have been an abrogation of such a constitutional right, held that it fell within the accepted limitations for derogations from constitutional rights in Jamaica, that is, it was 'reasonably required in the interests of public order' and 'for the purpose of protecting the rights and freedoms of others'.[14] This was because trial by jury was an 'essential part of the law administered' in the circuit courts of Jamaica. Somewhat paradoxically, therefore, while trial by jury may not be a constitutional right, it is sufficiently important to dislocate constitutional rights.

CIVIL TRIALS

Trial by jury in civil cases appears to be declining more rapidly than in criminal cases. However, although seldom used, the jury is still available in Caribbean territories for civil cases. The exceptions are in St Lucia and Guyana. There is also an alternative to the civil jury in the form of trial in the Supreme Court. Trials by jury in civil cases, except for those of a specified nature, such as defamation or fraud, are within the discretion of the judge if good cause is shown.[15]

The status of trial by jury in civil matters was discussed in *Miller v Dunkley*,[16] where a full court in Jamaica held that, where a statute does not prescribe any definite mode of trial, there is no right to trial by jury in civil matters. Further, in *Boos v Ambard*,[17] it was held that the grant of a jury in civil matters lay entirely within the jurisdiction of the judge where statute is silent. Typically, the rules of court are that civil trials are by a judge only unless the party applying for a jury can show sufficient cause why there should be a jury trial. This was outlined in the case of *Morales v Morales*.[18]

---

12 The constitutional status of the gun court was itself the subject of constitutional litigation in the famous case of *Hinds v R* [1976] 1 All ER 353; [1976] 2 WLR 366.
13 (1974) 22 WIR 323.
14 *Ibid*, p 326. See the Constitution, s 21(1) and 21(6).
15 See, eg, the Jury Act of Grenada, s 242. Trial by jury in civil trials is abolished, except in exceptional circumstances by discretion of the judge.
16 [1933] 1 JLR 8.
17 (1915) 2 Trin LR 327.
18 (1962) 5 WIR 235, Trinidad.

THE ELECTION TO SUMMARY TRIAL

Even for indictable offences, there has been a growing tendency to allow an alternative to jury trial. This is achieved by allowing certain indictable offences to be tried before inferior courts and widening the jurisdiction of such courts by extending the number of summary offences to be tried there, sometimes called 'hybrid offences', discussed in Chapter 15 ('The Court System of the Commonwealth Caribbean'). This latter method logically results in a diminution of jury trials.

The first attempt to interfere with the jurisdiction of inferior courts with regard to trials by jury was in Guyana. There, in certain cases, the accused may elect to be tried by jury upon indictment, or by the district court under summary jurisdiction. These provisions relate to offences not punishable by death or terms exceeding seven years.[19]

This experiment sparked off a growing trend in Caribbean jurisdictions. The fact that non-jury trials attract a lighter sentence perhaps explains the preference for the choice against jury trial in such situations. Yet there are those, for reasons to be discussed further in this chapter, who will prefer to take their 'chances' with what they perceive as a sympathetic jury.

THE REPRESENTATIVE NATURE OF THE JURY

The juror in the common jury can be viewed as the epitome of the reasonable man, the man on Broad Street, Frederick Street, or in Half-Way Tree.[20] This is founded on the democratic principles that a person is to be judged by his or her own peers and that ordinary citizens should play a part in the administration of justice. Ironically, however, few of the above may actually qualify for jury service, and the ideal is often different from reality. The functions, composition and role of the jury are spelt out under statute. They are substantially similar within the Commonwealth Caribbean.

In earlier times, in order to have qualified for jury service, the citizen had to be a property holder. It was felt that such a person would be less susceptible to corruption and more easily punishable by fine. Nowadays, however, the qualifications for jurors relate mainly to income brackets. As a general rule, the law seeks to choose jurors representative of the middle, perhaps lower middle class of society. As such, job specifications and educational requirements are specified. Legislation prescribes the qualifications to be met before one can serve on a jury. In Barbados, under the Juries Act,[21] to qualify for jury service a person must be between 18 and 60 years, a citizen, and literate. He or she should also meet the income or property requirements set out in the Act.[22]

Statute also provides for the disqualification of persons from jury service. For example, s 5 of the Barbados Juries Act states that persons convicted of any misdemeanour or felony in respect of which they have been sentenced to imprisonment

---

19 See the Jury Act of Guyana.
20 These are all names of well known streets and places in the Caribbean.
21 Cap 115B.
22 See, also, the Juries Act 1989 of Antigua and Barbuda; the Juries Act 1988 of the Bahamas; the Jury Act, Cap 151 of Grenada; the Jury Act 1973 of Jamaica; the Criminal Code, revised (1992) Part III, Arts 786–841 of St Lucia and the Jury Act, Cap 211, revised laws 1990 of St Vincent.

are disqualified. So, too, are the illiterate and persons who are deaf, blind, bankrupt, or of unsound mind. The above provisions are fairly typical of the region. Further, in the Commonwealth Caribbean, there are wide scale exemptions allowed for jury service. Such exemptions include public officers, doctors, clergymen, lawyers, schoolmasters and persons employed in essential services. Even businessmen who can make a good case for exemption can be excused from jury service. This leads to the criticism that only a narrow group of people actually sit on the jury. This may have significant implications for the impartiality and efficiency of trial by jury, discussed below, p 386.

CHALLENGES TO THE JURY

To attain the ideals of representativeness, objectivity and impartiality in jury trials, there is a process known as challenging the jury. In this process, if it is believed that a particular juror is biased in any way, either through intimate knowledge of the circumstances of the case, or prejudice, he may be challenged and asked to step down if the challenge is found by the court to be justified.[23]

There are two types of challenge to the jury, 'challenge for cause' and 'peremptory challenge'. A reason for the challenge is not necessary when the right to peremptory challenge is being exercised, but a good reason, such as suspicion of bias, must be advanced before one may challenge or question a juror for cause. A limited number of peremptory challenges is allowed for each matter. The conditions for challenging jury selection are expressed under statute. Legislation also makes provision for the numerical limit for peremptory challenges. For example, under s 28 of the Juries Act 1989 of Barbados, a person may object by way of peremptory challenge to not more than seven persons selected. By amendment, the Jury Act of Trinidad and Tobago now permits peremptory challenges on a number of specified grounds, including the situations where a juror has been sentenced to death or imprisonment, is an alien or has no knowledge of the English language.[24] The judge has a discretion either on his own or on application from counsel to order that the jury be composed of men or women only.[25]

A juror may also be challenged for cause. This is a challenge without numerical restriction on the part of either the defence or prosecution, alleging some good reason why the juror should not be empanelled. Common reasons are bias on grounds of knowledge of the defendant, some other involvement with the case, or prejudice such as race or pre-trial publicity. The judge must then decide whether to allow the challenge. In *R v Kray*,[26] the notorious murderers, the Kray brothers, were on trial. Because of the widespread publicity afforded this case, challenges for cause were successfully made on the ground of pre-trial publicity.[27]

While courts appear willing to allow challenges on grounds of publicity or bias in the interest of impartiality, they appear less willing to allow challenges to protect the

---

23 See the Juries Act 1989 of Barbados, s 25.
24 See the Jury (Amendment) Act 1996 of Trinidad and Tobago.
25 See the Barbados Juries Act 1989, s 26. But see the discussion on 'Gender Equality and the Jury' below.
26 (1969) 53 Cr App R 412.
27 See the discussion on pre-trial publicity and jury impartiality below, p 398.

notion of the representativeness of the jury. This is a live issue in multiracial societies such as those in the Commonwealth Caribbean and the USA. It has been argued, for example, that a jury should reflect the racial type of the accused. Such a composition, apart from ensuring a more equitable representation, may alleviate perceived problems of racial bias towards an accused. A similar argument may be made on the basis of gender. These arguments have not, however, been very successful in the region, perhaps because Caribbean jurisprudence relies heavily on English case law which has not yet fully accepted such propositions. For example, in *R v Broderick*,[28] a request for an all black jury in Britain in a case concerning a black accused person was refused. Race here was not seen as a legitimate reason for a challenge for cause.[29]

A note of caution of a pragmatic nature is warranted here. In the Commonwealth Caribbean, jury selection based on race may be justifiable due to the cosmopolitan nature of the various societies. However, coupled with the wide exemptions for jury service, such a criterion for jury selection will reduce even more the numbers of persons available as jurors. This will further undermine the representative nature of the jury. Does challenge on the basis of race or other such criteria make a nonsense of jury selection? We will return to this question later in the chapter.

DISCHARGING THE JURY

The discharge of the jury or individual jurors is another mechanism to protect the impartiality of the jury process. An inefficient, non-representative or biased juror may not be identified in the challenge process. In general, a juror may be discharged if he commits some irregularity which may prejudice the fairness of the trial.

It is within the discretion of the judge to decide whether a juror's misconduct, irregular behaviour or circumstance sufficiently prejudices the trial enough to discharge him. Every accused in the Commonwealth Caribbean has a constitutional right to a fair trial. Discharging jurors or juries who may prejudice that trial is in keeping with this principle.

It is important to note that the discretion given to a judge, to decide whether prejudice has occurred sufficient to discharge a juror, is wide. In many cases a judge may decide that although an irregularity has occurred, it is not serious enough to warrant a discharge, or, further, a new trial. This is illustrated in *Gibson v R*.[30] Here, after the commencement of a murder trial, the court discovered that one of the jurors was the brother of the deceased. The juror was immediately discharged and the trial heard by the remaining 11 jurors. On being found guilty, the accused appealed on the ground that, as the juror who was discharged sat together with the rest of the jurors, he had the opportunity to influence them, thus laying the grounds for bias. The court held that a fundamental principle was raised, ie, that justice must not only be done but must be seen to be done. However, in this instance, the court did not find that the right to a fair trial had been prejudiced.

---

28 [1970] Crim LR 155.
29 We can contrast this with the now infamous murder trial of OJ Simpson in the USA, where race was the main ground for successful juror challenges, a factor which caused a substantial delay in the trial.
30 (1963) 5 WIR 450.

A leading case is *R v Spencer*.[31] This case concerns a popular ground for discharge, that is, where a juror discusses the case with someone else, or, more seriously, with a witness. The case concerned alleged mistreatment of mental patients. The juror was found to have a wife who worked at a mental hospital. He discussed the case with his wife. The judge then warned him not to discuss it further with the other jurors, but he did. The juror was discharged as the court found that there was a real risk of prejudice.

The judge must hold a proper inquiry where such contamination of the case has been alleged. In *Papan v The State*,[32] the father of the deceased in a murder case had a conversation with the jury foreman. The judge inquired into the matter but did not dismiss the juror or the jury. However, he made no findings or written notes. The juror admitted that he knew the deceased's father and frequently had coffee with him. In the absence of information due to the lack of notes, the Privy Council decided to remit the matter to the Court of Appeal.

Nevertheless, not every case of a juror discussing the case with someone else will amount to a discharge. In *Chaitlal v The State*,[33] for example, a Trinidad case, a juror was allegedly seen speaking during the break. The judge invited counsel to his chambers and conducted an inquiry into the occurrence. He decided that the evidence was not sufficiently credible to raise the possibility of a miscarriage of justice. The court held that the fact that one of the jurors had held a conversation with a witness was not itself fatal to the trial, once the judge had investigated the possibility of a miscarriage and had in his discretion decided. The juror was not discharged.

Similar circumstances occurred in *R v Sawyer*.[34] Again, the question was whether there was any real danger to the fairness of the trial. The court disagreed with counsel for the defence: that the mere fact of speaking to a witness could influence a juror, who is presumed to be a reasonable man:

> It seems to us that that is not crediting the jury with any wisdom at all. It is unbelievable that the mere exchange of words 'Good morning' or 'I am having my breakfast' could in any way influence the jury.

Indeed, it was just such an innocuous remark which formed the basis of the complaint in *Jordan v R*,[35] where a juror was overheard describing counsel as 'slow and boring'. This was not sufficient for a discharge as it did not speak to the merits or final outcome of the trial and therefore did not constitute prejudice.

The case of *R v Stewart, Cunha, Burges and Donegan*[36] formulated the broad principle in this way:

> A juror will be discharged . . . if there is a reasonable concern that he might be biased . . . by a personal relationship or acquaintance with a defendant or other person whose actions are significant to the trial . . . There need not be a firm basis for the conclusion that the juror might be biased in favour of the interests of his acquaintance. Circumstances imposing pressure on him to become predisposed against his acquaintance or placing him in a general quandary threatening his impartiality will suffice.[37]

---

31   [1986] 3 WLR 348.
32   (1999) 54 WIR 451 (PC, Trinidad and Tobago).
33   (1985) 39 WIR 295.
34   (1980) 71 Cr App R 28.
35   Civ App No 321 of 1996, dec'd August 2000 (CA, Barbados).
36   [2002] CILR 18.
37   *Ibid.*

Where a juror merely has moral or other qualms about the nature of a sentence, this is not a sufficient ground for discharge. In *Hinds (Rodney) v R*,[38] the judge asked the jurors in a murder case whether any of them would feel 'too uncomfortable' trying a murder case, since a guilty verdict would mean capital punishment.

DISCHARGE OF THE ENTIRE JURY

In certain cases, on the grounds of pre-trial prejudice, such as where there has been widespread publicity of a case, an entire jury may be prevented from hearing the trial. This is in the situation where the court finds that the minds of the jury have been so prejudiced against an accused as to prevent them from coming to an impartial decision. Where this occurs, the trial may even be moved to another town or city in an attempt to overcome this prejudice.

This practice is in keeping with the fundamental right entranched in Caribbean Constitutions of a right to a fair trial. The difficulties inherent in the practice of relocating juries in small jurisdictions such as the Caribbean are, however, to be noted.

The jury should also be discharged if their impartiality has been compromised during the trial. An extreme case of this is seen in *Arthurton v R*.[39] In this case, the jury had been exposed to a witness statement that the accused, on trial for unlawful sexual intercourse, had been charged for a similar offence. The judge did not discharge the jury and merely told them to remove the disclosure from their minds. The Court of Appeal quashed the conviction. While reiterating that the decision to discharge a jury was a discretion given to the trial judge which an appellate court would not lightly interfere with, the information disclosed was so prejudicial as to make the trial unfair.

Where a jury fails to reach a unanimous or majority verdict as required by law, they may also be discharged. While a judge has a wide discretion to discharge jurors, he cannot do so arbitrarily or for trivial reasons. An example of this is seen in *Abdool Salim Yaseen and Thomas v The State*.[40] The trial judge in this case discharged several jurors merely because they said that they did not want to be 'kept together for the duration of the trial'. The Court of Appeal found that although the Jury Act states that a judge may discharge or excuse 'for any reason which it deems sufficient', there must be a good reason. Good reasons may have been a pressing business commitment or poor health. In this instance, there had been an 'arbitrary exercise of the judge's discretion'. This amounted to 'much more than an irregularity. For wholly insufficient reasons he deprived the appellants of the services of persons who were selected according to law and whom they may have wished to have sit in their own cause'.[41] Accordingly, a re-trial was ordered.

Where a juror dies or becomes incapable of serving, it is not necessary to discharge the entire jury or replace that juror and the verdict may proceed.[42]

---

38   (1999) 58 WIR 38 (CA, Barbados).
39   [2005] I LRC 210 (Privy Council, BVI).
40   (1990) 44 WIR 219.
41   *Ibid*, p 229.
42   *Spence (Newton) v R* (1999) 59 WIR 216.

Jury confidentiality

Every attempt is made to protect the confidentiality of the jury process. We see this in the way in which juries are kept separate and cloistered and are prevented from speaking to others about the trial. Even after the trial is over, the jury's deliberations are to be kept confidential. A breach of this may result in a contempt of court action. This was confirmed in *AG v Scotcher*,[43] where even a desire by a former juror to prevent a miscarriage of justice was not sufficient to undermine this duty of confidentiality. A door was opened in *Re Nanan*,[44] when the Privy Council said:

> It is, of course, entirely consistent with this principle that evidence may be given that the verdict was not pronounced in the sight and hearing of one or more members of the jury, who did not in fact agree with that verdict, or who may not have done so... In such a case, the confidence of the jury room can be breached in so far as a juryman, outside whose sight and hearing the verdict was pronounced, may give evidence whether he did or did not agree with that verdict.

SIZE OF THE JURY

There is no special size for a jury nor for the number of jurors required to constitute a legitimate verdict. However, for capital offences, the number is usually 12 jurors. For non-capital offences, the magic number of 12 is often dispensed with and a lower number, such as nine, may be acceptable. The St Vincent legislation gives an illustration: By ss 12 and 13 of the Jury Ordinance 1938, provision is made for different modes of trial by jury for capital and non-capital offences:

> **12.** A jury in a criminal trial other than for a capital offence shall consist of nine persons to be selected by ballot.
>
> **13.** A jury in a criminal trial for a capital offence shall consist of twelve persons to be selected by ballot.

EXAMINING THE MERITS OF TRIAL BY JURY

The efficiency and desirability of trial by jury is an ongoing debate. Several criticisms may be levelled appropriately at the system of trial by jury, no doubt lending support to its decline. In this section we will examine the most important of these and weigh them against the advantages of the system.

Perhaps the most popular criticism made against the jury is the accusation that their verdicts often run counter to the evidence presented in court. Deosaran sees this as one of the most crucial issues facing the jury system in the Commonwealth Caribbean. He identifies a tension area between strict areas of law on one hand and jury 'common sense' or 'compassion' on the other.[45]

Several reasons may be advanced for the apparent inconsistency between the verdict and the evidence – Chief of these is the extent to which a jury is able to follow a

---

43 [2005] 1 WLR 1867 (HL).
44 (1986) 35 WIR 358 (Privy Council, Trinidad and Tobago) at 367.
45 Deosaran, R, *Trial by Jury – A Case Study*, 1980, Trinidad and Tobago: ISER, UWI.

judge's instructions. It should be recalled that the jury's function is to arbitrate on the facts and not the law. The point of departure is the judge's instructions. It is there that the judge directs where matters of fact are to be separated from matters of law, and where the substantive areas for jury deliberations are identified. If the jury is unable to appreciate these sometimes esoteric distinctions, the jury process is corrupted. If the judge misdirects the jury as to its areas for consideration, the process is similarly flawed.

Determining the difference between fact and law

The jury system expects that the jury verdict would reflect appropriate judicial direction. However, it is often difficult to distinguish between fact and law. The legal system, in effect, gives to the jury the power, if not the right, in reaching its verdict, to refuse the substantive rules of law given to it by the judge. This explains supposedly erroneous verdicts. One good example of the difficulty in separating fact from law occurred in *Sookram v R*.[46] The defendant was charged with wounding with intent. He attempted to establish a plea of self-defence. The trial judge left it up to the jury to decide whether the issue of self-defence arose. On appeal, this was held to be a misdirection, an erosion of the judicial function. The court held that the question whether there is sufficient evidence to raise or support an issue of self-defence is within the province of the judge to decide. This was not a question to be left to the jury. It was a question of law which was part of the judicial function.

In contrast, the question whether, on the facts, the defendant had acted in self-defence was for the jury to decide. Here, there was a thin line between the question of law and the question of fact. A close examination of the trial judge's words reveals the difficulty:

> You will have to examine the evidence very carefully to see if you can find self-defence *raised* in the defence. If you find that you must consider the question of self-defence, then I will give you certain directions. I will give you directions on the law relating to self-defence, that is, if you are going to consider self-defence. That is a matter entirely for you [emphasis added].[47]

The court found that the trial judge's approach was totally wrong and could cause a serious upset in the process of proper adjudication if adopted. What issues are fit to be left for the jury's consideration is a matter of law for the judge to determine. How those issues should be decided is for the jury. It is part of the judicial function to instruct on the capacity of the evidence to lead to a particular conclusion. After this direction, the factual evaluation of the evidence falls within the province of the jury.

Incompetence and ignorance

Other factors may explain the apparent conflict between verdict and evidence. A popular complaint is the alleged incompetence and even ignorance of jurors. The case of *Nanan v The State* emanating from Trinidad and Tobago is perhaps not typical, but

---

46   (1971) 18 WIR 195.
47   *Ibid*, p. 209.

is nevertheless instructive. In that case, after a unanimous verdict of 'guilty' in a trial for murder, four members of the jury swore on affidavit that the verdict was not unanimous since the foreman had not known the meaning of the word. Consequently, he had erroneously informed them that a majority verdict was what was required.[48]

Indeed, we could argue that illiteracy and low educational levels are major obstacles to the proper functioning of the jury system in the Commonwealth Caribbean. Perhaps a minimum educational standard for the juror is necessary to be an efficient representative of the reasonable man. To substantiate this, in a study done in Trinidad and Tobago, one lawyer's response was:

> Today's requirements of re-sifting of evidence, understanding of directions and summing up, demand much more than mere literacy.[49]

Another response went even further:

> In modern times, the literate juror has to cope with matters which have political and social overtones and are not easily divorced from right and wrong.[50]

Those who emphasise educational criteria believe that adjudicators of facts need formal education to be efficient. In addition, the ideal modern juror requires much more than basic literacy and even common sense. It is to be noted that common sense has traditionally been felt to be the fundamental tool of the juror.

Certainly, the jury function requires its members to wade through complicated, detailed facts and law and rely on overall impressions. They must weigh the evidence after long periods without the benefits of taking notes, as does a judge. Although they are allowed to question witnesses, they seldom do so. It is therefore unsurprising, especially in complex cases, or where, for example, there is more than one issue involved, or more than one defendant, that the jury's task is burdensome and difficult.

Oppenheimer argues:

> We commonly strive to assemble 12 persons colossally ignorant of all practical matters, fill their vacuous heads with law which they cannot comprehend, obfuscate their seldom intellects with testimony which they are incompetent to analyse or unable to remember, permit partisan lawyers to bewilder them with their meaningless sophistry, then lock them up until the most obstinate of their numbers coerce the others into submission or drive them into open revolt.[51]

Still, the fact that judges, lawyers or even the public at large may disagree with the verdict of a jury is not of itself an indication that the verdict is not properly based on the evidence. Assessments of credibility and the drawing of inferences from proven facts are areas in which there is much room for honest differences of opinion.[52]

---

48   [1986] 35 WIR 358 (PC, Trinidad and Tobago).
49   *Op cit*, Deosaran, fn 45.
50   *Ibid.*
51   Oppenheimer, P, 'Trial by jury' (1937) 11 Cincinnati ULR 142.
52   See Georges J, 'Is the jury trial an essential cornerstone of justice?', in Proceedings and Papers of the Seventh Commonwealth Law Conference, 1985, Hong Kong, p 33.

Perception and emotional considerations

Jurors are also accused of being too easily swayed by sympathy rather than the hard facts of the evidence. Feelings of compassion for the prisoner or of repugnance to the punishment which the law awards may overpower their sense of duty. On the other hand, Baldwin and McConville believe that sympathy may be destructive in the opposite way, in that a jury 'will on other occasions wrongly convict for those same reasons of compassion, and repugnance'.[53]

Juries may also ignore evidence on grounds of conscience, or in special circumstances. An example may be where there is evidence of hostility towards the police by an accused and the jury believes that the police generally engage in police brutality. This tradition of 'jury sovereignty' may be criticised as leading to an unfair lack of uniformity in decisions and to an unpredictability in the law, since 'jury law' will change from case to case and from jury to jury. It is unlike the certainty of a judicial precedent which is followed on points of legal principle.

Further, certain sensitive issues may have an emotional effect on jurors, bringing to the fore certain prejudices or strong feelings. Common examples cited are women jurors in rape or obscenity cases, or male jurors in homosexual cases. In such situations, jurors may lack the objectivity of a seasoned professional. In societies where there is a strong sense of community norms such as exist in the Caribbean, these problems may be exacerbated.

In addition, the logical result of the wide exemptions to jury service, coupled with a general reluctance to serve on juries, has led to a shortage of jurors in some jurisdictions, notably Trinidad and Tobago.

Perhaps one of the more important criticisms against the system is that members of the legal profession appear to hold it in low esteem. This can undermine confidence in the ability of the legal system to deliver justice. One study illustrates that as a high a proportion as 84% of the members of the legal profession expressed dissatisfaction with the way the system operates in Trinidad and Tobago.[54] This is a view that is echoed in jurisdictions outside the region.

PROBLEMS WITH THE REPRESENTATIVENESS OF THE JURY

Criticism can also be levelled at the composition of the jury in several respects. Often, the jury is not as representative of the society as is desired. The very selection process of the system comes into question in this regard. First, the wide exemptions allowed under the system mean that there is an even narrower margin for choosing one's peers and attaining a representative ideal. Indeed, after such wide exemptions, one may well wonder how much choice is left? This is particularly true in small, multicultural societies such as those in the Commonwealth Caribbean.

Inequality as regards the composition of the jury defeats the ideal of peerage and representative justice, since one of the fundamental concepts of trial by jury, that is, that a man should be judged by his peers, is undermined, as the choice for the selection of jurors is limited.

---

53   Baldwin, J and McCorville, M, 'Jury, foreman and verdicts' [1980] Journal of Criminology 352.
54   *Op cit*, Deosaran, fn 45.

Yet, the answer to the question of who are our peers may be difficult. As seen above, jury qualifications militate that it is basically a lower-middle income person who will serve on the jury. Indeed, Lord Devlin complains that jurors are 'predominantly male, middle aged, middle minded and middle class'.[55]

The experience in the Commonwealth Caribbean has been that jurors often come from a lower income bracket than that of their English counterparts. This is due partly to the early abolition of property qualifications. Yet the problem still remains. It is still a fairly uniform class of persons who will represent the system. This uniform class may seldom be representative of the accused.

However, Devlin's complaint about the character of the jury is not shared universally. For example, Georges, speaking on the Caribbean, argues that the jury should indeed represent a 'broadly based middle class sense of values generally accepted in the community'.[56] Still, in the heterogeneous societies that form the Caribbean, with their multiracial and varying cultural groupings, it is questionable whether such generally acceptable values may be achieved within the jury system. Differing cultural values as exist in the Caribbean may undermine the representativeness and even the impartiality of the jury system. At minimum, there must be a broad bedrock of shared beliefs for the jury to function efficiently.

QUESTIONS OF RACE AND ETHNICITY

As we saw earlier, race is not as yet an acceptable criterion for jury selection. Indeed, the question whether race is an important variable in the jury process is a controversial one. Should the composition of the jury be based on ethnicity in multiracial societies; black jurors for black accused, Indians for Indians, Chinese for Chinese, etc? Much has been written concerning this issue as it relates to jury trials in the USA, particularly in relation to black persons. Those who advocate a racially stratified jury argue that certain accused are not able to obtain real justice because of the racial prejudice of jurors of different ethnic backgrounds.[57] Deosaran, in his study on Trinidad and Tobago, notes that:

> Trinidad and Tobago, like many parts of the Caribbean, is a multiracial country and as such the variable of physical appearance, be it through physiognomy or culture, becomes quite relevant.[58]

Several studies have shown that ethnic minorities tend to be more easily convicted by juries. This is a problem, for example, for young, black males in countries where they are minorities.[59] The problem of racial stereotyping is therefore a real one for trials by jury. We are not free of the problem of racial stereotyping in our multiethnic 'rainbow' societies of the Caribbean.[60] Only limited research has been done on this particular

---

55 *Op cit*, Devlin, fn 3, p 20.

56 *Op cit*, Georges, fn 52.

57 See Alker, HR and Bernard, J, 'Procedural and social biases in the jury selection process' (1978) (3) The Justice System Journal 220.

58 *Op cit*, Deosaran, fn 45, p 8. Recall, also, the case of *R v Broderick*, concerning the desire for an all black jury, discussed above, p 277.

59 See, eg, Mills, CJ and Bohannon, WE, 'Character and jury behaviour: conceptual and applied implications' [1980] J of Personality and Social Psychology 25. Dashwood, A, 'Juries in a multiracial society' [1972] Crim LR 85.

60 This is the description given to Trinidad and Tobago by Bishop Tutu of South Africa on his historic visit in 1993.

issue.[61] Nevertheless, the few studies carried out point to potential problems of racial conflict. In addition, comprehensive studies done on race and politics and other social relations add to the evidence that there is a possible problem.[62]

How in the region should we deal with the problem of race? Should we, as happened in the *OJ Simpson* case, attempt to ensure a certain racial format in the jury?

There is historical justification for juries tailored to address possible prejudices against minority groups. For example, in medieval times, juries were chosen from among resident aliens where an alien was on trial. These were the juries *de medietate linguae*, which consisted of half of the numbers from foreign communities and half of Englishmen.[63] Interestingly, Caribbean statutes still make reference to such juries.[64]

Nonetheless, distinguished jurists in the Commonwealth Caribbean have expressed reservations as to whether the jury in the region is in any way less effective for the purpose which it is intended to serve because it is not an accurate sample of the community from which it is drawn.[65]

GENDER EQUALITY

Gender inequality as regards the composition of the jury also defeats the notion of peerage and representative injuries. Studies show that women jurors are underrepresented in the Caribbean.[66] This finding is compatible with those done in the USA, where it was found that the young, the old and black males were seriously underrepresented and that women were generally underrepresented.[67]

In a path breaking case from Gibraltar, a jurisdiction which also utilises the Privy Council as a final court, thereby making the decision in effect, binding on Privy Council jurisdictions in the region, the issue of gender was successfully raised as a constitutional challenge to jury trials. In *Rojas v Berllaque (AG Intervening)*,[68] the Privy Council declared a practice under the Supreme Court Ordinance of Gibraltar which regulated the eligibility of men and women for jury service, to be in violation of the right to a fair trial. Although jurors were chosen at random from a jury list, in practice, juries were all male because men and women were treated differently in the compilation of the jury list. Subject to exemptions, all men between 18 and 65 were liable to compulsory jury service but, while women were liable to jury service, it was not compulsory for them.[69]

---

61   See, eg, Deosaran, R, 'The jury system in a post-colonial multi-racial society – problems of bias' (1981) 21 Br Jr of Criminology 305.

62   Ryan, S, *Race and Nationalism in Trinidad and Tobago – A Study of Decolonisation in a Multi-Racial Society*, 1974, Mona: ISER, UWI. See, also, La Guerre, T, 'Race and colour' [1974] Caribbean Issues 1 and Malik, YK, *East Indians in Trinidad*, 1971, London: OUP.

63   See 'Ordinance of the Staples', 27 Edw 3, st 2, c 8 (1353) and 28 Edw 3, c 13 (1354).

64   Note, eg, s 44 of the Jury Act 1992 (rev) of Antigua and Barbuda, which states 'no alien shall be entitled to be tried by jury *de medietate linguae*, but every alien shall be triable by jury empanelled and sworn under this Act, in the same manner as if he were a citizen of Antigua and Barbuda'.

65   *Op cit*, Georges, fn 52, p 31.

66   *Op cit*, Deosaran, fn 61.

67   See, eg: Zeisel, H, 'Dr Spock and the case of the vanishing women jurors', 1986, Centre for the Study of Criminal Justice, Chicago; and *op cit*, Alker and Bernard, fn 57.

68   [2004] 1 LRC 296 (PC, Gibraltar).

69   Section 19(2) of the Supreme Court Ordinance of Gibraltar.

In practice, few women volunteered, rendering the jury practically all male, as there were approximately 6,000 men on the jury list and only approximately 25 women. The Privy Council agreed that where a jury mode of trial was in place, the method by which the jury was selected had to be one which accorded citizens a fair trial. A non-discriminatory method of compilation of the jury lists was an essential ingredient of a fair trial by jury, a principle inherent in the concept of a fair trial by an impartial jury. Such fairness was achieved in the composition of a jury by random selection. Where the list was compiled on a basis, without objective justification, which excluded virtually half of the otherwise eligible population, this was an unfairly constituted list which did not satisfy the constitutional requirement of a fair trial by an independent and impartial court.

This far-reaching judgment paves the way for challenges to be made on the basis of other discriminatory criteria to juries which follow a certain pattern in relation to their makeup, whether in terms of ethnicity, religion and so on. The judgment is sensitive to principles found in anti-discriminatory law, where *de facto* situations, such as a pattern of conduct, can constitute discrimination if a category of discrimination can be identified.[70]

The judgment thus relaxes the approach to jury challenges on the basis of gender, race and other such criteria and may ground further developments in this area.

MISDIRECTIONS TO THE JURY – PROCEDURAL IRREGULARITIES

Not all irregularities in a trial are the fault of the jury. Often, it is the judge's mistake. He may, for example, misdirect the jury. Yet even here, we see that the jury's ignorance of the law places a greater burden on the judge and the trial to avoid a miscarriage of justice.

There are instances where a verdict will be overturned and a new trial ordered. When this happens we can see that the system is protecting the integrity of jury trial by compelling the court to allow the jury and not the judge to be the deciders of the facts.

There are several categories of misdirections and improper instructions or influences which come from a judge and which can have the effect of a mistrial.[71]

(a) The judge may make inappropriate comments which can influence the jury during the trial. For example, he may be antagonistic to counsel and unduly criticise him.

(b) The judge may also inadvertently or deliberately seek to influence the jury in his summing up. For example, he may seem to point the verdict in a particular direction.

(c) The judge may mistakenly leave an issue of law for the jury to decide, as we saw in *Sookram*,[72] or fail to leave a question of fact for the jury to decide.

---

70   See, eg, *Re Bilka Kaufhaus* [1986] IRLR 317.
71   Given the high number of cases dealing with misdirections by judges to the jury, some thought should be given to specialist training for judges similar to what obtains under the civil law tradition.
72   (1971) 18 WIR 195.

(d) More commonly than is believed, the judge may misrepresent the status of the law when attempting to guide the jury on a question of law.

The following examples illustrate these various defects in judges' directions. In *Seneviratne v R*,[73] a case from Ceylon, the appellant was charged with murder of his wife. From the evidence, it was unclear whether it could be suicide, and the medical experts could not agree on the point. In his direction, the judge said:

> He [the appellant] has got to explain . . . In the absence of explanation, the only inference is that he is guilty . . .[74]

On appeal, it was found that the judge had misdirected the jury as to the status of law. In law, in a criminal prosecution, the onus of proof is upon the prosecution. There is no obligation placed upon an accused to prove facts, especially within his own knowledge, as the judge seemed to suggest.

The case of *Berry Linton v R*[75] provides another example of a misdirection of the status of the law. This was a murder case where the defence was accident. There were many discrepancies in the evidence. The judge, in summing up, failed to point out to the jury that the appellant's good character was primarily relevant to the question of his credibility. The conviction was quashed and a new trial ordered. This was on the basis that it was not inevitable that the jury would have convicted if they had had a proper direction on the law. However, while the judge has a duty to summarise the evidence and comment fairly upon it, he is not required to construct a positive defence for the benefit of the defendant.[76]

In a Jamaican case, *Daley and Another v The Queen*,[77] the Privy Council overturned the convictions of two appellants who had been convicted for capital murder committed in the course or furtherance of an act of terrorism. The Privy Council found that the trial judge had failed in his duty to direct the jury on certain fundamental aspects of the offence, such as the level of participation sufficient to amount to a capital offence and whether the notion of 'violence' required physical contact with the victim. Similarly, in *Rahming v R*,[78] the Privy Council quashed a conviction when the judge's direction indicated erroneously that reckless killing could constitute murder and not manslaughter.

The case of *Sookram v R*,[79] discussed above, p 384, on the difference between law and fact with respect to the issue of self-defence, is also relevant here.[80]

In such cases, the judge has a duty to explain to the jury the legal issue, such as self-defence, provocation and the like, in clear and simple terms. This was not done in *Shaw v R*,[81] where the Privy Council complained that the 'rudiments of that defence, [self-defence] should have been stated in clear and simple terms which left no room

---

73   [1936] 3 All ER 36.
74   *Ibid.*
75   (1992) 41 WIR 244.
76   See *Byers v The Queen* (1997) 2 Carib LB 85.
77   [1998] 1 WLR 494.
78   [2003] 1 LRC 357 (PC, The Bahamas).
79   (1971) 18 WIR 195.
80   *Ibid,* p 135. See, also, *Sukhram Sewpersad and Persaud v The State* (1993) 44 WIR 400.
81   (2001) 59 WIR 115.

for doubt'[82] The judge failed to explain that the appellant had to honestly believe that he needed to defend himself.[83]

More entertaining is the Barbadian case of *Thomas v R*.[84] This is a good example of inappropriate judicial comments which may influence a case. The attorney for the defence here was a leading political activist, who apparently was unpopular with the judge, perhaps because he was of a different political persuasion. Throughout the trial the judge made insulting and highly uncomplimentary remarks about counsel, including the remark that he was 'putting stupidness' to the witness. He interrupted further, saying, 'I am not subjecting the jury to any more of this stupidity'. This was held to be sufficient to order a new trial, as it placed undue influence on the jury. There was a danger that it could have made them decide in a particular way. It also indicated to the jury that the judge himself had already come to a particular decision. This is a usurpation of the jury's function to decide the case.

Similarly, in *Parchment v R*,[85] it was held that:

> ... where a judge comments on the witnesses and the presentation of the defence case in such a way as to reveal his own opinion and heavily influence the jury to reach a decision according to that opinion, his summing up is fundamentally unbalanced and a conviction pursuant to it should be set aside.

A contrasting decision is that of *Bucket v R*.[86] The appellant shot the deceased through the window of the bedroom of his house. He claimed that he had not seen him. As there was apparently no intent to kill, the offence of manslaughter was raised. The trial judge then withdrew the question of manslaughter from the jury by directing them that it was a case of 'murder or nothing'. When the jury failed to reach a verdict after three hours he directed them to retire again and try to 'reach a verdict'. He further admonished the jury that was it was unreasonable for a jury 'to take a stand one way or other and refuse to listen to reasonable discussion'.

On appeal, it was held that the question of manslaughter was rightly withdrawn from the jury as the reasonable man would have foreseen harm. The jury in this case had not been misdirected as the words used to make them retire again were words of 'exhortation' rather than words of coercion.[87]

Similarly, if the trial judge merely makes reference to a fact, even if that fact is prejudicial to the defence, this is not improper, as juries are arbiters of fact. This occurred in *Davis, Bush, Smith and Brown v R*.[88] The trial judge referred to the fact that he had rejected the appellants' submissions of no case to answer. This was held not to render the verdicts of the jury unsafe or unsatisfactory, since defence counsel had already mentioned this and the judge had taken the opportunity to remind the jury of its role as the arbiter of fact.

---

82 *Ibid*, at p 124.

83 Cf *Jacob v R* (1997) 56 WIR 255 (CA, Grenada), where the judge interrupted the psychiatrist while giving evidence on a plea of automatism and insanity and failed to direct the jury on the burden of proof for such defences. But the Court of Appeal felt the judge's actions were not prejudicial and no reasonable jury properly directed could have reached any different conclusion.

84 (1992) 44 WIR 76.

85 [1994–95] CILR N-12.

86 (1963) 6 WIR 285.

87 See also, *R v Warwar* (1969) 15 WIR 298.

88 [1996] CILR 123, p 135.

In some contexts, the directions which a judge is required to give are akin to a literary formula. Consider, for example, *Cooper v The State*.[89] The court held that the following words, advising the jury on the unanimity of the verdict, were inaccurate: '[Your] verdict must be unanimous one way or the other . . . When you are all agreed . . . and that is, all of you must agree to the verdict, that is the meaning of unanimous.' This, the court found, was different to the words: 'You cannot . . . return to give your verdict before three hours unless all of you are agreed on the verdict one way or another. That is the meaning of the word unanimous.' The first formula constituted a trespass upon the jury's alienable right to disagree among themselves as to the ultimate verdict.[90]

Certain kinds of misdirections are more likely to have the effect of a mistrial or unsafe verdict. A popular category is the failure of a judge to warn a jury where the evidence is based wholly or substantially on identification. The judge in such a case must warn the jury that identification evidence is unreliable. This is a common problem in West Indian courts. The general rule on directions on identification evidence is that, unless there are exceptional circumstances to justify a failure to warn of its dangers, the conviction will be quashed. To do otherwise would result in a substantial miscarriage of justice.[91] The vulnerability of such evidence to error and the consequent duty of the judge was noted in *Freemantle v R:*[92]

> . . . whenever the case against the accused is based wholly or substantially on the disputed correctness of a visual identification of the accused . . . the judge should warn the jury of the danger of convicting and of the special need for caution . . .[93]

A similar situation occurred in *Bernard v K*.[94] Here, the possibility of mistaken identity was enhanced because of circumstances which terrified and distressed the identifying witnesses. There was even more of a need for a warning to the jury.[95] A further example is where the evidence is inadmissible or uncorroborated.[96]

Sometimes, it is difficult to tell why a direction is misleading. In some cases, the fault in the judge's direction is not so much particular words used or incorrect statements, but rather the effect of the direction when taken as a whole. In *Bernard*, for example, the Privy Council held that the trial judge, in directing on the accused's character, did so in a manner which 'was calculated to prejudice him seriously' in the jury's eyes. In some aspects the direction was admirable, but the overall effect was prejudicial. What the trial judge had given 'in one breath she had taken away with the next'. In directing the jury on the question of an alibi, the trial judge had said:

---

89   (1990) 43 WIR 400.
90   *Ibid*, p 404.
91   *Freemantle v R* (1994) 45 WIR 312. The court followed *Whylie v R* (1989) 37 WIR 346. This rule is known as the *Turnbull* principle. But see *Commr of Police v Hall* (1996) 1 Carib LB 99. A *Turnbull* direction is only necessary in a case of mistaken identity. See also *Pop v R* (2003) 62 WIR 18 (PC, Jamaica); and *Roberts v The State* [2003] 5 LRC 138 (PC, Trinidad and Tobago).
92   *Ibid*, p 314.
93   *Ibid*.
94   (1994) 45 WIR 296.
95   *Ibid*. The *Bernard* case also establishes that a jury should be properly directed as to the impact of an alibi and an accused's character. The judge should have pointed out in her direction that the appellant had a good character, and that disproof of an alibi did not corroborate identification evidence.
96   See, eg, *Fanus v The Queen* Cr Appeal No 8 of 1999, dec'd 2 Feb 2001, CA, Barbados.

> There is no burden on him to show . . . that he was at his shop or he was by a domino
> game. The burden is on the prosecution . . . So you can't convict him unless you def-
> initely reject his story . . .[97]

The Privy Council in this case found that these words gave rise to an inference
that if the alibi was rejected he was guilty. This, however, was wrong in law. The
failure to establish an alibi is not enough to convict for murder. The judge went on to
say:

> If you reject what he says . . . if you say he is a liar . . . You still have to go back and look
> and look and see whether or not the prosecution has satisfied you on a complete review
> of the evidence . . .[98]

While the second passage was a correct direction, the first passage undermined the
second. Even though the judge went on to explain herself properly, the *overall*
effect was prejudicial. The two directions, read together, were likely to give the jury
the impression that they could convict merely for disproof of alibi. The Privy
Council held that there had been a miscarriage of justice, and quashed the trial.
The cases illustrate that the appeal court will carefully examine the judge's direction.
The judge must not create a wrong impression in the minds of the jurors. Similarly,
the judge cannot exert pressure on a jury to quickly arrive at a verdict. This was
explored in *R v Tommy Walker*.[99] In this case the judge became unusually impatient
with the inability of the jury to reach a unanimous verdict, as was required, saying
to them:

> It is getting late in the evening but it does not exclude you from giving due consider-
> ation to the charge . . . I hope that you all can agree . . . You try to come back well before
> midnight, you see.

The jury returned an hour later and were still divided. The judge admonished them:

> Don't tell me that it going to happen for the second time . . . This has never happened in
> any parish . . . I did tell you before . . . that you have to try and all of you agree because
> it's not a charge where you can take a majority verdict . . .

The jury retired a third time and within 12 minutes returned a unanimous verdict. The
Court of Appeal held that this was a result of the judge administering 'pressure' on
the jury to arrive at a verdict[100] which made the trial unfair.

However, a procedural irregularity may not be sufficient to ground a miscarriage
of justice. This is seen when we contrast the identification cases above with that of
Ashby v The State.[101] Here, the judge failed to direct the jury on the issue of law relating
to accomplices. While this is often detrimental to a trial, in this instance, the Court of
Appeal felt that the evidence against the accused was so cogent and overwhelming
that no miscarriage of justice had occurred. The conviction was upheld.

---

97   (1994) 45 WIR 296, p 303.
98   *Ibid*, p 304.
99   Cr Appeal No 105 of 2000, dec'd 20 December 2001, CA, Jamaica.
100 The court reiterated the principle in *R v McKenna* [1960] 1 All ER 326 at 330 F '. . . it is of
     fundamental importance that in their deliberations a jury should be free to take such time as
     they feel they need, subject always . . . to the right of a judge to discharge them if protracted
     consideration still produces disagreement.'
101 (1994) 45 WIR 360.

Judge to present a balanced direction to jury

Finally, on this point, there need not even be a specific misdirection on a point of law for a miscarriage of justice to occur. If, on looking at the trial as a whole, the court finds that the defendant's case was not fairly placed before the jury, the conviction may be quashed. This is so even if it were counsel's fault. This was seen in *Crosdale v R*.[102] Instrumental to the finding of a miscarriage of justice was that the judge commented unfairly in his summing up on certain discrepancies in the evidence. He remarked on the improbabilities of the defence. Counsel for the defence had mentioned a knife, which had not been discussed elsewhere in the evidence. The judge criticised this omission:

> ... you must ask yourself the question, why is the defence so insincere ... He is asking you to say that is how the knife reached his leg ... It's a matter for you because you are sensible people ...[103]

He then compounded his suggestion that the defence's case was weak by asking the jury whether they wanted to retire. The implication was that they had no need to retire as the accused was clearly guilty. The essential question was whether the accused had had the substance of a fair trial. The appeal court decided in the negative. The judge had painted an unfair and unbalanced picture of the case. The jury would not have understood that it was counsel's fault for not establishing a proper defence with regards to the knife. This was sufficient to quash the conviction. An equally extreme example is found in *John v The State*.[104] Chief Justice de la Bastide sought to explain the way in which the judge failed to approach this direction fairly:

> ... the trial judge ... stepped over the line which separates legitimate and permissible criticism and comment ... the summing up in this case was fundamentally unbalanced and unfair, as a result of the cumulative effect of a number of passages which it contains, some of which, if looked at individually, might not even have merited attention ... Their overall effect, however, was to deny the appellant an integral element of due process under our system, that is a summing-up which was fair and balanced, even if unfavourable.[105]

Other procedural irregularities may impugn the trial by a jury. For example, the very process of cloistering the jury is an important one to the process and must be approached judiciously.

Curiously, given the adversarial nature of our judicial system, speech by prosecuting counsel can also be viewed as being so influential on the jury and so prejudicial as to constitute a material irregularity and unfairness in the trial process, rendering the verdict unsafe.[106]

---

102   (1995) 46 WIR 278.
103   *Ibid*, pp 282–83. See, also, *Sankar v The State* [1995] 1 All ER 236 and *Mears v R* (1993) 42 WIR 284.
104   (2001) 62 WIR 314 (CA, Trinidad & Tobago).
105   *Ibid*, at p 317.
106   Se *Ramdhani et al v The State* (2005) 67 WIR 340 (PC, Trinidad and Tobago).

QUESTIONING THE VALIDITY OF THE VERDICT

Strictly speaking, the jury derives all its power from the judge and his willingness to accept the verdict. In theory, even today, a trial judge may refuse to accept a verdict, although this is practically unheard of. In reality, all that this means is that the jury's verdict has no legal effect until judgment is pronounced upon it.

Different rules apply in varying jurisdictions as regards the jury verdict and where these rules are not obeyed, either by the letter, or in spirit, the verdict, and thus the trial may be vulnerable to challenge. Some countries insist on complete unanimity, whilst others accept a majority verdict.[107] Some countries provide for a proviso for a majority verdict in special circumstances. For example, in St Vincent, s 12 of the Jury Ordinance 1938 stipulates that in non-capital offences the 'verdict shall be unanimous if delivered within two hours of its consideration but if delivered more than two hours after its consideration the verdict of seven jurors shall be received as the verdict in the cause.' However, under s 13, in a criminal trial for a capital offence, 'the verdict shall be unanimous. Provided that in trials for murder after two hours of its consideration a verdict of ten jurors convicting the accused of any offence less than murder of which they are entitled by law to convict him shall be received as the verdict in the cause.'

In addition, juries are usually given time limits during which they must come to a verdict. However, even the time which a jury is granted for its deliberations may be questioned. In *Alleyne v R*,[108] a challenge was made to s 41 of the Juries Act CAP 115B of Barbados on the ground that the three-hour limit which it prescribed in jury deliberations was unconstitutional, having regard to s 18(1) of the Barbados Constitution, which provides:

> If any person is charged with a criminal offence ... the case shall be afforded a fair hearing within a reasonable time by an independent and impartial court established by law ...

The Court of Appeal conceded that there appeared to be a 'good reason' for amending the section to permit longer jury deliberations. However, it was unprepared to rule on the constitutional question without full argument which was not forthcoming in the instant case.

Protecting the essence of the jury system also means protecting the integrity of the verdict. After examining the many difficulties with jury trials, at what point can we question a conviction and declare a verdict unsafe? Only in extreme cases would a jury verdict be disturbed. For the verdict to be disturbed, it must be considered unsafe and unsatisfactory and must have prejudiced the constitutional right to a fair trial.

Nanan v The State[109] illustrates that the finality of a verdict is important to the administration of justice process. In that case, even though the jury foreman gave evidence after the verdict was pronounced, that he did not know the meaning of the word 'unanimous' and believed that it was sufficient to reach a majority verdict in a

---

107 See *Nanan v The State, above*, fn 44, illustrating that an unanimous verdict is expected for a murder trial in Trinidad and Tobago. Cf, eg, s 40(1) of the Juries Act of Barbados, Cap 115B: 'A judge shall not accept a majority verdict unless the foreman of the jury has stated in open court the number of jurors who respectively agreed to and dissented from the verdict.'

108 (2001) 61 WIR 47 (CA, Barbados).

109 *Above*, fn 44 at pp 366–67.

murder case, this was not enough to overturn the verdict. The Privy Council explained:

> If a juryman disagrees with the verdict pronounced by the foreman of the jury on his behalf, he should express his dissent forthwith; if he does not do so, there is a presumption that he assented to it. It follows that, where a verdict has been given in the sight and hearing of an entire jury without any expression of dissent by any member of the jury, the court will not thereafter receive evidence from a member of the jury that he did not in fact agree with the verdict, or that his apparent agreement with the verdict resulted from a misapprehension on his part. . . .

Two reasons of policy have been given as underlying the principle as stated above. The first is: 'the need to ensure, that decisions of juries are final; the second is the need to protect jurymen from inducement or pressure either, to reveal what has passed in the jury-room, or, to alter their view.'[110]

The presumption that a juror assented to a verdict, is however, rebuttable in appropriate circumstances such as where the juror did not understand the proceedings.[111]

One common reason for disturbing the verdict is where the jury has been misdirected on a question of law or where the judge sought to influence the verdict. We have already discussed this.

Interestingly, the cases show that even some situations which may have been sufficient to challenge a juror for cause, such as alleged bias, may not be sufficient to ground a mistrial later, once the verdict has been given.

One of the most vivid examples is *R v Box and Box*.[112] There, the verdict of guilty was upheld, despite the fact that it was discovered afterwards that the foreman knew that the accused persons were ex-burglars, villains and associates of prostitutes, and had said that 'he did not need to hear the evidence' and 'would get them 10 years'. This would have been sufficient to ground a successful challenge for cause.

Similarly, in *R v Chapman and Lauday*,[113] even though it was discovered afterwards that one of the jurors was deaf and had heard only half the evidence and none of the summing up, the verdict stayed.

In *Sanker and Pitts v R*,[114] the jury reached a verdict of guilty and were discharged. After the discharge, but before the judge could give the sentences, one of the jurors alleged that the verdict had not been reached as stated by the foreman. In effect, he

---

110 Relying on *Boston v Bagshaw* [1966] 1 WLR 1135 at p 1136: 'It would be destructive of all trials by jury if we were to accede to this application. There would be no end to it. You would always find one juryman who said: "That is not what I meant" and you would have to start the whole thing anew. *Interest reipublicae ut sit finis litium.*'

111 *Nanan, above,* fn 44, relying on *Ellis v Deheer* [1922] 2 KB 113 at p 120: '. . . there will in such circumstances be "a *prima facie* presumption that all assented to it, but that presumption may be rebutted. Circumstances may arise in connection with the delivery of the verdict showing that they did not all assent." Evidence may also be led that a juryman was "not competent to understand the proceedings" in which event, if such evidence is accepted, the ordinary course would be to award a *venire de novo*. In such a case, as Lord Atkin pointed out in *Ras Behari Lal v R* (1933) 50 TLR 1 at p 2, "The objection is not that he did not assent to the verdict, but that he so assented without being qualified to assent". That case shows, however, that the mere fact that a verdict had been pronounced in the sight and hearing of all the jury without protest, does not lead to an irrebuttable presumption of assent.' *Nanan, ibid* at p 367.

112 [1964] 1 QB 430.

113 (1976) 63 Cr App R 75.

114 (1982) 33 WIR 64.

had misrepresented the verdict. However, the appeal court held that when a verdict is delivered by a foreman in the sight and hearing of all the jurors without their protest, their assent must be conclusively inferred. The verdict remained.

THE THRESHOLD FOR OVERTURNING A VERDICT

We have seen from the cases above how difficult it is to disturb a verdict. The baseline is whether there was some serious error in the trial such as to produce a serious miscarriage of justice.

The courts will conform to the policy that they will not attempt to speculate what happened in a jury room, even if an irregularity is suspected. Consequently, the threshold for determining what is an 'unsafe' or unsatisfactory verdict is an extremely high one. Yet it is correct legal principle that a verdict should not be easy to overturn, as it is in the public interest that jury verdicts should be treated with respect. To hold otherwise would undermine public confidence in the jury system.

The burden of proof is on the defence to prove that there was an irregularity in the trial. For example, the evidence of some biased belief held by a juror does not necessarily mean that he or she was not able to function objectively in the case before him or her. It must be demonstrated that the juror would have arrived at some other verdict and was in fact prejudiced.

Where some irregularity occurs, such as a juror discussing the case, and the judge examines the juror but finds no danger of bias and does not discharge him, the court will rarely disturb the discretion of the judge by overturning the verdict. For example, in *R v Flack*,[115] in a case concerning alleged racism, the trial was allowed to continue although it was discovered that one juror had been dismissed from his job for calling someone a 'black bastard'. This was not sufficient to overturn the verdict.

Most important, a Court of Appeal has a wide discretion to overturn a verdict if it is found to be unsafe and unsatisfactory. This is so even if there is no irregularity in the trial.

A recent case illustrates this, that of *Henry and Emmanuel v R*.[116] This was a murder trial. The facts were that there was a dispute between cooking vendors in St Vincent. The deceased harassed the appellants by plastering faeces all over the wall near the appellants' cooking pot and also spat in the appellants' pot. The appellant, in response, decided to 'just chop he and not stop chop he if he say he pit in a we pot' or to just 'chop he, chop he till he dead'. The evidence showed that there was a scuffle and that the deceased had not been blameless. Nevertheless, on a point of law, the Court of Appeal did not believe that provocation could stand as a defence since there had been a cooling off period. The judge's direction on this point had been correct. Consequently, there were no procedural irregularities in the trial at first instance.

Despite this, the Court of Appeal had a 'general feeling of unease' about the case that 'created lurking doubt in our minds as to the accuracy of the jury's verdict on murder'.[117] Because of this doubt, the Court of Appeal found the verdict of murder unsafe and unsatisfactory and reduced it to manslaughter. The substance of this

---

115　[1985] Crim LR 160.
116　(1993) 46 WIR 135.
117　*Ibid*, p 141. The court relied on the English rule *R v Cooper* (1968) 53 Cr App Rep 82.

'feeling of doubt' needs some explanation. The court explained that this 'lurking doubt' is a 'reaction which may not be based strictly on the evidence as such; it is a reaction which can be produced by the general feeling of the case as the court experiences it'. It is a 'subjective reaction' after the court has appraised the admissible evidence. These questions are 'not solved by rules of thumb . . . they are largely by the experience of the judges concerned and the feeling which the case has for them'.[118]

A verdict should also be set aside if there is fresh evidence such that, had it been before the jury, it might have caused a reasonable jury to acquit.[119]

The case illustrates the wide margin of discretion given to an appeal judge with regard to the viability of a jury verdict.

THE ISSUE OF SIZE – PRE-TRIAL PREJUDICE AND OTHER PROBLEMS

Certain problems inherent in jury trials are magnified in small jurisdictions such as those in the Commonwealth Caribbean. In particular, difficulties with the impartiality of the process are exacerbated. This is due to a number of factors. For example, the danger of prejudice is greater in small jurisdictions, due to such factors as local knowledge of the accused, of the crime, and difficulty in ordering a change of venue for the trial. Consequently, the right to a fair trial may be seriously undermined. Where a small jurisdiction is also stratified along class and ethnic lines, these problems are further complicated. A verdict may also be held to be inconsistent. In *Minott et al v The State*,[120] it was explained that a complaint of an inconsistent verdict may be raised in a case where a single defendant is charged with more than one count or where several accused are tried on the same charge. As in this case, where the jury considered that certain evidence was not sufficiently reliable to convict on one charge, but relied on that same evidence, or evidence from the same source, to convict another defendant or on another charge, such a verdict is inconsistent.[121]

However, there is no right to have an inconsistent verdict quashed. The appellant needs to be satisfied that no reasonable jury applying their minds to the evidence could have arrived at the impugned verdict and that such verdict was so unsafe or unsatisfactory that it should not be allowed to stand. While each case depends on its facts, the appellant court will not interfere where some reasonable explanation for the verdict is apparent.[122]

The Jamaican case of *Grant v DPP*[123] outlines some of these difficulties. At the inquest, in a trial for murder, the jury brought in a verdict of murder but was unable to name the guilty persons. This was strongly criticised in certain newspapers, which thereupon named 10 persons as the murderers and demanded that they be brought to trial. Indictments were subsequently brought against the named 10. They responded by way of originating notice of motion for certain declarations including a declaration

---

118   (1993) 46 WIR 135, relying on *R v Lake* (1976) 64 Cr App Rep 172, p 177, *per* Lord Widgery CJ.
119   See *DPP's Reference No 2 of 2001* (2002) 63 WIR (CA, Barbados).
120   (2001) 62 WIR 347 (CA, Trinidad and Tobago).
121   *Ibid*, pp 353–54.
122   *Ramjattan v The State* (2001) 62 WIR 340 (CA, Trinidad and Tobago).
123   [1981] 3 WLR 352, Jamaica. See also the Privy Council appeal: *Grant v DPP* [1982] AC 190 (PC, Jamaica).

that their constitutional right to a fair hearing had been, or was likely to be prejudiced by the massive pre-trial publicity. Yet, the cases demonstrate that the courts have been reluctant to translate these concerns into legal principle.

A rather strict approach to the question of impartiality was given in the Court of Appeal. Carberry JA said:

> It is not sufficient for them to establish . . . that there has been adverse publicity which is likely to have a prejudicial effect on the minds of potential jurors. They must go further and establish that prejudice is so widespread and so indelibly impressed on the minds of potential jurors that it is unlikely that a jury unaffected by it can be obtained.[124]

The potential for pre-trial prejudice in small jurisdictions was discussed in *Stephens v R*.[125] Here, there was a population of only 5,000. The accused had been sentenced for assault on his wife, and was now on trial for the murder of an officer. Defence counsel said:

> Those events are as true today in the minds of islanders as if they had happened yesterday.

The judge rejected the argument that knowledge of such events, so acquired, should, in the ordinary way, produce a case of probable bias against jurors. However, he conceded that in particular cases, depending on the kind or degree of the prejudice, it might so do. The case was, however, lost on its merits.

The high threshold required for a finding of pre-trial publicity sufficient to vitiate a trial is also seen in *Boodram v AG and Another*.[126] This was a murder trial in Trinidad. The court relied expressly on *Grant* and considered whether the pre-trial publicity had been 'indelibly impressed' upon the minds of the jurors. Interestingly, the court paid homage to the cultural mores of Trinidadian society in considering the question:

> . . . we have often described ourselves as a people who thrive on sensationalism, who have a special penchant for *mauvaise langue* [character assassination and ill-speaking] . . . Yet, by the same token, it has also been accepted that . . . we as a people have short memories. We forget easily, as if this were a collective act of atonement to salve our conscience for having indulged ourselves for vitriolic behaviour.[127]

Accordingly, the court found no evidence of prejudice. It also held *per curiam* that where a motion of pre-trial publicity was filed, there was a presumption that it was a delay tactic.

Notwithstanding the high threshold for demonstrating pre-trial prejudice sufficient for a constitutional violation, the State, through the DPP or appropriate officer:

> owes a heavy responsibility towards the court, the defendants and the community at large to play [their] part in keeping (as Lord Diplock put it in *Grant v DPP* [1982] AC 190, 206) 'the springs of justice undefiled'.[128]

Thus, the DPP has the power to cite those who prejudice the trial for contempt. This does not mean that he will act on every complaint 'however trifling.' Rather, 'alertness

---

124   *Ibid.*
125   [1985] LRC (Crim) 17, p 21.
126   (1994) 47 WIR 459. Upheld by the Privy Council in [1996] AC 842 (PC). See also *Hayward v The Queen* Cr Appeal No 18 of 2001, dec'd 2 April 2002, CA, Bermuda.
127   *Ibid*, p 480.
128   *Boodram*, [1996] AC 842, p 853.

on his part to guard against serious risk that trial by jury will develop into trial by media is an important function of his office.'[129]

Importantly, the Privy Council in *Boodram* emphasised that it is only if due process or 'protection of the law' with regard to jury trial is threatened that the issue of constitutional violation may be raised. Mechanisms exist to protect the trial from outside influences. These mechanisms form part of the 'protection of the law'.[130] There was a distinction to be made between pre-trial prejudice which could prejudice the 'existence' of the constitutional right to fair trial and that which prejudiced the exercise of that right:

> It is only if it can be shown that the mechanisms themselves (as distinct from the way in which, in the individual case, they are put into practice) have been, are being or will be subverted that the complaint moves from the ordinary process of appeal into the realm of constitutional law.[131]

In *Grant*, Carberry JA also referred to the 'remedial measures' available under the common law to address such a problem. This included a change of venue to a parish distant from the area where the incident took place and postponement of the trial to allow the adverse publicity to subside.

The question of size arose again in *R v Teare*,[132] a case from the Isle of Man, a small British territory similar in size to countries in the Commonwealth Caribbean. This was a murder trial which generated much publicity. The defence submitted that there was a real prejudice or serious risk of prejudice and asked that the trial be transferred to England.

The application was refused, although such a transfer was provided for under the law. The court held that a fair trial was possible in the circumstances. The test for granting a 'stay' of the trial and the consequent transfer was where the circumstances were 'exceptional'. Here, newspaper coverage had not been misleading. A serious risk of prejudice had not been created. Once again, the high threshold which a court requires before a finding of possible prejudice sufficient to stay proceedings or declare a mistrial was confirmed.

However, the remedial measure of a transfer, although it may be available, is not always practical or even possible in such small jurisdictions. It is to be noted that Jamaica is one of the largest jurisdictions in the region. Such measures are much more difficult in other islands of the Caribbean, which are smaller. Spry, in his study of the effects of jury trials in small jurisdictions states:

> The ordering of a change of venue ... is barely possible or practicable in the small territories. It is obviously impossible in a territory with only one substantial centre of population. It is impracticable between islands where the means of communication are such that the delays and expense would be wholly unreasonable.[133]

The smaller the jurisdiction, the longer it will take for some event to be forgotten. The danger of pre-trial prejudice is more likely to endure.

---

129 *Ibid*. The Privy Council also emphasised that the proper forum for a complaint about pre-trial publicity is the trial court where the judge can assess the circumstances which exist. Remedial measures such as challenge to the jury may be utilised. *Boodram, PC, ibid*, p 855.

130 *Ibid*, p 854.

131 *Ibid*.

132 [1993–95] Manx LR 212; [1995] CLB 445.

133 Spry, J, 'Problems of Jury Trials in Small Jurisdictions', 1985, London, Commonwealth Secretariat Report.

The small choice available for jury service could also exacerbate the problem of size. The lesser the number of persons available for jury service, the greater the danger or lack of obscurity or representativeness and impartiality. Patchett[134] argues that there is a:

> ... small and close-knit group [of jurors] and in these communities news and opinions, particularly of notorious crimes, will spread quickly. It is by no means inconceivable that several members of the jury will have some prejudice grounded on personal knowledge of the events and people involved.

We can elaborate on this point. Criminologists have often made the connection between crime and lower income groups. We know that jury service tends to be targeted at those in lower income to lower middle income groups. This makes it even more likely that there will be some connection between jurors and accused.

The setting up of constitutional procedures which will allow the transfer of cases where there is potential prejudice to other Caribbean jurisdictions is an innovative means of combating the limitation of size. This mechanism already exists in some jurisdictions. As we saw in *R v Teare*,[135] the possibility was discussed, but the court refused the transfer. It felt that the proper course, if prejudice had been established, was not a transfer but a stay of proceedings. This shows the reluctance of local courts to transfer cases out of their jurisdiction. As we are moving toward a more integrated judicial system in the region, with the advent of the CCJ, there is an opportunity to begin dialogue toward the introduction of such transfers for first instance courts.

LOCAL KNOWLEDGE OF THE JURY

The question of prejudice is also relevant as it relates to local knowledge of the issues or events. The point is well illustrated in *R v Minto*,[136] a case from the Falklands, a jurisdiction with approximately 2,000 people only. The accused submitted that he believed his trial was prejudiced because he was unpopular in the community and did not feel he would get a fair trial in that jurisdiction.

Although the judge disagreed with the accused on the question of prejudice, he acknowledged the problem of partiality in small jurisdictions. He said:

> It may be true that in a small community ... a number of jurors in any trial are likely to know an accused person personally or by reputation, but it does not necessarily follow that they will be incapable of reaching an impartial verdict.[137]

In small jurisdictions, people tend to know each other or even be related. This makes the composition of an impartial jury even more difficult. We saw this earlier in *Gibson v R*,[138] where one of the jurors was the brother of the deceased. In Nevis, this problem was just as vividly demonstrated in the case of *R v Browne and Barry*.[139] This was a trial for armed robbery. Sitting on the jury were a brother and sister who were related to

---

134   Patchett, KW, 'English Law in the West Indies' (1963) 12 ICLQ 15, p 17.
135   [1995] CLB 445.
136   Unreported Criminal Case No 1 of 1981, Falkland Islands. Noted in *op cit*, Spry, fn 133, p 9.
137   *Ibid*.
138   (1963) 5 WIR 450.
139   Unreported No 20 of 1995, Sup Ct, St Kitts and Nevis.

the accused. The jury, apparently against the weight of the evidence, returned a verdict of not guilty.[140]

Such occurrences have moved Mr Justice Barcilon of Bermuda to remark:

> The principle of the jury system is fine, but it cannot work in a community as small as Bermuda where so many people know each other.[141]

In the case of *Elroy Howe v R*[142] from St Vincent, some of the jury empanelled to try the appellant had been present when he had been convicted of rape not long before. The trial judge warned the jury that they should not allow any knowledge that they had of the appellant to prejudice their minds against him. Notwithstanding, the Court of Appeal felt that this was not sufficient. Lewis CJ said:

> In our view, however, his decision to proceed with the trial and to give the warning to the jury which he did, unfortunately only served to emphasise the prejudicial situation which had earlier arisen and this resulted in an irregularity so grave as to vitiate the trial.[143]

The conviction was quashed and a new trial ordered.

Another case from the Seychelles, that of *AG v Dolnischeck*, is also instructive.[144] The Seychelles is a small population of only 64,000. There was an attempted *coup* which generated substantial adverse publicity. This was a case 'likely to create an atmosphere of public emotion not conductive to the weighing of the evidence'.[145] While there was much discussion on the possibility of pre-trial prejudice, the court held that it was not impossible to empanel an unbiased jury.

The *Dolnischeck* case is similar to the now well-known Trinidadian cases of *Phillip et al v DPP*[146] and *Lasalle v AG*.[147] Both these cases concerned socio-political uprisings in Trinidad and Tobago. The latter arose out of the 'black power' movement, while the former concerned an attempted political coup. Unlike *Dolnischeck*, however, the courts in both decisions were more sensitive to public sentiment which, in these instances, were sympathetic to the militants. Interestingly, all of those persons could have been held for treason, but to date none has been so convicted.

This leads to another telling point about the politics of size and small community. Often, there is a large measure of sympathy for accused persons who belong to the particular community or who are known in the small society. They may be seen as 'boys on the block' and persons in the society may identify with them. In contrast, in a large country or city, the community is more distanced and alienated from the accused.

In attempting to uphold the constitutional right of a fair trial, a purposive approach must be adopted, as illustrated in *Howe v R*.[148] Although a State cannot guarantee an impartial jury, it has a duty to do everything in its power to provide one.

140　The population of Nevis is approximately 8,800.
141　As reported in the *Bermuda Royal Gazette*, 17 February 1984.
142　(1972) 19 WIR 517.
143　*Ibid*, p 520.
144　(1982) 8 Carib LB 1360.
145　*Op cit*, Spry, fn 133, p 6.
146　[1992] 1 AC 545, PC, Trinidad and Tobago; see, also, *AG v Phillips* [1995] 1 All ER 93, related litigation.
147　(1971) 18 WIR 379.
148　(1972) 19 WIR 517.

It is in this respect that decisions like *Grant v DPP*[149] should be criticised. It may not be enough that the accused, if convicted, will have a right of appeal, for if the scales of justice were tipped by prejudice, the appeal may be equally worthless. Nevertheless, with respect to size and pre-trial publicity, it is perhaps easy to exaggerate the problems of small jurisdictions. We are not contending that pre-trial publicity is a factor only in small jurisdictions, only that it will tend to be exacerbated. In a modern context, dominated by aggressive media, the evidence is that such problems are just as problematic elsewhere, as seen in the *OJ Simpson* trial.

Another important point may be what some claim to be added pressures on jurors in small jurisdictions. Particularly in relation to some offences, such as drug offences, jurors feel pressured into acquitting. The reasons may be either intimidation, fear for self or family, or embarrassment. The latter may be because a juror may be related to another juror and he may not wish to disagree.

In addition, there may be feelings of loyalty to the community, the accused, the family or a particular societal group. A conviction might, therefore, be seen as betrayal. This may also happen elsewhere, but the social bonds may be stronger in small communities. We should not discount this easily. One hears, for example, of lawyers in the region refusing to take certain cases for fear of antagonising others in the community or being ostracised when they do so. At minimum, it is perhaps more difficult to divorce oneself from the social context when one practises, adjudicates or does jury service in a small jurisdiction.

OTHER JURY INFLUENCES

Juries are also believed to be greatly affected by the manner, dress, class, etc, of the accused or witnesses. For example, defendants are commonly advised to wear sober colours such as navy blue, while women should not wear provocative dresses. Similarly, in the Caribbean, it is commonly believed that members of the Rastafarian community are poorly received by juries and in the criminal justice system.[150] A telling example is a recent documentary about a region in Barbados called the Pine. It is claimed that, over the years, enforcement officers, juries and adjudicators have labelled persons from this area as social deviants: 'P' for Perry, 'P' for Pine and 'P' for Prison. This is yet another illustration of the politics of small communities.[151]

ALTERNATIVES TO JURY TRIALS

There are credible alternatives to trial by jury without abolishing the concept altogether. For example, a panel comprising advisory assessors, made up of lay persons whose function is merely to *advise* the judge on a verdict, is one option. This system operates in Tanzania. Alternatively, a panel of assessors who are lay persons with special expertise may be chosen to assist the judge. This is the Zimbabwe approach.[152]

---

149 (1981) 3 WIR 352, Jamaica.
150 The Rastafarian community is a religious sect which is distinguished by its 'dreadlocks' hairstyle, which is a form of hairdress that is uncombed, long and knotted.
151 Caribbean Broadcasting Unit: Documentary, 15 December 1997, 'The Pinelands'.
152 See *op cit*, Georges, fn 52 for an appraisal of these approaches.

A more radical option is to abolish jury trials entirely but increase the number of judges who will sit at first instance. Instead of a single judge, three or even four judges may hear the case. To those who advocate the need for legally skilled personnel to decide cases, this may be an attractive approach. It suffers, however, from some of the defects discussed earlier. Further, the judicial and economic resources of the region may not permit such an exercise.[153]

ADVANTAGES OF THE JURY SYSTEM

Many of the accusations thrown at the jury system may be seen to be flawed when examined more closely.

The assertion that juries are inefficient because of poor educational standards, and their resultant inability to understand questions of law, is exposed when one recalls their sole function as arbitrators of facts. The jury's primary tool is common sense. Surely one does not need formal training to acquire this. Is education really necessary to separate fact from law? It is likely that more highly educated jurors will place greater emphasis on procedure and instructions than those with only grade school education. The latter might be more interested in opinions, testimony, and personal experiences, but it is these which most concern the jury. It is the jury's task to assess the truth of witness statements and adjudicate on the facts. It is only common sense that is needed here.

The fact that judges and lawyers may disagree with a jury's verdict does not necessarily mean that it was not based on the evidence and is wrong. The nature of the jury's task, for example, assessing the credibility of witnesses, leaves room for differences of opinion, at least a margin of error. Indeed, Lord Devlin believes that the jury is best suited to decide upon such 'primary facts', as a judge 'may fail to make enough allowance for the behaviour of the stupid'.[154]

Similarly, the lack of legal training on the part of jurors allows them to bring to the trial a fresh outlook, as opposed to the professional opinion of a judge who may have become hardened and cynical after years of experience. Although this lack of legal of legal sophistication may at times mean that the jury may be at the mercy of the cunning and manipulative accused person, it can also be its special virtue, as it allows the jury to decide as the community itself would decide. It is also debatable whether a judge or attorney is any more adept at identifying cunning persons. As Weeramantry argues:

> The myth has long been propagated that judges, with a lifetime of experience, have a special skill in assessing demeanour . . . On this line of reasoning the judge can spot a liar, a rogue, or a prevaricator with the same ease as an experienced doctor can spot a slipped disc . . . But is this so? Take that same judge . . . pitted against an artful rogue in real life. The long judicial experience affords no special insurance against . . . 'being taken for a ride'. Indeed, the insulation he has had from ordinary problems which beset the ordinary citizen may make him less discerning of these problems in real life when they do occur.[155]

---

153 Other variations are possible, such as a panel of both judges and attorneys.
154 *Op cit*, Devlin, fn 3, p 168.
155 Weeramantry, CG, 'Judicial reasoning in the common law', Ninth Commonwealth Law Conference, 1990, New Zealand: Commerce Clearing House, p 86.

The sheer size of the jury is also an advantage in that it is unlikely that individual prejudices could significantly affect the verdict. Both judge and jury can fall prey to social, political and other biases but, with the jury system, the citizen has additional protection. His fate is not being decided by a single individual. It may also be of psychological significance to the judge, who is relieved of this heavy burden.

The jury's size also means that there is safety in numbers with regard to potential corruption in the system. Indeed, the image of the infallible and incorruptible judge is erroneous. Recently, in the Commonwealth Caribbean, there have been instances of corrupt judges.[156] Trial by jury can therefore help to uphold the independence and integrity of the justice system.

Another important feature of the jury system is that it can dispose of 'hard cases' without changing the law. Where it seems that the proper application of legal principles leads to a conclusion of guilt, but the verdict does not reflect this, a judicial precedent is not created. Verdicts and the judicial pronouncements make no impact on the law itself as do binding precedents emanating from a judge. The flexibility of the jury system therefore allows a decision away from the rigidity of the law, without injuring the fabric of the law.

The jury's verdict is also the expression of the community's conscience, in that it reflects the society's ideals and feelings on particular issues. For example, a jury's refusal to convict can be an expression of their revulsion towards the death penalty or police brutality. Hence, the jury may be the yardstick of public feeling and a safety valve against unpopular law. The jury tradition is thus as much outside the law as in it. These extra-legal functions are occasionally urged as the jury's chief justification. It assists in bringing the law, often accused of being alien and unfeeling, in touch with social reality.

Participatory justice

The jury brings acceptability to the system of justice, a stamp of public approval on the result reached. It represents a democratic commitment which is also popular among the masses, and has an emotional appeal to those who mistrust the administration of justice. It also avoids a paternalistic approach to justice.

The jury's justice is therefore popular justice, not justice meted out by judges who are often divorced from the ideals of the common man. Lord Devlin has remarked that the common man can get the kind of justice he likes, and not the kind governments and legal experts think is good for him.

Concepts of shared decision making and public participation are worthy and essential ideals in a democratic society. Trial by jury is characteristic of such a society. In the Commonwealth Caribbean, where the complaint that the citizen is not part of the decision-making process is often raised, the jury system plays an even more important role. It helps to inculcate a desirable participatory culture in the society. Problems of a passive type of democracy, where individuals are merely 'governed', and are alienated from the decision-making process, often thought to be a hangover

---

156   See, eg, newspaper reports of judges and justices of the peace being investigated and prosecuted for corruption in Trinidad and Tobago: (1997) *The Trinidad Express*, 12 May.

from colonial rule, can be considerably diminished. The jury system is, therefore, an important societal tool.[157]

The important point as seen by Johnny Cochran, Jr, a leading attorney in the controversial *OJ Simpson* case, is that:

Juries that include all of a community's people, that allow for the expression of all their informed consciences, and take into account the sum of all their historical experiences, simply are more competent to dispense justice. And if that justice is not always perfect – well, neither is anything else this side of the grave.[158]

The jury system has survived many changes in the legal system. It has weathered the several attacks made against its hallowed walls, but few have been radical enough to suggest total abolition. The desirability and efficiency of trial by jury is an ongoing debate. Some view jury trials as an essential feature of democracy which allow our peers to judge us. Others view them as robbing a trial of the opportunity to benefit from judicial expertise, greater education, technical expertise and unemotional adjudication, which, they argue, would characterise trial by judges or legal personnel. Many studies have shown the inconsistencies that may occur within jury trials. Just as many, however, have concluded that jurors are expected to judge fact and not law, and that the best person to judge facts, the defendant's character and other such 'common sense' matters, is the common man. Despite its shortcomings, it has been, as stated in *Ward v James*:[159]

... the bulwark of our liberties too long for any of us to seek to alter it. ... when one or other party must be deliberately lying, trial by jury has no equal.

Trial by jury is 'more than one wheel of the Constitution, it is the lamp that shows that freedom lives'.[160]

---

157 See Chapter 20 ('The Office of the Ombudsman').
158 Cochran, J, *Journey To Justice*, 1996, New York: One World Ballantine.
159 [1965] 1 All ER 563.
160 *Op cit*, Devlin, fn 3, p 164.

CHAPTER 20

THE OFFICE OF THE OMBUDSMAN

INTRODUCTION

The most popular alternative dispute mechanism in the Commonwealth Caribbean is the office of the Ombudsman. This office was established to address those abuses which the ordinary courts cannot adequately handle, or which are not convenient for resolution before the courts. The office of the Ombudsman thus performs a quasi-judicial function. Thus, in a modern day context, the office of the Ombudsman is viewed as an alternative or supplement to the court system, as a means to bridge the ever-increasing gap between the bureaucracy and the citizenry, and to protect the citizen from the abuses of the 'machinery of the State'. It is, in fact, a tool to facilitate good governance.

The concept of the Ombudsman is a relatively new concept in the Commonwealth Caribbean. Although a phenomenon which has been transplanted from outside the region, the ideals of the institution can be seen to be particularly well suited to the Commonwealth Caribbean. Perhaps this is because the problems of administration which the office is designed to correct are magnified in Commonwealth Caribbean societies.

Why the need for an Ombudsman? The rise of the 'administrative State' has had a tremendous impact on public life and the citizen. The contemporary State, with its accompanying tentacles of expanded bureaucracies, increased executive power and regulatory and administrative functions, now encroach on every aspect of the citizen's life. This increasingly poses threats to individuals' rights and liberties. The rapid and vast expansion of the bureaucracy has inevitably resulted in the potential for inefficiency, injustice and the alienation of the State from the individual. As the actions of the bureaucracy 'more and more affect the life and livelihood of the individual, the problem of exercising effective control over officialdom becomes increasingly important but at the same time more intractable'.[1] The role of the Ombudsman thus emerges as a protector of the citizens against the inherent abuses of the machinery of such complex and powerful public administration. His or her office is an additional weapon in the battle for the protection of citizens' rights and future protection against administrative error, inefficiency and abuse of power. The office of the Ombudsman, therefore, represents one more step in the democratic process and the administration of justice.

Notwithstanding the lofty ideals of the institution of the Ombudsman, the question has often been posed as to its suitability for Commonwealth Caribbean jurisdictions. Transplantation of the office would appear to be on fertile ground if one examines the historical context evident in Caribbean societies.

As we saw in Chapter 1, the rise of the independent political States in the Caribbean was an outgrowth of slave and colonial societies. Such societies were characterised by alienation of the masses from the bureaucracy. The change in formal

---

1   Gregory, R et al, *The Parliamentary Ombudsman: A Study in the Control of Administrative Action*, 1975, London: Allen & Unwin (for the Royal Institute of Public Administration), p 15.

political structure was not accompanied by real change in this regard. Indeed, many have argued that Caribbean society, by and large, retained the social, political and administrative structures and tendencies towards excessive centralisation. More importantly, there is a lack of participation in constitutional politics by the majority of the population and a 'remoteness' of the governors from the governed, which has been linked to the colonial and Third World experience. Elsewhere in the developing world, this has been noticed: '. . . government is very remote from the people who understand little of its structure, let alone its decisions. The Ombudsman's office may serve an explanatory or mediating role'.[2] The introduction of the Ombudsman to the Caribbean can thus be viewed as a means to counteract this 'remoteness', the inheritance of plantation and colonial societies.

Other problems inherent in our ex-plantation societies, such as functional illiteracy, racial prejudice, dependency, partisan and race politics, have served only to exacerbate this characteristic remoteness, thereby undermining true democracy.

It is precisely these types of challenges of the modern administrative State that the institution of the Ombudsman is designed to meet, enabling individuals to participate meaningfully in the democratic process and sensitising State bureaucracies to considerations of individual fairness.

NATURE OF THE OFFICE – APPOINTMENT AND REMOVAL

The idea of an Ombudsman for the protection of citizens' rights has taken firm hold in the Commonwealth Caribbean. The model followed is that of the 'classical Ombudsman', which is based on the Scandinavian Ombudsman institution. The first office of the Ombudsman was created in 1967 in Guyana, its birth supported by the idealism surrounding the initial post-independence period. More particularly, the office was viewed not only as a method to address administrative abuse, but also as a means of dealing with Guyana's serious social problems, particularly with regard to allegations of racial imbalances in its security services and public services and other allegations of discrimination practised in public office.

The concept soon spread and, to date, the countries where the office may be found include Antigua and Barbuda, Jamaica, Barbados, St Lucia, Trinidad and Tobago, Belize and Dominica. Indeed, the notion of the Ombudsman sometimes called the Parliamentary Commissioner, such as in Saint Lucia and Belize, proved so attractive in Jamaica that the island has no fewer than four Ombudsmen, including a Contractor General, which may be viewed as an Ombudsman-type office. Thus, the Jamaican experience provides for a Parliamentary Ombudsman, a Political Ombudsman, an Ombudsman for contracts and an Ombudsman for public utilities.

The office of the Political Ombudsman in Jamaica appears to be unique in the Caribbean and was born out of the saga of political violence in that country. It is therefore an attempt on the part of both leading political parties to appoint a conciliator to help reduce political terror and conflict. It is, however, the office of the Parliamentary Ombudsman which has found a home elsewhere in the Commonwealth Caribbean and indeed in most of the world.

---

2   Scott, I, 'The Ombudsman in Fiji: Patterns of Mediation and Institutionalisation' [1982] The Ombudsman Journal 218.

The International Bar Association defines the office of the Parliamentary Ombudsman in the following way:

> An office provided for by the Constitution or by action of the legislature or Parliament and headed by an independent high level public official who is responsible to the legislature or Parliament, who receives complaints from aggrieved persons against government agencies, officials and employees or who acts on his own motion and who has the power to investigate, recommend corrective action and issue reports.[3]

The nature of the office is essentially investigatory, with a view to addressing relevant complaints. To this end, the Ombudsman is given wide powers and protection to enable him to carry out his duties successfully.

The office of the Ombudsman may be established either by the Constitution or by ordinary statute. In the Commonwealth Caribbean Antigua, Dominica, Trinidad and Tobago, St Lucia and Guyana have set up the office by way of constitutional provision.[4] Conversely, in Jamaica and Barbados the office of the Ombudsman is set up by an Ombudsman Act.[5]

Comment may be made on the relative strength of appointment under the Constitution as opposed to an appointment by way of Act of Parliament or legislature. When one considers the entrenchment provisions in Caribbean Constitutions and their general stature, it would seem that the advantages of appointment by Constitution are obvious. However, as yet there has been no testing ground to determine whether the differences in appointment are in name only.

With regard to appointment and removal in the Caribbean, the status of the office holder is akin to that of a Justice of Appeal or High Court judge. He is generally a legal person and is appointed by the Head of State in consultation with the Leader of the Opposition, or on the recommendation of the Prime Minister after consultation with the Leader of the Opposition. One can see, in the provisions relating to consultation in appointment, the desire for the element of impartiality and non-partisanship which is so vital to the office.

His appointment is for a specific period, usually for a period ranging between five and seven years, as in St Lucia and Guyana respectively. There are strict provisions relating to removal, similar to those relating to judges. This is to ensure independence and impartiality of the office based on the idea of the separation of powers doctrine. Thus, the Ombudsman may only be removed for the inability to perform the function of his office or for misbehaviour after the matter has been referred to a tribunal appointed by the Head of State.

Further, the terms of service of the Ombudsman cannot be altered to his disadvantage. The security of tenure and independence afforded to this high level public official is easily understood if one recalls the nature of his function, which is to act as mediator between citizen and State. The Ombudsman is thus independent of the bureaucracy and reports only to Parliament and to the public.

---

3 Owen, P, 'Current Ombudsman issues – an international perspective', seminar papers, *The Role of the Ombudsman in the Commonwealth Caribbean*, 1989, Barbados: ISER, UWI, p 3.

4 See, eg, the Constitutions of Antigua, s 66; Trinidad and Tobago, s 91; St Lucia, s 110; Dominica, s 108; and Guyana, Art 191.

5 Act No 23 of 1978 and Ch 8A of 1989 respectively.

Consensual and accessible approach

In keeping with his role as a mediator, the character of the office is epitomised by a consensual and investigatory approach as opposed to an adversarial one, the latter being exemplified in the court system. Indeed, this is a fundamental difference between these two systems of administration of justice. Therefore, in the Caribbean, the Ombudsman, after his investigation, can only recommend. He cannot, as can his French counterpart, overturn administrative demands, as may a court. The consensual and investigatory approach is also reflected in the informal procedure which characterises the office.

The real attempt made by the office to reach the citizen and involve him in the democratic process is evidenced by the fact that there is usually no charge for the service, or if there is a charge, it is only a minimum fee, as in Barbados. This is clearly in contrast with the characteristic expense of court proceedings. Further, the less formal structure of the Ombudsman as compared to the judicial system enables him to be easily accessible to the citizen.

JURISDICTION AND FUNCTIONS

The Ombudsman's function is called into operation where a citizen or body of citizens suffers an injustice due to a fault in administration, or from administrative action or inaction. The word 'injustice' is to be interpreted in a wide sense, hence, an injustice covers not only injury repressible in a court of law, but also a sense of outrage aroused by unfair or incompetent administration. This includes the situation where the complainant has suffered no actual loss.

Administrative authorities to which the Ombudsman must turn for his investigation include local statutory authorities or other bodies established for the purpose of the public service, local government; more generally, bodies or authorities involved in public administration. It may include such bodies or authorities where the majority of members are appointed by the Head of State or a minister; where revenues consist wholly or mainly of moneys provided out of public funds, any authority empowered to determine the entering into of contracts by or on behalf of the government and such other authorities as may be prescribed.

The category of bodies which may be described as 'public authorities' involved in public administration may be broader than first realised. Recent trends in administrative law indicate that bodies whose activities do not normally come under judicial review because they are not statutory or public authorities may now come under such supervision where these bodies exert undue influence over the public, even if such entities are private. This was seen, for example, in the landmark case of *R v Panel on Mergers ex p Datafin*,[6] followed in a number of Commonwealth Caribbean cases.[7] Consequently, such bodies will also come under the purview of the Ombudsman.

The Ombudsman's sphere of reference is administrative, not Executive action, hence the Ombudsman cannot usually inquire into Executive decisions or policy, but only administrative action or fault. The latter function is procedural, while the former

---

6   [1987] QB 814; [1987] 1 All ER 504.
7   See, eg, *Griffith v Barbados Cricket Association* (1989) 41 WIR 48, where the Barbados National Cricketing Authority was susceptible to judicial review.

is substantive. Indeed, it would be surprising if the Ombudsman were allowed to question the decision or policy of a minister of government, for this would be undermining the concept of ministerial responsibility. It is imperative, therefore, in defining the jurisdiction of the Ombudsman, to make this distinction between the administrative process and the legislative and executive processes.

The relevant legislation defining the jurisdiction of the Ombudsman allows him to inquire into 'administrative action' and a 'fault' in administration. However, the actual terms are not defined and it is often difficult to distinguish between the administrative, legislative and executive functions.

Indeed, the parameters of the term 'administration' and consequently, the boundaries of the Ombudsman's jurisdiction are often difficult to identify and may be quite contentious. In *Re British Columbia Development Corporation and Friedman*,[8] Dickson J of the Supreme Court of Canada explained that the 'words "administration" or "administrative" . . . are fully broad enough to encompass all conduct engaged in by a governmental authority in furtherance of governmental policy, business or otherwise'. SA de Smith,[9] has also attempted to define the terms and has argued that an administrative act 'includes the adoption of a policy, the making and issue of a specific direction, and the application of a general rule to a particular case in accordance with the requirements of policy or expediency or administrative practice.'

While the Ombudsman cannot therefore inquire directly into the merits or demerits of a governmental or administrative policy, he or she may examine and challenge the administration of that policy.

This difficulty can be overcome somewhat once the Ombudsman is allowed to investigate the advice or recommendation made to a minister upon which he based his decision. This apparent loophole is by way of certain sections of the various Constitutions, such as s 93 of the Trinidad and Tobago Constitution or the identical provision in St Lucia.[10] This may in fact allow for a full investigation while still preserving ministerial responsibility. However, this conjures up the difficulty of deciding how much of the decision was based on such advice. Because of this difficulty, it is largely left up to the initiative of the Ombudsman to determine whether a decision can be said to be due to administrative action or fault.

The Caribbean Ombudsman, not unlike his British counterpart, tends to foil any attempt at formally defining the scope of his authority. This is to prevent a rigid operation of the framework of that authority or terms of reference. Rather, he reveals a preference for a flexible approach which in effect means the scope of his authority and operation is left to evolve from dealing with actual cases. This is a logical development from the state of affairs whereby questions relating to his jurisdiction and competence under the Constitution are left largely to discretion. It is due to this vagueness in assessing jurisdiction that the office can be described as having a flexible jurisdiction. Nevertheless, it is clear that executive policy and inquiry into the merits of a decision are outside the bounds of the Ombudsman's jurisdiction. However, the present President of the International Ombudsman Association, Stephen Owen, makes an exception for the situation where legislation offends established principles of fairness.

---

8   (1985) 14 DLR (4th) 129, at 137.
9   *Judicial Review of Administrative Action*, 4th edn (1980), Oxford: OUP, pp 68–71.
10   See the Constitution Order 1978 of St Lucia, s 112.

In this situation he feels that the Ombudsman has a responsibility to enter the debate.[11]

Perhaps this is the rationale behind the Jamaican provision, under s 21(5) of the Ombudsman Act 1978, where it allows the Ombudsman to recommend that an enactment, rule or regulation which causes or may cause injustice be altered. This provision seems to encourage investigation into the substantive merits of legislative and executive actions, but is nevertheless justified by the 'fairness' rationale. Further, the existence of written Constitutions in the Commonwealth Caribbean, such Constitutions being supreme law against which all other laws are measured, means, in effect, that any statute may be challenged as being *ultra vires* the Constitution, thus giving *locus standi* to any citizen, and indeed the Ombudsman, to embark upon such inquiry.

Apart from the above limited situations, however, it is only administrative policy which concerns the Ombudsman. This involves the translation and application of broad legislative policy to individual situations. It describes method and not purpose, and it requires the exercise of discretion by public servants which is *prima facie* arbitrary or may create the potential for arbitrariness.

The administrative fault, action or inaction which concern the Ombudsman may include delay, bias, unfair discrimination, whether based on race, politics or otherwise, failing to give proper advice, harassment, failing to follow proper procedure, rash, unworkable procedure, neglect, failure to take relevant considerations into account or considering irrelevant ones, or even mere discourtesy. The list is not exhaustive and it is obvious that the Ombudsman would certainly not want for complaint in the Commonwealth Caribbean, a region which is noted for its informal approach (to say the least) to public office.

In *R v Local Commission for Administration for the North and East Area of England, ex p Bradford Metropolitan County Council,*[12] the English Court of Appeal pronounced upon the meaning of administrative fault or maladministration within the context of the UK Ombudsman Act, a statute which is very similar to legislation in the Commonwealth Caribbean. Denning MR affirmed in principle the long list mentioned above, including 'incompetence, inaptitude, perversity, turpitude, arbitrariness and so on'.[13] However, Denning emphasised that the list was 'open-ended, covering the manner in which a decision is reached . . . but excluding the merits of the decision itself or of the discretion itself.'

It follows that a 'discretionary decision, properly exercised, which the complainant dislikes but cannot fault the manner in which it was taken, is excluded.'[14]

It is clear, therefore, that the Ombudsman is no mere lobbyist. Nevertheless, from an examination of administrative law and the principles of judicial review, which form the ground rules for determining the concepts of administration and maladministration, it is clear that the tools of the inquiry open to investigate decision-making can come very close to resembling inquiry into the merits of a decision, act or even policy. The infamous line of English cases beginning with *Bromley LBC v GLC,*[15] etc demonstrates this thin line between procedure and substance.

---

11   *Op cit*, Owen, fn 3, p 6.
12   (1979) 2 All ER 881.
13   *Ibid*, pp 897–98.
14   *Ibid*.
15   [1982] AC 768. See also *R v LTE ex parte GLC* [1983] 2 WLR 702.

In these cases government's polices, which were described as philanthropist and socialist by the court, were not only frowned upon, but the courts were able to use seemingly procedural mechanisms, such as the doctrine of irrelevant considerations, to determine that the decisions or policies were unlawful. The reader will note that the determination of what is relevant or irrelevant lies within the realm of the court. The Commonwealth Caribbean response to these cases is found in *C O Williams*,[16] where the then governmental policy of wanting to improve the lot of the 'black masses' in Barbados, was undermined by the courts when it manifested itself in the award of contracts. Could not, for example, the Ombudsman, had he been asked to examine the cases in question, have legitimately argued that there was administrative fault on the ground that there was bias?

It is these fine distinctions which placed one Barbados Ombudsman in controversy when he set about investigating issues related to the apparent phenomenon of private beaches and the usage of the beaches in general. The Ombudsman took a wide view of 'administration' and argued further that it was governmental departments which had the responsibility for regulating the beaches.[17]

The Jamaican Ombudsman has been even more interventionist, speaking out (but not investigating) the economic role of males in Jamaican society.

It has been judicially noted too that the concept of administration includes the 'proprietary or business decisions of governmental organisations'.[18]

The Ombudsman may also have special jurisdiction with respect to public officers. For example, he has the authority in Trinidad and Tobago and St Lucia, to investigate conditions arising from, or facilitating corruption in the Public Service and to report any evidence to the appropriate authority.[19] Further, in Trinidad and Tobago, Antigua and Barbuda, Belize and Jamaica, where he unearths evidence of misconduct, breach of duty or criminal conduct by any public officer, he has authority to refer the matter to the relevant authority.[20]

THE OMBUDSMAN'S JURISDICTION IN PROTECTING HUMAN RIGHTS

In recent times, the Ombudsman has been called upon to assume an important role in the protection of fundamental rights. In the Commonwealth Caribbean, Ombudsmen are not usually endowed with a specific human rights jurisdiction. Such a jurisdiction is found in many other parts of the world, with the advent of what has been termed the 'hybrid Ombudsman' model. The Commonwealth Caribbean models do, however, make room for some overlap.

In addition to the avenue via the High Court for redress of the abrogation of rights provided for in Caribbean Constitutions, it is specifically provided in Jamaica that the

---

16   *C O Williams Construction Ltd v AG of Barbados* [1985] 1 WLR 102; (1994) 45 94.
17   Ombudsman Carl Ince, Lecture on 'The Role of the Ombudsman' 5 November 2003, Faculty of Law, UWI, Barbados.
18   *Friedman, above*, fn 8.
19   Ss 94 (2) and 113(2) and (3) respectively.
20   Ss 3(4), 7(4), 22(1) and 22 respectively.

citizen may, in addition, or in the alternative, complain to the Ombudsman.[21] In other countries this aspect of the jurisdiction is less explicit.

Since the Ombudsman is the bulwark against abuses of the State and the watchdog for citizens' fundamental rights, he may not be prevented from investigating a matter, by reason only that a complainant could apply to the Supreme Court for redress of the abrogation of fundamental rights.[22]

This is a special provision in addition to the general proviso that the Ombudsman cannot investigate judicial proceedings which are, or are likely to be in train. For example, s 113 of the St Lucia Constitution Order 1979 provides:

> (4) The Parliamentary Commissioner shall not investigate –
>   (a) any action in respect of which the complainant has or had:
>   (i) a remedy by way of proceedings in a court of law; or
>   (ii) a right of appeal, reference or review to or before an independent and impartial tribunal other than a court of law; . . .
> (5) Notwithstanding the provisions of subsection (4) of this section the Parliamentary Commissioner –
>   (a) may investigate a matter notwithstanding that the complainant has or had a remedy by way of proceedings in a court of law if satisfied that in the particular circumstances it is not reasonable to expect him to take or to have taken such proceedings:
>   (b) is not in any case precluded from investigating any matter by reason only that it is open to the complainant to apply to the High Court for redress under section 16 of this Constitution [which relates to the enforcement of the fundamental rights and freedoms].

It cannot be argued however, that the Ombudsman in the Commonwealth Caribbean has a primary jurisdiction with respect to human rights as is the case for some of his counterparts worldwide. The Ombudsman is, however, to be concerned with human rights in the carrying out of his functions. His role in relation to human rights may be best described as 'indirect'.

Certainly, this can be seen as the *raison d'être* of the office. Indeed, the Ombudsman in Jamaica has argued that as long as citizens in the Caribbean are deprived of basic human rights, such as lack of education, food, work, or housing, there is justification for the office of the Ombudsman.

Proponents of a more interventionist role for human rights by the Ombudsman argue that he or she should be concerned with promulgating both domestic and international human rights norms in their investigations where no redress exists in relation to those norms.[23] The Jamaican Ombudsman has noted, for example, that the Ombudsman is 'very often called upon to investigate complaints for which no action at law lies'.[24]

---

21 See the Ombudsman Act, s 12(1).
22 See, eg, Dominica, s 111(5); Trinidad and Tobago, s 94 (5); Guyana, Art 53(3); and St Lucia, s 113.
23 See L Reif, 'Ombudsman and human rights protection and promotion in the Caribbean: issues and strategies' in Ayeni, V, Reif, L and Thomas, H *Strengthening Ombudsman and Human Rights Institutions in Commonwealth Small and Island States*, Commonwealth Secretarial, 2000, pp 160 at 164.
24 'Strengthening Ombudsman and Human Rights – Report of the Commonwealth Regional Workshop' Antigua, March 1998, p 11.

If we are to give serious thought to a more proactive role in human rights for the Ombudsman, we will have to consider the particular deficiencies in our constitutional protection of human rights, since the Constitution is the focus of human rights redress in our respective countries. It is perhaps in this context that the Ombudsman can be most useful.

Our Constitutions are not complete documents with respect to human rights, nor have they always been interpreted liberally in this regard. Rights such as discrimination on grounds of gender, HIV/AIDS and the like, can be seen to be poorly protected, either because of inadequate provisions or restrictive interpretations of those Constitutions. In addition, if we consider the restrictive *Harikisson*[25] approach to constitutional access to human rights, there is further empathy for the enlargement of the Ombudsman's purview. In *Harikisson*, the Privy Council said that it is not every case against a public authority that should involve an application to the High Court for redress of human rights and that 'the value of the Constitution will be diminished if it is to be allowed to be misused as a general substitute for the normal procedures for invoking judicial control of administrative action.'[26] While the courts have retreated somewhat from this restrictive position, it is clear that there is a role, perhaps a more useful role, for other mechanisms devoted purely to examining administrative action. The Ombudsman could be useful in this regard.

The UN has also championed the elevation of the Ombudsman function to include human rights: 'An Ombudsman . . . may be engaged in a broad range of promotional and protective activities generally recognised as characteristic of a [human rights] commission'.[27]

Certainly, in the traditional work of any Ombudsman, contact will be made with many matters which have human rights aspects or implications. Government departments or public authorities may engage in discriminatory treatment, inappropriate police treatment, privacy intrusions and so on. Reif also points out that while some of these rights may not be located within the domestic sphere, they may arise as a result of rights under customary law, which is enforceable.[28]

At minimum, the Ombudsman may have to engage, at least indirectly, in the resolution of these matters. Many have done so. The Ombudsman of Saint Lucia, for example, has given concrete examples of such cases. These complaints of maladministration or injustice indirectly involve human rights issues. She reports, for example, complaints from the mother of a wrongfully arrested accused murderer, who had received no information about her son's status. While the Ombudsman could not inquire into the legality of the arrest, she was able to obtain information about the status of the accused.[29]

---

25 *Harrikisoon v AG of Trinidad and Tobago* [1997] 3 WLR 62 (PC, Trinidad and Tobago). The issues are discussed in Chapter 7 ('The Written Constitution as a Legal Source').

26 *Ibid*, at p 64.

27 *A Handbook on the Establishment and Strengthening of National Institutions for the Promotion and Protection of Human Rights*, NY/Geneva: UN Centre for Human Rights, 1995, p 7. See also the OAS General Assembly's recognition of the 'increasingly important role of the Ombudsman in consolidating the promotion and dissemination of citizens' rights' OAS General Assembly 27th Session, OEA/Ser P, AG/doc 3599/97, 5 June 1977.

28 Reif, *above*, fn 23, p 166.

29 L Laurent, 'The Promotion and Protection of Human Rights in the Caribbean – A Case Study of Saint Lucia' in Ayeni, *above*, fn 23, 198, at 199–200.

She argues that 'we, the Ombudsmen of the Caribbean, may have to rethink our role and either reinterpret or adapt our mandate to adequately fulfil our task of ensuring the provision of good governance.'[30]

This new role may extend to petitions on the behalf of groups of citizens to international bodies such as the Inter-American Court on Human Rights or to a petition for mercy as has occurred in Jamaica.[31] At minimum, the Ombudsman can be instrumental in making the public more aware of human rights.

Nevertheless, it is difficult to see how an office which is essentially concerned with administrative action can have such a far-reaching influence on fundamental rights, except those which are more logically linked to administrative abuse, such as discrimination in employment or housing.

Notwithstanding the above, legislative provisions allowing the Ombudsman to have regard to the protection of human rights are a welcome addition to societies where the constitutional redress in the High Court for abrogation of such rights are often inaccessible to the masses. The informality, accessibility and lack of cost of the office of the Ombudsman may prove to be a more important weapon in this regard.

Exclusions from jurisdiction

Except in a matter concerning fundamental rights, as described above, the Ombudsman is generally precluded from investigating any matter for which a remedy exists by court proceedings, or which may be the subject of appeal or review by a tribunal. Thus, his jurisdiction is not as wide as, for example, the Swedish Ombudsman. Once again, one may note the flexibility of the jurisdiction, however, for he has a discretion to investigate, where he determines that the particular circumstances point to the unreasonableness of recourse to the courts and it would be more equitable to allow recourse to the Ombudsman's office.[32] An example of the above would be where the judicial remedy is too difficult or too expensive to pursue. Section 12(5) of the Jamaican Act is noteworthy in this regard. It provides that the fact that a matter has come before a court does not prevent an investigation unless the court so directs.

Certain matters are absolutely precluded from the Ombudsman's sphere of investigation. Generally, these are matters which would prejudice the security or defence of the State, matters relating to foreign affairs and relations, and matters which are precluded from the jurisdiction of the ordinary courts via the Constitution. Further, investigations which would involve the deliberations of Cabinet or which would be injurious to the public interest may be excluded from the exercise of the jurisdiction. It should be noted, however, that these exclusions should not be taken as an indication that the office is not authoritative. They are, in the main, matters which are also precluded from the courts of law.

It was held in *R v Parliamentary Commissioner ex p Dyer*[33] that the Ombudsman is subject to judicial review by the courts.

---

30   *Ibid*, p 200.
31   See the Report of the Jamaican Ombudsman in Ayeni, *above*, fn 23, p 121.
32   See, eg, the Trinidad and Tobago Constitution, s 94(5).
33   [1994] 1 All ER 375.

PROCEDURE

In carrying out his investigative functions, the Ombudsman in the Caribbean has three methods at his disposal. First, he may investigate upon receipt of a letter of complaint from an individual or body of persons. This is in keeping with the aim of accessibility of the office to the citizen. It represents an attempt to restrict rigid procedures, such as leave requirements or writs, which characterise other forms of administrative complaints, such as judicial review. A complaint to the Ombudsman is inadmissible if it is frivolous, trivial, vexatious or anonymous.

Secondly, in certain jurisdictions, notably, Trinidad and Tobago, Dominica and Guyana, the Ombudsman may commence an investigation upon request from a Member of Parliament, on the grounds that a person specified in the request may have sustained an injustice. Parliament may also refer a matter to the Ombudsman if it seems that there are reasons of special importance which may make such an investigation desirable in the public interest. Finally, the Ombudsman may also conduct an investigation *ex proprio motu*, that is, on his own initiative. This is in circumstances where he considers that some person or body of persons has suffered an injustice and it is in the public interest to do so.

In relation to *locus standi* in the Caribbean, the Ombudsman can only investigate a complaint if the complainant has a 'sufficient interest' in the matter. This limitation suffices even in the situation of an *ex proprio motu* motion, for here the motion must be on someone's behalf who has such interest in an alleged injustice, whether potential or in fact.

This restriction would seem to rule out the possibility of the Ombudsman inquiring into complaints of a general public nature, as is allowed in the Nordic countries. Yet, an ambitious Ombudsman might be able to carve out an extended role for himself in this regard. The *ex proprio motu* power allows investigation not only on behalf of an individual but a 'body' of persons. Interpreted broadly, this might infer a general public interest. Coupled with the relaxation of *locus standi* requirements in administrative law, this is a plausible interpretation.[34]

There is no set manner for conducting investigations. Indeed, one Ombudsman has acclaimed this feature:

> The method of dealing with a complaint is intended to provide a result that is swift and equitable. Members of my staff have been directed not to allow themselves to be bogged down in red tape and formal trappings of procedure and instead, they must rely on their ability to influence by means of logical persuasion that has its grounding in accurate, thorough research.[35]

The elements of informality and accessibility are evident in the Trinidad context, where the investigative process is brought to the people by means of mobile units.

The Ombudsman has powerful tools for investigation. He can inspect agency premises, examine agency records, and summon and examine witnesses and documents, as does a judge. Further, the Ombudsman can commit for contempt any

---

34 See, eg, the exploits of Blackburn, who has been called the 'public spirited taxpayer' in cases such as *R v Greater London Council ex p Blackburn* [1976] 1 WLR 550. Blackburn lacked specific interest in these matters, such as preventing a local authority from licensing indecent films, but the court found that he had sufficient interest and standing.

35 Rees, J, 'The role of the Ombudsman in Trinidad and Tobago', *op cit*, seminar papers, fn 3, p 21.

person who obstructs him in his duties. Indeed, the Barbadian Ombudsman recently threatened to commit for contempt those public servants who appear to be ignoring his communications.

The Ombudsman has an absolute discretion to decide whether he will initiate, continue, or cease any investigation. At the conclusion of an investigation by the Ombudsman, he must inform the authority concerned of the result of his investigation.

If he forms the opinion that an injustice has been suffered, he must communicate the reasons for that finding to the relevant authority and provide an opportunity for them to be heard. The Ombudsman is also required to give to the complainant the results of his investigation. In the cases of Jamaica and Guyana, even where no finding of injustice is found, he must also communicate the reasons for the finding.[36]

The next step in the process is a waiting period, during which the Ombudsman's recommendations are expected to be heeded. Where no remedial action has taken place within the specified time, or a reasonable time, the Ombudsman may have the sanction of a Special Report to be laid before Parliament. The use of the Special Report may also be made in certain jurisdictions, for example, in Dominica and Trinidad and Tobago, where the matter is of sufficient 'public importance'. This provision operates regardless of whether there has been a finding of injustice or not.

Ultimately, the Ombudsman's weapon for redress is publication of his report and the recommendations therein. Thus, he submits his report to the media for publication and to Parliament. Of course, his report to Parliament must go through the usual channels. For example, it must be laid before the House of Parliament, an important consideration which will be examined further below, p 420.

PROBLEMS WITH THE OMBUDSMAN'S OFFICE

Transplantation of the institution of the Ombudsman has certainly not been problem-free. The difficulties range from structural and institutional problems to those that strike at the very ideology of the office and its compatibility with the Commonwealth Caribbean experience.

The office of the Ombudsman is such as to make it highly personal in nature. Hence, the strengths and weaknesses of the person of the Ombudsman are the strengths and weaknesses of the office. He is, indeed, the alter ego of the institution. This has potential difficulties for the office where the Ombudsman is not strong enough to stand up to the bureaucracy in his role as watchdog of the citizens' rights.

Such a role requires men and women:

> ... who substitute resolution for faint-heartedness and are of a determined and courageous mind, with firm opinions and the will to assert and pursue them; men and women strong enough to look politicians in the eye and destroy their peremptory commands to sweep under the carpet the refuse from the Aegean stables, and independent enough to resist their invitation for reward, to turn the lamp of scrutiny into other than dark, shadowy, obscure places . . . to let justice roll down as waters.[37]

---

36   See s 21(4)(b) and Art 54(2)(b), respectively.
37   Ombudsman Greene, G, of Jamaica, 'The role of the Ombudsman in Jamaica', *op cit*, seminar papers, fn 3.

Indeed, for the office to succeed, citizens must have confidence in the Ombudsman himself. This willingness and courage to represent citizens against the State is vital to the success of his office. So, too, is the citizens' trust in his impartiality in dispersing justice to them. As illustrated earlier, the Ombudsman has an absolute discretion to initiate, continue, or cease investigations. A timid Ombudsman would easily frustrate the ideals of the office.

The emphasis on the personal character of the office can have a negative effect in Commonwealth Caribbean societies, which are often characterised by racial hetero-geneity. It is instructive to recall that one of the reasons for the creation of the Ombudsman in Guyana was to address this very problem of racial discrimination in the Public Service.

Perhaps it is not the variable of race that has the greatest potential of undermining the success of the institution, but rather the lack of awareness of the very existence of the office and the consequent lack of stature.

In societies where citizens are not noted for being aware of their rights, avenues for problem solving are not often pursued. The office of the Ombudsman is no excep-tion. The Ombudsman therefore needs to educate the public on his role via the media and the publication of his reports. However, where illiteracy is still very much a problem, such methods are often prone to being ineffective. It is therefore left up to the Caribbean Ombudsman to create indigenous methods to reach the public. An interesting experiment has been carried out by Ombudsman Greene of Jamaica in this regard, where, in conjunction with a voluntary organisation, the Jamal Foundation, he was able to inform citizens of the existence of the office by allowing the foundation to reprint a brochure describing the nature of his office in local dialect.

The practice of literally taking the office to the public, by way of mobile units, as practised in Trinidad and Tobago, can also help counteract this problem. This also helps to alleviate the problems of physical distance and poverty, which can under-mine the investigative process. It is noteworthy that, in the Caribbean, the institution has attracted mainly those from the lower income brackets of society. An exception appears to be Trinidad and Tobago, where complaints are received 'from every social group, race and class'.[38] It thus represents the voice of the ordinary man. However, real attempts must be made to overcome the problems of illiteracy, poverty and inaccessibility due to physical distance.

As always in Third World economies, the lack of finance is a potential problem. The office of the Ombudsman is accorded a low priority with regard to goods and services. This serves to exacerbate the problems of ineffectiveness. The result is inadequate facilities and staffing, a problem not alleviated by the current economic recession in the region and the phenomenon of persistent poverty. This is exemplified in Guyana, where the state of the economy has led to a disruption of the functions of the institution as a result of it being 'financially starved'.

The fact that the office usually has to depend on the Ministry of Finance for the allocation of its budget further emphasises the problem. Indeed, the Minister of Finance also generally determines the number of staff members and terms and conditions of employment.

---

38   Justice George A Edoo, 'Types of Complaints and the Complaint Handling Process' in Ayeni, V, Reif, L and Thomas, H, *Strengthening Ombudsman and Human Rights Institutions in Common-wealth Small and Island States*, Commonwealth Secretariat, 2000, p 91.

In Trinidad and Tobago, provision is made in the Constitution for the office to have adequate staffing for the efficient discharge of his functions. This may account for the Trinidad and Tobago Ombudsman office having relatively high numbers of complaints which are investigated. There are also sub-offices in other parts of the island.[39]

Further, the office is totally dependent for goods and services on the relevant government department. This also has the effect of giving the impression that the Ombudsman is directly controlled by the bureaucracy and is just a token complaint organisation. The result is an undermining of confidence in the institution on the part of the citizen. It creates the uncomfortable situation of a supposedly independent institution which may be called upon to investigate objectively the very authority which it depends upon for its existence. There is therefore a great need for the office to have an independent budget.

Additionally, the sphere of the Ombudsman's authority may include such matters which are not essentially the result of maladministration but rather the problems peculiar to Third World countries. When this occurs, it is problematic, since it involves the Ombudsman in a self-defeatist and often frustrating role, which only serves to make the office lose face. For example, problems such as delays in housing, general infrastructure and poor public service utilities, may be in reality due to the political problems of a lack of adequate funds and a shortage of goods and services. Such problems are beyond the control of the bureaucracy and certainly beyond the scope of the Ombudsman's power.

A drastic example of this phenomenon has been seen in the Guyana experience, where the administrative system lost its capacity to perform due to a combination of serious social, economic and political factors. The office of the Ombudsman cannot thrive in an environment where institutions are so seriously starved of resources.

Other features of the institution which may be viewed as problematic are the lack of power to question decisions and the lack of effective sanctions, the latter being very different from the court system. In general, the fact that the institution is modelled on a consensual approach, rather than an adversarial approach, means that it relies for its effectiveness on persuasion and reasoning. The bureaucracy must be persuaded to take corrective action outlined in recommendations and cannot therefore be coerced. As a result, the Ombudsman is often accused of lacking 'teeth' or of being a 'toothless bulldog'. If Parliament fails to act on his recommendations, he is deprived of his sanction. It is common for reports of the Ombudsman to be shelved and never debated before Parliament.

In societies where partisan politics are often viewed as being the order of the day, and where Members of Parliament are seldom independent or courageous enough to speak out against the bureaucracy, one wonders if the consensual model is appropriate for Caribbean societies. This pessimism is not shared by the President of the International Ombudsman Association, however, who sees the lack of coercion as its central strength, rather than a weakness.[40]

This lack of independent sanction is further highlighted when one considers the other avenue for publication, the media. Can this avenue truly be seen as a weapon in exposing abuses of the bureaucracy in such small societies as those in the Caribbean

---

39   *Ibid.*
40   *Op cit*, Owen, fn 3.

often where there is an absence of competitive media? These societies are character-ised by media monopolies, and the media has even been accused of being politically influenced. Often, there is only one newspaper, radio and television station in the jurisdiction and this may be government controlled. The fact that it is not uncommon for reports of the Ombudsman to be printed in tiny print in obscure sections of the newspaper supports this view.

But, perhaps, the most fundamental and all-pervasive problem relating to the transplantation of the institution is the fact that Commonwealth Caribbean societies do not exhibit the tendencies of a well developed bureaucracy and State. This is significant, for it is precisely in such an environment that the institution works best, although, paradoxically, it is in less politically developed States such as ours where it is most needed.

Caiden has explained this phenomenon, questioning whether the institution could operate successfully:

> ... where political stability was low, democracy precarious, public maladministration rife, and the ethics of the Public Service within the public bureaucracy underdeveloped, the Ombudsman would only work where its position within the government system was assured, where the political system respected individual liberties and rights, where public administration operated well and incorporated sufficient safety checks and where public officials were sensitive to disclosures of arrogance and poor service.[41]

He concluded that few developed democracies, let alone developing democracies, could satisfy the above precondition. Hence the problems often alluded to in the Caribbean, such as partisan politics, victimisation, unfair allocation of public resources and corruption in public life are relevant in this context. Such personalised politics would also tend to produce citizens who are reluctant to speak out, for fear of victimisation. The 'remoteness' inherent in Caribbean societies alluded to earlier also describes a population unaccustomed to participating in the democratic process, and even unaware of their rights and their role in such a process.

POSITIVE FEATURES OF THE INSTITUTION AND TRENDS FOR THE FUTURE

Although the problems facing the institution of the Ombudsman are many, the idea is still popular in most jurisdictions. Both the Trinidad and Tobago and Jamaican Ombudsmen, for example, are extremely enthusiastic, the latter proclaiming it as being 'essential to the well being of the Jamaican society'.[42]

Certainly, the idea of an office which is the bulwark against abuses of power and the watchdog of citizens' rights is attractive. The simple procedures, easy accessibil-ity, flexibility and lack of cost also seem to be advantages in societies such as ours. Further, the informality and the personal touch which characterises the office cannot help but appeal to a people known for their warmth, openness and easy-going manner.

The office brings to the citizen an impartial agent without personal cost, or delay.

---

41 Caiden, G, 'Ombudsman in developing countries: comment' [1984] 1 International Review of Administrative Science 221.

42 *Op cit*, Ombudsman Greene, fn 37.

It further eradicates the need for costly counsel. It is not an office constrained by legal technicalities, as is the case in an adversarial system. Rather, the ideal Ombudsman is an arbitrator who seeks truth.

This human and consensual approach, as opposed to a rigid, legalistic, adversarial one, could indeed present advantages of the Ombudsman's institution over the judicial system. Accountability is an essential element in a democratic society and it is clear that the rise of the public sector has outgrown the potential of traditional control systems to perform this function.

Further, the traditional political process is not sufficiently finely tuned to monitor individual concerns about inappropriate administrative action, nor is the expensive, slow and sometimes impotent judicial system. An unreliable media, sometimes controlled by government, can exacerbate centralist tendencies in government. This can further frustrate the seeming irrelevance and unresponsiveness of public services. Thus, traditional parliamentary theory and the separation of powers doctrine may be insufficient to counteract partisan politics in the region.

It can also be noted that, in the Caribbean, there are no administrative law courts. Further, judicial review of administrative action, following the English jurisprudence, had until recently been given a rather restrictive interpretation by courts, both in terms of procedure and substance. The recent progressive developments in administrative law are changing this; yet gaps and defects in remedies for administrative fault remain.

The consensual approach may, therefore, be a major advantage to the institution of the Ombudsman. This approach requires vigorous analysis of all issues and the application of reason. One view is that the results of such an approach are 'infinitely more powerful than through the application of coercion', for coercion creates a 'loser' who will be unlikely to embrace the recommendations in future actions.[43] By contrast, where changes result from a reasoning process, it changes a way of thinking. The difficulties underlying this optimistic approach to the consensus method as it relates to the Caribbean have already been discussed above.

The Ombudsman can, however, have an educative function, both in making the citizen aware of his rights and participatory role in the democratic process, and also to point out to him the legitimate problems of government, as opposed to government inefficiency and abuse.

Whatever the limitations of the institution, it seems spearheaded for take-off the world over. Indeed, the scope of the office seems to be expanding and the current trend in public administration is heading towards preventative action. This preventative approach sees the future of the Ombudsman not only in the traditional role of responding to individual complaints, but also in attempting to put structures and systems in place to prevent future administrative abuses and inefficiencies.

Some of these systems include clear foundational links between policy and practice so that lawful authority is apparent, principled codes of service to emphasise the responsibility of public officials to ensure fairness, structured criteria against which discretion is exercised to ensure uniformity in decision making, the giving of reasons for discussion and the creation of opportunities for meaningful participation in administrative decision making.

---

43   See *op cit*, Owen, fn 3.

IMPACT AND CONCLUSION

An examination of the office of the Ombudsman in the Commonwealth Caribbean creates the impression that the institution is here to stay. With the notable exception of Guyana (which saw an initial rise, then a steady decline), the office seems to be growing slowly but steadily throughout the region, notwithstanding the scepticism surrounding it. Certainly, some countries have felt its impact more forcefully than others. The Jamaican Ombudsman argues:

> As long as due process of law remains (because of its exorbitant costs) outside the reach of so many members of the developing world, the Ombudsman institution would remain a welcome haven for great hordes of human beings.[44]

But can we say that the institution has achieved real goals, or is it merely of cosmetic effect, or worse, a propaganda tool to give the appearance of meaningful democracy? Perhaps we can only judge the usefulness and impact of the institution by examining the extent to which it has been used. In Trinidad and Tobago the annual average of complaints numbers 1,200. This is viewed as a success by that country's Ombudsman. Similarly, in Jamaica, after 10 years, 1,813 complaints were received by the Parliamentary Ombudsman.[45] Many successes have been recorded. For example, the Ombudsmen there have helped change laws through advocacy, and have identified serious flaws in policy and practice.[46]

Elsewhere, however, there is not much evidence of success. The institution may still have much more growth to do before it can take its rightful place in West Indian society. Perhaps it is fairer to say that there is a mixed response to the question of success. Few will disagree that the Ombudsman can quite easily achieve minor successes and trivial victories, but the substantial challenges of administration have yet to be faced. Ultimately, whether the Ombudsman can be an effective watchdog of citizens' rights depends not merely on the powers and character of the office holder, or on the willingness of Parliament to make the office work, but also on the willingness of the Executive and indeed, the society to let the office flourish.

Although the institution has been given a superficial welcome in the Commonwealth Caribbean, we may still question whether the region is ready for its full implications, or is merely content to give the appearance of meaningfulness, while allowing only a marginal contribution to the alleviation of the fundamental problems in West Indian society.

In the words of the President of the International Ombudsman Institute:

> The Ombudsman holds a mirror up to public officials, and makes visible possible shortcomings and bottlenecks in the performance of their duties. This is an impetus for repair and improvement. . .[47]

It is up to us to allow these reflections.

---

44 *Op cit*, Ombudsman Greene, fn 37, p 3.
45 See *op cit*, seminar papers, fn 3.
46 See *op cit*, Ombudsman Greene, fn 37.
47 Martin Oosting 'Quality of the Ombudsman' (1998) 4(3) *International Ombudsman Institute Newsletter*, p 1.

CHAPTER 21

ALTERNATIVE DISPUTE MECHANISMS – ARBITRATION, NEGOTIATION AND COMMISSIONS OF INQUIRY

ARBITRATION, NEGOTIATION AND CONCILIATION

Arbitration, conciliation and negotiation are important alternative dispute mechanisms. These procedures may be utilised for virtually any subject area as a replacement to the court procedure. However, they are most often used in commercial law and labour law. In commercial law matters, an arbitration clause will usually be inserted into the relevant commercial contract. In contrast, in labour law matters, arbitration, where it exists, is often effected by statute. Although beyond the scope of this book, we should note that more recently, even the courts in the region have moved to a system whereby mediation is used as a mandatory, preliminary mechanism for settling certain disputes.[1]

Arbitration, conciliation and negotiation describe processes whereby two or more parties in a dispute attempt to reach a consensus without recourse to the courts in an environment of compromise. The process may be facilitated by an independent third party, in which instance, it is more accurately described as arbitration. The essence of such processes is that the parties are not bound by strict or rigid rules of procedure but are guided by principles of appropriate conduct such as 'good faith' bargaining. A distinct feature of these procedures is that the strength of any one party rather than what is a correct rule will often determine the outcome.

An arbitration does not preclude the inherent jurisdiction of a superior court to review the proceedings. Such a review can extend to an inquiry into the conduct of the arbitration. One such instance is found in the case of *Re Heirs of Stanley Malaykhan*.[2] The court accepted that an arbitrator could misconduct himself or herself by presiding over an irregularity in the proceedings, such as a failure to give notice of the time and place of meetings or by acting unfairly towards the parties by, for example, hearing one party but refusing to hear the other. In the instant case, the court found that the arbitrator was indeed guilty of misconduct, and declared the arbitration award null and void since the arbitration was a nullity.

In the Commonwealth Caribbean, arbitration and negotiation are used most often in labour law matters, although this is slowly changing. Consequently, in order to demonstrate the principles of arbitration and negotiation as a quasi-judicial process, our discussion will be confined to this area of dispute solving. It should be noted too, that under the CARICOM Treaty of Chaguaramas, which lays down the parameters of regional integration, there is a mechanism for arbitration in commercial disputes.[3]

---

1 Discussed in Chapter 14 ('The Court System of the Commonwealth Caribbean').
2 LC 2001 HC 29.
3 See the discussion of the CARICOM treaty in Chapter 12 ('International Law as a Source of Law').

ARBITRATION AND NEGOTIATION IN LABOUR RELATIONS

Industrial relations has traditionally been characterised by negotiation. The two parties, the employer and the employee, through their representative, the union, seek to come to agreeable terms about the terms and conditions of the contract of employment and the work environment in general. Despite the term 'negotiation', this is not always a peaceful process. Where two such parties attempt to negotiate matters relevant to work, the process is labelled collective bargaining.

Arbitration and negotiation procedures are found in all the industrial systems in the region. These measures are utilised to settle industrial disputes and are supported by either the unwritten common law or statute. In some countries, notably Trinidad and Tobago, Antigua and the Bahamas, the State has intervened to a much greater degree into the industrial relations sphere than in other countries in the region.

There are two main approaches to arbitration and negotiation in the region. They are (a) compulsory arbitration mechanisms effected by statute and (b) voluntary arbitration, often codified under statute, or negotiation as exemplified under the common law. A few countries take a compromise position between these two main approaches. For example, in Antigua, Jamaica, Dominica and St Kitts there are features of both the voluntary and compulsory systems.

A third category can be established for special situations and specified types of industrial disputes. In the main, this group concerns disputes in the essential services or which it is in the public or national interest to regulate. Where arbitration occurs here, it is of the compulsory type.

VOLUNTARY ARBITRATION AND NEGOTIATION

The typical method for problem solving in industrial disputes under the common law is by collective bargaining, which is a process of negotiation. This is a voluntary method where the parties to a dispute, that is, the employer and the union/workers, negotiate or attempt to negotiate satisfactory solutions to their problems. This is sometimes called a *laissez-faire* approach to collective bargaining. The common law has evolved by custom a concept of 'good faith', which means that these parties must genuinely attempt to come to a solution and should not merely go through the motions of negotiation.

While collective bargaining is supposed to be a consensus approach, in practice it is characterised by confrontation, particularly in the Commonwealth Caribbean. Often, negotiations fail or break down, hence the phenomenon of strikes or work stoppages. In theory, the law is supposed to be divorced from this voluntary process. In practice, in contemporary labour law, it has devised minimal procedures, which are designed to facilitate, but not to intervene in this process. In the main, this refers to the establishment of labour law departments in the Ministry of Labour or relevant ministry, which perform a quasi-judicial role in settling disputes or otherwise assist in negotiation.

In addition, disputes may be referred to a designated arbitrator or arbitration tribunal with the consent of both parties to the dispute. This is the case, for example, in Belize, Barbados, Grenada, Montserrat, Guyana, St Kitts, St Lucia and

St Vincent.[4] Such a tribunal may be given investigative powers, but it is merely consensual and has no coercive function. The parties, however, undertake to abide by the decisions of the arbitrator or arbitrators.

COMPULSORY ARBITRATION

The mechanism of compulsory arbitration for industrial relations represents a significant deviation from the voluntary or *laissez-faire* approach of the common law. Compulsory arbitration for dispute settlement in industrial relations was first introduced to the region in 1965 by Trinidad and Tobago.[5] The rationale for this legislation was to dampen the wide industrial conflict that the country was experiencing, in particular, the high incidence of strike activity. This intervention was proclaimed as being necessary for industrial stability and socio-economic development. The measure has not been without its critics, however. For example, one eminent legal practitioner of Trinidad and Tobago, Douglas Mendes, has maintained that the system of compulsory arbitration was really a mechanism to undermine the strength of trade unions. Ultimately, of course, this would mean an erosion of their effectiveness in bringing about gains for the working masses.[6] Certainly, the very concept of an arbitration which is compulsory and reinforced by law instead of by agreement by the parties sits somewhat awkwardly with our traditional notions of consensus-driven alternative dispute mechanisms. In effect, the mechanism aborted the industrial action until a statutorily determined time, forcing the parties to arbitrate instead of strike or lock out when disputes arose. In contrast, under the voluntary approach of the common law, the union retains its ultimate bargaining weapon, the strike, in the contest of power between the two parties.

The modern procedures for compulsory arbitration in the Trinidad and Tobago model are contained under the Industrial Relations Act 1972. The model envisages different procedural steps. First, there must be an attempt at negotiation. If this fails, the dispute must be reported to the minister. After this report the minister can refer it to arbitration. Under s 60 of the Act, for example, strikes and lockouts are prohibited unless a dispute has been reported to the minister and the statutory time allowed for conciliation has elapsed with no successful result.

The Trinidad and Tobago Act makes a differentiation between 'rights' disputes and 'interests' disputes. Rights disputes, which are disputes concerning the application to any worker of any existing terms and conditions, must be referred to the industrial court where the matter is resolved.

The regime is followed fairly closely in the Bahamas under the Industrial Relations Act and the Fair Labour Standards Act.[7] The procedure is similar to Trinidad and Tobago. Dispute resolution is initiated by the filing of a notice of a trade dispute with the Department of Labour. If unresolved, a dispute, other than one relating to essential services, is referred to compulsory arbitration. Alternatively, an action in the

---

4   See, eg, the Trade Disputes (Arbitration and Inquiry) Acts of the relevant countries.
5   Under the Industrial Stabilisation Act 1965, now replaced by the Industrial Relations Act 1972.
6   Douglas Mendes, SC, Lecture entitled 'The Industrial Relations Model of Trinidad and Tobago', Faculty of Law, UWI, September 2001, Barbados.
7   However, the system in the Bahamas is in a state of flux since it was declared unlawful by the Supreme Court. As yet, there is no viable alternative, except recourse to the court.

Supreme Court can be commenced. The latter mechanism attempts to satisfy the legality of the proceedings in the absence of consent by the parties to arbitration as required by the Supreme Court.

In Antigua, the relevant legislation is found under Division K12 of the Antigua Labour Code. However, elements of the voluntary approach have been retained. The parties must request such arbitration except where it is determined to be a 'major trade dispute' as defined by the Act, in which case the minister has the sole discretion to decide whether to refer to compulsory arbitration or not.

In Jamaica and Dominica, the minister has a discretion to force compulsory arbitration in certain kinds of disputes.[8]

The determination of the arbitrator in compulsory arbitration is conclusive. However, as with all inferior tribunals or offices, judicial review is available and there may be an appeal on a point of law.

Compulsory arbitration mechanisms, where they exist in the region, are complemented, as of necessity, by statutory provisions for the recognition of trade unions, thus deeming them legitimate parties to arbitration. They are also supported by provisions ensuring the enforceability of the collective agreement, thereby conferring validity on the outcome of the arbitration process. Both of these supplementary provisions represent further deviations from the common law.

ARBITRATION FOR DISPUTES AGAINST THE PUBLIC OR NATIONAL INTEREST AND ESSENTIAL SERVICES

Some of the jurisdictions in the region make statutory provision for the compulsory settlement or arbitration of industrial relations disputes where it is determined that a dispute is not in the public or national interest.[9] In these instances, the minister or designated authority is given a discretion to determine when a dispute is against the public or national interest.

Provision is also made in some jurisdictions for compulsory arbitration for disputes in the essential services.[10] With regard to what is an essential service, this is defined by statute. It will usually include industries like health, water, electricity and sometimes the industry deemed to be the mainstay of the economy.

COMMISSIONS OF INQUIRY

Nature and functions of Commissions of Inquiry

All jurisdictions in the region make provision for the setting up of Commissions of Inquiry to investigate or advise on matters deemed to be within the stated terms of reference. Originally, the power to appoint a Commission of Inquiry vested in the

---

8   See, eg, the Industrial Relations (Consolidation) Act 1986 of Dominica.

9   See, eg, the Industrial Relations Act of the Bahamas, s 80; the Antigua Labour Code, Division K20; the Industrial Relations (Consolidation) Act of Dominica, s 59; the Labour Relations and Industrial Disputes Act of Jamaica, s 10; and the Industrial Relations Act of Trinidad and Tobago, s 65A.

10   See, eg, the Essential Services Acts of Barbados, Montserrat, St Lucia, St Vincent, the Public Health Services Arbitration Act of Guyana and the legislation of Dominica, Trinidad and Tobago, Jamaica and Antigua, *ibid*.

Prerogative. Today, however, it is grounded in statute.[11] Commissions of Inquiry are valuable investigatory tools. Their findings could lead to subsequent court proceedings. Often, an Inquiry is established as an initial step to inquire into matters where there is not enough evidence to ground a court trial in the first instance. Perhaps a more important reason for such Commissions is to give the public an opportunity to participate in the process of justice or some issue of public importance, as they are usually open to the public and anyone may be summoned to give evidence, or more accurately, information.

Sir Louis Blom Cooper, on assuming his duties as the Commissioner in an investigatory Commission of Inquiry in St Lucia in 1998, helpfully explained the nature and functions of a Commission of Inquiry:[12]

> The primary object [of an Inquiry] is not to attribute fault or blame for what occurred in any of the events enunciated in the separate terms of reference. It is primarily to identify what happened and why it happened . . .[13]

Consider also Lord Scarman's description of a Commission of Inquiry:

> . . . this is an Inquiry, not a piece of litigation. It is not the sort of adversary type confrontation between parties with which we English are familiar.[14]

The procedure of a Commission of Inquiry is characterised by flexibility and informality. It is 'not a trial with its predetermined rules of evidence or of practice and procedure'.[15] The Inquiry should be dictated by the fundamental principles of fairness as people's reputations or employment may be at risk. For example, although there is no legal right to legal representation or cross-examination, the Commissioner has a discretion to allow these in the interests of fairness. Similarly, the Commissioner has a wide power to determine which witnesses will be called and to what matters their evidence will be directed. Witnesses will be called to the extent that they are helpful to the information gathering purpose of the Inquiry. It is not bound by strict legal requirements of *locus standi* or standing. As Lord Denning said, in *Miller Ltd v Minister of Housing and Local Government*,[16] a public inquiry is 'master of its own procedure'. The original source of this power to determine procedure may be statute.[17]

Blom Cooper was of the view that statutory provisions determining the subjects of an Inquiry[18] should:

> . . . not be narrowly interpreted. The words 'concerned in the matter under inquiry' are of wider import than 'implicated', and that concern has no connotation of fault, but merely imports a direct interest.[19]

---

11 See, eg, the Commission of Inquiry Act 1911 of the Bahamas, recently the subject of litigation.
12 Commissioner's Statement on the Proposed Procedure for Conducting the Commission of Inquiry Ordered by the Governor General, 4 June 1998. The Commission was established by the Government to investigate allegations of impropriety into public life by the previous administration.
13 *Ibid*, p 4.
14 All Souls-Justice Report 1974.
15 *Ibid*, Commissioner's Statement, p 5.
16 [1968] 1 WLR 992.
17 See, eg, the Commission of Inquiry Act of St Lucia, s 10, which gives the Commission of Inquiry the power to summon witnesses, and s 9, which gives the Commissioner the authority to make such rules for the conduct and management of the proceedings.
18 Under the Commission of Inquiry Act of St Lucia, s 18.
19 *Op cit*, Commissioner's Statement, fn 12, p 7.

Although there is no restriction on the subject nature of such Commissions, they have tended to focus on political matters.[20] These Commissions are of an inquisitorial, not an accusatorial nature. They do not have jurisdiction akin to a criminal court, even where they are investigating matters which relate to criminal activity. Such Commissions do not grant penalties in the sense of a court. Their prime purpose is information gathering.

Not surprisingly, as Commissions of Inquiry are inevitably controversial, litigation arising from such Inquiries has come before the courts, some aspects of which are considered below as they contain important principles about the nature, functions and procedures of such Commissions.

APPOINTMENT OF COMMISSIONS OF INQUIRY

The very appointment of the Commission of Inquiry may be contentious. The source of authority for the appointment of the Commission is statute, and such legislation is to be construed strictly. In *Simmonds and Others v Williams and Others (No 2)*,[21] the question was whether statutory modes of appointment had displaced the previous source of appointing Commissions of Inquiry by virtue of the Prerogative.

The new Commission of Inquiry (Amendment) Act 1996, Cap 288 provided for the appointment by the Governor General, as before, but also indicated the requirement of the Minister's signature. The court disagreed that this was a change in substance, holding that it was a matter of form only and did not vitiate the appointment which had been made solely by the Governor General. The court was fortified in its opinion by the provision in the Act which stated that 'Any of the powers in this form [ie a commission] may be struck out by the Governor-General at his discretion.' Thus, the power of the Governor-General to appoint a Commission of inquiry remained 'whole and inviolable and unaffected by the amendment, which merely prescribes the form which the Commission should follow, subject to such modification by way of striking out of powers which the Governor General in his absolute discretion thinks fit. He who gives may take away.'[22]

Further, the terms of reference of the Commission must be unambiguous. In *Tudor v Forde v Others*,[23] for example, there was a successful contest to the validity of the appointment of the Commission on the grounds that the Governor General had not validly constituted it as an investigatory commission under the Commission of Inquiry Act, Cap 112 of Barbados. Allowing the appeal, the Court of Appeal noted that the Act, which conferred authority to constitute Commissions of Inquiry, allowed for the Constitution of both advisory and investigatory Commissions.[24] The Act made it clear that the Commission must be 'designated', that 'whoever is appointed as a Commission must be specified, or called, or ... identified, as either an advisory

---

20 Some welcome exceptions include the Commissions to inquire into a prison revolt and subsequent setting on fire of the prison, and into the nature and suitability of the Cable and Wireless monopoly over telephone services, both in Barbados.

21 (1999) 57 WIR 95 (CA, St Christopher and Nevis).

22 *Ibid*, p 104.

23 (1997) 55 WIR 88 (CA, Barbados).

24 Section 3(1) of the Act.

commission or an investigatory Commission.' The nature of the Commission could not, therefore, be inferred.[25]

This was no academic or legalistic point. The terms of reference for the different Commissions are not identical. As the Court pointed out, were there to be doubt as to whether the Commission was investigatory or advisory, it would:

> create considerable difficulties and dangers for a number of persons, including the Commission itself . . . For example, a person who has been summoned before a Commission would be uncertain whether he has to obey the subpoena . . . whether he can give evidence freely and without fear of incriminating himself or exposing himself to civil litigation in the form of an action for defamation; and a person who is faced with a warrant for a search of his property would not be sure whether he could safely resist.[26]

The warrant of appointment was therefore found to be void for uncertainty.

In contrast, in *Simmonds*,[27] the appointment of the Commission was not to be voided for uncertainty in its terms of reference merely because the Governor General had left it up to the Commission to specify details of the terms of reference, which it had done.[28]

Impartiality of Commissioners

Persons appointed to a Commission must also be free from bias or appearance of bias. It appears that the narrower test of bias is favoured with respect to such Commissions of Inquiry, that is, that bias must not only be done, but must be seen to be done.[29] This was the test adopted in *Simmonds*, finding that legal counsels to the Commission, who were political opponents of the person being interrogated before the Commission, successfully raised the issue of bias. In truth, while seeming to adopt the narrow test of justice must be seen to be done, the Court of Appeal found a real danger of bias,[30] saying 'As to the legal advisors to the Commissioner, I am of the view that the advice tendered to him if based on a biassed view of the facts could and would most likely result in a biassed conclusion being reached by the fact-finding body.'[31]

In contrast, it was clear in the case of *Compton v AG of St Lucia*,[32] that there was no real danger of bias from the Commissioner. The only assertion was that she had been a judge previously and her appointment had not been renewed during the time when the person appearing before the Commission had been Prime Minister. Nevertheless, the court allowed the appeal on the test of 'justice must be seen to be done'.

---

25   *Ibid*, p 93.

26   *Ibid*, p 94.

27   *Above*, fn 21.

28   Relying on *Bethel v Douglas* (1995) 46 WIR 15 (PC, The Bahamas), considered further below.

29   From the much criticised case of *R v Sussex Justices, ex p McCarthy* [1924] 1 KB 256. Many other courts have chosen to follow the broader test of actual bias, as laid down, for example, in *R v Gough* [1993] 2 All ER 724, or a real danger of bias.

30   The 'real danger test' was used directly in *Sandiford v Thompson, Audain and Luke* (Unreported), No 222 of 1999, decided 10 March 1999 (HC, Barbados), pp 15–16.

31   *Above*, fn 21, p 109.

32   Unreported, Civil Appeal No 14 of 1997, decided 9 February 1998, CA, St Lucia. See also the discussion of this case in Chapter 15 ('Specialised Courts, Tribunals and Functions').

NATURAL JUSTICE AND PROCEDURE BEFORE COMMISSIONS OF INQUIRY

Unlike a court of law, Commissions of Inquiry are characterised by informal and flexible procedures. Notwithstanding such informality, however, they are informed by the rules of natural justice and fairness in procedure, principles associated with judicial review and administrative law.

The rules of natural justice and fairness as identified in administrative law are themselves quite dynamic and allow for the particular circumstances of a case. The principles of natural justice in administration are to be distinguished from the rules of natural justice which apply to a court of law. The latter are stricter and more rigid. It is the more 'liberal' adherence to natural justice which Commissions of Inquiry must follow, so as not to get bogged down with technical rules of procedure. In fact, Commissions are essentially self-regulatory, their terms of reference often specifying that the Commission may make rules for the conduct and management of the proceedings as they see fit.

The extent to which rules of natural justice associated with court proceedings are to be applied to the proceedings of Commissions has been explored in a number of cases. In *Seaga and McKenzie v AG of Jamaica et al*,[33] the applicants sought judicial review of a ruling made by the Chairman of a Commission established to inquire into events which took place in Kingston. They argued that the decision of the Commission to prevent the attorneys representing the applicants from cross-examining witnesses was a breach of the principles of natural justice and of the duty to act fairly.

The court emphasised the self-regulatory nature of the Commission under s 9 of the Commission of Inquiry Act:

> The Commission ... may make such rules for their own guidance, and conduct and management of proceedings before them ... as they may from time to time think fit ...[34]

Further, the Commission had made it clear from the outset that the 'duplicating' of cross-examination would not be permitted and no one had objected to this rule.

After reviewing the case law, the court confirmed two important principles: (1) that the principles of natural justice were not rigid; and (2) that natural justice and fairness did not demand that there be an automatic right to cross-examination of witnesses at a Commission of Inquiry but, instead, the matter of cross-examination is within the discretion of Commissions.[35]

Quoting from the *Re Erebus Royal Commission, Air New Zealand v Mahon (No 2)*,[36] the court said:

> The concept of natural justice does not rest upon carefully defined rules or standards that must always be applied in the same fixed way nor is it possible to find answers to issues which really depend on fairness and commonsense by legalistic or theoretical approaches. What is needed is a broad and balanced assessment of what has happened and been done in the general environment of the case under consideration.[37]

---

33   Unreported, No M134 of 2001, decided 8 October 2001 (SC, Jamaica).
34   *Ibid*, p 2.
35   *Ibid*, p. 8.
36   [1981] 618 (CA).
37   *Op cit, Seaga*, p 4.

Moreover, the court was mindful of the greater flexibility which is to be accorded to Commission proceedings as opposed to a court of law, even in the face of the need to observe the rules of natural justice. Indeed, relying on certain court rules, such as the right to cross-examine, could actually make the Commission of Inquiry unfair. Thus, a ruling against cross-examination, Wolfe, CJ opined, could be said to be 'protective of such parties. It has been my experience that cross-examination can have the effect of unearthing damaging evidence against a party who was not implicated by the examination in chief.'[38] Indeed, 'to "overjudicialise" the inquiry by insisting on observation of the procedures of a court of justice which professional judges alone are competent to operate effectively in the interests of their clients would not be fair.'[39]

In this case, the court relied substantially on what may now be regarded as the cardinal principles on the procedures to be observed in Commissions of Inquiry, as identified in the Salmon Report.[40] These principles have been adopted and applied by Commonwealth Caribbean courts consistently. While they are not reproduced in full here, we may note the following:

(1) the undesirability of entrenching rigid rules of procedure, whether by statute or otherwise, for Commissions of Inquiry;

(2) although matters before Tribunals or Commissions of Inquiry may contain inherent risks of personal hurt to persons involved, it is in the public interest that truth should be established; and

(3) a witness should have the opportunity of testing by cross-examination any evidence which may affect him. However, the principle has been elaborated and it is explained that there are circumstances where cross-examination is inappropriate and there is no right to cross examine.[41]

These Salmon principles were applied in the case of *Small, Rouse et al v Belgrave*,[42] where the interest of flexibility was underlined. Accordingly, notices containing allegations together with summaries of the evidence were not to be construed as findings or prejudgment of the issue such as to necessitate the *audi alteram partem* rule. This confirmed the *dicta* in *Public Disclosure Commission v Isaacs*,[43] that statute did not require the Commission, after it had formed an opinion that a complaint should be investigated, to give the complainant the opportunity to rebut any case. There, too, the *audi alteram partem* rule was found to have no application to matters arising under the Act, other than where the Commission was required to report that the complaint was groundless.

The court also approved the Canadian approach saying:

An illustration as to the nature and extent of the powers of a Commission may be gleaned from *Beno v Canada (Commission and Chairperson, Commission of Inquiry Into the Deployment of Canadian Forces to Somalia . . .* A public inquiry is not equivalent to a civil

---

38   *Ibid*, p 7, *per* Wolfe, CJ.

39   *Ibid*, p 6, quoting from Lord Diplock in Cross and Tapper on Evidence, 8th edn, at p 18.

40   *Report of the Royal Commission on Tribunals of Inquiry, under the Chairmanship of the Rt Hon Lord Justice Salmon*, Cmnd. 3121 UK, 1966.

41   Six Salmon principles have been enunciated by Richard Scott PC, Vice Chancellor of the Supreme Court of England, 'Six Cardinal principles of Lord Salmon' [1995] 3 LQR 3 upheld, eg, in *Bushell v Secretary of State for the Environment* [1980] 2 All ER 608 (HL).

42   (Unreported) Civ Appeal No 23 of 2000, decided 16 February 2001 (CA, Barbados).

43   [1988] 37 WIR 1 (PC).

or criminal trial. In a trial, the judge sits as an adjudicator, and it is the responsibility of the parties alone to present the evidence. At an inquiry, the Commissioners are endowed with wide-ranging investigatory powers . . .[44] There is no plaintiff or defendant . . . . there are no . . . charges, indictment or depositions. The inquiry may take a fresh turn at any moment. It is therefore difficult for persons involved to know in advance of the hearing what allegations may be made against them.[45]

In contrast to *Small*, in *Re the Matter of the Commission of Inquiry Relating to the St Joseph Hospital*,[46] Payne, J took a stricter view of notices containing allegations. He accepted first that the principles of judicial review applied to Commissions because, although their findings had no legal consequences, they had public attention and could impact greatly on personal reputation. Allegations contained in notices, while not findings, provided for no alternative remedies made available to those against whom the allegations were made. Their only course was to present to the Commission but, if the Commission failed to accept their submissions not to proceed with the allegations, such allegations could find their way into the report of the Commission and be made public. Even then, no right of appeal was available. As such, the court felt compelled to examine the evidence upon which the allegations in the notice were brought, and finding them lacking, viewed the allegations as 'unreasonable in the *Wednesbury* sense and therefore in excess of the Commission's jurisdiction.'[47]

This seems to fly in the face of the *dicta* of the Privy Council in the Bahamas case of *Douglas v Pindling*,[48] where the court was of the opinion that although a Commission may not be able to 'prove all the links in a suspected chain of events . . . if the Commission bona fide seeks to establish a relevant connection between certain facts and subject matter, it should not be regarded as outside of its terms of reference . . . This flows from the very nature of the inquiry being undertaken.'[49] More importantly, 'a court, if it has power to do so, should be *very slow to restrain a Commission* from pursuing a particular line of questioning and should not do so unless it is satisfied, in effect, that the Commission is going off on a frolic of its own. If there is a real, as distinct from a fanciful possibility that a line of questioning may provide information . . . such a line of questioning should . . . be treated as relevant.'[50]

Access to the public

The public nature of a Commission of Inquiry was underscored in *Gomes et al v AG of Jamaica*,[51] where in issue, was the legality of a ruling by the Commission that the members of the public were precluded from taking notes of the Commission's proceedings. The court observed that although a Commission had authority to make rules for its proceedings, such rules were to be within the province of the law, and in particular, had to accord with the protections under the Constitution, in this case the provision against discrimination. Precluding some persons from taking notes was

---

44   *Ibid*, p 52.
45   *Ibid*.
46   (Unreported), No 1137 of 2000, decided 27 June 2001 (HC Barbados).
47   *Ibid*, p 23.
48   [1996] 3 LRC 460 (PC, the Bahamas).
49   *Ibid*, p 470.
50   *Ibid*, p 471.
51   (Unreported) No M 063 of 2000, decided 3 July 2000 (SC, Jamaica).

discriminatory. Further, there was a presumption that the legislative authority intended that the public should enjoy access to Commissions as the 'purpose of issuing a Commission to hold this enquiry is for the public welfare.'[52]

Witnesses before Commissions of Inquiry

Commissions of Inquiry have wide power to summon witnesses. This was explored in the case of *Bethel v Douglas*,[53] where the integrity of a Commission was challenged on several grounds, including its power to summon witnesses.

The Privy Council in *Bethel* also held that the Commission had a valid power to summon witnesses under the relevant statute, the Commission of Inquiry Act 1911. More important, it confirmed the alternative dispute status of such Commissions and their inquisitorial nature. It found that the Commission as established did not supersede the ordinary courts of justice as the Commission had no power to find anyone guilty of an offence. Similarly, it could not be equated to a criminal trial. As such, it did not violate the necessary procedures for establishing a court of justice.

Where witnesses are brought before a Commission of Inquiry, provision may be made for any incriminating evidence of the summoned witnesses to be prohibited from use in criminal proceedings in the future.[54] Public servants, who are often witnesses in such Inquiries, may also be protected from disciplinary proceedings on the basis of any evidence or assistance which they gave to the Inquiry.

This leads to an interesting ancillary point about Commissions of Inquiry, also brought out by the *Bethel* case. Persons coming before such Commissions are not entitled to avail themselves of the constitutional protection against self-incrimination. This is a right which allows an accused to remain silent when he is called upon to testify or produce documents in a trial where he believes that the evidence so compelled is likely to incriminate him. The privilege, as it is often called, is not available in Commissions of Inquiry precisely because they are not criminal trials. In the Commonwealth Caribbean, unlike the UK, the privilege against self-incrimination is only available in criminal trials.[55]

Commissions of Inquiry may be the subject of judicial review proceedings as seen in the litigation against the Commissions of Inquiry mentioned above.

---

52   *Ibid*, p 3.
53   (1995) 46 WIR 15 (PC, the Bahamas).
54   *Bethel v Douglas* (1995) 46 WIR 15, p 22.
55   See, eg, the Constitution of the Bahamas, s 20(7), and *Bethel v Douglas* (1995) 46 WIR 15, p 21. 'No person who is tried for a criminal offence shall be compelled to give evidence at the trial.' See also, the Constitutions of St Kitts and Nevis, s 10(7); Belize, s 6(6); Barbados, s 18(7); Antigua and Barbuda, s 15(7); and the Montserrat Constitution Order 1989, s 57(7).

BIBLIOGRAPHY

Akzin, A, 'Legislation: nature and functions' (1968) 9 International Encyclopedia of Social Sciences 221

Alexis, F, *Changing Caribbean Constitutions*, 1983, Bridgetown: Antilles Publications.

Alexis, F, 'When is an Existing Law Saved?' (1975) PL 256.

Alexis, F, White, D and Menon, PK (eds), *Commonwealth Caribbean Legal Essays*, 1982, Cave Hill, Barbados: UWI

Alker, HR and Bernard, J, 'Procedural and social biases in the jury selection process' (1978) (3) The Justice System Journal 220

Allott, AN, *The Limits of Law*, 1980, London: Butterworths

An Overview of the Report of the West Indian Commission – Time For Action, 1992, Barbados: West Indian Commission Secretariat

Anaya, J, 'Indigenous Peoples' Participatory Rights in Relation to Decisions About Natural Resource Extraction: The More Fundamental Issue of what Rights Indigenous Peoples have in Lands and Resources' (2005) 22 Ariz J Int'l & Comp Law 7.

Anaya, J, 'Maya Aboriginal Land and Resource Rights and the Conflict Over Logging in Southern Belize' [1998] 1 Yale H R Dev & Dev L J 17.

Anthony, KD, 'Approaches to the Common Law Trust in Codified Mixed Jurisdictions' in McBride, J (ed) *Droit Sans Frontieres, Essays in Honour of L. Neville Brown*, 1991, Birmingham: Holdsworth Club.

Anthony, KD, *Comparative Law Studies*, 1986, Washington: OAS, General Secretariat

Anthony, K and Ventose,E, 'St Lucia' in Kritzer, H (ed), *Legal Systems of the World – A Political, Social and Cultural Encyclopedia, Vol 1*, 2002, USA: ABC-CLIO.

Antoine, R-MB, *Trusts and Related Tax Issues in Offshore Financial Law*, 2005, Oxford: Oxford University Press.

Antoine, R-MB, *Confidentiality in Offshore Financial Law*, 2002, Oxford: Oxford University Press.

Antoine, R-MB, 'Opting out of the Optional Protocol: The UNHRC on death row – is this humane?' (1998) 3 Carib LB 30

Antoine, R-MB, 'The exhaustion of local remedies rule and death row appeals' [1993] Revue de droit internationale 33

Antoine, R-MB, 'The Judicial Committee of the Privy Council: An inadequate remedy for death row prisoners' (1992) 41 ICLQ 179

Antoine, R-MB, 'International law and the right of legal representation in capital offence cases – a comparative approach' (1992) 12 OJLS 293

Antoine, R-M B, 'UNICEF Ratification on the Convention on the Rights of the Child in the Commonwealth Caribbean', 1992, Barbados.

Antoine, R-MB, 'Law and the Caribbean man – a means of progress. Social engineering in a Caribbean context' [1986] Stud LR 24

Aquinas, T (St), *Summa Theologica*, 1942, London: Burns, Oates and Washbourne

Atkinson, L-G (ed), *The Earliest Inhabitants – The Dynamics of the Jamaican Taino*, 2006, Kingston, Jamaica: UWI Press.

Austin, J, *The Province of Jurisprudence Determined*, 1954, London: Weidenfeld and Nicolson

Ayeni, V, Reif, L and Thomas, H, *Strengthening Ombudsman and Human Rights Institutions in Commonwealth Small and Island States*, 2000, Commonwealth Secretariat.

Baldwin, J and McCorville, M, 'Jury, foreman and verdicts' [1980] Journal of Criminology 352

Beckford, G, *Persistent Poverty: Underdevelopment in Plantation Economies in the Third World*, 1972, New York: ISER

Beckford, G, *The Caribbean Economy*, 1975, London: Penguin

Bell, J and Engle, G (eds), *Cross on Statutory Interpretation*, 3rd edn, 1995, London: Butterworths

Ben Israel, R, *International Labour Standards: The Case of the Freedom To Strike: A Study Prepared for the ILO*, 1988, Deventer, Antwerp, London, New York: Kluwer

Brereton, B, *Law Justice and Empire – The Colonial Career of John Gorrie 1829–1892*, 1997, Jamaica: UWI Press.

Brierley, J, *The Law of Nations – An Introduction to the International Law of Peace*, 6th edn, 1963, Oxford: OUP

Burgess, A, 'Judicial precedent in the West Indies' (1978) 7 Anglo-Am LR 113

Burns, A, *History of the West Indies*, 1954, London: Allen & Unwin

Campbell, C, 'The transition from Spanish law to English law in Trinidad' (1989) 3 The Lawyer 15

Carey, B, *The Maroon Story*, 1977, Jamaica: Agouti Press.

Clarke, E, 'Land tenure and the family in four communities of Jamaica' (1953) 1 Social and Economic Studies 43

Clarke, E, *My Mother Who Fathered Me*, 1957, Kingston: Randell

Cochran, J, *Journey To Justice*, 1996, New York: One World Ballantine

Cotran, E and Rubin, N, *Readings in African Law*, 1970, London: Cass

Crabbe, VCRAC, 'Custom and the statute law' [1991] Stat LR 90

Cross, R and Harris, JW, *Precedent in English Law*, 4th edn, 1991, Oxford: Clarendon Press.

Curtain, P, *Two Jamaicas*, 1955, Cambridge, Mass: Harvard UP

Dashwood, A, 'Juries in a multi-racial society' [1972] Crim LR 85

David, R and Brierley, J, *Major Legal Systems in the World Today*, 3rd edn, 1985, London: Stevens

de la Bastide, J, 'The case for a Caribbean Court of Appeal' (1995) 5 Carib LR 401

DeMerieux, M, 'The codification of constitutional conventions in the Commonwealth Caribbean' (1982) 32 ICLQ 263

DeMerieux, M, *Fundamental Rights in Commonwealth Caribbean Constitutions*, 1992, Barbados: UWI

Denning, A, *Landmarks in the Law*, 1984, London: Butterworths

Deosaran, R, 'The jury system in a post-colonial multi-racial society – problems of bias' (1981) 21 Br Jr of Criminology 305

Deosaran, R, *Trial by Jury – A Case Study*, 1980, Trinidad and Tobago: ISER, UWI

Devlin, P (Sir), *Trial by Jury*, 1956, London: Stevens

Dicey, A, *Introduction to the Study of the Law of the Constitution*, 10th edn, 1959, London: Macmillan

Doucet, M and Vanderlinden, J (eds), *La Réception des Systèmes Juridiques*, 1994, Brussels: Bruylant

Dworkin, K, *Taking Rights Seriously*, 1977, London: Duckworth

Ewing, KD, 'Rights and immunities in British labour law' [1988] Comp Lab LJ 35

Ewing, KD and Gearty, CA, *Freedom under Thatcher – Civil Liberties in Modern Britain*, 1990, Oxford: Clarendon Press.

Fanon, F, *Black Skin, White Masks*, Lam Markmann C (trans), 1986, London: Pluto.

Fiadjoe, A, *Commonwealth Caribbean Public Law*, 2nd edn, 1999, London: Cavendish Publishing

Fuller, R, *Anatomy of the Law*, 1971, Harmondsworth: Penguin

Fuller, R, *The Morality of Law*, 1969, London, Yale UP

Funk, DA, 'Seven major functions of law' (1972) 23:2 Case Western Reserve L Rev 257

Gilmore, G, 'Legal realism: Its cause and cure' (1961) 70 Yale LJ 1037

Goveia, E, *Slave Society in the British Leeward Islands*, 1969, New Haven: Yale UP

Gregory, R *et al*, *The Parliamentary Ombudsman: A Study in the Control of Administrative Action*, 1975, London: Allen & Unwin

Griffiths, JAG, *Politics of the Judiciary*, 1986, London: Fontana

Hafard, J, Butler, W and Maggs, P, *The Soviet Legal System*, 3rd edn, 1977, New York: Oceana

Hall, CG, *Contemporary Caribbean Legal Issues*, No 2, 1997, Cave Hill, Barbados: UWI

Hall, HL, *The Colonial Office, A History*, 1937, London: Longmans, Greene

Harris, L, *Legal Philosophies*, 1980, London: Butterworths.

Hart, HLA, *The Concept of Law*, 1981, Oxford: Clarendon

Haynes, J, *Proceedings of the International Anniversary of the Abolition of Slavery in the Anglophone Caribbean*, 1984, Georgetown: Guyana Printers

Henriques, CGK, *Juvenile Delinquency and the Law*, 1958, London: Eyre and Spottiswoode

Higgins, R, 'The relationship between international and regional human rights norms and domestic law' [1992] CLB 1268

Hollis (Chalkdust) Liverpool, *Rituals of Power and Rebellion –The Carnival Tradition in Trinidad and Tobago 1732 -1962*, 2001, Chicago, USA: Research Associates School Times Publications/Frontline Distribution International Inc.

Jackson, M, *The Machinery of Justice in England*, 7th edn, 1977, Cambridge: CUP

James, RW, 'Land Tenure: Tradition and Change' (2001) 2 Carib LR 163.

Jane, C, *The Four Voyages of Columbus*, 1988, New York: Douer.

Jennings, R and Watts, A (eds), *Oppenheims's International Law*, 1992, London: Longman

Kahn-Freund, O, *Labour and the Law*, 6th edn, 1997, London: Stevens

Kasunmu, J and James, J, *Alienation of Family Property in Southern Nigeria*, 1966, Idaban: Idaban UP

Kelsen, H, *General Theory of Law and State*, 1961, Wedber, H (trans), New York: Russel and Russel

Kodilinye, G and Menon, PK (eds), *Commonwealth Caribbean Legal Studies*, 1992, London: Butterworths

Kodilinye, G, *Commonwealth Caribbean Law of Trusts: Text, Cases and Materials*, 1996, London: Cavendish Publishing

La Guerre, T, 'Race and colour' [1974] Caribbean Issues 1

Landry, RA and Caparros, E (eds), *Essays on the Civil Codes of Quebec and St Lucia*, 1984, Ottawa: Ottawa UP

Laurent, L, 'The promotion and protection of human rights in the Caribbean – A case study of Saint Lucia' in Ayeni, V, Reif, L and Thomas, H, *Strengthening Ombudsman and Human Rights Institutions in Commonwealth Small and Island States*, 2000, Commonwealth Secretariat.

Liverpool, N, 'Dominica' in Kritzer, H (ed), *Legal Systems of the World – A Political, Social and Cultural Encyclopedia*, Vol 1, 2002, USA: ABC-CLIO.

Long, E, *History of Jamaica*, 1774, London: Lowndes, repr in *Slaves, Free Men, Citizens: West Indian Perspectives*, 1973, USA: Anchor

Macmillan, W, *The Road to Self-Rule*, 1959, London: Faber and Faber

Maine, HS, *Ancient Law*, 1888, New York: Henry Helt

Malik, YK, *East Indians in Trinidad*, 1971, London: OUP

Marshall, OR, 'West Indian land law: Prospectus and reform' (1971) 20 Social and Economic Studies 1

Maxwell, R, *Maxwell on the Interpretation of Statutes*, 11th edn, 1980, London: Sweet & Maxwell

McIntosh, S, *Judicial Rights and Democratic Governance – Essays in Caribbean Jurisprudence*, 2005, Jamaica: The Caribbean Law Publishing Company.

Miers, D and Page, A, *Legislation*, 1990, London: Sweet & Maxwell

Mill, JS, *Utilitarianism*, 1979, USA: Hackett Publishing.

Millet, Lord, 'Construing Statutes' (1999) 20 SLR 107.

Mills, CJ and Bohannon, WE, 'Character and jury behaviour: conceptual and applied implications' [1980] J of Personality and Social Psychology 25

Mohammed, P and Shepherd, C (eds), *Gender in Caribbean Development*, 1988, St Augustine: UWI

Moore, T and Wilkson, T, *The Juvenile Court: A Guide to Law and Practice*, 1984, Chichester: Barry Rose

Morrison, D, 'The reception of law in Jamaica' (1979) 2 WILJ 43

Munneke, H and Kekker, AJ, 'Suriname' in Kritzer, H (ed), *Legal Systems of the World – A Political, Social and Cultural Encyclopedia, Vol IV*, 2002, USA: ABC- CLIO.

Munroe, T and Lewis, G (eds), *Readings on Government and Politics of the West Indies*, 1986, Mona, Jamaica: UWI

Nettleford, R (ed), *Mirror, Mirror: Identity, Race and Protest in Jamaica*, 1970, Jamaica: Collins and Sangster

Newton, V, 'An historical perspective of law reporting in the English-speaking Caribbean: A case for regional law reporting' (1979) 7 International J of Law Libraries 1

Newton, V, *Information Needs and Research Practices of the Commonwealth Caribbean Legal Profession*, 1981, Barbados: UWI

Okpaluba, C, *Essays in Law and Trade Unionism*, 1975, Trinidad: Key Caribbean

Oosting, M, 'Quality of the Ombudsman' (1998) 4(3) *International Ombudsman Institute Newsletter.*

Oppenheimer, P, 'Trial by jury' (1937) 11 Cincinnati ULR 142

Patchett, KW, 'Legal problems of the mini-State: The Caribbean experience' [1975] Cambrian L Rev 57

Patchett, KW, 'The reception of law in the West Indies' [1973] Jamaican Law Journal 17

Patchett, KW, 'English law in the West Indies' (1963) 12 ICLQ 15

Patterson, O, *The Sociology of Slavery*, 1973, London: Granada Publications Ltd.

Pollard, D. *The Caribbean Court of Justice, Closing the Circle of Independence*, 2004, Kingston, Jamaica: The Caribbean Law Publishing Co.

Pound, R, *Contemporary Justice Theory*, 1940, London: Banton

Pound, R, *Social Control Through Law*, 1968, Hamden: Archow

Radcliffe (Lord), *The Law and Its Compass*, 1961, London: Faber and Faber

Ratcliffe, P (ed), *The Good Samaritan and the Law*, 1966, London: Doubleday

Rawlins, H *'The Caribbean Court of Justice, A History and Analysis of the Debate'*, 2000, Guyana: CARICOM.

Rawlins, Berry and Antoine, 'Caribbean Justice For All - The Case For a Caribbean Regional Court', 2000 (3) Contemporary Legal Issues.

Rheddock, R, *Feminism and Feminist Thought: An Historical Overview*, 1986, Trinidad: UWI

Roberts-Wray, K, *Commonwealth Colonial Law*, 1966, London: Stevens

Rogowski, R, 'Civil Law' in Kritzer, H (ed), *Legal Systems of the World – A Political, Social and Cultural Encyclopedia, Vol I*, 2002, USA: ABC-CLIO.

Roth, WE, 'An introductory study of the arts, crafts and customs of the Guiana Indians (1916–17)' [1924] 38 Bureau of Amerindian Ethnology 58, Washington

Rouse, I, *The Tainos: Rise and Decline of the People who Greeted Columbus*, 1992, New Haven: Yale University Press.

Ryan, S, *Race and Nationalism in Trinidad and Tobago – A Study of Decolonisation in a Multi-Racial Society*, 1974, Mona: ISER, UWI

Scott, I, 'The Ombudsman in Fiji: Patterns of mediation and institutionalisation' [1982] The Ombudsman Journal 218

Sewell, G, *The Ordeal of Free Labour*, 1862, repr 1968, London: Sampson Low

Shahabuddeen, M, *The Legal System of Guyana*, 1973, Georgetown: Guyana Printers

Smith, MG, *The Plural Society in the British West Indies*, 1965, Los Angeles: California UP

Smith, R, 'Land tenure in three villages in British Guiana' (1955) 4 Social and Economic Studies 64

de Smith, SA, *Judicial Review of Administrative Action*, 4th edn, 1980, Oxford: Oxford University Press.

Spry, J, 'Problems of jury trials in small jurisdictions', 1985, London: Commonwealth Secretariat Report

Steyn, Lord, '*Pepper v Hart* – A re-examination' (2001) 21 OJLS 59.

Steyn, Lord, 'The Intractable Problem of the Interpretation of Legal Texts' (2003) 25 Sydney LR.

Stone, J, *Precedent and Law: Dynamics of Common Law Growth*, 1985, London: Butterworths

Thompson, AO (ed), *In the Shadow of the Plantation – Caribbean History and Legacy*, 2002, Jamaica: Ian Randle Publishers.

Tucker, SG (ed), *Blackstone's Commentaries* (1803), 1969, New York: Kelley

Tuitt, P, *Race, Law, Resistance*, 2004, Australia: GlassHouse Press.

Vogenauer, S, 'A Retreat from *Pepper v Hart*? A Reply to Lord Steyn' [2005] 25 OJS 629

Walker, R and Ward R, *Walker and Walker's English Legal System*, 7th edn, 1994, London: Butterworths

Wedderburn, KW, *The Worker and the Law*, 3rd edn, 1986, Harmondsworth: Penguin

White, D, 'Some problems of a hybrid legal system: a case study of St Lucia' (1981) 30 ICLQ 862

Williams, E, *The Negro in the Caribbean*, 1944, Manchester: Panaf Service

Williams, E, *Capitalism and Slavery*, 1964, London: André Deutsch

Wright (Lord), *Legal Essays and Addresses*, 1939, London: Butterworths

Yiannopoulas, AN (ed), *Civil Law in the Modern World*, 1965, Louisiana: Louisiana State UP

Zander, M, *A Bill of Rights*, 1975, London: Barry Rose

Zander, M, *The Law Making Process*, 4th edn, 1994, London: Butterworths

Zeisel, H, 'Dr Spock and the case of the vanishing women jurors', 1986, Chicago: Centre for the Study of Criminal Justice

Zweigert, K and Kotz, H, *An Introduction to Comparative Law, Vol 1*, 1977, Amsterdam: North Holland

INDEX